New Dictionary of Scientific Biography

Published by special arrangement with the American Council of Learned Societies

The American Council of Learned Societies, organized in 1919 for the purpose of advancing the study of the humanities and of the humanistic aspects of the social sciences, is a nonprofit federation comprising thirty-three national scholarly groups. The Council represents the humanities in the United States in the International Union of Academies, provides fellowships and grants-in-aid, supports research-and-planning conferences and symposia, and sponsers special projects and scholarly publications.

MEMBER ORGANIZATIONS

American Philosophical Society, 1743
American Academy of Arts and Sciences, 1780
American Antiquarian Society, 1812
American Oriental Society, 1842
American Numismatic Society, 1858
American Philological Association, 1869
Archaeological Institute of America, 1879
Society of Biblical Literature, 1880
Modern Language Association of America, 1883
American Historical Association, 1884
American Economic Association, 1885
American Folklore Society, 1888
American Society of Church History, 1888
American Dialect Society, 1889
American Psychological Association, 1892
Association of American Law Schools, 1900
American Philosophical Association, 1900
American Schools of Oriental Research, 1900
American Anthropological Association, 1902
American Political Science Association, 1903
Bibliographical Society of America, 1904
Association of American Geographers, 1904
Hispanic Society of America, 1904
American Sociological Association, 1905
American Society of International Law, 1906
Organization of American Historians, 1907
American Academy of Religion, 1909
College Forum of the National Council of Teachers of English, 1911
Society for the Advancement of Scandinavian Study, 1911
College Art Association, 1912
National Communication Association, 1914
History of Science Society, 1924
Linguistic Society of America, 1924
Medieval Academy of America, 1925
American Association for the History of Medicine, 1925
American Musicological Society, 1934
Economic History Association, 1940

Society of Architectural Historians, 1940
Association for Asian Studies, 1941
American Society for Aesthetics, 1942
American Association for the Advancement of Slavic Studies, 1948
American Studies Association, 1950
Metaphysical Society of America, 1950
North American Conference on British Studies, 1950
American Society of Comparative Law, 1951
Renaissance Society of America, 1954
Society for Ethnomusicology, 1955
Society for French Historical Studies, 1956
International Center of Medieval Art, 1956
American Society for Legal History, 1956
American Society for Theatre Research, 1956
African Studies Association, 1957
Society for the History of Technology, 1958
Society for Cinema and Media Studies, 1959
American Comparative Literature Association, 1960
Law and Society Association, 1964
Middle East Studies Association of North America, 1966
Latin American Studies Association, 1966
Association for the Advancement of Baltic Studies, 1968
American Society for Eighteenth Century Studies, 1969
Association for Jewish Studies, 1969
Sixteenth Century Society and Conference, 1970
Society for American Music, 1975
Dictionary Society of North America, 1975
German Studies Association, 1976
American Society for Environmental History, 1976
Society for Music Theory, 1977
National Council on Public History, 1979
Society of Dance History Scholars, 1979

New Dictionary of Scientific Biography

VOLUME 8
INDEX

Noretta Koertge

EDITOR IN CHIEF

CHARLES SCRIBNER'S SONS

An imprint of Thomson Gale, a part of The Thomson Corporation

THOMSON
™
GALE

Detroit • New York • San Francisco • New Haven, Conn. • Waterville, Maine • London

New Dictionary of Scientific Biography
Noretta Koertge

LIBRARY OF CONGRESS CATALOGING-IN-PUBLICATION DATA

New dictionary of scientific biography / Noretta Koertge, editor in chief.
   p. cm.
   Includes bibliographical references and index.
   ISBN 978-0-684-31320-7 (set : alk. paper)—ISBN 978-0-684-31321-4 (vol. 1 : alk. paper)—ISBN 978-0-684-31322-1 (vol. 2 : alk. paper)—ISBN 978-0-684-31323-8 (vol. 3 : alk. paper)—ISBN 978-0-684-31324-5 (vol. 4 : alk. paper)—ISBN 978-0-684-31325-2 (vol. 5 : alk. paper)—ISBN 978-0-684-31326-9 (vol. 6 : alk. paper)—ISBN 978-0-684-31327-6 (vol. 7 : alk. paper)—ISBN 978-0-684-31328-3 (vol. 8 : alk. paper)
   1. Scientists—Biography—Dictionaries. I. Koertge, Noretta.

Q141.N45 2008
509.2'2—dc22
[B]

2007031384

Editorial Board

Editorial and Production Staff

Table of Contents

List of Contributors

W. Abikoff
University of Connecticut,
Department of Mathematics
Professor
  LIPMAN BERS

Pnina G. Abir Am
Brandeis University, Women's Studies
Research Center and the Hadassah-
Brandeis Institute
Senior Research Fellow
  ERWIN CHARGAFF
  DOROTHY MOYLE NEEDHAM
  JOSEPH NEEDHAM

Charles I. Abramson
Oklahoma State University,
Laboratory of Comparative Psychology
and Behavioral Biology, Departments
of Psychology and Zoology
Professor
  CHARLES HENRY TURNER

Helmut A. Abt
Kitt Peak National Observatory
Astronomer Emeritus
  LUDWIG FRANZ BENEDIKT
  BIERMANN

Fabio Acerbi
Centre National de la Recherche
Scientifique (CNRS), UMR 8163
Savoirs, textes, langage
Researcher
  APOLLONIUS OF PERGA
  ARCHIMEDES
  DAMIANUS OF LARISSA

HERO OF ALEXANDRIA
HYPATIA

Peter Achinstein
Johns Hopkins University,
Department of Philosophy
Professor
  JOHN STUART MILL

Pascal Acot
Centre National de la Recherche
Scientifique, University of Paris 1
Researcher, Professor
  JOSIAS BRAUN-BLANQUET

Walter Wade Adams
Rice University, Richard E. Smalley
Institute for Nanoscale Science and
Technology
Director
  RICHARD ERRETT SMALLEY

George Adelman
Massachusetts Institute of Technology,
Department of Brain and Cognitive
Sciences
Research Affiliate
  FRANCIS OTTO SCHMITT

Duncan Carr Agnew
University of California San Diego,
Scripps Institution of Oceanography
Professor
  VICTOR HUGO BENIOFF
  HENRY WILLIAM MENARD
  CHARLES FRANCIS RICHTER

Marianne Gosztonyi Ainley
University of Northern British
Columbia, University of Victoria
Adjunct Professor
  CATHARINE PARR TRAILL

Kenneth Aizawa
Centenary College of Louisiana
Professor
  KORBINIAN BRODMANN
  WARREN STURGIS
  MCCULLOCH

Atsushi Akera
Rensselaer Polytechnic Institute,
Department of Science and
Technology Studies
Assistant Professor
  JOHN WILLIAM MAUCHLY

Douglas Allchin
University of Minnesota, Program in
the History of Science, Technology
and Medicine
  ALBERT LESTER LEHNINGER
  ALEX BENJAMIN NOVIKOFF
  EFRAIM RACKER
  ALBERT IMRE SZENT-GYÖRGYI

Garland E. Allen
Washington University, St. Louis,
Department of Biology
Professor
  HAMPTON LAWRENCE
  CARSON
  VIKTOR HAMBURGER

David K. Allison
Smithsonian National Museum of American History, Division of Information Technology and Communications
Chair and Curator
  J. (JOHN ADAM) PRESPER ECKERT, JR.

Ralph D. Amado
University of Pennsylvania, Department of Physics
Professor Emeritus
  HENRY PRIMAKOFF

Kevin Amidon
Iowa State University, Department of World Languages and Cultures
Assistant Professor
  (LEOPOLD FRANZ) EUGEN FISCHER

Kirsti Andersen
University of Aarhus, Steno Department for Studies of Science and Science Education
Associate Professor
  GUIDOBALDO, MARCHESE DEL MONTE
  PIERO DELLA FRANCESCA

Warwick Anderson
University of Wisconsin-Madison; University of Sydney
Professor; Chair
  RENÉ JULES DUBOS

Aitor Anduaga
Independent Scholar
  VICENTE INGLADA

Peder Anker
University of Oslo, Forum for University History, Department of Archaeology, Conservation and Historical Studies
Researcher
  JAN CHRISTIAN SMUTS

Henryk Anzulewicz
Albertus-Magnus-Institut, Bonn, Germany
Editor and scholarly collaborator
  SAINT ALBETUS MAGNUS

Adam Jared Apt
Independent Scholar
Manager, Peabody River Asset Management LLC
  JOHN GREAVES

Efstathios Arapostathis
Independent Scholar
  VERNER EDWARD SUOMI

Mitchell Ash
University of Vienna, Department of History
Professor
  KURT LEWIN

Oliver Ashford
World Meteorological Organisation
Emeritus, Jehuda Neumann Memorial Prize winner
  LEWIS FRY RICHARDSON

Robert Auerbach
University of Wisconsin, Madison, Department of Zoology and Institute on Aging
Professor Emeritus
  CLIFFORD GROBSTEIN

Massimiliano Badino
Max Planck Institute for the History of Science
Post-Doctoral Research Fellow
  LUDWIG EDUARD BOLTZMANN

Roland Baetens
University of Antwerp, Belgium
Professor Emeritus
  PAUL ADRIAAN JAN JANSSEN

Victor R. Baker
University of Arizona, Department of Hydrology and Water Resources
Professor
  RALPH ALGER BAGNOLD
  J. HARLAN BRETZ

Ugo Baldini
University of Padua, Faculty of Political Sciences, Department of Historical and Political Studies
Professor
  GIOVANNI ALFONSO BORELLI

John Bancroft
The Kinsey Institute for Research in Sex, Gender and Reproduction
Senior Research Fellow, previously Director
  ALFRED CHARLES KINSEY

Christina Helena Barboza
Museum of Astronomy and Related Sciences, Department of History of Science, Rio de Janeiro

Professor
  EMMANUEL-BERNARDIN LIAIS

John Barnett
University of Oxford, Department of Atmospheric, Oceanic & Planetary Sciences, Clarendon Laboratory
Senior Academic Staff
  GORDON MILLER BOURNE DOBSON

James R. Bartholomew
Ohio State University, Department of History
Professor
  KEN-ICHI FUKUI

Ofer Bar-Yosef
Harvard University, Department of Anthropology
Professor
  DOROTHY ANNIE ELIZABETH GARROD

Hyman Bass
University of Michigan, Department of Mathematics and School of Education
Professor
  SAMUEL EILENBERG

Giovanni Battimelli
Università La Sapienza, Dipartimento di Fisica
Associate Professor
  EDOARDO AMALDI

Elena Zaitseva
Moscow State University, Chemistry Department
Senior Researcher
  GEORGIĬ KONSTANTINOVICH BORESKOV
  GEORGIĬ NIKOLAEVICH FLEROV
  NIKOLAĬ NIKOLAEVICH SEMENOV
  NIKOLAY DMITRIEVICH ZELINSKIĬ

Betty M. Bayer
Hobart and William Smith Colleges, Department of Women's Studies, The Fisher Center for the Study of Women and Men
Associate Professor, Director
  LEON FESTINGER

Donald deB. Beaver
Williams College, Department of
History of Science
Professor
  SARAH EGLONTON WALLIS
    BOWDICH LEE
  DEREK JOHN DESOLLA PRICE

Antonio Becchi
Max Planck Institute for the History
of Science, Berlin
Visiting Scholar
  BERNARDINO BALDI

William Bechtel
University of California, San Diego,
Department of Philosophy and
Science Studies Program
Professor
  DAVID EZRA GREEN
  KEITH ROBERTS PORTER
  TORBJÖRN OSKAR
    CASPERSSON

Silvio A. Bedini
Smithsonian Institution
Historian Emeritus
  BENJAMIN BANNEKER

Colin Beer
Rutgers University, Department of
Psychology
Professor
  DANIEL SANFORD LEHRMAN
  THEODORE CHRISTIAN
    SCHNEIRLA

Bernadette Bensaude-Vincent
University of Paris X, Department of
Philosophy
University Professor
  ROBERT COLLONGUES

Marco Beretta
Institute and Museum of History of
Science, Florence, University of
Bologna
Vice-Director, Professor
  ANTOINE-LAURENT LAVOISIER

Paul Berg
Stanford University
Professor Emeritus
  GEORGE WELLS BEADLE

J. Lennart Berggren
Simon Fraser University, Department
of Mathematics

Professor Emeritus
  DIODORUS OF ALEXANDRIA
  IBRĀHĪM IBN SINĀN IBN
    THĀBIT IBN QURRA
  ABŪ SAHL WAYJAN IBN
    RUSTAM AL-QŪHĪ
  SHARAF AL-DĪN AL-MUẒAFFAR
    IBN MUḤAMMAD IBN AL-
    MUẒAFFAR AL-ṬŪSĪ

Carlo Bernardini
Università di Roma, La Sapienza,
Department of Physics
Professor Emeritus
  BRUNO TOUSCHEK

Sylvia Berryman
University of British Columbia,
Philosophy Department
Assistant Professor
  STRATO OF LAMPSACUS

Richard H. Beyler
Portland State University, History
Department
Associate Professor
  WALTER MAURICE ELSASSER
  ERNST PASCUAL JORDAN

John Bickle
University of Cincinnati, Department
of Philosophy and Neuroscience
Graduate Program
Head of Department, Professor
  ALAN HODGKIN
  ULF SVANTE VON EULER

Hinrich Biesterfeldt
University of Bochum, Seminar für
Orientalistik
Professor
  ABŪ BAKR MUḤAMMAD IBN
    ZAKARIYYĀ' AL-RĀZĪ

Norman Biggs
London School of Economics,
Department of Mathematics
Professor
  WILLIAM THOMAS TUTTE

Ken Binmore
University College of London,
Economics Department
Emeritus Professor
  JOHN FORBES NASH, JR.

Thomas Blass
University of Maryland, Baltimore
County, Department of Psychology

Professor
  STANLEY MILGRAM

Birger Blombäck
Karolinska Institutet, Solna, Sweden
Professor Emeritus
  PEHR VICTOR EDMAN

Marika Blondel-Mégrelis
Centre National de la Recherche
Scientifique, Paris, Institut d'Histoire
et Philosophie des Sciences et des
Techniques
Researcher (Retired)
  AUGUSTE LAURENT

Arthur L. Blumenthal
Graduate Faculty, The New School
Adjunct Professor
  WILHELM WUNDT

Stephen Bocking
Trent University, Environmental and
Resource Studies Program
Professor
  PIERRE MACKAY DANSEREAU
  CHARLES SUTHERLAND ELTON

Jim Bogen
University of Pittsburgh, Department
of HPS
Adjunct Professor
  BERNARD KATZ
  WILDER GRAVES PENFIELD

James J. Bohning
Lehigh University, Department of
Chemistry
Center for Emeritus Scientists in
Academic Research (CESAR) Fellow
  HERMAN F. MARK

Marvin Bolt
Adler Planetarium and Astronomy
Museum
Curator
  JOHN HERSCHEL

Mark Borrello
University of Minnesota, Program in
History of Science, Technology and
Medicine, Department of Ecology,
Evolution and Behavior
Assistant Professor
  PETR ALEKSEYVICH
    KROPOTKIN
  VERO COPNER WYNNE-
    EDWARDS

Soraya Boudia
Université Louis Pasteur (Strasbourg), Institut de recherches interdisciplinaires sur les sciences et la technologie
Associate Professor in History of Sciences
MARGUERITE CATHERINE PEREY

Joanne Bourgeois
University of Washington, Seattle, Department of Earth and Space Sciences
Professor
ROBERT SINCLAIR DIETZ

Jean-Pierre Bourguignon
Institut des Hautes Études Scientifiques, Centre National de la Recherche Scientifique
Director, Director of Research
ANDRÉ LICHNÉROWICZ

Peter J. Bowler
Queen's University, Belfast, School of History and Anthropology
Professor
CHARLES ROBERT DARWIN

Donald W. Boyd
University of Wyoming, Department of Geology and Geophysics
Emeritus Professor
NORMAN DENNIS NEWELL

Michael Bradie
Bowling Green State University, Department of Philosophy
Professor
EDMUND BRISCO FORD

Ronald Brashear
Chemical Heritage Foundation, Othmer Library
Director
HORACE WELCOME BABCOCK

Patrice Bret
Centre National de la Recherche Scientifique, Centre Alexandre Koyré, Centre de recherché en histoire des sciences et des techniques, Paris
Associate Researcher
MARIE GENEVIÈVE CHARLOTTE THIROUX D'ARCONVILLE
CLAUDINE PICARDET

Willam H. Brock
University of Leicester, Department of History
Emeritus Professor
THOMAS ARCHER HIRST
(FRIEDRICH) AUGUST KEKULE VON STRADONITZ
JUSTUS VON LIEBIG

Nathan Brooks
New Mexico State University, Department of History
Associate Professor
ALEKSANDR MIKHAILOVICH BUTLEROV
GEORGIĬ NIKOLAEVICH FLEROV
DMITRII IVANOVICH MENDELEEV

Richard E. Brown
Dalhousie University, Department of Psychology
Professor
DONALD HEBB

Theodore L. Brown
University of Illinois, Urbana-Champaign, Department of Chemistry and Beckman Institute
Professor Emeritus, Emeritus Director
ARNOLD ORVILLE BECKMAN

Rod Buchanan
University of Melbourne, Department of History and Philosophy of Science
Research Associate
HANS JÜRGEN EYSENCK

Hugh Buckingham
Louisiana State University, Department of Communication Sciences & Disorders
Professor
ALEXANDER ROMANOVICH LURIA

Bernd Buldt
Indiana University - Purdue University Fort Wayne, Department of Philosophy
Professor, Chair
PAUL RUDOLF CARNAP

David R. Bundle
University of Alberta, Department of Chemistry
Professor
RAYMOND URGEL LEMIEUX

Richard W. Burkhardt
University of Illinois at Urbana-Champaign, Department of History
Professor
WALLACE CRAIG
HENRY ELIOT HOWARD
JEAN-BAPTISTE LAMARCK
KONRAD ZACHARIAS LORENZ
MARGARET MORSE NICE

Charles Burnett
University of London, Warburg Institute
Professor
ADELARD OF BATH

Martha Cecilia Bustamante
Université Paris 7 Denis-Diderot, Laboratoire REHSEIS UMR CNRS 7596
Associate Researcher
GIUSEPPE OCCHIALINI

Heiderose Brandt Butscher
York University, Humanities Division, Arts Department
Lecturer
LORENZ OKEN

Charles W. Byers
University of Wisconsin, Madison, Department of Geology & Geophysics
Professor
LAURENCE LOUIS SLOSS

W. Malcolm Byrnes
Howard University College of Medicine, Department of Biochemistry and Molecular Biology
Assistant Professor
ERNEST EVERETT JUST

Gerhard C. Cadée
Royal Netherlands Institute for Sea Research
Researcher
LAMBERTUS MARIUS JOANNES URSINUS VAN STRAATEN

Joe Cain
University College London, Department of Science and Technology Studies
Senior Lecturer
ARTHUR JAMES CAIN

Jane Callander
DOROTHY ANNIE ELIZABETH GARROD

Werner Callebaut
Hasselt University, Belgium, Faculty of
Sciences, and Konrad Lorenz Institute
for Evolution and Cognition Research,
Austria
Professor, Scientific Manager
DONALD THOMAS CAMPBELL

Antoine Calvet
REVUE CHRYSOPIA (CNRS,
Centre d'Histoire des Sciences et des
Doctrines)
ARNALD OF VILLANOVA
(PSEUDO)
RAMON LULL

Laura Cameron
Queen's University, Ontario,
Department of Geography
Assistant Professor
SIR ARTHUR GEORGE
TANSLEY

Michele Camerota
University of Cagliari, Dipartimento
di Scienze Pedagogiche e Filosofiche
Professor
GIROLAMO BORRO
FRANCESCO BUONAMICI
GALILEO GALILEI

Martin Campbell-Kelly
University of Warwick, Department of
Computer Science
Professor
CHRISTOPHER STRACHEY

Stefano Caroti
University of Parma, Department of
Philosophy
Professor
BLASIUS OF PARMA
NICOLE ORESME

Albert V. Carozzi
University of Illinois, Urbana-
Champaign
Emeritus Professor
HORACE BÉNÉDICT DE
SAUSSURE

Alan B. Carr
Los Alamos National Laboratory
Historian
ROBERT BACHER
ROBERT SERBER

Jacqueline Carroy
École des Hautes Études en Sciences
Sociales, Centre Alexandre Koyré

d'Histoire des Sciences et des
Techniques, Paris
Director of Studies
PIERRE JANET

Cathryn Carson
University of California, Berkeley,
Department of History
Associate Professor
WOLFGANG PAULI

Christine Cole Catley
Cape Catley Ltd, Auckland, NZ
Publisher
BEATRICE TINSLEY

Marta Cavazza
University of Bologna, Department of
Philosophy
Associate Professor
LUIGI FERDINANDO MARSILI

Beate Ceranski
University of Stuttgart, Historisches
Institut, Geschichte der
Naturwissenschaften und Technik
Adjunct Professor
LAURA MARIA CATERINA
BASSI VERATI

Ku-Ming (Kevin) Chang
Academia Sinica, Institute of History
and Philology
Assistant Professor (Research Fellow)
GEORG ERNST STAHL

Michelle Chapront-Touzé
SYRTE, Observatoire de Paris, CNRS,
UPMC
Researcher
JEAN LE ROND D'ALEMBERT

François Chast
Hotel-Dieu Hospital, Paris,
Department of Toxicology, Pharmacy
and Pharmacology
Director
GERTRUDE BELLE ELION

John Robert Christianson
Luther College, Department of
History
Professor Emeritus
TYCHO BRAHE

Frederick B. Churchill
Indiana University, Bloomington,
Department of History and
Philosophy of Science

Professor Emeritus
AUGUST FRIEDRICH
WEISMANN

Eugene Cittadino
New York University, The Gallatin
School
Adjunct Professor
HENRY CHANDLER COWLES

George W. Clark
Massachusetts Institute of Technology,
Department of Physics
Professor Emeritus
BRUNO BENEDETTO ROSSI

Richard D. Clark
Millersville University, Department of
Earth Sciences
Professor, Chair
HANS ARNOLD PANOFSKY

Neil Clayton
University of Otago, Dunedin, New
Zealand
LEONARD COCKAYNE

Claudine Cohen
L'Ecole des Hautes Etudes en Sciences
Sociales, Paris
Maître de conférences
HENRI VICTOR VALLOIS

Clive Cohen
Imperial College, London, Centre for
the History of Science, Technology
and Medicine
Honorary Research Associate
WARREN KENDALL LEWIS

Alan Collins
Lancaster University, Department of
Psychology
Doctor
FREDERIC CHARLES BARTLETT

Andrew M. Colman
University of Leicester, School of
Psychology
Professor
AMOS TVERSKY

Nathaniel Comfort
Johns Hopkins University,
Department of History of Medicine
Associate Professor
BARBARA MCCLINTOCK

Roger Cooke
University of Vermont
Professor Emeritus
SOFYA VASILYEVNA
KOVALEVSKAYA

Edgar E. Coons
New York University, Department of
Psychology
Professor
NEAL ELGAR MILLER

Leo Corry
Tel Aviv University, Cohn Institute for
History and Philosophy of Science and
Ideas
Director
NICOLAS BOURBAKI

Carl F. Craver
Washington University, St. Louis,
Philosophy-Neuroscience-Psychology
Program
Associate Professor
JULIUS AXELROD

Angela N. H. Creager
Princeton University, Department of
History
Professor
CHRISTIAN B. ANFINSEN

Robert P. Crease
Stony Brook University, Department
of Philosophy
Professor, Chair
MILTON STANLEY
LIVINGSTON

Julie Roberta Cribb
UHl Millenium Institute, Learning
and Information Services Department
Development Programmes Manager
NIKOLAY SERGEYEVICH
SHATSKIY

Eileen Crist
Virginia Tech, Department of Science
and Technology in Society
Associate Professor
DONALD REDFIELD GRIFFIN

Paul Croce
Stetson University, Program in
American Studies
Professor
WILLIAM JAMES

Maurice Crosland
University of Kent, School of History
Professor Emeritus
JEAN-BAPTISTE-ANDRE
DUMAS
CLAUDE LOUIS BERTHOLLET

James F. Crow
University of Wisconsin, Madison,
Laboratory of Genetics
Professor Emeritus
MOTOO KIMURA

Mary Cubitt
University of Warwick, Department of
Computer Science
Honorary Research Fellow
DOUGLAS RAYNER HARTREE
JAMES HARDY WILKINSON

Gregory T. Cushman
University of Kansas, Department of
History
Assistant Professor
JEROME NAMIAS
BENITO VIÑES

Per Dahl
Lawrence Berkeley National
Laboratory
Retired Physicist and Visiting Scientist
GREGORY BREIT

Gianni Dal Maso
International School for Advanced
Studies, Trieste, Functional Analysis
Sector
Research Staff
ENNIO DE GIORGI

Andrew I. Dale
University of KwaZulu-Natal, School
of Statistics and Actuarial Science
Professor Emeritus
THOMAS BAYES

Dane T. Daniel
Wright State University, Lake Campus
Assistant Professor
THEOPHRASTUS PHILIPPUS
AUREOLUS BOMBASTUS VON
HOHENHEIM PARACELSUS

Joseph Dauben
City University of New York, Herbert
H. Lehman College, Department of
History; The Graduate Center, Ph.D.
Program in History
Professor

GEORG FERDINAND LUDWIG
CANTOR

Keay Davidson
San Francisco Chronicle
Science Writer
CARL EDWARD SAGAN

Martin Davis
New York University, University of
California, Berkeley
Professor Emeritus, Visiting Scholar
JULIA BOWMAN ROBINSON

Deborah Day
University of California, San Diego,
Scripps Institution of Oceanography
Archives
Archivist
ROGER RANDALL DOUGAN
REVELLE

Soraya de Chadarevian
University of California, Los Angeles,
Department of History, Center for
Society and Genetics
Professor
MAX FERDINAND PERUTZ

Alexis De Greiff A.
Universidad Nacional de Colombia,
Departmento de Sociología/Centro de
Estudios Sociales, Bogotá
Associate Professor
MUHAMMAD ABDUS SALAM

Peter Dear
Cornell University, Departments of
History and Science and Technology
Studies
Professor
NICCOLÒ CABEO

Jacek Dębiec
New York University, Center for
Neural Science; New York University
School of Medicine, Department of
Psychiatry
Researcher, Trainer
JAMES WENCESLAS PAPEZ

Ute Deichmann
University of Cologne Institute for
Genetics, Leo Baeck Institute London
Research Group Leader, Research
Professor
ERNST DAVID BERGMANN
CARL ALEXANDER NEUBERG

Robert J. Deltete
Seattle University, Philosophy
Department
Professor
    FRIEDRICH WILHELM
        OSTWALD

S. Demidov
S.I. Vavilov Institute for the History of
Science and Technology of the Russian
Academy of Sciences; M. V.
Lomonosov Moscow State University
Director; Professor
    LEV SEMIONOVICH
        PONTRYAGIN
    I. M. VINOGRADOV

Adrian Desmond
University College London,
Department of Biology
Honorary Research Fellow
    THOMAS HENRY HUXLEY

David C. Devonis
Graceland University, Department of
Psychology
Professor
    PAUL EVERETT MEEHL

Melanie DeVore
Georgia College & State University,
Department of Biological &
Environmental Sciences
Associate Professor
    ARTHUR CRONQUIST

David H. DeVorkin
National Air and Space Museum,
Smithsonian Institution, Division of
Space History, History of Astronomy
and the Space Sciences
Senior Curator
    HERBERT FRIEDMAN
    DONALD HOWARD MENZEL
    MARTIN SCHWARZSCHILD
    LYMAN SPITZER, JR.
    RICHARD TOUSEY
    JAMES A. VAN ALLEN
    JAMES A. WESTPHAL
    FRED LAWRENCE WHIPPLE

Donald A. Dewsbury
University of Florida, Department of
Psychology
Professor Emeritus
    FRANK AMBROSE BEACH, JR.

Marie A. DiBerardino
Drexel University, College of Medicine

Professor Emeritus
    ROBERT W. BRIGGS

Michael R. Dietrich
Dartmouth College, Department of
Biological Sciences
Associate Professor
    JOHANNES HOLTFRETER
    MOTOO KIMURA

Igor S. Dmitriev
D. I. Mendeleev Museum and
Archives, St. Petersburg State
University
    ALEKSANDR NIKOLAEVICH
        NESMEJANOV

Ronald E. Doel
Oregon State University, Department
of History and Department of
Geosciences
Associate Professor
    MARION KING HUBBERT
    GERARD PETER KUIPER
    MARIE THARP

Aude Doody
University College Dublin, School of
Classics
Lecturer
    PLINY THE ELDER

R. H. Drent
University of Groningen, Dierecologie
Center for Ecological and
Evolutionary Studies
Professor
    GERARD PIETER BAERENDS

Steffen Ducheyne
Ghent University, Centre for Logic
and Philosophy of Science, Centre for
History of Science
Member, Doctor
    JOHANNES BAPTISTA VAN
        HELMONT

Michael Eckert
Deutsches Museum, Munich
Researcher
    ARNOLD JOHANNES WILHELM
        SOMMERFELD

Matthew D. Eddy
Durham University, Department of
Philosophy
Lecturer
    WILLIAM CULLEN
    JOHN WALKER

Ellery Eells
University of Wisconsin, Madison
Professor Emeritus, deceased
    ROBERT NOZICK

Frank N. Egerton
University of Wisconsin, Parkside,
Department of History
Professor Emeritus
    ARTHUR DAVIS HASLER
    AUGUST FRIEDRICH
        THIENEMANN

Jean Eisenstaedt
Observatoire de Paris, Centre National
de la Recherche Scientifique
Research Director
    ROBERT BLAIR

Ernest L. Eliel
University of North Carolina at
Chapel Hill, Department of
Chemistry
Professor Emeritus
    VLADIMIR PRELOG

Alan C. Elms
University of California, Davis,
Psychology Department
Professor Emeritus
    ERIK HOMBURGER ERIKSON

Stefan Emeis
Forschungszentrum Karlsruhe GmbH,
Institute of Meteorology and Climate
Research, Atmospheric Environmental
Research, University of Cologne
Adjunct Professor, Lecturer
    RICHARD ASSMANN

Irving R. Epstein
Brandeis University, Department of
Chemistry and Volen Center for
Complex Systems
Professor
    ILYA PRIGOGINE

Germana Ernst
Università di Roma Tre, Italy,
Department of Philosophy
Professor
    TOMMASO CAMPANELLA

Andrea Falcon
Concordia University, Montreal,
Department of Philosophy
Assistant Professor
    PLATO
    XENARCHUS

İhsan Fazlioğlu
Istanbul University, Department of
Philosophy
Associate Professor
ALI AL-QŪSHJĪ (ABŪ AL-
QĀSIM ALĀʾ AL-DĪN ALĪ
IBN MUHAMMAD QUSHJĪ-
ZĀDE)

Anne Fellinger
Université Louis Pasteur (Strasbourg),
Institut de recherches
interdisciplinaires sur les sciences et la
technologie
MARGUERITE CATHERINE
PEREY

Giovanni Ferraro
University of Molise, Faculty of
Mathematical, Physical and Natural
Sciences
Professor
LEONHARD EULER

Paula Findlen
Stanford University, Department of
History
Professor
ATHANASIUS KIRCHER

James Fleming
Colby College, Science, Technology,
and Society Program
Professor
GUY STEWART CALLENDAR

Pedro Navarro Floria
Consejo Nacional de Investigaciones
Científicas y Técnicas (CONICET),
Argentina
HERMANN KARL KONRAD
BURMEISTER

George W. Ford
University of Michigan, Department
of Physics
Professor Emeritus
GEORGE UHLENBECK

John Forrester
University of Cambridge, Department
of History and Philosophy of the
Sciences
Professor
SIGMUND FREUD

Marye Anne Fox
University of California, San Diego,
Department of Chemistry and
Biochemistry

Chancellor
MICHAEL J. S. DEWAR

Tibor Frank
LEO SZILARD

Henry Frankel
University of Missouri at Kansas City,
Department of Philosophy
Professor
ALLAN VERNE COX
JAN HOSPERS
JOHN TUZO WILSON

Craig Fraser
University of Toronto, Institute for the
History and Philosophy of Science and
Technology
Historian
AUGUSTIN-LOUIS CAUCHY

David W. Frayer
University of Kansas, Anthropology
Department
Professor
DRAGUTIN (KARL)
GORJANOVIĆ-KRAMBERGER
JAN JELÍNEK

Lucio Fregonese
University of Pavia, Department of
Physics, Museo per la Storia
Associate Professor, Scientific
Consultant
ALESSANDRO GIUSEPPE
ANTONIO ANASTASIO VOLTA

Anthony P. French
Massachusetts Institute of Technology,
Department of Physics
Professor Emeritus
PHILIP MORRISON

Robert Marc Friedman
University of Oslo, Department of
History
Professor
TOR HAROLD PERCIVAL
BERGERON
VILHELM BJERKNES

Bernhard Fritscher
University of Munich, Institute for the
History of Science
Adjunct Professor
OTTO AMPFERER
ARTHUR LOUIS DAY
ALFRED FERDINAND
RITTMANN

Iris Fry
Tel Aviv University, The Cohn
Institute for the History and
Philosophy of Science and Ideas
Doctor
STANLEY LLOYD MILLER

Yasu Furukawa
Nihon University, College of
Bioresource Sciences
Professor
WALLACE HUME CAROTHERS
ICHIRO SAKURADA

Louis Galambos
Johns Hopkins University,
Department of History, and the
Institute for Applied Economics and
the Study of Business Enterprise
Professor
KARL AUGUST FOLKERS

George Gale
University of Missouri, Kansas City,
Department of Philosophy
Professor
WILLIAM HUNTER MCCREA

Enrico Gamba
GUIDOBALDO, MARCHESE DEL
MONTE

Daniel Garber
Princeton University, Department of
Philosophy
Professor, Chair
RENÉ DU PERRON DESCARTES

Derek Gatherer
Medical Research Council Virology
Unit, Institute of Virology, University
of Glasgow
Senior Computer Officer
WALTER MAURICE ELSASSER

Jean Gaudant
Comité français d'Histoire de la
Géologie
Vice President, Secretary
JEAN PIVETEAU

Jean-Paul Gaudillière
CERMES, Institut National de la
Santé et de la Recherche Médicale
Senior Researcher
ADOLF FRIEDRICH JOHANN
BUTENANDT

Kostas Gavroglu
University of Athens, Department of
History and Philosophy of Science
Professor
　FELIX BLOCH

Clayton A. Gearhart
College of St. Benedict/St. John's
University, Department of Physics
Professor
　MAX PLANCK

Enrico R. A. Giannetto
University of Bergamo, Dipartimento
di Science della Persona
Professor
　GIORDANO BRUNO

Philip D. Gingerich
University of Michigan, Department
of Geological Sciences, Museum of
Paleontology
Professor, Director
　GEORGE GAYLORD SIMPSON

Owen Gingerich
Harvard University, Harvard-
Smithsonion Center for Astrophysics
Professor Emeritus
　CECILIA HELENA PAYNE-
　　GAPOSCHKIN

Sander Gliboff
Indiana University, Department of
History and Philosophy of Science
Assistant Professor
　HEINRICH GEORG BRONN
　PAUL KAMMERER

Stephen Glickman
University of California, Berkeley,
Department of Psychology
Professor
　DONALD HEBB

André Goddu
Stonehill College, Department of
Physics and Astronomy
Professor
　NICHOLAS COPERNICUS
　WILLIAM OF OCKHAM

Hubert Goenner
Universität Göttingen, Institute for
Theoretical Physics
Professor Emeritus
　OTTO HERMANN LEOPOLD
　HECKMANN

Jan Golinski
University of New Hampshire,
Department of History
Professor, Chair
　JANE HALDIMAND MARCET

José María Gondra
University of the Basque Country,
Department of Basic Psychological
Processes
　CLARK LEONARD HULL

Gregory A. Good
West Virginia University, Department
of History
Associate Professor
　STANLEY KEITH RUNCORN

Graeme Gooday
University of Leeds, Department of
Philosophy, Division of History and
Philosophy of Science
Senior Lecturer
　GEORGE CAREY FOSTER

Matthew R. Goodrum
Virginia Tech, Department of Science
and Technology in Society
Visiting Assistant Professor
　CARLETON STEVENS COON
　JOHN DESMOND CLARK
　RAYMOND ARTHUR DART

David L. Goodstein
California Institute of Technology
Vice Provost, Professor of Physics and
Applied Physics
　CARL DAVID ANDERSON
　WILLIAM A. FOWLER

Judith Johns Goodstein
California Institute of Technology
Faculty Associate
　CARL DAVID ANDERSON
　WILLIAM A. FOWLER

Gennady Gorelik
Boston University, Center for
Philosophy and History of Science
Research Fellow
　ANDREI DMITRIYEVICH
　　SAKHAROV

Leon Gortler
Brooklyn College of the City
University of New York, Department
of Chemistry
Professor Emeritus
　HERBERT CHARLES BROWN
　LOUIS PLACK HAMMETT

Constantin Goschler
Ruhr-University, Bochum
Professor
　RUDOLF CARL VIRCHOW

Jeremy Gray
The Open University, Department of
Mathematics
Professor
　LARS AHLFORS
　PAUL ERDOS
　DAVID HILBERT
　KUNIHIKO KODAIRA
　MARSTON MORSE
　ANTONI ZYGMUND

David H. Green
The Australian National University,
Research School of Earth Sciences
Professor Emeritus
　ALFRED EDWARD RINGWOOD

Mott T. Greene
University of Puget Sound, Honors
Program, Program in Science,
Technology and Society
Professor
　WLADIMIR PETER KÖPPEN
　ALFRED LOTHAR WEGENER

David A. Grier
George Washington University, Elliott
School of International Affairs
Associate Professor, Associate Dean
　CHARLES BABBAGE
　ADA AUGUSTA KING,
　　COUNTESS OF LOVELACE

William P. Griffith
Imperial College London, Department
of Chemistry
Senior Research Investigator
　SIR GEOFFREY WILKINSON

Tom Griffiths
Australian National University,
Canberra, Research School of Social
Sciences
Professor of History
　FRANCIS NOBLE RATCLIFFE

Shi-jie Guo
The Institute for the History of
Natural Science
　HOU TE-PANG (DEBANG
　　HOU)

Jeremiah Hackett
University of South Carolina,
Department of Philosophy
Professor, Chair
ROGER BACON

Petr Hadrava
Astronomical Institute, Academy of
Sciences of the Czech Republic,
Department of Galaxies and Planetary
Systems
Researcher
CRISTANNUS DE PRACHATICZ

Alena Hadravová
Institute for Contemporary History,
Academy of Sciences of the Czech
Republic, Department for the History
of Science
Researcher
CRISTANNUS DE PRACHATICZ

Jürgen Haffer
A. Koenig Zoological Research
Institute and Zoological Museum,
Section of Biology and Phylogeny of
Tropical Birds
Research Associate
ERNST WALTER MAYR

Joel B. Hagen
Radford University, Biology
Department
Professor
WARDER CLYDE ALLEE
FREDERIC EDWARD CLEMENTS
HOWARD THOMAS ODUM
EUGENE PLEASANTS ODUM

Alan Hájek
The Australian National University,
Philosophy Program, Research School
of Social Sciences
Professor
DAVID LEWIS

Karl Hall
Central European University,
Budapest, History Department
Assistant Professor
ARKADY BENEDIKTOVICH
MIGDAL

Brian K. Hall
Dalhousie University, Department of
Biology
University Research Professor
Emeritus
CONRAD HAL WADDINGTON

Jacob Darwin Hamblin
Clemson University, Department of
History
Assistant Professor
GEORGE EDWARD RAVEN
DEACON
KONSTANTIN NIKOLAYEVICH
FEDOROV

Richard Hamblyn
University of Nottingham, School of
Geography
Postdoctoral Research Fellow
LUKE HOWARD

Thomas L. Hankins
University of Washington,
Department of History
Professor Emeritus
WILLIAM ROWAN HAMILTON

R. J. Hankinson
University of Texas at Austin,
Department of Philosophy
Professor
GALEN

Peter Hannaford
Swinburne University of Technology,
Centre for Atom Optics and Ultrafast
Spectroscopy
Professor, Director
ALAN WALSH

Valerie Gray Hardcastle
University of Cincinnati, McMicken
College of Arts and Sciences
Dean
PATRICIA SHOER GOLDMAN-
RAKIC
WALTER RUDOLF HESS
HEINRICH KLÜVER
DAVID COURTNAY MARR

Russell Hardin
New York University, Department of
Politics
Professor
MANCUR OLSON, JR.

Kristine C. Harper
New Mexico Institute of Mining and
Technology, Socorro
Assistant Professor
JULE GREGORY CHARNEY
JOSEPH SMAGORINSKY
MARIE THARP

Geoffrey Harper
Royal Botanic Garden Edinburgh
Research Associate
VLADIMIR VLADIMIROVICH
STANCHINSKIY

Ronald Harstad
University of Missouri, Columbia
J. Rhoads Foster Professor of
Economics
WILLIAM SPENCER VICKREY

Harry Heft
Denison University, Department of
Psychology
Professor of Psychology
JAMES JEROME GIBSON

Colin Hempstead
University of Teesside, Middlesbrough,
UK, School of Arts and Media
Reader (Retired)
SIR RUDOLF ERNEST PEIERLS
SIR ALAN HERRIES WILSON

Pamela M. Henson
Smithsonian Institution Archives
Institutional History Division
Director
ALFRED EDWARDS EMERSON

Klaus Hentschel
University of Stuttgart, History of
Science & Technology, Historical
Institute
Professor
ALBRECHT OTTO JOHANNES
UNSÖLD

Christine Hertler
Johann Wolfgang Goethe University,
Biosciences
Faculty
GUSTAV HEINRICH RALPH
VON KOENIGSWALD
FRANZ WEIDENREICH

Norriss Hetherington
University of California, Berkeley,
Office for History of Science and
Technology
Visiting Scholar
GEORGE CUNLIFFE MCVITTIE
IOSIF SAMUILOVICH
SHKLOVSKII

Gerhard Heywang
Bayer Industry Services, Leverkusen
OTTO GEORG WILHELM
BAYER

Ellen McNiven Hine
York University, Humanities and
Women's Studies
Professor Emerita
JEAN-JACQUES DORTOUS DE
MAIRAN

Nigel J. Hitchin
Oxford University, Mathematical
Institute
Professor
SHIING-SHEN CHERN

Lillian Hoddeson
University of Illiniois at Urbana-
Champaign, Department of History
Professor
JOHN BARDEEN
ROBERT RATHBUN WILSON

Darleane C. Hoffman
University of California, Berkeley,
Department of Chemistry and
Lawrence Berkeley National
Laboratory
Professor
GLENN THEODORE SEABORG

Dieter Hoffmann
Max Planck Institute for the History
of Science
Research Scholar
MAX PLANCK

Charles H. Holbrow
Colgate University, Department of
Physics and Astronomy
Professor Emeritus
CHARLES CHRISTIAN
LAURITSEN

Ernst Homburg
Universiteit Maastricht, Department
of History
Professor
JOHANNES MARTIN BIJVOET
JAN HENDRIK DE BOER
DIRK WILLEM VAN KREVELEN

R. W. Home
University of Melbourne
Professor Emeritus
FERDINAND JAKOB HEINRICH
VON MUELLER

Annie Hor
California State University, Stanislaus
Acquisitions Librarian
PEI WENZHONG

Michael Hoskin
Churchill College, Cambridge, St.
Edmund's College, Cambridge
Fellow, Emeritus Fellow
CAROLINE LUCRETIA
HERSCHEL
WILLIAM HERSCHEL

Richard Howarth
University College London,
Department of Earth Sciences
Honorary Professor
HAROLD JEFFREYS

Wolfgang Hübner
University of Münster, Department of
Classical Philology
Professor
VETTIUS VALENS

Karl Hufbauer
University of California, Irvine,
Department of History
Professor Emeritus
BENGT EDLÉN

David L. Hull
Northwestern University, Department
of Philosophy
Professor Emeritus
STEPHEN JAY GOULD

Paul Humphreys
University of Virginia, Department of
Philosophy
Professor
ANDREI NIKOLAEVICH
KOLMOGOROV

Michael Hunter
University of London, Birkbeck
College, School of History, Classics
and Archaeology
Professor of History
ROBERT BOYLE

Graeme K. Hunter
University of Western Ontario,
Schulich School of Medicine and
Dentistry
Professor
DOROTHY MARY CROWFOOT
HODGKIN
MICHAEL SMITH

Sarah Hutton
University of Wales, Aberystwyth,
Department of English
Professor
ANNE CONWAY

P. K. Ingle
National Chemical Laboratory, Pune,
Publication and Science
Communication Unit
Scientist
KRISHNASAMI VENKATARAMAN

Bruna Ingrao
Università di Roma, Department of
Economics
Professor
VILFREDO PARETO

Brad Inwood
University of Toronto, Departments of
Classics and Philosophy
Professor
CHRYSIPPUS

Gürol Irzik
Bogazici University, Department of
Philosophy
Professor
THOMAS SAMUEL KUHN

Konstantin Ivanov
Tula State Pedagogical University,
Russia, Department of Theoretical
Physics
Dotsent
MSTISLAV VSEVOLODOVICH
KELDYSH

Roman Jackiw
Massachusetts Institute of Technology
Professor
JOHN S. BELL

Lothar Jaenicke
University of Cologne, Institute of
Biochemistry
Professor Emeritus
FRITZ ALBERT LIPMANN

Frank A. J. L. James
The Royal Institution, London
Professor
HUMPHREY DAVY
GEORGE PORTER

Michel Janssen
University of Minnesota, School of
Physics and Astronomy
Associate Professor
  HENDRIK ANTOON LORENTZ

Yang Jing-Yi
Institute for History of Natural
Sciences, Chinese Academy of Sciences
Professor
  HUANG JIQING (TE-KAN)

Jeffrey Allan Johnson
Villanova University, Department of
History
Professor
  FRITZ HABER

Sean F. Johnston
University of Glasgow
Reader
  GERHARD HERZBERG

Alexander Jones
University of Toronto, Department of
Classics
Professor
  APOLLINIARIUS
  HIPPARCHUS
  LEPTINES
  MARINUS OF TYRE
  PTOLEMY
  TIMOCHARIS

Paul Josephson
Colby College, Department of History
Associate Professor
  GERSH ITSKOVICH BUDKER
  PETR LEONIDOVICH KAPITSA

Jim Joyce
University of Michigan, Department
of Philosophy
Professor, Chair
  RICHARD CARL JEFFREY

Michael Kaasch
German Academy of Sciences
Leopoldina, Halle
Editor
  EMIL ABDERHALDEN

David Kaiser
Massachusetts Institute of Technology,
Program in Science, Technology, and
Society
Associate Professor
  RICHARD PHILLIPS FEYNMAN

VICTOR FREDERICK
  WEISSKOPF

Masanori Kaji
Tokyo Institute of Technology,
Graduate School of Decision Science
and Technology
Associate Professor
  TETSUO NOZOE

Andreas Karachalios
Mainz University, Institute for History
of Mathematics and Natural Sciences
Lecturer
  ERICH ARMAND ARTHUR
  HÜCKEL

Shaul Katzir
Leo Baeck Institute, London/Tel Aviv
University, The Cohn Institute for the
History and Philosophy of Science and
Ideas
Research Fellow
  WOLDEMAR VOIGT

George B. Kauffman
California State University, Fresno,
Department of Chemistry
Professor Emeritus
  WILLARD FRANK LIBBY
  AXEL CHRISTIAN KLIXBÜLL
  JØRGENSEN

Keiko Kawashima
Omohi College, Nagoya Institute of
Technology
Associate Professor
  MARIE-ANNE-PIERETTE
  PAULZE-LAVOISIER

Sean P. Keating
University of Cincinnati, Department
of Philosophy
  ALAN HODGKIN

Brian L. Keeley
Pitzer College, Philosophy, and
Science, Technology & Society Field
Groups
Associate Professor
  THEODORE HOLMES
  BULLOCK

Drew Keeling
University of Zurich, Department of
History
Instructor
  CHARLES DAVID KEELING

Ken Kellerman
National Radio Astronomy
Observatory; University of Virginia,
Astronomy Department
Senior Scientist, Research Professor
  JOHN GATENBY BOLTON

Diana E. Kenney
Marine Biological Laboratory at
Woods Hole
Science Writer
  GEORGE WALD

Michael Kessler
Museum of Pharmacy at the
University of Basel, Switzerland
  TADEUS REICHSTEIN

Daniel J. Kevles
Yale University
Professor
  MAX LUDWIG HENNING
  DELBRÜCK

Yoshiyuki Kikuchi
The Graduate University for Advanced
Studies, Sokendai, Hayama Center for
Advanced Studies
Researcher
  SAN-ICHIRO MIZUSHIMA

Helen King
University of Reading, Department of
Classics
Professor, Head of Department
  HIPPOCRATES OF COS

John A. Kington
University of East Anglia, Climatic
Research Unit, School of
Environmental Sciences
Visiting Fellow
  HUBERT HORACE LAMB

Chigusa Ishikawa Kita
Kansai University, Faculty of
Informatics
Associate Professor
  JOSEPH CARL ROBNETT
  LICKLIDER

Tinne Hoff Kjeldsen
Roskilde University, IMFUFA,
Department of Science, Systems, and
Models
Associate Professor
  ALBERT WILLIAM TUCKER

Matthew Klingle
Bowdoin College, Department of
History and Environmental Studies
Program
Assistant Professor
WALLIS THOMAS
EDMONDSON

David Knight
Durham University, Department of
Philosophy
Professor
JAMES FINLAY WEIR
JOHNSTON

Charles M. Knobler
University of California, Los Angeles,
Department of Chemistry and
Biochemistry
Professor Emeritus
RICHARD BARRY BERNSTEIN

Alexei Kojevnikov
University of British Columbia,
Department of History
Associate Professor
NIKOLAI NIKOLAEVICH
BOGOLUBOV
PAVEL ALEKSEYEVICH
CHERENKOV

Adrienne W. Kolb
Fermi National Accelerator Laboratory
Archivist
ROBERT RATHBUN WILSON

Klaus Peter Köpping
University of Heidelberg, Institut für
Ethnologie
Professor Emeritus
ADOLF BASTIAN

Gerhard Kortum
Geographical Institute of the Christian
Albrechts University of Kiel
GEORG WÜST

Russell D. Kosits
Redeemer University College,
Department of Psychology
Professor
WILLIAM BENJAMIN
CARPENTER

A. J. Kox
University of Amsterdam, Institute for
Theoretical Physics
Professor

HENDRIK BRUGT GERHARD
CASIMIR
HENDRIK ANTOON LORENTZ

Helge Kragh
University of Aarhus, Steno
Department for Studies of Science and
Science Education
Professor
HERMANN BONDI
WILLEM DE SITTER

Regina A. Kressley
Johann Wolfgang Goethe-University,
Department of Developmental
Psychology
Scientific Staff
MATHILDE CARMEN HERTZ

Henri Krop
Erasmus University, Rotterdam
Tenured Lecturer
FRANK PIETERSZOON
BURGERSDIJK

Hans Kruuk
University of Aberdeen, School of
Biological Sciences
Honorary Professor
NIKOLAAS TINBERGEN

Radha Kumar
Jamia Millia Islamia, New Delhi,
Nelson Mandela Centre for Peace and
Conflict Resolution
Professor, Director
KRISHNASAMI VENKATARAMAN

Jan Lacki
University of Geneva, School of
Physics, History and Philosophy of
Science
Lecturer, Researcher
LOUIS (VICTOR PIERRE
RAYMOND) BROGLIE

James T. Lamiell
Georgetown University, Department
of Psychology
Professor
LOUIS WILLIAM STERN

Hannah Landecker
Rice University, Department of
Anthropology
Assistant Professor
EDMUND VINCENT COWDRY

Y. Tzvi Langermann
Bar-Ilan University, Department of
Arabic
Professor
RABBI MOSES BEN MAIMON
MAIMONIDES

Pierre Laszlo
University of Liège and École
Polytechnique, Palaiseau
Professor Emeritus
EDGAR LEDERER
DONALD J. CRAM

James M. Lattis
University of Wisconsin, Madison,
Department of Astronomy
Director, UW Space Place
CHRISTOPH CLAVIUS

Roger D. Launius
National Air and Space Museum,
Smithsonian Institution
Curator
HOMER EDWARD NEWELL JR.
GERALD ALAN SOFFEN

Goulven Laurent
Comité Français d'Histoire de la
Géologie; l'Académie Internationale
d'Histoire des Sciences et des
Techniques
Science Historian, Vice President
ETIENNE GEOFFROY SAINT-
HILAIRE

F. W. Lawvere
University at Buffalo, Department of
Mathematics
Professor Emeritus
SAUNDERS MAC LANE

Homer E. Le Grand
Monash University, Department of
Philosophy and Bioethics
Professor
SAMUEL WARREN CAREY

David E. Leary
University of Richmond
Professor
ERNEST ROPIEQUET HILGARD

Joseph LeDoux
New York University, Center for
Neural Science
Professor, Director
JAMES WENCESLAS PAPEZ

William H. K. Lee
U. S. Geological Survey
Emeritus Scientist
  KEIITI AKI

G. Jeffery Leigh
University of Sussex, Department of
Chemistry
Professor Emeritus
  JOSEPH CHATT

James Lennox
University of Pittsburgh, Department
of History and Philosophy of Science
Professor
  ARISTOTLE

Walter Lenz
University of Hamburg, Institute of
Oceanography
Oceanographer
  PAUL GERHARD SCHOTT

Mark Lepper
Stanford University, Department of
Psychology
Professor
  ROBERT PAUL ABELSON

Elena S. Levina
Russian Academy of Sciences, S.I.
Vavilov Institute for the History of
Science & Technology
Professor
  YURY ANATOLYEVICH
  OVCHINNIKOV

Raphael D. Levine
University of California, Los Angeles,
Department of Chemistry and
Biochemistry
Professor
  RICHARD BARRY BERNSTEIN

David H. Levy
Jarnac Observatory
Astronomer
  BARTHOLOMEUS (BART) JAN
  BOK
  EUGENE MERLE SHOEMAKER

Ruth Prelowski Liebowitz
U.S. Air Force Electronic Systems
Center, Hanscom Air Force Base,
Massachusetts
Chief, ESC History Office
  HELMUT ERICH LANDSBERG

Mary Susan Lindee
University of Pennsylvania,
Department of History and Sociology
of Science
Professor
  JAMES VAN GUNDIA NEEL

Richard A. Littman
University of Oregon, Department of
Psychology
Professor Emeritus
  JOHN BROADUS WATSON

Maiken Lykke Lolck
University of Aarhus, Steno
Department for Studies of Science and
Science Education
PhD Student
  INGE LEHMANN

Malcolm S. Longair
University of Cambridge, Astrophysics
Group, Cavendish Laboratory
Professor
  MARTIN RYLE

Pierre Lory
Sorbonne, École Pratique des Hautes
Etudes, Section des Sciences
Religieuses
Director of Studies
  JĀBIR IBN HAYYĀN

Cornelia Lüdecke
University of Hamburg, Centre for
History of Natural Sciences,
Mathematics, and Technology
Privatdozent
  SOPHIE C(H)ARLOTTE
  JULIANE MOELLER

A. J. Lustig
University of Texas, Austin,
Department of History
Assistant Professor
  WILLIAM DONALD HAMILTON

Christoph Lüthy
Radboud University Nijmegen,
Faculty of Philosophy and Faculty of
the Sciences
Professor
  SÉBASTIEN BASSON (BASSO)
  DAVID GORLAEUS

John M. Lynch
Arizona State University, Barrett
Honors College

Honors Faculty Fellow
  PETER BRIAN MEDAWAR

Kirk Allen Maasch
University of Maine, Climate Change
Institute and Department of Earth
Sciences
Professor
  BARRY SALTZMAN

Ian Maclean
University of Oxford, All Souls
College, Faculty of History
Professor
  GIROLAMO CARDANO
  PETER RAMUS

Brenda Maddox
Journalist
  ROSALIND ELSIE FRANKLIN

Kazuaki Maenaka
Hanazono University, Faculty of
Letters
Professor
  MATUYAMA MOTONORI

Jane Maienschein
Arizona State University, School of
Life Sciences, Center for Biology and
Society
Professor
  THOMAS HUNT MORGAN

Patrick S. Market
University of Missouri, Columbia,
Department of Soil, Environmental
and Atmospheric Sciences
Associate Professor
  BERNHARD HAURWITZ

Gerald Markowitz
City University of New York, John Jay
College, Interdisciplinary Studies
Program
Professor
  KENNETH AND MAMIE CLARK

Ben Marsden
University of Aberdeen, Department
of History
Lecturer
  JOHN AITKEN

Ursula B. Marvin
Harvard-Smithsonian Center for
Astrophysics

Senior Geologist Emeritus
DIMITRI SERGEYEVICH
KORZHINSKII

J. N. Mather
Princeton University, Department of
Mathematics
Professor
JÜRGEN K. MOSER

Christina Matta
University of Wisconsin, Madison,
Department of the History of Science
SIMON SCHWENDENER

Jean Mawhin
University of Louvain, Department of
Mathematics
Professor
JEAN LERAY

J. P. May
University of Chicago, Department of
Mathematics
Professor
JOHN FRANK ADAMS

Innocenzo Mazzini
University of Macerata
CORNELIUS CELSUS

Massimo Mazzotti
University of Exeter, Department of
Sociology and Philosophy
Lecturer
MARIA GAETANA AGNESI

Charles McCarty
Indiana University, The Logic Program
Professor
ALFRED TARSKI

John McCleary
Vassar College, Department of
Mathematics
Professor
HASSLER WHITNEY

W. Patrick McCray
University of California, Santa
Barbara, Department of History
Professor
LEO GOLDBERG
JESSE LEONARD GREENSTEIN

Robert McCutcheon
Independent Scholar
VIKTOR AMAZASPOVICH
AMBARTSUMIAN

Colin McLarty
Case Western Reserve University,
Department of Philosophy
Chair
GARRETT BIRKHOFF
CLAUDE CHEVALLEY
JEAN DIEUDONNÉ
SAUNDERS MAC LANE
ANDRÉ WEIL

Michael McVaugh
University of North Carolina,
Department of History
Professor Emeritus
ARNALD OF VILLANOVA

Roger Meade
Los Alamos National Laboratory
Archivist
ROBERT SERBER

Christoph Meinel
University of Regensburg, Institute of
Philosophy
Professor
JOACHIM JUNGIUS

Michèle Mertens
University of Liège, Département des
Sciences de l'Antiquité
Conservator
ZOSIMOS OF PANOPOLIS

Ad Meskens
Departement Bedrijfskunde,
Lerarenopleiding en Sociaal Werk
MICHIEL COIGNET

Josef Michl
University of Colorado, Department
of Chemistry and Biochemistry
Professor
MICHAEL J. S. DEWAR

Ronald Mickens
Clark Atlanta University, Physics
Department
Professor
ELMER SAMUEL IMES

Heikki Mikkeli
University of Helsinki, Renvall
Institute for European Area and
Cultural Studies
Docent, Researcher
JACOPO (GIACOMO)
ZABARELLA

Hans Mikosch
Technical University Vienna, Institut
für Chemische Technologien und
Analytik
Assistant Professor
ERIKA CREMER

Sara Joan Miles
Eastern University, Esperanza College
Dean Emeritus
CLÉMENCE-AUGUSTE ROYER

Sari Miller-Antonio
California State University, Stanislaus,
Department of Anthropology and
Geography
Professor, Chair
PEI WENZHONG

Eric Mills
Dalhousie University, Department of
Oceanography
Professor Emeritus
HILDEBRAND WOLFE HARVEY
GORDON ARTHUR RILEY

Peter Milne
University of Stirling, Department of
Philosophy
Professor
KARL RAIMUND POPPER

Henry L. Minton
University of Windsor, Department of
Psychology
Professor Emeritus
LEWIS MADISON TERMAN

Simon Mitton
University of Cambridge, St Edmund's
College
Fellow
FRED HOYLE

Amirouche Moktefi
University of Strasbourg, IRIST;
University of Nancy 2, LPHS-AHP
CHARLES LUTWIDGE
DODGSON

Georgina M. Montgomery
Montana State University, Department
of History
Visiting Assistant Professor
CLARENCE RAY CARPENTER
DIAN FOSSEY

Michel Morange
École Normale Supérieure, Centre
Cavaillès
Professor
    ROBERT WILLIAM HOLLEY

Cathleen Synge Morawetz
New York University, Courant
Institute of Mathematical Sciences
Professor Emerita
    OLGA ALEXANDROVNA
        LADYZHENSKAYA
    OLGA ARSENIEVNA OLEINIK

Edward K. Morris
University of Kansas, Department of
Applied Behavioral Science
Professor
    BURRHUS FREDERIC (B. F.)
        SKINNER

Peter J. T. Morris
Science Museum, London
Manager
    DEREK HAROLD RICHARD
        BARTON
    PAUL JOHN FLORY
    ARCHER JOHN PORTER
        MARTIN
    WALTER JULIUS REPPE

Vivian Moses
Queen Mary University London;
King's College London; University
College London
Professor Emeritus
    MELVIN CALVIN

Ken Mowbray
American Museum of Natural History,
Department of Anthropology
Research Associate
    MARY DOUGLAS NICOL
        LEAKEY

Douglas J. Mudgway
National Aeronautics and Space
Administration: Jet Propulsion
Laboratory (retired)
Tracking and Data Systems Manager
    WILLIAM HAYWARD
        PICKERING

Axel Mueller
Northwestern University, Department
of Philosophy
Assistant Professor
    NELSON HENRY GOODMAN

Staffan Müller-Wille
University of Exeter, Department of
Sociology and Philosophy
Research Fellow
    CARL LINNAEUS
    GREGOR MENDEL

Shawn Mullet
Harvard University, Department of
the History of Science
PhD Student
    DAVID JOSEPH BOHM
    EDWARD TELLER

Walter Munk
University of California, San Diego,
Scripps Institution of Oceanography
Research Professor
    ROGER RANDALL DOUGAN
        REVELLE

Anne Mylott
Indiana University, Department of
History and Philosophy of Science
    MATTHIAS JACOB SCHLEIDEN

Christine Nawa
University of Regensburg, Lehrstuhl
für Wissenschaftsgeschichte
    ROBERT WILHELM EBERHARD
        BUNSEN

Paul Needham
Stockholm University, Department of
Philosophy
Professor
    PIERRE-MAURICE-MARIE
        DUHEM

Clifford M. Nelson
U.S. Geological Survey
Geologist
    CLARENCE RIVERS KING
    JOHN WESLEY POWELL

Gareth Nelson
University of Melbourne, School of
Botany
Research Fellow
    COLIN PATTERSON

Michael J. Neufeld
Smithsonian Institution, National Air
and Space Museum
Chair and Museum Curator
    WERNHER VON BRAUN

Peter M. Neumann
The Queen's College, Oxford, and the
University of Oxford Mathematical
Institute
Fellow
    WALTER FEIT
    DANIEL GORENSTEIN
    PHILIP HALL

William Newman
Indiana University, Department of
History and Philosophy of Science
Professor
    ISAAC NEWTON
    DANIEL SENNERT

Ian A. M. Nicholson
St. Thomas University, Department of
Psychology
Professor
    GORDON WILLARD ALLPORT
    ABRAHAM MASLOW

Richard G. Niemi
University of Rochester, Department
of Political Science
Professor
    WILLIAM HARRISON RIKER

Alfred Nordmann
Technische Universität Darmstadt,
Institut für Philosophie
Professor
    HEINRICH RUDOLF HERTZ

David Norman
University of Cambridge, Department
of Earth Sciences, Sedgwick Museum
Director
    YANG ZHONGJIAN

Joseph A. November
University of South Carolina,
Department of History
Assistant Professor
    GEORGE ELMER FORSYTHE

Igor Novikov
Niels Bohr Institute for Astronomy,
Physics, and Geophysics
Professor Emeritus
    YAKOV BORISOVICH
        ZELDOVICH

Vivian Nutton
University College London, Wellcome
Trust Centre for the History of
Medicine
Academic Staff
    RUFUS OF EPHESUS

Mary Jo Nye
Oregon State University, Department
of History
Professor
   PATRICK MAYNARD STUART
     BLACKETT
   LINUS CARL PAULING
   MIHÁLY (MICHAEL) POLÁNYI

Lynn K. Nyhart
University of Wisconsin, Madison,
Department of the History of Science
Professor
   ERNST HAECKEL
   MORITZ WAGNER

Gerhard Oberkofler
Universität Innsbruck,
Universitätsarchiv
Professor
   ERIKA CREMER

Roderick O'Donnell
Macquarie University, Department of
Economics
Professor
   JOHN MAYNARD KEYNES

Robert C. Olby
University of Pittsburgh, Department
of History and Philosophy of Science
Research Professor
   WILLIAM BATESON
   FRANCIS HARRY COMPTON
     CRICK
   GREGOR MENDEL

David Oldroyd
University of New South Wales,
School of History and Philosophy
Honorary Visiting Professor
   JAMES HUTTON
   DARASHAW NOSHERWAN
     WADIA

Lennart Olsson
Friedrich-Schiller-Universität Jena,
Institut für Spezielle Zoologie und
Evolutionsbiologie
Professor
   SVEN OTTO HÖRSTADIUS

Donald L. Opitz
DePaul University, School for New
Learning
Assistant Professor
   EDGAR DOUGLAS ADRIAN

ANDREW CROSSE
JOHN WILLIAM STRUTT

Wayne Orchiston
James Cook University, Centre for
Astronomy
Senior Lecturer
   JOHN GATENBY BOLTON

Vítězslav Orel
Mendelianum in the Moravian
Museum, Brno
Director Emeritus
   GREGOR MENDEL

Naomi Oreskes
University of California, San Diego,
Department of History
Professor
   HENRY MELSON STOMMEL

Eduardo L. Ortiz
Imperial College, Department of
Mathematics
Professor Emeritus
   JOSÉ MARÍA DE LANZ
   ANTÓNIO A. MONTEIRO

Michael A. Osborne
University of California, Santa
Barbara, Program in History of
Science, Technology, and Medicine
Associate Professor
   ISIDORE GEOFFROY SAINT-
     HILAIRE
   ÉDOUARD-MARIE HECKEL

Carla Rita Palmerino
Radboud University Nijmegen,
Faculty of Philosophy
Professor
   PIERRE GASSENDI

Maria K. Papathanassiou
National and Kapodistrian University
of Athens, Faculty of Mathematics
Assistant Professor
   STEPHANUS OF ALEXANDRIA

Hyung Wook Park
University of Minnesota, Program in
History of Science, Technology, and
Medicine
PhD Student
   FRANK MACFARLANE BURNET

Armando J. Parodi
Fundación Instituto Leloir

President
   LUIS FEDERICO LELOIR

Karen Hunger Parshall
University of Virginia, Departments of
Mathematics and History
Professor
   JAMES JOSEPH SYLVESTER

Cesare Pastorino
Indiana University, Department of
History and Philosophy of Science
PhD Student
   FRANCIS BACON

J. M. S. Pearce
Department of Neurobiology, Hull
Royal Infirmary, East Yorkshire
Emeritus Consultant Neurologist
   GORDON MORGAN HOLMES

Carl Pearson
Indiana University, Department of
History and Philosophy of Science
Visiting Professor
   JOHN PHILOPONUS

Volker Peckhaus
University of Paderborn, Institut für
Humanwissenschaften: Philosophie
Professor
   FRIEDRICH LUDWIG GOTTLOB
     FREGE

Phillip James Edwin Peebles
Princeton University, Department of
Physics
Professor Emeritus
   ROBERT HENRY DICKE

S. George Pemberton
University of Alberta, Department of
Earth & Atmospheric Sciences
Professor, Research Chair
   RUDOLF RICHTER

Jon V. Pepper
University College London,
Department of Mathematics
Honorary Research Fellow
   THOMAS HARRIOT

Anthony L. Peratt
Los Alamos National Laboratory,
Applied Physics Division
Guest Scientist
   HANNES OLOF GOSTA
     ALFVÉN

Stefano Perfetti
University of Pisa, Department of
Philosophy
Professor
AGOSTINO NIFO

Anders Persson
Swedish Meteorological and
Hydrological Institute, Meteorological
Analysis and Prediction Section
Researcher
ERIK HERBERT PALMÉN
SVERRE PETTERSSEN
REGINALD COCKCROFT
SUTCLIFFE

Aleksandar Petrovic
Serbian Academy of Science and Arts
MILUTIN MILANKOVIĆ

Steve Philips
Ghent University, Centre for History
of Science, Department of Early
Modern History
PhD Student
JODOCUS HONDIUS
PETRUS PLANCIUS

Gualtiero Piccinini
University of Missouri, St. Louis,
Department of Philosophy
Assistant Professor
ALLEN NEWELL

Anne D. Pick
University of Minnesota, Institute of
Child Development
Professor Emerita
ELEANOR JACK GIBSON

Herbert L. Pick
University of Minnesota, Institute of
Child Development
Professor
ELEANOR JACK GIBSON

Kathleen E. Pigg
Arizona State University, School of
Life Sciences
Associate Professor
KATHERINE ESAU

Brian Pippard
University of Cambridge, Department
of Physics, Cavendish Laboratory
Professor Emeritus
NEVILL FRANCIS MOTT

Régine Plas
Université Paris V René Descartes,
Centre de Recherces Psychotropes,
Santé Mentale, Société
Professor
PIERRE JANET

Irina Podgorny
Universidad Nacional de La Plata,
Facultad de Ciencias Naturales y
Museo de La Plata, Archivo Histórico
CONICET Investigadora
ROBERT LEHMANN-NITSCHE
FRANCISCO PASCASIO
MORENO

John A. Pojman
The University of Southern
Mississippi, Department of Chemistry
& Biochemistry
Professor
ILYA PRIGOGINE

Theodore M. Porter
University of California, Los Angeles,
Department of History
Professor
KARL PEARSON

Lawrence M. Principe
Johns Hopkins University,
Department of the History of Science
and Technology and Department of
Chemistry
Professor
WILHELM HOMBERG

Gregory Radick
University of Leeds, Department of
Philosophy, Division of History and
Philosophy of Science
Senior Lecturer, Chair
WILLIAM HOMAN THORPE

Leo Radom
University of Sydney, School of
Chemistry
Professor
JOHN ANTHONY POPLE

Jakov Radovčić
Croatian Natural History Museum,
Krapina Collection
Curator
DRAGUTIN (KARL)
GORJANOVIĆ-KRAMBERGER

F. Jamil Ragep
McGill University, Institute of Islamic
Studies
Research Chair
QUṬB AL-DĪN MAḤMŪD IBN
MASʿŪD IBN AL-MUṢLIḤ AL-
SHĪRĀZĪ

Sally Ragep
McGill University, Institute of Islamic
Studies
Senior Researcher
SHARAF AL-DĪN MAḤMŪD IBN
MUḤAMMAD IBN ʿUMAR AL-
JAGHMĪNĪ

Peter J. Ramberg
Truman State University, Division of
Science
Associate Professor
JAMES MASON CRAFTS

Pierre Rat
University of Burgundy
Honorary Professor
HENRI TINTANT

Simon Olling Rebsdorf
University of Aarhus, Steno
Department for Studies of Science and
Science Education
Associate Professor
BENGT GEORG DANIEL
STRÖMGREN

Brian Regal
Kean University, Department of
History
Assistant Professor
HENRY FAIRFIELD OSBORN

Karin Reich
University of Hamburg, Department
of Mathematics
Professor
MARCEL GROSSMANN

Carsten Reinhardt
University of Bielefeld, Institute for
Science and Technology Studies
Professor
HERBERT SANDER GUTOWSKY

Maria Rentetzi
National Technical University of
Athens, School of Applied
Mathematics and Physics
Assistant Professor
MARIETTA BLAU

Martin Reuss
U. S. Army Corps of Engineers, Office
of History
Senior Historian (retired)
ROBERT ELMER HORTON

Hans-Jörg Rheinberger
Max Planck Institute for the History
of Science, Berlin Director
ALBERT CLAUDE

Robert C. Richardson
University of Cincinnati, Department
of Philosophy
Professor
BORIS EPHRUSSI
EDWARD LAWRIE TATUM

Olivier Rieppel
The Field Museum, Department of
Geology
Curator and Chair
OTTO HEINRICH
SCHINDEWOLF

John S. Rigden
Washington University in St. Louis,
Department of Physics
Professor
EDWARD MILLS PURCELL
ISIDOR ISAAC RABI

Michael Riordan
University of California, Santa Cruz,
Department of Physics
Adjunct Professor
WILLIAM BRADFORD
SHOCKLEY

Gerrylynn K. Roberts
The Open University, Faculty of Arts,
Department of History of Science,
Technology & Medicine
Senior Lecturer
CHISTOPHER KELK INGOLD

Libby Robin
Australian National University, Fenner
School of Environment and Society;
National Museum of Australia
Senior Fellow; Senior Research Fellow
FRANCIS NOBLE RATCLIFFE

Eleonora Rocconi
University of Pavia, Faculty of
Musicology
Researcher
DIDYMUS

PORPHYRY
PTOLEMAIS OF CYRENE

Michel Rochas
Conseil Général des Ponts et
Chaussées
Ingénieur général
LÉON PHILIPPE TEISSERENC
DE BORT

Alan Rocke
Case Western Reserve University,
Department of History
Professor
JONS JACOB BERZELIUS
ADOLF WILHELM HERMANN
KOLBE
ADOLPHE WURTZ

Raul Rojas
Freie Universität Berlin, Fachbereich
Mathematik und Informatik, Institut
für Informatik
Professor
KONRAD ZUSE

Nils D. Roll-Hansen
University of Oslo, Department of
Philosophy, Classics, History of Art
and Ideas
Professor Emeritus
LOUIS PASTEUR

Joandomènec Ros
University of Barcelona, Faculty of
Biology, Department of Ecology
Professor
RAMON MARGALEF

Rachael Rosner
Independent Scholar
CARL RANSOM ROGERS

Donald K. Routh
University of Miami, Department of
Psychology
Professor Emeritus
ROGER WOLCOTT SPERRY

David Rowe
Johannes Gutenberg Universitat
Mainz, Geschichte der Mathematik
und der Naturwissenschaften
Professor
SOPHUS LIE

David Rudge
Western Michigan University,
Department of Biological Sciences,

Mallinson Institute for Science
Education
Associate Professor
HENRY BERNARD DAVIS
KETTLEWELL

Martin J. S. Rudwick
University of Cambridge, Department
of History and Philosophy of Science
Affiliated Research Scholar
GEORGES CUVIER

William McKinley Runyan
University of California, Berkeley,
School of Social Welfare
Professor
HENRY ALEXANDER MURRAY

Nicolaas A. Rupke
Göttingen University, Institute for the
History of Science
Professor and Director
RICHARD OWEN

Colin A. Russell
The Open University, Department of
History of Science, Technology and
Medicine
Professor Emeritus
EDWARD FRANKLAND
ROBERT ROBINSON
ALEXANDER ROBERTUS TODD

Klaus Ruthenberg
Coburg University of Applied
Sciences, Faculty of Science and
Technology
Professor
FRIEDRICH ADOLF PANETH

Abdelhamid I. Sabra
Harvard University, Department of
the History of Science
Professor Emeritus
ABU 'ALI AL-HASAN IBN AL-
HASAN IBN AL-HAYTHAM

Dorothy Sack
Ohio University, Department of
Geography
Professor
ARTHUR NEWELL STRAHLER

Cihan Saclioglu
Sabanci University, Istanbul, Faculty
of Engineering and Natural Science
Professor
FEZA GÜRSEY

Cora Sadosky
Howard University, Department of
Mathematics
Professor
ALBERTO PEDRO CALDERÓN

Klaus Sander
University of Freiburg, Faculty of
Biology
Professor
HILDE MANGOLD

Lisa T. Sarasohn
Oregon State University, Department
of History
Professor
MARGARET CAVENDISH

Helga Satzinger
University College London, Wellcome
Trust Centre for the History of
Medicine
Reader
CÉCILE AND OSKAR VOGT

Wolfgang Scherer
Universidad Central de Venezuela,
Department of Geology
Professor
WILLIAM CHRISTIAN
KRUMBEIN

Londa Schiebinger
Stanford University, Department of
History and the Clayman Institute for
Gender Research
Professor
MARIA SIBYLLA MERIAN
MARIA MARGARETHA
WINKELMANN

Judith Johns Schloegel
Independent Scholar
HERBERT SPENCER JENNINGS
TRACY SONNEBORN

Wolfgang Schlote
Johann Wolfgang Goethe-University
Frankfurt Main, Edinger Institute
Professor Emeritus
LUDWIG EDINGER

Florian Schmaltz
Johann Wolfgang Goethe University
Frankfurt am Main, History of
Science Working Group
RICHARD KUHN

Warren Schmaus
Illinois Institute of Technology, Lewis
Department of Humanities
Professor
ROBERT K. MERTON

Gail K. Schmitt
Princeton University, Department of
History, Program in the History of
Science
PhD Student
RUTH SAGER

Erhard Scholz
University of Wuppertal, Department
C - Mathematics
Professor
FELIX HAUSDORFF
HERMANN CLAUS HUGO
WEYL

Jay Schulkin
Georgetown University, Department
of Physiology and Biophysics
Research Professor
CURT P. RICHTER

David M. Schultz
University of Helsinki, Division of
Atmospheric Sciences; Finnish
Meteorological Institute
TOR HAROLD PERCIVAL
BERGERON

Hans-Werner Schütt
Technical University Berlin, Institute
of Philosophy and History of Science
Professor
EILHARD MITSCHERLICH

Vera Schwach
Norwegian Institute for Studies in
Research and Higher Education,
Center for Innovation
Senior Researcher
SVEN OTTO PETTERSSON

Joel S. Schwartz
City University of New York, College
of Staten Island, Department of
Biology
Professor Emeritus
ROBERT CHAMBERS

Silvan S. Schweber
Brandeis University, Martin A. Fisher
School of Physics
Professor
HANS ALBRECHT BETHE

J. ROBERT OPPENHEIMER
JULIAN SCHWINGER

Jérôme Segal
École Normale Supérieure de Paris,
Centre Cavaillès
Assistant Professor
CLAUDE SHANNON

Gino Segrè
University of Pennsylvania,
Department of Physics
Professor
HENRY PRIMAKOFF

Robert Seidel
University of Minnesota, Department
of History of Science, Technology and
Medicine
Professor
LUIS WALTER ALVAREZ
EMILIO GINO SEGRÈ

Rena Selya
University of California, Los Angeles,
Department of History
Lecturer
SALVADOR EDWARD LURIA
MAURICE HUGH FREDERICK
WILKINS

Dennis L. Sepper
University of Dallas, Department of
Philosophy
Professor
JOHANN WOLFGANG VON
GOETHE

Reinhard W. Serchinger
SePhys, Consultant in Applied Physics
Owner
WALTER HANS SCHOTTKY

Eldar Shafir
Princeton University, Department of
Psychology and the Woodrow Wilson
School of Public and International
Affairs
Professor
AMOS TVERSKY

Sonu Shamdasani
University College London, Wellcome
Trust Centre for the History of
Medicine
Reader
CARL GUSTAV JUNG

Michael H. Shank
University of Wisconsin, Madison,
Department of the History of Science
Professor
JOHANNES REGIOMONTANUS

Gordon M. Shepherd
Yale University School of Medicine,
Department of Neurobiology
Professor
JOHN CAREW ECCLES

Abner Shimony
Boston University, Departments of
Philosophy and Physics
Professor Emeritus
JOHN S. BELL

Martin Shubik
Yale University, Department of
Economics
Professor
OSKAR MORGENSTERN

Gerold Siedler
Kiel University, Leibniz Institute for
Marine Sciences
Professor
ALBERT JOSEPH MARIA
DEFANT

Ruth Lewin Sime
Sacramento City College, Department
of Chemistry
Professor Emeritus
OTTO HAHN

Ana Simões
Universidade de Lisboa, Centro de
História das Ciências
Professor
ROBERT SANDERSON
MULLIKEN

Maxine Singer
Carnegie Institution of Washington;
National Institutes of Health
President Emeritus; Scientist Emeritus
GEORGE WELLS BEADLE

Rivers Singleton
University of Delaware, Departments
of Biological Sciences and English
Associate Professor
HERMAN MORITZ KALCKAR
SEVERO OCHOA
HARLAND GOFF WOOD

S. Sivaram
National Chemical Laboratory, Pune
Director
KRISHNASAMI VENKATARAMAN

Robert A. Skipper
University of Cincinnati, Department
of Philosophy
Professor
RONALD AYLMER FISHER
SEWALL WRIGHT

Nancy Slack
The Sage Colleges, Department of
Biology
Professor Emeritus
G. EVELYN HUTCHINSON

Leo B. Slater
Johns Hopkins University, Institute for
Applied Economics and the Study of
Business Enterprise
Fellow
ROBERT BURNS WOODWARD

Phillip R. Sloan
University of Notre Dame,
Department of History
Professor
GEORGE-LOUIS LE CLERC,
COMTE DE BUFFON

Chris Smeenk
University of California, Los Angeles,
Department of Philosophy
Assistant Professor
DENNIS WILLIAM SCIAMA

Barry H. Smith
Weill Medical College of Cornell
University, Department of
Neuroscience
Professor, Attending Surgeon
FRANCIS OTTO SCHMITT

Charles H. Smith
Western Kentucky University,
Department of Library Public Services
Professor, Science Librarian
ALFRED RUSSEL WALLACE

John K. Smith
Lehigh University, Department of
History
Associate Professor
PAUL HUGH EMMETT
EUGÈNE JULES HOUDRY

Justin E. H. Smith
Concordia University, Department of
Philosophy
Associate Professor
GOTTFRIED WILHELM
LEIBNIZ

Pamela H. Smith
Columbia University, Department of
History
Professor
JOHANN JOACHIM BECHER

Robert W. Smith
University of Alberta, Department of
History and Classics
Professor
JAN HENDRIK OORT

Vassiliki Betty Smocovitis
University of Florida, Departments of
Zoology and History
Professor
I. MICHAEL LERNER
GEORGE LEDYARD STEBBINS,
JR.

Walter Sneader
University of Strathclyde, Institute of
Biomedical Sciences
Honorary Lecturer
ARTHUR EICHENGRÜN

Thomas Söderqvist
University of Copenhagen
Professor, Director
NIELS KAJ JERNE

Michael M. Sokal
Worcester Polytechnic Institute,
Department of Humanities and Arts
Professor Emeritus
JAMES MCKEEN CATTELL

Marianne Sommer
Eidgenössische Technische Hochschule
Zürich, Chair of Science Studies
Privatdozentin
WILFRID EDWARD LE GROS
CLARK
KENNETH PAGE OAKLEY

Henrik Kragh Sørensen
University of Aarhus, Steno
Department for Studies of Science and
Science Education
Post Doc
NIELS HENRIK ABEL

Sverker Sörlin
Royal Institute of Technology,
Stockholm, Division for History of
Science and Technology
Professor
 SVANTE AUGUST ARRHENIUS

Theodore L. Sourkes
McGill University, Department of
Psychiatry
Professor Emeritus
 JOHANN LUDWIG WILHELM
 THUDICHUM

P. E. Spargo
University of Cape Town, Department
of Physics
Associate Professor Emeritus
 JAMES LEONARD BRIERLY
 SMITH

T. A. Springer
Utrecht University, Mathematics
Institute
Professor
 ARMAND BOREL

John Stachel
Boston University, Department of
Physics, Center for Einstein Studies
Professor Emeritus
 ALBERT EINSTEIN

Ida H. Stamhuis
Vrye University, Faculty of Exact
Sciences
Professor
 JANTINA TAMMES
 HUGO DE VRIES

Matthew Stanley
Michigan State University,
Department of History
Professor
 ARTHUR STANLEY
 EDDINGTON

Richard Stanley
Massachusetts Institute of Technology,
Department of Mathematics
Professor
 GIAN-CARLO ROTA

Carlos Steel
University of Leuven, Institute of
Philosophy
Professor
 JOHANNES SCOTTUS
 ERIUGENA

Hubert Steinke
University of Bern, Institute for the
History of Medicine
Research Associate
 ALBRECHT VON HALLER

Friedrich Steinle
Bergische Universität Wuppertal,
Faculty of Humanities
Professor
 MICHAEL FARADAY

Lester D. Stephens
University of Georgia, Department of
History
Professor Emeritus
 JOHN EDWARDS HOLBROOK
 JOSEPH LeCONTE
 ALFRED GOLDSBOROUGH
 MAYOR

Thomas F. Stocker
University of Bern, Physics Institute
Professor
 HANS OESCHGER

Soňa Štrbáňová
Academy of Sciences of the Czech
Republic, Institute for Contemporary
History
Associate Professor
 MARJORY STEPHENSON

James E. Strick
Franklin and Marshall College,
Department of Earth and
Environment
Assistant Professor
 HENRY CHARLTON BASTIAN
 NORMAN HAROLD HOROWITZ
 HAROLD P. KLEIN

Jeffrey L. Sturchio
Merck & Co., Inc.
Vice President
 KARL AUGUST FOLKERS

Yasumoto Suzuki
Geological Survey of Japan, Geological
Information Center
Retired Member
 KIYOO WADATI

Edith Dudley Sylla
North Carolina State University,
Department of History
Professor
 JAKOB BERNOULLI
 THOMAS BRAWARDINE

WALTER BURLEY
JOHN DUMBLETON
RICHARD SWINESHEAD AND
ROGER SWYNESHED

Scott Tanona
Kansas State University, Department
of Philosophy
Assistant Professor
 NIELS HENRIK DAVID BOHR

Ian Tattersall
American Museum of Natural History,
Division of Anthropology
Curator
 MARY DOUGLAS NICOL
 LEAKEY

Pierre Teissier
University of Paris X, Nanterre,
Centre d'histoire et de philosophie des
sciences
PhD Student
 ROBERT COLLONGUES

Joachim Telle
University of Heidelberg and
University of Freiburg/Breisgau,
Germanistische Seminare
Professor
 ADAM OF BODENSTEIN
 ALEXANDER VON SUCHTEN

Roger Temam
Indiana University, Bloomington,
Institute for Scientific Computing and
Applied Mathematics
Professor
 JACQUES-LOUIS LIONS

Mary Terrall
University of California, Los Angeles,
Department of History
Associate Professor
 PIERRE LOUIS MOREAU DE
 MAUPERTUIS

Tosun Terzioğlu
Sabanci University
President
 CAHIT ARF

Bert Theunissen
Utrecht University, Institute for the
History and Foundations of Science
Professor
 MARIE EUGÈNE FRANÇOIS
 THOMAS DUBOIS

Denis Thieffry
Université de la Méditerranée, Faculté des Sciences de Luminy, Département de Biologie
Professor
JEAN LOUIS BRACHET

Jacques Thierry
University of Burgundy, Laboratory of Biogeosciences
Professor Emeritus
HENRI TINTANT

Johannes M. M. H. Thijssen
Radboud University Nijmegen, Faculty of Philosophy
Professor
ALBERT OF SAXONY
JOHN BURIDAN

Anne Tihon
Université Catholique de Louvain, Department of Greek, Latin and Oriental Studies, Institut Orientaliste
Professor
GEORGE CHIONIADES
THEODORE MELITENIOTES
MANUEL MOSCHOPOULOS
GEORGES PACHYMERES
ISAAC ARGYRUS

Werner Tochtermann
Christian-Albrechts-Universität zu Kiel, Institut für Organische Chemie
Professor Emeritus
GEORG WITTIG

Daniel P. Todes
Johns Hopkins University, School of Medicine, Department of the History of Medicine
Professor
IVAN PETROVICH PAVLOV

Hugh Torrens
Keele University, United Kingdom, School of Earth Sciences and Geography
Professor Emeritus
JOHN FAREY

Alain Touwaide
Smithsonian Institution, National Museum of Natural History, Department of Botany
Historian of Sciences
NICOLÒ LEONICENO
GUILLAUME PELLICIER

Anthony S. Travis
The Hebrew University of Jerusalem, Sidney M. Edelstein Center
Professor
ERNST DAVID BERGMANN
CHARLES BLACHFORD MANSFIELD

Simon Trépanier
University of Edinburgh, School of History, Classics, and Archaeology
Lecturer
EMPEDOCLES OF ACRAGAS

François Treves
Rutgers University, Department of Mathematics
Professor
LAURENT SCHWARTZ

Virginia Trimble
University of California, Irvine, Department of Physics and Astronomy
Professor
JOHN NORRIS BAHCALL
THOMAS GOLD

Roger Turner
University of Pennsylvania, History and Sociology of Science Department
PhD student
HORACE ROBERT BYERS
FRANCIS WILTON REICHELDERFER

Susan Turner
Monash University, Department of Geosciences, and Queensland Museum, Paleontology and Geology Section
Honorary Senior Research Associate
DOROTHY HILL

Ryan D. Tweney
Bowling Green State University, Department of Psychology
Professor Emeritus
DONALD ERIC BROADBENT

Monica Ugaglia
LEONARDO GARZONI, S.J.

Peter Ullrich
Universität Koblenz-Landau, Campus Koblenz, Mathematisches Institut
Professor
GEORG FRIEDRICH BERNHARD RIEMANN

Melvyn C. Usselman
University of Western Ontario, Department of Chemistry
Professor
WILLIAM HYDE WOLLASTON

Ezio Vaccari
Università dell'Insubria (Varese, Italy), Dipartimento di Informatica e Comunicazione
Professor
GIOVANNI ARDUINO

Adrienne van den Bogaard
Delft University of Technology, Faculty of Technology, Policy and Management, Department of Philosophy
Assistant Professor
WYBE EDSGER DIJKSTRA

Philip van der Eijk
Newcastle University, School of Historical Studies
Professor
DIOCLES OF CARYSTUS

René van der Veer
Leiden University, Department of Education and Child Studies
Professor
LEV SEMYONOVICH VYGOTSKY

Ton van Helvoort
Independent Scholar, The Netherlands
A. HUGO T. THEORELL

David Van Reybrouck
Independent Scholar and Author, Brussels
SHERWOOD LARNED WASHBURN

Hugo van Woerden
University of Groningen, Kapteyn Astronomical Institute
Professor
HENDRIK CHRISTOFFEL VAN DE HULST

Veeravalli Varadarajan
University of California, Los Angeles, Department of Mathematics
Professor
HARISH-CHANDRA

Hemmo J. Veenstra
LAMBERTUS MARIUS JOANNES URSINUS VAN STRAATEN

Cristina Viano
Centre National de la Recherche
Scientifique, Université de Paris-
Sorbonne
Senior Research Fellow
OLYMPIODORUS OF
ALEXANDRIA
OLYMPIODORUS OF THEBES

Fernando Vidal
Max Planck Institute for the History
of Science
Senior Research Scholar
JEAN PIAGET

Bernard Vitrac
Centre National de la Recherche
Scientifique, UMR 8667, Centre
Louis Gernet, Paris
Director of Research
EUCLID

James R. Voelkel
Massachusetts Institute of Technology
Senior Fellow
JOHANNES KEPLER

Annette B. Vogt
Max Planck Institute for the History
of Science, Berlin Research Scholar
TATIANA A. EHRENFEST-
AFANAS'EVA
LINA SOLOMONOVNA SHTERN

Hans Volkert
Deutsches Zentrum fur Luft und
Raumfahrt (DLR), Institut fur Physik
der Atmosphare (IPA)
Staff Scientist
FELIX MARIA VON EXNER-
EWARTEN

Craig B. Waff
Air Force Research Laboratory,
History Office
Historian
GEORGE BIDDELL AIRY

Kameshwar C. Wali
Syracuse University, Department of
Physics
Professor Emeritus
SUBRAHMANYAN
CHANDRASEKHAR

Scott Walter
University of Nancy, Department of
Philosophy

Maître de conférences
JULES HENRI POINCARÉ

Jessica Wang
University of British Columbia
Associate Professor
EDWARD UHLER CONDON

Zuoyue Wang
California State Polytechnic
University, Pomona, Department of
History
Associate Professor
WU CHIEN-SHIUNG
ZHONGYAO ZHAO
ZHU KEZHEN

Walter Warwick
Micro Analysis & Design Principal
Research Analyst
ALAN MATHISON TURING

A. M. C. Waterman
University of Manitoba; St. John's
College, Winnipeg
Professor Emeritus; Retired Fellow
THOMAS ROBERT MALTHUS

C. Kenneth Waters
University of Minnesota, Department
of Philosophy, Minnesota Center for
Philosophy of Science
Professor, Director
JULIAN HUXLEY

Bruce H. Weber
California State University Fullerton,
Bennington College
Professor Emeritus
PETER DENNIS MITCHELL

Nadine M. Weidman
Harvard University, History of Science
Lecturer
KARL SPENCER LASHLEY

Stephen J. Weininger
Worcester Polytechnic Institute,
Department of Chemistry &
Biochemistry
Professor Emeritus
PAUL DOUGHTY BARTLETT

Paul Weirich
University of Missouri-Columbia,
Department of Philosophy
Professor
BRUNO DE FINETTI
FRANK PLUMPTON RAMSEY

LEONARD JAMES SAVAGE
HERBERT ALEXANDER SIMON

Rainer Weiss
Massachusetts Institute of Technology,
Department of Physics
Professor Emeritus
DAVID TODD WILKINSON

Kathleen Wellman
Southern Methodist University,
Department of History
Professor
JULIEN OFFRAY DE LA
METTRIE

Simone Wenkel
Universität zu Köln, Institut für
Genetik
PhD Candidate
CARL ALEXANDER NEUBERG

Catherine Westfall
Michigan State University, Lyman
Briggs College
Visiting Associate Professor
EUGENE WIGNER

John A. Weymark
Vanderbilt University, Department of
Economics
Professor
JOHN CHARLES HARSANYI

E. O. Wiley
University of Kansas, Department of
Ecology and Evolutionary Biology;
Biodiversity Research Center
Professor, Senior Curator
(EMIL HANS) WILLI HENNIG

Alan F. Williams
University of Geneva, Department of
Inorganic Chemistry
Professor
AXEL CHRISTIAN KLIXBÜLL
JØRGENSEN

Kathleen Broome Williams
Cogswell Polytechnical College,
General Education Program
Director and Professor
GRACE HOPPER

David B. Wilson
Iowa State University, Department of
History
Professor
WILLIAM WHEWELL

Richard Wilson
Harvard University, Department of
Physics
Professor
   KENNETH (KEN) TOMPKINS
     BAINBRIDGE

Andrew S. Winston
University of Guelph, Department of
Psychology
Professor
   EDWIN GARRIGUES BORING

Judith E. Winston
Virginia Museum of Natural History,
Marine Biology
Curator
   LIBBIE HENRIETTA HYMAN

Rega Wood
Stanford University, Department of
Philosophy
Research Professor
   RICHARD RUFUS OF
     CORNWALL

Walter W. Woodward
University of Connecticut,
Department of History

Assistant Professor
   JOHN WINTHROP, JR.

Robert H. Wozniak
Bryn Mawr College, Department of
Psychology
Professor
   JOHN BROADUS WATSON

Franz M. Wuketits
University of Vienna, Institute for
Philosophy of Science
Professor
   OTTO KOEHLER
   ERICH VON HOLST

Sepideh Yalda
Millersville University, Department of
Earth Sciences
Professor
   TETSUYA THEODORE FUJITA
   CHARLES WARREN
     THORNTHWAITE
   GILBERT THOMAS WALKER
   HARRY WEXLER

Ellis Yochelson
National Museum of Natural History,
Department of Paleobiology
Research Associate, deceased

HARRY STEPHEN LADD
CURT TEICHERT

Zhendong You
China University of Geosciences,
Faculty of Earth Sciences
Professor
   DING WENJIANG (V. K.
     TING)
   YIN ZANGXUN

Christian C. Young
Alverno College, Division of Natural
Sciences, Mathematics & Technology
Professor
   ALDO LEOPOLD

Palle Yourgrau
Brandeis University, Department of
Philosophy
Professor
   KURT FRIEDRICH GÖDEL

Li Zhang
Chinese Academy of Sciences,
Institute for the History of Natural
Science
Professor
   PETER P. T. SAH

List of Scientists by Field

Scientists treated in the *New DSB* are here broken out according to the discipline(s) to which each has contributed. The order of sciences moves, however imperfectly, from the mathematical and logical through the physical and organic realms to areas of specific human application.

Mathematics

Probability / Decision and Game Theory

Logic

Computer Science

Cosmology

Astronomy

Astrophysics

Space Science

Classical Physics

Thermodynamics / Statistical Mechanics

Theoretical Physics

Nuclear Science/Radioactivity

Particle / High-Energy Physics

Condensed Matter / Solid State Physics

Alchemy / Chymistry

General Chemistry

Theoretical Chemistry

Physical Chemistry

Analysis / Spectroscopy

Inorganic Chemistry

Organic Chemistry

Biochemistry

Geology

Geophysics / Plate Tectonics

Oceanography

Meteorology

Climatology

Paleontology

Paleoanthropology / Physical Anthropology

Natural History

Evolutionary Biology

Ecology

Physiology

Cellular / Developmental Biology

Genetics

Molecular Biology

Ethology / Animal Behavior

Psychology

Cognitive Science

Neuroscience

Medical Science

Technology / Engineering

Nature of Scientific Inquiry

Science Pedagogy / Popularization

Science Policy

List of Scientists by Field

MATHEMATICS

Abel, Niels Henrik
Adams, John Frank
Agnesi, Maria Gaetana
Ahlfors, Lars
Albert of Saxony
Apollonius of Perga
Archimedes
Arf, Cahit
Argyrus, Isaac
Babbage, Charles
Bacon, Roger
Baldi, Bernardino
Bernoulli, Jakob (Jacob, Jacques, James) I
Bers, Lipmann
Birkhoff, Garrett
Bogolubov, Nikolai Nikolaevich
Borel, Armand
Borelli, Giovanni Alfonso
Bourbaki, Nicolas
Bradwardine, Thomas
Calderón, Alberto Pedro
Cantor, Georg Ferdinand Ludwig
Cardano, Girolamo
Cauchy, Augustin-Louis
Chandrasekhar, Subrahmanyan
Chern, Shiing-Shen
Chevalley, Claude
Clavius, Christoph
Coignet, Michiel

d'Alembert (Dalembert, D'Alembert), Jean Le Rond
de Finetti, Bruno
De Giorgi, Ennio
Descartes, René Du Perron
Didymus
Dieudonné, Jean
Dijkstra, Wybe Edsger
Dodgson, Charles Lutwidge
Ehrenfest-Afanas'eva, Tatiana A.
Eilenberg, Samuel
Erdos, Paul
Euclid
Euler, Leonhard
Farey, John
Feit, Walter
Fisher, Ronald Aylmer
Forsythe, George Elmer
Frege, Friedrich Ludwig Gottlob
Gödel, Kurt Friedrich
Gorenstein, Daniel
Grossmann, Marcel
Hall, Philip
Hamilton, William Rowan
Harish-Chandra
Harriot (or Hariot), Thomas
Hartree, Douglas Rayner
Hausdorff, Felix
Hero of Alexandria
Hilbert, David
Hipparchus

Hirst, Thomas Archer
Hondius, Jodocus
Hypatia
Ibn al-Haytham, Abu 'Ali al-hasan Ibn al-hasan
Ibrāhīm Ibn Sinān Ibn Thābit Ibn Qurra
Inglada, Vicente
Jeffreys, Harold
Jungius, Joachim
Keldysh, Mstislav Vsevolodovich
Kepler, Johannes
King, Ada Augusta, the Countess of Lovelace
Kodaira, Kunihiko
Kolmogorov, Andrei Nikolaevich
Kovalevskaya, Sofya Vasilyevna (Sonya)
Ladyzhenskaya, Olga Alexandrovna
Lanz, José María de
Leibniz, Gottfried Wilhelm
Leray, Jean
Lichnérowicz, André
Lie, Sophus
Lions, Jacques-Louis
Mac Lane, Saunders
Mauchly, John William
Maupertuis, Pierre Louis Moreau de
McCrea, William Hunter
McVittie, George Cunliffe
Milanković, Milutin

Monte, Guidobaldo, Marchese del
Monteiro, António A.
Morse, Marston
Moschopoulos, Manuel
Moser, Jürgen K.
Nash, John Forbes, Jr.
Newell, Homer Edward, Jr.
Newton, Isaac
Oleinik, Olga Arsenievna
Oresme, Nicole
Pachymeres, Georges
Pearson, Karl
Piero della Francesca
Poincare, Jules Henri
Pontryagin, Lev Semionovich
Prachaticz, Cristannus de

Ptolemais of Cyrene
Ptolemy
Qūhī (or al-Kūhī), Abū Sahl Wayjan
    Ibn Rustam al-
Ramsey, Frank Plumpton
Ramus, Peter, also known as Pierre de
    la Ramee
Regiomontanus, Johannes
Richardson, Lewis Fry
Robinson, Julia Bowman
Rota, Gian-Carlo
Savage, Leonard James
Schwartz, Laurent
Seaborg, Glenn Theodore
Stephanus of Alexandria
Sylvester, James Joseph

Tarski, Alfred
Tucker, Albert William
Turing, Alan Mathison
Tūsī, Sharaf al-Dīn al-Muzaffar Ibn
    Muhammad Ibn al-Muzaffar al-
Tutte, William (Bill) Thomas
Tversky, Amos
Valens, Vettius
Vinogradov, I. M.
Walker, Gilbert Thomas
Weil, André
Weyl, Hermann Claus Hugo
Whitney, Hassler
Wigner, Eugene
Wilkinson, James Hardy
Zygmund, Antoni

PROBABILITY/DECISION AND GAME THEORY

Bayes, Thomas
Bernoulli, Jakob
Broadbent, Donald Eric
Buffon, George-Louis Le Clerc,
    Comte de
Carnap, Paul Rudolf
de Finetti, Bruno
Dodgson, Charles Lutwidge
Fisher, Ronald Aylmer
Gödel, Kurt Friedrich
Goodman, Nelson Henry
Harsanyi, John Charles

Jeffrey, Richard Carl
Jeffreys, Harold
Keynes, John Maynard
Kolmogorov, Andrei Nikolaevich
Kuhn, Thomas Samuel
Lewis, David
Mill, John Stuart
Morgenstern, Oskar
Nash, John Forbes, Jr.
Nozick, Robert
Olson, Mancur, Jr.
Pareto, Vilfredo

Pearson, Karl
Popper, Karl Raimund
Ramsey, Frank Plumpton
Riker, William Harrison
Savage, Leonard James
Schwartz, Laurent
Simon, Herbert Alexander
Tarski, Alfred
Tucker, Albert William
Tversky, Amos
Vickrey, William Spencer

LOGIC

Albert of Saxony
Buridan, John (Jean)
Burley, Walter
Carnap, Paul Rudolf
Chrysippius
Dijkstra, Wybe Edsger
Dodgson, Charles Lutwidge
Frege, Friedrich Ludwig Gottlob

Galen
Gödel, Kurt Friedrich
Goodman, Nelson Henry
Jungius, Joachim
Lewis, David
Ockham, William of
Popper, Karl Raimund
Ramsey, Frank Plumpton

Ramus, Peter, also known as Pierre de
    la Ramee
Rāzī, Abū Bakr Muhammad Ibn
    Zakariyyā', Al-
Robinson, Julia Bowman
Tarski, Alfred
Turing, Alan Mathison
Zuse, Konrad

COMPUTER SCIENCE

Babbage, Charles
Dijkstra, Wybe Edsger
Eckert, J. (John Adam) Presper, Jr.
Forsythe, George Elmer
Hopper, Grace

King, Ada Augusta, the Countess of
    Lovelace
Licklider, Joseph Carl Robnett
Newell, Allen
Mauchly, John William

Shannon, Claude
Strachey, Christopher
Turing, Alan Mathison
Wilkinson, James Hardy
Zuse, Konrad

NATURAL PHILOSOPHY

Adelard of Bath
Albertus Magnus, Saint
Ali al-Qūshjī, Abū al-Qāsim Alā' al-
  Dīn Alī ibn Muhammad Qushjī-
  zāde
Bacon, Francis
Bacon, Roger
Basson (Basso), Sébastien (Sebastian,
  Sebastiano)
Blasius of Parma
Borro, Girolamo
Boyle, Robert
Bradwardine, Thomas
Bruno, Giordano
Buffon, George Louis Le Clerc,
  Comte de
Buonamici, Francesco
Burgersdijk, Frank Pieterszoon

Buridan, John (Jean)
Burley, Walter
Cabeo, Niccolò
Campanella, Tommaso
Cavendish, Margaret, Duchess of
  Newcastle
Conway, Anne
Descartes, Rene Du Perron
Dumbleton, John
Empedocles of Acragas
Eriugena, Johannes Scottus
Gassendi, Pierre
Gorlaeus (van Goorle, van Gooirle),
  David
Helmont, Johannes (Joan) Baptista
  Van
John Philoponus
Jungius, Joachim

Leibniz, Gottfried Wilhelm
Maupertuis, Pierre Louis Moreau de
Newton, Isaac
Nifo, Agostino
Olympiodorus of Alexandria
Oresme, Nicole
Paracelsus
Plato
Rufus, Richard of Cornwall
Stephanus of Alexandria
Strato of Lampsacus
Volta, Alessandro Giuseppe Antonio
  Anastasio
Winthrop, John, Jr.
Xenarchus
Zabarella, Jacopo (Giacomo)

COSMOLOGY

Alfvén, Hannes Olof Gosta
Aristotle
Bacon, Francis
Bondi, Hermann
Brahe, Tycho
Bruno, Giordano
Chrysippus
Clavius, Christoph
Copernicus, Nicholas
Dicke, Robert Henry

Eddington, Arthur Stanley
Gold, Thomas
Heckmann, Otto Hermann Leopold
Herschel, William
Hoyle, Fred
Jordan, Ernst Pascual
Kuiper, Gerard Peter
McCrea, William Hunter
McVittie, George Cunliffe
Morrison, Philip

Newton, Isaac
Ptolemy
Ryle, Martin
Sakharov, Andrei Dmitriyevich
Sciama, Dennis William
Sitter, Willem de
Tinsley, Beatrice
Wilkinson, David Todd
Zeldovich, Yakov Borisovich

ASTRONOMY

Airy, George Biddell
Ali al-Qūshjī, Abū al-Qāsim Alā' al-
  Dīn Alī ibn Muhammad Qushjī-
  zāde
Ambartsumian Amazaspovich, Viktor
Apolliniarius
Argyrus, Isaac
Babcock, Horace Welcome
Bacon, Roger
Bahcall, John Norris
Banneker, Benjamin
Bernoulli, Jakob (Jacob, Jacques,
  James) I
Biermann, Ludwig Franz Benedikt
Bok, Bartholomeus (Bart) Jan
Bolton, John Gatenby

Borelli, Giovanni Alfonso
Brahe, Tycho
Chandrasekhar, Subrahmanyan
Chioniades, George (or Gregory)
Clavius, Christoph
Copernicus, Nicholas
d'Alembert (Dalembert, D'Alembert),
  Jean Le Rond
Diodorus of Alexandria
Eddington, Arthur Stanley
Edlén, Bengt
Euler, Leonhard
Galilei, Galileo
Gassendi, Pierre
Gold, Thomas
Greaves, John

Greenstein, Jesse Leonard
Harriot (or Hariot), Thomas
Heckmann, Otto Hermann Leopold
Herschel, Caroline Lucretia
Herschel, John
Herschel, William
Hipparchus
Hoyle, Fred
Ibn al-Haytham, Abu 'Ali al-hasan
  Ibn al-hasan
Ibrāhīm Ibn Sinān Ibn Thābit Ibn
  Qurra
Jaghmīnī, Sharaf al-Dīn Maḥmūd ibn
  Muḥammad ibn 'Umar al-
Kuiper, Gerard
Leptines

Liais, Emmanuel-Bernardin
McCrea, William Hunter
McVittie, George Cunliffe
Meliteniotes, Theodore
Menzel, Donald Howard
Monte, Guidobaldo, Marchese del
Newton, Isaac
Oort, Jan Hendrik
Payne-Gaposchkin, Cecilia Helena
Prachaticz, Cristannus de
Ptolemy
Purcell, Edward Mills
Runcorn, Stanley Keith

Qūhī (or al-Kūhī), Abū Sahl Wayjan
    Ibn Rustam al-
Quṭb al-Dīn Maḥmūd ibn Masʿūd
    ibn al-Musliḥ al-Shīrāzī
Ramus, Peter
Regiomontanus, Johannes
Ryle, Martin
Sagan, Carl
Schwarzschild, Martin
Shklovskii, Iosif Samuilovich
Sitter, Willem de
Spitzer, Lyman
Stephanus of Alexandria

Strömgren, Bengt Georg Daniel
Timocharis
Tinsley, Beatrice
Ṭūsī, Sharaf al-Dīn al-Muzaffar Ibn
    Muḥammad Ibn al-Muzaffar al-
Unsöld, Albrecht Otto Johannes
Valens, Vettius
Van de Hulst, Hendrik Christoffel
Westphal, James A.
Whewell, William
Whipple, Fred Lawrence
Winkelmann, Maria Margaretha
Xenarchus

ASTROPHYSICS

Ambartsumian, Viktor Amazaspovich
Babcock, Horace Welcome
Bahcall, John Norris
Biermann, Ludwig
Bok, Bartholomeus (Bart) Jan
Bolton, John
Bondi, Hermann
Chandrasekhar, Subrahmanyan
Eddington, Arthur Stanley
Edlén, Bengt
Fowler, William A.
Friedman, Herbert
Gold, Thomas
Greenstein, Jesse Leonard

Heckmann, Otto Hermann Leopold
Herzberg, Gerhard
Hoyle, Fred
Jeffreys, Harold
Kuiper, Gerard Peter
Lauritsen, Charles Christian
McCrea, William Hunter
Menzel, Donald Howard
Morrison, Philip
Newell, Homer Edward, Jr.
Oort, Jan Hendrik
Payne-Gaposchkin, Cecilia Helena
Purcell, Edward Mills
Ryle, Martin

Sagan, Carl
Schwarzschild, Martin
Sciama, Dennis William
Shklovskii, Iosif Samuilovich
Spitzer, Lyman, Jr.
Strömgren, Bengt Georg Daniel
Tinsley, Beatrice
Unsöld, Albrecht Otto Johannes
Van de Hulst, Hendrik Christoffel
Westphal, James
Whipple, Fred
Wilkinson, David Todd
Zeldovich, Yakov Borisovich

SPACE SCIENCE

Bahcall, John Norris
Friedman, Herbert
Goldberg, Leo
Horowitz, Norman Harold
Keldysh, Mstislav Vsevolodovich
Klein, Harold P.
Kuiper, Gerard Peter

Miller, Stanley Lloyd
Newell, Homer Edward, Jr.
Pickering, William Hayward
Rossi, Bruno Benedetto
Sagan, Carl Edward
Shoemaker, Eugene Merle
Soffen, Gerald Alan

Spitzer, Lyman, Jr.
Tousey, Richard
Van Allen, James A.
von Braun, Wernher
Westphal, James A.
Whipple, Fred Lawrence

CLASSICAL PHYSICS

Archimedes
Baldi, Bernardino
Bassi Verati (Veratti), Laura Maria
    Caterina
Bernoulli, Jakob (Jacob, Jacques,
    James) I
Blair, Robert

Borelli, Giovanni Alfonso
Cabeo, Niccolò
Cauchy, Augustin-Louis
Crosse, Andrew
d'Alembert (Dalembert, D'Alembert),
    Jean Le Rond
Damianus of Larissa

Descartes, René Du Perron
Duhem, Pierre-Maurice-Marie
Euler, Leonhard
Faraday, Michael
Foster, George Carey
Galilei, Galileo
Garzoni, Leonardo S. J.

Gassendi, Pierre
Hamilton, William Rowan
Hero of Alexandria
Hertz, Heinrich Rudolf
Ibn al-Haytham, Abu 'Ali al-hasan
    Ibn al-hasan
Keldysh, Mstislav Vsevolodovich

Kepler, Johannes
Leibniz, Gottfried Wilhelm
Mairan, Jean-Jacques Dortous de
Maupertuis, Pierre Louis Moreau de
Milanković, Milutin
Monte, Guidobaldo, Marchese del
Moser, Jürgen K.

Newton, Isaac
Poincaré, Jules Henri
Ramus, Peter
Voigt, Woldemar
Volta, Alessandro Giuseppe Antonio
    Anastasio
Wollaston, William Hyde

THERMODYNAMICS/STATISTICAL MECHANICS

Boltzmann, Ludwig Eduard
Ehrenfest-Afanas'eva, Tatiana A.
Flory, Paul John
Korzhinskii, Dimitri Sergeyevich

Odum, Howard Thomas

Prigogine, Ilya

Schottky, Walter Hans

Touschek, Bruno

Uhlenbeck, George

Voigt, Woldemar

THEORETICAL PHYSICS

Bell, John Stewart
Bethe, Hans Albrecht
Bloch, Felix
Bogolubov, Nikolai Nikolaevich
Bohm, David Joseph
Boltzmann, Ludwig Eduard
Bondi, Hermann
Broglie, Louis (Victor Pierre
    Raymond)
Casimir, Hendrik Brugt Gerhard
Condon, Edward Uhler
Dicke, Robert Henry
Eddington, Arthur Stanley
Einstein, Albert
Feynman, Richard Phillips
Gödel, Kurt Friedrich
Gursey, Feza

Hartree, Douglas Rayner
Hückel, Erich Armand Arthur
Jordan, Ernst Pascual
Lichnérowicz, André
Lorentz, Hendrik Antoon
Mairan, Jean-Jacques Dortous de
Menzel, Donald Howard
Morrison, Philip
Oppenheimer, J. Robert
Pauli, Wolfgang
Pauling, Linus Carl
Poincaré, Jules Henri
Popper, Karl Raimund
Sakharov, Andrei Dmitriyevich
Salam, Muhammad Abdus
    (Abdussalam)
Schwinger, Julian

Sciama, Dennis William

Shklovskii, Iosif Samuilovich

Sommerfeld, Arnold Johannes
    Wilhelm

Spitzer, Lyman, Jr.

Strutt, John William, third Baron
    Rayleigh

Teller, Edward

Touschek, Bruno

Uhlenbeck, George

Voigt, Woldemar

Weisskopf, Victor Frederick

Weyl, Hermann Claus Hugo

Wigner, Eugene

Zeldovich, Yakov Borisovich

NUCLEAR SCIENCE/RADIOACTIVITY

Amaldi, Edoardo
Bacher, Robert
Blackett, Patrick Maynard Stuart
Blau, Marietta
Bohr, Niels Henrik David
Cherenkov, Pavel Alekseyevich
Flerov, Georgiï Nikolaevich
Fowler, William A.

Hahn, Otto
Lauritsen, Charles Christian
Libby, Willard Frank
Livingston, Milton Stanley
Oppenheimer, J. Robert
Perey, Marguerite Catherine
Primakoff, Henry
Rabi, Isidor Isaac

Segrè, Emilio Gino
Serber, Robert
Szilard, Leo
Uhlenbeck, George
Weisskopf, Victor Frederick
Wilkinson, Sir Geoffrey
Wu Chien-Shiung
Zhao, Zhongyao

PARTICLE/HIGH-ENERGY PHYSICS

Alfvén, Hannes Olof Gosta
Alvarez, Luis Walter

Bell, John Stewart
Breit, Gregory

Budker, Gersh Itskovich
Cherenkov, Pavel Alekseyevich

Feynman, Richard Phillips
Goldberg, Leo
Hoyle, Fred
Migdal, Arkady Benediktovich
Morrison, Philip

Occhialini, Giuseppe
Primakoff, Henry
Salam, Muhammad Abdus
  (Abdussalam)
Schwinger, Julian

Seaborg, Glenn (Glen) Theodore
Spitzer, Lyman, Jr.
Touschek, Bruno
Wilson, Robert Rathbun

CONDENSED MATTER/SOLID STATE

Bardeen, John
Bloch, Felix
Collongues, Robert
Condon, Edward Uhler

Friedman, Herbert
Kapitsa (or Kapitza), Petr Leonidovich
Migdal, Arkady Benediktovich
Mott, Nevill Francis

Primakoff, Henry
Schottky, Walter Hans
Shockley, William Bradford
Wilson, Sir Alan Herries

ALCHEMY/CHYMISTRY

Arconville, Marie Geneviève Charlotte
  Thiroux d'
Arnald of Villanova (Pseudo)
Becher, Johann Joachim
Bodenstein, Adam of
Boyle, Robert
Helmont, Johannes (Joan) Baptista
  Van
Homberg, Wilhelm

Jābir ibn Hayyān
Jungius, Joachim
Lull, Ramon
Newton, Isaac
Olympiodorus of Alexandria
Paracelsus, Theophrastus Philippus
  Aureolus Bombastus von
  Hohenheim

Rāzī, Abū Bakr Muḥammad Ibn
  Zakariyyā', al-
Stahl, Georg Ernst
Suchten, Alexander von
Stephanus of Alexandria
Winthrop, John, Jr.
Zosimos of Panopolis

GENERAL CHEMISTRY

Arconville, Marie Geneviève Charlotte
  Thiroux d'
Becher, Johann Joachim
Berzelius, Jons Jacob
Cullen, William
Crosse, Andrew
Davy, Humphrey
Foster, George Carey

Frankland, Edward
Helmont, Johannes (Joan) Baptista
  Van
Homberg, Wilhelm
Lavoisier, Antoine-Laurent
Mitscherlich, Eilhard
Picardet, Claudine
Paulze-Lavoisier, Marie-Anne-Pierette

Porter, George
Sennert, Daniel
Stahl, Georg Ernst
Suchten, Alexander von
Volta, Alessandro Giuseppe Antonio
  Anastasio
Walker, John
Winthrop, John, Jr.

THEORETICAL CHEMISTRY

Dewar, Michael J. S.
Fukui, Ken-ichi
Hahn, Otto
Hartree, Douglas Rayner
Hückel, Erich Armand Arthur
Ingold, Chistopher Kelk

Kekule von Stradonitz (Kekulé),
  (Friedrich) August
Mendeleev, Dmitrii Ivanovich
Mulliken, Robert Sanderson
Paneth, Friedrich Adolf
Pauling, Linus Carl

Pople, John Anthony
Prelog, Vladimir
Prigogine, Ilya
Smalley, Richard Errett
Wigner, Eugene

PHYSICAL CHEMISTRY

Arrhenius, Svante August
Bartlett, Paul Doughty
Bernstein, Richard Barry

Bijvoet, Johannes Martin
Boer, Jan Hendrik de
Boreskov, Georgiĭ Konstantinovich

Cremer, Erika
Dewar, Michael J. S.
Duhem, Pierre-Maurice-Marie

Flory, Paul John
Franklin, Rosalind Elsie
Gutowsky, Herbert Sander
Hammett, Louis Planck
Herzberg, Gerhard
Hückel, Erich Armand Arthur
Jørgensen, Axel Christian Klixbüll

Mark, Herman F.
Mizushima, San-ichiro
Mulliken, Robert Sanderson
Ostwald, Friedrich Wilhelm
Pauling, Linus Carl
Polányi, Mihály (Michael)

Pople, John Anthony
Porter, George
Prigogine, Ilya
Semenov, Nikolaĭ Nikolaevich
Smalley, Richard Errett
Theorell, A. Hugo T.

ANALYSIS/SPECTROSCOPY

Bainbridge, Kenneth Tompkins
Barton, Derek Harold Richard
Beckman, Arnold Orville
Condon, Edward Uhler
Cremer, Erika
Edlén, Bengt
Frankland, Edward

Franklin, Rosalind Elsie
Gutowsky, Herbert Sander
Harvey, Hildebrand Wolfe
Herzberg, Gerhard
Hodgkin, Dorothy Mary Crowfoot
Imes, Samuel Elmer

Jørgensen, Axel Christian Klixbüll
Lemieux, Raymond Urgel
Liebig, Justus von
Martin, Archer John Porter
Polányi, Mihály (Michael)
Walsh, Alan

INORGANIC CHEMISTRY

Boer, Jan Hendrik de
Brown (Brovarnik), Herbert Charles
Chatt, Joseph
Emmett, Paul Hugh
Frankland, Edward

Haber, Fritz
Jørgensen, Axel Christian Klixbüll
Libby, Willard Frank
Nesmejanov, Aleksandr Nikolaevich
Paneth, Friedrich Adolf

Perey, Marguerite Catherine
Pettersson, Sven Otto
Wilkinson, Sir Geoffrey
Wittig, Georg

ORGANIC CHEMISTRY

Bartlett, Paul Doughty
Barton, Derek Harold Richard
Bayer, Otto Georg Wilhelm
Beckman, Arnold Orville
Bergmann, Ernst David
Brown (Brovarnik), Herbert Charles
Bunsen, Robert Wilhelm Eberhard
Butlerov, Aleksandr Mikhailovich
Carothers, Wallace Hume
Crafts, James Mason
Cram, Donald J.
Dewar, Michael J. S.
Edman, Pehr Victor
Eichengrün, Arthur
Flory, Paul John
Folkers, Karl August
Frankland, Edward
Fukui, Ken-ichi

Gutowsky, Herbert Sander
Haber, Fritz
Hammett, Louis Plack
Holley, Robert William
Houdry, Eugéne Jules
Ingold, Chistopher Kelk
Kekule von Stradonitz (Kekulé),
 (Friedrich) August
Kolbe, Adolf Wilhelm Hermann
Kuhn, Richard
Laurent, Auguste
Lemieux, Raymond Urgel
Liebig, Justus von
Mansfield, Charles Blachford
Mark, Herman F.
Nozoe, Tetsuo
Ovchinnikov, Yuri Anatolyevich

Pasteur, Louis
Prelog, Vladimir
Reichstein, Tadeus
Reppe, Walter Julius
Robinson, Robert
Sah, Peter P.T.
Sakurada, Ichiro
Smalley, Richard Errett
Smith, Michael
Todd, Alexander Robertus (Baron
 Todd)
Van Krevelen, Dirk Willem
Venkataraman, Krishnasami
Wittig, Georg
Woodward, Robert Burns
Wurtz, Adolphe
Zelinskiĭ, Nikolay Dmitrievich

BIOCHEMISTRY

Abderhalden, Emil
Anfinsen, Christian B.
Axelrod, Julius

Bijvoet, Johannes Martin
Butenandt, Adolf Friedrich Johann
Calvin, Melvin

Caspersson, Torbjörn Oskar
Chatt, Joseph
Delbrück, Max Ludwig Henning

Edman, Pehr Victor
Elion, Gertrude Belle
Hodgkin, Alan
Hodgkin, Dorothy Mary Crowfoot
Folkers, Karl August
Green, David Ezra
Holley, Robert William
Horowitz, Norman Harold
Kalckar, Herman Moritz
Klein, Harold P.
Kuhn, Richard
Lederer, Edgar
Lehninger, Albert Lester
Leloir, Luis Federico

Lemieux, Raymond Urgel
Lipmann, Fritz Albert
Martin, Archer John Porter
Miller, Stanley
Mitchell, Peter Dennis
Needham, Dorothy
Neuberg, Carl Alexander
Novikoff, Alex Benjamin
Ochoa, Severo
Ovchinnikov, Yuri Anatolyevich
Pauling, Linus Carl
Racker, Efraim
Reichstein, Tadeus

Sah, Peter T. T.
Schmitt, Francis Otto
Shtern, Lina Solomonovna
Smith, Michael
Soffen, Gerald Alan
Stephenson, Marjory
Szent-Györgyi, Albert Imre
Tatum, Edward Lawrie
Theorell, A. Hugo T.
Todd, Alexander Robertus
Wald, George
Wood, Harland Goff
Zelinskiĭ, Nikolay Dmitrievich

GEOLOGY

Arduino (or Arduini), Giovanni
Bretz, J Harlan
Chambers, Robert
Crosse, Andrew
Darwin, Charles Robert
Ding Wenjiang (V. K. Ting)
Farey, John

Goethe, Johann Wolfgang von
Hutton, James
King, Clarence Rivers
Lavoisier, Antoine-Laurent
LeConte, Joseph
Linnaeus, Carl
Menard, Henry William

Mitscherlich, Eilhard
Powell, John Wesley
Richter, Rudolf
Rittmann, Alfred (Alfredo) Ferdinand
Van Straaten, Lambertus Marius
  Joannes Ursinus
Walker, John

GEOPHYSICS/PLATE TECTONICS

Aki, Keiiti
Alvarez, Luis Walter
Ampferer, Otto
Benioff, Victor Hugo
Blackett, Patrick Maynard Stuart
Carey, Samuel Warren
Cox, Allan Verne
Day, Arthur Louis
Dietz, Robert Sinclair
Elsasser, Walter Maurice
Gold, Thomas

Hospers, Jan
Huang Jiqing (Te-Kan)
Hubbert, Marion King
Inglada, Vicente
Jeffreys, Harold
Krumbein, William Christian
Landsberg, Helmut Erich
Lehmann, Inge
Matuyama Motonori
Milanković, Milutin
Richter, Charles Francis

Ringwood, Alfred Edward
Runcorn, Stanley Keith
Shatskiy, Nikolay Sergeyevich
Sloss, Laurence Louis
Strahler, Arthur Newell
Van Allen, James A.
Wadati, Kiyoo
Wadia, Darashaw Nosherwan
Wegener, Alfred Lothar
Westphal, James A.
Wilson, John Tuzo

OCEANOGRAPHY

Baerends, Gerard Pieter
Deacon, George Edward Raven
Defant, Albert Joseph Maria
Dietz, Robert Sinclair
Edmondson, Wallis Thomas
Fedorov, Konstantin Nikolayevich
Harvey, Hildebrand Wolfe
Margalef, Ramon

Marsili (or Marsigli), Luigi Ferdinando
Mayor (formerly Mayer), Alfred
  Goldsborough
Moeller, Sophie C(h)arlotte Juliane
Namias, Jerome
Palmén, Erik Herbert
Pettersson, Sven Otto

Revelle, Roger Randall Dougan
Riley, Gordon Arthur
Schott, Paul Gerhard
Stommel, Henry Melson
Tharp, Marie
Wüst, Georg

METEOROLOGY

Aitken, John
Aristotle
Assmann, Richard
Bergeron, Tor Harold Percival
Bjerknes, Vilhelm
Byers, Horace Robert
Charney, Jule Gregory
Defant, Albert Joseph Maria
Dobson, Gordon Miller Bourne
Exner-Ewarten, Felix Maria von
Fujita, Tetsuya Theodore
Haurwitz, Bernhard
Herschel, John

Horton, Robert Elmer
Howard, Luke
Köppen, Wladimir Peter
Lamb, Hubert Horace
Liais, Emmanuel-Bernardin
Mauchly, John William
Mendel, Johann Gregor
Namias, Jerome
Palmén, Erik Herbert
Panofsky, Hans Arnold
Petterssen, Sverre
Picardet, Claudine

Reichelderfer, Francis Wilton
Richardson, Lewis Fry
Saltzman, Barry
Saussure, Horace Bénédict de
Smagorinsky, Joseph
Suomi, Verner Edward
Sutcliffe, Reginald Cockcroft
Teisserenc de Bort, Léon Philippe
Viñes, Benito
Walker, Gilbert Thomas
Wexler, Harry
Zhu Kezhen

CLIMATOLOGY

Arrhenius, Svante August
Callendar, Guy Stewart
Keeling, Charles David
Köppen, Wladimir Peter

Lamb, Hubert Horace
Landsberg, Helmut Erich
Milanković, Milutin
Namias, Jerome

Saltzman, Barry

Thornthwaite, Charles Warren

Zhu Kezhen

PALEONTOLOGY

Bronn, Heinrich Georg
Burmeister, Hermann Karl Konrad
Cuvier, Georges
Dubois, Marie Eugène François
  Thomas
Gorjanović-Kramberger, Dragutin
  (Karl)
Gould, Stephen Jay
Hill, Dorothy
Huxley, Thomas Henry
Jelínek, Jan

Koenigswald, Gustav Heinrich Ralph
  von
Ladd, Harry Stephen
Lamarck, Jean-Baptiste
Moreno, Francisco Pascasio
Newell, Norman Dennis
Oakley, Kenneth Page
Osborn, Henry Fairfield
Owen, Richard
Patterson, Colin

Pei Wenzhong
Piveteau, Jean
Richter, Rudolf
Schindewolf, Otto Heinrich
Simpson, George Gaylord
Teichert, Curt
Tintant, Henri
Wadia, Darashaw Nosherwan
Yang Zhongjian
Yin Zanxun

PALEOANTHROPOLOGY/PHYSICAL ANTHROPOLOGY

Bartlett, Frederic Charles
Bastian, Adolf
Callendar, Guy Stewart
Campbell, Donald Thomas
Clark, John Desmond
Clark, Wilfrid Edward Le Gros
Coon, Carleton Stevens
Dart, Raymond Arthur
Dubois, Marie Eugène François
  Thomas

Fischer, (Leopold Franz) Eugen
Garrod, Dorothy Annie Elizabeth
Gorjanović-Kramberger, Dragutin
  (Karl)
Jelínek, Jan
Koenigswald, Gustav Heinrich Ralph
  von
Leakey, Mary Douglas Nicol
Lehmann-Nitsche, Robert
Libby, Willard Frank

Moreno, Francisco Pascasio
Oakley, Kenneth Page
Pei Wenzhong
Piveteau, Jean
Vallois, Henri Victor
Virchow, Rudolf Carl
Walker, John
Washburn, Sherwood Larned
Weidenreich, Franz

NATURAL HISTORY

Arduino (or Arduini), Giovanni
Aristotle
Bodenstein, Adam of
Buffon, George-Louis Le Clerc, Comte de
Burmeister, Hermann Karl Konrad
Cronquist, Arthur
Cullen, William
Geoffroy Saint-Hilaire, Étienne
Geoffroy Saint-Hilaire, Isidore
Goethe, Johann Wolfgang von
Haller, [Victor] Albrecht von

Heckel, Édouard-Marie
Holbrook, John Edwards
Hutton, James
Hyman, Libbie Henrietta
Kinsey, Alfred
LeConte, Joseph
Lee, Sarah Eglonton Wallis Bowdich
Linnaeus, Carl
Marsili (or Marsigli), Luigi Ferdinando
Mayr, Ernst Walter
Merian, Maria Sibylla

Mueller, Ferdinand Jakob Heinrich von
Oken (or Okenfuss), Lorenz
Piaget, Jean
Pliny the Elder (Gaius Plinius Secundus)
Ratcliffe, Francis Noble
Saussure, Horace Bénédict de
Smith, James Leonard Brierly
Traill, Catharine Parr
Walker, John

EVOLUTIONARY BIOLOGY

Anfinsen, Christian B.
Baldwin, James Mark
Bronn, Heinrich Georg
Cain, Arthur James
Campbell, Donald Thomas
Carson, Hampton Lawrence
Chambers, Robert
Darwin, Charles Robert
Emerson, Alfred Edwards
Fisher, Ronald Aylmer
Geoffroy Saint-Hilaire, Isidore
Gould, Stephen Jay
Haeckel, Ernst
Hamilton, William Donald
Hennig, (Emil Hans) Willi
Huxley, Julian

Huxley, Thomas Henry
Kammerer, Paul
Kettlewell, Henry Bernard Davis
Kimura, Motoo
Kinsey, Alfred
Koenigswald, Gustav Heinrich Ralph von
Kropotkin, Petr Alekseyvich
Ladd, Harry Stephen
Lamarck, Jean-Baptiste
Lerner, I(sadore) Michael
Mayr, Ernst Walter
Osborn, Henry Fairfield
Owen, Richard
Patterson, Colin
Piaget, Jean

Popper, Karl Raimund
Royer, Clémence-Auguste
Schindewolf, Otto Heinrich
Simpson, George Gaylord
Smuts, Jan Christian
Sonneborn, Tracy Morton
Stebbins, George Ledyard, Jr.
Tintant, Henri
Waddington, Conrad Hal
Wagner, Moritz
Wallace, Alfred Russel
Washburn, Sherwood Larned
Weidenreich, Franz
Weismann, August Friedrich Leopold
Wright, Sewall
Wynne-Edwards, Vero Copner

ECOLOGY

Allee, Warder Clyde
Braun-Blanquet, Josias
Clements, Frederic Edward
Cockayne, Leonard
Cowles, Henry Chandler
Dansereau, Pierre Mackay
Dubos, René Jules
Edmondson, Wallis Thomas
Elton, Charles Sutherland
Emerson, Alfred Edwards

Harvey, Hildebrand Wolfe
Hasler, Arthur Davis
Heckel, Édouard-Marie
Hutchinson, G. Evelyn
Ladd, Harry Stephen
Lee, Sarah Eglonton Wallis Bowdich
Leopold, Aldo
Margalef, Ramon
Mayor (formerly Mayer), Alfred Goldsborough

Nice, Margaret Morse
Odum, Eugene Pleasants
Odum, Howard Thomas
Oeschger, Hans
Ratcliffe, Francis Noble
Riley, Gordon Arthur
Stanchinskiy, Vladimir Vladimirovich
Tansley, Sir Arthur George
Thienemann, August Friedrich
Wynne-Edwards, Vero Copner

PHYSIOLOGY

Abderhalden, Emil
Adrian, Edgar Douglas, first Baron Adrian of Cambridge

Aristotle
Bastian, Henry Charlton
Borelli, Giovanni Alfonso

Carpenter, William Benjamin
Cullen, William
de Vries, Hugo

Descartes, René Du Perron
Eccles, John Carew
Elsasser, Walter Maurice
Ephrussi, Boris
Galen
Gold, Thomas
Goldman-Rakic, Patricia Shoer
Haller, [Victor] Albrecht von
Hasler, Arthur Davis
Hertz, Mathilde Carmen
Hess, Walter Rudolf
Hodgkin, Alan
Holmes, Gordon Morgan
Jennings, Herbert Spencer

Katz, Bernard
Koehler, Otto
La Mettrie, Julien Offray de
Lashley, Karl Spencer
Lavoisier, Antoine-Laurent
LeConte, Joseph
Luria, Alexander Romanovich
McCulloch, Warren Sturgis
Paracelsus, Theophrastus Philippus
   Aureolus Bombastus von
   Hohenheim
Pavlov, Ivan Petrovich
Richter, Curt P.
Sah, Peter P. T.

Schleiden, Matthias Jacob
Schwendener, Simon
Shtern, Lina Solomonovna
Suchten, Alexander von
Tatum, Edward Lawrie
Volta, Alessandro Giuseppe Antonio
   Anastasio
Von Euler, Ulf Svante
von Holst, Erich
Winthrop, John, Jr.
Wollaston, William Hyde
Wundt, Wilhelm

CELLULAR/DEVELOPMENTAL BIOLOGY

Aristotle
Baldwin, James Mark
Bastian, Henry Charlton
Bateson, William
Brachet, Jean Louis
Briggs, Robert W.
Carson, Hampton Lawrence
Caspersson, Torbjörn Oskar
Claude, Albert
Cowdry, Edmund Vincent
Dubos, René Jules
Ephrussi, Boris
Esau, Katherine
Grobstein, Clifford

Haeckel, Ernst
Haller, [Victor] Albrecht von
Hamburger, Viktor
Holley, Robert William
Holtfreter, Johannes
Hörstadius, Sven Otto
Huxley, Julian
Just, Ernest Everett
Klein, Harold P.
Luria, Salvador Edward
Mangold, Hilde
Maupertuis
McClintock, Barbara

Morgan, Thomas Hunt
Novikoff, Alex Benjamin
Oken, Lorenz
Pasteur, Louis
Porter, Keith Roberts
Purcell, Edward Mills
Sager, Ruth
Schleiden, Matthias Jacob
Schwendener, Simon
Sonneborn, Tracy Morton
Stephenson, Marjory
Tatum, Edward Lawrie
Waddington, Conrad Hal

GENETICS

Bateson, William
Beadle, George Wells
Briggs, Robert W.
Caspersson, Torbjörn Oskar
Delbrück, Max Ludwig Henning
de Vries, Hugo
Ephrussi, Boris
Fischer, (Leopold Franz) Eugen
Ford, Edmund Brisco
Hamilton, William Donald
Horowitz, Norman Harold

Huxley, Julian
Jennings, Herbert Spencer
Kettlewell, Henry Bernard Davis
Kimura, Motoo
Lerner, I(sadore) Michael
Luria, Salvador Edward (Salvatore)
McClintock, Barbara
Mendel, Johannes Gregor
Morgan, Thomas Hunt
Neel, James Van Gundia

Pearson, Karl
Sager, Ruth
Schmitt, Francis Otto
Shockley, William Bradford
Sonneborn
Tammes, Jantina
Tatum, Edward Lawrie
Weismann, August Friedrich Leopold
Wright, Sewall
Waddington, Conrad Hal

MOLECULAR BIOLOGY

Anfinsen, Christian B.
Brachet, Jean Louis
Chargaff, Erwin

Crick, Francis Harry Compton
Delbrück, Max Ludwig Henning
Franklin, Rosalind Elsie

Holley, Robert William
Jerne, Niels Kaj
Jordan, Ernst Pascual

Kalckar, Herman Moritz
Luria, Salvador
Ochoa, Severo

Pauling, Linus Carl
Perutz, Max Ferdinand
Sagan, Carl Edward

Schmitt, Francis Otto
Smith, Michael
Wilkins, Maurice Hugh Frederick

ETHOLOGY/ANIMAL BEHAVIOR

Allee, Warder Clyde
Nice, Margaret Morse
Baerends, Gerard Pieter
Beach, Frank Ambrose Jr.
Carpenter, Clarence Ray
Craig, Wallace
Fossey, Dian
Griffin, Donald Redfield

Hertz, Mathilde Carmen
Howard, Henry Eliot
Huxley, Julian
Jennings, Herbert Spencer
Koehler, Otto
Lehrman, Daniel Sanford
Lorenz, Konrad Zacharias

Schneirla, Theodore Christian
Thorpe, William Homan
Tinbergen, Nikolaas
Turner, Charles Henry
von Holst, Erich
Watson, John Broadus
Wynne-Edwards, Vero Copner

PSYCHOLOGY

Abelson, Robert Paul
Allport, Gordon Willard
Aristotle
Baldwin, James Mark
Bartlett, Frederic Charles
Bastian, Adolf
Beach, Frank Ambrose Jr.
Boring, Edwin Garrigues
Broadbent, Donald Eric
Campbell, Donald Thomas
Carpenter, William Benjamin
Cattell, James McKeen
Chrysippius
Clark, Kenneth and Mamie
Cullen, William
Erikson, Erik Homburger
Eysenck, Hans Jürgen
Festinger, Leon
Freud, Sigmund
Galen

Gibson, Eleanor Jack
Gibson, James Jerome
Hebb, Donald
Hertz, Mathilde Carmen
Hilgard, Ernest Ropiequet
Hull, Clark Leonhard
James, William
Janet, Pierre
Jung, Carl Gustav
Klüver, Heinrich
Kinsey, Alfred
La Mettrie, Julien Offray de
Lashley, Karl Spencer
Lehrman, Daniel Sanford
Lewin, Kurt
Luria, Alexander Romanovich
Maslow, Abraham
Meehl, Paul Everett
Milgram, Stanley
Miller, Neal Elgar

Murry, Henry Alexander
Nifo, Agostino
Pavlov, Ivan Petrovich
Piaget, Jean
Richardson, Lewis Fry
Richter, Curt P.
Rogers, Carl Ransom
Rufus, Richard of Cornwall
Schneirla, Theodore Christian
Simon, Herbert Alexander
Skinner, Burrhus Frederic
Sperry, Roger Wolcott
Stern, Louis William
Tansley, Arthur George
Terman, Louis Madison
Tversky, Amos
Vogt, Cécile and Oskar
Vygotsky, Lev Semyonovich
Watson, John Broadus
Wundt, Wilhelm

COGNITIVE SCIENCE

Abelson, Robert Paul
Babbage, Charles
Bartlett, Frederic Charles
Festinger, Leon
Hebb, Donald
Hull, Clark Leonard
James, William
Kuhn, Thomas Samuel

Lashley, Karl Spencer
Luria, Alexander Romanovich
Marr, David Courtnay
McCulloch, Warren Sturgis
Newell, Allen
Penfield, Wilder Graves
Piaget, Jean

Shannon, Claude
Simon, Herb
Sperry, Roger Wolcott
Turing, Alan Mathison
Tversky, Amos
Vygotsky, Lev Semyonovich
Wundt, Wilhelm

NEUROSCIENCE

Adrian, Edgar Douglas, first Baron
   Adrian of Cambridge

Axelrod, Julius
Bastian, Henry Charlton

Brodmann, Korbinian
Bullock, Theodore Holmes

Clark, Wilfrid Edward Le Gros
Crick, Francis Harry Compton
Eccles, John Carew
Edinger, Ludwig
Goldman-Rakic, Patricia Shoer
Hamburger, Viktor
Hebb, Donald

Holmes, Gordon Morgan
Katz, Bernard
Klüver, Heinrich
Lashley, Karl Spencer
Luria, Alexander Romanovich
Marr, David Courtnay
McCulloch, Warren Sturgis

Papez, James Wenceslas
Penfield, Wilder Graves
Schmitt, Francis Otto
Sperry, Roger Wolcott
Thudichum, Johann Ludwig Wilhelm
Vogt, Cécile and Oskar
Vygotsky, Lev Semyonovich

MEDICAL SCIENCE

Abderhalden, Emil
Arconville, Marie Geneviève Charlotte
  Thiroux d'
Arnald of Villanova
Assmann, Richard
Axelrod, Julius
Bacon, Francis
Bodenstein, Adam of
Borelli, Giovanni Alfonso
Borro, Girolamo
Buonamici, Francesco
Burnet, Frank Macfarlane
Cardano, Girolamo
Carpenter, William Benjamin
Claude, Albert
Cowdry, Edmund Vincent
Diocles of Carystus
Dubos, René Jules
Edinger, Ludwig
Eichengrün, Arthur

Elion, Gertrude Belle
Elsasser, Walter Maurice
Galen
Helmont, Johannes (Joan) Baptista
  Van
Hippocrates of Cos
Howard, Luke
Janssen, Paul Adriaan Jan
La Mettrie, Julien Offray de
Leoniceno, Nicolò
Linnaeus, Carl
Luria, Salvador Edward (Salvatore)
Maimonides, Rabbi Moses Ben
  Maimon
Medawar, Peter Brian
Nifo, Agostino
Paracelsus, Theophrastus Philippus
  Aureolus Bombastus von
  Hohenheim
Pasteur, Louis

Pellicier, Guillaume
Prachaticz, Cristannus de
Purcell, Edward Mills
Quṭb al-Dīn Maḥmūd ibn Masʿūd
  ibn al-Muṣliḥ al-Shīrāzī
Rāzī, Abū Bakr Muḥammad Ibn
  Zakariyyāʾ, al-
Reichstein, Tadeus
Rufus of Ephesus
Sah, Peter P. T.
Sennert, Daniel
Stahl, Georg Ernst
Starkey, George
Stephanus of Alexandria
Suchten, Alexander von
Virchow, Rudolf Carl
Von Euler, Ulf Svante
Wilson, Alan Herries

TECHNOLOGY/ENGINEERING

Aitken, John
Blau, Marietta
Boer, Jan Hendrik de
Boreskov, Georgiĭ Konstantinovich
Butenandt, Adolf Friedrich Johann
Callendar, Guy Stewart
Condon, Edward Uhler
Cremer, Erika
Eckert, J. (John Adam) Presper, Jr.
Frankland, Edward

Horton, Robert Elmer
Hou Te-pang (Debang Hou)
Houdry, Eugéne Jules
Kapitsa, Petr Leonidovich
Lewis, Warren Kendall
Licklider, Joseph Carl Robnett
Milanković, Milutin
Pickering, William Hayward
Reichstein, Tadeus
Reppe, Walter Julius

Sakharov, Andrei Dmitriyevich
Schottky, Walter Hans
Shannon, Claude
Smalley, Richard Errett
Smith, Michael
Turing, Alan Mathison
Van Krevelen, Dirk Willem
von Braun, Wernher
Wigner, Eugene
Wilson, Sir Alan Herries

NATURE OF SCIENTIFIC INQUIRY

Aristotle
Babbage, Charles
Bacon, Francis
Bohr, Niels Henrik David
Boring, Edwin Garrigues

Borro, Girolamo
Descartes, René Du Perron
Duhem, Pierre-Maurice-Marie
Galilei, Galileo
Goethe, Johann Wolfgang von

Goodman, Nelson Henry
Gould, Stephen Jay
Herschel, John
Jennings, Herbert Spencer
Kuhn, Thomas Samuel

La Mettrie, Julien Offray de
Lewin, Kurt
Liais, Emmanuel-Bernardin
Meehl, Paul Everett
Merton, Robert K.
Mill, John Stuart

Paneth, Friedrich Adolf
Poincaré, Jules Henri
Polányi, Mihály (Michael)
Price, Derek John DeSolla
Royer, Clémence-Auguste
Sagan, Carl Edward

Schindewolf, Otto Heinrich
Schleiden, Matthias Jacob
Weyl, Hermann Claus Hugo
Whewell, William
Zabarella, Jacopo (Giacomo)

SCIENCE PEDAGOGY/POPULARIZATION

Bastian, Adolf
Bergmann, Ernst David
Bretz, J Harlan
Campbell, Donald Thomas
Cattell, James McKeen
Chambers, Robert
Clavius, Christoph
Ding Wenjiang (V. K. Ting)
Ehrenfest-Afanas'eva, Tatiana A.
Eysenck, Hans Jürgen
Forsythe, George Elmer
Foster, George Carey
Frankland, Edward
Gould, Stephen Jay
Hennig, (Emil Hans) Willi
Hilgard, Ernest Ropiequet

Hirst, Thomas Archer
Huxley, Julian
Huxley, Thomas Henry
Imes, Elmer Samuel
Jelínek, Jan
Johnston, James Finlay Weir
Mac Lane, Saunders
Marcet, Jane Haldimand
Mark, Herman F.
Morrison, Philip
Namias, Jerome
Needham, Joseph
Newell, Norman Dennis
Odum, Eugene Pleasants
Oken (or Okenfuss), Lorenz
Prachaticz, Cristannus de

Purcell, Edward Mills
Sagan, Carl Edward
Saussure, Horace Bénédict de
Seaborg, Glenn Theodore
Sonneborn, Tracy Morton
Terman, Lewis Madison
Tinbergen, Nikolaas
Tinsley, Beatrice
Turner, Charles Henry
Vygotsky, Lev Semyonovich
Whewell, William
Wilson, Alan Herries
Yin Zanxun
Zhu Kezhen

SCIENCE POLICY

Abderhalden, Emil
Amaldi, Edoardo
Bacher, Robert
Bahcall, John Norris
Bergmann, Ernst David
Bondi, Hermann
Fossey, Dian

Grobstein, Clifford
King, Clarence Rivers
Marsili (or Marsigli), Luigi Ferdinando
Neel, James Van Gundia
Pickering, William Hayward
Price, Derek John DeSolla

Rabi, Isidor Isaac
Revelle, Roger Randall Dougan
Seaborg, Glenn (Glen) Theodore
Teller, Edward
Vickrey, William Spencer
Zhu Kezhen

List of Nobel Prize Winners

NOBEL PRIZE IN PHYSICS

Hendrik Antoon Lorentz, 1902
Max Planck, 1918
Albert Einstein, 1921
Isidor Isaac Rabi, 1944
Wolfgang Pauli, 1945
Edward Mills Purcell, 1952
William Bradford Shockley, 1956
Pavel Alekseyevich Cherenkov, 1958
Emilio Gino Segrè, 1959
Eugene Wigner, 1963
Richard Phillips Feynman, 1965
Julian Schwinger, 1965
Martin Ryle, 1974
Nevill Francis Mott, 1975
Muhammad Abdus Salam, 1979
Ken-ichi Fukui, 1981
Subrahmanyan Chandrasekhar, 1983
William A. Fowler, 1983

NOBEL PRIZE IN MEDICINE

Ivan Petrovich Pavlov, 1904
Thomas Hunt Morgan, 1933
Albert Imre Szent-Györgyi, 1937
Walter Rudolf Hess, 1949
Tadeus Reichstein, 1950
Fritz Albert Lipmann, 1953
A. Hugo T. Theorell, 1955
Edward Lawrie Tatum, 1958
Severo Ochoa, 1959

Peter Brian Medawar, 1960
Francis Harry Compton Crick, 1962
Maurice Hugh Frederick Wilkins, 1962
John Carew Eccles, 1963
Alan Hodgkin, 1963
George Wald, 1967
Robert William Holley, 1968
Max Ludwig Henning Delbrück, 1969
Salvador Edward Luria, 1969
Bernard Katz, 1970
Ulf Svante Von Euler, 1970
Konrad Zacharias Lorenz, 1973
Nikolaas Tinbergen, 1973
Albert Claude, 1974
Roger Wolcott Sperry, 1981
Barbara McClintock, 1983
Niels Kaj Jerne, 1984
Gertrude Belle Elion, 1988

NOBEL PRIZE IN CHEMISTRY

Friedrich Wilhelm Ostwald, 1909
Fritz Haber, 1918
Richard Kuhn, 1938
Otto Hahn, 1944
Robert Robinson, 1947
Glenn Theodore Seaborg, 1951
Archer John Porter Martin, 1952
Linus Carl Pauling, 1954
Nikolaï Nikolaevich Semenov, 1956
Willard Frank Libby, 1960

Max Ferdinand Perutz, 1962
Dorothy Mary Crowfoot Hodgkin, 1964
Robert Burns Woodward, 1965
Robert Sanderson Mulliken, 1966
George Porter, 1967
Luis Federico Leloir, 1970
Gerhard Herzberg, 1971
Geoffrey Wilkinson, 1973
Paul John Flory, 1974
Vladimir Prelog, 1975
Ilya Prigogine, 1977
Peter Dennis Mitchell, 1978
Georg Wittig, 1979
Donald J. Cram, 1987
Michael Smith, 1993
Richard Errett Smalley, 1996
John Walker, 1997
John Anthony Pople, 1998

NOBEL PRIZE IN ECONOMICS

Herbert Alexander Simon, 1978
John Charles Harsanyi, 1994
John Forbes Nash, Jr., 1994
William Spencer Vickrey, 1996

NOBEL PEACE PRIZE

Andrei Dmitriyevich Sakharov, 1975

List of Articles

VOLUME 1

A

ABDERHALDEN, EMIL
ABEL, NIELS HENRIK
ABELSON, ROBERT PAUL
ADAMS, JOHN FRANK
ADELARD OF BATH
ADRIAN, EDGAR DOUGLAS, FIRST
   BARON ADRIAN OF CAMBRIDGE
AGNESI, MARIA GAETANA
AHLFORS, LARS
AIRY, GEORGE BIDDELL
AITKEN, JOHN
AKI, KEIITI
ALBERT OF SAXONY
ALBERTUS MAGNUS, SAINT
ALFVÉN, HANNES OLOF GOSTA
ALI AL-QUSHJI, ABU AL-QASIM ALA'
   AL-DIN ALI IBN MUHAMMAD
   QUSHJI-ZADE
ALLEE, WARDER CLYDE
ALLPORT, GORDON WILLARD
ALVAREZ, LUIS WALTER
AMALDI, EDOARDO
AMBARTSUMIAN, VIKTOR
   AMAZASPOVICH
AMPFERER, OTTO
ANDERSON, CARL DAVID
ANFINSEN, CHRISTIAN B.
APOLLINARIUS
APOLLONIUS OF PERGA
ARCHIMEDES
ARCONVILLE, MARIE GENEVIÈVE
   CHARLOTTE THIROUX D'
ARDUINO, GIOVANNI

ARF, CAHIT
ARGYRUS, ISAACC
ARISTOTLE
ARNALD OF VILLANOVA
ARNALD OF VILLANOVA (PSEUDO)
ARRHENIUS, SVANTE AUGUST
ASSMANN, RICHARD
AXELROD, JULIUS

B

BABBAGE, CHARLES
BABCOCK, HORACE WELCOME
BACHER, ROBERT FOX
BACON, FRANCIS
BACON, ROGE
BAERENDS, GERARD PIETER
BAGNOLD, RALPH ALGER
BAHCALL, JOHN NORRIS
BAINBRIDGE, KENNETH (KEN)
   TOMPKINS
BALDI, BERNARDINO
BALDWIN, JAMES MARK
BANNEKER, BENJAMIN
BARDEEN, JOHN
BARTLETT, FREDERIC CHARLES
BARTLETT, PAUL DOUGHTY
BARTON, DEREK HAROLD RICHARD
BASSI VERATI (VERATTI), LAURA
   MARIA CATERINA
BASSON (BASSO), SÉBASTIEN
   (SEBASTIAN, SEBASTIANO)
BASTIAN, ADOLF
BASTIAN, HENRY CHARLTON
BATESON, WILLIAM
BAYER, OTTO GEORG WILHELM
BAYES, THOMAS

BEACH, FRANK AMBROSE, JR.
BEADLE, GEORGE WELLS
BECHER, JOHANN JOACHIM
BECKMAN, ARNOLD ORVILLE
BELL, JOHN STEWART
BENIOFF, VICTOR HUGO
BERGERON, TOR HAROLD PERCIVAL
BERGMANN, ERNST DAVID
BERNOULLI, JAKOB (JACOB, JACQUES,
   JAMES) I
BERNSTEIN, RICHARD BARRY
BERS, LIPMAN
BERTHOLLET, CLAUDE LOUIS
BERZELIUS, JÖNS JACOB
BETHE, HANS ALBRECHT
BIERMANN, LUDWIG FRANZ
   BENEDIKT
BIJVOET, JOHANNES MARTIN
BIRKHOFF, GARRETT
BJERKNES, VILHELM
BLACKETT, PATRICK MAYNARD
   STUART
BLAIR, ROBERT
BLASIUS OF PARMA
BLAU, MARIETTA
BLOCH, FELIX
BODENSTEIN, ADAM OF
BOER, JAN HENDRIK DE
BOGOLUBOV, NIKOLAI NIKOLAEVICH
BOHM, DAVID JOSEPH
BOHR, NIELS HENRIK DAVID
BOK, BARTHOLOMEUS (BART) JAN
BOLTON, JOHN GATENBY
BOLTZMANN, LUDWIG EDUARD
BONDI, HERMANN
BOREL, ARMAND

BORELLI, GIOVANNI ALFONSO
BORESKOV, GEORGIĬ
  KONSTANTINOVICH
BORING, EDWIN GARRIGUES
BORRO, GIROLAMO
BOURBAKI, NICOLAS
BOYLE, ROBERT
BRACHET, JEAN LOUIS
BRADWARDINE, THOMAS
BRAHE, TYCHO
BRAUN-BLANQUET, JOSIAS
BREIT, GREGORY
BRETZ, J HARLEN
BRIGGS, ROBERT W.
BROADBENT, DONALD ERIC
BRODMANN, KORBINIAN
BROGLIE, LOUIS (VICTOR PIERRE
  RAYMOND) DE
BRONN, HEINRICH GEORG
BROWN, HERBERT CHARLES
BRUNO, GIORDANO
BUDKER, GERSH ITSKOVICH
BUFFON, GEORGES-LOUIS LECLERC
  COMTE DE
BULLOCK, THEODORE HOLMES
BUNSEN, ROBERT WILHELM
  EBERHARD
BUONAMICI, FRANCESCO
BURGERSDIJK, FRANK PIETERSZOON
BURIDAN, JOHN (JEAN)
BURLEY, WALTER
BURMEISTER, HERMANN KARL
  KONRAD
BURNET, FRANK MACFARLANE
BUTENANDT, ADOLF FRIEDRICH
  JOHANN
BUTLEROV, ALEKSANDR
  MIKHAILOVICH
BYERS, HORACE ROBERT

VOLUME 2

C

CABEO, NICCOLÒ
CAIN, ARTHUR JAMES
CALDERÓN, ALBERTO PEDRO
CALLENDAR, GUY STEWART
CALVIN, MELVIN
CAMPANELLA, TOMMASO
CAMPBELL, DONALD THOMAS
CANTOR, GEORG FERDINAND
  LUDWIG PHILIP
CARDANO, GIROLAMO
CAREY, SAMUEL WARREN
CARNAP, PAUL RUDOLF
CAROTHERS, WALLACE HUME
CARPENTER, CLARENCE RAY

CARPENTER, WILLIAM BENJAMIN
CARSON, HAMPTON LAWRENCE
CASIMIR, HENDRIK BRUGT GERHARD
CASPERSSON, TORBJÖRN OSKAR
CATTELL, JAMES MCKEEN
CAUCHY, AUGUSTIN-LOUIS
CAVENDISH, MARGARET, DUCHESS
  OF NEWCASTLE
CELSUS, CORNELIUS (AULUS)
CHAMBERS, ROBERT
CHANDRASEKHAR, SUBRAHMANYAN
CHARGAFF, ERWIN
CHARNEY, JULE GREGORY
CHATT, JOSEPH
CHERENKOV, PAVEL ALEKSEYEVICH
CHERN, SHIING-SHEN
CHEVALLEY, CLAUDE
CHIONIADES, GEORGE (OR
  GREGORY)
CHRYSIPPUS
CLARK, JOHN DESMOND
CLARK, KENNETH BANCROFT AND
  MAMIE PHIPPS CLARK
CLARK, WILFRID EDWARD LE GROS
CLAUDE, ALBERT
CLAVIUS, CHRISTOPH
CLEMENTS, FREDERIC EDWARD
COCKAYNE, LEONARD
COIGNET, MICHIEL (MICHAËL)
COLLONGUES, ROBERT
CONDON, EDWARD UHLER
CONWAY, ANNE
COON, CARLETON STEVENS
COPERNICUS, NICHOLAS
COWDRY, EDMUND VINCENT
COWLES, HENRY CHANDLER
COX, ALLAN VERNE
CRAFTS, JAMES MASON
CRAIG, WALLACE
CRAM, DONALD J.
CREMER, ERIKA
CRICK, FRANCIS HARRY COMPTON
CRONQUIST, ARTHUR
CROSSE, ANDREW
CULLEN, WILLIAM
CUVIER, GEORGES

D

D'ALEMBERT (DALEMBERT), JEAN LE
  ROND
DAMIANUS OF LARISSA
DANSEREAU, PIERRE MACKAY
DART, RAYMOND ARTHUR
DARWIN, CHARLES ROBERT
DAVY, HUMPHREY
DAY, ARTHUR LOUIS
DE FINETTI, BRUNO
DE GIORGI, ENNIO
DEACON, GEORGE EDWARD RAVEN

DEFANT, ALBERT JOSEPH MARIA
DELBRÜCK, MAX LUDWIG HENNING
DESCARTES, RENE DU PERRON
DEWAR, MICHAEL J. S.
DICKE, ROBERT HENRY
DIDYMUS
DIETZ, ROBERT SINCLAIR
DIEUDONNÉ, JEAN
DIJKSTRA, WYBE EDSGER
DING, WENJIANG (V. K. TING)
DIOCLES OF CARYSTUS
DIODORUS OF ALEXANDRIS
DOBSON, GORDON MILLER BOURNE
DODGSON, CHARLES LUTWIDGE
DUBOIS, MARIE EUGÈNE FRANÇOIS
  THOMAS
DOBOS, RENÉ JULES
DUHEM, PIERRE-MAURICE-MARIE
DUMAS, JEAN-BAPTISTE-ANDRÉ
DUMBLETON, JOHN

E

ECCLES, JOHN CAREW
ECKERT, J. (JOHN ADAM) PRESPER, JR.
EDDINGTON, ARTHUR STANLEY
EDINGER, LUDWIG
EDLÉN, BENGT
EDMAN, PEHR VICTOR
EDMONDSON, WALLIS THOMAS
EHRENFEST-AFANAS'EVA, TATIANA A.
EICHENGRÜN, ARTHUR
EILENBERG, SAMUEL
EINSTEIN, ALBERT
ELION, GERTRUDE BELLE
ELSASSER, WALTER MAURICE
ELTON, CHARLES SUTHERLAND
EMERSON, ALFRED EDWARDS
EMMETT, PAUL HUGH
EMPEDOCLES OF ACRAGAS
EPHRUSSI, BORIS
ERDÖS, PAUL (PÁL)
ERIKSON, ERIK HOMBURGER
ERIUGENA, JOHANNES SCOTTUS
ESAU, KATHERINE
EUCLID
EULER, LEONHARD
EXNER-EWARTEN, FELIX MARIA VON
EYSENCK, HANS JÜRGEN

VOLUME 3

F

FARADAY, MICHAEL
FAREY, JOHN
FEDOROV, KONSTANTIN
  NIKOLAYEVICH
FEIT, WALTER

FESTINGER, LEON
FEYNMAN, RICHARD PHILLIPS
FISCHER, (LEOPOLD FRANZ) EUGEN
FISHER, RONALD AYLMER
FLEROV, GEORGIĬ NIKOLAEVICH
FLORY, PAUL JOHN
FOLKERS, KARL AUGUST
FORD, EDMUND BRISCO
FORSYTHE, GEORGE ELMER
FOSSEY, DIAN
FOSTER, GEORGE CAREY
FOWLER, WILLIAM A.
FRANKLAND, EDWARD
FRANKLIN, ROSALIND ELSIE
FREGE, FRIEDRICH LUDWIG
    GOTTLOB
FREUD, SIGMUND
FRIEDMAN, HERBERT
FUJITA, TETSUYA THEODORE
FUKUI, KEN'ICHI

G

GALEN (GALÊNOS)
GALELEI, GALILEO
GARROD, DOROTHY ANNIE
    ELIZABETH
GARZONI, LEONARDO S. J.
GASSENDI, PIERRE
GEOFFROY SAINT-HILAIRE, ÉTIENNE
GEOFFROY SAINT-HILAIRE, ISIDORE
GIBSON, ELEANOR JACK
GIBSON, JAMES JEROME
GÖDEL, KURT FRIEDRICH
GOETHE, JOHANN WOLFGANG VON
GOLD, THOMAS
GOLDBERG, LEO
GOLDMAN-RAKIC, PATRICIA SHOER
GOODMAN, NELSON HENRY
GORENSTEIN, DANIEL
GORJANOVIĆ-KRAMBERGER,
    DRAGUTIN (KARL)
GORLAEUS (VAN GOORLE, VAN
    GOOIRLE), DAVID
GOULD, STEPHEN JAY
GREAVES, JOHN
GREEN, DAVID EZRA
GREENSTEIN, JESSE LEONARD
GRIFFIN, DONALD REDFIELD
GROBSTEIN, CLIFFORD
GROSSMAN, MARCEL
GÜRSEY, FEZA
GUTOWSKY, HERBERT SANDER

H

HABER, FRITZ
HAECKEL, ERNST
HAHN, OTTO
HALL, PHILIP

HALLER, (VICTOR) ALBRECHT VON
HAMBURGER, VIKTOR
HAMILTON, WILLIAM DONALD
HAMILTON, WILLIAM ROWAN
HAMMETT, LOUIS PLACK
HARISH-CHANDRA
HARRIOT (OR HARIOT), THOMAS
HARSANYI, JOHN CHARLES
HARTREE, DOUGLAS RAYNER
HARVEY, HILDEBRAND WOLFE
HASLER, ARTHUR DAVIS
HAURWITZ, BERNHARD
HAUSDORFF, FELIX
HEBB, DONALD OLDING
HECKEL, ÉDOUARD-MARIE
HECKMANN, OTTO HERMANN
    LEOPOLD
HELMONT, JOHANNES (JOAN)
    BAPTISTA VAN
HENNIG, (EMIL HANS) WILLI
HERO OF ALEXANDRIA
HERSCHEL, CAROLINE LUCRETIA
HERSCHEL, JOHN
HERSCHEL, WILLIAM
HERTZ, HEINRICH RUDOLF
HERTZ, MATHILDE CARMEN
HERZBERG, GERHARD
HESS, WALTER RUDOLF
HILBERT, DAVID
HILGARD, ERNEST ROPIEQUET
HILL, DOROTHY
HIPPARCHUS
HIPPOCRATES OF COS
HIRST, THOMAS ARCHER
HODGKIN, ALAN
HODGKIN, DOROTHY MARY
    CROWFOOT
HOLBROOK, JOHN EDWARDS
HOLLEY, ROBERT WILLIAM
HOLMES, GORDON MORGAN
HOLTFRETER, JOHANNES
HOMBERG, WILHELM
HONDIUS, JODOCUS
HOPPER, GRACE MURRAY
HOROWITZ, NORMAN HAROLD
HÖRSTADIUS, SVEN OTTO
HORTON, ROBERT ELMER
HOSPERS, JAN
HOU TE-PANG (DEBANG HOU)
HOUDRY, EUGÈNE JULES
HOWARD, HENRY ELIOT
HOWARD, LUKE
HOYLE, FRED
HUANG JIQING (TE-KAN)
HUBBERT, MARION KING
HÜCKEL, ERICH ARMAND ARTHUR
HULL, CLARK LEONARD
HUTCHINSON, G. EVELYN
HUTTON, JAMES

HUXLEY, JULIAN
HUXLEY, THOMAS HENRY
HYMAN, LIBBIE HENRIETTA
HYPATIA

VOLUME 4

I

IBN AL-HAYTHAM, ABU ʿALĪ AL-
    HASAN IBN AL-HASAN
IBRĀHĪM IBN SINĀN IBN THĀBIT IBN
    QURRA
IMES, ELMER SAMUEL
INGLADA, VICENTE
INGOLD, CHRISTOPHER KELK

J

JĀBIR IBN ḤAYYĀN
JAGHMĪNĪ, SHARAF AL-DĪN MAḤMŪD
    IBN MUḤAMMAD IBN ʾUMAR AL-
JAMES, WILLIAM
JANET, PIERRE
JANSSEN, PAUL ADRIAAN JAN
JEFFREY, RICHARD CARL
JEFFREYS, HAROLD
JELÍNEK, JAN
JENNINGS, HERBERT SPENCER
JERNE, NIELS KAJ
JOHN PHILOPONUS
JOHNSTON, JAMES FINLAY WEIR
JORDAN, ERNST PASCUAL
JØRGENSEN, AXEL CHRISTIAN
    KLIXBÜLL
JUNG, CARL GUSTAV
JUNGIUS, JOACHIM
JUST, ERNEST EVERETT

K

KALCKAR, HERMAN MORITZ
KAMMERER, PAUL
KAPITSA (OR KAPITZA), PETR
    LEONIDOVICH
KATZ, BERNARD
KEELING, CHARLES DAVID
KEKULE VON STRADONITZ (KEKULÉ),
    (FRIEDRICH) AUGUST
KELDYSH, MSTISLAV
    VSEVOLODOVICH
KEPLER, JOHANNES
KETTLEWELL, HENRY BERNARD
    DAVIS
KEYNES, JOHN MAYNARD
KIMURA, MOTOO
KING, ADA AUGUSTA, COUNTESS OF
    LOVELACE
KING, CLARENCE RIVERS
KINSEY, ALFRED CHARLES

KIRCHER, ATHANASIUS
KLEIN, HAROLD P.
KLÜVER, HENRICH
KODAIRA, KUNIHIKO
KOEHLER, OTTO
KOLBE, HERMANN
KOLMOGOROV, ANDREI
   NIKOLAEVICH
KÖPPEN, WLADIMIR PETER
KORZHINSKII, DIMITRI
   SERGEYEVICH
KOVALEVSKAYA, SOFYA VASILYEVNA
   (SONYA)
KROPOTKIN, PETR ALEKSEYEVICH
KRUMBEIN, WILLIAM CHRISTIAN
KUHN, RICHARD
KUHN, THOMAS SAMUEL
KUIPER, GERARD PETER

L

LA METTRIE, JULIEN OFFRAY DE
LADD, HARRY STEPHEN
LADYZHENSKAYA, OLGA
   ALEXANDROVNA
LAMARCK, JEAN-BAPTISTE
LAMB, HUBERT HORACE
LANDSBERG, HELMUT ERICH
LANZ, JOSÉ MARÍA DE
LASHLEY, KARL SPENCER
LAURENT, AUGUSTE
LAURITSEN, CHARLES CHRISTIAN
LAVOISIER, ANTOINE-LAURENT
LEAKEY, MARY DOUGLAS NICOL
LECONTE, JOSEPH
LEDERER, EDGAR
LEE, SARAH EGLONTON WALLIS
   BOWDICH
LEHMANN, INGE
LEHMANN-NITSCHE, ROBERT
LEHNINGER, ALBERT LESTER
LEHRMAN, DANIEL SANFORD
LEIBNIZ, GOTTFRIED WILHELM
LELOIR, LUIS FEDERICO
LEMIEUX, RAYMOND URGEL
LEONICENO, NICOLÒ
LEOPOLD, ALDO
LEPTINES
LERAY, JEAN
LERNER, I(SADORE) MICHAEL
LEWIN, KURT
LEWIS, DAVID
LEWIS, WARREN KENDALL
LIAIS, EMMANUEL-BERNARDIN
LIBBY, WILLARD FRANK
LICHNÉROWICZ, ANDRÉ
LICKLIDER, JOSEPH CARL ROBNETT
LIE, MARIUS SOPHUS
LIEBIG, JUSTUS VON
LINNAEUS, CARL

LIONS, JACQUES-LOUIS
LIPMANN, FRITZ ALBERT
LIVINGSTON, MILTON STANLEY
LORENTZ, HENDRIK ANTOON
LORENZ, KONRAD ZACHARIAS
LULL, RAMON
LURIA, ALEXANDER ROMANOVICH
LURIA, SALVADOR EDWARD
   (SALVATORE)

VOLUME 5

M

MAC LANE, SAUNDERS
MAIMONIDES, RABBI MOSES BEN
   MAIMON
MAIRAN, JEAN-JACQUES DORTOUS
   DE
MALTHUS, THOMAS ROBERT
MANGOLD (NÉE PROSCHOLDT),
   HILDE
MANSFIELD, CHARLES BLACHFORD
MARCET, JANE HALDIMAND
MARGALEF, RAMON
MARINUS OF TYRE
MARK, HERMAN F.
MARR, DAVID COURTNAY
MARSILI (OR MARSIGLI), LUIGI
   FERDINANDO
MARTIN, ARCHER JOHN PORTER
MASLOW, ABRAHAM
MATUYAMA, MOTONORI
MAUCHLY, JOHN WILLIAM
MAUPERTUIS, PIERRE LOUIS MOREAU
   DE
MAYOR (FORMERLY MAYER), ALFRED
   GOLDSBOROUGH
MAYR, ERNST WALTER
MCCLINTOCK, BARBARA
MCCREA, WILLIAM HUNTER
MCCULLOCH, WARREN STURGIS
MCVITTIE, GEORGE CUNLIFFE
MEDAWAR, PETER BRIAN
MEEHL, PAUL EVERETT
MELITENIOTES, THEODORE
MENARD, HENRY WILLIAM
MENDEL, JOHANN GREGOR
MENDELEEV, DMITRII IVANOVICH
MENZEL, DONALD HOWARD
MERIAN, MARIA SIBYLLA
MERTON, ROBERT KING
MIGDAL, ARKADY BENEDIKTOVICH
MILANKOVIĆ (MILANKOVITCH),
   MILUTIN
MILGRAM, STANLEY
MILL, JOHN STUART
MILLER, NEAL ELGAR

MILLER, STANLEY LLOYD
MITCHELL, PETER DENNIS
MITSCHERLICH, EILHARD
MIZUSHIMA, SAN-ICHIRŌ
MÖLLER, SOPHIE C(H)ARLOTTE
   JULIANE (LOTTE)
MONTE, GUIDOBALDO, MARCHESE
   DEL
MONTEIRO, ANTÓNIO A.
MORENO, FRANCISCO PASCASIO
MORGAN, THOMAS HUNT
MORGENSTERN, OSKAR
MORRISON, PHILIP
MORSE, MARSTON
MOSCHOPOULOS, MANUEL
MOSER, JÜRGEN K.
MOTT, NEVILL FRANCIS
MUELLER, FERDINAND JAKOB
   HEINRICH VON
MULLIKEN, ROBERT SANDERSON
MURRAY, HENRY ALEXANDER

N

NAMIAS, JEROME
NASH, JOHN FORBES, JR.
NEEDHAM, DOROTHY MOYLE
NEEDHAM, JOSEPH
NEEL, JAMES VAN GUNDIA
NESMEJANOV, ALEKSANDR
   NIKOLAEVICH
NEUBERG, CARL ALEXANDER
NEWELL, ALLEN
NEWELL, HOMER EDWARD, JR.
NEWELL, NORMAN DENNIS
NEWTON, ISAAC
NICE, MARGARET MORSE
NIFO, AGOSTINO
NOVIKOFF, ALEX BENJAMIN
NOZICK, ROBERT
NOZOE, TETSUO

O

OAKLEY, KENNETH PAGE
OCCHIALINI, GIUSEPPE PAOLO
   STANISLAO
OCHOA, SEVERO
OCKHAM, WILLIAM OF
ODUM, EUGENE PLEASANTS
ODUM, HOWARD THOMAS
OESCHGER, HANS
OKEN (OR OKENFUSS), LORENZ
OLEINIK, OLGA ARSENIEVNA
OLSON, MANCUR, JR.
OLYMPIODORUS OF ALEXANDRIA
OLYMPIODORUS OF THEBES
OORT, JAN HENDRIK
OPPENHEIMER, J. ROBERT
ORESME, NICOLE

OSBORN, HENRY FAIRFIELD
OSTWALD, FRIEDRICH WILHELM
OVCHINNIKOV, YURY ANATOLYEVICH
OWEN, RICHARD

VOLUME 7

P

PACHYMERES, GEORGES (OR
    GEORGE)
PALMÉN, ERIK HERBERT
PANETH, FRIEDRICH ADLOF
PANOFSKY, HANS ARNOLD
PAPEZ, JAMES WENCESLAS
PARACELSUS, THEOPHRASTUS
    PHILIPPUS AUREOLUS BOMBASTUS
    VON HONENHEIM
PARETO, VILFREDO
PASTEUR, LOUIS
PATTERSON, COLIN
PAULI, WOLFGANG
PAULING, LINUS CARL
PAULZE-LAVOISIER, MARIE-ANNE-
    PIERETTE
PAVLOV, IVAN PETROVICH
PAYNE-GAPOSCHKIN, CECILIA
    HELENA
PEARSON, KARL
PEI WENZHONG
PEIERLS, RUDOLF ERNST
PELLICIER, GUILLAUME
PENFIELD, WILDER GRAVES
PEREY, MARGUERITE CATHERINE
PERUTZ, MAX FERDINAND
PETTERSSEN, SVERRE
PETTERSSON, SVEN OTTO
PIAGET, JEAN
PICARDET, CLAUDINE
PICKERING, WILLIAM HAYWARD
PIERO DELLA FRANCESCA
PIVETEAU, JEAN
PLANCIUS, PETRUS
PLANCK, MAX
PLATO
PLINY THE ELDER (CAIUS PLINIUS
    SECUNDUS)
POINCARÉ, JULES HENRI
POLÁ, MIHÁLY (MICHAEL)
PONTRYAGIN, LEV SEMIONOVICH
POPLE, JOHN ANTHONY
POPPER, KARL RAIMUND
PORPHYRY
PORTER, GEORGE
PORTER, KEITH ROBERTS
POWELL, JOHN WESLEY
PRACHATICZ, CRISTANNUS DE
PRELOG, VLADIMIR

PRICE, DEREK JOHN DESOLLA
PRIGOGINE, ILYA
PRIMAKOFF, HENRY
PTOLEMAIS OF CYRENE
PTOLEMY (OR CLAUDIUS
    PTOLEMAEUS)
PURCELL, EDWARD MILLS

Q

QŪHĪ (OR AL-KŪHĪ), ABŪ SAHL
    WAYJAN IBN RUSTAM AL-
QUTB AL-DĪN MAHMŪD IBN MASʿŪD
    IBN AL-MUSLIH AL-SHĪRĀZĪ

R

RABI, ISIDOR ISAAC
RACKER, EFRAIM
RAMSEY, FRANK PLUMPTON
RAMUS, PETER
RATCLIFFE, FRANCIS NOBLE
RĀZĪ, ABŪ BAKR MUHAMMAD IBN
    ZAKARIYYAʾ AL-
REGIOMONTANUS, JOHANNES
REICHELDERFER, FRANCIS WILTON
REICHSTEIN, TADEUS
REPPE, JULIUS WALTER
REVELLE, ROGER RANDALL DOUGAN
RICHARDSON, LEWIS FRY
RICHTER, CHARLES FRANCIS
RICHTER, CURT P.
RICHTER, RUDOLF
REIMANN, GEORG FRIEDRICH
    BERNHARD
RIKER, WILLIAM HARRISON
RILEY, GORDON ARTHUR
RINGWOOD, ALFRED EDWARD (TED)
RITTMANN, ALFRED (ALFREDO)
    FERDINAND
ROBINSON, JULIA BOWMAN
ROBINSON, ROBERT
ROGERS, CARL RANSOM
ROSSI, BRUNO BENEDETTO
ROTA, GIAN-CARLO
ROYER, CLÉMENCE-AUGUSTE
RUFUS OF EPHESUS
RUFUS, RICHARD OF CORNWALL
RUNCORN, STANLEY KEITH
RYLE, MARTIN

S

SAGAN, CARL EDWARD
SAGER, RUTH
SAH, PETER P. T.
SAKHAROV, ANDREI DMITRIYEVICH
SAKURADA, ICHIRO
SALAM, MUHAMMAD ABDUS
    (ABDUSSALAM)
SALTZMAN, BARRY

SAUSSURE, HORACE BÉNÉDICT DE
SAVAGE, LEONARD JAMES
SCHINDEWOLF, OTTO HEINRICH
SCHLEIDEN, MATTHIAS JACOB
SCHMITT, FRANCIS OTTO
SCHNEIRLA, THEODORE CHRISTIAN
SCHOTT, PAUL GERHARD
SCHOTTKY, WALTER HANS
SCHWARTZ, LAURENT
SCHWARZSCHILD, MARTIN
SCHWENDENER, SIMON
SCHWINGER, JULIAN SEYMOUR
SCIAMA, DENNIS WILLIAM
SEABORG, GLENN (GLEN) THEODORE
SEGRÈ, EMILIO GINO
SEMENOV, NIKOLAÏ NIKOLAEVICH
SENNERT, DANIEL
SERBER, ROBERT
SHANNON, CLAUDE ELWOOD
SHATSKIY, NIKOLAY SERGEYEVICH
SHKLOVSKII, IOSIF SAMUILOVICH
SHOCKLEY, WILLIAM BRADFORD
SHOEMAKER, EUGENE MERLE
SHTERN, LINA SOLOMONOVNA
SIMON, HERBERT ALEXANDER
SIMPSON, GEORGE GAYLORD
SITTER, WILLEM DE
SKINNER, BURRHUS FREDERIC (B. F.)
SLOSS, LAURENCE LOUIS
SMAGORINSKY, JOSEPH
SMALLEY, RICHARD ERRETT
SMITH, JAMES LEONARD BRIERLEY
SMITH, MICHAEL
SMUTS, JAN CHRISTIAN
    (CHRISTIAAN)
SOFFEN, GERALD ALAN
SOMMERFELD, ARNOLD JOHANNES
    WILHELM
SONNEBORN, TRACY MORTON
SPERRY, ROGER WOLCOTT
SPITZER, LYMAN, JR.
STAHL, GEORG ERNST
STANCHINSKIY, VLADIMIR
    VLADIMIROVICH
STARKEY, GEORGE
STEBBINS, GEORGE LEDYARD, JR.
STEPHANUS OF ALEXANDRIA
STEPHENSON, MARJORY
STERN, LOUIS WILLIAM
STOMMEL, HENRY MELSON
STRACHEY, CHRISTOPHER
STRAHLER, ARTHUR NEWELL
STRATO OF LAMPSACUS
STRÖMGREN, BENGT GEORG DANIEL
STRUTT, JOHN WILLIAM, THIRD
    BARON RAYLEIGH
SUCHTEN, ALEXANDER VON
SUOMI, VERNER EDWARD
SUTCLIFFE, REGINALD COCKCROFT

SWINESHEAD (SWYNESHED, SUICET,
     ETC.), RICHARD
SWYNESHED (SWINESHEAD), ROGER
SYLVESTER, JAMES JOSEPH
SZENT-GYÖRGYI, ALBERT IMRE
SZILARD, LEO

VOLUME 7

T

TAMMES, JANITA
TANSLEY, SIR ARTHUR GEORGE
TARSKI, ALFRED
TATUM, EDWARD LAWRIE
TEICHERT, CURT
TEISSERENC DE BORT, LÉON
     PHILIPPE
TELLER, EDWARD
TERMAN, LEWIS MADISON
THARP, MARIE
THEORELL, AXEL HUGO THEODOR
THIENEMANN, AUGUST FRIEDRICH
THORNTHWAITE, CHARLES WARREN
THORPE, WILLIAM HOMAN
THUDICHUM, JOHANN LUDWIG
     WILHELM
TIMOCHARIS
TINBERGEN, NIKOLAAS (NIKO)
TINSLEY, BEATRICE MURIEL HILL
TINTANT, HENRI
TODD, ALEXANDER ROBERTUS
     (BARON TODD)
TOUSCHEK, BRUNO
TOUSEY, RICHARD
TRAILL, CATHARINE PARR
TUCKER, ALBERT WILLIAM
TURING, ALAN MATHISON
TURNER, CHARLES HENRY
ṬŪSĪ, SHARAF AL-DĪN AL-MUẒAFFAR
     IBN MUḤAMMAD IBN AL-
     MUẒAFFAR, AL-
TUTTE, WILLIAM (BILL) THOMAS
TVERSKY, AMOS

U

UHLENBECK, GEORGE EUGENE

UNSÖLD, ALBRECHT OTTO
     JOHANNES

V

VALENS, VETTIUS
VALLIOS, HENRI VICTOR
VAN ALLEN, JAMES A.
VAN DE HULST, HENDRIK
     CHRISTOFFEL
VAN KREVELEN, DIRK WILLEM
VAN STRAATEN, LAMBERTUS MARIUS
     JOANNES URSINUS
VENKATARAMAN, KRISHNASAMI
VICKREY, WILLIAM SPENCER
VIÑES MARTORELL, CARLOS BENITO
     JOSÉ
VINOGRADOV, IVAN MATVEEVICH
VIRCHOW, RUDOLF CARL
VOGT, CÉCILEAUGUSTINE MARIE
     (NÉE MUGNIER) AND OSKAR VOGT
VOIGT, WOLDEMAR
VOLTA, ALESSANDRO GIUSEPPE
     ANTONIO ANASTASIO
VON BRAUN, WERNHER MAGNUS
     MAXIMILIAN FREIHERR
VON EULER, ULF SAVANTE
VON HOLST, ERICH
VON KOENIGSWALD, GUSTAV
     HEINRICH RALPH
VRIES, HUGO DE
VYGOTSKY, LEV SEMYONOVICH

W

WADATI, KIYOO
WADDINGTON, CONRAD HAL
WADIA, DARASHAW NOSHERWAN
WAGNER, MORITZ
WALD, GEORGE
WALKER, GILBERT THOMAS
WALKER, JOHN
WALLACE, ALFRED RUSSEL
WALSH, ALAN
WASHBURN, SHERWOOD LARNED
WATSON, JOHN BROADUS
WEGENER, ALFRED LOTHAR
WEIDENREICH, FRANZ
WEIL, ANDRÉ

WEISMANN, AUGUST FRIEDRICH
     LEOPOLD
WEISSKOPF, VICTOR FREDERICK
WESTPHAL, JAMES A.
WEXLER, HARRY
WEYL, HERMANN CLAUS HUGO
WHEWELL, WILLIAM
WHIPPLE, FRED LAWRENCE
WHITNEY, HASSLER
WILKINS, MAURICE HUGH
     FREDERICK
WILKINSON, DAVID TODD
WILKINSON, GEOFFREY
WILKINSON, JAMES HARDY
WILSON, ALAN HERRIES
WILSON, JOHN TUZO
WILSON, ROBERT RATHBUN
WINKELMANN, MARIA MARGARETHA
WINTHROP, JOHN, JR.
WITTIG, GEORG
WOLLASTON, WILLIAM HYDE
WOOD, HARLAND GOFF
WOODWARD, ROBERT BURNS
WRIGHT, SEWALL
WU CHIEN-SHIUNG
WUNDT, WILHELM
WURTZ, ADOLPHE
WÜST, GEORG
WYNNE-EDWARDS, VERO COPNER

X

XENARCHUS

Y

YANG ZHONGJIAN
YIN ZANXUN

Z

ZABARELLA, JACOPO (GIACOMO)
ZELDOVICH, YAKOV BORISOVICH
ZELINSKIĬ, NIKOLAY DMITRIEVICH
ZHAO ZHONGYAO
ZHU KEZHEN
ZOSIMOS OF PANOPOLIS
ZUSE, KONRAD
ZYGMUND, ANTONI

A Note on the Index

In compiling the Index for the *New Dictionary of Scientific Biography* the following criteria have been adopted:

Alphabetization: This index is sorted in word-by-word order. This means that spaces between words are included in the sort and that headings beginning with the same word are sorted together. For example, the heading for "Mariner, Ruth" will be found *after* "Marine science" in the list below:

Marine ecosystems

Marine science

Mariner, Ruth

Mariner space probes

Diacritical marks are ignored for sorting purposes. Punctuation is sorted before numbers, and numbers are sorted before letters. Initial articles in both English and foreign languages (the, an, das, les) are ignored for sorting purposes.

Person names starting with Mac- and Mc- have all been sorted together under Mac-.

Alphabetization of subheadings is by principal words, ignoring leading prepositions.

Inclusion: All substantial mentions of persons, works, organizations, places and concepts, including branches of science from the essays in this encyclopedia have been included in this index. The content of the front matter, the back matter, and the bibliographic material is not included in this index. This index is designed to steer users of the print version of the *New Dictionary of Scientific Biography* quickly to all substantial information contained herein regarding a topic. However, it is worth mentioning that those users who seek all possible mentions of a topic may be well advised to consult the electronic version of this work in the Gale Virtual Reference Library.

Page References: The volume number precedes the page reference the first time that the volume number is used, e.g. 8:123, 157 or 12:15-27, 145. Bolded page references refer to a main essay on a topic and italicized page references refer to an image. For example, in the entry for Newell, Homer Edward, Jr., 3:80, 5:259, *259,* **259–264,** 6:100, 102, an image appears on page 259 of Volume 5 and the entry from pages 259 to 264 of Volume 5 is the main entry.

Names: Person names with surnames are generally inverted and appear as they have been listed in their main essay in the encyclopedia, e.g. Marcet, Jane Haldimand, 5: **20–22,** 21. Person names consisting of forenames only are in natural order as in Adelard of Bath, 1: **13–15.** *See* references have also been created for alternate names, so that all of the page references for a person are gathered under a single heading.

Work Names: Titles of works such as novels, newspapers, monographs, and other longer works have been italicized, e.g. *Optical Lectures* (Newton), 5:269. Most work names have received a parenthetical qualifier to distinguish them from similarly titled works. Headings for foreign-language works may appear in either English or the language of origin and will reflect the version of the title was used in the text. Where variant titles have been used, *See* references have been created between the English and foreign-language versions.

Term Selection, Inversions and Natural Word Order: The terms selected for headings and subheadings in this index reflect the terms and concepts used in the essays themselves and seek to replicate them as closely as possible. Wherever practical, concept terms appear in natural word order, e.g. "Marine ecosystems" instead of "Ecosystems, marine."

John A. Magee
Manager, Book & Database Indexing, Cengage Learning

Index

A

A-4 rockets, 7:173–174

A-bombs. *See* Atomic bombs

A-S Reaction Study (Allport), 1:52

ABA (Association for Behavior Analysis), 6:465

Abauzit, Firmin, 5:11

Abbe, Ernst, 3:69, 6:370

ABCC (Atomic Bomb Casualty Commission), 5:242

abcdef system, 6:544

'Abd al-'Alī al-Birjandī. *See* al-Birjandī, 'Abd al-'Alī

Abderhalden, Emil, 1:**1–5**, *2*, 2:349

Abderhalden reaction, 1:2

Abdussalam. *See* Salam, Muhammad Abdus

Abegg, Richard Wilhelm Heinrich, 4:288

Abel, Niels Henrik, 1:**5–8**, *7*

    Abelian categories, 5:2

    integrals, 7:254

Abel, Nils. *See* Abel, Niels Henrik

Abel, Othenio, 7:142

Abeles, Francine F., 2:310

Abelian categories, 5:2–3

Abelian functions, 1:5, 6:251, 252

Abelian groups, 3:213, 214, 241, 243

Abelian integrals, 1:6–7, 7:254

Abelson, Philip H., 1:55, 6:402

Abelson, Robert Paul, 1:**8–11**

Aberhalden-Fanconi syndrome, 1:2

Ability grouping, 7:26, 27

ABMA (Army Ballistic Missile Agency), 7:174–175

About Behaviorism (Skinner), 6:465

Abri Zumoffen (Lebanon), 3:106

Abriss der Naturphilosophie (Oken), 5:331

The Abruptly Ended Discourse in the College of France (Bruno), 1:424–425

Absolon, Karel, 4:42

Absolute dating techniques, 3:155, 5:299

Absorption

    energy

        Franck-Condon principle, 2:165

        gamma rays, 7:398–399

    light

        photosynthesis, 2:14–15

        transition metals, 4:60

        vision, 7:214, *214*

Absorption and Density Distribution in the Galactic System (Oort), 5:343

Abstract (Hutton), 3:419

Abū Ḥātim al-Rāzī. *See* al-Rāzī, Abū Ḥātim

Abū l-'Abbās al-Irānshahrī, 6:213–214

Abū al-Qāsim Alā' al-Dīn Alī ibn Muhammad Qushjī-Zāde. *See* Alī al-Qūshjī

Abū Ma'shar. *See* Abū Ma'shar al-Balkhī, Ja'far ibn Muhammad

Abū Ma'shar al-Balkhī, Ja'far ibn Muhammad, 1:14, 145

Abundance Project, 3:175–176

Abwehrfermente. See Defense enzymes

Abystoma mexicanum, 1:399–400

Accelerators

    Cockcroft-Walton, 1:392

    electrostatic

        China, 7:400

        resonance phenomena and, 3:60

    heavy ion, 3:35–36

    linear, 6:409

Accelerators, *continued*
> particle
>> atomic weapons and, 2:110, 7:329–331
>> betatron, 7:69
>> colliding-beam, 1:425–429, *426,* 7:70–72
>> development of, 1:237, 4:328–333, 7:69, 70–71
>> diagram of, 4:*329, 330*
>> field theory and, 1:238
>> synchrotron, 2:110
Accommodation, 1:169, 171–172, 2:26
According to the Action (Zosimus), 5:338
Accretion, 3:388, 389
Acetates, 7:347–348
Acetic acid, 3:168
Acetyl-CoA, 3:170, 171
Acetylcholine (ACh), 4:86, 87–88, 90
Acetylene, 6:230–231, 233
Acetylene and Carbon Monoxide Chemistry (Copenhaver and Bigelow), 6:232
Ach, Narziss, 4:279
ACh (Acetylcholine), 4:86, 87–88, 90
Achard, Franz Karl, 1:95
Achievement tests, 7:26
Achromatism, 1:295
Acids
> gas chromatography, 5:40
> Hell-Volhard-Zelinskiĭ reaction, 7:395
> water effect on, 3:238–239
Ackermann, R., 4:231
Ackermann, Wilhelm, 3:309
Ackroyd, Peter, 4:347
Acoustics
> air particle elasticity, 5:10, 11
> experimental, 6:549
> psychoacoustics, 4:303–304
> underwater, 6:500
Acquired immunodeficiency syndrome (AIDS)
> acyclovir and, 2:377
> aspergillus in, 4:33
> origin of, 3:234
Across the Space Frontier (Whipple), 7:287
Acrylate esters, 6:231
Acrylonitrile, 1:217–218
Acta Crystallographica, 1:285
Acta Mathematica, 2:32
Actinide concept, 6:401, 403, *403,* 404
Action potentials, 3:328–332, *329,* 329–332
> axons, 6:362
> neurotransmitters, 4:89–90
Actualistic paleontology, 6:249
Actuarial science, 6:566
Actuogeology, 6:248, 249
Acyclovir, 2:373, 376–377
Ad Apollinem in catarrho pestilentiali (Suchten), 6:552

AdA (Anello di Accumulazione) particle collider, 7:70–71
Adadurov, Ivan Evgrafovich, 1:352
Adair, Eleanor, 5:151
Adair, Robert K., 1:392
Adam of Bodenstein. *See* Bodenstein, Adam of
Adamantane, 1:200, 6:*156*
Adami, Tobias, 2:20
Adams, Charles C., 2:198
Adams, Francis, 3:322
Adams, John Couch, 1:25–26, 7:320
Adams, John Frank, 1:*11,* **11–13**
Adams, Mark, 4:163
Adams, Roger, 3:197, 200
Adam's Ancestors (Leakey), 4:221
Adams conjecture, 1:11, 12
Adams operations, 1:11, 12
Adams spectral sequence, 1:11, 12
Adamson, Robert, 1:142
Adaptation
> behavioral, 3:184, 408
> biosocial theory of individual, 1:168, 171–172
> extinction and, 1:416
> natural selection, 7:226–227
> punctuational model of, 3:161
> selection and, 2:5
> taste aversion, 6:245–246
Adaptation and Intelligence (Piaget), 6:94
Adaptation and Natural Selection (Williams), 1:48, 3:229, 7:379
Adaptive optics, 1:131
Adaptive variation, 1:210–211
Addis, Thomas, 6:39
Addison's disease, 6:568
Additions to the Data (al-Qūhī), 6:186
Addresses to the German Nation (Fichte), 5:331
Adelard I, Elements (Euclid) translation, 1:14
Adelard II, Elements (Euclid) translation, 1:14
Adelard III, Elements (Euclid) translation, 1:14
Adelard of Bath, 1:**13–15**
Adenosine, 2:375–376, 7:*67*
Adenosine diphosphate (ADP), 5:309–310
Adenosine triphosphate (ATP)
> formation from ADP, 4:324–325, *325,* 326–327
> in glycolysis, 6:197, 198
> in muscle contraction, 5:231, 232, 6:571
> in photosynthesis and phosphorylation, 5:161–163, 7:67
> in pyruvate oxidation, 5:307, 309–310
> synthesis of, 6:312
Adet, Pierre Auguste, 4:216
ADH (Alcohol dehydrogenase), 7:34–35
Adie, William J., 3:345
Adkins, Homer, 3:41, 42, 43

Adler, Alfred, 2:135
Adler, Hanna, 4:232, 233
Administrative Behavior (Simon), 6:449
Admirandi Archimedis Syracusani monumenta omnia mathematica quae extant ex traditione Maurolyci (Borelli), 1:349
Adone (particle collider), 7:71, 72
Adorno, Theodor, 6:135
ADP (adenosine diphosphate), 5:309–310
Adrenal cortical hormones, 6:227
Adrenal glands, 6:568–569
Adrenaline, 7:178, 179
Adrian, Edgar Douglas, First Baron Adrian of Cambridge, 1:**15–19**, *16, 185*
Adsorption, 1:313–314
Advanced Inorganic Chemistry (Wilkinson), 7:312–313
The Advancement of Learning (Bacon, Francis), 1:140
Advances in Enzymology and Related Areas of Molecular Biology (Lipmann), 4:325
Advances in Mathematics, 6:286
Advances in Prospect Theory (Tversky and Kahneman), 7:94
Advances in the Study of Behavior (Lehrman), 4:243
Adventures and Discoveries (Coon), 2:175
Adventures with the Missing Link (Dart), 2:241–242
Advertissements sur la reformation de l'université de Paris, au Roy (Ramus), 6:205
AEC. *See* Atomic Energy Commission
Aepinus, Franz Ulrich Theodosius, 7:167, 169
Aerodynamics
    interstellar, 7:128
    mathematics of, 1:261, 5:335–336
Aerology
    air pollution, 6:7–8
    jet stream, 6:86
    U. S. Navy, 6:220
Aeronautics
    aircraft construction, 4:101–104
    observatories, 1:116–117
Affection, Cause, Treatment (Diocles of Carystus), 2:302
Affine connection, 2:367–368
Affò, Ireneo, 1:168
Affordances, perception of, 3:122, 125, 129
Afzelius, Johan, 1:266
Against Averroës (Rufus of Cornwall, Richard). *See Contra Averroem* (Rufus of Cornwall, Richard)
Against the Christians (Porphyry), 6:137
Against the Fifth Substance (Xenarchus), 7:381
Agassiz, Alexander, 5:59
Agassiz, Jean Louis Rodolphe, 4:224
    catastrophism theory of evolution, 1:416
    systematics, 6:32
The Age of Lamarck (Corsi), 4:190–191
Agenda for Progressive Taxation (Vickery), 7:150

Aggregates, 1:205
Aging
    arteriosclerosis, 2:184–185
    immunity and, 1:458
    See also Gerontology
AGK2 star catalog, 3:275–276
AGK3 star catalog, 3:276
Agnesi, Maria Gaetana, 1:**19–21**, *20*
Agricola, Georgius, 1:110
Agriculture
    ancient, 2:82
    chemical principles in, 2:218, 4:54
    energy capture and, 6:511
    farming practices, 3:420
    maize cytogenetics, 5:68–69
    and other scientific disciplines, 3:6–7
Agrippa, Heinrich Cornelius, 1:309
Agron-37, 1:158–159
AGU (American Geophysical Union), 3:374
Aharonov, Yakir, 1:324
Aharonov-Bohm effect, 1:324
Ahlfors, Lars, 1:**21–24**, *22*, 262, 263
Ahmadiyya-Jammat, 6:335
AIDS. *See* Acquired immunodeficiency syndrome (AIDS)
AIGT (Association for the Improvement of Geometrical Teaching), 3:327
Aiken, Howard, 7:409
    computing machine design, 1:129
    electromechanical relay machine, 3:357–358
Air, 7:169–170
Air defense weapons, 4:211–212
    acoustical systems, 2:110
    Semi-Automatic Ground Environment, 4:303
Air masses, 1:248
Air pollution
    automobile emissions, 1:235, 3:383
    industrial melanism, 4:109–110
    ozone, 1:235
Air pumps, 3:353
Air traffic control, 5:255
Airs, Waters, and Places (Hippocrates), 1:82, 3:325, 6:291
Airy, George Biddell, 1:**24–26**, *25*
    on calculators, 1:128
    conical refraction, 3:236
Airy disk, 1:25
Aitken, John, 1:**27–30**
Aitken, Robert Grant, 5:112
Akademogorodok. *See* Insitute of Nuclear Physics (Akademogorodok)
Akerlof, George, 7:150
Akers, Wallace, 2:103
Akert, Konrad, 3:304–305
Aki, Keiiti, 1:**30–34**

Aksakov, Alexander N., 1:467
AKZO Research and Engineering, 7:138
Alanine, 3:341–342
Albert, Abraham, 3:194
Albert, Duke of Prussia, 6:550, 551
Albert, Richard David, 7:366
Albert Einstein College of Medicine, 5:282
Albert of Saxony, 1:*34,* **34–36**
Albert the Great. *See* Albertus Magnus, Saint
Alberti, Michael, 6:506
Albertini, Fritz Alleman von, 1:388
Albertus Magnus, Saint, 1:**36–40,** *37,* 38, 104
Albrecht of Prussia, Duke. *See* Albert, Duke of Prussia
Albritton, Claude Carrol, 3:398
Alchemy
    chemistry *vs.,* 4:249–250, 6:506–507, 511–513
    Christian, 7:333–335
    Egyptian, 7:406–407
    Greek, 5:338–339, 7:406–407
    Islamic, 4:19–20, 6:212–213
    medicine and, 1:230, 231–232, 6:511–513, 551,
        552
    metallurgy and, 4:346–348, 5:273–275, 6:418–419
    natural philosophy and, 3:110
    philosopher's stone, 6:506
    Pseudo-Arnald corpus, 1:108–110, 309
    speculative science, 1:367–369
    works, 6:517–518
Alcibiades I (Olympiodorus, the Younger, of Alexandria),
    5:338
Alcocke, John, 6:512
Alcohol dehydrogenase (ADH), 7:34–35
Alcoholic fermentation
    molecular dissymetry and, 6:22–24
    perglycerine and perkaglycerine, 5:251–252
Aldehydes, 1:214
Aldosterone acetate, 1:198
Aldrin, Buzz, 6:444–445
Aleksandrov, Pavel Sergeevich, 7:292
Alembert, Jean le Rond d'. *See* d'Alembert, Jean le Rond
Alexander, James W., 7:292
Alexander, Richard D., 3:231
Alexander of Aphrodisias, 1:442
*The Alexandrian Philosopher Olympiodorus on the Book
    Katenergeian* (Zosimus), 5:338, 339, 340
Alexandroff, P. S. *See* Aleksandrov, Pavel Sergeevich
Alfonsi, Petrus. *See* Petrus Alphonsus
Alfrey, Turner, 5:31
Alfvén, Hannes Olof Gosta, 1:**40–45,** *44,* 2:379, 6:434
Algae
    biochemical reactions, 2:15
    eutrophication and, 2:354–355
    lichens, 6:389

Algebra
    Boolean, 6:425
    class field theory, 2:117–118
    current, 1:238
    elliptic functions, 4:159–160, 7:254–258
    geometric, 5:4, 269
    group theory, 3:212–214, 4:56
    homological
        Abelian categories, 5:2–3
        Bourbaki group, 1:366, 2:361
        medieval, 1:13
    introductory textbooks, 1:19–20
    logic, 5:178–179
        axiomatization, 6:134–135
        set theory and, 5:3–4
    nonassociative, 4:56
    oscillations, 6:127–128
    singular integral operators, 2:8–9
    symbolic, 3:69–70, 236
    theory of equations, 1:5–7, 3:245–246
    theory of errors, 2:77
    transcendental numbers, 2:30–31
    universal, 1:286–287
An Algebra for Theoretical Genetics (Shannon), 6:425
The Algebraic Eigenvalue Problem (Wilkinson), 7:316
Algebraic geometry
    complex function theory, 4:144–146
    curvature, 2:114–115
    finite groups, 3:152–154
    group theory, 3:152, 153
    Lie groups, 2:119–120
    scheme theory, 2:292
    topology, 4:144–146
Algebraic topology
    Arf invariant, 1:97
    arithmetic properties in, 5:179
    axiomatic method, 5:2–3
    Bourbaki text, 2:290–291, 360–362, 7:255, 257
    cohomology, 4:151, 272–273
    duality law, 6:127
    Lie groups, 1:343–345
    manifold, 5:195, 7:291–292
    Riemann-Roch theorem, 4:144–146
    stable homotopy theory, 1:11–13
Algemene Geologie (Pannekoek), 7:142
Algire, Glenn, 3:187
ALGOL programming language, 2:296–297
Algorismus prosaycus (Prachaticz), 6:153
Algorithms
    ALGOL, 2:297
    error analysis, 7:316–317
    See also Mathematics
Algué, José, 7:154

Alhazen. *See* Ibn al-Haytham, Abū ʿAlī al-Hasan Ibn al-Hasan
Alhazen's problem, 3:246
Alī al-Qūshjī, 1:**45–47**, 6:217
Alien life. *See* Extraterrestrial life
Alikhanov, Abram Isaakovich, 4:102
Alkaloid chemistry, 3:57
Alkaloids
    phenolic, 1:198
    structure, 6:269, 270, 271, 273
Alkemade, Kees, 7:229
All-embracing Book (Rāzī). *See Kitāb al-Hāwī* (Rāzī)
All-sky camera, 3:174
Allais, Maurice, 6:350
Allais's paradox, 6:350, *350*
Allan, Bromley A., 1:392
Allard, William K., 2:259
Allchin, Douglas, 4:110
Allee, Warder Clyde, 1:**47–49,** 2:389, 390, 391
Allen, Albert D., 2:105
Allen, Edgar Johnson, 3:258, 259
Allen, Eugene T., 2:254
Allen, Garland E., 5:183, 184, 185–186
Allen, Geoffrey, 3:39
Allen, Thomas, 2:326
Allergies, drugs, 4:33
Allerhand, Adam, 3:199
Allgemeine Handatlas (Andree), 7:246
Allgemeine Meereskunde (Dietrich), 5:172
Allgemeine Naturgeschichte für alle Stände (Oken), 5:332
Allgemeine Psychologie auf personalistischer Grundlage (Stern), 6:525
Allgemeine Zoologie (Bronn), 1:416
Allison, Anthony, 5:242
Allometry, 3:424–425
Allopatric speciation, 3:159–160
Allosteric effects, 7:34–35
Allport, Floyd, 1:50, 52
Allport, Gordon Willard, 1:**49–54,** *51,* 6:525–526
    humanism, 5:217
    traits and personality psychology, 2:428
Almagest (Ptolemy), 6:174, 175–177
    astronomy, 5:95, 6:216, 217
    manuscripts, 3:166
    mathematical proofs, 3:285
    proofreading of, 3:436
    trigonometry, 3:320, 321
Almanacs, 1:175–176
Almgren, Frederick J., 2:259
Alperin, J. L., 3:153
Alpetragius. *See* al-Biṭrūjī al-Ishbīlī, Abū Isḥāq
Alpha particles, 1:299
Alpher, Ralph Asher, 2:281
Alpinotype tectonics, 1:*70,* 70–71

Alps, 6:346, 347–349
Alston, Charles, 7:221
Altenburger, Kamillo, 1:299
Alternative energy, 6:306
Altmann, Jeanne, 7:236
Altmann, Simon L., 3:236
Altmann, Stuart, 7:236
Altruism, 3:226–232
Altum, Bernard, 3:385
Alvarez, Luis Walter, 1:**54–59,** *56,* 2:65
    fusion weapons, 7:22
    implosion bomb physics, 6:422
    linear accelerators, 6:409
    resonance method, 1:305
Alzheimer, Alois, 1:407
Alzheimer's disease, 5:42
Alzire (Voltaire), 5:10
Amado, R. D., 6:171
Amaldi, Edoardo, 1:**59–64,** 6:407, 410, 7:72
Amateur Telescope Making (Westphal), 7:269
Amazing Stories (magazine), 5:112
Ambartsumian, Viktor Amazaspovich, 1:**64–68**
Ambros, Otto, 6:230, 232, 233
Ambrosianus, 2:121
Ambrosio, Luigi, 2:258
Ameghino, Florentino, 1:453, 5:181
American Geophysical Union (AGU), 3:374
American Journal of Human Genetics, 5:242
American Mesozoic Mammalia (Simpson), 6:453
American Nautical Almanac, 1:128–129
American Psychological Association (APA)
    bylaws and organization, 3:314
    unification with other psychological organizations, 1:360
American Science and Engineering, Inc., 6:283
American Society of Human Genetics, 5:242
The American Species of Crepis: Their Interrelationships and Distribution as Affected by Polyploidy and Apomixi (Stebbins), 6:514–515
Amerindian groups, 5:243–244
Ames, Joseph Sweetman, 1:391
Ames, Oakes, 6:514
Amino acids
    configuration, 4:258–259
    degradation, 2:351–352
    essential, 5:247
    in molecular evolution, 4:116
    nutrition and, 1:2
    paper chromatography, 5:39–40
    protein synthesis, 1:78
    structure, 2:348, *348,* 348–352, 5:363–364
Aminoglycoside antibiotics, 1:198–199
Ammon, Otto, 7:261

Ammonia
    inversion spectrum, 7:101
    nitrogen fixation, 2:104–105
    synthetic, 3:203–204
Ammonia process, 3:378–379
Ammonites, 7:62
Ammonius, 2:235–6, 4:51
Amnesia, 4:27
Amory, Copley, 2:385
Amos, Max, 7:231
Ampferer, Otto, 1:**69–72**
Amphibians
    nervous system, 6:495
    organ development, 3:349, 350, 351
    skeleton formation, 3:369
    taxonomy, 3:339
Amplifiers, field-effect, 1:180–181
Analemma (Diodorus of Alexandria), 2:305
Anales del Museo Publico de Buenos Aires (Burmeister),
    1:452
Analgesics, 1:118–119, 2:358–359, 4:31
Analysis of Development (Holtfreter and Hamburger),
    3:351
Analysis of the Problem of Space (Weyl). *See*
    Mathematische Analyse des Raumproblems (Weyl)
The Analysis of Verbal Behavior, 6:464
Analytic geometry, 6:54
Analytic number theory, 2:404–405, 7:155–157
Analytical chemistry
    bacterial, 2:94, 4:229
    electricoconductivity, 7:396
    instrumental techniques, 1:439–440
    thermometry, 2:194–195
The Analytical Chemistry of Synthetic Dyes
    (Venkataraman), 7:148
Analytical Engine, 1:127–129
Analytical psychology
    development of, 4:62–64
    social change, 2:135–136
Analytical school, 1:125–126
Anarchy, State, and Utopia (Nozick), 5:286
Anatomical Study of the Articulation of the Primate Knee
    (Vallois). *See Étude anatomique de l'articulation du
    genou chez les primates* (Vallois)
Anatomy
    ancient, 3:93–94
    animal, 2:340–342, 3:115–116, 118
    blood circulation, 3:110, 302–303
    brain
        animal, 2:340–342
        circuitry, 6:10–13
        epilepsy, 6:69–74
        functional, 6:*71, 72*
        histology, 3:304–305

    regions, 1:406–409
    cytology and, 2:183
    female, 1:91–92
    fossil, 6:107–108
    functional, 7:113–114
    heart, 1:103
    knee joint, 7:113–114
    paleoanthropology, 2:137–139, 238, 239
    plant, 2:413–415, 6:389–391
    skeletal system, 1:91–92, 7:249–250
    See also Comparative anatomy; Morphology;
        Neuroanatomy; Teratology
Anatomy (Diocles of Carystus), 2:302
Anatomy of Seed Plants (Esau), 2:413
Anatomy of the Human Bones (Arconville), 1:91–92
Ancient Medicine in Its Socio-Cultural Context (van der
    Eijk), 3:323
Andersen, C. M., 6:170
Andersen, Per, 2:332
Anderson, Carl David, 1:**72–76,** *74*
    cloud chamber, 1:291, 7:399
    cosmic rays, 6:99
    electron-positron pairs, 5:302
Anderson, Ernest C., 4:297
Anderson, George C., 2:354
Anderson, Hamilton H., 6:322, 323
Anderson, Herbert, 6:169, 7:328
Anderson, Johan Gunnar, 2:299
Anderson, John, 2:218
Anderson, Philip W., 5:200, 203–204
Anderson, Thomas, 4:356
Ando, Rikichi, 5:290
Andrade, Edward, 6:140, 142
Andree, Richard, 7:246
Andrews, Roy Chapman, 5:355
Andromeda Galaxy, 1:130–131
Andronov, Aleksandr Aleksandrovich, 1:317, 6:127
Andronov, Alexander. *See* Andronov, Aleksandr
    Aleksandrovich
Androsterone, 1:460
Anecdotes of the Habits and Instincts of Animals (Lee),
    4:232
*Anecdotes of the Habits and Instincts of Birds, Reptiles, and
    Fishes* (Lee), 4:232
Anello di Accumulazione (AdA) particle collider,
    7:70–71
Anemia, sickle-cell, 5:242, 6:39, 42
Anemometers, 6:553
Anesthesia, 4:33
*Anfänge der Reifezeit: Ein Knabentagebuch in
    psychologischer Bearbeitung* (Stern), 6:522
Anfinsen, Christian B., 1:**76–82,** *79*
Angell, James Rowland, 7:239
Angiogenesis, 3:188

Aniceto Monteiro, António. *See* Monteiro, António A.
Anima, 6:505–506
Animal behavior, 3:385
    autonomic response control, 5:150
    behaviorism, 7:242
    birds, 2:196–198, 4:244–246, 336–345, 5:277–279
    comparative psychology, 6:366–369
    drive-reduction hypothesis, 5:148–149
    environmental influence on, 1:148–153
    ethology, 7:181–182
    isopods, 1:47–48
    Klüver-Bucy syndrome, 4:142
    navigation, 3:177–178
    nervous system, 1:438
    neuroanatomy, 2:341
    primate, 2:50–54, 3:54–55
    problem-solving, 3:294–296
    protozoans, 4:44–45
    reasoning, 3:407
    sensory physiology, 1:436, 3:222–223, 4:147–148
    sexual selection, 3:384–385
    See also Ethology; Instinct
Animal Communities in Temperate America (Shelford), 2:382
Animal Dispersion in Relation to Social Behavior (Wynne-Edwards), 7:376, 378
Animal Ecology (Elton), 2:382, 383–384, 386
Animal Ecology and Evolution (Elton), 2:384
Animal electricity, 7:170–172
The Animal Mind (Washburn), 7:241
Animal Minds (Griffin, 1992), 3:180
Animal Minds-Beyond Cognition to Consciousness (Griffin, 2001), 3:181
Animal Nature and Human Nature (Thorpe), 7:44
Animal physiology, 4:224–225
Animal psychology
    behaviorism, 7:241–242
    birds, 2:196–198, 4:244–247, 336–342
    experimental, 6:47
    neuroanatomy, 2:341
    See also Animal behavior
Animal Species and Evolution (Mayr), 5:63, 6:351
Animal Species and Their Evolution (Cain), 2:4, 6
Animal Thinking (Griffin), 3:180
Animals
    adaptation, 2:5, 4:77–78
    Aristotelian theory, 1:101–104
    consciousness, 3:180–182
    domestication, 3:116, 6:245–246
    ecology, 2:382–388
    experimentation, 3:215
    instinct, 6:368–369, 7:50, 52–53
    minds, 3:177, 180–182
    motion, 1:349

populations
    communities, 2:382–383
    ecological communities, 2:384–386
    natural selection, 7:377–380
    transgenic, 1:399
    unity of plan, 3:118–119
    See also Anatomy; Morphology; Zoology
Annalen der Chemie (journal), 5:107
Annales de chimie, 1:264
Annis, Martin, 6:283
Anomalous scattering, 1:283–284
Anomia, 4:352
Anschauliche Quantentheorie (Jordan), 4:56
Ant lions, 7:86
The Antarctic Circumpolar Ocean (Deacon), 2:263
Antarctica, ice cores, 5:328
The Antecedents of Man (Clark), 2:140
Antennas, Yagi, 1:333
Anthes, Richard A., 6:8
Anthocyanins
    research, 6:271, 272
    synthesis, 7:64–65
Anthologiai (Valens), 7:111–112
Anthony, Raoul, 7:114, 115
Anthropogenic climate change, 2:12–13
Anthropogenic nature, 7:4
Anthropogenie (Haeckel), 3:208, 209
Anthropologie de la population francaise (Vallois), 7:115
Anthropology
    cultural
        evolution, 2:173–175
        personality psychology and, 5:44
    dating techniques, 5:295, 296–299
    diffusionism, 1:184, 185
    language, 7:222–223
    physical
        archaeology, 2:123–127
        Argentina, 4:236–237, 5:180–181
        development, 7:234–238
        ethnography, 2:172–175
        ethnology, 4:236–237
        France, 7:113, 117
        heredity, 3:26–28
    racism, 7:158–159
    teratology, 3:116
    See also Ethnology; Paleoanthropology
Anthropomorphism, 3:182
Anthropopithecus, 2:313
Anti-aircraft weapons
    ballistic calculations, 3:253
    differential analyzers, 3:255
    radar, 1:292
    research, 6:425
Anti-ballistic missile defense, 6:327

Anti-knock agents, 3:381, 382
Antibiotics
    aminoglycoside, 1:198–199
    microchemistry, 3:43
    resistance to, 6:318
Antibodies
    clonal selection theory, 1:458
    diversity, 4:49–50
    host-parasite interactions, 1:455
    monoclonal, 4:50
    natural selection theory, 4:47–50
    self and not-self theory, 1:457
Anticyclones, 5:223, 6:559–560
Antidarrheal drugs, 4:32
Antifreeze, 6:229
Antifungal drugs, 4:32–33
Antigens, 4:261, *262*
Antihistamines, 4:33
Antileukemic drugs, 2:374–375
Antimetabolites, 2:374
Antimonii mysteria gemina (Suchten), 6:552
Antimony, 6:552
Antimycotic drugs, 4:33
Antiparticles, 6:325–326, 410, 7:264
Antiprotons, 6:410
Antireductionism (biology), 7:43–44
Antisemitism
    Austria, 7:69
    Hungary, 7:20
    Poland, 7:10
    Russia, 6:224
    Soviet Union, 1:426–427
    suicides, 3:266
    Switzerland, 6:226
    United States, 5:282
    USSR, 6:434, 447–448
    women, 3:294
Antispasmodic drugs, 4:31
Antiviral drugs, 2:373–374, 375–377
Anton, Carl, 1:288
Ants, army, 6:367–368
APA (American Psychological Association), 1:360, 3:314
Ape and Superape (film), 1:153
Aperture synthesis, 6:302–306
Apes. *See* Primatology
Apes, Giants, and Man (Weidenreich), 7:252
Aphasia
    brain anatomy, 6:73
    syndromes of, 4:350–354
Aphorismi de gradibus, Medicationis parabole (Arnald of
    Villanova), 1:107
Aphorisms (Hippocrates), 3:323, 6:68
Apollinarius, 1:**82–83,** 6:7
Apollo Project, 5:262–263, 7:175–176

Apollonius of Perga, 1:**83–85,** 3:436
    commentaries on, 4:5
    commentaries on Euclid, 2:418
    influence of, 4:1, 6:185, 186
    influences on, 2:302
Apologia (Suchten), 6:551
Apologia pro Galileo (Campanella), 2:21
Apotelesmatika (Ptolemy), 7:111
Apotelesmatike Pragmateia, 6:518
L'apparition de l''homme (Piveteau), 6:108
Appetite, 5:*148,* 148–149, 151
Appetites and Aversion as Constituents of Instincts (Craig),
    2:197
Appleby, Louis, 2:431
Appleton, Edward, 3:254, 7:321
Appleton-Hartree equation, 3:254
Applications Technology Satellite (ATS), 6:555–556
Applied chemistry, 4:53–54
Applied ecology, 6:208–210
*An Approach to the Sediment Transport Problem from
    General Physics* (Bagnold), 1:156
An Approach toward a Rational Classification of Climate
    (Thornthwaite), 7:39
*Approaches to the Bargaining Problem before and after the
    Theory of Games* (Harsanyi), 3:250
Approximation, 1:221
Aptitude testing, 3:405
Aptitude Testing (Hull), 3:406
ab'Aquapendente, Fabricius. *See* Fabrici, Girolamo
Aquatic ecosystems, 5:322–325
    analytical chemistry, 3:257–259
    tidal flats, 7:142
Aquatic insects, 3:411
Aquilani, Scipione, 1:443
Aquinas, Saint Thomas
    astronomy, 2:21
    big bang theory, 1:43
    followers of, 1:36, 37
    mixture theory, 6:418
    natural philosophy, 5:313
    philosophy and theology, 1:444
Arabic astronomy, 6:187, 188
    cosmology, 4:20–21
    medieval, 1:13
    observational, 1:47
    sundials, 4:4–5
    translations, 1:14–15
    trigonometry, 6:185
Arago, François, 1:264, 295
Arbouzov, Yury A., 5:360
Archaeology
    Argentina, 5:180–181
    China, 6:57–61
    ethnography, 2:173

excavations, 3:103–107
fossil hominid culture, 5:295–296
physical anthropology, 2:123–127
prehistoric, 4:42–43, 221
radiocarbon dating, 4:297–298
Archestratos, 2:284
Archimedes, 1:**85–91,** *86*
commentaries on, 5:175, 176
extrusion, 1:443
influence of, 6:185, 186
influence on Hypatia, 3:436
mechanical problems, 1:167
translations of, 6:218
Archimedes in the Middle Ages (Clagett), 1:85
Architecture, naval, 6:470
The Architecture of Mathematics (Dieudonné), 1:365
Archiv für Hydrobiologie, 7:36, 37
Arconville, Marie Geneviève Charlotte Thiroux d', 1:**91–93**
Arctic expeditions, 5:*57,* 57–58
Ardrey, Robert, 2:54, 141
Arduini, Giovanni. *See* Arduino, Giovanni
Arduino, Giovanni, 1:**93–96**
Are Theories of Learning Necessary? (Skinner), 6:463
Are We Retrogressing in Science? (Hubbert), 3:398
Arf, Cahit, 1:**96–98**
Argentina, 1:452–453, 4:236–237
Argyrus, Isaac, 1:**98–99**
Aristogenesis, 5:355
Aristotelianism
astronomy, 2:21
celestial physics, 7:381–382
Christian natural philosophy, 4:51–52
commentaries by Dumbleton, John, 2:327
Copernicanism, 2:177–178
dissection practice, 1:104
evidence for, 6:540
Italy, 7:387–390
mathematics application to nature, 1:105
mixtures, 2:322, 6:418–419
motion, 1:441–442
natural philosophy, 2:272–273, 6:292–296
nature, 1:361–362
ncoplatonism and, 6:137
physics, 1:424, 445–446, 5:7
Quṭb al-Dīn Maḥmūd Ibn Masʿūd Ibn al-Muṣliḥ al-Shīrāzī, 6:187
scholarship, 1:104–105
shortcomings of, 4:65–66
Telesian philosophy, 2:19–20
Aristotle, 1:**99–107,** *101*
alchemical commentaries on, 5:338–339
Calvinism and, 1:204–205
citations of Empedocles by, 2:396

commentaries on, 5:175, 313–314, 6:517
expositions, 1:449, 450
medicine, 5:280
natural philosophy, 1:34, 35, 38, 296, 5:350–351
cosmology, 2:122, 5:176
Dominicans study of, 2:19
influence of, 4:171
intelligent design, 3:94
Jesuits, 3:97
Logic, 6:1
Lyceum, 2:303
magnetism, 2:1–2
mechanical problems, 1:167
medicine, 3:95
meteorology, 2:1
natural philosophy, *1*:388–389
natural science foundations, 1:101–102
pneuma, 2:123
publication of works, 4:264
questions on, 1:143
rainbows, 1:146
scholarship on, 1:104–105
scientific investigations, 1:102–104
theology and science, 1:37
theory of science, 1:99–100
transition states, 1:378
translations, 1:14
See also Aristotelianism
Aristoxenus, 2:284, 6:173
Aristyllus, 7:47
Arithmetic
groups, 1:345–346
language of, 6:265–267
Paris Problems, 3:308–309
Arithmetic (Nikomachus), 4:51
Arithmetica (Diophantus), 3:436
Arithmetica Universalis (Newton), 5:269
Arkwright, J. A., 1:454
Arminian conflict, 3:157–158
Arminius, Jacob, 3:157–158
Arms and Insecurity (Richardson), 6:240
Arms race
policy development, 7:24
quantitative research methods, 6:240
Armstrong, David M., 4:284
Armstrong, Marvin, 1:120
Armstrong, Neil, 6:444–445
Armstrong, William, 3:430
Army ants, 6:367–368
Army Ballistic Missile Agency (ABMA), 7:174–175
Arnald of Villanova, 1:*107,* **107–108,** 4:347
Arnald of Villanova (Pseudo), 1:**108–111**
Arnau de Vilanova. *See* Arnald of Villanova

Arnauld, Antoine, 4:250

Arndt, Fritz, 6:37

Arndt, Uli, 3:338

Arnold, James R., 4:297

Arnold, Matthew, 3:432

Arnold, Thomas, 3:423

Arnold, Vladimir Igorevich, 4:151, 273, 5:198

Arnold and Mabel Beckman Foundation, 1:235–236

Aromatic compounds

    benzene, 3:*402*

    cyclopropenyl cation, 3:*404*

    electron states, 3:*403*

    molecular structure, 6:272

    nonbenzenoid, 5:287, *289,* 289–292

    quantum theory, 3:401–404

    substition reactions, 1:421

Arons, Arnold, 6:529–530

Aronson, Lester, 6:10

Arrhenius: From Ionic Theory to the Greenhouse Effect (Crawford), 1:111

Arrhenius, Svante August, 1:**111–113,** *112,* 2:12, 4:91, 288

    dilute solutions, 7:189

    molecular dissociation, 6:88

    physical chemistry, 5:356

Arrow, Kenneth, 7:150

Arroway, Ellie, 6:314

Ars Conjectandi (Bernoulli), 1:254–255

Ars Eudoxi (Leptines), 4:271

Ars magna (Cardano), 2:36

Arsberättelser över vetenskapernasframsteg (Berzelius), 1:267

Art, 2:362–363, 4:42–43

Art Forms in Nature (Haeckel). *See Kunstformen der Natur* (Haeckel)

The Art of Computer Programming (Knuth), 2:296, 3:51

Arte de navegar (Medina), 2:157

Arteriosclerosis, 2:184–185

Arteriosclerosis: A Survey of the Problem (Cowdry), 2:184

Arthrology, 7:113–114

Artificial Cloud Nucleation Project, 1:470

Artificial food, 5:247

Artificial intelligence

    computational neuroscience and, 5:34–36

    computer science, 7:83–84

    development, 5:255–257, 258, 6:427–429, 449

    founder of, 5:254

    man-computer interactions, 4:305

Artificial Intelligence, Military Intelligence, and Command and Control (Licklider), 4:305

Artillery, 7:120

Artin, Emil, 2:117

Artis Analyticae Praxis (Harriot), 3:246

Artostenone, 1:198

Artsimovich, Lev Andreevich, 4:102

Asaf, Neta. *See* Bahcall, Neta Asaf

Asch, Solomon, 5:137

Aschbacher, Michael, 3:153

Ascher, Marcia, 3:50

Ascidians, 3:429

Ascorbic acid, 6:322

Aselli, Gaspare, 3:110

Asensio, Carlos, 5:311

Ashby, W. Ross, 2:23, 5:255

Asmundson, Vigfus F., 4:275

Aspergillus, 4:33

Aspirin

    discovery, 2:358–359

    manufacture, 4:150

Assassin bugs, 3:183

The Assayer (Galilei), 3:96, 98–100

The Assessment of Men (Murray), 5:217, 218

Assmann, Richard, 1:**113–118,** 7:18, 19

Assmann psychrometers, 1:114–116, *115*

Association (cognitive), 1:171

Association for Behavior Analysis (ABA), 6:465

Association for the Improvement of Geometrical Teaching (AIGT), 3:327

Association of Polymer Chemistry, 6:334

Association of Universities for Research in Astronomy (AURA)

    formation, 3:143

    Kitt Peak National Observatory, 6:546

    leadership, 3:177

Assumption and Myth in Physical Science (Bondi), 1:342

Astbury, William Thomas, 6:39, 40

Astell, Caroline, 6:480, 482

Astemizole, 4:33

Asteroids, 6:445–446

The Astonishing Hypothesis (Crick), 2:212

Astrobiology

    exobiology, 3:364–365

    genetics, 3:361

    interstellar matter, 3:391

    NASA, 6:484, 486–487

    origin of life research, 5:157–158

Astrogeology, 6:442–446

Astrolabes, 6:153–154, 7:88, *88*

Astrologicorum libri (Campanella), 2:21

Astrology

    alchemical commentaries on, 5:338

    alchemy and, 6:517–518

    Greek, 7:111–112

    horoscopes, 2:37

    Inquisition, 2:20–21

    Islamic, 1:145

    mathematics, 6:2

    medicine and, 5:280

opposition to, 5:8, 6:314
Astrometry, 3:273–274, 6:541
Astronomia Magna (Paracelsus), 6:15
Astronomia Nova (Kepler), 4:105, 106–107
Astronomiae Pars Optica (Kepler), 4:106
Astronomical Advantages of an Extra-Terrestrial Observatory (Spitzer), 6:501
Astronomical Tribiblos (Meliteniotes), 2:121, 5:95
Astronomische Gesellschaft, 6:541
Astronomy, 1:375
    alchemy and, 6:517–518
    almanacs, 1:128–129
    Arabic, 6:187, 188
        cosmology, 4:20–21
        medieval, 1:13
        observational, 1:47
        sundials, 4:4–5
        translations, 1:14–15
        trigonometry, 6:185
    astrolabes, 6:153–154
    astrometry, 3:273–274
    astrophysics, 7:105–107
    Babylonian, 3:320–321
    cameras, 3:174
    comets, 7:283, 284–285
    Copernicanism, 2:177–178
    cosmic microwave background, 7:393–394
    cosmology, 2:149–150, 5:73–74
    Difference Engine, 1:127
    earth orbit, 5:133–134
    ephemeris, 1:174–176
    galaxy formation, 7:57–61
    galaxy shapes, 1:328–332, 5:342–343
    Germany, 7:332–333
    Greek
        calendars, 1:98–99
        moon, 1:82–83
        records, 7:47
        sun, 1:85
        uranography, 2:304–305
        works, 4:271, 6:173–174, 175–177
    historical, 3:166–167
    humanism, 1:380–381
    impetus theory, 1:423–424
    influential figures, 6:498–502
    instrumentation, 1:382–383, 7:271–272
    Jesuits, 3:109
    linear astrolabes, 7:88
    magnetism, 1:130–132, 3:137–139
    mathematics, 3:288–289, 5:82–84
    motion, 2:230–231
    National Observatory (Brazil), 4:293–294
    natural history, 3:289–291
    nebulae, 3:286–287

    observational, 1:24–26, 381, 3:165, 166–167
    optics, 3:111–112, 142
    Persian, 2:120–121
    philosophy, 1:445
    planetary motion, 1:138–139, 4:105–106
    popular, 6:309–315
    Ptolemaic, 6:216–218
        astrolabes, 6:153–154
        calendars, 1:98
        The Copernican Revolution (Kuhn), 4:175
        Copernicanism, 2:177
        cosmology, 2:149–150, 4:20–21
        errors and contradictions in, 4:2
        mathematics, 6:2
        translations, 1:14
    Rees-Sciama effect, 6:399–400
    religion and, 1:147
    Schwarzchild, Martin, 6:382–387
    solar neutrinos, 1:158
    solar physics, 3:141–144
    solar system, 4:179–180
    spectral lines, 7:126–131
    spectroscopy, 2:343–345
    stars, 2:87–92, 6:50–51, 541–546
    steady state theory, 3:135
    treatises on, 5:95
    x-ray, 1:159–160
        development, 6:280, 283–284
        stars, 1:159
    See also Copernicanism; Cosmology; Radio astronomy
Astronomy and General Physics, Considered with Reference to Natural Theology (Whewell), 7:280
Astrophysics
    artificial satellites, 5:260–263
    black holes, 5:348, 6:399–400
    chemistry, 6:49–52
    cosmic rays, 5:300, 304, 7:120–125, 303–305
    cosmology and, 7:392–394
    influential figures, 6:397, 498–503
    inverse problems of, 1:64–67
    light nuclei in, 4:211
    magnetism, 1:42–43
    mathematics and, 5:111–112
    molecular spectra, 3:300–301
    motion and resistance, 5:270
    nuclear magnetic resonance, 6:181
    Project West Ford, 3:143
    quantum mechanics, 7:104–108
    quasars, 3:173
    relativistic, 2:91–92
    relativity, 1:340, 342
    rocket design, 1:274
    solar neutrinos, 1:157–161

Astrophysics, *continued*
    spectral lines, 7:126–131
    spectroscopy, 2:343–347
    stars, 3:174–176, 6:541–546
    steady state theory, 3:388–392
    stellar dynamics, 3:274–275
    stellar models, 2:339
    stellar structure, 2:87–92, 4:177–181
    supernovae, 1:276–278
    thermonuclear processes, 3:61–62
    USSR, 6:432–436
Asymmetric information, 7:149–150
Asymmetry, baryon, 6:324, 325–326
Asymptotic Approximations (Jeffreys), 4:40
Atanasoff, John, 2:335, 5:52, 53, 7:409
Ateismo trionfato (Campanella), 2:20
The Athanasius Kircher Correspondence Project, 4:131
Atheism vanquished (Campanella). *See Ateismo trionfato*
  (Campanella)
Atheismus triumphatus (Campanella), 2:21
Atiyah, Michael, 1:12
Atiyah-Singer index theorem, 7:415
Atkins, William Ringrose Gelston, 3:258, 5:306
Atkinson, Edmund, 3:58
Atlantic Ocean, 6:370–372
Atlas of African Prehistory (Clark), 2:126
The Atmosphere (Panofsky), 6:8
Atmospheric chemistry, 4:91–95, 7:169–170
Atmospheric circulation, 7:17–19
Atmospheric diffusion, 6:239
Atmospheric nuclear testing, 7:24
Atmospheric refraction, 5:352
Atmospheric science
    carbon dioxide rise, 2:12–13, 4:91–95
    climatology, 6:341–345
    continental drift, 7:245–248
    development, 6:559–561
    diagnosis and prediction, 1:289
    dynamic meteorology, 2:99, 7:17–19
    electricity, 2:215–216
    geophysics, 1:390–391
    global warming, 2:10–11
    hurricanes, 7:274–275
    instrumentation, 1:114–117
    large-scale waves, 2:99–101
    Mars, 6:313
    mathematics, 6:469–472
    nuclear weapons, 6:315
    observational methods, 4:197
    oceanography, 2:264–265
    ozone, 2:306–309
    primordial, 5:*155,* 155–156
    Smithsonian Astrophysical Observatory, 7:288
    societies and organizations, 1:470
    space-based telescopes, 6:502
    surface pressure, 2:*425,* 425–427
    tholins, 6:314
    tropical cyclones, 3:262–264
    turbulence, 2:*426*
    Venus, 6:310–311
    See also Meteorology
Atmospheric Turbulence (Panofsky), 6:9
Atom, Man, and the Universe (Alfvén), 1:43
Atom-Molecule Collision Theory (Bernstein), 1:259
Atombau und Spektrallinien (Sommerfeld), 6:491
Atomic absorption spectroscopy, 7:229–232
Atomic Bomb Casualty Commission (ABCC), 5:242
Atomic bombs
    critical mass, 1:274
    cyclotrons and, 1:164–165
    development, 5:190, 6:195–196, 421–422, 573,
      7:295–296, 298, 328–329
    explosion, 5:191, 6:415–416
    first test, 1:162, 164
    fission, 1:57, 6:64–65
    genetic effects, 5:242–243
    high energy physics, 1:425
    nuclear physics, 6:419
    oceanographic effects, 6:235
    opposition to, 1:292, 327–328, 5:191
    particle physics, 3:20
    plutonium, 1:134–135, 6:401, 402–403
    reduction efforts, 1:269
    Soviet, 3:34–35
    testing, 6:283
    See also Hydrogen bombs; Manhattan Project;
      Nuclear weapons
Atomic energy. *See* Nuclear energy
Atomic Energy (Peierls), 6:65
Atomic Energy Commission
    accelerators, 7:329
    establishment, 1:135–136, 165, 6:196
    investigations by, 6:422
    leadership, 6:405
    McMahon bill, 2:167–168
Atomic Energy States, as Derived from the Analyses of
  Optical Spectra (Bacher and Goudsmit), 1:133
Atomic Forces and Adsorption (Boer), 1:313
Atomic mass, 1:265
Atomic model. *See* Atomic theory
Atomic physics, 5:200, 7:302
Atomic Spectra and Atomic Structure (Herzberg),
  3:300–301
Atomic spectrum, 1:133–135
Atomic Structure and Spectral Lines (Sommerfeld), 2:88
Atomic theory
    Arminian conflict, 3:157–158
    Boscovichian, 3:289

carbon chains, 4:98–99
chemical, 1:268
hidden variables, 1:322–323
molecular spectra and structure, 3:298
nature, 6:288
relativity, 6:489, 490
religion and, 1:205
translations, 1:265
wholeness, 1:327
x-rays, 1:410–411
Atomic weights
    isomorphism, 5:166
    periodic table, 5:105–108, *107*
Atomism
    anti-atomism, 2:320–321
    Arminian conflict, 3:157–158
    belief in, 4:1
    chemistry, 7:344
    Eucharist and, 3:98–100
    heliocentrism, 2:21
    Jesuits, 3:109
    materialism, 2:80
    mechanics, 3:112
    medicine, 6:418–419, 7:342
    microscopes, 3:110–111
    theory of impetus, 1:423–424
Atoms
    behavior and structure, 4:206
    muon capture, 6:170–171
    quantum mechanics, 6:126
Atomspektren und Atomstruktur (Herzberg), 3:300–301
ATP. *See* Adenosine triphosphate (ATP)
ATPases, 6:199
ATS (Applications Technology Satellite), 6:555–556
Atten, Mark van, 3:131
Attending Marvels (Simpson), 6:453
Attention
    double theory, 1:404
    filter theory, 1:401, 403–405, *404*
    voluntary, 1:171
Attis, David, 3:236
Attitude-Interest Analysis Test, 7:28
Attraction, gravitational, 5:11–12
Atwood, Wallace W., 1:357
L'aube du savoir (Duhem), 2:319
Auctions, second-price, 7:150
Audouze, Jean, 7:61
The Aufbau (Carnap), 2:44
AURA (Association of Universities for Research in
    Astronomy), 3:143, 177, 6:546
Aurelianus, Caelius, 2:302
Auschwitz, 1:463
Ausführliches Lehrbuch der Organischen Chemie
    (Bergmann and Schlenk; 1932), 1:250

Ausführliches Lehrbuch der organischen Chemie (Kolbe;
    1854-1878), 4:149
Austin, James M., 6:342
Australia
    botany, 5:204–208
    ecology, 6:207, 208–210
    geology, 2:39
    nuclear energy, 6:260–261
    prehistoric art, 4:42
    zoology, 6:207–210
Australian Academy of Science, 6:210
Australian Conservation Foundation, 6:210
Australian Fossil Corals in Relation to Evolution (Hill),
    3:316
Australian National University, 6:258
Australopithecus, 2:238–241, *241*, 4:223, 7:116–117,
    188, 235–236
Austria, 7:69, 70
Authentic Memoirs (Zosimos of Panopolis), 7:406
The Authoritarian Personality (Eysenck), 2:430
Autism, 7:55
"Autistic" Children: New Hope for a Cure (Tinbergen and
    Tinbergen), 7:55
Autoimmunity, 1:458
Automatic control, theory of, 6:127–128
L'Automatisme psychologique (Janet, Pierre), 4:26
Automobile emissions, 3:383
Automobile industry, industrial chemicals, 6:229–230
Automobiles, engine knock, 3:381, 382
Autoneuralization, 3:350
Autonomic nervous system
    brain regions, 3:302–305
    learnable voluntary control of, 5:150–151
Auwers, Karl Friedrich von, 7:336
Availability heuristic, 7:94
Ave Maria Aristotle Quires (Rufus of Cornwall, Richard),
    6:292
Averaging of Income for Income-Tax Purposes (Vickery),
    7:151
Averroës. *See* Rushd, Abu'l-Walīd Muḥammad ibn
    Aḥmad ibn Muḥammad,Ibn
Avery, Oswald T., 2:95, 317, 7:299
Aviation
    aircraft design, 4:101–102
    chemistry, 2:358, 359
    condensation, 2:308
    safety, 3:83–84
    World War II, 2:11–12
Avicenna. *See* Sīnā, Abū ʿAlī al-Ḥusayn, Ibn
Avoidance behavior, 5:146, *146*
Axelrod, Julius, 1:**118–123**, *119*, 7:178, 179
Axelrod, Robert, 3:231–232, 232
Axiomatics, 3:307
    algebraic topology, 5:2–3

Axiomatics, *continued*
    Bourbaki group, 2:290
    geometry, 3:71
    simplifying role, 2:289
Axonologists, 6:361
Axons, 6:362–364
Ayer, A. J., 5:88
Ayrton, Hertha, 6:549
Ayrton, William, 3:58

B

B2FH paper, 3:391
Baade, Wilhelm Heinrich Walter, 6:51
    colleagues of, 3:276, 389
    influence of, 5:346
    Schwarzchild, Martin, 6:386
Babbage, Charles, 1:**125–130,** *128,* 2:310
    acquaintances of, 4:231
    influence of, 4:119–120
Babbage, Henry Prevost, 1:129
Babcock, Ernest Brown, 4:275–276, 6:514–515
Babcock, Harold Delos, 1:130, 7:105
Babcock, Horace Welcome, 1:*130,* **130–133**
Babylonian astronomy, 3:320–321
Bacastow, Robert, 4:95
Bacher, Robert Fox, 1:**133–137,** *135*
    colleagues of, 3:24
    Los Alamos National Laboratory, 7:329
    nuclear physics, 1:271
Bachman, John, 3:339
Back, Kurt, 3:15
Backer, Hilmar J., 1:310
The Backtracking Fallacy (Horowitz), 6:350–351
The Backwoods of Canada (Traill), 7:78–79
Bacon, Francis, 1:**137–142,** *140*
    influence of, 4:65, 66, 314
    natural history, 1:368
Bacon, Roger, 1:**142–148,** *143,* 4:347, 6:293, 296
Bacteria
    antibiotics, 2:318
    antimetabolites, 2:374
    extraterrestrial, 3:364–365
    genetics
        controlling elements in, 5:71
        fluctuation test, 4:356–357
    lipids and, 4:228–229
    metabolism, 6:519–520
    phage research, 2:270
    propionic acidp, 7:346–347
    resistant, 2:268–269
    sex, 7:14–15
    spores, 1:209
    transport in, 5:160
    virology, 4:358

    vitamins, 7:12
The Bacterial Cell (Dubos), 2:318
Bacterial enzymology, 6:519–520
Bacterial infections, 1:454–455
Bacterial membranes, 5:160–162
Bacterial Metabolism (Stephenson), 6:519–520
Bacteriohodopsin, 5:364
Bacteriology, 6:519–521
Bacteriophages
    assay system, 4:47
    genetics of, 1:374, 454–455, 2:210, 268, 4:356–358
    reproduction of, 2:374
Baer, Karl Ernst von, 2:246, 5:331, 332
Baerends, Gerard Pieter, 1:**148–154,** *152,* 4:247, 7:51, 56
Bagley, William C., 7:27
Bagnold, Enid, 1:156
Bagnold, Ralph Alger, 1:**154–157,** *155*
Bahcall, John Norris, 1:**157–162,** *158, 160*
Bahcall, Neta Asaf, 1:157, 160–161
Bahcall, Safi, 1:157
Bailey, Percival, 4:141
Baily, Walter L., 1:346
Bainbridge, John, 3:165
Bainbridge, Kenneth Tompkins, 1:**162–166,** *164,* 6:179
Bairstow, Leonard, 3:253
Baker, Herbert, 6:515
Baker, James G., 7:285
Baker, John Randal, 2:3, 383, 387
Baker, Wilson, 7:144
Baker-Venkataraman rearrangement, 7:144, *144*
Balance of Wisdom (al-Khāzinī), 6:186
Balance theory, 1:9
Balard, Antoine Jérome, 4:205
Baldi, Bernardino, 1:**166–168**
Baldini, Ugo, 2:150
Baldwin, George C., 5:128
Baldwin, James Mark, 1:**168–173,** *170,* 2:74, 6:92
Baldwin effect, 1:168, 172
Balfour, Arthur, 1:213, 6:548
Ballistic missiles, 7:173–175
Ballistics, 3:253
Balloons, meteorological, 7:18–19
Baltzer, Fritz, 5:16
Banding, chromosome, 2:71–72
The Bandwagon (Shannon), 6:427
Banks, Edwin, 1:48
Banks, Joseph
    library of, 4:231
    patronage of geology, 3:6, 7
    promotion of science by, 2:250
Banks, M. L., 4:166
Banneker, Benjamin, 1:**173–177,** *176*
Bannister, Robert, 2:247

Barbaro, Daniele, 6:106
Barber, Bernard, 5:124
Barber, Elinor, 5:124
Barber, Sherman, 6:341
Barcroft, Joseph, 6:81
Bard, Philip, 6:11
Bardeen, John, 1:*178*, **178–184**, 4:*103*
    superconductivity, 1:318, 5:129
    transistors, 6:437, 438
Bardeen-Cooper-Schrieffer theory, 1:182
Bareš, Jan, 3:40
Bargaining, rational
    cooperative games, 3:249–250
    decision making, 5:225–226
    Nash equilibrium, 5:227
A Bargaining Model for the Cooperative n-Person Game
    (Harsanyi), 3:248
The Bargaining Problem (Nash), 3:249
Bargmann, Valentine, 3:242
Barium-alumino-vanadium (BAV), 1:352
Barium-tin-vanadium (BOV), 1:352
al-Barjandī, ʿAbd al-ʿAlī, 4:21
Barker, Andrew, 2:418
Barker, George, 1:119
Barker, Horace Albert, 7:347
Barker, Jane, 3:187
Barkhausen, Heinrich Georg, 6:375
Barkley, Theodore, 2:214
Barlow, Peter, 1:295
Barlow, William, 2:158
Barnard, Edward Emerson, 1:330
Barnes, Charles R., 2:189
Barnes, S. Barry, 1:211, 4:176, 5:125
Barnett, Muriel McClure. *See* Beadle, Muriel McClure
    Barnett
Barometrographia (Howard), 3:387
Baron Todd. *See* Todd, Alexander Robertus
Barrett, Gary, 5:319
Barrett, Tony, 1:200–201
Barron, David, 6:534
Barry, Herbert, 5:149
Bartels, Julius, 5:51–52, 7:118
Barth, Lester, 3:350
Bartlett, Frederic Charles, 1:**184–189**, *185*, 402, 405
Bartlett, George, 1:190
Bartlett, Jame Holley, 2:379
Bartlett, Paul Doughty, 1:**189–195**, 420–421
Bartley, William W., 2:311, 6:135
Bartling, Gottlob, 6:356
Barton, Derek Harold Richard, 1:**195–202**, *197*, 6:158,
    7:350, 353
Barton, Ruth, 3:431
Barton-McCombie deoxygenation, 1:199
Baruch, Bernard, 5:348–349

Bary, Anton de. *See* De Bary, Heinrich Anton
Baryon asymmetry, 6:324, 325–326
Basalt, 5:49, *49*, 6:348
Les bases de la météorologie dynamique (Teisserenc de Bort
    and Hildebrandsson), 7:19
BASF AG, 6:229, 232–233
Basic Botany (Cronquist), 2:214
Basic Inorganic Chemistry (Wilkinson), 7:313
Basic Methods for Experiments on Eggs of Marine Animals
    (Just), 4:68
Basic Questions in Paleontology (Schindewolf), 6:351
The Basis of Dynamic Meteorology (Teisserenc de Bort
    and Hildebrandsson). *See Les bases de la météorologie*
    dynamique (Teisserenc de Bort and Hildebrandsson)
The Basis of Sensation (Adrian), 1:17
Basolo, Fred, 7:310
Bassham, James A., 2:17
Bassi Verati, Laura Maria Caterina, 1:**202–204**, *203*
Basso, Sebastian. *See* Basson, Sébastien
Basson, Sébastien, 1:**204–206**
Bastian, Adolf, 1:**206–208**, *207*
Bastian, Charlton. *See* Bastian, Henry Charlton
Bastian, Henry Charlton, 1:**208–210**, *209*, 6:28–29
Batchelor, George Keith, 2:379
Bate, Dorothea, 3:106
Bateson, Gregory, 7:202, 227
Bateson, William, 1:**210–214**, *212*, 4:79
    Mendelian genetics, 5:101–102
    on Vries, Hugo de, 7:190
Bats, 3:177
al-Battānī, Abū ʿAbd Allāh Muḥammad ibn Jābir ibn
    Sinān al-Raqqī al-Ḥarrānī al-Ṣābiʾ, 6:7–8
Battelli, Federico, 6:447, 448
Batteries
    efficiency, 2:12
    invention of, 7:170–172, *171*
Battro, Antonio, 6:94
Bauch, Bruno, 2:43
Bauer, Friedrich, 2:296
Bauer, Georg. *See* Agricola, Georgius
Bauer, John, 2:375, 376
Baum, William, 6:386
Baumrind, Diana, 5:142
Baur, Erwin, 3:28, 6:317–318
Bautz, Mark, 7:305
BAV (barium-alumino-vanadium), 1:352
Bayer, Friedrich, 1:215
Bayer, Otto Georg Wilhelm, 1:**214–219**, *215*
Bayer AG, 1:215
Bayes, Thomas, 1:**219–220**
Bayesian rationality, 3:248–249, 250
Bayesian statistics
    development, 6:349–351
    methods, 4:40

Baylen, Sarah, 1:418–419
Bayley, Donald, 7:119
Beach, Frank Ambrose, Jr., 1:**220–224**
    colleagues of, 6:367
    learning and perception, 3:270
Beach barriers, 7:142
Beadle, George Wells, 1:**224–229,** *225, 227*
    amino acids, 6:318
    colleagues of, 7:15
    Drosophila research, 1:463
    Mendelian genetics, 2:399–400
    Tatum, Edward Lawrie, 7:12–14
Beadle, Muriel McClure Barnett, 1:227, 228
Beagon, Mary, 6:117, 118
Beans, Hal, 3:238
Bear, Richard, 6:362
Beard, George M., 4:27
Bearden, Joyce Alvin, 3:78
Beaton, John, 1:198
Beautiful Black Bronzes (Hunter), 7:407
A Beautiful Mind (film), 5:225
Bebee, William, 2:389
Because That's My Way (film), 6:278
Beccaria, Giambatista, 4:214
Becher, Johann Joachim, 1:**229–232,** *231*
    alchemy, 6:506
    experimental method, 3:278
    phlogiston, 6:505
Beck, William S., 6:454
Becker, George Ferdinand, 2:253
    geology, 6:151
    Merton Thesis, 5:122
Becker, Gerald, 4:241
Becker, Karl, 7:173
Becker, Richard, 7:294
Becker, Theodor, 2:359
Beckit, Robert, 2:158
Beckman, Arnold Orville, 1:*233,* **233–236,** 6:39
    centrifuges, 1:373–374
    semiconductors, 6:440
Becoming (Allport), 1:52
Bedancken von der Gold-macherey (Stahl), 6:506
Beddoes, Thomas, 6:97
Bednorz, J. Georg, 5:204
Bee wolves, 7:49–50
Beer, Colin, 3:182
Beer, Gillian, 2:247
Bees
    dance language, 3:179, 180, 183
    visual perception, 3:294–296, *296*
Bees: Their Vision, Chemical Senses, and Language
    (Frisch), 3:179
Beevers, Arnold, 3:335
Begg, Geoffrey, 2:351

Beggren, John, 1:87
Beginning of the Age of Mammals in South America
    (Simpson), 6:453
Beginselen der natuurkunde (Lorentz), 7:99
Begriffsschrift (Frege), 3:69, 70
Behavior
    animal
        autonomic response control, 5:150
        behaviorism, 7:242
        birds, 2:196–198, 4:244–246, 336–345,
            5:277–279
        comparative psychology, 6:366–369
        domestication and, 6:245–246
        drive-reduction hypothesis, 5:148–149
        emotional, 3:268
        environmental influence on, 1:148–153
        ethology, 7:181–182
        isopods, 1:47–48
        Klüver-Bucy syndrome, 4:142
        navigation, 3:177–178
        nervous system, 1:438
        neuroanatomy, 2:341
        primates, 2:50–54, 3:54–55
        problem-solving, 3:294–296
        protozoans, 4:44–45
        reasoning, 3:407
        sensory physiology, 1:436, 3:222–223,
            4:147–148
        sexual selection, 3:384–385
    avoidance, 5:146, *146*
    genetics
        homeostasis, 4:277
        importance of, 4:203–204
    hormones, 1:221
    infant, 1:168
        experimental study of, 1:170
        reflexes, 6:246
    innate
        environmental influence on, 1:150
        homeostasis, 6:245–246, 247
    instinctive action, model of, 4:*343*
    learned
        cognitive ethology, 3:182
        foresight and, 5:145
        social contexts and, 5:147
    neuroembryology, 3:222–223
    organizational, 5:254–255
    political, 6:254–255
    sexual
        animals, 1:222–223, 3:384–385
        humans, 4:124–129
        humans *vs.* primates, 5:44
        plants, 4:316
        psychoanalysis, 3:73–75

social
adaption and, 1:171–172
animals, 1:48
birds, 2:196–198
group dynamics, 3:14–15
humans, 4:127
natural selection, 7:376
primates, 2:50–54
psychoanalysis and, 5:146, *146*
segregation, 2:129–131
social Darwinism, 2:244–245
theory of, 3:405, 407–409
therapy, 2:429–430
verbal, 6:462, 464
See also Ethology
Behavior: An Introduction to Comparative Psychology (Watson), 7:241
Behavior and Evolution (Piaget), 6:94
The Behavior of Organisms (Skinner), 6:462
Behavior of the Lower Organisms (Jennings), 4:44–45
The Behavior of the Rat: A Study of General and Specific Activities (Richter), 6:244
A Behavior System (Hull), 3:408, 409
Behavioral ecology, infant development, 3:123–124
Behavioral endocrinology, 1:220, 221–223
Behavioral pharmacology, 6:462, 463
Behavioral physiology, 6:459, 7:180, 181–183
Behavioral psychology, 3:405–409
consciousness in, 4:28–29
development, 6:458–466
field theory, 4:279–282
genetics in, 4:203–204
Klüver-Bucy syndrome, 4:141–143
Meehl, Paul Everett on, 5:93–94
personality psychology and, 5:44–47
therapy, 2:429–430
Behavioral technology, 6:464
Behaviorism
animal behavior, 7:50
child psychology, 4:281, 7:243–244
development, 6:458–466, 7:241–243
perception, 3:125
psychobiology, 6:243–247
Behaviorism (Watson), 7:244
Behaviour (journal), 1:151, 222
Behaviour Research and Therapy (Eysenck), 2:430
Behind Appearance (Waddington), 7:203
Die beiden Grundprobleme der Erkenntnistheorie (Popper), 6:133–134
Beinert, Helmut, 3:170
Beiträge (Oken), 5:331
Beiträge zur Kenntnis devonischer Trilobiten aus dem Rheinischen Schiefergebirge (Richter), 6:248
Beiträge zur Physiologie des Hirnstammes (Hess), 3:304

Bekhterev, Vladimir Mikhailovich, 7:243
Bekoff, Marc, 3:180
Belambre, Jean Baptiste, 3:321
Belief in the Law of Small Numbers (Tversky and Kahneman), 7:93
Belief systems modeling, 1:9
Bell, Eric Temple, 2:34, 4:158
Bell, Gordon, 5:257
Bell, John Stewart, 1:**236–243,** 325
Bell, Mary Ross, 1:237
Bell-Jackiw-Adler anomaly, 1:236
Bell Laboratories, 1:180–181
Bellhouse, David R., 1:221
Bellman, Richard, 5:187
Bello, Francis, 6:182
Bell's inequalities, 1:240
Bells' theorem, 1:239
Beloff, Ruth Hirsch. *See* Grobstein, Ruth Hirsch Beloff
Belopolskii, Aristarkh A. *See* Belopolsky, Aristarkh Apollonovich
Belopolsky, Aristarkh Apollonovich, 1:65
Belousov, Boris, 6:166
Beltrami coefficients, 1:262
Ben-Gurion, David, 1:251–252
Bénard, Jacques, 2:160
Benedict XIV, Pope, 1:202
Benedict, Ruth, 5:44
Benioff, Victor Hugo, 1:**243–245,** *244,* 6:241, 242, 7:200
Benjamin Banneker's Pennsylvania, Delaware, Maryland and Virginia Almanak, and Ephemeris for the Year of Our Lord 1792 (Banneker), 1:175–176
Bennett, H. S., 2:331
Bennett, John Hughes, 1:209
Bennett, Ralph, 4:208, *210*
Bennett, William H., 3:59
Bensley, Robert, 2:144
Benson, Andrew A., 2:17, 18
Bentham, George, 5:206
Benton, Arthur F., 2:393–394
Benzene
aromaticity, 3:401–403, 404
Cram's rule, 2:200–201
electron states, 3:*402*
inclusion complexants, 2:203–204
organometallic chemistry, 7:*339,* 339–340, *340*
pioneering research with, 5:19
structure of, 4:13, 15–17, 99, 6:272
synthesis of, 5:166
Beranek, Leo, 4:303
Berchet, Gerard Jean, 2:50
Berg, Howard, 6:182
Berg, Paul, 1:236

Bergen school
    cyclone model, 1:289–290
    meteorology, 1:246–247, 468, 6:220
Berger, Hans, 3:269
Bergeron, Tor Harold Percival, 1:**245–250,** 6:85
    colleagues of, 6:220
    influence of, 6:558–559
Bergeron-Findeisen process, 1:245, 248, *248*
Berggren, J. L., 2:416
Bergman, Max, 2:349
Bergman, Torbern Olof, 6:349
Bergmann, Ernst David, 1:**250–254**
Bergmann, Felix, 1:251
Bergson, Henri Louis, 5:355
    acquaintances of, 4:25
    influence of, 4:64, 6:109
    life, 6:91
    religion and science, 6:92
Beria, Lavrenty, 1:426–427, 4:84
Berkhoff, Gé, 7:134
Berlage, Hendrick Petrus, 7:200
Berlekamp, Elwyn R., 3:153, 6:429
Berlin, Ted, 7:103
Berlin Academy of Sciences, 7:332, 333
Berlin school (mathematics), 6:251
Bernal, John Desmond, 3:67
    colleagues of, 5:237
    influence of, 6:39
    on social responsibility of scientists, 1:293
    students of, 3:334, 335
    x-ray crystallography, 6:79, 7:298
Bernard, Claude, 6:46
Bernardini, Gilberto, 5:301
Bernays, Paul, 3:309
Bernheim, Hippolyte, 3:406, 4:25
Bernoulli, Jacob. *See* Bernoulli, Jakob I
Bernoulli, Jakob I, 1:**254–257,** *255,* 2:423, 5:56
Bernoulli, James. *See* Bernoulli, Jakob I
Bernoulli, Jaques. *See* Bernoulli, Jakob I
Bernoulli, Johann I, 1:254, 255–256, 2:423
    and Maupertuis, Pierre Louis Moreau de, 5:59
    vis viva controversy, 5:10–11
Bernoulli, Nikolaus (1687-1769), 1:254
Bernoulli, Nikolaus I (1687-1759), 1:254–255
Bernstein, Elliott, 6:473
Bernstein, Harold, 4:259–260
Bernstein, Jeremy, 1:237, 6:170
Bernstein, Norma Olivier, 1:260
Bernstein, Richard Barry, 1:**257–260**
Berreman, Joel V., 3:311–312
Berrill, John, 3:350
Berry, Arthur, 3:213
Berry, Clifford, 5:52
Bers, Lipman, 1:22, 23, **260–263,** *261*

Berson, Jerome, 3:404
Bertani, Giuseppe, 4:356
Bertholet, Marcelin, 2:321
Berthollet, Claude Louis, 1:**263–266,** *264,* 4:216
Bertius, Petrus, 3:354
Bertomeu, Carlos A., 5:182
Bertrand, Joseph, 5:188
Berzelius, Jöns Jacob, 1:**266–269,** *267,* 4:53
    electrochemical dualism, 2:324
    students of, 5:166
Berzelius' Werden und Wachsen, 1779-1821 (Söderbaum),
    1:266
Besomi, Ottavio, 3:96
Bessarion, Basilius, 6:216, 217, 218
The Best Doctor Is Also a Philosopher (Galen), 3:92–93
BET equation, 2:393–394
Beta decay, 7:102, 366–367
Betal Cutters from the Samuel Eilenberg Collection
    (Brownrigg), 2:363
Betatrons, 7:69, 71
Bethe, Hans Albrecht, 1:**269–276,** *275,* 4:59, 209,
    7:106
    atomic bombs, 6:65
    carbon-nitrogen reaction, 3:60
    colleagues of, 3:20, 21, 6:337, 393–394, 419, 7:20,
        21, 266
    Delbrück scattering, 2:268
    influence of, 4:332
    negative hydrogen ion, 2:90
    nuclear physics, 6:62, 64
    plasticity, 7:182
    scope of nuclear physics and, 1:133, 134
    stellar energy, 6:543, 7:119
    stellar structure, 6:385
Between Two Wars (Baldwin), 1:170
Betz, Vladimir, 1:407
Beurlen, Karl, 6:352
Beurling, Arne, 1:23
Bevan, Benjamin, 3:6
Beyond Freedom and Dignity (Skinner), 6:465
*Beyond the Gene: Cytoplasmic Inheritance and the Struggle
    for Authority in Genetics* (Sapp), 5:69
Beyond the Gene (Sonneborn), 6:493
Bèze, Théodore de, 1:309
Bezold, Johannes Friedrich Wilhelm von, 7:246
Bhabha, Homi Jehangir, 1:293
Biagioli, Mario, 3:100–101
Biases, 7:93–94
Bibliografi över J. J. Berzelius (Holmberg), 1:266
Biblioteca Comunale (Arnald of Villanova, Pseudo),
    1:108
Bibliotheca (Photius), 5:340–341
Bieberbach, Ludwig, 2:289
Biel, William C., 5:255

Bielawski, Jozef, 4:240

Bien, Frederic, 1:345

Bierens de Haan, Johan, 7:50

Biermann, Ludwig Franz Benedikt, 1:**276–279**

Big bang theory
    Aquinas theology and, 1:43
    expansion of the universe, 2:108, 3:139
    helium, 1:277–278
    matter creation, 3:389–390
    skepticism about, 5:75
    steady state theory, 1:341, 3:136–137

Bigelow, Julian, 5:78

Bigelow, Maurice, 6:232

Bijvoet, Johannes Martin, 1:**279–286**

Bikini Atoll, 4:186–187, 5:254, 6:235

Billingham, Rupert, 5:87–88

Binet, Alfred, 4:26, 6:92, 7:25

Binney, George, 2:382

Binomial nomenclature, 2:6–7, 7:221

Bio-Ecology (Clements and Shelford), 2:390, 3:414

Biocenology, 6:509–510

Biochemical Journal. See Biochemische Zeitschrift

Biochemische Zeitschrift, 5:250, 252–253

Biochemistry, 1:1
    blood-brain barrier, 6:447, 448
    carotenes, 4:227
    chemical warfare, 4:167–170
    dynamic, 5:250
    embryology and, 5:236–237
    enzymology, 3:167–172, 340–343, 5:305, 306–309, 7:31–35
    genetics and, 1:228, 3:361–364, 5:309–310, 7:12–15
    in Germany, 5:250–253
    history, 5:238
    influential figures, 7:345–348
    interdisciplinary approach, 5:236–237
    intermediary metabolism, 5:305, 306–309
    mechanist-vitalist debate, 5:236
    metabolic enzymology, 4:323–327
    microbial, 6:519–521
    mitochondria, 4:238–242
    modern medicine, 6:567–572
    molecular structure, 6:38–39
    muscles, 5:231–234
    nucleotide sugars, 4:253
    oxidative phosphorylation, 4:72–76, 5:160–163
    pharmacology, 1:118–120, 4:30–33
    photosynthesis, 2:15–17
    physiology, 2:218–219, 5:306
    proteins, 1:1–4
    ribonuclease, 1:77–80
    steroid hormones, 1:459–464
    synthesis, 7:64–68

visual perception, 7:211–215

Biochemistry (Lehninger), 4:238, 242

Biochemistry and Morphogenesis (Needham), 5:236, 237

Biochemistry of Muscle (Needham), 5:232

Biodiversity, 3:416–417

Bioenergetics, 6:569–571

Bioenergetics (Lehninger), 4:240

Bioethics, 3:186, 188–189

Biofeedback, 5:150–151

Biogenetics law, 3:207

Biogeochemistry
    ecology, 3:410
    ecosystems, 5:322
    population ecology, 3:413–414

The Biogeochemistry of Vertebrate Excretion (Hutchinson), 3:413

Biogeography
    biodiversity, 3:416–417
    ethnography, 7:210
    plant ecology, 2:235–236
    plant taxonomy, 6:514

Biogeography: An Ecological Perspective (Dansereau), 2:235–236

Biographical Memoir (Hutchinson and Wilson), 3:416

Biological Aspects of Infectious Disease (Burnet), 1:455

The Biological Basis of Personality (Eysenck), 2:429

Biological Chemistry and Physics of Sea Water (Harvey), 3:258

Biological clocks, 6:244

Biological oxidation, 6:569–571

Biological Principles (Woodger), 5:236

Biological psychology. *See* Psychobiology

Biological weapons, 5:361

Biology
    Aristotelian, 1:100–102
    comparative, 1:436–438
    developmental
        cell and tissue differentiation, 3:187–188
        cranial neural crest, 3:368–369
        cytology, 2:398–399
        experimental, 3:366
        fertilization, 4:67–70
        morphology, 6:355
    ecology, 6:509–510
    education, 3:189
    evolutionary
        birds, 5:61–62
        dinosaurs, 2:86
        downward causation, 2:24
        gall wasps, 4:124–125
        influential figures, 5:63–64, 7:224–227
        Lamracksim, 4:189–190
        mammals, 2:86
        mollusks, 2:3–7

Biology, *continued*
    philosophy, 7:63
    primatology, 7:236–238
    protein chemistry in, 1:80
    social behavior, 7:378–380
    superorganism concept, 2:391–392
  fixism theory, 1:452–453
  history and philosophy, 5:64–66, 236
  mathematical, 3:415
  molecular
    atomic physics, 2:267–271
    DNA base ratios, 2:93–97
    DNA synthesis, 6:478–482
    embryology, 1:370–376
    enzymology, 3:340–343
    foundation of, 5:305–311
    genetics and, 1:228, 5:310
    hemoglobin, 6:81–83
    protein chemistry, 6:360, 361–365
    ribonuclease, 1:79–80
    virology, 1:463–464
    x-ray crystallography, 2:207–209
  nitrogen fixation, 2:104–105
  physiochemical, 5:359–364
  plants, 2:413–415
  space, 4:137–140, *138*
  teleology, 3:93–94
  theoretical
    embryology, 7:201–205
    palingenesis, 4:250–251
    rationality, 2:379–381
    scientific inquiry and, 5:88–89
  See also Astrobiology; Cytology; Psychobiology
Biology and Knowledge (Piaget), 6:94
The Biology of Mind (Hess), 3:305
A Biology of the British Hemiptera-Heteroptera (Butler), 3:411
The Biology of the Cell Surface (Just), 4:68, 69
Biomechanics, 1:349
Biomedical computing, 3:51
Biomes, 5:317
Biometrika, 6:54
Biometry, 6:53–55
Bioorganic chemistry, 5:359–364
Biophysical Science: A Study Program (Schmitt), 6:362
Biophysics
  amplifier theory, 4:55–56
  development, 6:360, 362
  x-ray crystallography, 7:298–300
La Biosfera: Entre la termodinámica y el juego (Margalef), 5:24
Biosfera (Vernadskiy), 6:509
Biospecies, 3:159
Biosphere, 6:509

Biostratigraphy
  evolution, 6:351–355
  geological mapping, 3:393
Biosystematics
  botany, 6:515
  evolutionary biology, 6:353, 354
Biot, Jean-Baptiste, 4:205, 6:22, 23
Biotechnology, 6:478–482, *481*
Biotheoretical Gathering, 5:237
Birch, Albert Francis, 4:234, 6:259
Birch, Thomas, 1:367
Bird, Kai, 5:348
Bird, R. Byron, 7:135
Bird Island (Tinbergen). *See Vogeleiland* (Tinbergen)
Bird-Song: The Biology of Vocal Communication and Expression in Birds (Thorpe), 7:43
Birds
  ancestors, 3:431
  Anecdotes of the Habits and Instincts of Birds, Reptiles, and Fishes (Lee), 4:232
  behavior
    comparative psychology, 6:369
    courtship, 3:384–385, 424
    environmental influence on, 1:148–153
    evolution, 3:425
    instinctive, 4:336, 337–338
    interacting causes, 4:244–246
  consciousness, 3:180–181, 183
  cytogenetics, 2:59
  ecology, 2:7, 3:370
  evolution, 2:4, 5:61–62
  flight, 7:182
  heart rate, 5:317
  migration, 5:277–278
  natural selection, 3:183, 184, 185, 7:377–378
  navigation, 3:177–178, 5:322
  nesting, 5:277
  songs, 7:42–43
  territoriality
    British warblers, 5:278
    courtship, 3:384–385
  See also specific birds; Ornithology
The Birds of Oklahoma (Nice), 5:277
Birdsell, Joseph, 2:174
Birge, Edward Asahel, 2:353, 3:260
Birge, Raymond T., 2:165, 5:210
al-Birjandī, ʿAbd al-ʿAlī. *See* al-Barjandī, ʿAbd al-ʿAlī
Birkeland, Olaf Kristian, 1:41
Birkhoff, Garrett, 1:**286–288**, 5:2
  influence of, 5:178
  universal algebra lattice, 3:213
Birkhoff, George David, 5:198
Birkhoff variety theorem, 1:286, 287
Birth defects, radiation-associated, 5:242–243

Bis-(4-aminophenyl)-sulfone, 6:323

Bishop, George, 6:361

Bismarck, Otto Eduard Leopold von, 7:159

Bitableaux, 6:286

al-Bitrūjī, Nur al-Din Abu Ishāq. *See* al-Bitrūjī al-Ishbīlī, Abū Ishāq

al-Bitrūjī al-Ishbīlī, Abū Ishāq, 1:138, 6:216

Bivalvia, 5:265, 266

Bjerknes, Jacob Aall Bonnevie, 1:247, 249, 289, 2:99
    atmospheric science, 6:3
    cyclogenesis, 6:220
    meteorology, 6:85
    Pacific Basin climate variation, 5:223
    Southern Oscillation, 7:218

Bjerknes, Vilhelm, 1:246, **288–290,** 2:100, 426
    atmospheric science, 6:3, 5
    cyclogenesis, 6:220
    meteorology, 6:85, 88, 471
    weather forecasting, 6:470

Bjerrum, Jannik Nielsen, 4:59

Bjorken, James, 3:24

Blaauw, Adriaan, 6:456, 7:131–132

Black, Davidson, 2:239
    colleagues of, 7:251
    paleoanthropology, 6:57, 58

Black, James, 2:373

Black, Joseph, 2:217, 218, 219, 3:420
    colleagues of, 7:222
    combustion, 6:507

Black body radiation
    black holes, 6:400
    wave theory, 1:411

Black-Body Theory and the Quantum Discontinuity, 1894-1912 (Kuhn), 4:175, 6:112

The Black Cloud (Hoyle), 3:391

Black holes
    black body radiation, 6:400
    formation of, 5:348
    Kerr solution, 6:399
    mathematical theory, 2:92
    physics, 2:370
    properties, 7:393–394

Black terns, 1:151

Blackadar, Alfred, 6:8, 9

Blackett, Patrick Maynard Stuart, 1:**290–294,** *291*
    attempted poisoning of, 5:348
    cloud chambers, 1:289–291, 5:301–302, *302*
    colleagues of, 6:337, 7:66
    earth's magnetism, 2:379
    geophysics, 2:191
    influence of, 5:303
    magnetic fields, 6:299, 300
    and McCrea, William Hunter, 5:74
    particle physics, 6:282

positrons, 1:73, 7:399

Blackman, Richard B., 6:425

Blagden, Charles, 1:265

Blair, Archibald, 1:295

Blair, Robert, 1:**294–296**

Blanckaert, Claude, 3:116

Blaschke, Wilhelm Johann Eugen, 2:111

Blasius of Parma, 1:**296–298**

Blastomeres, 3:*367*

Blastulae, 3:*368*

Blau, Marietta, 1:**298–302,** *300*

The Blazing World (Cavendish), 2:80

Bletchley Park cryptographic headquarters, 7:89–90

Bleuler, Eugen, 4:63, 64, 6:92

Blind-variation-and-selective-retention, evolutionary, 2:23, 26

Blink machines, 1:336

Bloch, André, 1:23–24

Bloch, Felix, 1:55, **303–308,** *305*
    condensed matter physics, 6:169
    electrical conductivity, 3:401
    nuclear magnetic resonance, 3:196, 199, 6:181
    solid-state physics, 5:201, 6:63

Bloch, Konrad, 7:350

Bloch equation, 1:306

Bloch-Nordsieck method, 7:69

Bloch wall, 1:304

Bloch's constant, 1:23

Bloch's principle, 1:24

Bloembergen, Nicolaas, 3:197

Blombäck, Birger, 2:352

Blombäck, Margareta, 2:350

Blood
    antigens, 4:261, *262*
    hemoglobin, 6:39, 42
    physics, 1:445

Blood-brain barrier, 6:447, 448

Blood circulation. *See* Circulatory system

Blood groups, 3:47, 7:114

Bloor, David, 3:236, 4:176

Blos, Peter, 2:407

Blum, Harold F., 6:485

Blum, Joseph, 6:145–146

Blum-Bergmann, Ottilie, 1:251

Blumenbach, Johann Friedrich, 2:223, 5:368

Blumenthal, Arthur, 7:368–369

Blundell, Thomas, 3:338

Blundeville, Thomas, 2:157

Boas, Franz, 2:74

Bochner, Salomon, 6:380

Bodansky, David, 1:165

Bode, Hendrik, 6:425

Bodenstein, Adam of, 1:**308–310**

Bodenstein, Max, 5:167

Boderman, Alvin, 3:17
Boer, Jan Hendrik de, 1:281, **310–316,** 5:203, 7:133, 136
Boerhaave, Hermann, 2:218
    influence of, 4:314
    translations of, 4:183, 184
    writings of, 5:37
Bogen, Joseph E., 6:496
Bogoliubov, Nikolai Nikolaevich. *See* Bogolubov, Nikolai Nikolaevich
Bogolubov, Nikolai Nikolaevich, 1:**316–321,** *320*
Bogolyubov, Nikolai. *See* Bogolubov, Nikolai Nikolaevich
Bohlin, Birger, 6:58
Bohm, David Joseph, 1:**321–326,** *324*
    Bardeen, John, 1:181
    Copenhagen Interpretation, 1:409
    hidden variables, 1:239
    nonlocal theory, 1:413
Bohr, Niels Henrik David, 1:**326–328,** *327*
    acquaintances of, 2:205, 357, 4:71–72, 83, 6:134, 192
    atomic bombs, 6:65
    atomic theory, 1:411, 6:37, 489, 490
    colleagues of, 2:343, 6:195, 282
    Copenhagen Interpretation, 2:380
    hydrogen, 6:62
    influence of, 3:254, 4:55, 209, 233, 7:100
    Lehmann, Inge, 4:232
    physicists network, 2:269
    quantum mechanics, 3:21, 6:35
    students of, 2:64, 267–268, 3:400, 5:200
Bohr-Kramers-Slater theory, 1:327
Bohr-Sommerfeld quantization scheme, 1:411
Boilot, Jean-Pierre, 2:163
Bok, Bartholomeus Jan, 1:**328–332,** *329,* 7:286
    colleagues of, 6:383
    on Oort, Jan Hendrik, 5:342
    students of, 6:500
Bok, Priscilla, 1:331, 332
Bokhoven, Cornelis, 1:283
Boland, Edward, 5:264
Bolívar, Simón, 4:202
Bolker, Ethan, 4:35
Bolognese University, 1:202
Bolognian stone, 3:352, 353
Bolsheviks, 6:326–327
Bolton, John Gatenby, 1:**332–337,** *335,* 3:137, 6:304
Boltyanskii, Vladimir G., 6:128
Boltzmann, Ludwig Eduard, 1:**337–339,** *338,* 2:320, 7:99, 100
    integral equations, 3:307
    quantum mechanics, 6:112
    statistical mechanics, 2:356

Bolyai, Farkas, 3:246
Bombieri, Enrico, 2:259
Bombs
    atomic
        critical mass, 1:274
        cyclotrons and, 1:164–165
        development, 5:190, 6:195–196, 421–422, 573, 7:295–296, 298, 328–329
        explosion, 5:191, 6:415–416
        first test, 1:162, 164
        fission, 1:57, 6:64–65
        genetic effects, 5:242–243
        high energy physics, 1:425
        Manhattan Project, 4:291
        nuclear physics, 6:419
        oceanographic effects, 6:235
        opposition to, 1:292, 327–328, 5:191
        particle physics, 3:20
        plutonium, 1:134–135, 6:401, 402–403
        reduction efforts, 1:269
        Soviet, 3:34–35
        testing, 6:283
    hydrogen
        development, 1:57, 6:421, 7:21–24
        ethics, 6:196
        fusion, 6:501–502
        schematic, 7:*22*
        strategic value, 1:136
        Ulam-Teller mechanism, 1:274
        USSR, 6:325
    neutron, 1:392
Bombsights, 1:292
Bonaparte, Napoléon. *See* Napoléon I, Emperor of France
Bondaryuk, Mikhail M., 4:103
Bondi, Christine Stockman, 1:340
Bondi, Hermann, 1:**339–343,** *341,* 3:136, 137, 6:80
    colleagues of, 3:389
    influence of, 6:398
    steady state theory, 5:74
    on Van de Hulst, Hendrik, 7:130
Bonds (chemical)
    aluminum alkyls, 3:195–196
    benzene, 3:198
    double, 3:400–404, *403, 404*
Bonhoeffer, Karl Friedrich, 2:205, 267, 270
Bonhoeffer, Otto, 2:359
Bonner, Elena, 6:327, 328
Bonnet, Charles, 4:250
Bonneville, Mary A., 6:147
Bonnin, Louis-Armand, 3:352
Book of Mercy (Jābir Ibn Ḥayyān), 4:19
Book of Seventy (Jābir Ibn Ḥayyān), 4:19
Book of Sophe (Zosimos of Panopolis), 7:406

Book of Spiritual Physick (Rāzī), 6:213
Book of the Fifty (Jābir Ibn Ḥayyān), 4:20
Book of the Solution of the Difficulties in Euclid (Hero of
    Alexandria), 3:284–285
Booklet on Geology (Heimans). *See Het Geologieboekje*
    (Heimans)
Boole, George, 2:310, 3:70
Boolean algebra, 6:425
Boolos, George, 4:35
Boomerangs (Walker), 7:217
Boore, David M., 1:31
Boos, Winfried, 4:75, 76
Boot, John T., 1:55
Booth, David, 5:151
Borck, Stanislaus von, 6:551
Bordet, Jules, 1:455
Borel, Armand, 1:**343–348,** 2:361
    Bourbaki group, 1:364
    semisimple groups, 3:244
    theory of automorphic forms, 1:346
Borel, Émile, 3:265, 6:123
Borel-Moore homology, 1:345
Borel-Weil theorem, 1:344–345
Borelli, Giovanni Alfonso, 1:**348–351,** *349*
Boreskov, Georgiĭ Konstaninovich, 1:**351–356**
Borgesius, A. H., 7:99
Boring, Edwin Garrigues, 1:**356–361,** 5:217, 7:368
Born, Hedwig, 4:57
Born, Max, 4:57
    axiomatics, 3:307
    colleagues of, 5:348
    firing of, 3:275
    quantum mechanics, 2:165
    students of, 2:378, 3:400
Boron, 1:418–420, 421–422
Borrichius, Olaus, 6:512
Borro, Girolamo, 1:**361–363,** 442
Borromeo, Carlo, 1:167
Borst, Arno, 6:119
Borsuk, Karol, 2:360
Bos, Gerrit, 5:8
Bosch, Carl, 3:203–204
Boscovich, Ruggiero Giuseppe, 7:167
Botanical nomenclature, 1:386, 387–388
Botany
    Australia, 5:204–208
    Canada, 7:78–79
    developmental morphology, 6:356–359
    ecology, 2:188–189, 7:3–5
    economic, 3:272
    ecosystems, 7:6–8
    Enlightenment, 7:221–222
    evolution, 2:154–157
    experimental, 3:133

genetics, 6:513–516, 7:1–2
Mendelian genetics, 7:189–191, *191*
nomenclature, 1:386, 387–388
plant anatomy, 2:413–415, 6:389–391
plant communities, 2:152–154
plant hybridization, 1:211–212, 5:98–100
South Africa, 6:483–484
steroid synthesis, 6:227–228
taxonomy, 2:213–214, 4:314–315
Bothe, Walther Wilhelm Georg, 2:*65,* 5:128, 301,
    6:280–281
Bott, Raoul, 1:12, 2:115
Botvinik, Mikhail, 6:429
Boudini, Paolo, 6:338
Boule, Marcellin, 6:107, 108, 7:115
Boullay, Polydore, 2:323
*The Boundary Correspondence under Quasiconformal
    Mappings* (Ahlfors and Beurling), 1:23
Boundary Layer Meteorology (Wyngaard), 6:9
Bounded rationality, 6:449–450
Bourbaki, Nicolas, 1:**363–366,** 6:379
Bourgeois, Jean-Pierre, 3:147
Boussingault, Jean Baptiste Joseph Dieudonné, 4:202
BOV (Barium-tin-vanadium), 1:352
Boveri, Theodor, 7:261
Bowden, Philip, 5:39
Bowdich, Thomas Edward, 4:230–231
Bowditch, Henry Pickering, 1:16
Bowditch, Sarah. *See* Lee, Sarah Eglonton Wallis
    Bowdich
Bowen, Alan, 2:418
Bowen, Ira Sprague, 1:131, 132, 2:343, 344, 345, 3:61,
    7:398–399
Bowen, Taffy, 1:334
Bowen, Vaught T., 3:414
Bowen, William, 2:418
Bower, Ernest Clare, 7:284
Bower, Gordon H., 3:312
Bowers, Joy, 6:130
Bowker, Albert H., 3:51
Bowler, Peter J., 1:210, 2:244, 246, 4:191
Bowles, Chester, 6:575
Bowman, Julia. *See* Robinson, Julia Bowman
Boyce, Frederick M., 6:498–499
Boyce, Joseph, 2:344
Boyd, David R., 4:13
Boyd, Robert Neilson, 2:200
Boyer, Paul, 5:162, 163
Boyer, Raymond, 5:32
Boyle, Robert, 1:28, **366–370,** *368,* 6:6
    acquaintances of, 5:273
    alchemy, 7:335
    atomism, 6:419
    colleagues of, 3:352

Boyle, Robert, *continued*
  experimental method, 3:278
  influence of, 2:171, 6:512
  patron to, 6:511
  phlogiston, 6:505
  Pietism, 6:506
Boynton, Paul, 7:303, 305
Brachet, Albert, 1:370, 372–373
Brachet, Jean Louis, 1:**370–377**, *371*, 2:145
Brackenridge, Bruce, 5:270
Bradbury, Norris E., 1:306
Braddick, Henry John James, 1:292
Bradley, Francis H., 2:310
Bradley, Giles, 5:33
Bradley, James, 1:25, 2:230
Bradwardine, Thomas, 1:297, **377–380**, 2:325, 327,
  6:562
Bragg, Sir William Lawrence, 2:211
  Cavendish Laboratory, 3:66–67
  crystal structure, 1:280
  DNA structure, 2:208
  International Union of Crystallography, 1:285
  molecular structure, 6:64
  research support by, 5:202
  Royal Institution, 6:141, 142
  scientists recruited by, 1:271
  students of, 7:299
  successors, 1:291
  x-ray crystallography, 6:40, 79, 81
  x-ray data interpretation, 2:207
Bragg, William Henry
  crystal structure, 1:280
  influence of, 3:333
  x-ray crystallography, 3:334
  x-ray diffraction, 3:335
Braham, Roscoe, 1:470
Brahe, Tycho, 1:**380–385**, *382*, 2:320, 413
  cosmology, 3:113
  influence of, 4:105, 107
  nova, 2:150
Brain
  anatomy
    animal, 2:340–342
    circuitry, 6:10–13
    epilepsy, 6:69–74
    functional, 6:*71, 72*
    histology, 3:304–305
    regions, 1:406–409
  behavior control
    behaviorism, 7:242–243
    learning, 5:150–151
  cephalization, 2:315
  cerebellum, 2:332, 5:33
  cerebral hemispheres, 6:496–498

cingulate cortex, 6:11–12, *12*
computational neuroscience, 5:32–36
consciousness
    mathematical modeling, 2:210–211
    shrinking field of, 4:26–27
diseases, 2:341–342
drive-reduction hypothesis and, 5:148–149
electrophysiology
    epilepsy, 6:69–74
    experimental, 1:15
    valve amplification, 1:17–18
hippocampus, 6:*12*
    comparative anatomy, 2:341
    emotions, 6:11–12
    inhibitory circuits, 2:332
histopathology, 1:408
hypothalamus, 5:148–149, 6:11–12, *12*
mapping, 7:161–163
neurochemistry, 1:120–122, 7:45–46
neurolophysiology, 3:345–346
neurotransmitters, 1:121
physiology, 5:76–79
prefrontal cortex, 3:145–148
psycholinguistics, 4:350–354
psychoneurology, 7:195–196
research, 6:363–364
surgery, 6:69–71
synapses, 2:329–333
temporal lobe, 4:142–143
See also Mind-brain connection
Brain (journal), 3:347
Brain injuries
  research, 6:495–497
  wartime, 3:345
Brain Mechanisms and Intelligence (Lashley), 4:203
Branched chain reactions, 6:411–415
Brand, Martin, 4:240
Brandt, Karl, 3:258, 4:169
Brannigan, Augustine, 5:100
Brans, Carl Henry, 2:282, 4:56
Branson, Herman, 6:39, 427
Brasavola, Antonius Musa, 4:265
Brattain, Walter
  Bell Laboratories, 1:178
  transistors, 1:180, 182, 6:437, 438
Braude, Ernest, 1:198
Brauer, Richard, 3:12, 153
Brault, James, 2:282
Braun, Ferdinand, 6:375
Braun, Josias. *See* Braun-Blanquet, Josias
Braun, Julius von, 1:214
Braun, Wernher Magnus Maximilian Freiherr. *See* von
  Braun, Wernher Magnus Maximilian Freiherr
Braun-Blanquet, Josias, 1:**385–389**, 2:235

Braun-Menéndez, Eduardo, 4:253
Bravard, Auguste, 1:452
Bray, William Crowell, 6:166
Brazilin, 6:269
Breast cancer, 6:320
The Breast Cancer Book: What You Need to Know to Make Informed Decisions (Grobstein), 3:190
Breathnach, Caoimhghin S., 3:345
Breaths (Hippocrates), 3:322–323
Breeding, selective, 1:211–212
Brehm, Alfred, 5:332, 7:181
Brehm, Jack, 3:17
Brehm's Tierleben (Brehm), 5:332
Breit, Gregory, 1:**389–393,** 2:166
    acquaintances of, 7:119
    retirement, 3:194
    students of, 6:393
Breland, Keller, 6:462, 463
Breland, Marian, 6:462
Brender à Brandis, Gerard A., 7:137–138
Brenner, Sydney, 2:210, 211
Brent, Leslie, 5:87, 88
Breslow, Ronald, 3:404
Brester, James, 1:422
Bretz, J Harlan, 1:**393–397,** 6:537
Breuer, Josef, 3:75, 4:27, 28
Breuil, Henri Édouard Prosper, 3:104, 6:58
Brewer, Alan W., 2:308
Brewer, David, 1:295
Brewster, David, 2:244, 4:53, 7:280
Brewster, Jonathan, 7:335
Brézis, Haim, 4:273, 319
Briançon, Daniel, 2:162
Briar, Glenn, 6:8
Bridges, Calvin Blackman, 1:212
Bridgman, Percy Williams, 7:135
    operationalism, 3:196
    physicalism, 1:359
    physics of high pressure, 1:179
Briefe and True Report of the New Found Land of Virginia (Harriot), 3:246
Briggs, Robert W., 1:*397,* **397–401**
Briggs Committee, 6:408
Brillouin, Marcel Louis, 1:338, 6:63
Brink, Royal Alexander, 5:70
Briquet, John, 1:386
Briscoe, Henry V. A., 7:309
Britain and Atomic Energy (Gowing), 6:65
British Catalogue (Flamsteed), 3:287
British Dyestuffs Corporation, 6:271
The British Islands and Their Vegetation (Tansley), 7:7
The British Warblers: A History with Problems of Their Lives (Howard), 3:384–385
Broadbent, Donald Eric, 1:**401–406**

Brobeck, William M., 6:410
Broca, Pierre Paul, 1:408, 3:161
    anthropology, 3:116
    anthropometric data collection, 5:181
    limbic cortex, 6:11
Broca's area
    motor aphasia, 4:352–353
    speech, 6:73–74
Brock, Laurence, 2:330
Brock, Thomas, 4:357
Brock, William H., 4:311
Brodbeck, May, 3:17
Brodie, Bernard B., 1:118–119
Brodmann, Korbinian, 1:**406–409,** 7:162
Broecker, Wallace, 5:329
Broekhoff, Hans, 1:314
Broglie, Louis de, 1:323, **409–415,** *412*
Broglie, Maurice de, 1:409, 410, 411
Broili, Ferdinand, 7:184
Brongniart, Alexandre, 2:225, 325, 4:205
Bronk, Detlev, 6:148
Bronn, Heinrich Georg, 1:**415–418**
Bronowski, Jacob, 2:210
Bronshtein, M. P., 5:127
Brønsted, Johannes Nicolaus, 3:239
Brooke, John, 1:268
Brookhaven National Laboratory, 1:135, 6:196
Brooks, Charles F., 5:221
Brooks, Frederick Phillip, Jr., 2:295–296
Brooks, John L., 3:411
Brooks, R. L., 7:89
Broom, Robert, 2:138–139, 239–240
Brostow, Witold, 3:40
Brouwer, Dirk, 6:501
Brouwer, Hendrik A., 1:281
Brouwer, Luitzen Egbertus Jan, 3:310, 7:277
Brovarnik, Herbert C. *See* Brown, Herbert Charles
Browder, Felix, 4:319
Brown, A. W., 7:231
Brown, Alexander Crum, 4:98–99
Brown, Ben C., 3:376
Brown, Frank Burch, 2:246
Brown, Gerald, 1:275, 392
Brown, Harrison, 4:91, 7:270
Brown, Herbert Charles, 1:194, **418–423,** *419,* 2:200–201, 7:337
Brown, Lindor, 2:329
Brown, Paul K., 5:16, 17
Brown, Robert, 4:231, 5:206, 6:357
Brown, Roger, 5:137
Brown, Sanger, 4:143
Brown, Stephen, 1:449
Brown, Weldon, 1:421
Brown v. Board of Education, 2:129–130

Browne, Janet, 2:242
Brownian motion, 7:101
Brownrigg, Henry, 2:362–363
Brück, Hermann A., 7:105
Brückner, Eduard, 5:133
Bruckshaw, G. M., 3:376
Bruhat, François, 6:381
Brunauer, Stephen, 2:393, 394
Bruner, Jerome, 5:137
Brunfels, Otto, 6:68
Brunner, Konrad, 3:303
Bruno, Giordano, 1:205, **423–425,** *424,* 4:131
Brunswik, Egon, 2:23
Brunt, David, 6:341
Bryan, Alice, 1:359–360
Bryan, Walter H., 3:317
Bryennius, Manuel, 6:2
Bryson, Reid A., 6:553
Bubble chambers, 1:57, 6:76
Buchan, Alexander, 6:371
Buchner, Eduard, 5:251
Buck, Dean Paul, 5:115, 116
Buckland, William, 2:225, 5:366
Buckyballs. *See* Fullerenes
Bucquet, Jean-Baptiste Michel, 6:44
Bucy, Paul, 4:142–143, 6:12
Budker, Gersh Itskovich, 1:**425–430,** 5:128
Bueche, Arthur, 3:40
Bueker, Elmer, 3:220
Buffon, Georges-Louis Leclerc, Comte de, 1:**431–436,** *433,* 2:224, 4:314
   influence of, 6:349
   unity of organic life, 4:185
   works of, 6:109
Buffon: Les Époques de la nature (Roger), 1:431, 433, 434
Bühler, Karl, 4:336, 6:133
Buisson, Henri, 2:307, 308
Bukhārī, Shams, 5:95
Bukharin, Nikolai, 4:83, 5:237
Buldt, Bernd, 3:131
Bullard, Edward Crisp, 1:293, 6:299, 7:323
Bullock, Theodore Holmes, 1:**436–439**
Bulman, Oliver Meredith Boone, 3:316
Bundberg tragedy, 1:454–455
Bundy, McGeorge, 7:287
Bunge, Gustav von, 1:1, 2
Bunn, Charles, 3:336
Bünning, Erwin, 4:55
Bunsen, Robert Wilhelm Eberhard, 1:*439,* **439–441,** 3:203–204, 7:105
   alkaloid chemistry, 3:57
   influence of, 4:150
   theory of derived radicals, 4:206
Bunte, Hans, 3:203–204

Buonamici, Francesco, 1:362, **441–444,** 442
Burbidge, E. Margaret, 3:61
   colleagues of, 3:390–391
   formation of elements in stars, 1:157
   stellar energy, 1:277
Burbidge, Geoffrey R., 1:157, 3:61, 177, 390–391
Burchenal, Joseph, 2:374
Burgers, Johann Martinus, 7:128
Burgers, Willy, 1:285
Burgersdijk, Frank Pieterszoon, 1:**444–446**
Buridan, Jean. *See* Buridan, John
Buridan, John, 1:34, 35, **446–448,** 5:350
Burke, Philip, 1:237
Burkhardt, G. N., 3:239
Burkhardt, Richard W., Jr., 3:424
Burkitt, Miles, 2:123
Burks, Arthur W., 2:294
Burley, Walter, 1:**448–452**
   existence of hot and cold, 1:297
   logic, 6:563
   misattributed works, 6:292
Burmeister, Hermann Karl Konrad, 1:**452–454**
Burnet, Frank Macfarlane, 1:**454–459,** *455,* 2:318,
   4:48–49, 5:86, 88
Burnette, Donald, 2:153
Burnside, William, 3:12, 13, 213
Burny, Arsene, 1:375–376
Burrau, Oyvind, 6:37
Burt, Cyril, 2:431, 3:161
Burton, Arthur, 5:91
Burton, Dan, 5:352
Burton, William, 3:381
Bury, Richard de, 1:448
Bush, Vannevar, 2:334
   differential analyzers, 3:253, 254, 357, 6:383
   inventions by, 5:53
   Office of Scientific Research and Development, 7:119
   students of, 6:425, 426
   weapons, 6:440
Butadiene, 3:383, 6:230–231
Butenandt, Adolf Friedrich Johann, 1:**459–465,** *461*
   eye color, 7:13
   Kaiser Wilhelm Society, 5:253
Butler, Clifford, 1:291
Butler, Edward A., 3:411
Butlerov, Aleksandr Mikhailovich, 1:**465–468,** *466,* 4:99
Butterflies, Common Morpho, 5:*119*
Butyl alcohol, 1:466, 6:229, 232
Butynediol, 6:230–231, 233
Buxton, John, 6:534
Byerly, Perry, 2:191
Byers, Horace Robert, 1:**468–471,** 5:222
Bykov, G. V., 1:465

Bykov, K. M., 5:150
Byram, Edward Taylor, 3:79, 80
Byrd, Richard E., 2:287
Byrnes, James F., 6:574
Byzantine medicine, 6:290–291
 See also Islamic medicine

C
C. W. Thornthwaite Associates, 7:40
C programming language, 6:534
Cabeo, Niccolò, 2:**1–3,** 3:108
Cabib, Enrico, 4:256
Cabibbo, Nicola, 7:70
Caccioppoli, Renato, 2:258
Cadogan, John, 1:200
Cadwalader, Charles, 5:*65*
Caffeine, 3:272
Cahir, John J., 6:8
Cahn, Robert S., 4:17
Cain, Arthur James, 2:**3–7,** 4:314
Cairns, John, 4:357
Calcium, 4:241
Calcium chloride, 3:353
Calcium homeostasis, 6:245
Calculating Instruments and Machines (Hartree), 3:257
Calculationes (Swineshead). *See Liber Calculationium* (Swineshead)
Calculators
 computer science and, 2:334
 as computers, 7:409–410
 differential analyzers, 3:254–256
 early, 3:357
 numerical analysis, 3:257
 numerical Archimedes, 6:541
Calculus
 analysis, 2:76
 development, 5:269
 of functions, 1:125–126, 126
 geometry and, 1:20
 infinitesimal, 4:201
 mathematics education, 7:281
 tensor, 3:190, 192
 textbooks, 1:19, 6:565
 of variations, 2:258–260, 423, 5:195
Calderón, Alberto Pedro, 2:**7–10,** *9,* 7:414, 415
Calendars
 astronomical, 7:332–333
 Callippic, 7:47
 Gregorian, 2:150
 solar and lunar cycles, 1:99
California Institute of Technology
 administration, 1:227, 228
 research prominence, 1:136
Callendar, G. S. *See* Callendar, Guy Stewart

Callendar, Guy Stewart, 1:113, 2:**10–13,** *11,* 4:91
Callendar Steam Tables (Callendar), 2:11
Callippic calendar, 7:47
Caltech. *See* California Institute of Technology
Calvert, Frederick Crace, 5:20
Calvert, Phillip, 5:*65*
Calvin, Melvin, 2:**13–19,** *14,* 6:199
Calvinism
 Aristotelianism, 1:204
 Paracelsianism, 1:309
 philosophy, 1:444–445
Calwagen, Ernst, 1:248
Cameras
 all-sky, 3:174
 Faint Object Camera, 7:130
 spin-scan, 6:555–556
Camerini, Ugo, 5:303
Cameron, Donald, 4:276
Cameron, Ewan, 6:42
Cammas, Raoul, 7:116
Camoeracensis Acrotismus (Bruno), 1:425
Campanella, Tommaso, 1:348, 2:**19–22**
Campanus of Novara, 6:218
Campbell, Bernard Grant, 5:299
Campbell, Dan, 6:39
Campbell, Donald Thomas, 2:**22–29**
Campbell, Kenton S., 3:317, 318
Camplani, Alberto, 7:407
Campomar, Jaime, 4:254, 256
Can Quantum-Mechanical Description of Physical Reality Be Considered Complete? (Einstein et al.), 1:240 241, 323, 325, 326–327
Can the Maximin Principle Serve as a Basis for Morality? A Critique of John Rawls's Theory (Harsanyi), 3:249
Canada, natural history, 7:78–79
The Canadian Settler's Guide (Traill), 7:79
Canadian Wild Flowers (Traill), 7:79
Canalization, 7:205
Cancer
 cell division, 3:343
 clonal selection theory, 1:458
 cytology, 2:142–147
 neuronal growth rate, 3:220–221, *222*
 personality and, 2:431
 pharmacology, 2:373–375
 radiation therapy, 1:298, 4:208, 210
 research, 2:185, 6:200, 201
 viruses and, 4:358
 See also specific types of cancer
Cancer Cells (Cowdry), 2:185
Cancer genetics, 6:319–320
Candelas, Philip, 6:400
Candidates, Issues, and Strategies (Pool, Abelson, and Popkin), 1:9

Canfield, Richard, 3:78
Cannabis, 2:214
Cannibalism, 3:154, 155
Cannizzaro, Stanislao, 1:466
Cannon, Walter Bradford, 2:244–245, 3:408, 4:276, 6:11
Canobic Inscription (Ptolemy), 6:173–174, 177
Canon of Insolation and the Ice-Age Problem (Milanković), 5:132
Cantacuzenus, John, 1:98
Cantlie, Mrs., drawings by, 6:*71,* 72, *72*
Canton, John, 1:221
Cantor, Georg. *See* Cantor, Georg Ferdinand Ludwig Philip
Cantor, Georg Ferdinand Ludwig Philip, 2:**29–36,** *31,* 3:265–266, 5:4
Capacity, infiltration, 3:373, 374
Capella, Martianus. *See* Martianus Capella
Caputto, Ranwel, 4:254, *254,* 255
Car emissions, 3:383
Carathéodory, Constantin, 1:286, 3:307
Caravan: The Story of the Middle East (Coon), 2:175
Carbap, Rudolf, 7:10
Carbenium ions, 2:278
Carbocation
    nonclassical ions, 1:420–421
    reactions, 1:192, *192*
Carbohydrates, 4:136–137
Carbon
    atoms, tetrahedron, 6:*155*
    compounds
        benzene, 7:*339, 340*
        chemistry, 5:250
        fermentation analysis, 5:252
        nitrogen fixation, 2:104
        organometallic chemistry, 7:338–341
        phenyllithium, 7:*338*
        structure of, 4:13
    conformational analysis, 1:197–198
    dating techniques, 5:299
    fixation, 2:16
    optical activity, 4:17
    origin of, 3:390
    radioactivity
        dating techniques, 4:295
        half-life, 4:296–297
        photosynthesis, 2:14–15
    stereoisomers, 2:201
Carbon-14, 4:295–298
Carbon cycle, 5:326, 328
Carbon dating. *See* Radiocarbon dating
Carbon dioxide
    artificial, 2:10–11
    atmospheric, 4:91–97, 7:169–170

climate change and, 5:328–329, 6:344
    measurement, 5:326–327, 7:275
    oceanography, 6:236
    rise of, 4:91–95
  global warming, 2:10–11, 12–13
  isolation, 2:217, 218
  Keeling Curve, 4:*92*
  on Mars, 4:138–139, 178
  photosynthesis, 2:15–16
Carbon nanotubes, 6:473, 474–475
Carbonate sedimentology, 5:266
Carbonylation, 6:231
Carboxylase, 5:252
Card, Stuart, 5:257
Cardano, Girolamo, 2:**36–38,** *37,* 5:175
Cardinal numbers, 2:32–33
Cardinal utility, 3:248–249
Cardinal Utility in Welfare Economics and in the Theory of Risk-Taking (Harsanyi), 3:249
Cardinal Welfare, Individualistic Ethics, and Interpersonal Comparisons of Utility (Harsanyi), 3:249
Cardini, Carlos, 4:254
The Care of the Geriatric Patient (Cowdry), 2:185
Carey, Samuel Warren, 2:**38–43**
Carey, Sorcha, 6:118
Carey, William, 7:343
Carlin, J. R., 1:302
Carlisle, Harry, 1:198, 3:335
Carlson, Rae, 5:219
Carlyle, Thomas, 3:326
Carmichael, Leonard, 5:116, 7:287
Carmona, Alfred, 5:150
Carnap, Paul Rudolf, 2:**43–47,** *45,* 4:34
    postivism, 6:136
    unified science, 4:279
Carnap, Rudolph. *See* Carnap, Paul Rudolf
Carnegie (ship), 6:234
Carnegie Institution of Washington (CARSO), 1:132
Carnesecchi, Pietro, 1:361
Carothers, Wallace Hume, 1:215, 2:**47–50,** *48, 49*
    commentaries on, 5:31
    polymers, 6:332
Caroti, Stefano, 6:562
Carpenter, Clarence Ray, 2:**50–55,** 7:234, 236
Carpenter, Ray. *See* Carpenter, Clarence Ray
Carpenter, William Benjamin, 2:**55–58,** *56*
    fossil sequences, 2:246
    ocean currents, 6:528
Carr, Harvey, 7:242
Carr-Saunders, Alexander, 2:382, 384
Carrel, Alexis, 2:183, 317, 5:215
Carriero, Michele, 2:260
Carroll, Lewis. *See* Dodgson, Charles Lutwidge
CARSO (Carnegie Institution of Washington), 1:132

Carson, Cathryn, 5:349
Carson, Hampton Lawrence, 2:**59–64**
Carson, Rachel, 2:318, 3:416, 4:270
Cartan, Élie, 2:111–112, 3:242
    influence of, 4:301
    Lie groups, 6:127
Cartan, Henri, 1:364, 2:118, 119, 6:379
    acquaintances of, 2:290
    homology, 2:361
Cartan subgroups, 3:243–244
Carter, Brandon, 6:399
Carter, Jimmy, 3:398, 5:32
Carter, K. Codell, 3:75
Cartesian Tensors (Jeffreys), 4:40
Cartier, Pierre, 2:290
Cartography
    Croatian, 3:156
    Dutch, 6:110–111
    geodesy, 1:383
    geological, 3:393
    Mercator Atlas, 3:354–356
    seafloor mapping, 2:*41*, 42, 7:29–31
    tectonic, 1:69–70, 6:431
    U.S., 6:149–152
Cartwright, D. E., 5:270
Cartwright, Dorwin, 3:14
Carus, Carl Gustav, 5:366
Carus, J. Victor, 1:417
Casanovas, Juan, 2:150
Casaubon, Isaac, 4:133
Case Histories in Clinical and Abnormal Psychology (Harris), 5:91
Casimir, Hendrik Brugt Gerhard, 2:**64–67,** *65*
Casimir, Henk, 1:313
Casimir effect, 2:66
Caspari, Ernst Wolfgang, 2:399
Caspersson, Torbjörn Oskar, 1:373, 2:**67–73,** *68*
Casselman, W., 1:346
Cassini, Giandomenico, 1:350
Cassini, Jacques
    earth's shape, 5:10
    on Maupertuis, Pierre Louis Moreau de, 5:57
Cassini, Jean-Dominque, 2:231
Cassirer, Ernst, 4:278
Cast elastomers, 1:216
Castelnuovo, Guido, 4:146
Castle, William Ernest, 7:357
Cataclysmic floods, 1:393–395, *395, 396*, 6:537
Catalase, 5:283
A Catalog of Magnetic Stars (Babcock), 1:131
Catalogue des hommes fossiles (Vallois and Movius), 5:299
Catalogue of Fossil Hominids (Oakley et al.), 5:299
A Catalogue of the Books in Natural History with a Few Others (Eliot), 7:223

A Catalogue of the Mesozoic Mammalia in the Geological Department of the British Museum (Simpson), 6:453
Catalysis
    characteristics of catalysts, 1:351–355
    chemistry, 7:311–312
    cracking, 3:381–383
    crystals, 1:311–312
    Dutch School of, 1:313–314
    enzymes, 4:74–75
    fluidized bed, 4:290
    heterogeneous, 6:416
    hydration reactions, 2:205–206
    iron, 2:393–394
    petroleum cracking, 3:380
    rhodium, 7:*311*
Catalysis in the production of sulfuric acid (Boreskov). *See Kataliz v proizvodstve sernoi kisloty* (Boreskov)
Catalysis Then and Now (Emmett), 2:394
Catarole process, 1:251
Catastrophism
    evolution, 1:416
    flooding, 1:395
    geology, 3:398, 7:280
Catechism of Agricultural Chemistry and Geology (Johnston), 4:54
Categories (Aristotle), 5:338
Categories for the Working Mathematician (Mac Lane), 5:2
Category theory, 5:4–5
Catholicism
    Aristotelianism, 2:19–20
    atomism, 3:98–100
    cognition and, 2:332
    cosmology, 3:113
    mathematics, 2:33–34, 150–151
    natural sciences, 1:37–38
    patronage, 3:100–101
    philosophy, 1:444–445, 4:133
    spiritualism *vs.*, 6:15
    See also Christianity; Jesuits
Caton-Thompson, Gertrude, 4:221
Catoptrica (Euclid), 2:417, 3:284
Cats, domestic, 1:153
Cattabriga, Lamberto, 2:259
Cattell, James McKeen, 1:169, 2:*73*, **73–75,** 428
Cauchy, Augustin-Louis, 1:6–7, 2:**75–79,** *77*
Cauchy distribution, 2:78
Cauchy-Kovalevskaya theorem, 4:158–159
Cauchy problem, 6:380
Cauchy-Riemann equations, 1:261
Causal Embryology (Brachet), 1:372
Causality, 1:324
Causality and Chance in Modern Physics (Bohm), 1:324
The Cause (Costelloe), 6:532

The Causes of Evolution (Fisher), 3:31
Cave art, 4:42–43
Cavell, Stanley, 4:172
Cavendish, Henry, 4:215
  combustion, 6:507
  electricity, 7:167
  electrostatic theory, 7:169
Cavendish, Margaret, Duchess of Newcastle, 2:*79,*
  79–81
Cavendish Laboratory, 5:301–302
Caves, 1:395–396
Caves of Missouri (Bretz), 1:396
Cayley, Arthur, 2:310, 311, 6:566
Cayley, Dorothy, 1:213
CDWs (Charge density waves), 1:182–183
Céa, Jean, 4:320
Celestial mechanics, 4:101–102, 5:197–199
Celestial physics
  Aristotelianism, 7:381–382
  stellar structure, 2:87–90
Celestial sphere
  Aristotelian physics, 1:382
  theory of impetus, 1:424
Cell biology. *See* Cytology
Cell Heredity (Sager and Ryan), 6:320
The Cell in Development and Heredity (Wilson), 2:183
Cell nucleus
  cytoplasm, 1:*372,* 4:67–69
  DNA, 1:370–371
  regions, 2:68–72
  transplantation, 1:398–399
Cell theory, 6:357–358
Cellini, Benvenuto, 6:128
Cellio, Marco Antonio, 3:352
Cellit, 2:359
Cells
  differentiation, 3:187–188
  division, 3:343, 5:102–103
  endoplasmic reticulum, 6:145–146
  energy, 6:569–571
  epigenetics, 7:204–205
  infections, 2:182
  membranes
    action potentials, 3:329–332
    cytology, 6:197–202
    ion-transporting proteins in, 5:364
  microtrabecular lattice, 6:147–148
  microtubules, 6:146–147
  mitochrondia, 4:239–241
  transplantation, 5:17–18
Cells and Organelles (Novikoff and Holtzman), 5:284
Cellulose, 6:332
Celsus, Aulus Cornelius, 2:**81–84,** *82*
Cenozoic Era, 6:343–345, 453

Centers of action, 7:18
Centiloquium (Pseudo-Ptolemy), 1:14
Central nervous system
  physiology, 7:183
  psychology, 3:268–269
  synapses, 2:329–333
Centrifugation, differential, 2:144–145, *145*
Centrifuges, 6:572
  See also Ultracentrifuges
Centuriae (Poliziano), 4:264
Cephalization, 2:315
Cephalopod fossils, 7:15–17
Cepheids, 6:382, 384
Cerebellum, 3:345–346
  cognition, 2:332
  function of, 5:33
The Cerebellum as a Neuronal Machine (Eccles), 2:332
Cerebral cortex, 1:407
Cerebral Cortex, 3:148
The Cerebral Cortex and the Internal Organs (Bykov),
  5:150
Cerebral hemispheres, 6:495–497
CERN (Conseil Européen pour la Recherche Nucleaire),
  6:196
Certain Philosophical Questions (Newton), 5:273
Certain Physiological Essays (Newton), 5:274
Ceruzzi, Paul, 2:297
Chadwick, James, 1:73
  atomic bombs, 6:64
  neutrons, 6:407
Chadwick, John, 4:82
Chaffinches, 7:42–43
Chagnon, Napoleon, 5:244
Chain, Ernst, 3:336
Chain reactions
  branched, 6:411–415
  nuclear, 6:573–575
Challenge for Survival (Dansereau), 2:236
The Challenge of Man's Future (Brown), 4:91
Challenger Expedition, 6:371
Challis, James, 1:26
Chalmers, Thomas, 4:54, 5:14, 6:574
Chamaecyparis taiwanensis, 5:289
Chamberlain, Owen, 1:62, 6:409, 410
Chamberland, Charles Edouard, 6:27
Chamberlin, Thomas Chrowder, 2:186, 187, 4:91
Chambers, Carl, 2:334
Chambers, Robert, 2:**84–87,** *85,* 216
  criticism of, 3:430
  enzymology, 3:167
  evolution model, 1:208, 4:162
Chambers's Edinburgh Journal (Chambers), 2:84, 85
Chance, 1:324
Chance, Britton, 4:239, 6:200

Chandler, Thomas, 3:429
Chandrasekhar, Subrahmanyan, 2:**87–93,** *88*
   acquaintances of, 6:383, 384
   colleagues of, 6:499, 7:128
   Milky Way brightness, 1:65
   Nobel Prize, 3:59
   principle of invariance, 1:66
   rivals of, 2:339
   stellar structure, 6:385
   students of, 6:310
Chang, Hsichun, 6:323
The Channeled Scablands of the Columbia Plateau (Bretz),
   1:394
Chant of Pleasant Exploration (Clark), 2:141
Chantrenne, Hubert, 1:374, 375–376, 2:145
Chaos in cosmic selection (Hausdorff). *See Das Chaos in
   kosmischer Auslese* (Hausdorff)
Das Chaos in kosmischer Auslese (Hausdorff), 3:265
Chaos theory, 6:166–167, 343
Chapman, Orville L., 2:204
Chapman, Robert, 5:255
Chapman, Sidney, 1:278, 7:118
Chappell, Brian, 5:162
Chapters to Eusebia (Zosimos of Panopolis), 7:406
Chapters to Theodore (Zosimos of Panopolis), 7:406
Character species, 1:387–388
Characterisation of Organic Compounds (Wilde), 6:322
Charcot, Jean-Martin, 4:25, 26
Chargaff, Erwin, 2:**93–98,** *95,* 208, 7:299–300
Charge-coupled devices, 7:305
Charge density waves (CDWs), 1:182–183
Charlesworth, H. A. K., 3:376
Charlotte, Elizabeth, 3:354
Charney, Jule Gregory, 2:**98–102,** 6:470, 471
Charpa, Ulrich, 6:358
Charraud, Nathalie, 2:34
Chase, Alston, 5:320
Chase, Martha, 1:374, 4:358
Chasles, Michel, 3:327
Châtelet, Gabrielle-Émilie Le Tonnelier de Breteuil,
   Marquise du, 1:92, 5:11
Chatt, Joseph, 2:**102–106,** 7:310
Chaucer, Geoffrey, 1:110, 6:162
Chauvon, Elisabeth, 6:517
Cheadle, Vernon, 2:415
Check-List of Birds of the World (Peters), 5:61
Chelintsev, Gennadi V., 5:248
Chelomey, Vladimir N., 4:104
Chemical Bonding as an Electrostatic Phenomenon (Boer).
   See Chemische binding als electrostatisch verschijnsel
   (Boer)
Chemical bonds. *See* Bonds (chemical)
Chemical Effects of Steric Strains (Brown), 1:420
Chemical elements. *See* Elements

Chemical Embryology (Needham), 1:372, 5:236, 237
Chemical energy, 6:165–166
Chemical engineering
   catalytic cracking, 3:381–383
   development, 7:133–139
   educational methods, 4:287–292
   petroleum cracking, 3:380
   Solvay process, 3:377–380
Chemical Engineering Science, 7:136
Chemical Engineer's Handbook (Perry), 4:289
Chemical evolution, 3:363
Chemical Kinetics and Chain Reactions (Semenov), 6:414
Chemical microbiology, 6:519–521
Chemical physics
   bonds, 3:195–196
   branched chain reactions, 6:411–415
   hydrodynamics, 7:391–392
   spectroscopy, 6:473
Chemical physics (periodical), 6:412
Chemical Physics Letters, 1:260
Chemical physiology, 4:14–15, 6:447–448
Chemical reactions
   adenosine trisophate (ATP), 4:*325*
   with benzene, 5:19
   branched chain reactions, 6:411–415
   catalytic hydration, 2:205–206
   chain-mechanisms, 2:205
   chemical affinity, 1:265
   electronic theory, 4:14
   energy cycles, 4:324–327
   fluidized catalyst bed, 4:289–290
   hydrochloric acid, 2:195
   kinetics, 1:354
   lasers, 1:259–260
   lectures on, 6:141
   mechanics of molecular collisions, 1:258–259
   nucleophilic substitution, 1:*191*
   organic, 1:*190,* 190–193, 2:277–278, 4:14, 15
   peptide synthesis, 4:*326*
   physical chemistry, 6:126
   protein chemistry, 2:349–351
   quantum mechanics, 3:87–88
   ribonuclease, 1:79–80
   stereochemistry, 6:156–160
   structure-reactivity, 3:238–240, *239*
   theory of chemical heat, 4:217–218
Chemical technology. *See* Industrial chemistry
Chemical weapons
   development of, 4:167–170
   nitrogen fertilizers, 3:204
   See also specific chemical weapons
Chemiosmotic theory, 6:197, 199, 200, 201
Chemische Annales (Lavoisier), 4:216

Chemische binding als electrostatisch verschijnsel (Boer),
1:311
Chemische Studien (Kekulé), 4:99
*A Chemist in the White House: From the Manhattan
Project to the End of the Cold War* (Seaborg), 6:406
Chemistry
    alchemy *vs.,* 4:249–250, 6:506–507, 511–513
    analytical
        bacterial, 2:94
        electroconductivity, 7:396
        instrumental techniques, 1:439–440, 4:229
        qualitative analysis, 2:194–195
    applied, 4:53–54
    atmospheric, 4:91–95, 7:169–170
    bioorganic, 5:359–364
    chemical affinity, 1:265
    colloids
        crystals, 1:311–312
        polymers, 6:330–332
    combustion, 6:504, 505
    computers in, 6:131
    coordination
        ferrocene, 7:308–309, *309*
        nickel, 7:*308*
        rhodium, 7:310–311
        transition metals, 2:102–103, 4:59–60
    economics and, 2:218–219
    education
        introductory textbooks, 5:21
        popular, 3:64
    experimental
        metabolic enzymology, 4:323
        organic chemistry, 2:277–278
        oxidative phosphorylation, 5:160–163
        primordial atmosphere, 5:155–156
        transition metals, 4:61
        translations, 1:92
        on water, 4:215
    fullerenes, 6:473–474
    geochemistry, 6:258–261
        solar system, 4:179–180
        volcanology, 6:263
    high-temperature, 2:161
    industrial
        catalysis, 1:352–355, 7:311–312
        chemical synthesis, 7:349, 350–352
        decomposition, 1:233–234
        dyes, 6:271, 7:144–145
        educational methods, 4:287–292
        metals separation and purification, 1:310–314
        organic, 6:228–233
        platinum, 7:342–343
        research and development, 7:321–322
        Solvay process, 3:377–380

        synthetic ammonia, 3:203–204
    inorganic
        analysis methods, 4:312
        iron monoxide, 2:160–161
        philosophy of science, 6:6
        radiochemistry, 7:306, 307–308
        synthesis, 2:160, 4:149
        transition metals, 2:102–104, 4:58–61
    matter theory, 1:229–230
    medicine and, 6:418–419
    metaphyics, 3:158
    neurochemistry
        modern medicine, 7:45–46
        sympathomimetic amines, 1:120–122
    Newton's theory of, 5:273–274, 274–275
    nuclear
        plutonium, 6:408–409
        radioactivity, 6:75–78
        transuranium elements, 6:401–406
    nuclear magnetic resonance, 3:195, 196–197
    optical materials, 2:162–163
    organic
        acids, 3:237
        aromatic compounds, 1:250
        behavior of matter, 4:205–206
        benzene structure, 4:98–99
        boron, 1:418–423
        carbohydrates, 4:258–263
        chemical shifts, 3:197–200, *198*
        combustion method of analysis, 1:268
        conformational analysis, 1:200
        crystallography, 6:21–22
        cyclohexane, 1:199, *199*
        dyes, 1:214–218
        flavones, 7:143–148
        France, 7:371–372
        free radical polymerization, 1:*194*
        gravimetric analysis, 4:311–312
        history, 1:194, 195–196
        hydrogenation, 3:41–43
        industrial, 6:228–233
        influential figures, 7:336–341, 349–356
        Japan, 5:287–292
        Kolbe-Frankland theory, 4:149
        molecular orbitals, 2:276–278
        nucleophilic substitution, 1:*191*
        origin of life, 5:156–157
        physical, 1:189, 195–201, 2:199–204, 4:12, 14
        radioactivity, 2:14–15
        reactions, 1:*190*, 190–195
        research, 2:323–324, 6:223–228
        rotenone, 1:459–460
        stereochemistry, 6:154–161
        stoichiometry, 1:268

structure-reactivity relationships, 3:238–240, *239*
synthesis, 6:268–273, 321–324, 7:64–68
water analysis, 3:63–64
organometallic, 5:246–249
  coordination, 2:102–103
  ferrocene, 7:*309*
  phenyllithiium, 7:338–339
  transition metals, 2:102–103, 7:308–310, *310*
  water analysis, 3:63–64
origin of life, 5:154–158
periodic table, 5:105–108, *107*
physical
  acids, 3:237
  atomism, 2:320–322
  catalysis, 2:205–206
  chemical reactions, 6:126
  experimental, 3:57–58
  founding of, 5:356–357
  greenhouse effect, 1:112–113
  molecular structures, 5:167–170
  oceanography, 6:88–90
  organic, 3:86–88
  radar, 6:139–140
  structure-reactivity relationships, 3:238–240
  systematization of, 4:14–15
pigments, 2:14
pneumatic, 6:507
professional societies, 2:250–252
protein, 1:*77*
  amino acids, 2:348–352
  biosynthesis, 4:326–327
  chain folding, 1:76 80
  hemoglobin, 6:81–83
  molecular structure, 6:38–40, 360, 361–365
  nucleic acids, 2:68–69
  oligosaccharide recognition, 4:261–263
  peptides, 1:1, 2, 4:*326*
  physical chemistry and, 5:170
  synthesis, 2:209–210
quantum
  beginning of, 5:211–212
  computers, 6:129–132
  internationalization of, 5:212–214
  molecular structure, 6:37–40
  resonance theory dispute, 5:248
  wave mechanics, 7:104
research, 2:323–325
revolution, 6:44
solid-state
  chemical reactions, 6:126
  crystal growth, 2:161–162
speculative, 1:367
structural, 1:465–467

advances in, 5:29
theory, 1:465–466
synthesis, 7:349, 350–352
theoretical
  bonds, 6:37
  computers in, 6:131–132
  organic chemistry, 2:277–278, 4:205–206
translations, 6:97–98
transmutation, 3:352–354
x-rays, 3:333–334
See also specific chemical processes; Biochemistry; Geochemistry; Stereochemistry
The Chemistry and Fertility of Sea Waters (Harvey), 3:259
Chemistry for the Modern World (Porter), 6:140
The Chemistry of Common Life (Johnston), 4:54
The Chemistry of Muscular Contraction (Szent-Györgyi), 6.571
The Chemistry of Synthetic Dyes (Venkataraman), 7:147–148
Chemistry of Vegetable and Animal Physiology (Mulder), 4:54
Chemostat, 6:576
Chen Ning Yang. *See* Yang, Chen Ning
Chengzi, Hu, 7:187
Cherenkov, Pavel Aleksandrovich. *See* Cherenkov, Pavel Alekseyevich
Cherenkov, Pavel Alekseyevich, 2:**106–111,** *110*
Chern, Shiing-Shen, 2:**111–116,** *113*
  Chern-Weil homomorphism, 7:256
  mathematical analysis, 5:199
Chern-Weil homomorphism, 7:256
Cherwell, Lord. *See* Lindemann, Frederick Alexander
Chess, 6:428, 429
Chevalier, J. P., 3:317
Chevalley, Claude, 2:112, **116–120,** 290, 291
  algebraic groups, 1:345
  Bourbaki groups, 1:364
Chew, Geoffrey, 6:396
Chicago school of ecology, 2:390–391
Chicken embryos
  cell theory, 5:332
  developmental biology, 3:217
  microsurgery, 3:*219,* 219–221, *220*
  sensory development, 3:222–223
Chien-Shiung Wu. *See* Wu, Chien-Shiung
Child, Charles Manning, 3:434, 435
Child, Robert, 7:334
Child development
  adaptation and, 1:171–172
  biosocial theory, 1:169
  communication, 6:*93*
  intelligence, 6:91–95, 522
  See also Child psychology
Child guidance movement, 6:275

Child psychology, 1:169
    behaviorism, 4:281, 7:243–244
    intelligence, 6:91–96, 522
    psychoanalysis, 2:408–409
    race and, 2:128–129
    segregation and, 2:128
Childhood and Society (Erikson), 2:409–410
Children, John George, 2:216
Children's Speech (Stern and Stern). *See Die Kindersprache*
    (Stern and Stern)
The Child's Conception of Number (Piaget), 6:95
Chile, observatories, 1:132
Chimeric vesicles, 6:197, 200, 201
La chimie au Moyen Âge (Duval), 7:406
Chimpanzees
    emotional behavior, 3:268
    stimulus-response connection, 3:407
    See also Primatology
China
    geology, 2:299–300, 7:385–386
    meteorology, 7:402–405
    paleontology, 7:251–252, 383–384
    pharmaceutical industry, 4:30
    science in, 5:235, 238–239
China monumentis illustrata (Kircher), 4:131, 134
Chinese Academy of Sciences, 7:404–405
Chinese hamster embryo cells, 6:320
Chioniades, George, 2:**120–122**
Chiral ionophores, 6:160, *160*
Chlamydomonas, 6:316–317, 318–319
Chlorine
    discovery, 1:265
    gas, 3:204–205
Chlorine-37, 1:158–159
Chlorophyll
    oxidized, 2:16–17
    synthesis, 7:351–352
Chloroplasts, 6:316–319
Chlorvinylketones, 5:246–247
Chlorvinyls, 5:246–247
Choice
    behavior, 7:92–95
    impartial observer theory, 3:249
    rational choice theory, 3:227, 231–232
    See also Decision making
Choices, Values, and Frames (Kahneman and Tversky),
    7:95
Cholera
    1849 London epidemic, 5:20
    sanitary reform, 4:54
Chomsky, Noam, 4:50, 6:464
Choucroun, Nine, 4:228
Chouet, Bernard, 1:32
Chow, Wei-Liang, 4:146

Christian IV, King of Denmark, 1:383
Christianity
    aristogenesis and, 5:355
    Aristotelianism, 6:295
    astronomy, 1:423–424
    of Charles Darwin, 2:247
    client-centered psychology, 6:278
    dualism, 3:214–215
    evolution, 6:109
    McCrea, William Hunter on, 5:75
    pagan natural philosophy, 4:51–52, 133
    political economics, 5:13–14
    Protestantism, 6:206
    science and, 5:121–122
    social gospel, 6:275
Christiansen, Wilbur Norman, 5:345
Christianson, J. R., 1:380
Christoffersson, Anders, 1:32
Christofilos, Nicholas, 4:333
Christol, Jules de, 2:226
Christy, Robert F., 5:190
Chromatography
    gas
        development of, 5:40
        experimental and theoretical, 2:206
    paper
        development of, 5:39–40
        photosynthesis, 2:15–16
    partition
        development of, 5:39
        rediscovery of, 4:226
Chromodynamics, quantum, 5:130–131
Chromomictors, 1:28
Chromosomes
    banding, 2:71–72
    gene expression and, 2:68–70
    mapping, 1:225
    Mendelian genetics, 1:212
    ploidy, 1:397–398
Chrysippus, 2:**122–123,** 3:321
Chrysococces, George, 5:95
Chrysopoeia, 5:273, 6:512
Chubb, Talbot, 3:80
Chun, Carl, 6:370
Chung-ho Chen, 4:241
Chung Yao Chao. *See* Zhao, Zhongyao
Church, Alonzo, 5:4, 7:83
Church-Turing thesis, 7:83
Churchill, Winston, 6:65, 81, 7:68
Chymistry. *See* Chemistry
Chymistry of Isaac Newton, 5:274
Ciarlet, Philippe, 4:320
Cingulate cortex, 6:11–12, *12*
Circadian rhythms, 6:244–245

Circles, Arabic mathematics, 6:186

Circuits, 6:425

Circular Causal Systems in Ecology (Hutchinson), 3:413, 415

Circulation
atmospheric, 7:17–19
ocean, 6:*529*

Circulatory system, 3:110
blood flow, 3:303–304
physics, 1:445

Cirrostratus clouds, 7:154

Cities, psychology of living in, 5:140–141

Citric acid cycle. *See* Krebs cycle

Citroni Marchetti, Sandra, 6:118

Città del Sole (Campanella), 2:20

Cittadino, Eugene, 6:390, 391

City of the Sun (Campanella) *See Città del Sole* (Campanella)

Civil engineering, 5:132

Civil rights, 6:483, 7:84, 85, 86

Civilized Man's Eight Deadly Sins (Lorenz), 4:345

Cladistics
bottom-heavy, 3:160
development, 3:281–282
paleontology, 6:30–33

Clagett, Marshall, 1:85

Clairaut, Claude, 2:231

Claparède, Édouard, 6:91

Clapp, Phil, 5:223

Clark, Alvin, 4:276

Clark, Desmond. *See* Clark, John Desmond

Clark, Grahame, 2:123

Clark, John Desmond, 2:**123–127,** *124,* 7:236

Clark, Kenneth Bancroft, 2:**128–137,** *130*
Northside Center, 2:129
race and academics, 2:131–132
school integration, 2:129–131
theoretical analysis of inequailty, 2:135–136
war on poverty, 2:132–135

Clark, Mamie Phipps, 2:**128–137,** *133*
Northside Center, 2:129
school integration, 2:129–131
war on poverty, 2:133–134

Clark, Wilfrid Edward Le Gros, 2:**137–142,** 138–141, 5:296

Clarke, Arthur C., 4:117, 5:82

Clarke, George, 2:354

Class field theory, 2:117–118

Classes and Orders of the Animal Kingdom (Bronn). *See Klassen und Ordnungen des Thierreiches* (Bronn)

Classical genetics, 6:493–494

The Classical Groups (Weyl), 7:277

Classification
animals, 2:222–223
geological, 1:93–95
insects, 2:389–390
invertebrates, 4:190
natural
Aristotelian theory, 1:102–104
universe, 2:320
plants
Linnaean, 4:316
relationships, 2:214
varying approaches to, 5:206
stars, 6:544, 546
See also Nomenclature; Taxonomy

Claude, Albert, 2:69, **142–148,** *143,* 3:169, 6:143–145

Claudii Ptolemaei Alexandrini geographicae libri octo graecog latini (Hondius), 3:355

Claudius Galen. *See* Galen

Claudius Ptolemaeus. *See* Ptolemy

Clausen, Roy Elwood, 4:276

Clausius, Julius Emanuel, 6:165

Clave, Étienne de, 3:353

Clavius, Christoph, 1:105, 2:**148–152,** *149,* 5:176

Clayton, H. H., 5:221

Cleanthes (Homer), 7:112

Clear air turbulence, 6:8

The Clear Mirror (Hutchinson), 3:412

Clegg, John A., 2:191

Clements, Frederic Edward, 2:**152–154**
bioecology, 5:317
botany, 1:388, 7:4, 5, 7
letter to, 7:6
plant ecology, 2:187, 188, 3:414

Clerk, John, 3:419

Clerk, John, Jr., 3:419

Cleveland, Grover, 6:150

Client-centered psychology, 6:274–279

CLIMAP (Climate: Long-Range Investigation, Mapping, and Prediction), 6:343

Climate: Long-Range Investigation, Mapping, and Prediction (CLIMAP), 6:343

Climate: Present, Past and Future (Lamb), 4:195

Climate, urban, 3:386, 387

Climate change
abrupt, 5:328–329, *329*
anthorpogenic, 2:12–13
Dansgaard-Oeschger Events, 5:326
experimental physics, 5:327–330
impact of, 4:193–195
oceanography, 5:329, 6:236
theory, 6:341, 343–345

The Climate of London (Howard), 3:386, 387

Climatic Systems Analysis (Saltzman), 6:343

Climatology
Aristotelian, 1:100
atmospheric science, 6:341–345

Climatology, *continued*
    clouds, 3:386–387
    computer modeling, 2:100–101
    cosmic, 5:132–135
    descriptive, 4:152–155
    development, 7:38–40
    El Niño, 5:223–224
    Fujita scale, 3:83
    global warming, 2:10–11, 12–13, 4:91–95
    historical, 4:193–195
    legitimization of, 5:221
    mathematics, 3:50
    observatories, 1:116–117
    oceanic fronts, 3:11
    physical, 4:197–199
    surface pressure, 2:425–427
    tornadoes, 3:82–85
    See also Meteorology; Paleoclimatology; Weather
Climbing Our Family Tree (Novikoff), 5:284
The Clinical Treatment of the Problem Child (Rogers), 6:275
Clinical vs. Statistical Prediction (Meehl), 5:92–93, 94
Clonal selection theory, 1:458
Cloning, 1:398–399, 400
Clossius, Johann F., 2:84
Cloud chambers
    alpha particles, 1:290–291
    China, 7:400
    cosmic rays, 5:301–303, *302*
    dust counters and, 1:28–29
    gamma rays, 7:399
    particle physics, 6:283
Clouds
    cirrostratus, 7:154
    classification, 3:386–387
    formation, 7:219
    Oort, 5:*344*, 346
    physics, 1:470
    seeding
        Australia, 1:334
        development, 6:222
        ice crystals, 1:249
        weather modification, 1:469–470, 5:223
    solar energy, 6:555
CMB (Cosmic microwave background), 7:303–304, 393–394
Cnide et Cos? (Thivel), 3:324
Co-Ching Chu. *See* Zhu Kezhen
CoA (coenzyme A), 3:170, 171, 4:322, *325*
Coachman, L. K., 5:328
Coal
    gasoline from, 3:381
    hydrocarbons from, 5:19
    mining, 2:250, 300
    science, 7:133–139
Coal: Typology, Chemistry, Physics, Constitution (Van Krevelen), 7:137
Coal gas, 7:134–136
Coal Science: Aspects of Coal Constitution (Van Krevelen), 7:137
Coalitions, political, 6:254
Coastline measurement, 6:240
Cobb, Judith, 1:200, 201
COBOL (Common Business Oriented Language), 3:356, 360
Cocconi, Giuseppe, 5:192, 6:310
Coche, André, 6:78
Coching Chu. *See* Zhu Kezhen
Cochran, William, 2:208, 4:125
Cockayne, Leonard, 2:**154–157**
Cockcroft, John D. *See* Cockroft, John Douglas
Cockroach mazes, 7:*85*, 85–86, *86*
Cockroft, John Douglas, 3:59
    influence of, 4:208, 331
    radar, 1:164
CODASYL (Committee on Data Systems Languages), 3:360
Code-breaking. *See* Cryptography
Coding theory, 3:153
Cody, Martin, 3:416
Coelacanths, 6:476, *476, 477*
Coelum philosophorum (Ulstad), 1:110
Coenen, Jacques, 1:313
Coenzyme A (CoA), 3:170, 171, 4:322, *325*
Coenzyme Q, 3:171
Coenzymes
    activation, 7:31, 33
    cyclophorase system, 3:169–171
    nucleotides, 7:67
    See also specific coenzymes
Coffee, artificial aroma, 6:225
Cognet, Christine, 1:199, 200, 201
Cognition
    perception and, 1:188
    quantitative methods, 6:239
    schema theory, 1:187
Cognitive development
    perceptual learning, 3:124
    visual processing, 2:210–211
Cognitive ethology, 3:177, 179–180
Cognitive neuroscience
    cerebral hemispheres, 6:495–497
    computational research in, 5:32–36
    consciousness, 6:498
    intelligence tests, 3:267
    prefrontal cortex, 3:145–148
Cognitive psychology
    behaviorism, 3:267–271, 6:466

cerebral hemispheres, 6:495–497
computer simulations in, 5:254, 255
education, 7:194–195
filter theory of attention, 1:403–405
ideo-motor action, 2:55–56
noise, 1:402, 403
unified theory of cognition, 5:257–258
Cognitive science
belief systems, 1:9–10
cognitive dissonance, 3:15–17
computational neuroscience, 5:32–36
Cohausen, Johann Heinrich, 6:512
Cohen, Ernst, 1:280
Cohen, I. Bernard, 5:268–269
Cohen, Seymour, 4:358
Cohen, Stanley, 3:217, 220–221
Cohen, Victor W., 6:193
Cohn, Ferdinand, 6:28
Cohn, Melvin, 4:50
Cohn, Mildred, 6:169
Cohomology, 1:345, 346, 4:151, 7:257
Coignet, Michiel, 2:**157–159**
Coincidence circuits, 6:281, 282
Colbert, Jean-Baptiste, 3:352
Colby, Walter F., 5:210
Cold fronts, 1:247–248
Cold War
air defense systems, 4:303
astrophysics, 3:176
intellectuals and, 5:349–350
investigations, 6:422–423
National Bureau of Standards, 2:168–169
nuclear physics policy, 2:168–170
nuclear weapons, 1:58, 6:315
politics, 6:574–575
rocketry, 4:180, 7:174–175
USSR, 6:326–328
Vista Project, 1:136
Cole, John F., 7:73
Cole, K. S. (Kacy), 3:329, 330–331
Cole, Michael, 4:350
Coleman, William, 1:212
Colennuccio, Pandolfo, 6:120
Collagen, 6:361–362
Collecta per magistrum Cristannum de Prachaticz de sanguinis et lunacionum (Prachaticz), 6:153
Collected Essays (Huxley), 3:432
The Collected Papers (Einstein), 2:363–364
Collected Works (Jung), 4:64
Collected Works of Mahatma Gandhi (Swaminathan), 7:144
Collection of Examples on the Integral Calculus (Sylvester), 6:565
Collectivized particles, 1:318

Collegium (Burgersdijk), 1:445
Collett, Robert, 2:383
Colliding-beam accelerators, 1:425, 426, *426,* 427, 428–429, 7:70–72
Collins, G. O., 6:471
Collins, Michael, 3:152, 6:444–445
Collins, Peter, 2:376
Collins, William Henry, 7:323
Colloids, 2:66
crystals, 1:311–312
polymers, 6:330–332
Collongues, Robert, 2:**159–164**
Colonialism, 1:230
Australia, 6:207–208, 209
ethnology and, 1:206–207
meteorology, 7:153
sugar growth and, 1:230–231
Coloniensis, A. *See* Albertus Magnus, Saint
Color
eyes, 1:225, 228, 2:399–400, 7:12–13
graph theory, 7:291
interference colors, 3:133
light and, 5:10
perception, 6:295
quantitative color theory, 5:356–357
Colp, Ralph, 2:247
Colthup chart, 3:199
Combes, Raoul, 1:388
Combinatorics
development, 6:285–286
mathematics, 6:203
Ramsey theory and random graphs, 2:405–406
Stoic logic, 3:321
Combined Programming Language (CPL), 6:534, 535, 536
Combustion, 1:268, 6:504, 507
air, 7:170
gases, 6:411, 415
Comets
astrogeology, 6:442, 445–446
cloud of, 5:346
nuclei, 7:283
observations, 1:382, 7:284–285
organic compounds, 3:391
reflectors, 3:286
structure, 7:286–287
tails, 1:278
Coming of Age: A Psychological Analysis of a Boy's Diary (Stern). *See Anfänge der Reifezeit: Ein Knabentagebuch in psychologischer Bearbeitung* (Stern)
Comita, Gabriel W., 2:354
Commandino, Federico, 1:166, 5:175, 176
Commelin, Caspar, 5:120
Commentaria de religione Christiana (Ramus), 6:206

Commentary in Four Books on Aristotle's Meteorology (Cabeo). *See In Quatuor libros meteorologicorum Aristolelis commentaria* (Cabeo)
Commentary on Aratus (Hipparchus), 3:321
Commentary on Plato's Parmenides (Porphyry), 6:137
Commentary on the Book 3 of Aristotle's De anima (Stephanus of Alexandria), 6:517
Commentary on the Handy Tables of Ptolemy (Stephanus of Alexandria), 6:517, 518
Commentary on the Harmonics of Ptolemy (Porphyry), 2:284, 6:172
Commentary on the Meteologica (John Philoponus), 4:51
Commentary on the Physics (Philoponus), 4:51
Commentary on the Sphere of Sacrobosco (Clavius), 2:149
Commerce, 1:230–231
Committee for Geophysics and Space Research (GROC), 7:130
Committee for the Scientific Investigation of Claims of the Paranormal (CSICOP), 6:314
Committee on Data Systems Languages (CODASYL), 3:360
Committee on Space Research (COSPAR), 7:130
Common Business Oriented Language (COBOL), 3:356, 360
Commoner, Barry, 6:41
Commonwealth Scientific and Industrial Research Organization (CSIRO) (Australia), 6:209
Communia mathematica (Bacon, Roger), 1:144
Communia naturalium (Bacon, Roger), 1:146
Communication, scientific, 1:330–331
Communication (language), 1:324–325
    milestone table (Piaget), 6:*93*
    science of, 6:424–427, 429
Communidades naturales (Margalef), 5:24
Communism (science norm), 5:123–124
Communist Party
    biologists, 5:282
    physicists, 1:322, 5:191, 348
    scientists, 1:371
Communities, plant, 1:385–388
Community Planning for Peacetime Living (Hilgard et al.), 3:314
Comparative anatomy
    Aristotelian theory, 1:102–104
    brain, 1:406–409
    embranchment, 2:222–223
    embryology, 3:116
    human evolution, 2:313–316
    primate, 2:140–141
    vertebrate paleontology and, 5:366–367
Comparative biology, 1:436–438
Comparative embryology, 3:207–209
Comparative Neurology (Papez), 6:10
Comparative physiology, 6:358

Comparative psychology
    animal behavior, 4:243–244, 6:366–369
    behaviorism, 7:241–242
    biology, 3:294
    figural quality, 3:296–297
    sexual behavior, 1:222–223
The Comparative Unimportance of Steric Strain in Unimolecular Olefin Eliminations (Ingold), 1:420
A Compend of Geology (LeConte), 4:224, 225
Compendium for al-Manṣūrī (Rāzī), 6:212, 213
Compendium of Meteorology (Haurwitz), 3:263–264
Competition, 3:416
Complex Analysis (Ahlfors), 1:21
Complex analytic functions, 2:423
    calculus, 2:76
    partial differential equations, 1:260–263
Complex function theory, 1:21–22, 23, 4:144–145
Complex Manifolds and Deformation of Complex Structures (Kodaira), 4:146–147
Complex numbers
    groups, 2:291
    polynomials, 2:229–230
Composition (Prachaticz), 6:153
Composition and Petrology of the Earth's Mantle (Ringwood), 6:259, 261
Comprehensive Coordination Chemistry (Wilkinson), 7:310, 313
Comprehensive Natural Products Chemistry, 1:199–200
Comprehensive Organic Chemistry, 1:199
Comprehensive Organometallic Chemistry (Wilkinson), 7:313
Comptes Rendus de l'Academie des Science (Chevalley), 2:117
Compton, Arthur Holly
    cosmic rays, 6:282
    influence of, 7:296
    Metallurgical Laboratory, 1:392
    plutonium, 1:56
    quantum electrodynamics, 7:398
    recruitment of Carl Anderson, 1:75
    students of, 7:400
    Washington University leadership, 2:170
Compton, Karl Taylor, 2:166, 4:291, 5:111
Compton effect
    confirmation of, 5:28
    cosmic rays, 6:170
    discovery, 2:107–108
Computability and Logic (Jeffrey), 4:35
Computable functions, 6:266
Computational neuroscience, 5:32–36
Computer architectures, 5:257
Computer languages. *See* Programming languages
Computer science, 4:304–305
    astronomy and, 1:127–129

biomedical, 3:51

COBOL, 3:356

companies, 2:335–337

development, 6:427–428, 429, 532–536, 7:82–84

Difference Engine, 1:*126*

early

    ENIAC, 2:333–337, 5:50, 53–54

    Germany, 7:409–413

    mathematics, 3:50–52

    numerical analysis, 7:314

    psychology and, 4:303–306

    textbooks, 2:294–295

human information processing and, 5:254–258

mathematics and, 1:286–288, 4:319–320

mechanical computing machines and, 1:125

meteorology, 6:561

numerical analysis, 3:256–257

operating systems, 2:295–296

Pilot ACE, 7:314–318

processors

    Germany, 7:410–411

    man-computer interaction, 4:305

programming languages, 3:357–361

satellites, 6:556–557

software, 2:294–295

UNIVAC, 2:336–337

x-ray diffraction, 3:338

See also Computers; Programming languages

Computer Science (Forsythe), 3:51

Computer simulation

    belief systems, 1:8, 9

    population genetics, 4:116

Computers, 1:*126*

    in chemistry, 6:131

    mechanical, 7:409–413

    meteorological, 6:556–557, 558, 561

    in physics, 5:51–52

    psychotherapy with, 6:279

    suitcased-sized, 5:*55*

    time-sharing, 6:533–534

Computus chirometralis (Prachaticz), 6:153

Comrie, Leslie John, 1:129

Comstock, Anna Botsford, 2:389

Comstock, John Henry, 2:389

Comte de Buffon. *See* Buffon, Georges-Louis Leclerc, Comte de

Comtino, Mordecai, 1:98–99

Conant, James Bryant, 5:115

    Harvard cyclotron, 1:164

    Harvard tenureship meetings, 5:217

    military explosives, 3:240

    physical organic chemistry techniques, 1:190

    students of, 3:238

The Concept of Affordances in Development: The Renascence of Functionalism (Gibson, Eleanor Jack), 3:122

The Concept of Integrative Levels and Biology (Novikoff), 5:284

The Concept of the Reflex in the Description of Behavior (Skinner), 6:461

Concepts of Particle Physics (Gottfried), 7:267

Concession to the Improbable (Simpson), 6:454

Concluding Remarks (Hutchinson), 3:415–416

Condensation

    Bose-Einstein, 7:101, 102

    pion, 5:130–131

Condensed matter physics, 6:169

Condillac, Étienne Bonnot de, 4:201, 5:11

Conditionals, counterfactual, 3:150–151

Conditioning

    emotional, 7:243–244

    olfactory, 7:41–42

    Pavlovian, 3:267, 407

    psychology, 3:311–312

Conditioning and Learning (Hilgard and Marquis), 3:312, 313

Condon, Edward Uhler, 2:**164–171**, *168*, 6:422

    National Bureau of Standards, 2:168–169

    nuclear research, 2:166–167

    nuclear weapons, 6:41

    quantum mechanics, 2:165–166

    radio wave propagation, 5:114

Condorcet, Marie-Jean-Antoine-Nicolas Caritat, Comte de, 2:229

Conduction aphasia, 4:353

Confessions of an English Opium Eater (De Quincey), 6:49

Confirmation, social, 1:172

Conformal groups, 3:193

Conformational analysis, 1:197–200, *199*, 4:259–263

Conforth, John W., 6:161

Congress for Cultural Freedom, 5:349

Congruence (psychology), 6:276, 277, 278

Conical refraction, 3:236

Conics (Apollonius), 1:83–84, 2:418, 3:436, 5:7, 6:7

Conjectures and Refutations (Popper), 6:135

Conjoint measurement theory, 7:92

Connotative concepts, 5:312, 313–314

Connstein, Wilhelm, 5:252

Conry, Yvette, 6:287

Conscious imitation, 1:171

Consciousness

    animal, 3:177, 180–182

    cognitive neuroscience, 6:498

    experimental psychology, 7:369

    levels, 3:310

    mathematical modeling, 2:210–211

Consciousness, *continued*
    mechanistic psychology, 7:370–371
    psychology, 3:312–313
    shrinking field of, 4:26–27
    social, 1:172
Consden, Raphael, 5:40
Conseil Européen pour la Recherche Nucleaire (CERN),
    6:196
Conservation
    botany, 2:189, 6:516
    Canada, 7:79
    ecology, 7:7–8
    nature, 2:387–388
    ornithology, 5:279
    primate, 3:56
    soil, 7:39
    wildlife, 4:268–269
        Australia, 6:207, 209–210
        evolution, 7:44
Conservation and Australia (Ratcliffe), 6:210
Conservation of energy, law of, 3:307
The Conservation of Orbital Symmetry (Woodward),
    7:355
The Conservation of the Wildlife of Canada (Hewitt),
    2:383
Conservation of vector current, 7:367
Considérations sur des Ossemens fossils (Geoffroy Saint-
    Hilaire, Isidore), 3:119
Constantine the African, 6:291
Constructing Scientific Psychology (Weidman), 4:203, 204
Construction of a Regular Heptagon in the Circle (al-
    Qūhī), 6:186
The Construction of Reality (Piaget), 6:93
Contact (Sagan), 6:314, 435
Contamination stars, 1:298
Contarini, Giacomo, 5:175–176
Continens (Rāzī). *See Kitāb al-Hāwī* (Rāzī)
Continental drift
    atmospheric science, 7:246–248
    disbelief in, 4:41
    earth's magnetism and, 1:292–293
    earth's pole movements and, 5:133
    geomagnetism, 6:299–300
    geophysics, 7:323–326
    mapping, 2:39–41, *40, 41*
    marine geology, 2:288
    mobilist view, 2:39–42
    paleomagnetism, 2:191–192
    See also Earth
Continuity of Solutions of Parabolic and Elliptic Equations
    (Nash), 5:229
Continuous media, 2:77–78
The Continuum (Weyl), 7:276, 277
Continuum hypothesis, 3:265–266

    mathematics, 3:130–131
    solution, 2:30, 33
    unified field theory, 2:370–371
Contra Aristotelem de aeternitate mundi (John
    Philoponus), 4:51, 52
Contra Averroem (Rufus of Cornwall, Richard), 6:294,
    295
Contra Proclum de aeternitate mundi (John Philoponus),
    4:51
Contrast model, 7:92–93
*Contribution à l'étude des propriétés et des modes de
    décomposition de la phase protoxyde de fer* (Collongues),
    2:160
Contributions of the Theory of Natural Selection (Wallace),
    7:226
Contributions to Optics (Goethe), 3:133
*Contributions to the Knowledge of Devonian trilobites from
    the Rheinische Schiefergebirge* (Richter). *See Beiträge zur
    Kenntnis devonischer Trilobiten aus dem Rheinischen
    Schiefergebirge* (Richter)
Control, social, 6:464
Convection, 1:277
Convention (Lewis), 4:284
Conversations on Chemistry (Marcet), 5:21
Conversations on Natural Philosophy (Marcet), 5:21
Conversations on Political Economy (Marcet), 5:21
Conversations on Vegetable Physiology (Marcet), 5:22
Conversations with Goethe (Eckermann), 4:63
Convexity theory, 7:81–82
Conway, Anne, 2:**171–172**
Conybeare, William Daniel, 2:225
Cook, Howard L., 3:374
Cook, J. W., 5:290, 291
Cooke, John Charles, 3:429
Cooke-Yarborough, E., 6:302
Coolidge, Harold J., 7:234
Coolidge, Julian, 2:111
Cooling
    electron, 1:429
    stochastic, 1:429
Coombs, John, 2:330
Coon, Carleton Stevens, 2:**172–176**, *174,* 7:237
Coons, Edgar, 5:149, 151
Cooper, Cecil, 4:239
Cooper, Leon Neil, 1:178, 181–182, 5:129
    superconductivity, 1:318
    teachers of, 6:423
Cooper, Leslie Hugh Norman, 3:259
Cooper, William S., 2:187
Cooperating Sequential Process (Dijkstra), 2:296
Cooperation, 3:231–232
Cooperation, international. *See* International cooperation
Cooperative games, 3:249–250
    bargaining theory, 3:248

incomplete information, 3:251
Cooperative Institute for Meteorological Satellite
  Studies, 6:555
Coordination chemistry
  ferrocene, 7:308–309, *309*
  nickel, 7:*308*
  rhodium, 7:310–311
  transition metals, 2:102–103, 4:59–60
Cope, Edward Drinker, 5:354
Copenhagen interpretation
  atomic phenomena, 1:322
  Bohr's quantum mechanics, 1:326–327
  pilot wave interpretation, 1:413
  supremacy, 1:323
Copenhaver, John W., 6:232
The Copernican Revolution (Kuhn), 4:172, 174–175
Copernican system. *See* Copernicanism
Copernicanism, 2:176–179, 320, 413
  The Copernican Revolution (Kuhn), 4:172, 174–175
  cosmology, 3:112–113
  Eucharist and, 3:98–100
  Itinerarium exstaticum (Kircher), 4:130
  mathematics, 2:149
  Mysterium cosmographicum (Kepler), 4:105–106
  natural classification, 2:320
  observational astronomy, 3:166
  patronage, 3:100–101
  physics, 1:445–446
  theory of impetus, 1:423–424
Copernicus, Nicholas, 2:**176–182**, *178*, 3:166, 6:217
Copleston, Edward, 5:14
Coral reefs, 5:59–60
  ecosystem development, 5:320
  formation of, 4:185–187
  metabolism, 5:318, 323
Corals, 3:315–317
Cordilleran Ice Sheet, 1:394
Cordura, 5:30
Corey, Robert, 2:96, 202, 6:39
Corey-Pauling-Koltun models. *See* CPK models
Cori, Carl, 4:72–73, 253, 5:307, 6:169
Cori, Gerty, 4:72–73, 253, 5:307
Corn, 5:68–71
  See also Maize
Cornetz, Victor, 7:85
Cornforth, John, 5:41
Cornog, Robert, 1:55, 6:408
Cornu, Alfred, 2:307
Cornubiensis, Richard Rufus. *See* Rufus of Cornwall,
  Richard
Corona, solar
  observation of, 5:113
  spectroscopy, 2:344–346
Coronagraphs, 7:77

Corpus Aristotelicum (Burgersdijk), 1:444, 445
Corpuscular theory, 1:295, 411, 5:273
  atomism, 6:418
  influence, 6:512
*Correlations between Molecularity and Energies of Reaction
  Activation in Forward and Reverse Directions*
  (Boreskov). *See Sootnoshenie mezhdu molekuliarnost' iu
  i energiiami aktivatsii v priamom i obratnom
  napravleniiakh* (Boreskov)
Correns, Carl, 6:317–318
The Correspondence of Isaac Newton, 5:268–269
Correspondence of Robert Boyle (Boyle), 1:367
Correspondence principle, 1:327, 411
Corrin nucleus, 3:333
Corsi, Pietro, 4:190–191
Corson, Dale, 6:408
La Corteza Terrestre (Inglada), 4:11
Corticosteroids, 6:227
Cortisol, 6:568
Cortisone, 7:350
Coryell, Charles, 6:38, 7:308
Cosans, Christopher, 3:430
The Cosmic Connection (Sagan), 6:313
Cosmic Gas Dynamics (Biermann and Schatzman), 1:278
Cosmic microwave background (CMB), 7:303–305,
  393–394
Cosmic rays, 6:99, 280–283
  archaeology, 1:58–59
  astrophysics, 7:120–125
  cloud chambers, 1:72–73, 5:301–303
  Compton effect, 6:170
  magnetism, 1:41
  particle physics and, 1:62, 5:303–304
  satellites, 3:80–81
  scattering, 7:399
  Wilson chamber detectors, 2:110
Cosmic Static (Reber), 7:127
Cosmic View (Morrison), 5:193
Cosmographic Mystery (Kepler). *See Mysterium
  cosmographicum* (Kepler)
Cosmography, 6:110–111
Cosmological Theory (McVittie), 5:81
Cosmology
  antiprotons, 6:410
  astrophysics and, 7:392–394
  baryon asymmetry, 6:324, 325–326
  Christian, 1:424
  Copernicanism, 2:177–178, 3:112–113
  elements, 2:122
  Empedoclean, 2:397
  evolutionary, 6:302, 305
  expanding universe, 2:283–284
  galaxy formation, 6:398–399, 7:57–61
  general relativity theory, 4:56

Cosmology, *continued*
 geo-heliocentrism, 2:413
 Jeans-Jeffreys theory, 4:39
 Mach's principle, 2:369–370
 mathematics and, 5:80–84
 matter creation, 3:389–390
 mechanical perspectives on, 5:176
 medieval, 5:5–7
 mind-body connection, 6:15–16
 models, 6:456–458
 and philosophy, 4:131
 planetary motion, 1:138–139
 Platonic, 6:115–116
 popular science and, 1:43
 relativistic, 1:340–342, 3:274, 275, 5:73–74
 renaissance of, 6:397
 steady state theory, 3:136–137, 388
 stellar dynamics, 3:274–275
 string theory, 3:131
Cosmology (Bondi), 1:342
Cosmos, the Story of Evolution (film), 3:425
Cosmos (television series), 6:312, 314
COSPAR (Committee on Space Research), 7:130
Coste, Pierre, 5:12
Costelloe, Ray, 6:532
Coster, Dirk, 1:280, 284, 311
COT (Cyclooctatetraene), 6:231, 233
Cotes, Roger, 5:270
Cotta, Georg von, 4:312
Cotton, F. Albert, 1:200, 7:307, 309, 312
Coulson, Charles Alfred, 5:212–213, 6:38
Coulter, John Merle, 2:187, 189
Council for Scientific and Industrial Research (CSIR) (Australia), 6:208
Counseling
 psychological, 6:274–279
 vocational, 3:313–314
Counterfactual conditionals, 3:150–151
Counterfactuals (Lewis), 4:286
Couper, Archibald Scott, 1:465
 chemical structure, 7:372
 influence of, 4:99
 theory of chemical structure, 4:149
Courant, Ernest, 4:333, 7:329
Courant, Richard, 3:86, 357
 acquaintances of, 7:254
 influence of, 4:320
 Primakoff waves, 6:170
Cournot, Antoine, 5:188
Cours d'Analyse Mathématique (Goursat), 2:290
Cours d'économie politique (Pareto), 6:17
Courses of Chemistry (Shaw), 1:92
Courtauld, Samuel, 7:321
Courtenay-Latimer, Marjorie, 6:477

Courtship, birds, 3:384–385, 424
Cousteau, Jacques-Yves, 2:287
Covián, Carmen García, 5:306
Covián, Francisco Grande, 5:306
Cowan, C. E., 6:170
Cowan, Eugene, 1:75
Cowdry, Edmund Vincent, 2:**182–186,** *185*
Cowels, Raymond B., 1:436
Cowgill, Ursula M., 3:413
Cowings, Patricia, 5:151
Cowles, Henry Chandler, 1:388, 2:152, **186–190,** 7:4
Cowling, Thomas G., 1:277
Cox, Allan Verne, 2:**190–194,** 5:50
Cox, E. Gordon, 2:104
CP violation, 6:326
CPK models, 2:201–202
CPL (Combined Programming Language), 6:534, 535, 536
The CPL Working Papers (Strachey), 6:535
Crab Nebula, 5:343, 6:432, 434
Crafts, James Mason, 2:**194–196**
Craig, David, 3:341
Craig, Harmon, 4:91
Craig, Lyman C., 3:341
Craig, Patricia, 2:153
Craig, Wallace, 2:**196–199,** 4:340, 5:279
Craige, Betty Jean, 5:319
Craik, Kenneth
 government research, 1:402
 human cognition and machines, 1:187
 Medical Research Council, 1:188
 science of psychology, 1:405
Cram, Donald, 2:**199–205,** *202*
Cramer, Gabriel, 2:229, 5:11
Crane, Fred, 3:170, 171
Crane, Horace R., 4:208, 7:302
Cranial neural crest, 3:366, 368–369
Craters, lunar, 2:286, 288, 6:443, 444–445
Crawford, David, 6:546
Crawford, Elisabeth, 1:111
The Crazy Ape (Szent-Györgyi), 6:572
Creatinine, 5:305–306
Creation
 dualism, 3:214–215
 education, 3:162
 evolution *vs.,* 5:365
 saltational theory, 5:367–368
Creation-Evolution Satiricon (Dietz), 2:288
Creationism, 3:162–163
 See also Evolution
Creative Evolution (Bergson), 6:91, 109
Creed, R. S., 2:329
Creighton, Harriet, 5:68
Crell, Lorenz, 4:216

Crelle, August Leopold, 1:5
Crelle's Journal, 1:5, 6, 2:30, 31, 4:26
Cremer, Erika, 2:**205–207**
Cremona, Luigi, 3:327
Crepis spp., 6:514–515
Crescimbeni, Giovan Mario, 1:168
Crich, David, 1:199
Crick, Francis Harry Compton, 2:**207–213,** *208,* 4:357
   base-pairings, 2:93
   cognitive neuroscience, 6:498
   criticisms of, 2:96
   DNA structure, 1:*374,* 2:270, 5:202, 6:478–479,
     7:67
     crystallography, 3:66, 7:298–300
     modeling, 6:40
   hemoglobin structure, 6:81, 83
   rivals of, 3:67
   RNA, 3:341
   wobble hypothesis, 3:342
Crieger, Rudolf, 1:194
Critchfield, Charles, 1:271–272, 278
Critchley, Macdonald, 3:347
Critical personalism, 6:522, 523
Critodemus, 7:112
Crofts, Anthony, 5:162
Croker, John Wilson, 2:251
Croll, James, 5:133, 6:528
Crombie, Alistair, 1:142–143, 2:151
Cromwell, Norman O., 2:199
Cronbach, Lee, 2:432
Croneis, Carey, 4:164–165
Cronin, Helena, 2:247
Cronquist, Arthur, 2:**213–215**
Cronshaw, James, 2:415
Cronstedt, Axel, 2:219
Crops, energy flow, 6:511
Cross-cultural psychology, 2:22
Crosse, Andrew, 2:**215–217**
Crosswhite, H. Milton, 7:229
Crow, James F., 4:115
Crowcroft, Peter, 2:382
Crowfoot, Dorothy. *See* Hodgkin, Dorothy Mary
   Crowfoot
Crowther, J. A., 4:55
Crozier, William, 6:461
The Crucial Year (Guerlac), 4:214
Cruls, Louis, 4:293
Cryptography
   research, 6:425–427
    World War II, 7:89–91
Cryptology, 5:113–114
*The Crystal Structure of Insulin I: The Investigation of Air-
   Dried Insulin Crystals* (Hodgkin), 3:335
Crystallography
   as analytical tool, 5:165–166
   atomic constitution, 4:53
   DNA, 3:66–67
   face-centered monoclinic, 3:67
   organic chemistry, 4:16, 6:21–22
   single crystal growth, 2:161–162
   x-ray, 2:9
     biophysics, 7:298–300
     chemical reactions, 6:126
     diffusion, 4:81
     DNA, 2:207–209
     hemoglobin, 6:79–80, 81–83
     insulin, 3:334–335
     molecualar configuration, 1:279–285
     protein chemistry, 6:39
     scientific method, 7:312
Crystals
   defects, 1:311
   electroconductivity, 6:375
   electrocrystallization, 2:215–216
   electronic processes, 5:201
   liquid, 2:278
   molecular structure, 6:37
   polymers, 3:39
   research, 7:164–166
CSICOP (Committee for the Scientific Investigation of
   Claims of the Paranormal), 6:314
CSIR (Council for Scientific and Industrial Research)
   (Australia), 6:208
CSIRO (Commonwealth Scientific and Industrial
   Research Organization) (Australia), 6:209
Ctenophores of the Atlantic Coast of North America
   (Mayor), 5:59
CTP theorem, 1:237, 238
Cuatrecases, Pedro, 1:80
Cuba, 7:153–155
Cubic equations, 7:87–88
Cuchet, Gaspard-Joseph, 4:216
Cuènot, Lucien, 7:117
Cullen, Esther, 7:53, 55
Cullen, William, 2:**217–221,** 7:220, 221–222
Cultural anthropology
   evolution, 2:173–175
   personality psychology and, 5:44
Cultural psychology, 7:192–196
Culture
   behaviorism, 6:465
   evolution
     human, 4:78–79
     Paleolithic, 5:296
   geography and, 1:206–207
   primitive
     archaeology, 2:124–127, 173
     cave art, 4:42–43

Culture, *continued*
    evolution, 2:173–175
    psychology, 1:185
  religion and, 4:251–252
Cunaeus, Petrus, 1:445
Cuprous-oxide junctions, 6:375–376
Curie, Marie, 5:231, 6:75–76, 78
Curie, Pierre, 7:165
Curious Naturalists (Tinbergen), 1:149
Curl, Robert, 6:473–474, 475
Current algebra, 1:238
  See also Quantum field theory
Currents, ocean, 2:260–264, 5:172, *173*, 329, 6:*528*, 528–531, *529*
Currey, John, 2:4
Curtis, Garniss, 2:192
Curtis, Howard, 3:329, 330
Curtius, Theodor, 7:340
Cusanus, Nicolas, 4:131
Cushing, Harvey Williams, 6:70–71
Cuvier, Georges, 2:**221–226**, *223*, 3:133
  antitransformism, 3:118
  embranchment theory, 2:222–223, 3:429
  evolution, 3:115, 6:109
  geohistory, 3:422
  human paleontology, 2:226
  illustrations for, 4:231
  influence of, 4:191, 5:366
  influences on, 5:332
  rivals of, 3:115
Cyanuric Chloride, a Useful Reagent for macrocyclic Lactonization (Venkataraman), 7:148
Cybernetics, 5:*77*, 77–79, *78*, 6:427
  See also Computer science
Cybernetics (Wiener), 5:255, 6:427, 532
Cyclic theory, 3:419–420
Cyclogenesis, 6:220
Cycloheptatriene, 3:*403*, 403–404
Cyclohexanes, 1:197, *199*
Cyclones
  atmospheric science, 6:3
  extratropical
    forecasting, 1:289–290
    life cycles, 1:245, *246, 247*
    mathematics, 2:99
    occlusion process, 1:246–247
  formation, 6:559–560
  laboratory production of, 1:28
  low-pressure, 6:559
  meteorology, 5:223, 6:86
  tropical
    formation, 6:559
    height, 3:262–263
    resonance theory, 3:264

  weather forecasting, 7:153–155
Cyclonic and Anticyclonic Development (Sutcliffe), 6:560
Cyclooctatetraene (COT), 6:231, 233
Cyclopaedia (Rees), 3:7
Cyclopentadiene, 3:*403*, 403–404
Cyclophanes, 2:203–204
Cyclophorase system, 3:168–169, 170–171
Cyclopropenyl, 3:404, *404*
Cyclostereoisomerism, 6:*160*
Cyclotrons
  applications, 6:179
  atomic bombs and, 1:164–165
  development of, 1:55, 163, 4:328–333
  heavy ion, 3:35–36
  neutron physics, 1:304–305
  nuclear physics, 7:328–329
  See also Accelerators; Particle accelerators
Cygnus A radio source, 6:302, *303*
Cystine storage disease, 1:2
Cytochrome *c*, 7:33, 34
Cytochromes, 3:168–169, 171
Cytogenetics
  birds, 2:59–61
  development, 6:514–515
  maize, 5:68–69
Cytology
  anatomy and, 2:183
  cancer, 2:143–147, 144–147
  cellular membranes, 6:197–202
  cytogenetics, 6:514–515
  DNA, 2:68–70
  electron microscopy, 2:143, 144–146, 6:143–148
  enzymology, 5:283–284, 285, 6:197, 198–202
  heterogeneity, 5:285
  histology, 7:249
  mitochondria, 4:238–241
  morphology, 2:182–184, 4:66–70
  ornithology, 2:59–61
  oxidative phosphorylation, 5:160–162
  pharmacology, 4:29–34
  RNA, 2:68–70
  somatic cell hybrids, 2:402
  spontaneous generation, 6:24
  tissue culture studies, 5:86
  See also Cells
Cytoplasmic Genes and Organelles (Sager), 6:320
Cytoplasmic inheritance
  cancer genetics, 6:319–320
  cell nucleus, 4:67–69
  experiments, 6:492–493
  plant genetics, 6:317–319
  self and not-self theory, 1:457
Czerwinska, Ewa, 5:357

D

Da Vinci, Leonardo. *See* Leonardo da Vinci

Dacey, Michael, 4:165

Dahlgren, Rolf, 2:214

Dainton, Fred, 6:139

Dakin, Henry, 3:43

Daktarin, 4:33

Dal Monte, Guidobaldo. *See* Monte, Guidobaldo, Marchese del

Dalcq, Albert, 1:370–371, 372

Dale, Henry Hallett, 1:119, 6:142, 568
    chemical transmitters, 2:329
    colleagues of, 2:332
    neurotransmitters, 7:178
    synaptic signaling, 4:87

d'Alembert, Jean le Rond, 2:**229–233**, *230,* 5:11, 270

Dalitz, Richard, 6:65, 66

Dall, William, 6:151

Dallinger, William Henry, 1:209

Dalrymple, G. Brent, 2:190, 193

Dalton, John, 2:324
    atomic theory, 1:265
    clouds, 3:386
    stoichiometry, 1:268

Damascius, 6:517

Dameshek, William, 2:375

Damianus of Larissa, 2:**233–234,** 3:284

Dan Sun, 2:111

Dana, Charles L., 6:11

Dance language, bees, 3:179, 180, 183

Dandolo, Vincenzo, 4:216

Danibius Pannonico-mysicus (Marsili), 5:37

Daniel Sieff Institute, 1:251

Danielli, James, 5:159

Daniels, T. C., 6:323

Dansereau, Pierre Mackay, 2:**234–237**

Dansgaard, Willy, 5:326, 328–329

Dansgaard-Oeschger Events, 5:328–329

Dantzig, George B., 7:80

Danziger, Kurt, 7:368

Dapivirine, 4:33

Darboux, Gaston, 4:308

Darcet, Jean, 4:215

Darcy's law, 3:396

Dark Ghetto (Clark), 2:134

Dark nebulae, 1:329–330

Darkness in El Dorado: How Scientists and Journalists Devastated the Amazon (Tierney), 5:244

Darlan, Jean-François, 2:173

Darlington, Cyril Dean, 1:213
    cytology and evolution relationship, 2:59
    genetic inertia, 4:276
    on Mendel, Johann Gregor, 5:97

Darmstaedter, Ernst, 4:19

Darrigol, Olivier, 1:411, 6:112

Dart, Raymond Arthur, 2:138–139, **237–242,** *241*

Darwin, Charles Galton, 3:254

Darwin, Charles Robert, 1:80, 2:86, 239, **242–249,** *245*
    acquaintances of, 2:310
    atoll shape, 4:187
    birds, 3:384
    colleagues of, 7:281
    commentaries on, 5:64–65
    criticisms of, 5:206, 7:378–379
    early career, 2:243
    evolution, 7:224
    fission, 6:260
    Griffin, Donald Redfield, 3:180
    humility, 5:124
    ideo-motor action criticisms, 2:57
    influence of, 2:246–247, 4:225, 5:354, 7:210, 223, 259
    influence on genetic theory, 2:390
    Mendel, Johann Gregor on, 5:104
    Mendelian genetics, 3:45–49, 5:102
    mutual aid theory, 4:160, 161–163
    natural selection, 1:415, 7:117, 226–227
    naturalism, 3:430–431
    niche concept, 2:383
    opponents of, 5:365
    paleoanthropology, 6:109
    philosophy, 3:287
    population genetics, 3:228
    rejection of, 3:289
    spontaneous generation, 1:208
    statistics, 6:54
    translations, 1:417, 3:272, 6:287, 288
    transmutation theory, 2:243–245
    on Whewell, William, 7:282

Darwin, Erasmus, 2:243

Darwin, Francis, 1:211–212

Darwinism
    creationism, 3:163
    embryology and, 1:210–211
    epistemology, 6:136
    fixism theory, 1:453
    morphology, 6:355
    naturalism, 3:430–431
    race, 3:208
    spontaneous generation, 1:208–210
    See also Darwin, Charles Robert

Das, Shamita, 1:32

Dastin, John, 4:347

Data (Euclid), 1:84, 2:306, 416, 3:436

Data Smoothing and Prediction in Fire-Control Systems (Shannon et al.), 6:425

Databases, Gmelin, 1:215

Dating techniques
    fossils, 3:155, 5:295, 296–299
    radiocarbon, 5:326–327
Datz, Sheldon, 1:258
Dauben, William G., 5:291
Daubenton, Louis-Jean-Marie, 1:433
Dautray, Robert, 4:320
Dauvillier, Alexandre, 1:410–411
Davenport, Charles B., 3:27, 5:59
Daves, Agnes, 5:231
David, Jacques-Louis, 4:215, 6:44
Davidson, Arnold I., 3:75
Davidson, Herbert, 6:6
Davidson, Julian, 1:221
Davie, Earl, 6:482
Davies, Llewelyn, 3:430
Davis, Arthur Powell, 3:374
Davis, Edward A., 5:204
Davis, George F., 4:288
Davis, Jack, 5:151
Davis, Leverett, Jr., 1:278
Davis, Martin, 6:267
Davis, Morris, 2:186–187
Davis, Raymond, Jr., 1:158–159, 2:213
Davis, William Morris, 3:374, 6:536–537
Davisson, Clinton Joseph, 1:270, 2:165, 378
Davy, Humphry, 2:85, **2:249–252,** 2:*251,* 4:54
    aquaintances of, 2:215
    chlorine, 1:265
    influence of, 3:1, 5:21
    Royal Institution, 6:141
    stoichiometry, 1:268
Dawkins, Richard
    altruism theory, 3:230
    criticism of Stephen Jay Gould, 3:162
    inclusive fitness theory, 3:225
    Nash equilibrium and evolution, 5:228
Dawson, Harry Medforth, 4:14
Dawson, John, 3:131
Day, Arthur Louis, 2:**252–255**
De aeternitate mundi: contra Aristotelem (Philoponus), 7:382
De alimento (Buonamici), 1:441
De anima (Aristotle). *See On the Soul* (Aristotle)
De Animalibus (Albertus Magnus), 1:104
De animorum immortalitate (Cardano), 2:37
De aqua vitae simplici et composita (Arnald of Villanova, Pseudo), 1:109
De aspectibus (Ibn al-Haytham), 1:145
De audibilibus (Porphyry), 6:138
De augmentis scientiarum (Bacon, Francis), 1:141
De Bary, Heinrich Anton, 6:389, 390
De Beer, Gavin, 2:242, 244, 3:369
    experimental biology, 3:425

    Mendelian genetics, 5:101, 102
    students of, 7:377
de Bruijn, Henk, 1:314, 315, 7:134
De caelo (Aristotle). *See On the Heavens* (Aristotle)
De causa Dei (Bradwardine), 1:378
De causis mirabilium (Oresme), 1:449–450
De chemische binding als electrostatisch verschijnsel (van Arkel and Boer), 7:133
De chymicorum cum Aristotelicis et Galenicis consensu ac dissensu (Sennert), 6:418
De consolatione (Cardano), 2:36
De continuo (Bradwardine), 1:379
De la dégénération des animaux (Buffon), 1:431
De diebus criticis (Nifo), 5:280
De divina proportione (Piero Della Francesca), 6:106
de Donder, Théophile, 6:165
de Duve, Christian, 1:374, 5:283, 285
De eodem et diverso (Adelard of Bath), 1:13, 14
de Finetti, Bruno, 2:**255–258**
De finitiones medicae (Celsus), 2:84
de Fossambruno, Angelus, 2:326
de Fourcroy, Antoine-François. *See* Fourcroy, Antoine-François de
de Fragata, Alférez, 4:201
de Giorgi, Ennio, 2:**258–260,** 5:199, 229
de Guevara, Giovanni, 1:167
de Hondt, Joost. *See* Hondius, Jodocus
de Houtman, Frederik, 6:111
De incipit et desinit (Bradwardine), 1:378, 379
De innumerabilibus, immenso et infigurabili (Bruno). *See The Immense Universe, the Numberless and Figureless Worlds* (Bruno)
De intensione et remissione formarum (Blasius of Parma), 1:297
De interioribus (Galen), 1:107
De interpretatione (Aristotle), 5:338
De Kepper, Patrick, 6:166
de la Roche, Antonio, 2:192
de Laguna, Grace Andrus, 2:197
De l'angoisse à l'extase (Janet), 4:28
De lapide philosophorum (Suchten), 6:552
de Launoy, Jean, 1:204
de Leeuw, W. C., 1:388
de Limpges, Pierre. *See* Peter of Limoges
De magnete (Gilbert), 2:1
De magnete (Peter Peregrinus), 1:146
De malo recentiorum medicorum medendi usu (Cardano), 2:36
de Martonne, Emmanuel, 2:235
De materia medica (Dioscorides), 4:265, 6:68
de Maupertuis, Pierre-Louis Moreau. *See* Maupertuis, Pierre Louis Moreau de
De medicina (Celsus), 2:82–84
De methodis (Zabarella), 7:388–389

De Methodis Serium et Fluxionum (Newton), 5:269

de Mirecourt, Jean. *See* John of Mirecourt

de Moivre, James Stirling-Abraham, 1:219

de Montmort, Pierre R., 1:255

De Morgan, Augustus, 4:119
    London Mathematical Society, 3:327
    students of, 6:565

De morte Petri Bembi (Suchten), 6:551

de Mortillet, Gabriel, 7:116

De motibus celorum (al-Biṭrūjī al-Ishbīlī), 1:138

De motibus naturalibus (Swyneshed), 6:563

De motu animalium (Borelli), 1:349, 350

De motu antiquiora (Buonamici), 1:442–443

De motu gravium et levium (Borro), 1:361, 362

De motu libri X (Buonamici), 1:362, 441–443

De motu terrae (Monte), 5:176

De multiplicatione specierum (Bacon, Roger), 1:143, 144

De natura acidorum (Newton), 6:512

De natura boni (Albertus Magnus, Saint), 1:38

De natura rerum (Paracelsus), 6:14

De naturalis scientiae constitutione (Zabarella), 7:388–389

De nostrarum calamitatum causis (Nifo), 5:280

De nuptiis (Capella), 2:412

De occulta philosophia (Agrippa), 1:309

De oculo morali (Peter of Limoges), 1:146

De opere astrolapsus (Adelard of Bath), 1:13

De opificio mundi (John Philoponus), 4:51, 52

De ortu et progressu chemiae: Dissertatio (Borrichius), 6:512

De partibus animalium (Aristotle). *See On the Parts of Animals* (Aristotle)

De phoenomenis in orbe lunae (Lagalla), 1:442

de Pieters, Honoré, 7:135

De placitis philosophorum qui ante Aristotelis tempora floruerunt (Aquilani), 1:443

De Plinii aliorumque in medicina erroribus (Leoniceno), 4:264

De Plinii et plurium aliorum in medicina erroribus (Leoniceno), 6:120

de Possel, René, 1:364, 2:118, 290

De praedestinatione (Eriugena), 2:412

De primo et ultimo ins (Burley), 1:450

De principiis (Damascius), 6:517

De proportionibus velocitatum in motibus (Bradwardine), 2:327, 6:562

De prospectiva pingendi (Piero Della Francesca), 6:105, 106

De Quincey, Thomas, 6:49

De quinta essentia (John of Rupescissa), 1:110

De radiis (al-Kindi), 1:145

De ratione medendi (Nifo), 5:280

De re metallica (Arnald of Villanova, Pseudo), 1:110

De resolutione et compositione mathematica (Ghetaldi), 1:348

De revolutionibus (Copernicus), 2:179, 3:166

de Robertis, Eduardo, 2:331

de Saussure, Horace-Bénédict. *See* Saussure, Horace Bénédict de

De scientia experimentali (Bacon, Roger), 1:146–147

De secretis antimonii (Suchten), 6:551

de Sepi, Giorgio, 4:134

De septem punctis (Paracelsus), 6:14

De signis (Bacon, Roger), 1:144

de Sitter, Willem. *See* Sitter, Willem de

De speculis (Hero of Alexandria), 3:283, 284

De sphaera (Sacro Bosco), 1:445

de Staël, Madame, 7:282

de-Stalinization reforms, 1:427

De subtilitate (Cardano), 2:37, 38

de Terra, Hellmut, 3:412

De triplici minimo et mensura (Bruno). *See The Threefold Minimum and the Measure* (Bruno)

De usu artis conjectandi in jure (Bernoulli), 1:255

de Valois, Louis. *See* Valois, Louis de

De velocitate motus alterationis (John of Casali), 2:326

De vera medicina (Suchten), 6:552

De verborum Vitruvianorum significatione (Baldi), 1:166

De vi attractiva ignis electrici ac Phaenomenis inde Pendentibus (Volta), 7:166–167, 168

De vijs mortis (Bacon, Francis), 1:138, 139

De visione stellarum (Oresme), 5:352

de Vries, Hugo. *See* Vries, Hugo de

Deacon, George Edward Raven, 2:**260–263**

Dean, Dennis R., 3:421

Dean-Jones, Lesley, 3:324

Debang Hou. *See* Hou Te-Pang

DeBenedetti, Sergio, 6:170

Debierne, André, 6:76, 77

Debus, Allen G., 1:229

Debye, Peter Joseph William, 1:280, 3:39, 40
    physical chemistry, 5:168, 170
    students of, 1:303, 3:400, 6:407, 491

Debye-Hückel theory, 3:400

Decarboxylation, 1:199

The Dechronization of Sam Magruder (Simpson), 6:455

Decision and Stress (Broadbent), 1:405

Decision making
    cooperative games, 3:249–250
    development, 7:91–96
    rational bargaining and, 5:225–226
    rational theory, 5:286–287

Decision problem. *See* Entscheidungsproblem

Decision theory, 4:35–36, 6:203–204, 349–351

Declinations (stars), 7:47

Dedekind, Richard, 1:287, 2:30, 31, 6:252

Dee, John, 4:133
    alchemy, 7:334
    influences on, 4:348

Deelder, Rob, 7:138
Deevey, Edward S., 3:411, 412–413
Defant, Albert Joseph Maria, 2:**263–267,** *264*
  acquaintances of, 5:172, 173
  colleagues of, 7:373, 374
  ocean circulation, 2:261, 6:529
Defant, Friedrich, 2:266
Defense enzymes, 1:1, 2–3
Defense industry. *See* Military sciences; Weapons
A Defense of Galileo (Campanella), 2:21
Defensio Theonis contra Georgium Trapezuntium
  (Regiomontanus), 6:216–218
Defensive ferments, 1:1, 2
Definitional operationalism, 2:24
Defloratio philosophorum (Arnald of Villanova, Pseudo),
  1:109
Dehydrobenzene and Cycloalkynes (Hoffmann), 7:339
Dejerine, Joseph, 7:162
Dejerine-Klumpke, Augusta, 7:162
Dekker, Maurits, 5:30
Del Castillo, José, 2:331, 4:89, 90
Del Monte, Guidobaldo. *See* Monte, Guidobaldo,
  Marchese del
Delbrück, Max Ludwig Henning, 2:**267–271,** *269*
  DNA structure, 6:40
  influence of, 4:48, 55, 56, 355–358
  molecular structure, 6:39
  mutations, 6:318
Deligne, Pierre, 7:257
Delineation of the Strata of England and Wales (Smith),
  3:7
Della forma et parti del compasso di Fabritio Mordente
  (Coignet), 2:158
Della Francesca, Piero. *See* Piero della Francesca
Della Porta, Giovan Battista, 3:108
Delle cagioni delle febbri maligne (Borelli), 1:348, 349
Dellinger, J. Howard, 5:114
Dels-Alder reaction, 1:193
Delsarte, Jean, 1:364, 2:118, 290, 291, 6:379
Deltete, Robert J., 5:356, 357
Deluc, Jean-André, 2:223
Dembo, Tamara, 3:14, 4:280
Demerec, Milislav, 4:356, 5:70
Dempster, Everett R., 4:275
Dennery, P., 6:171
Dennett, Dan, 3:162
Dennison, David, 7:101
Denny-Brown, Derek, 2:329
Denotational Semantics (Strachey), 6:535
Density, ocean currents, 6:528–530
Densmore, Dana, 5:270
Deoxygenation, Barton-McCombie, 1:199
Deoxyribonucleic acid. *See* DNA
Deperet, Charles, 7:117

Depew, David J., 2:243
Depreduntia eximia (Cardano), 2:38
Depsipeptides, 5:362–363
Depth perception, 3:121, 127–128
Derebus naturalibus (Zabarella), 7:389
Dererum natura iuxta propria principia (Telesio), 2:19
Dererum varietate (Cardano), 2:37
Derivative Hypothesis of Life and Species (Owen), 5:367
Derrida, Jacques, 3:76
DES (diethylstilbestrol), 1:462
Desaga, Peter, 1:440
Descartes, René du Perron, 2:**272–276**
  celestial motion, 5:270
  criticisms of, 2:274
  geometry, 6:54
  influence of, 4:66
  influences on, 3:158, 246
  mechanical philosophy, 1:204–205, 4:184
  on method, 1:432
  scientific method, 5:11
  theory of matter, 4:51
  theory of vision, 2:*275*
The Descent of Instinct (Beach), 1:222
Descent of Man (Darwin), 2:239, 244, 247
*Description of the Notions/Theorems Used in Astronomy
  and Geometry* (Ibrāhīm Ibn Sinān Ibn Thābit Ibn
  Qurra), 4:5
Descriptiones motuum (Swineshead), 2:326, 6:562, 563
Desegregation, school, 2:131
Desensu rerum et magia (Campanella), 2:20, 21
The Desert Fayum (Caton-Thompson), 4:221
Desiderali fato vitando (Campanella), 2:21
Design for a Brain (Ashby), 5:255
Desimplicium medicinarum noxa (Cardano), 2:36
Desmond, Adrian, 2:242, 244, 246, 3:432
Dessaignes, Victor, 6:22
Dessauer, Friedrich, 1:299, 4:55
Dessler, Alex, 1:41
Deszendenzlehre (Schindewolf), 6:353–354
Determinism, 2:365
Deterministic Nonperiodic Flow (Lorenz), 6:343
Detonation, gases, 6:411, 415
Detwiler, Samuel, 3:219, 7:235
Deuterons, 6:193–194
Deutsch, Morton, 3:15
Developing countries, 6:339
  See also names of specific countries
Development, child. *See* Child development
Development and Evolution (Baldwin), 1:172
Development of the Chick (Lillie), 3:223
Developmental biology
  cell and tissue differentiation, 3:187–188
  cranial neural crest, 3:368–369
  cytology, 2:398–399

experimental, 3:366
fertilization, 4:67–70
morphology, 6:355
See also Embryology
Developmental genetics
limb growth, 3:221–222
pathoclisis, 7:163
ploidy, 1:397–398
Developmental mechanics, 4:44
Developmental morphology, 6:356–359
Developmental psychology
perceptual learning, 3:121–124
personality development, 2:409–411
The Developmental Psychology of Jean Piaget (Flavell),
6:94
Devlin, Thomas, 4:239
Devonian System, 6:467
DeVore, Irven, 7:236, 237
Dew-point recorders, 6:553
Dewar, James, 6:37
Dewar, Michael J. S., 2:103, **276–280**, *277*, 5:290
Dewey, John, 2:74, 184, 7:239
Deyrup, Alden, 3:238
D'Herelle, Felix, 1:455
Das Di-Isocyanat-Polyadditionsverfahren (Bayer), 1:217
Diabetes mellitus, 5:243
Diaconis, Persi, 2:257
Dialectic, 6:205
Dialectica (Cardano), 2:37
Dialectica (Ramus), 6:205, 206
Dialogo del flusso e reflusso del mare (Borro), 1:361
Dialogue on the Two Chief Systems (Galilei), 3:96, 97
Diamond, Jared, 3:416
Diatomic molecules
infrared spectrum of, 4:6–9
spectra analysis, 5:210
Dibon, Paul, 1:444–445
Diccionario de epistemología genética (Battro), 6:94
Dichloroethanes, 1:196
Dicke, Robert Henry, 2:**280–284**, *281*, 4:56
colleagues of, 6:180
cosmic microwave background, 7:303
gravity, 7:302
Dickel, Ferdinand, 7:260
Dickinson, Roscoe Gilkey, 1:234, 6:37
Dickinson, William C., 3:197
Dictionary of Philosophy and Psychology (Baldwin), 1:169
Dictionnaire de chymie (Macquer), 7:169
Diderot, Denis, 4:213
Didymus, 2:**284–286**, 6:172
Diecke, Friedrich, 1:436
Dieckvoss, Wilhelm, 3:276
Dieke, Gerhard, 5:51, 7:229
Diels, Friedrich, 2:155

Diels, Hermann, 6:540
Diencephalon, 3:304–305
Dienert, F., 6:520
Diet and nutrition
calories, 3:64
evolution, 3:118
medicinal chemistry, 3:42–43
proteins in, 1:1, 2–3
selection, 6:244, 245
study of food, 1:441
Diethylstilbestrol (DES), 1:462
Dietrich, Gunter, 5:172
Dietz, Nicholas, 3:238
Dietz, Robert Sinclair, 2:**286–289**, *287*, 5:97, 7:325
Dieudonné, Jean, 1:364, 365, 2:**289–294**
on Claude Chevalley, 2:120
Lie groups, 2:119–120
on Poincaré, Jules Henri, 6:121
textbooks by, 2:118
Difference Engine, 1:*126*, 127, 129
Differential analyzers
circuits, 6:425
development, 3:253, 254–256, 357
Electronic Numerical Integrator and Computer and,
5:53–54
stellar structure calculations, 6:383
Differential centrifugation, 2:144–145, *145*
Differential equations
ballistics, 3:253
differential analyzers, 3:254
distribution theory, 6:379–382
integrals, 7:415
meteorology, 6:238, 343
partial, 5:335–336
analysis, 2:76
Cauchy-Kovalevskaya theorem, 4:158–159
computer science, 3:51
discrete mathematics, 2:404
elliptic, 2:258–259, 5:335
hyperbolic, 4:273
independent variables, 2:230
integrals, 2:76
nonlinear, 4:319, 5:229, 335
parabolic and elliptic, 4:187–189
singular integrals, 2:8–9
Differential geometry
algebraic topology, 2:112–115
holonomy groups, 4:300–301
Kleinian groups, 1:23
topology and, 5:194–195
value distribution theory, 1:22
Differential psychology, 6:522, 524
Differential topology, 1:12–13, 7:291–292
Differentiation, as perceptual learning, 3:120–123

Die Differentielle Psychologie in ihren methodischen Grundlagen (Stern), 6:524

The Difficult Art of Giving (Penfield), 6:74

Diffraction
electron
crystals, 1:410
nickel crystals, 1:270
x-ray
cellulose, 6:332
crystallography, 1:280
plant pigmets, 3:334

Diffused-base transistors, 6:440–441

Diffusionism, 1:184, 185

Digard, Jean-Pierre, 3:116

Digby, Kenelm, 2:326

Digestion
chemistry, 6:46–47
proteins, 1:1–4

Digger wasps, 7:49–50

Dij de Beesten af (film), 1:153

Dijksterhuis, Eduard Jan, 2:356, 357

Dijkstra, Wybe Edsger, 2:**294–299**

Diluvial man from Krapina in Croatia (Gorjanovic-Kramberger). *See Der diluviale Mensch von Krapina in Kroatien* (Gorjanovic-Kramberger)

Der diluviale Mensch von Krapina in Kroatien (Gorjanovic-Kramberger), 3:155

Dilworth, Constance Charlotte, 5:304

Dimensions of Personality (Eysenck), 2:428

Dines, William Henry, 2:306, 6:559–561

Ding Wenjiang, 2:**299–301**

Dingler, Hugo, 4:56

Dinneen, G. P., 5:255

Dinosaurs
birds, 3:431
extinction, 1:58–59
vertebrate paleontology, 7:383–384

Diocles of Carystus, 2:**301–304**

Diodes, 6:440

Diodorus of Alexandria, 2:**304–306**

Diogenes Laërtius, 2:395, 396

Dionysius the Areopagite, 2:413

Diophantine equations, 6:267

Diophantus, 3:436

Dioptra (Hero of Alexandria), 3:283–284

Dioptrics (Descartes), 2:272

Dioscorides, 4:264, 265
ancient medicine, 6:68
translations, 6:120

Diphtheria, 1:454–455, 4:47

Diptera, 3:281

Dirac, Paul Adrien Maurice, 1:73, 2:108, 3:21, 4:56, 7:398, 399
acquaintances of, 4:83

colleagues of, 3:388
distribution theory, 6:379–380
electron theory, 1:413, 7:278
Fermi-Dirac statistics, 2:92
gravity, 2:282, 7:325
influence of, 4:55
Kapitsa Club, 4:82
quantum electrodynamics, 7:264
quantum mechanics, 2:88
relativistic electrodynamics, 1:291
students of, 5:200, 6:335, 336, 398

Dirac-Fock-Podolsky theory, 1:304

A Direct Demonstration of the Phosphorous Cycle in a Small Lake (Bowen), 3:414

Direct realism, 3:125

Dirichlet, Peter Gustav Lejeune, 6:250, 252

Dirichlet principle, 6:251

DiSalle, Robert, 5:270

A Discipline of Programming (Dijkstra), 2:295, 297

Discontinuities in Waveguides (Schwinger and Saxon), 6:394

Discontinuous Solutions of Non-Linear Differential Equations (Oleinik), 5:335

Discorsi (Galileo), 2:274

Discorsi e dimostrazioni matematiche intorno a due nuove scienze (Galileo), 1:167, 349

Discorso sopra i due massimi sistemi del mondo (Galilei), 7:382

Discours préliminaire (La Mettrie), 4:185

Discours sur les figures des astres (Maupertuis), 5:57

Discourse on Bodies in Water (Galileo), 1:442

Discourse on the Cause of Gravity (Newton), 5:270

Discourse on the Comets (Galilei), 3:96

Discourse on the Natural Theology of the Chinese (Leibniz), 4:252

A Discourse on the Roman Foot and the Denarius (Greaves), 3:165

The Discovery of the Unconscious (Ellenberger), 3:74

Discrete mathematics, 2:403–406

Discrete Thoughts (Rota), 6:286

Diseases
ancient medicine, 3:95
brain, 2:341–342
epilepsy, 6:69–74
germ theory, 1:209
microbiology, 2:318–319
personality and, 2:431
treatises on, 4:184
See also Cancer; Medicine

Diseases (Hippocrates), 3:323

Diseases of Women (Hippocrates), 3:323

The Disjunction Effect in Choice under Uncertainty (Tversky and Shafir), 7:95

Disputationes contra deliramenta cremonensia
  (Regiomontanus), 6:218
Disquisitio metaphysica (Gassendi), 3:110, 112–113
Dissection, 3:94
Dissection of squares problem, 7:*87*, 89
Dissertation on Aristotle's Metaphysics (Rufus of Cornwall,
  Richard), 6:295, 296
Dissertation sur la glace (Mairan), 5:10, 11
Dissertations on Different Subjects in Natural Philosophy
  (Hutton), 3:420
Distemper, 3:95
The Distribution of the Stars in Space (Bok), 1:329–330
Distribution theory, 6:378–382
Disturbances of Vision by Cerebral Lesions (Holmes),
  3:346
Diversity. *See* Biodiversity
*Divided Consciousness: Multiple Controls in Human
  Thought and Action* (Hilgard), 3:312–313
Divine Benevolence (Bayes), 1:219
Division of labor, 1:127
Dix, C. Hewitt, 7:270
Dixon, Harold Baily, 6:269, 271
Dixon, Malcolm, 4:254, 5:159
Djerassi, Carl, 6:158
DNA
    base ratios, 2:93–97
    carbon-14 in, 4:298
    crystallography, 3:66–67
    cytology, 2:68–70
    discovery, 2:207, 4:358, 6:83
    helical theory, 3:67
    information storage, 2:380
    modeling, 6:40
    phage research, 2:269–270
    RNA and protein relationships, 1:*373*, 373–375,
        374, 5:310
    RNA polymerase, 5:363–364
    sequencing, 4:117
    structure, 1:374, 2:208–210, 270, 3:66, 5:202, 6:40,
        478–479, 7:67, 298–300
    synthesis, 6:478–482
    ultracentrifuge, 1:464
    virology, 4:357, 358
    See also Crick, Francis Harry Compton; Genetics;
        Watson, James Craig
Dobbs, Betty Jo Teeter, 5:273
Dobson, Gordon Miller Bourne, 2:**306–310**
Dobzhansky, Theodosius, 2:59–60, 62
    acquaintances of, 7:235
    colleagues of, 6:515
    evolution, 7:360, 362
    genetics, 6:494
    group selection, 7:379
    influence of, 4:114, 275, 276, 5:62, 63, 7:237

students of, 5:241
Doctor Universalis. *See* Albertus Magnus, Saint
A Documentary History of Biochemistry (Needham and
  Teich), 5:233
Dodds, Harold, 1:322
Döderlein, Lugwig, 3:294
Dodgson, Charles Lutwidge, 2:**310–312,** *311*
Dodson, Guy, 3:338
Doell, Richard, 2:190, 191, 192–193
Doering, William von Eggers, 5:291, 7:350
Doflein, Theodor, 4:148
Dogmatists (medicine), 2:302–303, 3:92–93
Dogs, experimentation, 6:47–48
Dolby, Alex, 5:125
Dole, Malcolm, 4:91
A Dollar to a Doughnut (Lewis), 4:289
Dollard, John, 5:146, 147
Dolley, Charles S., 2:73
Dolly (cloned sheep), 1:399
Domagk, Gerhard, 1:462
Domestication and behavior, 6:245–246
Domperidone, 4:32
Donald, Hugh P., 5:88
Donald Olding Hebb (Beach), 3:270
Donaldson, Henry H., 7:239, 240
Doncaster, Leonard, 1:211
Donnan, Frederick George, 4:15, 16
Donnino, Alfonso, 4:133
Dopamine receptors, 3:147
Doppler, Christian, 5:98
Doppler effect, 1:294–295, 2:280, 281, 282
D'Oresme, Nicole. *See* Oresme, Nicole
Dorfmeister, Georg, 7:260
Dorn, G., 1:309
Dornberger, Walter, 7:173, 174
Dosimeters, Lauritsen, 4:*209*
Double beta decay, 6:170, 171
Double bonds, 3:400–404, *403, 404*
The Double Helix (Watson), 3:68, 6:40, 83, 7:300
Double theory of attention, 1:404
Doubts Concerning Galen (Rāzī), 6:212
Douglas, Alex E., 3:300
Dow Chemical Company, 3:200
Down to Earth (Krumbein), 4:164, 165
The Dragons of Eden (Sagan), 6:313
Drainage basins, 3:371–374, 6:537–538
Drake, Frank, 5:193, 6:312, 313
Drake, Stillman, 3:96, 97, 98
Draper, George, 5:215
Drawing Two Lines from a Known Point (al-Qūhī), 6:186
Dream interpretation
    Freud's impact on, 4:63
    medicine and, 2:37
Dreiding, André S., 1:198, 2:*202*, 6:159–160, 161

Dreitlein, Joseph, 6:171
Drent, Rudi H., 1:151, 153
Drevermann, Fritz Ernst, 7:250
Drexler, Eric, 6:474
Dreyfus, D., 1:301
Drèze, Jacques, 7:151
Driesch, Hans, 4:45
Drifting sand, in Australia, 6:208–209
Dříza, Gothard J., 6:156
Drosophila
    Caspersson, Torbjörn Oskar, 2:69
    cytology, 2:59–63
    epigenetics, 7:204, 205
    eye color, 1:225, 228, 2:399–400, 7:12–13
    genetics, 2:268, 4:276, 5:185–186
    maternal genes, 1:400
    Mendelian genetics, 1:212
    mutations, 1:463
    statistical distribution, 7:362
    in USSR, 5:248
Drugs
    allergies, 4:33
    analgesic, 1:118–119, 2:358–359, 4:31
    ancient medicine, 3:94
    antibiotic, 1:198–199, 3:43, 6:318
    antidiarrheal, 4:32
    antifungal, 4:32–33
    antihistamine, 4:33
    antileukemic, 2:374–375
    antimetabolite, 2:374
    antimycotic, 4:33
    antispasmotic, 4:31
    antiviral, 2:373–374, 375–377
    aspirin
        discovery, 2:358–359
        manufacture, 4:150
    discovery, 2:358–359
    human immunodeficiency virus, 4:33
    manufacture of, 4:29–33
    marijuana, 2:214
    metabolism, 1:118–120
    neuroleptic, 4:31–32
    psychiatric, 1:118–120
    sympathomimetic, 1:119–120
    See also Pharmacology
Drummond, Jack, 6:361
Druyen, Ann, 6:314
Drysdale, Henry, 3:170
Drysdale, John, 1:209
DSM (Dutch State Mines), 7:133, 134
Du Bois, P. M., 2:191
du Châtelet, Émilie. *See* Châtelet, Gabrielle-Émilie Le
    Tonnelier de Breteuil, Marquise du
Du Moncel, Théodore Achille Louis, 4:294

Du Rietz, Gustav Einar, 1:388
Du Toit, Alexander Logie, 7:208
Du Vigneaud, Vincent, 4:323
Dualism, 3:214–215, 7:80–81
Duane, William, 5:28
Dubois, Eugène. *See* Dubois, Marie Eugène François
    Thomas
Dubois, Marie Eugène François Thomas, 2:239,
    312–316
    hominid fossils, 5:296, 7:252
    Pithecanthropus, 7:184, 185–186
    retirement from University of Amsterdam, 1:281
DuBois, W. E. B., 7:85
Dubos, René Jules, 2:**317–319**
DuBridge, Lee A., 1:56, 2:280
    administration, 6:42
    California Institute of Technology presidency, 3:174
    Vista Project, 1:136
Due lettere sopra varie osservazioni naturali (Arduino),
    1:93
Due trattati sopra la natura, e le qualità della calamita
    (Garzoni), 3:108
Dugan, Raymond Smith, 5:111
Duhem, Pierre-Maurice-Marie, 1:142, 2:**319–323**, *321*
    cosmology, 2:413
    on links between da Vinci and Baldi, 1:167
    on Monte, Guidobaldo, Marchese del, 5:174
Duijvestijn, Arie J. W., 2:296
Dulbecco, Renato, 4:356
Dumas, George, 4:26
Dumas, Jean-Baptiste-André, 2:*323*, **323–325**
    education, 1:265
    influence of, 4:205, 7:371
    Mémoires de physique et chimie (Lavoisier), 4:217
Dumbleton, John, 2:**325–327**
    influences on, 5:314
    natural philosophy, 6:562
DuMond, Jesse, 7:401
Dunbar, Carl O., 5:265
Dunbar, Maxwell J., 3:413
Dunes, sand, 1:155–156
Dunn, Leslie Clarence, 5:241
Dunsch, Lothar, 5:357
Dupont, Pierre Samuel, 4:217
Duppa, B. F., 6:22
Durkheim, Émile, 4:25, 5:123
Durnová, Helená, 2:297
Durrat al-tāj li-ghurrat al-dubāj (Quṭ al-Dīn), 6:188
Durst, Charles Sumner, 6:559
Dusser de Barenne, Johan Gregorius, 5:76
Dust, 1:27–29
Dust, interstellar, 7:127–128
Dutch State Mines (DSM), 7:133, 134
Dutton, Clarence, 6:149, 151

Dutton, John, 6:9
Duval, Rubens, 7:406
Duvaut, Georges, 4:319
Duyvendak, Jan Julius Lodewijk, 5:343
Dyatkina, Mirrah E., 5:248
The Dyer's Hand (Payne-Gaposchkin), 6:52
Dyes
    aldehyde, 1:214
    industrial chemistry, 6:271, 7:144–145
    synthetic, 7:143–148, *147, 148*
Dynamic aphasia, 4:353
Dynamic assessment, 7:193–194
Dynamic Basis of Geomorphology (Strahler), 6:538
Dynamic biochemistry, 5:250
Dynamic meteorology, 2:99
    atmospheric circulation, 7:17–19
    mathematics, 6:558 561
    numerical modeling, 6:469–472
    research, 6:341–342
    tropical cyclones, 3:262–263
    United States, 6:221–223
Dynamic Meteorology (Forsythe, Holmboe, and Gustin),
    3:50
Dynamic Meteorology (Haurwitz), 3:263
Dynamic relativity, 1:425
The Dynamical Character of Adsorption (Boer), 1:313
Dynamical Paleoclimatology (Saltzman), 6:345
Dynamics of a System of Rigid Bodies (Routh), 4:39
The Dynamics of Anxiety and Hysteria (Eysenck), 2:429
*The Dynamics of Insect and Bird Populations in Pine
    Wood* (Tinbergen), 1:151
Dynamics of the Interstellar Medium (Spitzer), 6:501
Dynamische Meteorologie (Exner-Ewarten), 2:425
Dynamische Ozeanographie (Defant), 2:261
Dynamogenesis, 1:171
Dyson, Freeman, 3:22, 6:336, 395
Dystrophy, 7:36

E

E. coli. See Escherichia coli
Eaborn, Colin, 2:104
Eames, Charles, 5:193
Earle, Wilton, 3:187
*Early Forerunner of Man: A Morphological Study of the
    Evolutionary Origin of the Primates* (Clark), 2:138, 140
The Early Growth of Logic in the Child (Piaget), 6:94
Early Papers on Diffraction of X-rays by Crystals (Bijvoet et
    al.), 1:285
Earth
    age
        earth's crust, 2:85
        fossil radiation, 2:283
        mass extinction and, 2:224–226
        thermal history, 4:40–41

    crust, 2:85, 7:324–325
    expansion
        geophysics, 7:324–325
        ocean ranges, 2:42
        plate tectonics, 2:38
        rift valleys, 4:56
    geochemistry, 4:179–180
    heat budgets, 6:554–555
    interior composition, 6:263
    magnetic fields
        atmospheric electricity and, 5:51–52
        continental drift and, 1:292–293, 6:298–300
        radiation, 6:99
        reverse, 3:375–377
        variations in, 5:48–49, *49*
    mantle, 4:187, 6:258–259
    motion
        d'Alembert's principle, 2:230–231
        Copernicanism, 2:176, 177–178
        modeling, 1:31
        testing, 6:188
    orbit, 4:105–106, 5:133–134
    origin, 5:*155,* 155–157
    plate tectonics
        continental drift, 4:40
        earth's magnetism, 1:292–293, 2:379
        expansion, 2:38
        paleomagnetism, 2:192
    primordial atmosphere, 5:*155,* 155–156
    rotation aperture synthesis, 6:305–306
    shape
        controversies, 5:10, 57
        spherical, 5:27
    structure, 2:274
        geomorphology, 1:94–95
        Lehmann discontinuity, 4:233–235
        prebiotic materials and, 5:156–157
        seafloor, 2:288
    surface pressure, 2:*425,* 425–426
    transform faults, 7:325–326
    See also Continental drift
Earth, Moon, and Planets (Whipple), 7:285
Earth, Universe, and Cosmos (Carey), 2:42
The Earth: Its Origin, History, and Physical Constitution
    (Jeffreys), 4:40
Earth sciences. *See specific earth sciences*
Earthquakes
    measurement, 6:241–243
    mountains, 6:348
    oceans, 7:199–200
    prediction, 1:30–32
    seismographs, 1:243–245
    See also Seismology
Earthquakes and Mountains (Jeffreys), 4:40

Earthworms, 7:181

East, Edward Murray, 5:68, 7:357

East-west effect, 6:282

Eastman, George, 4:288

Easton, Dexter, 2:330

Easton, Stewart C., 1:146–147

Eastwood, Bruce S., 6:119

EBA (Elimination by Aspects theory), 7:93

Ebblinghaus, Hermann, 3:406, 6:522, 523

Ebendal, Ted, 3:370

EBMs (Energy balance models), 6:343

Eccles, John Carew, 2:**329–333**, *331,* 4:87

Echardt, Georg, 6:523

Echinoderms, 3:366, *367,* 367–370, *368,* 370

Echolocation, bats, 3:177

Eckermann, Johann Peter, 4:63

Eckert, J. Presper, Jr., 2:**333–338**, *336,* 3:358–359, 5:50, 54–55, 7:315

Eckert, John Adam Presper, Jr. *See* Eckert, J. Presper, Jr.

Eckert, Wallace John, 3:50, 6:384

Eckert-Mauchly Computer Corporation (EMCC), 3:358–359

Eckhard, Rachel. *See* Matthews, Rachel Eckhard

Eckholm, Nils, 4:91

Eclipses, lunar, 3:283–284

L'ecologia (Margalef), 5:24

An Ecological Approach to Perceptual Learning and Development (Gibson, Eleanor Jack and Pick), 3:123–124

The Ecological Approach to Visual Perception (Gibson, James Jerome), 3:122, 125, 129

Ecological economics, 5:325, *325*

Ecological engineering, 5:324–325

Ecological genetics
    Darwinism, 3:45–49
    industrial melanism, 4:109–110

Ecological Genetics (Ford), 3:48

Ecological modeling, oceanography, 6:255–257

Ecological optics, 3:128

Ecological psychology
    perception, 3:125–130
    perceptual learning, 3:123–124

Ecology
    animal, 2:382–388
    animal behavior and, 1:48
    applied, 6:208–210
    Australia, 6:207, 208–210
    biogeochemistry, 3:410, 413–414
    biology, 6:509–510
    birds, 2:7, 3:370
    botany, 2:188–189, 7:3–5
    Braun-Blanquet, Josias, 1:386–388
    Canada, 7:78–79
    Chicago school, 2:390–391

    ecosystem, 5:315–321, 322–325
    holism, 6:484
    limnology, 2:355–356
    major scientists in, 5:22–26
    paleoecology
        carbonate sedimentology and, 5:266
        limnology, 3:412–413
        Pacific atolls, 4:185–187
    plant, 2:152–154, 188–189, 234–237
    population
        animals, 3:415–416
        biochemistry, 3:413–414
        limnology, 3:412–413
        natural selection, 7:377–380
    radiation, 3:414, 5:318–319
    See also Limnology

The Ecology of Animals (Elton), 2:384

The Ecology of Invasions by Animals and Plants (Elton), 2:387, 388

The Economic Consequences of the Peace (Keynes), 4:112

An Economical History of Hebrides (Walker), 7:221

Economics
    chemistry and, 2:218–219
    division of labor, 1:127
    ecological, 5:325, *325*
    equilibrium, 6:17–19
    freerider problem, 5:336–337
    game theory and, 5:187–188, 7:150
    Nash equilibrium, 5:228
    natural history and, 4:315–316
    political
        induction, 7:281
        introductory textbooks on, 5:21
        Keynesian, 4:111–113
        population dynamics, 5:13–14
    politics and, 5:337
    ratificationism, 4:36
    saving, 6:203
    social Darwinism, 2:244
    social theory, 7:225
    taxation, 6:203
    theoretical, 6:499, 7:149–152
    utilitarianism, 3:248–249

Ecosystems
    aquatic, 5:322–325
    botany, 7:6–8
    energy flow, 5:24–25, 316, 317, *324, 325*
        aquatic, 5:322–324, *323*
        theory, 6:509–511
    holism, 5:315–320
    information theory and, 5:24–25
    lake, 3:412–414
    marine
        analytical chemistry, 3:257–259

tidal flats, 7:142
thermodynamics, 5:324
Ectoderm, 3:350, 351
Eddington, Arthur Stanley, 1:65, 2:**338–340,** *339,* 4:38
    electromagnetic fields, 2:370
    general theory of relativity, 3:390–391
    influence of, 6:383
    irreversibility, 6:165
    relativity, 2:91, 6:49, 456, 457
    scientific authority, 2:89
    stellar model, 6:50, 385, 542
    students of, 1:340, 5:80–81, 6:499
    theorizing and, 5:112
    white dwarf configuration, 2:92
Edelman, Gerald, 4:49, 6:364
Edgeworth, Francis Ysidro, 5:186, 188, 6:53
Edinburgh Literary Amusement (Chambers), 2:85
Edinger, Ludwig, 2:**340–343,** 3:344, 345–346
Edinger, Tilly, 6:107
Edlén, Bengt, 2:**343–347,** *344*
Edman, Pehr Victor, 2:**347–353**
Edmondson, Frank Kelley, 3:195
Edmondson, Tommy. *See* Edmondson, Wallis Thomas
Edmondson, Wallis Thomas, 2:**353–356,** 3:412, 413
Edmondson, Yvette Hardman, 2:353, 355
EDSAC computer, 3:256
Education
    biology, 3:189
    chemistry
        introductory textbooks on, 5:21
        popular, 3:64
    cognitive psychology, 7:194–195
    dynamic assessment, 7:193–194
    environmental studies
        ecology, 2:189
        microbiology, 2:318–319
        urban, 2:236
    intelligence tests
        army program, 1:357
        child development, 6:92
        debate over, 7:27
        dynamic assessment, 7:193–194
        neuroscience, 3:267, 268
        personality psychology and, 1:51
        race and, 2:131–132, 6:441
        Stanford-Binet, 7:25–26
    mathematics
        calculus, 7:281
        Jesuits, 2:151–152
        organizational reform, 5:1–2
    reform, 6:205–206
    school desegregation, 2:131
    science
        Atomic Energy Commission, 6:405–406

    critiques of, 1:144
    introductory textbook writers, 5:20–22
    paleontology, 5:267
    popularization of, 7:159–160
    reform and advancement, 5:191–192,
        7:281–282
    teacher training, 3:431–432
    See also Learning
Edwards, Anthony, 3:32
Edwards, Don R., 2:304
Edwards, R. H., 3:313–314
Edwards, William F., 3:97
EEG (Electroencephalography)
    development, 1:18
    intelligence, 2:431
    seizures and, 6:71
Eells, Ellery, 4:35
EFCE (European Federation of Chemical Engineering),
    7:136
The Effect of Space Charge and Residual Gases on
    Thermionic Currents in High Vacuum (Langmuir),
    6:373–374
Effective temperature and precipitation, 7:39
The Effects of Personal Heterosuggestion and Two Forms of
    Autosuggestion upon Postural Movement (Hilgard and
    Berreman), 3:311–312
Egerton, Alfred Charles Glyn, 2:11
Eggen, Olin, 1:24, 25–26
Egger, David, 5:151
Egocentric speech, 7:195
Egodic hypothesis, 1:338
Egyptian pyramids, 3:166
Ehrenberg, Christian Gottfried, 3:429
Ehrenfest, Paul, 2:64, 6:37
    acquaintances of, 2:357, 378, 4:81
    crystal analysis, 1:281
    family life, 2:356–357
    industrial chemistry, 1:311
    quantum mechanics, 6:112
    students of, 1:389–390, 7:99
Ehrenfest-Afanas'eva, Tatiana A., 2:**356–358**
Ehresmann, Charles, 1:364
Ehrlich, Paul, 1:113, 4:31, 47
Eichengrün, Arthur, 2:**358–360**
Eidgenössische Technische Hochschule Zürich,
    6:224–226
Eigen, Manfred, 6:363
Eijkman, Christiaan, 6:568
Eilenberg, Samuel, 1:364, 2:*360,* **360–363,** 4:145, 5:1,
    2–3, 4
Eilenberg-Mac Lane, Collected Works (Eilenberg, Mac
    Lane), 2:362
Einmart, Georg Christoph, 5:37
Einmart, Maria Clara, 5:37

Einsele, Wilhelm G., 3:260
Einstein, Albert, 2:108, **363–373,** *366,* 3:24
    abstract conceptions, 3:400
    acquaintances of, 2:357, 6:7
    affine connection, 2:367–368
    black hole physics, 2:370
    colleagues of, 3:130–131, 191–192
    condensation, 7:100–101, 102
    Copenhagen Interpretation, 1:326–327
    cosmology and, 2:369–370, 3:274, 5:80, 6:456
    determinism, 2:365
    dual nature of light, 1:410
    earth's magnetism, 2:379
    electron spin, 7:100
    EPR paper, 1:240–241, 323, 325, 326–327
    family business, 2:363–364
    gas degeneracy, 2:378
    general relativity, 1:425, 2:338–339, 367,
        3:307–308, 6:34, 122, 399
    German Academy of Natural Sciences membership,
        1:4
    gravity, 2:282
    honors, 5:282
    influence of, 2:280, 4:335
    influences on, 6:252–253
    letter to Roosevelt, 6:421, 574
    light quantum hypothesis, 1:411, 2:364–365
    love affairs, 2:364
    Mach's principle, 6:398
    quantum gases, 1:412
    quantum mechanics, 2:365, 6:112
    relation between geometry and physics, 2:370
    response to John Nash, 5:228
    rivals of, 3:307–308
    special relativity, 2:365–367
    students of, 3:77–78, 6:499, 573
    tensor calculus, 3:190
    tests of general theory, 2:369
    unified field theory, 2:370–371
Einstein-Cartan-Sciama-Kibble theory, 6:399
Einstein—de Sitter model, 3:275, 6:457
Eisenbud, Leonard, 6:64
Eisenhart, Luther, 5:111
Eisenhower, Dwight D.
    advisors to, 6:182
    air defense systems, 4:211–212
    computer predictions, 2:336–337
    nuclear testing concerns, 7:24
    nuclear weapons, 6:41
    President's Science Advisory Committee, 1:275
    satellites, 7:174, 175
    school desegregation, 2:131
Eisenstein, Ferdinand Gotthold Max, 6:250
Eissler, Kurt, 3:73

Ekeberg, Anders, 1:266
Ekholm, Nils, 1:245
Eklund, Sigvard, 6:337–338
Ekman, Fredrik Laurentz, 6:89
Ekman, Gustaf, 6:89
Ekman, Vagn Walfrid, 6:89, 90
El Niño, 5:223–224
El-Wad (Palestine), 3:105, 106
Elasticity
    crystals, 7:165
    monotone operators, 4:272, 273
Elastomers
    cast, 1:216–217
    kinetics, 3:38–39
Eldredge, Niles, 3:159, 161
Elections
    elimination reactions, 4:15
    forecasting outcomes, 1:8, 9
Electric Excitation of Nerve (Katz), 4:86, 87
Electric Waves (Hertz), 3:291
Electrical engineering
    computer science, 2:333–334
    telegraphy, 3:58
Electrical measurements, 6:549
Electricity
    Aharonov-Bohm effect, 1:324
    atmospheric science, 2:215–217, 5:51–52
    batteries, 2:12, 7:170–172
    in chemical combinations and operations, 4:214
    experimental procedures, 3:2–3
    Franklin's theory of one electric fluidum, 1:202–203
    magnetism and, 2:1–2
    modeling, 7:167–168
    nuclear energy, 6:401
    pneumatic-attractive model, 7:167–169
Electricity and Light (Hertz), 3:292–293
Electricity and Magnetism (Purcell), 6:182
Electroconductivity
    analytical chemistry, 7:396
    Goldman-Hodgkin-Huxley equations, 4:87–89
    substitution reactions, 2:324
    theoretical physics, 6:373–377
Electrocrystallization, 2:215–216
Electrodynamics
    development, 6:123
    electromagnetic forces, 3:3–4
    electron scattering, 3:21–23
    quantum
        absorption, 7:398–399
        Bloch-Nordsieck method, 7:69
        development, 7:263–268
        electromagnetism, 6:336
        electron-positron emissions, 6:393
        electron scattering, 3:*21,* 21–23, *22*

limit of validity, 1:273
    particle collisions, 1:428
    refinement, 6:196
    renormalization, 6:394–395
    synchrotrons, 7:70
    theorem of corresponding states, 4:335
    thermonuclear reactors, 1:428
  radio waves, 3:291–293
  theorem of corresponding states, 4:333–335
Electroencephalography (EEG)
  development, 1:18
  intelligence, 2:431
  seizures and, 6:71
Electromagnetic radiation
  Cherenkov effect, 2:107–110
  cosmic rays, 1:40–41
  energetics, 2:320–321
  geometry, 2:370
  gravity, 2:282
Electromagnetism
  Einstein-Cartan-Sciama-Kibble theory, 6:399
  electrodynamics, 3:3–4
  gauge theory, 6:340
  hadronic SU(6) symmetry, 3:193
  quantum electrodynamics, 6:335
  United Kingdom, 6:549
Electrometers, 6:179, 7:169
Electron Emission and Adsorption Phenomena (Boer), 1:312
Electron microscopy, 2:*146*
  cytology, 2:143, 144–146, 6:143–148
  embryology, 2:145–146, *147*
  molecular biology, 6:362
  transmission, 1:374
Electron-positron annihilation, 7:70–71
Electron spectrography, 1:165
Electron transport particles (ETP), 3:171
Electron Tubes (Barkhausen). *See Elektronen-Röhren* (Barkhausen)
Electronic Numerical Integrator and Computer. *See* ENIAC (Electronic Numerical Integrator and Computer)
Electronic Processes in Ionic Crystals (Mott), 5:201
Electronic Processes in Non-crystalline Materials (Mott), 5:204
Electronic Spectra and Electronic Structure of Polyatomic Molecules (Herzberg), 3:301
Electronic switching systems, 6:438
Electronic theory, 6:272
The Electronic Theory of Organic Chemistry (Dewar), 2:276, 277, 279
Electrons
  collisions, 1:428–429
  conduction, 5:203–204

  cooling, 1:429
  correlation, 6:132
  diffraction, crystals, 1:270, 410
  energy, 7:263–265
  gravitational forces, 2:282
  metals, 1:303–304, 5:200–201
  polarization, 7:*263*, 263–264
  positrons as, 7:399
  quantum electrodynamics, 1:273–274
  quantum mechanics, 3:87–88
  scattering, 2:378, 3:*21*, 21–23
  spectroscopy
    inorganic chemistry, 2:103
    transition metals, 4:59–60
  spin
    discovery, 7:99–104
    Kondo effect, 2:65
    resonance, 3:155
  See also Atomic theory
Electrons and Holes in Semiconductors (Shockley), 6:440
Electrophorcsis, 7:33
Electrophoresis, gel
  genetic variability measurements, 3:47–48
  hemoglobin, 6:39
Electrophysiology, brain, 1:17–18
  epilepsy, 6:69–74
  experimental, 1:15
Electrostatic accelerators
  carbon-nitrogen cycle, 3:60
  China, 7:400
Electrostatic theory, 1:311, 312, 7:169
Electroweak theory, 6:396
Elegien (Suchten), 6:552
Elektrochemie: Ihre Geschichte und Lehre as *Electrochemistry: History and Theory* (Ostwald), 5:357
Elektronen-Röhren (Barkhausen), 6:375
Elektronentheorieder Metalle (Sommerfeld and Bethe), 1:270
Elementa physiologiae (Haller), 3:215
Elementary idea set, 1:207
Elementary particles
  Cherenkov radiation, 2:109
  field theory, 1:238–239
  fission, 7:392
  hadronic SU(6) symmetry, 3:193
  nonlinear chiral sigma model, 3:192, 193
  positrons, 1:73
  quantum field theory, 1:236, 6:394–396
Elementary Seismology (Richter), 6:242
Elementary Theory of the Category of Sets (Lawvere), 5:4
Elementary Treatise on Mechanics (Whewell), 7:281
Elemente der exakten Erblichkeitslehre (Johannsen), 5:102
Elemente Entwicklungsgeschichte der Menschheit (Wundt), 7:370

Elements
    atomic weights
        isomorphism, 5:166
        periodic table, 5:105–108, *107*
    heavy, 7:398–399
    ideal, 3:309
    motion of, 1:362, 442
    origin of, 3:390–391
    philosophy of science, 6:6
    radioactivity, 6:75–78
    synthesis, 3:35–36
    transition, 7:308–310
    transuranium, 6:401–406
Elements (Euclid), 1:13, 14, 83–84, 2:416, 417–418,
    3:284–285, 436
    Aristotelianism, 7:389
    commentaries on, 5:177, 6:137, 185–186
    Copernicanism, 2:176
    cosmology, 2:148
    mathematics, 2:149
    proportion theory and, 1:87
    translations of, 6:218
Elements According to Hippocrates (Galen), 3:93
Éléments d'analyse (Dieudonné), 2:292
Les Élements de géométrie algébrique (Dieudonné), 2:292
Eléments de mathématique (Bourbaki), 1:364–366
Elements of Agricultural Chemistry (Davy), 4:54
Elements of Agricultural Chemistry and Geology
    (Johnston), 4:54
Elements of Architecture (Wotton), 1:167
Elements of Cloud Physics (Nyers), 1:470
Elements of Electricity and Electro-Chemistry (Singer),
    2:216
Elements of Electro-biology (Noad), 2:216
Elements of Folk Psychology (Wundt). *See Grundlinien
    einer psychologishen Entwicklungsgeschichte der
    Menschheit* (Wundt)
Elements of Geology (LeConte), 4:224–225
Elements of Higher Mathematics (Vinogradov). *See
    Elementy vysshei matematiki* (Vinogradov)
Elements of Mathematics (Bourbaki), 2:118, 290,
    7:255–256
Elements of Natural History (Lee), 4:232
Elements of Number Theory (Vinogradov). *See Osnovy
    teorii chisel* (Vinogradov)
Elements of Physics (Lorentz). *See Beginselen der
    Natuurkunde* (Lorentz)
The Elements on Experimental Embryology (Huxley and
    De Beer), 3:425
Elementy vysshei matematiki (Vinogradov), 7:156
Elettricismo artificiale (Lavoisier), 4:214
Elhafez, Fathy Ahmed Abd, 2:201
Eliashberg, Gersim Matveevich, 5:129
Eliassen, Arnt, 2:100

Eliel, Ernst, 1:197–198
Elimination by Aspects (Tversky), 7:93
Elimination by aspects theory (EBA), 7:93
Elimination reactions, 4:15
Elion, Gertrude Belle, 2:**373–377,** *376*
Eliot, Christopher, 2:152
Eliot, George, 3:429
Eliot, John, 5:19, 7:218
ELIZA (computer program), 6:279
Elkington, Joseph, 3:6
Ellegard, Alvar, 2:247
Ellenberger, Henri F., 3:75, 4:29
Elles, Gertrude L., 3:316
Ellett, Alexander, 7:119
Ellicott, Andres, 1:174
Ellicott, George, 1:174, 177
Elliot Smith, Grafton
    acquaintances of, 2:238, 239
    Pithecanthropus, 2:314
    Sinathropus, 2:240
    treeshrew studies, 2:138
Elliott, Thomas Renton, 7:179
Elliptic functions
    integrals in, 1:6
    operators, 4:188
    partial differential equations, 2:258–259, 5:335
Ellis, Albert, 5:93
Ellis, Emery, 2:268
Ellis, James R., 2:355
Elms, Alan C., 5:219
Éloge de Homberg (Fontenelle), 3:352
Elsasser, Walter Maurice, 2:**378–381,** *380*
Elsmore, Bruce, 6:304
Elton, Charles Sutherland, 2:**382–388,** 3:413, 7:377
Elvehjem, Conrad Christian Thomas, 3:169, 170
Elvey, Christian, 6:544
EMB (Empire Marketing Board), 6:207–208
Embden, Gustav, 3:170
Embranchment, 2:222–223
Embryologie Chimique (Brachet), 1:371, 372
Embryology
    biochemical, 5:236–237
    blastomeres, 3:*367*
    blastulae, 3:*368*
    brain development, 1:408
    cell and tissue differentiation, 3:187–188
    cell nucleus, 1:*372*
    cell theory, 5:331, 332, 6:357
    chemical analysis, 1:372–373
    comparative, 3:116, 207–209
    cytology, 2:398–399
    DNA, 1:370–371
    electron microscopy, 2:145–146, *147*
    ethology, 3:423–424

evolution, 3:423–424

experimental, 3:348, *366–369, 425,* 4:67–70

genetics and, 1:210–213, 5:185

microsurgery, 3:*219, 220*

nervous system development, 3:217–224

nutrition, 1:441

organizer effect, 3:349–351, 5:15, 16–17, *17*

phylogeny and, 1:210–211

ploidy, 1:397–400

preformism, 3:216

theoretical biology, 7:201–205

Embryology and Genetics (Morgan), 5:185

EMCC (Eckert-Mauchly Computer Corporation), 3:358–359

Emden, Robert, 7:105

Emendatio et restitutio Conicorum Apollonii Pergaei (Maurolico), 1:348–349

Emergency Association of German Science. *See* Notgemeinschaft der Deutschen Wissenschaft

Emerson, A. E. *See* Emerson, Alfred Edwards

Emerson, Alfred Edwards, 1:48, 2:**389–393**

Emerson, Rollins A., 1:225, 5:68

Emery, K. O., 2:286

Emery, William J., 2:37

Emiliani, Cesare, 5:134

Emilsson, Tryggvi, 3:200–201

Emissions

automobile, 3:383

radio, 7:127, 128

Emlen, John, 3:54

Emmett, Paul Hugh, 2:**393–395**, 6:36

Emmons, Franklin, 6:151

Emotional behavior, chimpanzees, 3:268

Emotions

conditioning, 7:243–244

neuroanatomy, 6:10–13

Empedocles of Acragas, 2:**395–398**, *396*

Empire Marketing Board (EMB), 6:207–208

Empiricism, 2:44, 6:458

Empiricists (medicine), 3:92–93

Encyclopädie der Staatswissenschaften (Bronn), 1:415

Encyclopedia of Mathematical Sciences, 6:489

Encyclopedia of Physics, 2:266

Encyclopedias, 6:117–120

End plate potentials, 4:89–90

Endocrinology, behavioral, 1:220, 221–223

Endoderm, 3:350, 351

Endoplasmic reticulum, 5:283, 6:145–146

Energetics, 2:320–321

wavenumber, 6:342

as worldview, 5:356–357

The Energetics of the Larger Scales of Atmospheric Turbulence in the Domain of Wavenumber (Saltzman), 6:342

Energy

absorption

Franck-Condon principle, 2:165

gamma rays, 7:398–399

alternative, 6:306

cellular, 6:569–571

chemical, 6:165–166

consumption

catastrophism, 3:398

nanotechnology, 6:472, 474–475

cycles, in muscle contraction, 4:324–325

ecosystem, 5:24–25, 316, 317, *324, 325*

aquatic, 5:322–324, *323*

theory, 6:509–510, 511

electromagnetism, 6:549

Gibbs free, 7:136

law of conservation of, 3:307

light

quantum hypothesis, 2:364–365

Smith-Purcell effect, 6:182

metabolism, 6:197–202

nuclear, 1:165

atomic bombs, 6:422

Australia, 6:260–261

civilian control over, 1:165

ecology research and, 5:319

electricity, 6:401

explosion, 6:415–416

fusion, 6:384–385

Oppenheimer, J. Robert, on, 5:348–349

reactors, 1:314–315

USSR, 6:325

particle, 7:263–265, 267–268

rotational, 4:6–7

solar

catalysis, 6:416

clouds, 6:555

stellar

chain reactions, 1:271–272

helium, 1:277–278

Energy balance models (EBMs), 6:343

Energy Levels of Complexes and Gaseous Ions (Jørgensen), 4:60

Enewetak Atoll, 4:186–187, 5:318, 320, 323, 6:404

Engel, Friedrich, 4:308–310

Engelhardt, Dietrich von, 5:331

Engelhardt, Vladimir, 6:571

Engels, Friedrich, 3:2

Engine knock, 3:381, 382

Engineering

aviation, 4:101–102

chemical

catalytic cracking, 3:381–383

development, 7:133–139

Engineering, *continued*
    educational methods, 4:287–292
    petroleum cracking, 3:380
    Solvay process, 3:377–380
  civil, 5:132
  ecological, 5:324–325
  electrical
    computer science, 2:333–334
    telegraphy, 3:58
  genetic
    DNA synthesis, 6:478–482
    microbial synthesis and, 5:364
  mechanical, 7:409–413
  petroleum, 4:289–290
  rocket
    dynamics, 4:101–103
    early research, 5:259–260
    influential figures, 7:173–176
    World War II, 6:99
  steam, 2:11
Engler, Adolf, 2:154, 155, 156
Englert, Berthold-Georg, 6:397
Engstrom, Howard, 5:113
ENIAC (Electronic Numerical Integrator and
  Computer), 3:358
  development, 2:333, 334–336, 5:50, 53–54
  multipurpose capability, 3:357
  numerical analysis, 3:256
  Pilot ACE computer, 7:315
Enjoy Old Age (Skinner and Vaughan), 6:465
Enlightenment, 1:431–434, 4:185, 7:220–223
Enrico Fermi, Physicist (Segrè), 6:410
Enriques, Federigo, 4:146
Enthalpy, 7:136
Entomology
  cladistics, 3:281–282, 6:32
  cytogenetics, 2:59–63
  European, 5:118–120
  evolution, 2:389–391
  gall wasps, 4:124–125
  genetics and behavior, 4:277
  industrial melanism, 4:109–110
  South American, 1:452
  species, 7:41–42
Entropy
  axiomatics, 3:307
  cryptography, 6:426–427
  in filtration processes, 5:335
Entscheidungsproblem, 7:82–83
Die Entstehung der Kintinente und Ozeane (Wegener),
  7:247
*Entwurf einer verallgemeinerten Relativitätstheorie und
  einer Theorie der Gravitation* (Grossmann and
  Einstein), 3:192

Environment, Power, and Society (Odum), 5:322, 324
Environmental policy, 6:236
Environmental psychology. *See* Ecological psychology
Environmental studies
  ecology, 2:189
  microbiology, 2:318–319
  urban, 2:236
Environmentalism, 5:320
Enz, Charles P., 6:35
Enzensberger, Horst, 2:148
Enzyme, Antigen, and Virus (Burnet), 1:458
Enzymes
  bacterial membrane transport, 5:160–162
  function and pH, 1:76–77
  galactose metabolism, 4:73
  genetics, 7:13–14
  metabolism, 4:322–323
  methyl transferase, 1:120–121
  oxidation, 7:31–35
  proteins, 1:1–4
  stereochemistry, 6:160
Enzymes and Trace Substances (Green), 3:168
Enzymology
  bacterial, 6:519–520
  biochemistry, 3:167–172, 340–343, 5:305, 306–309,
    7:31–35
  cytology, 5:283–284, 285, 6:197, 198–202
  hydrolysis, 3:340
Eötvös, Roland, Baron von, 2:281–282
Ephrussi, Boris, 2:**398–403**, *401*
  Drosophila eye pigments, 1:225, 463, 7:12–13
  on *Embryology and Genetics* (Morgan), 5:185
Ephrussi-Taylor, Harriet, 1:376
Epicurus, 3:110, 111, 112, 113
Epidemics (Hippocrates), 3:323, 324, 325
Epigenesis
  animal behavior, 6:368, 369
  preformism, 3:216
Epigenetics, 7:201, 203–205
The Epigenetics of Birds (Waddington), 7:205
Epilepsy, 6:69–74
Epilepsy and the Functional Anatomy of the Human Brain
  (Penfield), 6:70
Epinephrine, 1:119–121
Epistemology
  belief is knowledge, 5:286
  child development, 6:94–95
  evolutionary, 2:23–26, 4:342–343, 345, 6:137
  medieval, 5:5–7
  principles of, 4:264–266
  rational choice theory, 4:35
  reliability, 6:204
*Epistola ad Jacobum de Toleto de distillatione sanguinis
  humani* (Arnald of Villanova, Pseudo), 1:109

Epistola Lucretiae ad Eurialum (Suchten), 6:551
Epistola super alchimia ad regem Neapolitanum (Arnald of Villanova, Pseudo), 1:109
Epistolae duae de motu impresso a motore translato (Gassend), 3:112, 113
Epistolica exercitatio (Gassendi), 3:110
Epitome (Regiomontanus), 2:178
Epitome of simplified theoretical astronomy. See *al-Mulakhkhaṣ fī al-hayʾa al-basīṭa* (Jaghmīnī)
Epitome of the Almagest (Regiomontanus), 6:216–217
Epitome Theatri Orbis Terrarum (Ortelius), 2:158
Époques de la Nature (Buffon), 1:432, 6:109
EPR paper. *See Can Quantum-Mechanical Description of Physical Reality Be Considered Complete?* (Einstein et al.)
Epstein, P. S., 1:281
Equations
    Abelian, 1:5
    BET, 2:393–394
    Bloch, 1:306
    Cauchy-Riemann, 1:261
    cubic, 7:87–88
    differential
        ballistics, 3:253
        differential analyzers, 3:254
        distribution theory, 6:379–382
        integrals, 7:415
        meteorology, 6:238, 343
        textbooks, 6:128
    differential, partial, 5:335–336
        analysis, 2:76
        Cauchy-Kovalevskaya theorem, 4:158–159
        computer science, 3:51
        discrete mathematics, 2:404
        elliptic, 2:258–259, 5:335
        hyperbolic, 4:273
        independent variables, 2:230
        integrals, 2:76
        nonlinear, 4:319, 5:229, 335
        parabolic and elliptic, 4:187–189
        singular integrals, 2:8–9
    differential analyzers, 3:254
    Diophantine, 6:267
    Hammett, 3:239
    Lotka-Volterra, 3:415
    Navier-Stokes, 3:263, 4:188–189, 272, 319
    nonlinear elliptical partial differential, 1:261–262
    quadratic, 7:87–88
    Quintic, 1:5
    Schrödinger, 1:241
    theory of, 1:5–6
    Tomonaga-Schwinger, 6:395
Equatorium of the Planetis (Chaucer), 6:162
Equilibrium

    economics, 6:17–19
    Nash, 3:250–251, 5:225, 227–228
    reflective, 3:151–152
    stellar, 2:91
    in thermodynamics, 6:164–167
The Equilibrium of Cognitive Structures (Piaget), 6:94
An Equilibrium-Point Interpretation of Stable Sets and a Proposed Alternative Definition (Harsanyi), 3:251
Erasistratus, 6:540
Erdös, Pál. *See* Erdös, Paul
Erdös, Paul, 2:**403–406,** *404*
Erdtman, Holger, 5:290
Ericson, Algot, 2:343
Erikson, Erik Homburger, 2:**406–412,** *408*
Erinnerung, Aussage und Lüge in der ersten Kindheit (Stern and Stern), 6:523
Eriugena, Johannes Scottus, 2:**412–413**
Erlander, Joseph, 6:361
Erlenmeyer, Richard August Carl Emil, 1:465
Eropkin, Dmitrii, 1:64, 67
Erosion
    geomorphology, 6:537
    rock cycle, 3:419–420
    soil, 3:371–374, 6:208, 209
Errera, Maurice, 1:374
Ersten Entwurf eines Systems der Naturphilosophie (Schelling), 5:331
ESA (European Space Agency), 7:130
Esau, Katherine, 2:**413–416**
Escalona, Sybille, 3:14
Eschenmoser, Albert, 7:352
Escher, B. G., 7:141, 142
Escherichia coli
    enzymology, 6:520
    genetics, 7:14
    mutations, 7:15
ESO (European Southern Observatory), 3:273, 276
ESRO (European Space Research Organisation), 5:304, 7:130
ESS (Evolutionarily Stable Strategy), 3:230, 5:228
Es-Skhul (Palestine), 3:105, 106
Essai d'arithmétique morale (Buffon), 1:432
Essai de cosmologie (Maupertuis), 5:58
Essai de statique chimique (Berthollet), 1:265
Essai d'une nouvelle théorie de la résistance des fluides (d'Alembert), 2:230
Essai sur la composition des machines (Lanz), 4:201
Essais de chimie (Homberg), 3:353
Essay d'analyse sur les jeux de hazard (de Montmort), 1:255
Essay of the Atomical Philosophy (Boyle), 6:419
Essay on Dew (Wells), 1:28
Essay on Phlogiston (Kirwan), 4:218, 6:44, 97
Essay on Population (Malthus), 5:13

Essay on the Distribution of Wealth and on the Sources of Taxation (Jones), 7:281

An Essay towards Solving a Problem in the Doctrine of Chances (Bayes), 1:219–220

Essays and Observations, Physical and Literary (Cullen), 2:219

Essays from the Edinburgh and Quarterly Reviews (Herschel), 3:288

Essays of a Biologist (Huxley), 3:425

Essays on Natural History and Rural Economy (Walker), 7:221

Essays on the Theory of Lie Groups and Algebraic Groups (Borel), 1:346–347

Essential amino acids, 5:247

The Essential Tension (Kuhn), 4:173, 175

Essentials of Behavior (Hull), 3:408, 409

Estlin, J, 2:57

Estrogen, 1:460–461

Et-Tabun (Palestine), 3:105, 106, 107

Ether, 5:274

Ethics
    hydrogen bombs, 6:196
    personality and, 1:52
    physicians, 3:93
    science and, 4:291–292
    social psychology and, 5:142
    See also Bioethics

Ethics (Kropotkin), 4:161

Ethik (journal), 1:3

Ethnic groups
    geography and, 1:206–207
    racial classification, 3:208–209, 7:114–115

Ethnography
    biogeography, 7:209–210
    culture and religion, 4:251–252

Ethnology
    anthropology, 3:118–119
    colonialism and, 1:206–207
    South American, 4:237

Ethology
    animal behavior, 7:181–182
    behavior, 1:222
    biology, 7:41–44
    cognitive, 3:177, 179–180
    embryology, 3:423–424
    field studies, 1:150–151, 153
    influential figures, 7:84–86, 180–184
    instinctive behavior, 4:343–344
    migration, 3:177
    See also Neuroethology

Ethylene glycol, 6:229

Ethynylation reaction, 6:230–231

Etomidate, 4:33

ETP (Electron transport particles), 3:171

Étude anatomique de l'articulation du genou chez les primates (Vallois), 7:113–114

Étude géologique de la Région Weissmies-Portjengrat (Huang Jiqing), 3:393

Études d'épistémologie génétique (Piaget), 6:94

Eucharist
    atomism and, 3:98–100
    spiritualism, 6:15, 16
    See also Religion and science

Euclid, 2:**416–421,** *417*
    alternative proofs of, 1:83–84
    Aristotelianism, 7:389
    commentaries on, 5:177, 6:137
        by Hero of Alexandria, 3:284–285
        by Theon of Alexander, 3:436
    Copernican motion, 2:176
    cosmology, 2:148
    geometry, 2:306, 310–311
    influence of, 4:1, 6:185–186
    mathematics, 2:149
    proportion theory and, 1:87
    reflection, 3:284
    translations, 1:13, 14, 6:218

Euclid and His Modern Rivals (Dodgson), 2:310–311

Euclidean geometry
    combinatorial techniques, 1:87–89
    Gauss-Bonnet theorem, 2:113–114
    heptagon, 1:*88*
    hyperbolic geometry and, 6:121–122
    influence of, 3:405
    space, 7:291–292
    tangent circles, 1:*89*
    theory of knowledge, 3:408
    translations, 1:13, 14

Eudiometry, 7:170

Eudoxus, 2:304

Eudoxus Papyrus. *See Ars Eudoxi* (Leptines)

Eugenics
    criticism of, 4:44, 45
    Darwinism, 3:209
    genetics and, 5:245, 7:2
    idiotypic network theory, 4:50
    medical ethics, 1:1, 3–4
    negative, 3:234
    reform, 3:426–427
    statistics, 6:54, 55

Euler, Leonhard, 1:7, 2:231, **421–424,** *422*
    acquaintances of, 2:229
    controversies, 5:11
    equations of motion, 4:159
    partial differential equations, 2:230

Euler, Ulf Svante von. *See* von Euler, Ulf Svante

Euler-Goldbach conjecture, 6:566

Eupsychian Management (Maslow), 5:46, 47

European Federation of Chemical Engineering (EFCE), 7:136
European Southern Observatory (ESO), 3:273, 276
European Space Agency (ESA), 7:130
European Space Research Organisation (ESRO)
    development, 5:304
    members of, 7:130
Eutocius of Ascalon, 1:83–84
Eutrophy, 7:36
Evans, Denis, 7:312
Evans, John W., 5:116
Evans, Lloyd Thomas, 2:244
Evans, Meredith G., 6:126
Evans, Robley, 4:332
Evapotranspiration, 7:39
Evarts, Edward, 1:120
Everaert, Merten, 2:157
Everard, John, 7:334
Evernden, Jack, 2:192
Evert, Ray F., 2:415
Evolution, 5:365
    allometry, 3:424–425
    Australopithecus, 2:238–241
    Baldwin effect, 1:168, 172
    behaviorism, 6:465
    big bang theory, 3:136–137
    biogeography, 7:210
    biological fixism, 1:452
    biostratigraphy, 6:351–355
    botany, 2:154–157
    brain, 1:408
    catastrophism, 1:416
    cave art, 4:42–43
    chemical, 3:363
    cladistics, 3:281–282, 6:32
    comparative anatomy, 2:313–316
    comparative embryology, 3:207–209
    controversy, 2:197
    creative, 5:354–355
    cultural anthropology, 2:173–175
    cultural progress, 4:78–79
    culture, 5:296
    earth, 1:415
    ecosystems and, 5:319
    embryology, 3:423–424
    epistemology, 2:23–26, 4:342–343, 345, 6:137
    ethics, 3:432
    fixism theory, 1:453
    founder-flush model, 2:62–63
    galaxies, 7:58–59, 60
    game theory, 3:232–233
    genetics
        birds, 2:59–61
        epigenetics, 7:203–205

eugenics, 3:32
    germplasm theory, 7:259–261
    Mendelian, 5:104
    of protozoa, 4:44–45
group selection, 7:378–380
hippocampus controversy, 5:368
holism, 6:484
hominid fossils, 7:184–188, *185, 186*
ideo-motor action, 2:57
industrial melanism, 4:109–110
intelligence and, 1:169–170, 6:91
Marxism and, 5:284
Mendelian genetics, 7:189–191
migration, 2:61–62
molecular, 4:116–117
mollusks, 2:4–7
Nash equilibrium and, 5:228
natural selection, 3:425–426
    adaptation, 7:226–227, *361*
    altruism, 9:226–229
    antibody formation, 4:48
    atomism, 3:289
    birds, 2:4–5
    consciousness, 3:183
    epistemology, 2:25–26
    eugenics, 3:234
    first species, 1:417
    flora and fauna, 1:415
    genetical theory, 3:31–32
    intelligence, 6:9
    physiological genetics, 7:358
    power of struggle, 2:246
    selection theory, 2:25–26
    shifting-balance theory, 7:358–362, *359, 360*
    social behavior, 7:376, 377–380
    social environment and, 2:243–247
    systematics, 2:7
    territoriality, 3:385
naturalism, 3:430–431
Neanderthal, 3:154, 155–156
nervous system, 1:438
non-Darwinian view of, 5:365–368
origin of, 1:208–210
paleoanthropology, 2:126, 4:42–43, 6:108–109, 7:115–117
Paleolithic cultures, 5:296
paleontology, 6:452, 453–455
parallel evolution, 2:138–141
Pithecanthropus, 7:185
plant, 6:513, 515
population genetics, 5:63–64, 243–244, 7:353–363
psychology, 3:162, 6:458
second law of thermodynamics, 6:485
sexual reproduction, 3:232–233

Evolution, *continued*
    shifting-balance theory, 7:358–360
    social, 3:226–232, 234
    speciation, 5:63–64
        allopatric, 3:159–160
        Drosophila, 2:62–63
        mammals, 2:86
    stages, 6:108–109
    teratology, 3:116
    vertebrate archetype, 5:367
    vision, 4:224–225
    zoology, 3:115–119, 133, 4:189–190, 7:259–260
    See also Darwinism; Fossils; Paleontology
Evolution: Its Nature, Its Evidences, and Its Relation to Religious Thought (LeConte), 4:42–43
Evolution, the Modern Synthesis (Huxley), 3:426
The Evolution and Classification of Flowering Plants (Cronquist), 2:214
Evolution and Ethics (Huxley), 3:432, 4:162
Evolution and Its Relation to Religious Thought (Le Conte), 4:224
Evolution and Modification of Behavior (Lorenz), 4:247
Evolution and the Genetics of Populations (Wright), 7:357, 362
Évolution créatice (Piveteau), 6:91, 109
The Evolution of Cooperation (Hamilton and Axelrod), 3:231
Evolution of Man (Haeckel). *See Anthropogenie* (Haeckel)
Evolution of Stars and Galaxies (Payne-Gaposchkin), 6:51
Evolution of the Stars and Gas in Galaxies (Tinsley), 7:58
Evolution Through Group Selection (Wynne-Edwards), 7:379
Evolutionarily stable strategy (ESS), 3:230, 5:228
Evolutionary biology, 3:159–162
    birds, 5:61–62
    dinosaurs, 2:86
    downward causation, 2:24
    gall wasps, 4:124–125
    influential figures, 5:63–64, 7:224–227
    Lamarckism, 4:189–190
    mammals, 2:86
    mollusks, 2:3–7
    philosophy, 7:63
    primatology, 7:236–238
    protein chemistry in, 1:80
    social behavior, 7:378–380
    superorganism concept, 2:391–392
Evolutionary cosmology, 6:302, 305
Ewald, Paul Peter
    education, 1:270
    International Union of Crystallography, 1:285
    students of, 1:237
Ewel, John, 5:322
Ewen, Harold I., 6:181

    radio astronomy, 5:345
    radio signals, 1:330
    spectral lines, 7:129
Ewens, Warren, 3:31–32
Ewing, W. Maurice, 2:354, 7:324
    colleagues of, 7:30, 31, 375
    earth's upper mantle, 4:234
    seismology, 7:323
Examen (Hobbes), 1:369
Exchangeability, probability, 2:256–257
Excursions in Madeira and Porto Santo (Bowdich), 4:231
Exercises (Blundiville), 2:157
Exercises in Experimental Geometry (Ehrenfest-Afanas'eva), 2:357
Exercitatio (Gassendi), 3:110
Exercitationes exotericae (Scaliger), 3:157
Exercitationes philosophicae (Gorlaeus), 3:157, 158
Exhaustive Treatise on Shadows (Saʿīd), 2:305–306
Existential definability, 6:267
Exner, Sigmund, 2:425
Exner-Ewartne, Felix Maria von, 2:**425–428**
Exobiology. *See* Astrobiology
The Expanding Earth (Carey), 2:42
Expanding universe, 6:457
Expected utility theory, 7:92, 94
Expected Utility Theory without the Independence Axiom (Machina), 6:350
Experiences of Collaborative Research (Kahneman), 7:94
Experimental Approaches to Psychoanalysis (Hilgard), 3:312
Experimental chemistry
    metabolic enzymology, 4:323
    organic chemistry, 2:277–278
    oxidative phosphorylation, 5:160–163
    primordial atmosphere, 5:155–156
    transition metals, 4:61
    translations, 1:92
    on water, 4:215
Experimental embryology, 3:348, 366–369, 425, 4:67–70
Experimental Essays (Arconville), 1:92
Experimental philosophy
    Aristotelian theory, 1:102–104
    manual work of artisans and, 1:231
    natural philosophy, 2:2
Experimental physics
    Cherenkov effect, 2:107–110
    climate change, 5:327–330
    nuclear magnetic resonance, 6:178, 179–182
    radiation, 2:108–110
    radiocarbon dating, 5:326–327
    superconductivity, 2:64–65
    telegraphy, 3:58
    United Kingdom, 6:548–549

Experimental psychology
    attention and perception, 1:401
    behaviorism, 6:244–247
    computing, 4:302–303
    conditioning and learning, 3:311–312
    consciousness, 7:369
    critical personalism, 6:523
    critique, 6:525
    history of, 1:357–359
    hypnosis, 3:312, 406
    hysteria, 4:25–26
    influential figures, 7:368–371
    laboratory procedures, 2:73–74
    learning research, 5:145–151
    obedience research, 5:137–140, *138, 139*
    operationalism, 2:24–25
    primitive culture, 1:185–186
    psychotherapy, 6:274–279
    scientific specialty, 1:405
    tendencies and, 1:185
    twin studies, 3:312
Experimental science
    Aristotelianism, 7:389–390
    early eighteenth-century, 5:36–37
    electricity, 3:2–3
    as hypothetico-deductive enterprise, 5:88–89
    philosophy, 2:171
    zoology, 4:43
    See also Scientific method
Experimental Studies in Ecology: I. The Magnesium Tolerance of Daphnidae and its Ecological Significance (Hutchinson), 3:414
Experiments and Observations on Different Kinds of Airs (Priestley), 7:169
Experiments and Observations on Electricity (Franklin), 7:167
Experiments and Observations on the Unequal Refrangibility of Light (Blair), 1:295
Experiments with People (Abelson, Frey, and Gregg), 1:10
Explicate order, 1:325
Explorations in Personality (Murray), 2:408, 5:214, 217
Explorations with Sugars, How Sweet It Was (Lemieux), 4:258
"Exploratory Behavior in the Development of Perceiving, Acting, and the Acquiring of Knowledge" (Gibson, Eleanor Jack), 3:123
Explorer space probes, 5:261, 7:122–123, 175
Explosives, thermal, 6:411
Expositio cum quaestionibus (Burley), 1:449
Exposition on Bloodletting by Master Cristannus de Prachaticz. See Collecta per magistrum Cristannum de Prachaticz de sanguinis et lunacionum (Prachaticz)
Expositiones on De generatione animalium (Nifo), 5:280
Expositiones on De partibus animalium (Nifo), 5:280

Expositiones on Historia animalium (Nifo), 5:280–281
Extensional versus Intuitive Reasoning (Tversky and Kahneman), 7:95
Extensive air showers, 6:283
External Human Fertilization (Grobstein), 3:188
Extinction
    catastrophism, 1:395, 416, 3:398, 7:280
    dinosaurs, 1:58–59
    mass, 2:224–226, 5:265, 266
Extraordinary Sex Ratios (Hamilton), 3:230
Extraterrestrial life
    genetics, 3:361
    Mars, 3:364–365, 6:435
    possibility of, 6:309–314, 435, 436, 485–487
    radio astronomy, 3:139
    works on, 6:432
Extratropical cyclones
    forecasting, 1:289–290
    life cycles, 1:245, *246, 247*
    mathematics, 2:99
    occlusion process, 1:246–247
Extreme ultraviolet spectroscopy, 7:77
Eyes
    color, 1:225, 228, 2:399–400, 7:12–13
    geometry and, 1:145
    movements and perception, 3:17
Eyring, Henry, 6:126
Eysenck, Hans Jürgen, 2:**428–433,** *431*

F

Fā' ida fi ishkal utārid (Ali al-Qūshjī), 1:47
Fa' alta fa-lā talum (Qut al-Dīn), 6:188
Faber, Alexander, 1:114
Faber, Sandra, 7:59, 61
Fabre, Jean Henry, 3:86
Fabrici, Girolamo, 1:104
Fabricius, David, 4:107
Fabry, Charles, 2:307, 308
Facets of Physics (Allan and Hughes), 1:392
Fact, Fiction, and Forecast (Goodman), 3:149
Fact and Theory in Cosmology (McVittie), 5:84
Factorization of graphs, 7:89, 90
Faddeev, Ludwig D., 5:129
Fagan, Brian, 2:125
Faint Object Camera (FOC), 7:130
Fairchild, Herman L., 4:225
Fairchild Semiconductor, 1:234
Fairey, John. *See* Farey, John
Faith and Physical Science (Van de Hulst). *See Geloof en Natuurwetenschap* (Van de Hulst)
Falk, K. G., 1:118
Fallout, radioactive, 1:165, 6:327
Familiar Lectures on Scientific Subjects (Herschel), 3:288
Family-habit hierarchies, 3:407

The Family of Man (Washburn), 7:236
Fan Xudong, 3:378, 379
Fano, Gino, 4:309
al-Fārābī, 6:6
Faraday, Michael, 1:28, 2:216, 3:**1–5,** *2*
  benzene, 5:166
  influence of, 7:281
  on Marcet, Jane Haldimand, 5:21
  Royal Institution, 6:142
  Royal Society, 2:251
Farben, I. G., 5:29
Farey, John, 3:**5–8**
Farbenindustrie AG, I.G. *See* I. G. Farbenindustrie AG
Farley, John, 6:26
Farmer, Erik, 1:188
Farming. *See* Agriculture
Farnsworth, Philo, 2:333
The Farther Reaches of Human Nature (Maslow), 5:47
Fasciolo, Juan C., 4:253
Fast ionization chambers, 6:283
Fatḥallāh al-Shirwānī, 4:21
al-Fathiyya fī ilm al-hay' a (Alī al-Qūshjī), 1:47
Fatt, Paul, 2:331, 4:87, 89
Fatty acids
  metabolism, 3:170, 171, 4:238–239, 254
  oxidation, 4:253
Faults, overthrust, 3:397
Faura, Federico, 7:154
Favaro, Antonio, 3:97
FDA (Food and Drug Administration), 1:400
Fear, War, and the Bomb (Blackett), 1:292
Features of Similarity (Tversky), 7:92
Fedigan, Linda, 2:52
Fedorov, Konstantin Nikolayevich, 3:**8–11**
Feenberg, Eugene, 6:169, 7:295
Feferman, Solomon, 3:130–131
Fefferman, Robert, 7:414
Fehler, Mike, 1:32
Fehrenbach, Charles, 3:273
Feigl, Herbert, 1:359, 5:90, 92, 6:133
Feijen, Wim, 2:295
Feinstein, Lillian, 6:384
Feit, Walter, 3:**11–13,** 153
Fejos, Paul, 7:235
Féjoz, Jacques, 5:198
Feldberg, Wilhelm, 2:329, 4:325
Feller, William, 3:50
*The Female Emigrant's Guide, and Hints on Canadian
  Housekeeping* (Traill), 7:79
Femininity and masculinity, 7:27–28
Feminism. *See* Feminist movement
Feminist movement
  academic life, 7:60
  France, 6:288

Lehrman, Daniel Sanford, 4:247
  Maslow's hierarchy of needs and, 5:46–47
  psychology, 1:359–360
Fenchel, Werner, 7:82
Feng, T. P., 2:330
Fenner, Frank J., 5:88, 6:209
Fentanyl, 4:31
Fermat's theorem, 3:309
Fermentation
  alcoholic, 5:251–252
  glucose, 7:347–348
  organic chemistry, 6:22–24
Fermi, Enrico, 2:88, 6:169, 7:328, 331
  acquaintances of, 7:100
  atomic bombs, 6:409, 7:266
  beta decay, 3:193, 7:102, 366
  boron absorption method, 1:134
  chain reactions, 7:295, 296
  colleagues of, 5:190, 6:384
  Fermi-Dirac statistics, 2:92
  finite Fermi systems, 5:129–130
  fission, 7:21
  hydrodynamic waves, 1:41
  hydrogen bombs, 6:196, 7:23
  influence of, 6:410, 411, 574
  magnetic fields, 2:91
  nuclear decay, 1:55
  nuclear physics, 6:407
  physics instruction by, 1:60–61
  students of, 1:270, 4:355, 7:365
  Teller, Edward, 7:22
Fermi National Accelerator Laboratory, 7:329–331
Fermi-Segré formula, 6:407
Fernald, Merritt Lyndon, 6:514
Fernández-Morán, Humberto, 2:70–71, 3:171–172
Ferns, 6:228
Ferrari, Valerie, 1:33, 2:92
Ferraro, V. C. A., 1:278
Ferrazzini, Valerie, 1:32
Ferrel, W., 6:559
Ferrocene, 7:308–309, *309,* 310
Ferrocerone, 5:247
Ferromagnetism, 1:304, 306, 2:191–192, 6:169–170
Ferster, Charles, 6:463
Fertilization, *in vitro,* 3:188–189
Fertilizers
  nitrogen
    chemical weapons, 3:204
    Solvay process, 3:379
  phosphate, 5:295
Feschbach, Herman, 7:267
Festinger, Leon, 3:**13–18,** *15*
Fetal research, 3:186, 188
Feyerabend, Paul, 5:93

Feynman, Richard Phillips, 3:**18–26,** *21, 22, 23*
    algebra, 6:286
    conservation of vector current, 7:367
    quantum electrodynamics, 7:266
    quantum mechanics, 6:395
    renormalization, 6:336
    theory of electromagnetic force, 1:428
Fibers, synthetic
    cellulose acetate, 2:359
    macromolecules, 2:49–50
    molecular structure research, 5:28–29
    rayon, 5:30
Fibonacci sequence, 6:267
Fibrinogen, 2:352
Fichera, Gaetano, 5:335
Fichte, Johann Gottlieb, 5:331, 6:55
Fichtner, Gerhard, 3:73
Ficino, Marsilio, 2:20
Ficq, Adrienne, 1:374
Fiedler, Wilhelm, 3:191
Field, Hartry, 4:37
Field, Richard M., 7:323
Field-effect amplifiers, 1:180–181
Field effects, 6:496
Field mapping, 1:69–70
Field theory
    formalism, 6:35
    in psychology, 4:279–280
    quantum
        elementary particles, 1:236
        gauge theory, 6:339–340
        mesons, 6:393
        particle physics, 1:238–239
        renormalization, 6:394
        source theory, 6:395–396
        superconductivity, 1:318–319
    unified, 2:370–371
Fieldwork, scientific, 2:51–54
Fieser, Louis, 1:196–197
Fifth substance, 7:381–382
Figural intensity, 3:296
Filament dissipation, 6:499, 500
La filosofia di Francesco Buonamici, professore di Galileo Pisa (Helbing), 1:441
Filter theory of attention, 1:401, 403–405, *404*
Filtration, 5:335
Final Count (Zosimos of Panopolis), 7:406
Finch, George I., 7:147
Finch, John, 2:171
Findeisen, Walter, 1:248
Finding the Missing Link (Broom), 2:139
Fine, Henry, 5:111
Finitary operation, 3:309

Finite-Difference Methods for Partial Differential Equations (Forsythe), 3:51
Finite groups, 3:152–154
Finkel, Miriam, 6:41
Finlay, Carlos, 7:153
Finocchiaro, Maurice, 3:97
Fire, motion of, 7:381–382
First Lines of the Practice of Physic (Cullen), 2:220
Fischbach, Ephraim, 6:171
Fischer, Albert, 2:144, 4:323
Fischer, Emil Hermann, 1:1
    influence of, 1:201
    organic molecular structure, 1:280
    students of, 5:250
Fischer, Ernst Otto, 7:309
Fischer, Ernst Peter, 2:270
Fischer, Eugen, 3:**26–29,** *27*
Fischer, Froese, 3:254
Fischer, Leopold Franz Eugen. *See* Fischer, Eugen
Fischer-Tropsch process, 2:394
Fish
    animal electricity, 7:171–172
    fossils, 6:31
    illustrations of, 4:231–232
    Indian Ocean, 6:476, 477
    neuroanatomy, 7:182
    physiology, 3:260–261
    taxonomy, 3:339–340
    vision, 7:213
    See also Ichthyology
Fish, Eleanor, 2:391
FISH and I (speech), 7:90
Fisher, Irving, 6:18, 7:225
Fisher, Ronald Aylmer, 3:*29,* **29–33,** 46, 4:47, 5:62
    colleagues of, 3:376
    continental drift, 6:300
    evolution, 7:356–357, 360–362
    influence of, 3:226
    mark-release-recapture method, 3:47
    on Mendel, Johann Gregor, 5:97
    statistics, 6:52–53
Fishes of Seychelles (Smith, James Leonard Brierley and Smith, Margaret), 6:477
Fission
    discovery, 3:210–212
    vs. fusion, 7:21
    hypothesis, 6:260
    plutonium, 6:408–409
    spontaneous, 3:35–36
    transuranium elements, 6:402
    uranium, 1:55
        discovery, 2:205
        elementary particles, 7:392
        implosion bombs, 1:56

Fission, *continued*
    neutron energy threshold, 2:166
    particle physics, 3:20
    spontaneous, 3:33
    xenon, 7:365
Fitness, inclusive, 3:225, 226–232
Fits, Passions, and Paroxysms (Shapiro), 5:269
Fitton, W. H., 3:7
Five Billion Vodka Bottles to the Moon: Tales of a Soviet Scientist (Shklovskii), 6:433
Five islands theorem, 1:24
Fixed forms, 6:294
Fixed-point theorems, 5:228
Fixism theory, 1:452, 453
    See also Evolution
Fizeau, Hyppolite, 2:365, 366, 367
Fjörtoft, Ragnar, 2:100
Der Flachsstengel: Eine statistisch-anatomische Monographie (Tammes), 7:1
Flahault, Charles, 1:387
Flame propagation theory, 7:392
Flamsteed, John, 3:287
Flanagan, John C., 5:147
Flatworms, taxonomy, 3:434
Flavell, John, 6:94
Flavones, 7:143–148, *144, 145, 146*
A Flavoprotein from Yeast (Green), 3:168
Flax, 7:1–2
The flax stalk: A statistical-anatomical monograph (Tammes). *See Der Flachsstengel: Eine statistisch-anatomische Monographie* (Tammes)
Flechsig, Paul, 7:162
Fleming, Alexander, 6:158
Fleming, John Ambrose, 1:391, 3:58, 7:119
    acquaintances of, 5:51
    colleagues of, 3:58
Fleming, Richard, 2:261
Flerov, Georgiï Nikolaevich, 3:**33–37**
Flesh of the Wild Ox (Coon), 2:173
Fletcher, James C., 5:262, 6:486
Fletcher, John, 4:131
Fletcher, Roslyn, 1:420
Fletcher, Walter Morley, 5:232
Flexner, Simon, 2:182
Flies, 3:281
    See also Drosophila
Flight, birds, 7:182
Flitner, Wilhelm, 2:43
Flohn, Hermann, 5:329
Floods, cataclysmic, 1:393–395, *395*, 396, 6:537
Flora Australiensis (Bentham), 5:206
Flora des Graubündens (Braun-Blanquet), 1:387
Flora Lapponica (Linnaeus), 4:316
Flora of Australia, 2:214

Flora of Idaho (Davis), 2:213
Flora of North America (Barkley), 2:214
Flora of the Great Plain (Barkley), 2:214
Florey, Howard, 5:86
Florkin, Marcel, 2:143
Flory, Paul John, 1:197, 3:**37–41,** *39*
Flos florum (Arnald of Villanova, Pseudo), 1:109
Flourens, Marie-Jean-Pierre, 6:73
Flournoy, Théodore, 4:64
Flow-Matic, 3:359
Flower, Michael, 3:188–189
Flowering Plants: Evolution above the Species Level (Stebbins), 6:515
Floyd, Robert, 5:257
Flu virus, 1:457–458
Flubendazole, 4:32
Fludd, Robert, 3:110
Fluid dynamics
    atmospheric science, 2:426
    geophysics, 3:395–396
    meteorology, 4:39
    missiles, 1:287–288
    sediment transport, 1:156
    two-dimensional subsonic flow, 1:261
Fluid mechanics, 4:272–273
Fluidization, 1:355, 3:383, 4:290
Fluidized bed technology. *See* Fluidization
Fluorine dating, 5:296–298, 299
Flürscheim, Bernard, 4:14
Fluxions (Newton), 1:432
Flygare, William H., 3:200
Flying Fox and Drifting Sand (Ratcliffe), 6:208–209
Flying foxes, 6:208
FOC (Faint Object Camera), 7:130
Fock, Vladimir, 2:108, 4:84
    acquaintances of, 4:80
    Hartree-Fock approximation, 3:253, 255
    students of, 5:127
Foerster, Ottfrid, 6:70, 71
Foëx, Gabriel, 6:78
Fog dispersal, 2:11–12
Folds, geologic, 3:394
Folk ideas, 1:206–207
Folkers, Karl August, 3:**41–45**
Folkman, Judah, 3:188
Fontana, Felice, 4:215
Fontéchevade skull, 5:298
Fontenelle, Bernard le Bouyer de, 3:352, 5:10
Food, artificial, 5:247
Food and Drug Administration (FDA), cloning, 1:400
Food chain, 5:322–323
For the Layman (Rufus of Ephesus), 6:291
For Those Who Have No Doctor to Hand (Rufus of Ephesus). *See For the Layman* (Rufus of Ephesus)

Forberger, G., 1:309
Forbes, Alexander, 1:16, 17
Forbes, Greg, 3:84, 85
Forbes, Stephen A., 7:37
Ford, Clellan S., 1:222
Ford, Edmund Brisco, 3:**45–49**
    colleagues of, 2:383
    evolution, 7:360–362
    on industrial melanism, 4:110
    students of, 7:377
Ford, George W., 7:102
Ford, Gerald, 6:102
Ford, James, 1:49
Forecasting, election outcomes, 1:8–9
Forecasting, weather. *See* Weather forecasting
Forel, August, 7:162
Föreläsningar i djurkemien (Berzelius), 1:267–268
Forestry, 4:267–270
Forests, 1:388
Forget-Me-Not (Ackermann), 4:231
Form and Causality in Early Development (Dalcq), 1:372
Formal Logic (Jeffrey), 4:35
Formal semantics. *See* Semantics
La formation du symbole chez l'enfant. See Play, Dreams,
    and Imitation (Piaget)
*Formation of Solid Particles and Condensation in
    Interstellar Space* (van de Hulst), 5:345
Formulas and Tables for Determinations of Parabolic Orbits
    (Strömgren), 6:541
Forster, Johann, 4:231
Forsythe, George Elmer, 3:**49–53**, 7:314
Forsythe, Sandra, 3:50, 51
Fortenbaugh, William, 1:104
Fortin, Nicolas, 4:215
FORTRAN, 3:360
    competition, 2:296
    development, 7:317
Fossey, Dian, 3:**53–57**, *55*, 7:236
The Fossil Evidence for Human Evolution (Clark),
    2:139–140
Les fossiles (Piveteau), 6:108
Fossils
    ammonites, 7:62, 201–202
    Australopithecus, 7:235–236
    biostratigraphy, 6:351–355
    bivalve mollusks, 5:265, 266
    cephalopods, 7:15–17
    excavation methods, 2:124–125
    extinction, 2:223–224
    fishes, 6:31
    geological strata dating, 1:415–416
    hominid
        Argentian, 4:236–237
        China, 6:57–60

    dating techniques, 5:296–299
    evolution, 5:354–355
    Neanderthal, 3:154, 155–156
    paleoanthropology, 7:115–117
    Pithecanthropus, 7:184–188, *185, 186*
    progressive evolution, 5:368
    Sinanthropus, 7:249–253
    homonid
        Olduvai Gorge (Tanzania), 4:222–223
    human evolution, 2:139–140
    insect, 3:281–282
    missing link, 2:313–316
    radiation, 2:283
    unity of plan, 3:116
    vertebrate, 5:366–368, 6:107–108
    See also Anthropology; *Australopithecus*
Fossils and the History of Life (Simpson), 6:455
Foster, George Carey, 3:**57–59**, *58*
Foucault, Michel, 3:75
Foundation of Morals (Whewell), 7:282
*Foundations of a Positive Theory of Choice Involving Risk
    and a Criticism of the Postulates and Axioms of the
    American School* (Allais), 6:350
Foundations of Algebraic Topology (Eilenberg), 2:361,
    4:145
The Foundations of Causal Decision Theory (Joyce),
    6:349–350
The Foundations of Ethology (Lorenz), 4:344
The Foundations of Geometry (Hilbert). *See Grundlagen
    der geometrie* (Hilbert)
The Foundations of Measurement (Krantz et al.), 7:92
Foundations of Modern Analysis (Dieudonné), 2:292
The Foundations of Statistics (Savage), 6:350
Founder-flush speciation, 2:62–63
Four humors. *See* Humorism
Four whys. *See* Tinbergen's four whys
Fourcroy, Antoine-François de, 1:264, 2:320
Fourier series
    3-D, 2:9
    development, 7:414–415
Fourier synthesis, 1:282, 283, 284, 3:241
Fowler, Alfred, 2:307
Fowler, Ernst Sondheimer, 7:319, 321
Fowler, L. R., 3:171
Fowler, Ralph Howard
    colleagues of, 3:253, 254
    influence of, 5:111
    statistical mechanics, 3:87
    students of, 1:270, 5:72, 6:499
    white dwarf configuration, 2:88–89
Fowler, Robert D., 6:401
Fowler, William A., 3:**59–62**, *60*, 390–391
    accelerators, 4:210
    formation of elements in stars, 1:157

Fowler, William A., *continued*
    light nuceli, 4:211
    Nobel Prize, 3:175
    solar neutrinos, 1:158–159
    stellar energy, 1:277
    students of, 3:176
Fox, David, 1:323
Fox, Leslie, 6:535
Fox, Thomas, 3:39, 40
Foxon, George Eric Howard, 6:30
Fractals, 6:240
Fractured forms, 6:294
Fraenkel-Conrat, Heinz, 3:364
Fragments biographiques (Geoffroy Saint-Hilaire,
    Étienne), 3:119
Frameworks for Dating Fossil Man (Oakley), 5:299
Framing effects, 7:94–95
The Framing of Decisions and the Psychology of Choice
    (Tversky and Kahneman), 7:94, 95
France
    Bourbaki pseudonym, 1:363–364
    feminist movement, 6:288
    organic chemistry, 7:371–372
    physical anthropology, 7:113, 117
    Vertebrate paleontology, 6:106–108
La France et la guerre (Baldwin), 1:170
Francesca, Piero Della. *See* Piero della Francesca
Francis, J. G. F., 7:317
Francium, 1:163
Franck, James, 1:57, 291, 2:165, 3:78
    acquaintances of, 7:294
    colleagues of, 2:378
Franck, Sebastian, 6:15
Frank, Albert Bernhard, 6:389
Frank, Ilia Mikhailovich, 2:109, 110
Frank, Lawrence K., 4:281
Frank-Kamenestkii, David Al'bertovich, 7:392
Frankland, Edward, 3:**62–65**, *64*, 7:309
    influence of, 4:99
    Kolbe-Frankland theory, 4:149
Franklin, Benjamin
    electricity, 7:167–168, 169
    theory of one electric fluidum, 1:202–203
Franklin, Rosalind Elsie, 2:208, 3:**65–69**, *67*
    DNA crystallography, 7:299–300
    DNA structure, 6:40
    molecular structure, 6:83
Franssila, Matti, 6:553
Franz, Shepherd Ivory, 1:357
Franz, Walter, 4:*103*
Franzoni, Tullio, 2:259
Fraser, Allan Cameron, 1:225
Fraser, Craig G., 3:236
Fraudulent research. *See* Research misconduct

Fraunhofer, Joseph von, 1:295
Fraunhofer lines, 7:105
Fréchet, Maurice, 5:178
Fredericq, Henri, 2:143
Frederik II, King of Denmark, 1:381, 382
Free discontinuity problems, 2:259–260
Free radicals
    in disease, 6:571
    molecular structure, 3:301
    polymerization, 1:189, *192*, 192–193, *193, 194*
    synthetic chemistry, 1:199
Free Research versus Design Research (Richter), 6:246
Freedman, David, 2:257
Freedom and the Control of Men (Skinner), 6:464
Freerider problem, 5:336–337
Frege, Friedrich Ludwig Gottlob. *See* Frege, Gottlob
Frege, Gottlob, 2:310, 3:**69–73**, 307
Frei Montalva, Eduardo, 1:132
Freidlina, Rachel H., 5:247
Fremlin, John H., 6:532
French, Bruce, 6:394, 7:266
French, Roger, 6:118
Frenkel, Yakov Ilyich, 2:108
    acquaintances of, 5:128
    collectivized particles, 1:318
    condensation, 6:413
    crystal models, 1:311
    quantum mechanics, 6:63
Fresenius, Carl Remigius, 4:312, 6:88
Fresh-Water Fishes of Great Britain (Lee), 4:231
Fresnel, Augustin-Jean, 2:78, 3:236
Freud: A Life for Our Time (Gay), 3:76
Freud, Anna, 2:407
Freud: Biologist of the Mind (Sulloway), 3:75
Freud, Sigmund, 3:**73–77**, *74*
    ego psychology, 2:407
    influence of, 1:49, 4:62–64, 5:90, 7:8
    influences on, 4:27, 28
    learned behavior and, 5:146, 147–148
    meeting with Gordon Allport, 1:50
    personality development, 2:409–410
    psychoanalysis, 7:5–6, 7, 162
    social change, 2:135
Freud: The Mind of the Moralist (Rieff), 3:76
Freud and His Followers (Roazen), 3:73
Freudenberg, Karl, 7:337
Freudenthal, Gad, 6:7
Freudenthal, Hans, 1:12, 2:356, 357, 3:309
Freundlich, Erwin Finlay, 7:105
Frey, Kurt, 1:10
Freyd, Peter, 2:360
Friday, Jim, 6:142
Friedan, Betty, 5:46
Friedel, Charles, 2:194, 195

Friedell, Hymer, 1:164
Friedel's law, 1:284
Friedman, Herbert, 3:**77–82**
Friedmann, Alexander Alexsandrovich, 2:108, 369, 3:274–275, 5:73
Friedmann, Robert Marc, 5:221
Friedrich, Walter, 1:280
Friedrich Wilhelm I, 6:504
Friedrichs, Kurt O., 6:170
Fries, Jakob Friedrich, 3:69, 6:357–358
Fries, Karl, 7:337
Frisch, Karl von, 4:147
    animal behavior, 1:151
    Griffin, Donald Redfield, 3:179
    Nobel Prize, 7:55
    students of, 3:260
    visual perception in honeybees, 3:295
Frisch, Otto Robert, 2:205, 3:211, 6:64
Frobenius, Georg Ferdinand, 3:12, 241, 4:310
Frobenius groups, 3:12–13
Frobenius-Weyl character theory, 3:242
Frogs
    cloning, 1:398–399
    developmental genetics, 1:397
    nervous system, 3:218
Fröhlich, Herbert, 1:181, 318
Frölicher, Alfred, 4:146
From, Harry, 5:141
From Anxiety to Ecstasy (Janet). *See De l'angoisse à l'extase* (Janet)
From Being to Becoming (Prigogine), 6:167
From Chance to Purpose: An Appraisal of External Human Fertilization (Grobstein), 3:189
From Head to Foot (Novikoff), 5:284–285
Fromageot, Claude, 4:227
Fromhertz, Konrad, 5:251
Frontal lobes, 3:145–148
Fronts (weather), 1:247–248
Frost, Robert, 6:460
Fruit flies. *See Drosophila*
Frustration and Aggression (Miller), 5:146
Fruton, Joseph S., 4:312
Fuchs, Klaus
    atomic bombs, 6:64–65
    colleagues of, 7:321
    internment, 6:80
Fuchs, Lazarus, 6:121
Fuchsian groups, 1:23
Fuel systems, 2:12
Fuel technology, 7:137–138
Fujioka, Yoshio, 5:169
Fujita, Ted. *See* Fujita, Theodore
Fujita, Tetsuya. *See* Fujita, Theodore
Fujita, Theodore, 3:**82–85**, *84*

Fukiwhara effect, 3:264
Fukui, Ken'ichi, 3:**85–89**
Fullam, Ernest, 2:145, 6:144
Fuller, George Damon, 2:189
Fuller, Steve, 5:100
Fullerenes, 6:473–474
Fullerton, George S., 2:73
Fulton, John Farquhar, 2:329
Function and Evolution in Behavior (Baerends), 1:151
Functional anatomy, 7:113–114
Functions (mathematics)
    analytical expressions, 2:421–422
    complex analytic
        differential calculus, 2:423–424
        integrals, 2:76
        partial differential equations, 1:260–263
    computable, 6:266
    elliptic, 1:5, 6
        operators, 4:188
        partial differential equations, 2:258–259
    Green's, 6:395
    Möbius, 6:285–286
    recursive, 6:266
Fundamenta Botanica (Linnaeus), 4:315
Fundamental Concepts of Programming Languages (Strachey), 6:535
Fundamental Equations of Physics (Hilbert), 3:308
Fundamentals of chemistry (Mizushima). *See Kagaku Honron* (Mizushima)
Fundamentals of Ecology (Odum), 1:48, 2:390, 5:316, 317, 318–319, 322
Fundamentals of the theory of phylogenetic systematics (Hennig). *See Grundzüge einer Theorie der Phylogenetischen Systematik* (Hennig)
Fungi, 6:389
Die funktionelle Organisation des vegetativen Nervensystems (Hess), 3:305
Fürbringer, Max, 2:312
Furman, Philip, 2:376
Furrer, Ernst, 1:387
Furry, Wendell, 6:170, 7:264
Furshpan, Ed, 2:331
Fuses
    radio proximity, 7:119–120
    variable time, 7:120
Fusion
    vs. fission, 7:21
    hydrogen bombs, 6:501–502, 7:21–24
    of lighter particles into heavier particles, 1:428
    magnetic traps, 1:426
    nuclear energy, 6:384–385
    USSR, 6:325
Fuson, Reynold C., 6:322

The Future of Fundamental Physics (Schwinger), 6:396
Fye, Paul, 6:530–531

G

G-stack project, 5:304
Gabriel, Peter, 5:4
GAC (General Advisory Committee)
    hydrogen bombs, 7:23
    members of, 6:196
GAD (geocentric axial dipole), 3:375, 376–377
Gaddum, John H., 7:178
GAF (General Aniline and Film Corporation), 6:232
Gaffron, Mercedes, 3:297
Gagarin, Yuri, 4:104
Gagnan, France, 2:287
Gaitskell, Hugh, 1:293
Gaius Plinius Secundus. *See* Pliny the Elder
Gajdusek, D. Carleton, 1:80
The Galactic Novae (Payne-Gaposchkin), 6:51
The Galactic System as a Spiral Nebula (Oort et al.),
    5:346, 7:129
Galactose metabolism, 4:73
Galaxies
    brightness, 1:65–66
    elliptical, 6:387
    evolution, 7:58–59, 60
    formation, 6:398–399
    radio astronomy and, 1:333, 5:345
    spectral lines, 7:126–131
    stars, 6:51
    structure of, 5:342–343
    telescopes, 7:271–272
    See also Milky Way galaxy
Galaxies and the Universe (Oort), 5:346
Galdikas, Biruté, 3:53
Gale, David, 7:80–81
Gale, Ernest F., 6:520
Galen, 3:**91–96**, *93*
    ancient medicine, 6:290, 291
    brain theory, 2:123
    commentaries on, 5:8
    diagnostics and pathology in medicine, 1:107
    dissection practice, 1:104
    influence of, 3:322–323, 324
    influences on, 2:84, 302
    medical authority of, 2:37
    medieval medicine, 6:212
    publication of works, 4:264
    Renaissance medicine, 5:280, 6:550, 552
    theoretical medicine, 3:325
Galênos. *See* Galen
Galilean Studies (Koyré), 4:172
Galilei, Galileo, 3:**96–103**, *3:99*, 4:51
    Aristotelianism, 7:389

Copernicanism, 2:177
cosmology, 3:112
criticisms of, 2:274
education of, 1:361
elements, 1:362
gravity, 2:2
heliocentrism, 2:20–21
influence of, 4:131–132, 7:382
mechanical problems, 1:167
motion, 1:442, 3:97
    animal, 1:349
    planetary, 1:139
    relativity of, 1:424
telescopes, 2:150
tides, 2:320
Galileo and His Sources (Wallace), 2:150
Galileo Courtier (Biagioli), 3:100–101
Galileo Galilei's Notes on Motion (Galilei), 3:97
Galileo's Early Notebooks (Galilei), 3:97
Galison, Peter, 1:300–301
Gall, Franz, 6:73
The Gall Wasp Genus (Kinsey), 4:124
Gall wasps, 4:124
Gallager, Robert G., 6:429
Galley Hill remains, 5:297
Galois, Evariste, 1:6, 4:310
Galois cohomology, 1:345
Galois theory, 5:3
Galton, Francis, 1:211, 2:431, 6:53, 54
Galvani, Luigi, 7:170, 171–172
Galvanometers, string, 1:17
Gambling
    Allais's paradox, 6:350
    information theory, 6:429
Game Management (Leopold), 4:269, 270
The Game of Logic (Dodgson), 2:311
Game theory
    analysis of conventions, 4:284
    cooperative games, 3:249–250
    development of, 5:187
    economics and, 5:187–188, 7:150
    linear programming, 7:80
    Nash equilibrium, 5:227–228
    organizational theory, 5:254
    political science, 6:254–255
    rational bargaining, 5:225–227
    rational choice theory, 3:231–232
    utilitarianism, 3:247, 248–249
Games
    cooperative, 3:248, 249–250, 251
    of incomplete information, 3:250–251
    non-zero-sum, 3:231–232
    noncooperative, 3:250–251, 5:227
    signaling, 7:150

Tit for Tat, 3:232

Games with Incomplete Information Played by Bayesian Players (Harsanyi), 3:250

Games with Randomly Disturbed Payoffs: A New Rationale for Mixed Strategy Equilibrium Points (Harsanyi), 3:251

Gamkrelidze, Revaz V., 6:128

Gamma-convergence, 2:259

Gamma rays
  absorption
    quantum electrodynamics, 7:398–399
    uranium fission, 2:166
  cancer treatment, 1:298
  radiation
    Cherenkov, 2:108–109
    energy measurement, 4:209

Gamow, George, 2:108, 166, 209, 4:82, 7:393
  colleagues of, 3:389, 7:21
  stellar structure, 6:385
  Strömgren, Bengt Georg Daniel, 6:543
  thermal radiation, 2:281
  Washington Conferences on Theoretical Physics, 1:271

Gandelman, G. M., 7:392

Gandhi, Mohandas, 2:410–411, 6:484

Gandhi's Truth (Erikson), 2:406, 410–411

Gangoiti, Lorenzo, 7:155

Ganshi, Mahatma. *See* Gandhi, Mohandas

Gantt, W. H., 5:150

GAP (glyceraldehyde-3-phosphate), 6:198

Gap junctions, 1:437

Gaposchkin, Sergei I., 6:51

Garbasso, Antonio, 5:301, 302

Garfield, Eugene, 6:163

Garn, Stanley, 2:174

GARP (Global Atmospheric Research Program), 6:471–472, 555, 556–557

Garrels, Robert, 4:166

Garrett, Henry, 2:129, 130

Garrod, Dorothy Annie Elizabeth, 3:**103–108,** *3:105*

Gärtner, Carl Friedrich, 5:99

Garzoni, Leonardo S.J., 3:**108–109**

Gas and Smoke in Interstellar Space (Van de Hulst), 7:127

Gas chromatography
  development of, 5:40
  experimental and theoretical, 2:206

Gas reserves, 3:397–398

Gases
  combustion and detonation, 6:411, 415
  degeneracy, 2:378
  dense, 7:103
  greenhouse, 1:113
  ideal, 1:318
  interstellar, 6:543–544

liquefacation, 4:83–84
  nerve, 4:169
  noble, 3:402
  physics, 1:202–203
  quantum, 1:412
  quantum mechanics, 6:112

Gasoline, 3:381–383

Gasometry, 1:439–440

Gassend, Pierre. *See* Gassendi, Pierre

Gassendi, Pierre, 3:**109–114,** *3:111,* 4:132

Gasser, Achilles Pirmin, 6:551

Gasser, Herbert Spencer, 3:329, 6:361

Gastrulation
  blastomeres, 3:367, *367*
  process, 3:350

Gati, Itamar, 7:92

Gatterman, Ludwig, 7:349

Gatti, Attilio, 2:12

Gatto, Raul, 7:70

Gauge theory, 6:337, 339–340

Gaule, Justus, 3:303

Gaunt, John A., 6:542

Gaupp, Ernst, 7:259

Gaurico, Luca, 1:309

Gaus, Wilhelm, 5:29

Gause, George F., 3:414, 415

Gauss, Carl Friedrich, 1:6, 2:117
  Beltrami coefficients, 1:262
  Gauss-Bonnet theorem, 7:256
  influences on, 3:246, 6:251
  surface theory, 3:191

Gauss-Bonnet theorem, 7:256

Gay, Peter, 3:76

Gay-Lussac, Joseph Louis, 4:206
  Annales de chimie, 1:264
  chlorine, 1:265
  criticisms of, 5:166

Gayon, Jean, 2:246

Gaza, Theodorus, 1:104

GCMs (general circulation models), 6:342, 344, 471, 472

GDNA (Gesellschaft Deutscher Naturforscher und Ärzte), 5:333

Gears from the Greeks (Price), 6:163

Geber Ibn Hayyān. *See* Jābir Ibn Ḥayyān

Gebhard, Paul, 4:124, 125, 129

Gébotanique Méditerranéenne et Alpine (SIGMA), 1:388

Gedanken eines Biologen (Abderhalden), 1:4

Geddes, Patrick, 1:388

Gee, Geoffrey, 3:39

Gegenbaur, Carl, 2:312, 3:209

Gehennical Fire (Newman), 6:512

Geiger, Hans Johannes Wilhelm, 5:301

Geiger, Rudolf, 4:155
Geiger counters. *See* Geiger-Müller counters
Geiger-Müller counters
    China, 7:400
    circuits, 6:280, 282
    construction of, 4:295
    cosmic rays, 5:301, 302, *302*
Geiser, Carl Friedrich. *See* Geiser, Karl Friedrich
Geiser, Karl Friedrich, 3:191
Geison, Gerald, 6:21, 26, 27
Gel electrophoresis, 3:47–48
Gel'fand, Israel M., 3:241, 242, 4:187–188, 7:415
Gell-Mann, Murray, 1:75
    conservation of vector current, 7:367
    current algebra, 1:238
    double beta decay, 6:171
    Fermi interaction, 3:24
    hadrons, 3:194
Gellner, Ernest, 3:76
Geloof en Natuurwetenschap (Van de Hulst), 7:131
Gender identity, 7:27–28
Genera Plantarum (Linnaeus), 4:314
General Advisory Committee (GAC)
    hydrogen bombs, 7:23
    members of, 6:196
General Aniline and Film Corporation (GAF), 6:232
General Chemistry (Pauling), 2:200, 6:43
General circulation models (GCMs)
    atmospheric science, 6:342
    climate change, 6:344
    development, 6:471
    Smagorinsky, Joseph, 6:472
General Cytology (Cowdry), 2:182–183
General Geology (Pannekoek). *See Algemene Geologie*
  (Pannekoek)
General Meteorology (Byers), 1:469
General natural history for all social classes (Oken). *See*
  Allgemeine Naturgeschichte für alle Stände (Oken)
General Problem Solver (GPS), 5:257, 258
General Purpose macrogenerator (GPM), 6:534
General relativity
    astrophysics, 1:340, 342
    covariant, 3:307–308
    dynamic, 1:425
    influential figures, 1:425, 2:338–339, 367, 6:34,
      122, 397, 399
    Mach's principle, 6:398
    quarks, 3:194
    stellar dynamics, 3:274–275
General Relativity and Cosmology (McVittie), 5:80, 84
General selection theory, 2:23
A General Statement on the Mining Industry of China
  (Ding Wenjiang), 2:299

The General Theory of Employment, Interest, and Money
  (Keynes), 4:112
A General Theory of Equilibrium Selection in Games
  (Harsanyi and Selton), 3:251
General View of the Agriculture and Minerals of Derbyshire
  (Farey), 3:7
General Virology (Luria), 4:358
General Zoology (Bronn). *See Allgemeine Zoologie* (Bronn)
Generalized Foreign Politics (Richardson), 6:240
Generation, spontaneous
    Darwinism and, 1:208–210
    metabolism, 3:363
Generators
    radioisotope thermoelectric, 7:124
    shock, 5:138, *138*
Generelle Morphologie (Haeckel), 3:207, 208, 431
Genes
    homeobox, 1:210
    maternal, 1:399–400
    origin of life, 3:363–364
    tumor suppressor, 6:320
Genetic Basis of Selection (Lerner), 4:275
Genetic code
    chemical analysis, 1:373–375
    RNA synthesis and, 5:309–310
    transfer RNA, 3:340
    wobble hypothesis, 3:342
Genetic engineering
    DNA synthesis, 6:478–482
    microbial synthesis and, 5:364
Genetic Homeostasis (Lerner), 4:274, 276
Genetic mutations. *See* Mutations
Genetic Theory of Reality, Being the Outcome of Genetic
  Logic as Issuing in the Aesthetic Theory of Reality
  (Baldwin), 1:169–170
The Genetical Evolution of Social Behaviour (Hamilton),
  3:227, 229, 230
The Genetical Theory of Natural Selection (Fisher), 2:18,
  3:31, 225
Genetically modified animals. *See* Transgenic animals
Genetics
    bacterial
        controlling elements in, 5:71
        fluctuation test, 4:356–357
    behavior
        in competition, 4:277
        importance of, 4:203–204
    biochemistry, 1:228, 7:12–15
    canalization, 7:205
    cancer, 6:319–320
    chemical analysis, 1:373–2576
    classical, 6:493–494
    code, 2:209–210
    cytology, 2:68–70

developmental
> limb growth, 3:221–222
> pathoclisis, 7:163
> ploidy, 1:397–398

DNA, RNA, and protein relationships, 1:*373, 374*

ecological
> diversity and population growth, 3:45–49
> industrial melanism, 4:109–110

embryology and, 1:210–213, 5:185

evolutionary
> biostratigraphy, 6:353
> birds, 2:59–61
> epigenetics, 7:203–205
> eugenics, 3:32
> germplasm theory, 7:260–261
> of protozoa, 4:44–45

gender identity, 7:28–29

history, 5:184–185

homeostasis, 4:274–277

intelligence, 7:26, 27, 29

Mendelian
> botany, 7:1–2, 189–191, *191*
> Darwinism and, 2:246
> diversity and population growth, 3:45–47
> founding of, 5:101–103
> influence of, 5:97
> physiological, 2:399–400, 7:358–360
> plant genetics, 6:317–319
> protozoa, 4:45
> rediscovery, 7:189
> segregation, 1:211–212
> sickle-cell anemia, 5:242
> theoretical population genetics, 3:29

microbial, 6:492–494

molecular
> metabolic reactions, 1:225–229
> mutations, 4:56
> *Neurospora,* 1:*226*
> neutral theory, 4:114–116
> phage research, 2:269–270
> protein production, 1:224

physiological
> *Drosophila,* 2:399–400
> evolution, 7:357–360
> Wright, Sewell, 7:*358*

plants
> chloroplasts, 6:316–319
> cytogenetics, 6:514–515
> evolution, 6:513
> homeostasis, 4:275–276
> hybridization, 1:211–212, 5:98–100
> maize, 5:68–71

polymorphism, 3:47
> natural selection, 3:48

neutral theory, 4:117

population
> adaptation, 7:*361*
> altruism, 3:226–229
> biological evolution and, 5:62
> diffusion equation approximations, 4:115
> diversity, 3:45–47
> evolution and, 5:63–64, 243–244
> homeostasis, 4:275–277
> mathematical, 7:356–363, *359, 360*
> theoretical, 3:29

radiation effects, 5:242–243

random drift
> neutral theory, 4:116
> population genetics, 3:29–30

shifting-balance theory, 7:358–360, *359, 360*

ultracentrifuge use, 1:464

variance
> assimilation, 7:205
> dominance, 3:30–31
> gel electrophoresis, 3:47–48

See also Natural selection

Genetics and the Origin of Species (Dobzhansky), 2:59, 4:114, 7:362

Genetics Epistemology (Piaget), 6:94

Genetics for Medical Students (Ford), 3:47

Genetics in the U.S.S.R (Lerner), 4:277

Genetics of Colonizing Species (Stebbins and Baker), 6:515

Genetics of Natural Populations (Dobzhansky), 7:362

Genotype, thrifty, 5:243–244

Gentner, Wolfgang, 5:128

Geocentric axial dipole (GAD), 3:375, 376–377

Geochemistry
> Ringwood, Alfred Edward, 6:258–261
> solar system, 4:179–180
> volcanology, 6:263
> *See also* Biogeochemistry

Geodesy
> Arctic expedition, 5:57, *57*
> earth density, 1:25
> earth's upper mantle, 4:234–235
> land surveying, 1:99
> lectures on, 4:10–11
> U.S. Geographical Survey, 4:121–122

Geodynamics, 4:38, 39

Geoffroy, Étienne-François, 3:353

Geoffroy Saint-Hilaire, Étienne, 3:*115,* **115–117,** 133
> affinity tables, 2:218
> embranchment theory, 2:222
> evolution, 6:109
> zoology, 2:226

Geoffroy Saint-Hilaire, Isidore, 3:**117–120**

Geographie des Indischen und Stillen Ozeans (Schott), 6:372

Geography
  ancient, 5:27
  Australian, 5:207
  China, 7:403
  climatology, 7:38–40
  ecology, 2:235–236
  folk ideas, 1:206–207
  Mercator Atlas, 3:354–356
  ornithology and, 5:61
  physical, 6:348–349
  plant, 2:186–188, 235–236, 7:3–4
  politics and, 5:37
  Roman empire, 6:118–119
  Siberia, 4:160–161
Geography (Ptolemy), 5:27
Geography of the Indian and Pacific Oceans (Schott). *See*
  Geographie des Indischen und Stillen Ozeans (Schott)
Geologic time, 6:468, *468*
Geological Map of China (Huang Jiqing), 3:393
Geological Map of Tsinling (Huang Jiqing), 3:393
Geological Reports of Dr. V. K. Ting (Huang Jiqing), 2:300
Geological Survey News. See Vijesti geoloskog povjerenstva
A Geologist's View of Cape Cod (Strahler), 6:538
Geology
  Alpine, 6:346–349
  China, 2:299–300, 7:383–384, 385–386
  classification systems, 1:93–95
  craters, 6:443–445
  evolution, 2:243, 4:189, 251
  expeditions, 5:181–182
  field research, 5:166, 265, 266–267
  fluid dynamics, 3:395–396
  geochronology, 2:190
  geomorphology, 6:536–539
  Germany, 6:248–250
  Huttonian, 2:85
  India, 7:207–209
  invertebrate paleontology, 3:315–319
  marine, 2:286–288, 5:96–97
  mathematical, 4:164
  mineralogy, 3:6–7, 7:222
  Pacific atolls, 4:185–187
  paleoanthropology, 6:57
  paleontology, 6:453
  petroleum instrumentation, 7:270–271
  petrology, 2:253–254
  plant, 2:186–188
  plate tectonics, 1:69–70, 2:38–42, 3:392–394
  reversals, 2:192–193
  rock cycle, 3:419–420
  sedimentology, 7:140–143
  stratigraphy, 1:415–416, 6:467–469, *468*
  structural, 5:37
  subsurface, 4:132
    techniques of, 4:10–11
  Teichert, Curt, 7:15–17
  textbooks on, 4:224–225
  time, 3:*419*, 419–420
  U.S., 6:149–152
  U.S. Geological Survey, 4:120–123
  USSR, 6:430–432
  See also Astrogeology
Geology of India for Students (Wadia), 7:207
Geology of Queensland (Hill), 3:317
Geology of Tsinlingshan and Szechuan (Huang Jiqing),
  3:393
Geomagnetic reversals, 3:375–377
Geomagnetism, 6:298–301, 7:118–120, 121–122
Geometria (Newton), 5:269
Geometria speculativa (Bradwardine), 1:379
Geometry
  algebraic
    complex function theory, 4:144–146
    curvature, 2:114–115
    finite groups, 3:152–154
    group theory, 3:153
    Lie groups, 2:119–120, 4:309
    scheme theory, 2:292
    topology, 4:144–146
  analytic, 2:421, 6:54
  artithmetic, 3:308–309
  astronomy, 3:245–246, 6:185
  axiomatics, 3:71
  Beltrami equation, 1:262
  category theory, 5:4–5
  circles, 6:186
  differential
    algebraic topology, 2:112–115
    holonomy groups, 4:300–301
    Kleinian groups, 1:23
    topology and, 5:194–195
    value distribution theory, 1:22
  equations, 1:19–21
  Euclidean
    combinatorial techniques, 1:87–89
    Gauss-Bonnet theorem, 2:113–114
    heptagon, 1:*88*
    hyperbolic geometry and, 6:121–122
    influence of, 3:405
    space, 7:291–292
    tangent circles, 1:*89*
    theory of knowledge, 3:408
    translations, 1:13, 14
  Gauss-Bonnet theorem, 2:113–114
  logic, 1:349
  mechanics, 3:292–293
  perspective, 5:176–177, *177*
  physics relationship

electromagnetic effects, 2:370
relativity, 7:277
research, 3:327–328
Riemann surface theory, 7:254–255
spherical, 1:14, 2:113, 4:4–5
symbolic mathematics *vs.,* 5:269
vision, 1:146
Geomorphic History of the Ozarks of Missouri (Bretz), 1:396
Geomorphic Terminology and Classification of Land Masses (Strahler), 6:537
Geomorphology
classification systems, 1:93
geology, 6:536–539
quantitative, 3:371–372
seafloor, 2:288
Siberia, 4:160–161
Geophysical Fluid Dynamics Laboratory (GFDL), 6:471
Geophysics
continental drift, 7:323–326
earthquake processes, 4:11
earthquakes, 1:30–33, 7:200
earth's age, 4:40–41
earth's upper mantle, 4:234–235
electromagnetic prospecting, 1:179
fluid dynamics, 3:395–399
geomagnetism, 5:48, 6:298–301, 7:118–120, 121–122
gravitational fields, 4:56
instrumentation, 7:270–271
Lehmann discontinuity, 4:233–235
magnetic fields, 3:375–377
methane, 3:139–140
Moon, 3:138
North American, 2:191
oceanography, 2:265–266
petroleum, 3:396–398
petrology, 2:253–254
radio waves, 1:390–391
thermal history of earth, 4:39
U.S. government programs in, 4:197–198
Geophysics and Warfare (Landsberg), 4:198
George C. Marshall Space Flight Center (MSFC), 7:175–176
George III, King of England, 3:290
George of Trebizond, 6:216, 217
George the Synkellos, 7:406
Georgi, Howard, 3:193
Geostrophy, quasi, 6:559
Geotectonic Map of China (Huang Jiqing), 3:393, 394
Geotectonics
polycyclic theory, 3:394
USSR, 6:430–431
Gerasimovich, Boris, 1:67

Gerhardt, Charles Frédéric, 2:323, 324, 7:371
Gerlach, Hans, 5:362, 6:160
Germ cells, 7:190, 259–260
Germ theory, 1:209
German Psychology of To-day (Robot), 1:169
Germany
astronomy, 7:332–333
biochemistry, 5:250–253
computer science, 7:409–413
geology, 6:248–250
medicine, 6:504–505
oceanography, 6:370–373
science education, 7:159–160
science in, 5:332–333
sedimentology, 6:248, 249
Virchow, Rudolf Carl, 7:158
See also National Socialism (Germany); World War II
Germany (de Staël), 7:282
Germer, Lester H., 1:270, 2:165
Germplasm theory, 7:259–261
Gernsback, Hugo, 5:112
Gerontology, 2:184–185
Gershtein, Simon Solomonovich, 7:392
Gerstner, Patsy A., 3:420
Die gesammelten Werke der Mathematiker und Physiker der Familie Bernoulli (Bernoulli), 1:254, 256
Der gescheiterte Aufstand (Jordan), 4:57
Geschichte des arabischen Schrifttums (Sezgin), 4:19
Geschwind, Norman, 6:362
Gesellschaft Deutscher Naturforscher und Ärzte (GDNA), 5:333
Das Gesetz der Serie (Kammerer), 4:79
Gessner, Konrad, 6:551
Gestalt theory
field effects, 6:496
nervous system, 3:269
visual perception, 3:294, 295
Getting, Ivan, 5:52
Geus, John, 1:313
Gezelius, Göran, 3:370
GFDL (Geophysical Fluid Dynamics Laboratory), 6:471
Ghetaldi, Marino, 1:348
Ghirardi, GianCarlo, 1:241
Ghiselin, Michael, 3:160
Giacconi, Riccardo, 3:80, 143, 6:283
Gibbs, Josiah Willard, 1:280, 4:156
Gibbs, Sharon, 6:163
Gibbs free energy, 7:136
Gibbs phase rule, 4:156–157
Gibelin, Jacques, 6:98
Gibney, Robert, 1:180
Gibraltar, excavations, 3:104
Gibson, David, 3:171
Gibson, Eleanor Jack, 3:**120–125,** 126, 127–128

Gibson, George Ernest, 6:401–402
Gibson, James Jerome, 3:120–121, 122, **125–130**
Gibson, Ralph, 7:121
Gibson, Thomas, 5:86
Gif system, 1:200
Giffard, John, 6:533
Giftedness, 7:26–27
Gilbert, Grove Karl, 6:149, 151
    craters, 6:443
    qualitative geomorphology, 3:374
Gilbert, Joseph Henry, 4:25
Gilbert, William, 2:1, 4:132
Gilchrist, Lachlan, 7:323
Gildenmeister, Martin, 4:86
Gill, Robert, 2:415
Gill, Stanley, 6:534
Gillam, Shirley, 6:480
Gilles, Jean-Claude, 2:163
Gillespie, Neal, 2:246
Gilliland, Edwin R., 4:290, 291
Gillispie, Charles, 4:191
Gilman, Henry, 7:338
Gilman, Robert, 6:398
Gilon, Chaim, 1:253
Gilson, Ralph, 7:66
Gingerich, Owen, 1:382–383, 4:106
Ginzburg, Anna I., 3:10, 11
Ginzburg, Vitaly Lazarevich, 6:325, 433, 434
Giorgi, Ennio de. *See* de Giorgi, Ennio
Giumlia-Mair, Alessandra, 7:407
Giusti, Enrico, 2:258
Glaciers, ice cores, 5:326, 327–330, *329*
Glaciology
    continental drift, 7:247–248
    earth's heat budget, 2:12
    sediment, 1:69–70
Gladstone, William Ewart, 5:366
Glansdorff, Paul, 6:165
Glaser, Donald, 1:57, 75
Glashow, Sheldon
    electromagnetism, 3:193, 6:335, 340
    electroweak theory, 6:396
Glass, 2:254
Glauber's salt, 7:396
Gleason, Andrew, 1:239
Gleason, Henry Allen, 1:387, 2:213–214
Gleditsch, Ellen, 1:301
Glennan, T. Keith, 5:261
Gliboff, Sander, 5:99, 103
Gliomas, 1:407
Gliozzi, Mario, 7:166
Global Atmospheric Research Program (GARP),
    6:471–472, 555, 556–557
Global carbon cycle, 5:326, 328

Global Positioning System, 2:369
Global warming, 4:91–95
    artificial carbon dioxide, 2:10–11, 12–13
    China, 7:405
    greenhouse gases, 1:113
Globular clusters, 3:274
Gloriosi, Giovanni Camillo, 1:348
Glowinski, Roland, 4:320
Glozel affair, 3:104
Gluckstern, Robert L., 1:392
Glucose
    fermentation, 7:347–348
    synthesis of, 4:254–255
Glueck, Bernard, 5:91
Glyceraldehyde-3-phosphate (GAP), 6:198
Glycerol, 5:252
Glycogen, 4:255–257, 5:232
Glycolysis
    adenosine triphosphate, 6:197, 198
    biochemical studies, 5:251–252
    muscles, 4:325, 5:232, 306
    oxidative phosphorylation, 4:72
    reversal, 2:16
Gmelin database, 1:215
Gnaphaeus, Gulielmus, 6:551
Gnosticism, 7:407
God
    atheism and, 3:131
    atomic theory and, 1:205
    in creation, 6:15–16
    evolution and, 4:225
    geology and, 7:280–281
    human knowledge and, 5:6–7
    metaphysics, 2:412–413
Godart, Odon, 6:560
Goddard, Henry H., 7:25
Gödel, Kurt Friedrich, 3:**130–132,** *3:131*
    colleagues of, 7:277
    infinite numbers, 2:30
    influence of, 3:309
    influences on, 4:35
    intuitionistic mathematics, 4:151
    theory of language, 2:44–45
Godet, Paul, 6:91
Godlewski, Emilie, 1:373
Godwin, Harry, 7:6, 8
Godwin, William, 5:13
Goebel, Karl Immanuel Eberhard Ritter von, 2:155
Goedart, Johann, 5:120
Goedel, Kurt, 6:265
Goeppert-Mayer, Maria, 2:379, 6:170
Goering, Hermann, 7:236
Goethe, Johann Wolfgang von, 3:**132–135,** *3:134,*
    3:387

developmental morphology, 6:358
  influences on, 4:65
  morphology, 6:356
  priority claim disputes, 5:332
Gold, alchemy, 5:273, 6:506, 512, 517
Gold, Thomas, 1:340, 341, 3:**135–141**, *3:136, 138*
  colleagues of, 3:389, 6:313
  influence of, 6:398, 399
  internment, 6:80
  steady state theory, 5:74
Goldammer, Kurt, 6:15
Goldberg, Leo, 3:**141–145,** 5:83, 116, 117, 6:500
  colleagues of, 6:501
  Harvard College Observatory, 7:289
Goldenberg-Oetker-Stiftung, 5:252
Goldfischer, Sidney, 5:283
Goldhaber, Gerson, 6:410
Goldhaber, Maurice, 6:63–64
Goldman, David, 4:88
Goldman-Hodgkin-Huxley equations, 4:86, 88–89
Goldman-Rakic, Patricia Shoer, 3:**145–148**
Goldschmidt, Richard Benedict, 4:68
  acquaintances of, 5:69
  biostratigraphy, 6:353
  colleagues of, 3:294
  genetics and development, 3:218
  influence of, 4:147, 276
  Schindewolf, Otto Heinrich, 6:354
Goldstein, Kurt, 2:342, 4:353, 354
Goldstine, Herman, 2:334–335
Goldstone, Geoffrey, 1:273
Goldwasser, Edwin, 7:330
Goldwater machine, 1:9
  See also Political psychology
Golgi, Camillo, 2:341
Golgi apparatus
  electron microscopy, 2:146–147
  function, 2:3
Golgi body, 5:281, 283
Golitsyn, Boris, 4:10
Golius, Jacobus, 3:165
Golub, Gene, 7:317
Gombrich, Ernst H., 6:313
Goodall, Alan, 3:56
Goodall, Jane, 3:53, 54, 7:236
Goodhart, Robert Stanley, 5:308
Gooding, David, 3:2
Goodman, Nelson Henry, 3:**148–152,** 4:284
Goodrich, Edwin Stephen, 2:382, 7:377
Goods, public
  allocation, 7:150
  freerider problem, 5:336–337
Goodspeed, Thomas Harper, 4:276
Goodwin, Astley John Hilary, 2:124, 4:221

Goodwin, Brian, 6:355
Gopfert, H., 2:330
Gorbachev, Mikhail, 6:328
Gordeladze, Sh. G., 1:65
Gordon, A. Hugh, 5:40
Gordon, Arnold L., 7:375
Gordon, Neil, 1:419
Goreau, Thomas, 3:411
Gorenstein, Daniel, 3:**152–154**
Gorenstein ring, 3:153
Gorgias (Plato), 5:338
Gorillas in the Mist (Fossey), 3:54, 55
Gorjanović-Kramberger, Dragutin, 3:**154–157**
Gorjanović-Kramberger, Karl. *See* Gorjanović-
  Kramberger, Dragutin
Gorlaeus, David, 3:**157–159**
Gorter, Cornelis Jacobus, 2:64–65
Gortler, Leon, 3:44
Gosling, Raymond, 2:208
  DNA crystallography, 3:66, 7:299, 300
  DNA research, 3:67
Gosset, William Sealey, 6:53
Gottfried, Kurt, 1:241, 7:267
Göttingen, Victor Meyer, 7:395
Göttingen school (mathematics), 6:251
Göttinger Universitätszeitung, 7:182
Göttingische Gelehrte Anzeigen (Haller), 3:216
Göttling, Johann Friedrich August, 7:170
Götz, Paul, 2:308
Goudsmit, Samuel Abraham, 1:133, 7:99, 100, *100*
Gough, David, 7:232
Gough, Philip B., 3:312
Gould, James, 3:185
Gould, John, 2:243, 246
Gould, Stephen Jay, 2:4, 246, 3:**159–165,** *160*
  education, 5:267
  on Lamark's philosophy of nature, 4:190
  on Schindewolf, Otto Heinrich, 6:351
  scientific method, 3:421
Goursat, Édouard Jean-Baptiste, 2:117, 118, 290
Gout, 2:375
Gowen, Olga, 7:251
Gowers, William, 3:347
Gowing, Margaret, 6:65
Goy, Robert W., 3:261
GPM (General Purpose macrogenerator), 6:534
GPS (General Problem Solver), 5:257, 258
Grabau, Amadeus William, 2:299–300
Gradient flows, 2:259–260
Graebe, Carl, 2:358
Graf, Samuel, 6:36
Graff, Maria Sybilla Merian. *See* Merian, Maria Sibylla
Graham, John, 2:191, 338
Graham, Ronald L., 2:403

Graham-Smith, Francis, 6:302, 303, 304, 306
The Grammar of Science (Pearson), 4:39, 6:55
Grand Canyon, 6:537
Grande, F., 5:311
Granger, Clive W. J., 5:187
Granick, Samuel, 6:318
Grant, Robert, 1:208, 2:243
Graph theory
    color, 7:291
    development, 7:89–91
Graph Theory as I Have Known It (Tutte), 7:90
*A Graphic Application of the Principle of the Equilateral
    Triangle* (Richter), 6:246
Graphomat, 7:412
Grasp reflex, 6:246
Grassé, Pierre-Paul, 6:77
Grasses, savanna, 6:483
Grassmann, Wolfgang, 5:253
Grave, Caswell, 6:361
Grave, Grigoriy Leonidovich, 6:510
Graves, Mary, 6:460
Graves, Robert Perceval, 3:235
Gravitational attraction, 5:11–12
Gravitational bending, 2:368–369
Gravitational radiation
    bending effect, 2:369
    cosmology, 2:283–284
    relativity, 1:342
Gravity
    alchemy and, 5:273
    cosmology, 3:275
    experimental philosophy, 2:2
    field equations, 3:192
    and geological substructure, 5:48
    and glacial ice deformation, 5:48
    mass and, 1:265
    mechanics, 3:112
    Newtonian theory of, 5:56–57, 270–271
    over the Japan Trench, 5:49–50
    physics
        acceleration, 2:281–283
        affine connection, 2:367–369
        measurement, 7:302–303
    relativity theory, 2:280, 6:456
    vector theory, 6:398
    white dwarf configuration, 2:89
Gray, Harry B., 1:236, 2:104
Gray, Jeffrey, 2:429, 432
Gray, Jeremy, 3:310
Gray, John Edward, 2:216
Graybill, Franklin, 4:164
Gray's Manual of Botany (Fernald), 6:514
Great Aletsch Glacier, 5:327–328
The Great Art of the Early Australians (Jelínek), 4:42

Great Barrier Reef, 3:429
The Great Computer (Alfvén), 1:43
Great Instauration (Bacon, Francis), 1:141
*Great Pictorial Atlas of Prehistoric Man. See Das Grosse
    Bilderlexikon des Menschen in der Vorzeit* (Jelínek)
Great Unified Theory, 6:340
Greatrakes, Valentine, 2:171
Greaves, John, 3:**165–167**
Greek alchemy, 7:406–407
Greek astronomy
    calendars, 1:98–99
    moon, 1:82–83
    records, 7:47
    sun, 1:85
    uranography, 2:304–305
    works, 4:271, 6:173–174, 175–177
Greek civilization, 5:340–341
Green, Ben, 2:405
Green, David Ezra, 3:**167–173**, 4:253, 303, 6:199
Green, Joseph Henry, 5:366
Green, William, 2:393
Green Musselman, Elizabeth, 3:288
Greenawalt, John, 4:241
Greenberg, Gary, 6:369
Greenberg, J. Mayo, 7:128
Greene, John, 1:433
Greenhouse gases
    global warming and, 1:113
    measurement, 5:326, 328
Greenland
    geology, 1:395–396
    ice cores, 5:326, 328, *329*
Green's functions, 6:395
Greenstein, Jesse Leonard, 3:61, **173–177**, *175*
    astronomy, 3:144, 6:502
    Crab Nebula, 6:434
    light scattering, 7:128
    stars, 6:50
    thermal radiation, 7:284
Greenwich Observatory, 1:24–26
Greenwood, Humphry, 6:31
Gregg, Aiden, 1:10
Gregg, Willis, 6:221
Gregorian Reform of the Calendar (Coyne), 2:150
Gregory, David, 1:219
Gregory, James, 1:219
Gregory, Margaret, 1:404
Gregory, Reginald Philip, 1:211
Gregory, William King, 7:235
Gren, Friedrich Albrecht Carl, 7:170
Grene, Marjorie, 6:354
Grensemann, Hermann, 3:323
Grey-Walter, William, 5:255
Gridgeman, Norman T., 2:310

Grierson, John, 3:425
Griffin, Donald Redfield, 3:**177–186,** *179*
Griffith, John S., 4:59
Griffiths, David E., 3:171
Griffiths, James H. E., 6:169
Griffiths, Phillip, 2:114
Grignard, Victor, 7:309
Grimaux, Edouard, 4:217
Grimoult, Cédric, 3:115
Grisebach, A. H. R., 1:386
Grobstein, Clifford, 3:**186–190,** *188*
Grobstein, Ruth Hirsch Beloff, 3:189–190
GROC (Committee for Geophysics and Space Research), 7:130
Groenwegen, Rinus, 7:138
Groes, Niels, 4:235
Grøndahl, Lars O., 6:375
Groombridge, Stephen, 1:25
Gross, Charles C., 3:430
Gross, Jerome, 6:361
Gross, Walter, 6:354
Grossarth-Maticek, Ronald, 2:431
Grosse, Aristide von, 4:297
Das Grosse Bilderlexikon des Menschen in der Vorzeit (Jelínek), 4:42
Grosse Männer (Ostwald), 5:357
Grosseteste, Robert, 1:15
    Franciscan order, 1:143 144
    geometry and natural philosophy, 5:351
    knowledge *vs.* fact, 1:450
Grossman, Evgeny P., 4:101
Grossman, Kenneth, 7:130
Grossman, Sebastian P., 5:151
Grossmann, Marcel, 3:**190–192,** *191*
Groth, Edward, 7:305
Grothendieck, Alexander, 1:346, 364, 2:289, 292
    algebraic geometry, 5:4
    Bourbaki group, 1:366
    cohomology, 7:257
    nuclear space, 2:291
Grotrian, Walter, 2:344, 345, 7:105
Grötzsch, Helmut, 1:262
Groundwater, 3:396, 397
Group dynamics
    Lewin, Lippitt, and White study, 4:281–282
    social psychology, 3:14–15
Group selection (evolution)
    ecosystems and, 5:319
    social behavior, 7:378–380
Group theory
    finite, 3:12–13
    Lie groups, 2:119
    quantum mechanics, 7:277–278, 294

Group Theory and Its Application to Quantum Mechanics (Wigner), 7:294
Groups (mathematics)
    arithmetic, 1:345–346
    Cartan, 3:243 244
    finite, 3:152–154, 213–214
    Lie, 1:343, 2:119–120
        algebraic topology, 1:344–345
        creation of, 4:307–310
        harmonic analysis, 3:241–244
        Jordan algebra, 3:194
        linear algebraic, 1:343
    linear algebraic, 1:345
    quasi-thing, 3:153
    Sylow, 3:153
    symmetry, 6:339–340
    universal algebra, 1:286–287
Groups (physics), conformal, 3:193
Groups (social), 5:336–337
Grover, Nathan C., 3:374
Groves, Leslie Richard, 2:167
    atomic bomb research, 4:291, 5:190
    Los Alamos colleagues, 5:348
    Manhattan Project, 7:266
    plans to commission scientists as officers, 1:134
    on Szilard, Leo, 6:575
Growth, 3:424–425
The Growth of Biological Thought (Mayr), 4:314, 5:64
The Growth of Logical Thinking from Childhood to Adolescence (Piaget), 6:94
Gruber, Howard, 2:243, 244
Grünbaum, Adolf, 3:75
Grunberg-Manago, Marianne, 5:305, 308, 309–310, 311
Grundbegriffe der Wahrscheinlichkeitsrechnung (Kolmogorov), 4:151
Grundfragen der Paläontologie (Schindewolf), 6:351, 352
Grundlagen (Cantor), 2:31–32, 34
Grundlagen der Arithmetik (Frege), 3:70
Grundlagen der Geometrie (Hilbert), 3:71, 308–309, 310
Grundlinien einer psychologishen Entwicklungsgeschichte der Menschheit (Wundt), 7:370
Grundmann, Christoph, 4:169
Grundriss der Naturphilosophie (Oken), 5:331
Grundzüge der Mengenlehre (Hausdorff), 3:265–266
Grundzüge der physiologischen Psychologie (Wundt), 7:369
Grundzüge einer Theorie der Phylogenetischen Systematik (Hennig), 3:281
Grunsky, Helmut, 1:23
Gu Jinghui, 7:365
Gudden, Bernhard, 7:320
Guettard, Jean Étienne, 4:213
Guggenheim, Harry, 6:220
Guide of the Perplexed (Maimonides), 5:5, 6–7, 9

A Guide to Newton's Principia (Cohen), 5:269
Guided missiles, 5:259–260, 6:99–100
Guillemin, Roger, 3:44
Guldberg, Cato Maximillan, 1:265
Gulf Stream, 6:529
Gulls
  behavior, 7:51, 53, 54
  herring, 1:148, 150–151, *152, 153*
Gunn, James, 7:59, 60, 272
Gunpowder, 1:264
Guns, anti-aircraft, 6:425
Günther, Hans F. K., 3:27
Gurdon, John, 1:376
Gurney, Ronald W., 2:165, 5:201–202
Gürsey, Feza, 3:**192–195**
Gustin, William, 3:50
Gutachten über Herrn Daniels Marsaly Process zur Tinctur
  (Becher), 1:230–231
Gutenberg, Beno, 1:31, 5:133
    colleagues of, 7:247
    International Union of Geodesy and Geophysics,
      4:233
    seismology, 4:234, 6:241–242, 7:200
Guth, Alan, 3:194
Guth, Eugene, 3:40
Guthrie, Edwin R., 5:145
Gutiérrez, Juan María, 1:452
Gutowsky, Herbert Sander, 3:**195–201**
Guyton de Morveau, Louis Bernard, 1:264, 4:216,
  6:97–98
Gwei-Djen, Lu. *See* Lu Gwei-Djen
Gyldenkerne, Kjeld, 6:544
Gynaecia Muscionis (Soranus), 2:84
Gypsum, 4:214

H
H-bombs. *See* Hydrogen bombs
Haanstra, Bert, 1:153
Haar, Carel ter, 7:184
Haas, Wander J. de, 1:311, 2:64, 65
Haavik, A. G., 3:171
Haber, Edgar, 1:79
Haber, Fritz, 3:**203–206,** *204,* 5:28
Haber-Bosch process, 3:204
Haberlandt, Gottlieb, 2:189, 6:390
Habermas, Jürgen, 6:135
Habilitation (Carnap), 2:44
Habilitation (Wittig), 7:336
Habilitation lecture (Riemann), 6:250, 252
Habing, Harm, 7:129, 131
Habit, 1:171
Hachette, Jean Nicolas Pierre, 4:201
Hackerman, Norman, 3:44
Haco AG, 6:226

Hadamard, Jacques-Salomon, 2:117, 289
    acquaintances of, 7:254
    influence of, 4:273, 5:194
    influences on, 4:158
    set theory, 5:4
Hadot, Pierre, 6:137
Hadrons, 3:193, 194
Haeckel, Ernst, 2:313, 314, 3:**206–210,** *208,* 4:44, 77
    colleagues of, 7:259–260
    holism, 6:484
    influences on, 5:332
    ontogeny, 1:408
    phylogeny, 1:408, 3:431
    spontaneous generation, 1:208
Haeckel, Ernst Heinrich Philipp August. *See* Haeckel,
  Ernst
Haffner, Hans, 3:274
Hafnium, 1:311
Hafstad, Lawrence, 1:391, 2:166
Hagedoorn, Anna C., 3:30
Hagedoorn, Arund L., 3:30
Hagen, Joel B., 4:110
Hager, Dorsey, 6:443
Hägg, Gunnar, 1:285
Hahn, Erwin, 3:199
Hahn, Julius, 4:153–154
Hahn, Martin, 2:94
Hahn, Otto, 1:55, 2:205, 3:20, **210–212,** *211,* 6:408
Hahn, Roger, 1:433
Hájek, Alan, 2:256
al-Hajjā, 2:418
Hajnal, John, 3:226
Hakfoort, Casper, 5:357
Haldane, John Burdon Sanderson, 3:29, 31, 227, 5:62
    embryology, 7:202
    evolution, 6:109, 7:356–357
    influence of, 5:39
    origin of life, 5:155, 157
Haldol, 4:31–32
Hale, George Ellery, 1:131
Hall, A. R., 5:269
Hall, Benjamin, 6:482
Hall, Brian K., 3:369
Hall, Cecil, 6:362
Hall, Granville Stanley
    experimental psychology, 1:357
    students of, 5:277, 7:25
Hall, Harvey Monroe, 2:153
Hall, James, 3:420
Hall, John S., 7:128
Hall, Marie Boas, 1:366, 367, 369
Hall, Marshall, 3:13
Hall, Philip, 3:153, **212–214**
Hall, Russell, 6:557

Hall ishkāl al-qamar, 1:46

Ḥall mushkilāt al-majisṭi (Quṭ al-Dīn), 6:188

Haller, Albrecht von, 3:**214–216**, *215*
    medicine, 6:506
    scientific hypotheses, 1:433

Haller, Victor. *See* Haller, Albrecht von

Halley, Edmond, 1:83

Hallum, Bink, 7:407

Haloperidol, 4:31–32

Halpern, Otto, 6:392

Halphen, Georges, 4:308

Halprin, Arthur, 6:170

Halsbury, Lord. *See* Giffard, John

Hamada, Yusaku, 4:273

Hamaker, H. C., 1:312

Hamburg, David, 7:237

Hamburg Thesaurus Linguae Graecae, 3:323

Hamburger, Hartog Jakob, 6:568

Hamburger, Viktor, 3:**216–225**, *221*, 351, 5:16

Hamburger-Hamilton stage series, 3:223

Hamermesh, Morton, 1:304–305

Hamilton, Howard, 3:223

Hamilton, N. T., 6:173–174

Hamilton, Richard S., 5:198

Hamilton, William Donald, 3:**225–234,** 7:379

Hamilton, William Rowan, 1:411, 3:*235*, **235–237**

Hammadi, Hag, 7:407

Hammarsten, Einar, 2:68, 69

Hammer, Wilhelm, 1:69, 70

Hammett, Louis Plack, 3:**237–240**, *239*

Hammett equation, 3:239

Hammond, George S., 2:200

Hanahan, Douglas, 3:188

Handbook for Automatic Computation (Wilkinson), 7:317

Handbook for Numerical Analysis (Lions), 4:320

A Handbook of Chemical Engineering (Davis), 4:288

Handbook of Experimental Psychology (Stevens), 4:303

Handbook of Natural Philosophy and Astronomy (Lardner), 3:58

Handbook of Psychology (Baldwin), 1:169

Handbuch der Biochemie des Menschen und der Tiere (Oppenheimer), 5:252

Handbuch der Geophysik (Gutenberg), 5:133

Handbuch der Klimatologie (Hahn), 4:153, 155

Handbuch der Ozeanographie (Krümmel), 6:371

Handbuch der Palaeontologie (von Zittel), 3:154, 6:108

Handbuch der pathogene Mikroorganismen (Koehler), 4:148

Handbuch der Physik (Pauli), 1:269, 3:86, 6:337

Handbuch der regionalen Geologie (Köppen), 4:155

Handbuch einer Geschichte der Natur (Bronn), 1:416

Handy Tables (Ptolemy), 1:82, 98, 3:436, 5:95, 6:174

Hankins, Thomas L., 3:235, 236

Hannaford, Peter, 7:232

Hansen, Brinch, 2:296

Hansen, William Webster, 1:306, 3:196, 6:181

Hanson, Jean, 3:66, 6:362

Haphazard Reality (Casimir), 2:64

Haple, Thomas, 5:357

Haploids, 1:398, 3:228–229

Harary, Frank, 7:102

Haraway, Donna, 2:53, 3:56

Harcourt, Alexander, 3:56

Hardy, Elmo, 2:61

Hardy, Godfrey Harold, 7:156
    colleagues of, 3:5
    students of, 7:314, 414, 415

Hardy, William H., 5:235

Harington, Charles, 5:40

Hariot, Thomas. *See* Harriot, Thomas

Harish-Chandra, 3:**241–245**
    distribution theory, 6:381
    semisimple groups, 3:244
    theory of automorphic forms, 1:346

Harkins, William Draper, 5:209

Harkness, William, 2:344

Harlow, Harry, 5:43

Härm, Richard, 6:386, 387

Harman, John W., 3:169

Harmonices mundi (Kepler), 4:107

Harmonics (Ptolemy), 6:137, 138, 173, 174–175

Der Harn sowie die übrigen Ausscheidungen und Körperflüssigkeiten von Mensch und Tier (Neuberg), 5:250

Harper, William, 2:186, 5:270

Harriman, W. Averell, 2:169

Harrington, Charles, 5:41

Harriot, Thomas, 3:**245–247**

Harris, D., 1:335–336

Harris, Daniel E., III, 4:178

Harris, Geoffrey, 4:245

Harris, Leslie J., 5:39, 6:569

Harris, Robert E., 5:91

Harris, Stan, 3:42

Harrison, Benjamin, 6:151

Harrison, Douglas Neill, 2:307

Harrison, Katherine Puening, 5:348

Harrison, Ross
    embryology, 3:411
    microsurgery, 3:369
    students of, 3:349–350

Harsanyi, John Charles, 3:**247–253**, *248*, 5:230, 7:150

Hart, Bernard, 7:5

Hart, Robert Brian, 2:193

Hartley, David, 6:534

Hartley, Walter, 2:307

Hartlib, Samuel, 1:369

Hartman, Willard, 3:411

Hartmann, Heinz, 5:146

Hartmann, Hermann, 4:59

Hartmann, Max, 4:55, 68

Hartmann, Robert, 1:206

Hartree, Douglas Rayner, 3:**253–257,** 6:397

Hartree, Edward, 3:168

Hartree-Fock approximation, 3:253, 254

Harvard College Observatory, 5:115–117, 7:284–285, 289

Harvey, Hildebrand Wolfe, 3:**257–260,** 6:256

Harvey, William, 1:104–105, 445

Harvill, Richard, 4:180

Haskins, Caryl, 3:179–180

Haslam, Robert, 4:290

Hasler, Arthur Davis, 3:**260–262**

Hasse, Helmut, 1:97, 2:117

Hassel, Odd, 1:197, 199

Hassenstein, Bernhard, 3:297

Hassid, W. Z., 4:256

Hasted, Henry, 7:342

Hatefi, Youssef, 3:171, 172

Hathaway, Starke Rosecrans, 5:90, 91

Hatschek, Berthold, 4:77

Die Hauptrichtungen der gegenwärtigen Psychologie (Müller-Freienfels), 6:525

Haurwitz, Bernhard, 3:*262,* **262–265**

Hausdorff, Felix, 3:**265–267**

Hauser, Fritz, 6:226

Hauser, Kaspar, 4:246

Haüy, R. J., 5:165

K. al-Hāwī (Rāzī). *See Kitāb al-Hāwī* (Rāzī)

Hawking, Stephen, 7:393, 394
    black holes, 6:400
    education of, 3:391
    general relativity, 6:399

Hawking-Penrose singularity theorems, 6:399

Hawkins, David, 6:452

Hawkins, Mike, 2:247

Hawkins, Thomas, 4:308

Hawkins-Simon theorem, 6:452

Haworth, R. D., 5:291

Haworth, Walter Norman, 7:33

Hay, John, 4:122

Hayden, Everett, 7:154–155

Hayden, Ferdinand Vandiveer, 4:120–122

Hayek, Friedrich von, 6:134

Haynes, Benarthur Castle, 6:553

Hays, James, 5:135

Ibn al-Haytham, Abū ʿAlī al-Hasan Ibn al-Hasan. *See* Ibn al-Haytham, Abū ʿAlī al-Hasan Ibn al-Hasan

Hazelhoff, Engel Hendrik, 1:149

Hazen, Harold, 5:53

Head, Henry, 1:186, 3:345–346, 4:352

Health. *See* Medicine

Health, James, 6:473

Hearing, physiology, 3:136

Hearnshaw, Leslie Spencer, 2:56

Heart
    anatomy, 1:103
    disease, 1:77, 78

Heart rate, birds, 5:317

Heat, 3:420

Heat transfer
    in chemical reactions, 4:217–218
    hydrodynamics, 7:391–392

Heath, Thomas L., 2:418

Heaviside, Oliver, 6:379

Heavy elements, energy absorption, 7:398–399

Hebb, Donald Olding, 3:**267–272,** *269*
    influence of, 5:34
    influences on, 5:91

Hebb, Malcolm, 6:179

Hebb synapse, 3:269, 270

Heberden, William, 7:342

Hecht, Selig, 5:14, 15

Heckel, Édouard-Marie, 3:**272–273**

Heckmann, Otto Hermann Leopold, 3:**273–277**

The Hedgehog, the Fox, and the Magister's Pox (Gould), 3:163

Hedlund, Gustav, 5:194

Hedvall, Johan, 2:160

Heezen, Bruce, 7:29, 30–31, 324

Hegel, George Wilhelm Friedrich, 2:413

Heiberg, Johan Ludvig, 1:88, 2:417, 419

Heidegger, Martin, 7:278

Heidenhain, Rudolf Peter Heinrich, 6:46

Heider, Fritz, 1:9, 3:17

The Height of Tropical Cyclones and of the Eye of the Storm (Haurwitz), 3:263

Heilbron, Ian, 1:196

Heilbron, John, 4:175, 331

Heimans, Eli, 7:141

Heine, Eduard, 2:31

Heinrich events, 6:344–345

Heinroth, Oskar, 4:336, 338

Heisenberg, Werner, 1:65, 2:88, 4:55, 57, 7:295
    acquaintances of, 6:192
    atomic bombs, 1:327–328
    colleagues of, 3:275, 400, 6:363, 7:69
    Copenhagen Interpretation, 1:326
    electrons, 6:37
    fundamental spinor field, 3:193
    quantum mechanics, 3:21, 5:200, 6:35, 62, 7:319
    students of, 1:303, 6:490, 7:20–21, 320
    theoretical physics, 1:391, 6:62–63
    theory of turbulence, 2:91
    uncertainty principle, 6:134

Heisenberg-Pauli theory, 1:304

Heitler, Walter Heinrich, 6:37
    colleagues of, 3:298
    quantum electrodynamics, 1:273
Helbing, Mario, 1:441, 3:96
Helfand, Michael S., 3:432
Helfer, H. Lawrence, 3:176
Helin, Eleanor, 6:445
Heliopot, 1:234
Helium
    isotopes, 1:55
    liquid, 4:83–84, 5:128
Hell-Volhard-Zelinskiĭ reaction, 7:395
Helland-Hansen, Björn, 7:373
Heller, Alex, 2:361, 362
Hellstrom, Gustaf, 1:293
Hellwinkel, Dieter, 7:341
Helm, Georg, 2:320, 5:357
Helmholtz, Hermann von, 3:4, 291, 292, 6:112, 121, 122
Helmont, Joan. *See* Helmont, Johannes Baptista van
Helmont, Johannes Baptista van, 3:**277–281**, *278,* 4:249
    chemistry, 6:512, 513
    compositional analysis, 1:367
    influence of, 5:273
Hemagglutination, 1:457–458
Hemianopsia, 7:342, 344
Hemicarcerands, 2:*203, 204*
Hemmer, Per C., 7:102
Hemodynamics, 3:303–304
Hemoglobin
    evolution, 6:42
    molecular structure, 6:39, 81–83
    x-ray crystallography, 6:79–80
Hempel, Carl Gustav, 4:34
Hen, Li, 6:385
Hencken, Hugh, 2:173
Henderson, Janice, 6:163
Hendry, John, 3:236
Henkel, Konrad, 4:169
Hennig, Emil Hans. *See* Hennig, Willi
Hennig, Willi, 3:**281–283**
Henri-Martin, Germaine, 5:298
Henriot, Émile, 1:373–374
Henry of Langenstein, 6:216
Henschel Flugzeugwerke, 7:409, 410
Henschen, Agnes, 2:352
Hensen, Victor, 3:258
Hentschel, E., 6:372
Henyey, Louis, 3:174
Hephaestio of Thebes, 7:112
Heptateuchon, 1:14–15
Heraclides Ponticus, 2:395
Herb, Ray, 1:392

Herbart, Johann, 7:370–371
Herbarum vivae eicones (Brunfels), 6:68
Herbert, Sandra, 2:243, 244
Herbrand, Jacques, 2:116, 117, 118
Herder, Johann Gottfried, 1:358, 434
Heredity
    botany, 7:1–2
    cytoplasm, 4:68
    environmental effects, 4:77–78
    and evolution, 4:45
    germplasm theory, 7:259–261
    Mendelian, 2:246
    natural selection, 7:362
    viruses, 4:357
    See also Genetics; Inheritance
Heredity, Evolution, and Society (Lerner), 4:277
Heredity and Its Variability (Lysenko), 4:357
Heredity in Man (film), 3:425
Heresthetics, 6:254
Heresy
    logic and natural philosophy, 5:313
    miracles, 1:361
    natural magic, 1:423
    Renaissance medicine, 6:552
Hergesell, Hugo, 1:114, 117
The Heritage of Experimental Embryology (Hamburger), 3:217, 223
Herlofson, Nicolai, 1:41
Herman, Michael, 5:198
Herman, Robert, 2:281, 6:166
Hermann of Carinthia, 1:14
Hermetism
    alchemy, 7:407
    Arabic, 1:46–47
Hermippus redivivus (Cohausen), 6:512
Hermite, Charles, 2:30
Hero of Alexandria, 2:418, 3:**283–286,** 6:540
Heron, William, 6:462
Heron, Woodburn, 3:270
Herophilus, 6:540
Herpes simplex virus, 2:376–377
Herpetology
    Anecdotes of the Habits and Instincts of Birds, Reptiles, and Fishes (Lee), 4:232
    taxonomy, 3:339
Herrick, Charles Judson, 4:143
    emergentism, 4:203–204
    neuroanatomy, 6:11
Herring, Conyers, 1:179
The Herring Gull and Its Egg (Baerends and Drent), 1:151, 153
Herring gulls, 1:148, 150–151, *152,* 153
Herringham, Christina J., 1:211
Herriot, John G., 3:50

Herschbach, Dudley R., 6:126
Herschel, Alexander, 3:290, 291
Herschel, Caroline Lucretia, 3:*286,* **286–287,** 289, 290
Herschel, Dietrich, 3:290
Herschel, John Frederick William, 1:28, 2:243,
    3:**287–289,** *288*
    Fresh-Water Fishes of Great Britain (Lee), 4:231
    friendship with, 1:125–126
Herschel, William, 3:**289–291,** *290*
    nebulae, 3:286–287
    theoretical speculation, 3:288
Hershey, Alfred, 1:374, 376, 4:355, 358
Hertz, Heinrich Rudolf, 3:**291–294,** *292,* 7:107
    children of, 3:294
    contiguous-action physics, 1:288
Hertz, Mathilde Carmen, 3:*294,* **294–298**
Hertzman, Max, 3:14
Hertzsprung, Ejnar
    directorships, 5:343, 345
    stellar evolution, 6:385–386
Hertzsprung-Russell diagram, 6:385–386
Herwath von Hohenburg, Johann Georg, 4:131
Herzberg, Gerhard, 3:**298–302,** *299,* 5:73
Herzl, Theodor, 4:86
Herzog, Reginald Oliver, 5:28
Hess, Harry Hammond, 2:288, 7:323, 325
Hess, Kurt, 6:330–332
Hess, Victor Franz, 1:72, 291, 5:301
Hess, Walter Rudolf, 3:*302,* **302–306,** 5:149
Hessen, Boris, 5:237
Heston, Walter, 3:187
Het Geologieboekje (Heimans), 7:141
Hétéerogénie ou traité de la génération spontanée
    (Pouchet), 6:24
Heuristics, 7:93–94
    computer science, 5:254, 255–257
    perceptual systems, 2:26
Hevesy, Georg Karl von, 1:311, 2:205
Hewett, Donnel Foster, 3:398
Hewish, Antony, 6:302, 304, 306
Hewitt, Abram, 4:120–121
Hewitt, C. Gordon, 2:383
Hexuronic acid, 6:568–569
Hey, J. S., 6:303
Heyden, Friedrich von, 4:149
Heydenburg, Norman P., 2:166, 7:119
Heyl, Dorothea, 3:43
Heymans, Corneel, 4:30
Heytesbury, William, 1:35, 2:325, 327
    influences on, 5:314
    limits of natural powers, 5:351
    natural philosophy, 6:562
Hgiwara, Susumu, 1:437
Hick, William Edmund, 1:402

Hickman, Roger, 1:163
Hidden variables
    non-separability and nonlocality in nature, 1:325
    quantum level, 1:322–323, 324
    quantum mechanics, 1:236–237, 239–241
Hieroglyphs, 4:131–132, 133
Hieronymus Fabricius. *See* Fabrici, Girolamo
Higashi, Ken-ichi, 5:169
Higgins, William, 2:320
High-energy physics
    accelerators, 5:304
    antiprotons, 6:410
    atomic bombs, 1:425
    electron-positron collisions, 1:428–430
    linear accelerators, 6:409
    parity nonconservation problem, 6:337
    relativistic plasmas, 1:426
High Resolution Spectroscopy (Tolansky), 7:229
High-temperature chemistry, 2:161
High velocity stars, 5:341–342
High Voltage Engineering Company, 7:400
Highberger, John, 6:361
Higman, Graham, 3:12, 13, 153, 213
Hilbert, David, 2:44, 117, 258, 404, 3:86, **306–310,**
    307
    axiomatics, 2:289, 3:71, 6:379, 7:277
    challenge problems
        computation, 7:82–83
        Diophantine equations, 6:267
    general relativity, 2:367
    influence of, 4:320
    probability theory, 4:151
    students of, 3:400, 5:73, 7:294
Hilbert transform, 7:415
Hilbert's problems
    of 1900, 6:267
    of 1928, 7:82–83
Hildebrandsson, Hugo Hildebrand, 7:18, 19, 218
Hiley, Basil, 1:324
Hilgard, Ernest Ropiequet, 3:271, **310–315**
Hilgard, Jack. *See* Hilgard, Ernest Ropiequet
Hilgard, Josephine R., 3:311, 312
Hill, Archibald Vivian, 4:86, 87, 5:306
Hill, Dorothy, 3:**315–320,** *318*
Hill, George William, 4:160
Hill, Julian, 2:49
Hill Tinsley, Beatrice. *See* Tinsley, Beatrice Muriel Hill
Hillarp, Niils-Åke, 7:178, 179
Hiltner, William Albert, 7:128
Himalyas, 7:208
Himmler, Heinrich, 7:173
Hinde, Robert, 4:245, 246
    criticism by, 4:344
    ornithology, 7:42

Hindman, J. V., 5:345

Hindsgaul, Ole, 4:262

Hinkle, Peter, 6:199

Hinokitiol, 5:287, 289, *289,* 290

Hinshelwood, Cyril Norman, 2:205, 6:140, 413

Hipparchus, 1:82, 85, 87, 3:*320,* **320–322**
    astronomy, 6:175, 176, 177
    Greek astronomy, 7:47

Hippocampus, 6:11–12, *12*
    controversy, 5:368
    emotions, 6:11–12
    inhibitory circuits, 2:332
    structure, 2:341

Hippocrates of Cos, 3:**322–326,** *323*
    ancient medicine, 6:290–291
    commentaries on
        Airs, Waters, and Places, 1:82, 3:325, 6:291
        Aphorisms, 3:323, 6:68
        by Diocles of Carystus, 2:303
        etiology of disease, 2:37
        by Galen, 3:92, 93, 94–95

The Hippocratic Tradition (Smith, Wesley), 3:322

Hippophagia, 3:116

Hirono, Takuzo, 7:200

Hiroshima bombing, 5:242, 6:422

Hirsch, Peter, 5:202

Hirschfelder, Joseph, 6:39

Hirschmüller, Albrecht, 3:75

Hirst, Edward Langley, 6:271

Hirst, Thomas Archer, 3:**326–328**

Hirzebruch, Friedrich, 1:344

His, Wilhelm, 3:369

Hisar, Remziye, 3:193

Hisinger, Wilhelm, 1:266–267

Histochemistry, 5:281–284

Histoire et théorie de la terre (Buffon), 1:432

Histoire naturelle, générale et particulière (Buffon), 4:314

Histoire naturelle (Buffon), 1:432, 433

Histoire naturelle de l'âme (La Mettrie), 4:185

Histoire Naturelle des Animaux san Vertèbres (Lamarck), 4:190

Histoire physique de la mer (Marisili), 5:37

Histology
    cell biology, 7:249
    morphology, 2:185
    zoology, 2:3–4

Historia et meteorologia incendii Aetnei (Borelli), 1:350

Historia Stirpium (Brunfels), 6:68

Historia vitae et mortis (Bacon, Francis), 1:137, 139, 140

Historical Accounts (Pachymeres), 6:1

History
    astronomy, 3:166–167
    biology, 5:64–66
    chemistry, 1:194, 195–196
    geology, 6:430, 431
    learning, 6:459–460
    mathematics, 2:292
    medicine, 6:290–291
    natural
        Canada, 7:78–79
        economics, 4:315–316
        Enlightenment, 1:431–434, 7:220–223
        evolution, 6:109
        illustrations, 4:230–232
        museums for, 5:366
        paleontological change, 1:415
        Paracelsianism, 1:308–309
        Renaissance medicine, 6:551–552
        Roman, 6:116–120
        systematics, 2:7
        utility, 1:368–369
        zoology, 1:416, 3:115
    psychology, 1:358, 6:94–95, 458–459
    scholarship in, 6:162–164
    science
        biochemistry, 5:233
        Chinese, 5:235, 239
        The Copernican Revolution (Kuhn), 4:174–175
        education, 6:1–2
        norms of science, 5:123–124
        physics, 6:411
    USSR, 7:157

History Is on Our Side (Needham), 5:237

History of Animals (Aristotle), 5:280

History of Creation (Haeckel). *See Natürliche Schöpfungsgeschichte* (Haeckel)

A History of Embryology (Needham), 5:236

History of Experimental Psychology (Boring), 1:357–358, 359

History of Life and Death (Bacon, Francis). *See Historia vitae et mortis* (Bacon, Francis)

History of Magic and Experimental Science (Thorndike), 1:108

History of Modern Computing (Ceruzzi), 2:297

A History of Psychiatry (Shorter), 3:75

History of Psychology (Baldwin), 1:170

The History of Sexuality (Foucault), 3:75

History of the Creation (Burmeister), 1:452

History of the Primates: An Introduction to the Study of Fossil Man (Clark), 2:137, 139, 5:296

History of the Royal Astronomical Society (Tayler), 5:75

Hitchcock, Frank L., 6:425

Hitchings, George H., 2:373–376

Hitler, Adolf
    ballistic missiles, 7:173
    German Academy of Natural Sciences and, 1:4
    See also National Socialism (Germany)

HIV (Human immunodeficiency virus), 4:33

Hlawaty, Franz, 5:28
HMO method, 3:401–404, *402*
Hoagland, Mahlon, 3:341
Hobbes, Thomas
    commentaries on, 2:80
    scientific controversies, 1:369
Hobby, George, 3:365
Hoch, Paul, 5:91
Hodge, Clifton F., 5:277
Hodge, Jonathan, 2:242, 243
Hodge, William V. D., 4:145
Hodgkin, Alan, 3:**328–333**, *329*
    action potentials, 2:331
    Goldman, Hodgkin, Katz (GHK) equations, 4:86
    Goldman-Hodgkin-Huxley equations, 4:88–89
    squid axon studies, 2:330
Hodgkin, Dorothy Mary Crowfoot, 1:282, 3:328, *333,*
    333–339, 6:39
    vitamin B12, 7:67
    x-ray crystallography, 6:79
Hodgkin, R. A., 6:126
Hodgkin, Thomas Lionel, 3:335, 338
Hoefert, Lynn, 2:415
Hoerr, Normand, 2:144
Hoffman, Abby, 5:47
Hoffman, Charles J., 3:197, 199
Hoffmann, Felix, 2:358–359
Hoffmann, Friedrich, 6:504
Hoffmann, Gerhard, 7:398
Hoffmann, Reinhard W., 7:339, 341
Hoffmann, Roald, 3:88, 5:214, 7:355
Hoffmann, Ulrich, 6:230
Hoffmann-La Roche, Inc., 6:226
Hoffmeister, J. Edward, 4:186
Hofmann, August Wilhelm, 2:358, 4:149, 5:19, 20
Hofmann, J. E., 1:254
Hofstadter, Richard, 2:247
Hofstadter, Robert, 1:304
Hoftijzer, Jan, 7:135, 139
Hoftyzer, Jan. *See* Hoftijzer, Jan
Hogeboom, George, 2:145, 3:169, 4:239
Holbach, Paul-Henri Thiry, Baron d', 4:185
Holborn, Ludwig Christian Friedrich, 2:253
Holbrook, John Edwards, 3:**339–340**
Holcomb, Donald F., 5:192
Holden, John C., 2:288
Holism
    botany, 6:483
    ecosystems, 5:315–320
    evolution, 6:484
    neuroembryology, 3:223
Holism and Evolution (Smuts), 6:484
Hollander, Samuel, 5:14
Holley, Robert William, 1:375, 3:**340–344**, *341*

Holliday, Read, 5:19
Hollinger, David, 5:43, 349
Holloway, Marshall, 5:190
Holm, Charles H., 3:199
Holm, Ragnar, 6:374–375
Holmberg, Arne, 1:266
Holmboe, Bernt Michael, 1:5
Holmboe, Jörgen, 2:99
Holmes, Arthur, 1:70, 2:39, 42, 4:40
Holmes, Frederic L., 5:184–185
Holmes, Gordon Morgan, 3:**344–348**
Holonyak, Nick, 1:181, 183
Holst, Erich von. *See* von Holst, Erich
Holst, Gilles
    colleagues of, 7:134
    industrial chemistry, 1:311
    Royal Netherlands Academy of Sciences, 1:312
Holstein, Theodore, 6:169–170
Holt, E. B., 3:125
Holtfreter, Johannes, 3:**348–352**
    amphibians, 3:187
    colleagues of, 3:218
    education of, 5:16
    influences on, 4:68, 69
Holtzer, Howard, 3:187
Holtzman, Eric, 5:284
Holway, Alfred, 1:358–359
Holweck, Fernand, 4:55, 356
Homage to Santa Rosalia (Hutchinson), 3:416
Homberg, Guillaume. *See* Homberg, Wilhelm
Homberg, Wilhelm, 3:**352–354**
Home, Henry, Lord Kames
    colleagues of, 7:220, 222–223
    soil fertility chemistry, 2:218
Homeobox genes, 1:210
Homeostasis
    behaviorism, 6:245
    calcium, 6:245
    genetics, 4:276
    innate behavior, 6:247
    phyletic gradualism, 3:159–160
    sleep, 6:244, 245
    sodium, 6:245
Homer, 7:112
Homes-Adie (myotonic) pupils, 3:345
Hominid fossils
    dating techniques, 5:296–299
    evolution, 5:354–355, 368
    Neanderthal, 3:154, 155–156
    paleoanthropology, 7:115–117
    Pithecanthropus, 7:184–188, *185, 186*
    Sinathropus, 7:249–253
Hominid phylogeny, 7:113–118
L'homme machine (La Mettrie), 4:183, 184

Les hommes fossiles (Boule), 7:115
Homo erectus, 7:184–188
Homoeomeries, 6:294
Homological algebra
    Abelian categories, 5:2–3
    Bourbaki group, 1:366, 2:361
    translations, 1:13
Homological Algebra (Eilenberg), 2:361
Homology, 1:11, 12–13
Homology (Mac Lane), 5:2
Homomorphism, 1:11, 12–13
Homosexuality, 4:125, 7:28
Homskaya, Eugenia D., 4:349, 354
Homunculi, 6:*71, 72*
Hondius, Jodocus, 3:**354–356,** *355*
Honeybees. *See* Bees
Hood, Thomas, 2:158
Hooft, Gerard, 6:396
Hooke, Robert, 3:419, 5:352
Hooker, Joseph Dalton, 2:156, 3:327
Hooper, Judith, 4:110
Hooton, Earnest A., 2:173, 7:234, 235
Hopf, Eberhard, 4:188
Hopf, Heinz, 1:344, 5:2, 7:257
Hopf invariant
    contributions to, 4:319
    stable homotropy theory, 1:11, 12
Hopkins, Frederick Gowland, 5:159
    acquaintances of, 6:568
    enzymology, 3:170
    influence of, 5:232, 233, 238, 6:519
    students of, 3:167, 5:231, 232, 235
Hopkins, Jeannette, 2:134
Hoppe, Ferdinand, 4:280
Hoppe-Seyler, Ernst Felix Immanuel, 5:253
Hopper, Grace Murray, 3:**356–361,** *359*
Hoquet, Thierry, 1:432
Horeau, Alain, 4:229
Horecker, Bernard, 4:74
Horiuchi-Boreslov correlations, 1:354
Horkel, Johann, 6:356, 357
Hormonal Factors Controlling the Differentiation,
    Development, and Display of Copulatory Behavior in the
    Ramstergig and Related Species (Beach), 1:223
Hormones
    behavior, 1:221, 4:245–246
    insect, 1:463
    sex, 1:459, 460–463
Hormones and Behavior (Beach), 1:221–222
Hormones and Behavior (journal), 1:221
Hornaday, William T., 4:268
Horoscope of Islam, 6:518
Horoscopes. *See* Astrology
Horoscopy, katarchic, 7:111

Horowitz, Gene, 2:128
Horowitz, Norman Harold, 3:**361–366,** *364,* 4:137
Horowitz, Paul, 7:305, 306
Horowitz, Ruth, 2:128
Horowitz, Tamara, 6:350–351
Horridge, G. Adrian, 1:437
Hörstadius, Greta Kjellström, 3:366
Hörstadius, Sven Otto, 3:**366–371,** 5:17
Horton, Robert Elmer, 3:**371–375,** 6:537, 538
Hospers, Jan, 2:191, 192, 3:**375–377**
Host-parasite interactions
    germ strains, 1:454–456
    lichens, 6:389
    speciation, 3:232
Hot Springs of the Yellowstone National Park (Day), 2:254
Hotchkiss, Rollin, 2:145, 318
Hotelling, Harold, 5:52
Hou Te-Pang, 3:**377–380**
Houben-Weyl Reference Series, 1:215
Houdrey, Eugène Jules, 3:**380–384**
Houdry Process, 3:381, 382–383
House Un-American Activities Committee, 2:169–170
Houssay, Bernardo Albertus, 4:253, 254, 256
Houtermans, Fritz Georg, 2:378
Houtgast, Jakob, 7:126
Houtman, Jan, 1:315
Houwink, Roelof, 5:29
Hovenier, Joop, 7:129, 132
The How and Why of Weather Knowledge (Reichelderfer),
    6:221
How Animals Develop (Waddington), 7:203
How Birds Live (Nicholson), 3:385
How to Pay for the War (Keynes), 4:113
How to Prepare for Our Future of Totally Unexpected
    Opportunities (Miller), 5:151
How to Solve It (Polya), 5:254
How to Teach Chemistry (Frankland), 3:64
Howard, Ebenezer, 7:225
Howard, Eliot. *See* Howard, Henry Eliot
Howard, Frank A., 4:290
Howard, Henry Eliot, 3:**384–386**
    bird courtship behavior, 3:424
    bird territoriality, 5:278
Howard, John Eliot, 3:387
Howard, Luke, 3:**386–388**
Howe, Herbert, 5:111
Howell, Francis Clark, 7:116
Howland, Arthur, 4:165, 166
Hoyle, Fred, 3:**388–392,** *390*
    acquaintances of, 6:499
    colleagues of, 7:60
    formation of elements in stars, 1:157
    radar, 1:340
    resonance phenomena, 3:61

Hoyle, Fred, *continued*
  Salam, Muhammad Abdus, 6:335
  solar corona, 3:137–138
  steady state theory, 1:341, 342, 3:136
  stellar model, 6:386
  students of, 3:176
  theoretical physics, 6:64
Hoyt, John C., 3:374
Hrdlička, Aleš, 2:239, 3:156
Hu Huanyong, 7:403
Hu Shi, 7:364, 365, 368
Huang, Tzu-ching, 6:323
Huang Jiqing, 2:300, 3:**392–395**
Huang Weiwen, 6:58
Huang Ziqing. *See* Huang, Tzu-ching
Huanyong, Hu. *See* Hu Huanyong
Hubbard, Jerry, 3:365
Hubbard, Ruth, 5:16
Hubbert, Marion King, 3:**395–400**
Hubble, Edwin Powell, 5:73, 81, 6:456
Hubble Space Telescope, 7:272
  development, 6:502, 7:130
  launch, 1:159–160
Hubel, David, 2:211, 3:146
Hubert, M. King, 4:164
Hückel, Erich Armand Arthur, 3:**400–405**
Huene, Friedrich Freiherr von, 7:384
Huez, Georges, 1:375–376
Huganir, Richard, 6:200
Huggins, Maurice, 3:38
Hughes, Alun, 2:241
Hughes, Arthur, 6:169
Hughes, Edward David, 4:15, 16, 17
Hughes, Vernon W., 1:392
Hugo, Marie-Chantal, 6:517
Hulbert, Henry S., 3:142
Hulburt, Edward O., 3:79, 7:74
Hull, Clark Leonard, 3:14, 120, **405–410**, *408*
  formalism, 2:429
  hypothetico-deductive method, 1:405
  intelligent behavior, 4:204, 245
  laws of behavior, 4:282
  laws of learning, 5:145, 146
Hull, David, 2:246, 3:160
Hull, McAllister H., 1:392
Human, Mary, 4:357
Human Biology and Racial Welfare (Cowdry), 2:183, 184
Human evolution. *See* Evolution
Human experimentation, National Socialism (Germany), 1:463
Human immunodeficiency virus, 4:33
The Human Legacy (Festinger), 3:17
The Human Mind (Meninger), 5:90
Human paleontology

  evolution, 6:108–109
  extinction, 2:226
Human Problem Solving (Simon and Newell), 6:452
Human Sexuality in Four Perspectives (Beach), 1:222
Humanism
  psychotherapy, 6:274
  scientific, 3:424, 427
Humanistic psychology, 5:45–47
Humanitarianism, 6:326–328
Humanities, 3:162–163
Humboldt, Friedrich Wilhelm Heinrich Alexander von, 2:266, 3:69, 7:209
  fieldwork, 1:206
  mentored by, 1:452
  natural history, 3:118
  plant community study, 1:386
  Stommel, Henry Melson, 6:528
Hume, David, 5:228
  empiricism, 3:421
  induction, 5:144, 6:133–134
  population dynamics, 5:13
Hume, Richard, 1:18
Hume, William, 1:28
Humidity
  distribution, 1:117
  isentropic analysis, 5:222
Humores minerales (Newton), 5:275
Humorism, 6:291
Humphrey, Rufus, 1:399–400
Hund, Friedrich, 3:275, 400, 5:210, 6:37
Hungary, 7:20
Hunger physiology, 5:*148*, 148–149, 151
Hunt, Edward, 2:175
Hunt, Eric, 6:477
Hunter, Ed, 4:253
Hunter, Erica C. D., 7:407
Huntress, Ernest H., 6:322
Hurricanes
  atmospheric science, 6:4, 7:274–275
  Fujita scale, 3:83
  weather forecasting, 7:153–155
  See also Cyclones
Husebye, Eystein, 1:32
Hussain, Chaudhri Muhammad, 6:335
Husserl, Edmund, 3:70, 131, 7:243
Hutchinson, Clyde, III, 6:480, 481
Hutchinson, G. Evelyn, 2:353, 3:**410–418**, *414*
  biogeochemistry, 3:413, 5:317, 322
  colleagues of, 5:316
  ecological theory, 2:386
  limnology, 6:256
  on Margalef, Ramon, 5:24
  students of, 3:414, 416
Hutton, James, 2:85, 3:*419*, **419–423**, *422*, 6:348

Huxley, Andrew Fielding, 2:331, 3:329
Huxley, Hugh E., 6:81, 362, 571
Huxley, Julian, 3:46, 64, **423–429,** *426*
　colleagues of, 2:382, 383, 3:385
　evolution, 5:284
　immunology, 1:456
　influence of, 2:384, 4:275
　students of, 7:377
Huxley, Thomas Henry, 2:86, 3:**429–434,** *431*
　anthropology, 7:116
　family of, 3:423
　hippocampus controversy, 5:368
　influences on, 2:246
　Kropotkin, Petr Alekseyevich, 4:161
　mutual aid theory, 4:162
　scientific humanism, 3:424
　scientific method, 6:28
　spontaneous generation, 1:208
　X-Club, 3:327
Huygens, Christiaan, 2:273
　inversion, 3:246
　on Newton, Isaac, 5:270–271
Hybridization, 1:211–212, 5:98–100
Hybridization of Somatic Cells (Ephrussi), 2:402
The Hydrides of Boron and Silicon (Stock), 1:418–419
Hydroboration, 1:422
Hydrocarbons
　aromatic, 1:251, 5:19, 20
　oil, 7:133
　oxidation, 1:200
　paraffin, 3:86
Hydrodynamic and Hydromagnetic Stability
　(Chandrasekhar), 2:91
Hydrodynamics
　boundary-layer theory, 5:335–336
　chemical physics, 7:391–392
　elasticity, 2:76–77
　magneto-, 2:91
　meteorology, 1:288
　oceanography, 1:288
　Turing patterns, 6:165–166
　weather prediction, 2:100
Hydrodynamics: A Study in Logic Fact, and Similitude
　(Birkhoff), 1:288
Hydrodynamics (Lamb), 4:193
Hydrogen
　activation, 2:14
　bonding
　　organic chemistry, 2:278
　　valence bond theory, 5:211–212
　conversion into helium, 3:60
　experiments, 6:193–194
　interstellar, 6:544, 7:126, 127–128, 129
　Lamb shift, 1:273–274

negative ion, 2:90–91
neutron scattering, 1:55
photochemistry, 1:234
spectrum
　measurement, 4:6–7
　research, 7:100
stellar, 6:542, 543
Hydrogen bombs
　development, 1:57, 6:421, 7:21–24
　ethics, 6:196
　fusion, 6:501–502
　schematic, 7:*22*
　strategic value, 1:136
　Ulam-Teller mechanism, 1:274
　USSR, 6:325
　See also Atomic bombs; Nuclear weapons
Hydrogen peroxide, 5:283
Hydrogen-sulfide, 7:397
Hydrogenation, 3:41–43
Hydrogenlyase, 6:520
Hydrographs, unit, 3:373
Hydrography of the Dutch Wadden Sea (Postma), 7:142
Hydrology
　fluid dynamics, 3:397
　geophysics, 3:395–396
　petroleum, 3:396
　soil erosion, 3:371–374
The Hydrology of the Southern Ocean (Deacon), 2:261
Hydromagnetic waves, 1:41
Hylleraas, Egil A., 2:90
Hyman, Libbie Henrietta, 3:*434,* **434–435,** 4:244
Hymenoptera, 3:228–229
Hypatia, 3:**435–437,** *436*
Hyperarithmetical sets of numbers, 6:266
Hyperbolas, 3:246, 7:89
Hypersurfaces, minimal, 2:259
Hypertension, 4:253
Hyperuricemia, 2:375
Hypnomidate, 4:33
Hypnosis
　behavior theory, 3:405
　Clark Hull on, 3:14
　consciousness, 3:310
　experimental psychology, 3:406
　for hysteria, 4:25–26
　post-hypnotic suggestion, 4:27
　psychology, 3:312–313
　Vogt, Oskar and Cécile, 7:162
Hypnosis and Suggestibility: An Experimental Approach
　(Hull), 3:14, 406
Hypnosis in the Relief of Pain (Hilgard and Hilgard),
　3:312
Hypnotic Susceptibility (Hilgard), 3:312
Hypothalamus, 5:*148,* 148–149, 6:11–12, *12*

Hypotheses, 1:433, 3:215
  catastropic, 4:39
  continental drift, 1:292
  continuum, 3:265–266
      mathematics, 3:130–131
      solution, 2:30, 33
      unified field theory, 2:370–371
  drive-reduction, 5:148–149
  egodic, 1:338
  fission, 6:260
  J.R., 6:267
  light quantum, 1:411, 2:364–365
  one gene-one enzyme, 7:14
  one gene-one polypeptide, 1:224, *226*, 227
  Riemann, 6:253
  wobble, 3:342
Hypothesis of Light (Newton), 5:274
Hypothetico-deductive method, 1:405
Hysteria, 4:25–29

I
I. G. Farbenindustrie AG, 6:229–232
I Wish I'd Made You Angry Earlier (Perutz), 6:84
IAEA (International Atomic Energy Agency), 6:338
Iagoge Eis Ten Apotelesmatiken Tou Ptolemaiou
    (Porphyry), 6:138
IArgentina, 5:180–181
Iatrochemistry, 6:550–551
Ibn. *See also* next element of name.
Ibn al-Haytham, Abū ʿAlī al-Hasan Ibn al-Hasan, 1:145,
    4:**1–4**
Ibrāhīm Ibn Sinān Ibn Thābit Ibn Qurra, 1:14, 2:305,
    419, 4:**4–5**
Icarus, 6:312
Ice ages
  curve of insolation and, 5:133
  flooding, 1:*395*
  geology, 1:393–395
  theory, 6:343–345
Ice cores, 5:326, 327–330, *329*
Iceland, lava flows, 3:375–377
ICES (International Council for the Exploration of the
    Sea), 6:371–372
Ichnology, 6:248, 249
Ichthyology
  illustrations, 4:231–232
  paleontology, 6:31
  South Africa, 6:475–477
  taxonomy, 3:339–340
  vision, 7:213
ICSN (Institut de Chimie des Substances Naturelles),
    1:200
ICSU (International Council of Scientific Unions),
    5:261

ICTP (International Centre for Theoretical Physics),
    6:338–339
Iddings, Joseph P., 2:254
Idea philosophiae moralis (Burgersdijk), 1:444, 445
Idea physicae (Gorlaeus), 3:157, 158
Ideal elements, 3:309
Ideal gases, 1:318
Idealistische Morphologie und Phylogenetik (Naif), 6:354
Idealphilosophie (Schelling), 5:331
Ideals and Realities (Salam), 6:339
Ideen zur Philosophie der Geschichte der Menscheit
    (Herder), 1:434
Ideler, Julius L., 6:517
Identification of Pure Organic Compounds (Huntress and
    Mulliken), 6:322
IGY (International Geophysical Year), 5:260–261, 6:236
Ikhitiyārāt-i muzaffarī (Quṭ al-Dīn), 6:188
Illusions, optical, 1:145–146
Ilse, Friedrich Ernst, 4:59
Images des mondes disparus (Piveteau), 6:108
The Imbedding Problem for Riemannian Manifolds
    (Nash), 5:229
Imbrie, John, 5:135
Imes, Elmer Samuel, 4:**6–9**
Imitation, conscious, 1:171
*The Immense Universe, the Numberless and Figureless
    Worlds* (Bruno), 1:424–425
Immerwahr, Clara, 3:205
Immunoadsorbents, 4:261
Immunology
  host-parasite interactions, 1:454–458
  idiotypic network theory, 4:47–50
  self and not-self theory, 1:455–457, 458
  transplantation, 5:86–89
Immunosuppression, 2:375
IMO (International Meteorological Organization), 6:223
Imodium, 4:32
Impetus theory, 1:423–424, 447
Implicate order, 1:325
Implosion, 6:422
*The Importance of Steric Strain in the Extent and
    Direction of Unimolecular Elimination* (Brown), 1:420
Imprinting, 2:197
In Aristotelis Mechanicas Commentarij (de Guevara),
    1:167
In De Anima Aristotelis (Rufus of Cornwall, Richard),
    6:295
In Defence of Empirical Psychology (Broadbent), 1:405
In Mechanica Aristotelis Problemata Exercitationes (Baldi),
    1:166, 167–168
In Physicam Aristotelis (Rufus of Cornwall, Richard),
    6:293
*In Quatuor Libros Meteorologicorum Aristolelis
    Commentaria* (Cabeo), 6:188

In the Surgery (Diocles of Carystus), 2:302
In vitro fertilization, 3:188–189
In vitro research, 3:187
Inanimate spirits, 1:139
Inchofer, Melchior, 3:100
Inclusive fitness, 3:225, 226–232
Incomplete information, 3:250–251
Index Chemicus (Newton), 5:274, 6:512
Index Hippocraticus, 3:323
India, 7:147, 207–209
India-rubber, 7:396
Indian Ocean
    fish, 6:476, 477
    oceanography, 6:372
Indians, American, 5:243–244
Indiscrete Thoughts (Rota), 6:286
Individual adaptation, 1:168, 171–172
The Individual and His Religion (Allport), 1:53
The Individual and Society (Baldwin), 1:170
Individual Differences in Susceptibility to Hypnosis
    (Hilgard), 3:312
Individuality
    critical personalism, 6:526
    differential psychology, 6:524
    zoology, 3:207
Individuality (Thorndike), 6:524
Induced mutations, 7:13, 14
Induction
    cell theory, 6:357–358
    controversy, 7:282
    political economics, 7:281
    probability, 1:432, 2:45–46
    riddle of, 3:149–151
Inductive philosophy, 5:143–144
Industrial chemistry
    catalysis, 1:352–355, 7:311–312
    chemical synthesis, 7:350–352
    decomposition, 1:233–234
    dyes, 6:271, 7:144–145
    educational methods, 4:287–292
    metallurgy, 1:310–314
    organic, 6:228–233
    photochemistry, 1:234
    platinum, 7:342–343
    research and development, 7:321–322
    Solvay process, 3:377–380
    synthetic ammonia, 3:203–204
Industrial Chemistry of Colloidal and Amorphous Materials
    (Lewis), 4:290
Industrial melanism, 4:109–110
Inertia, 6:398
Infant behavior
    evolutionary principles, 1:168
    experimental study, 1:170

reflexes, 6:246
Infant development, perceptual learning, 3:123–124
Infectious diseases, 1:454–458
Infiltration capacity, 3:373, 374
Infinite series (mathematics)
    continuum hypothesis, 2:30
    functions, 2:422–423
    John Philoponus, 4:52
    set theory, 2:30–32
Influenza virus, 1:457–458
Informatics, 4:320–321
Information
    asymmetric, 7:149–150
    attention and perception, 1:403–404
    incomplete, 3:250–251, 251
Information Processing Techniques Office (IPTO),
    4:302, 304–305
Information theory, 6:424, 426–427, 429
    ecosystems and, 5:24–25
Infrared and Raman Spectra of Polyatomic Molecules
    (Herzberg), 3:301
Infrared spectrophotometers
    design of, 4:6–7
    photochemistry, 1:234
Infrared spectroscopy
    applications, 7:352
    chemical shifts, 3:*198,* 198–199
    development, 7:228–229
    molecular structures, 5:170
    organic chemistry, 3:197
    scientific method, 7:312
Ingalls, Albert G., 7:269
Inge, L. D., 6:413
Inglada, Vicente, 4:**10–12**
Ingold, Christopher Kelk, 4:**12–18,** *13,* 6:37
    electronic theory, 3:87, 6:272
    organic reaction mechanisms, 1:191
    steric effects, 1:420
Ingold, Hilda, 4:13–14
Ingram, Vernon, 2:352
Inhelder, Bärbel, 6:92, 94
Inheritance
    Baldwin effect, 1:172
    cytoplasmic
        cancer genetics, 6:319–320
        experiments, 6:492–493
        plant genetics, 6:317–319
        self and not-self theory, 1:457
    See also Genetics
INHG (D-glucuronolactone isonicotinyl hydrazone),
    6:323
Injection molding, 2:358, 359
Inleiding tot de diersociologie (Tinbergen), 7:52

Innate behavior
  environmental influence on, 1:150
  homeostasis, 6:245–246, 247
  See also Instinct; Nature *vs.* nurture
The Innate Organization of Visual Activity (Hebb), 3:268
Inorganic chemistry
  analysis methods, 4:312
  iron monoxide, 2:160–161
  philosophy of science, 6:6
  radiochemistry, 7:306, 307–308
  synthesis, 2:160, 4:149
  transition metals, 2:102–104, 4:58–61
Inquisition
  Copernicanism, 3:98–100, 101
  physicians, 2:37
  relativity of motion, 1:424
  Telesian philosophy, 2:19–20
The Insect Societies (Wilson), 3:229
Insecticides, phosphoric acid esters, 1:218
Insects
  aquatic, 3:411
  behavior, 3:183
  classification, 2:389–390
  development, 1:452
  diversity, 3:416
  evolution
    biology, 2:389–390
    cytogenetics, 2:59–63
    genetics and behavior, 4:277
  hormones, 1:463
  navigation, 7:*85*, 85–86
  observation and illustration, 5:118–120, *119*
  phylogenetic systems, 3:281–282
  social, 3:228–229
  See also Entomology; *specific insects*
Insights and Illusions of Philosophy (Piaget), 6:94
Insitute of Nuclear Physics (Akademogorodok),
  1:427–430
Inskeep, Ray, 2:125
Insolation
  canon of, 5:133–134
  curve of, 5:133, *134*
Insolubilia (Swyneshed), 6:562, 563
Instinct
  animals, 6:368–369, 7:50, 52–53
  behavior, 3:296
  birds, 2:196–198, 4:339–341, 342–345
  cognitive ethology, 3:182
  hormones, 1:222
  model of instinctive action, 4:*343*
Institut de Chimie des Substances Naturelles (ICSN),
  1:200
Institute for Advanced Study, 1:160
Institute for Applied Psychology, 6:523

Institute of Actuaries, 6:566
Institute of Organic Chemistry, University of Basel,
  6:227
Institutes of Medicine (Cullen), 2:220
Institutes of Natural History (Walker), 7:220, 222
Institutio oratoria (Quintilian), 2:82
Institutiones calculi differentialis (Euler), 2:421
Institutiones mathematicae (Kircher), 4:131
Instituzioni analitiche ad uso della gioventù italiana
  (Agnesi), 1:19, 20
Instruction Set Processor (ISP), 5:257
Instrumentation
  analemma, 2:*305*, 305–306
  charge-coupled devices, 7:305
  chromomictors, 1:28
  electron microscopes
    cytology, 2:70–71, 143, 144–146, 6:143–148
    embryology, 2:*146, 147*
    light absorption errors, 2:68
  geophysics, 7:270–271
  history of science, 6:163–164
  koniscopes, 1:28
  microscopes, 5:23
  navigation, 2:157–158
  physics, 1:23
  psychrometers, 1:*115*
  seismographs, 1:243–245
  spectrophotometry
    development, 7:229–231, *230*
    ozone, 2:*307*, 307–308
  spinning cup, 2:351, *351*
  telescopes, 1:28
    Airy disk, 1:25
    charge-coupled device, 7:272
    gratings, 1:131
    radio, 5:83–84
    silicon-diode technology, 7:271–272
  thermometers, 1:114–116, 3:10
Insulators, 5:201–202
Insulin
  synthesis, 2:348
  x-ray crystallography, 3:334, 337–338
Integrals
  Abelian, 1:6–7
  differential calculus, 2:423–424
  harmonic, 4:144
  normal probability, 1:219
  polynomials, 2:229–230
  singular, 2:8–9, 7:415
Integrated circuits, 6:441, 442
An Integrated System of Classification of Flowering Plants
  (Cronquist), 2:214
Integration, school, 2:131
Intelligence

artificial
  computational neuroscience and, 5:34–36
  computer science, 7:83–84
  development, 5:255–257, 258, 6:427–429, 449,
    452
    founder of, 5:254
    man-computer interaction, 4:305
  child development, 6:91–95
  evolution and, 1:169–170, 6:91
  instinct, 3:296
  malnutrition, 5:245
  operationalism, 6:463
  race and, 2:430–431, 6:441
  testing, 3:406
  See also Intelligence quotient (IQ); Intelligence tests
Intelligence and Affectivity (Piaget), 6:95
The Intelligence Controversy (Eysenck), 2.431
Intelligence quotient (IQ)
  child development, 6:522
  defined, 7:25
Intelligence tests
  army program, 1:357
  child development, 6:92
  debate over, 7:27
  dynamic assessment, 7:193–194
  neuroscience, 3:267, 268
  personality psychology and, 1:51
  race and, 2:131–132, 6:441
  Stanford-Binet, 7:25–26
Intelligent design
  industrial melanism, 4:109–110
  medicine, 3:93–94
Intelligent Life in the Universe (Shklovskii and Sagan),
  6:313, 432, 435
Intensity, figural, 3:296
Interdisciplinary cooperation, 1:440, 5:236–237,
  238–239
Interferometry
  optical, 7:398
  radio
    radio astronomy, 6:302–304
    telescopes, 1:335–336
  Very Long Baseline, 3:139
Interferon, 5:364
El Interior de la Tierra (Inglada), 4:11
The Internal Constitution of the Stars (Eddington), 6:50,
  542
International Association for the Study of Fossil Cnidaria
  and Porifera, 3:317
International Association of Volcanology, 6:263
International Atomic Energy Agency (IAEA), 6:338
International Centre for Theoretical Physics (ICTP),
  6:338–339
International Cloud Year, 7:18

International cooperation
  Chinese science and, 5:238–239
  meteorology, 6:222–223
  oceanography, 6:236
International Council for the Exploration of the Sea
  (ICES), 6:371–372
International Council of Scientific Unions (ICSU),
  5:261
International Geophysical Year (IGY), 5:260–261, 6:236
International Meteorological Organization (IMO), 6:223
International Oceanographic Congress (IOC), 6:236
International Phytogeographical Excursions, 7:4
International Treatise on Invertebrate Paleontology (Hill),
  3:317
International Union of Crystallography (IUCr), 1:285
Internationale Vereinigung für Limnologie, 7:36
Interplanetary medium, 1:278
Interpolation, 4:319
Interstellar aerodynamics, 7:128
Interstellar magnetic fields, 1:278
Interstellar matter
  accretion, 3:388–389, 391
  field theory, 3:389
  gases, 6:543–544
Interstellar medium, 6:501, 502
Intracellulare Pangenesis (de Vries), 7:190
Intransitivity of Preferences (Tversky), 7:92
Introducción al estudio del plancton marino (Margalef),
  5:24
Introductio in analysin infinitorum (Euler), 2:421
Introduction to Animal Sociology (Tinbergen). *See
  Inleiding tot de diersociologie* (Tinbergen)
Introduction to Astronomy (Porphyry), 6:138
An Introduction to Biology (Kinsey), 4:124
Introduction to Clinical Neurology (Holmes), 3:345
An Introduction to Dynamic Meteorology (Panofsky), 6:8
Introduction to Meteorology (Petterssen), 6:85
An Introduction to Modern Genetics (Waddington), 4:114
Introduction to Nervous Systems (Bullock), 1:437
Introduction to Non-Linear Mechanics (Bogolubov), 1:317
An Introduction to Population Ecology (Hutchinson),
  3:414–415
Introduction to Psychology (Hilgard), 3:313
Introduction to Quantum Mechanics (Gutowsky and
  Pauling), 3:196, 6:38
An Introduction to Statistical Models in Geology
  (Krumbein), 4:164, 165
Introduction to the Art of Music (Bacchius), 2:284
Introduction to the Doctrine of Fluxions (Bayes), 1:219
An Introduction to the Fine Structure of Cells and Tissues
  (Porter), 6:147
Introduction to the Fine Structure of Plant Cells (Porter),
  6:147

An Introduction to the Study of Bird Behaviour (Howard), 3:385

An Introduction to the Study of Stellar Structure (Chandrasekhar), 2:89

An Introduction to the Study of the Ethology of Cichlid Fishes (Baerends), 1:151

Introductory Botany (Cronquist), 2:214

Introductory Science Primer (Huxley), 3:431

Invariants, 3:122, 6:285–286, 564, 566

Invasive species, 6:515

Invention and Economic Growth (Harsanyi), 3:248

Inversion spectrum, ammonia, 7:101

Invertebrate paleontology
    ammonites, 7:62
    classification, 4:190
    education, 5:267
    fossil bivalve mollusks, 5:265, 266
    geology, 3:315–319, 7:15–17

Invertebrate zoology
    influential figures, 7:84–86
    taxonomy, 3:434–435

Invertebrates, 4:190

The Invertebrates (Hyman), 3:434, 435

Investigation of the Ice Age (Kropotkin), 4:*161*

Investigation of the Principles of Knowledge (Hutton), 3:419, 420, 421, 422

Investigations on the developmental laws of the organic world during the formative period of our Earth's surface (Bronn). *See Untersuchungen über die Entwickelungs-Gesetze der organischen Welt während der Bildungs-Zeit unserer Erd-Oberfläche* (Bronn)

IOC (International Oceanographic Congress), 6:236

Ioffe, Abram F., 4:81, 6:412, 414

Ion pumps, 5:364, 6:200

Ionophores, 6:160, *160*

Ionosphere, 1:390

Ions
    accelerators, 3:35–36
    bonds, 6:37
    Goldman-Hodgkin-Huxley equations, 4:88–89
    nonclassical, 1:420–421, *421*, 2:200–201
    solar corona, 2:346

Ipatiev, Vladimir, 4:82

Ippolito, Felice, 7:72

IPTO (Information Processing Techniques Office), 4:302, 304–305

IQ (intelligence quotient), 6:522, 7:25

Irakiri, Hoshi, 6:485, 487

Iron
    deficiency, 5:247
    magnetism, 3:108–109
    monoxide, 2:160–161

Irreversibility, thermodynamics, 6:164–167

Irving, Edward A., 1:292, 6:299

Is Science Necessary? (Perutz), 6:84

Isaacs, John, 5:223

Isayev, Alexei M., 4:103

Isentropic analysis, 5:222

Ishida, Masahiro, 6:319

Isidore of Seville, 6:119

Isidorus of Miletus, 3:435

Ising, Gustaf, 1:293

Isis, 5:332–333

Islam
    Ahmadiyya Movement, 6:335
    alchemy, 4:19–20
    astronomy, 2:305–306
    cosmology, 6:213–215
    mathematics, 6:185–186
    philosophy, 6:187
    Shiite, 4:19–20

Islamic medicine, 5:8–9, 6:290–291

Islands (Menard), 5:96

Isoanomals, 7:17

Isochloranil, 6:323

Isoflavones, synthesis of, 7:*146*

Isomerism, 5:169–170

Isooctane, 1:*191*, 192

Isotopes
    nuclear taxonomy, 7:308
    philosophy of science, 6:6

Isotopes, radioactive. *See* Radioisotopes

ISP (Instruction Set Processor), 5:257

Israel, weapons development, 1:251–253

Italy, volcanology, 6:262–264

Itano, Harvey, 6:39

Itinerarium exstaticum (Kircher), 4:130, 133

Ito, Mansuke, 6:332

Ito, Masao, 2:332

It's a Long Way to Tipperary (Richter), 6:243

IUCr (International Union of Crystallography), 1:285

Ivanenko, Dmitrii, 1:64, 65

J

J-homomorphism, 1:11

Jābir Ibn Ḥayyān, 4:**19–20,** 6:517

Jac. Berzelius Bref (Söderbaum), 1:266

Jac. Berzelius Levnadsteckning (Söderbaum), 1:266

JAC (Jewish Anti-Fascist Committee), 6:447

Jac Berzelius, His Life and Work (Jorpes), 1:266

Jacchaeus, Gilbertus, 1:444, 445

Jackiw, Roman, 1:236, 238–239

Jackson, John Hughlings, 3:75, 347, 4:25

Jacob, Francois, 2:211, 5:71

Jacob, Teuku, 7:188

Jacobi, Carl Gustav Jacob, 1:7, 3:236, 4:308
    elliptic functions, 4:159
    students of, 7:254

Jacobsen, Jacob Christian, 1:76
Jacobson, Carl-Olof, 3:369–370
Jacyna, Stephen, 1:208
Jaeger, Frans Maurits
    students of, 1:310
    x-ray diffraction, 1:280
Jaeger, Siegfried, 3:294
Jaeger, Werner, 2:301
Jaffé, Aniela, 4:63
Jagendorf, André, 5:162
Jaghmīnī, Sharaf al-Dīn Maḥmūd Ibn Muḥammad
    Ibn 'Umar al-, 4:**20–22**
*Jahrbuch für Mineralogie, Geognosie Geologie, and
    Petrefaktenkunde* (Bronn), 1:415
Jahresberichte über die Fortschritte der physischen
    Wissenschaften (Berzelius), 1:267
Jakobson, Roman, 4:352, 354, 6:427
Jakus, Marie, 6:362
Jallabert, Jean, 5:10, 11
James, Preston E., 6:372
James, Tony, 5:40
James, William, 2:55, 57–58, 3:7, 4:**22–24,** *23*
    acquaintances of, 4:63, 64
    active constructive nature of mind, 1:186
    death of, 1:170
    influence of, 3:405, 5:92
    James-Lange theory of emotions, 6:11
    politics, 2:430
    reasoning, 3:406
James-Lange theory, 6:11
Jameson, Cynthia, 3:199
Jameson, Robert, 2:226, 3:419, 7:221
Jamin, Jules, 3:57
Janet, Paul, 4:25, 63
Janet, Pierre, 3:313, 4:**24–29,** *28,* 6:92
Janot, Maurice-Marie, 4:229
Jansky, Karl, 1:333, 3:173, 6:304
Jansky (unit), 6:304
Janssen, Paul Adriaan Jan, 4:**29–34,** *31*
Japan
    gravity over, 5:49–50
    organic chemistry, 5:287–292
Jardin du Roi, 1:433
Jardine, Nicolas, 2:149
Jarosik, Norman, 7:305
Jasper, Herbert, 6:70
Jastrow, Joseph, 3:406
Jaurès, Jean, 4:25
Jaynes, Julian, 1:222
Jeans, James Hopwood, 2:339
    influence of, 6:499
    scientific method, 6:542
Jeener, Raymond, 1:371, 374, 2:145
Jefferson, Thomas, 1:174–175

Jeffrey, Edward Charles, 6:514
Jeffrey, Richard Carl, 4:**34–38,** 285
Jeffreys, Harold, 2:40, 4:**38–42**
    earth's inner core, 4:235
    International Union of Geodesy and Geophysics,
        4:233
    psychoanalysis, 7:6
    students of, 7:323
    theoretical physics, 1:340
Jeger, Oskar, 7:350
Jelínek, Jan, 4:**42–43**
Jell, John S., 3:316, 317, 318
Jellyfish, 3:429, 5:59–60
Jenkin, Fleeming, 2:246
Jenkins, James, 4:276
Jennings, Herbert Spencer, 4:**43–46,** *44,* 6:492
Jensen, Arthur, 2:131–132, 3:161
Jensen, Hans, 2:379
Jerne, Niels Kaj, 1:458, 4:**46–51,** *48*
Jessenius, Johan, 6:418
Jesuits
    college education, 1:204
    influence of, 4:130–134
    mathematics, 2:150–151
    science and, 7:153
    See also Catholicism
Jet Propulsion Laboratory (JPL), 5:260, 6:99–103
Jeune, Francis, 3:430
Jewett, Frank B., 2:168
Jewish Anti-Fascist Committee (JAC), 6:447
Jia Lanpo
    paleoanthropology, 6:59, 60, 61
    Sinathropus, 6:58, 7:251
    students of, 7:384
Jiang Jieshi, 7:368
Jieshi, Jiang. *See* Jiang Jieshi
Jin, Anshu, 1:32
Jinghui, Gu. *See* Gu Jinghui
Jiong, Lü. *See* Lü Jiong
Jiqing, Huang. *See* Huang Jiqing
JMC (Joint Meteorology Committee), 6:221
Joergensen, Axel Christian Kluxüull. *See* Jørgensen, Axel
    Christian Klixbüll
Johannsen, Wilhelm Ludvig, 4:45
    biometry, 6:54–55
    Mendelian genetics, 5:102
John XXII, Pope, 5:313
John Innes Horticultural Institute, 1:212–213
John of Alexandria. *See* John Philoponus
John of Casali, 2:326
John of Damascus, 2:121
John of Dumbleton. *See* Dumbleton, John
John of Gmunden, 6:153
John of Holywood. *See* Sacro Bosco, Johannes de

John of Mirecourt, 5:350, 351
John of Rupescissa, 1:109, 110
John Paul II, Pope
    nuclear weapons, 6:315
    on science and faith, 3:101
John Philoponus, 4:**51–53**
John the Grammarian. *See* John Philoponus
Johnson, Douglas, 6:537
Johnson, Lyndon, 7:123
    Miller, Neal Elgar and, 5:149
    War on Poverty, 2:132
Johnson, Martin, 2:261
Johnson, Treat B., 3:42
Johnson, Virginia, 4:129
Johnson, W. H., 5:308
Johnson, William Ernest, 2:257
Johnson, William S., 3:40
Johnston, James Finlay Weir, 4:**53–55**
Johnston, John Black, 6:10
Johnstone, Pete, 5:4
Joint Meteorology Committee (JMC), 6:221
Joint Task Force One, 6:235
Joliot, Frédéric. *See* Joliot-Curie, Frédéric
Joliot-Curie, Frédéric, 3:211
    colleagues of, 2:379
    influence of, 4:331
    radioactivity, 6:77
Joliot-Curie, Irène, 4:227, 6:76, 77
Joly, Robert, 3:324
Jones, Alexander, 2:416
Jones, Ernest, 3:73, 7:5–6
Jones, Harry Clary, 5:200, 201, 6:63
Jones, J. A. A., 3:373
Jones, J. Eric, 2:148
Jones, Neville, 2:124
Jones, Richard, 7:280, 281
Jones, Tim, 1:196, 198
Jordan, David Starr, 7:210
Jordan, Edward C., 5:83
Jordan, Ernst Pascual, 3:21, 194, 4:**55–58**
    acquaintances of, 2:267
    influence of, 2:282
Jordan algebra, 3:194
Jordan-Brans-Dicke theory, 3:275
Jørgensen, Axel Christian Klixbüll, 4:**58–62**
Jörgensen, Christian Klixbüll. *See* Jörgensen, Axel
    Christian Klixbüll
Jorpes, Jhan Erik, 1:266, 2:347
Josefsson, Lars, 2:352, 3:368
Josephson, Brian, 1:182
Joubert, Jules François, 3:58
Journal für die reine und angewandte Mathematik. See
    Crelle's Journal
Journal für Hirnforschung, 7:164

Journal für Psychologie und Neurologie, 1:408
Journal of Applied Behavior Analysis, 6:465
Journal of Applied Psychology, 6:523
Journal of Combinatorial Theory, 6:286
Journal of Physical Chemistry (periodical), 6:412
Journal of the Experimental Analysis of Behavior, 6:464
Journey into Self (film), 6:278
The Joy of Insight (Weisskopf), 7:268
Joyce, James M., 4:36, 6:349–350
JPL (Jet Propulsion Laboratory), 5:260, 6:99–103
J.R. hypothesis, 6:267
Judaism
    astrology and, 5:8
    human knowledge and, 5:6–7
    Maslow, Abraham on, 5:43
    mathematics, 6:564–565
    Neuberg, Carl Sandel on, 5:251
    See also Antisemitism
Juday, Chancey, 2:353, 3:260
Judgment under Uncertainty: Heuristics and Biases
    (Kahneman, Tversky and Slovic), 7:94
Jukes, Tom, 4:116, 117
Julia, Gaston, 2:118
Jullien, Vincent, 2:149
Juncker, Johann, 6:506
Junction transistors, 6:438–440, 441
Jung, Carl Gustav, 2:428, 4:**62–65,** *64*
    influence of, 2:378, 5:215, 216
    opinion poll ranking, 5:47
    psychoanalysis, 6:35
Jungius, Joachim, 4:**65–66**
Jungle Laboratory (Robinson), 2:54
Jupiter, 6:442, 446
Just, Ernest Everett, 4:**66–70**
Justice
    politics and theory of, 5:337
    social, 5:236
Justification, 3:151–152
Juvenilia (Galilei). *See* *Galileo's Early Notebooks* (Galilei)

K

K. al-Hāwī (Rāzī). *See* *Kitāb al-Hāwī* (Rāzī)
K. al-Manṣūrī (Rāzī). *See* *Compendium for al-Manṣūrī*
    (Rāzī)
K theory, 1:11, 12
Kabachnik, Martin I., 5:248
Kac, Mark, 1:263, 2:405, 7:102, 103
Kadushin, Charles, 5:140
Kafuku, Kinzo, 5:288
Kagaku Honron (Mizushima), 5:167
Kagawa, Yasuo, 6:199, 200
Kahn, Boris, 7:102
Kahn, Theophile, 2:379
Kahneman, Daniel, 7:91, 93–95

Kainosho, Masayasu, 5:289
Kaiser Wilhelm Gesellschaft (KWG), 3:212
Kaiser Wilhelm Institute (KWI), 3:210
Kaiser Wilhelm Institute for Biochemistry (KWIB), 1:460–464, 464, 5:250–251
Kaiser Wilhelm Society for the Advancement of the Sciences, 3:205
Kakutani, Shizuo, 5:228
Kalambo Falls Prehistoric Site (Clark), 2:125
Kalckar, Herman Moritz, 4:**71–76,** *74*
Kaldor, Andrew, 6:473
The Kaleidoscope (Chambers), 2:85
Kallman, Frances, 3:188, 6:145
Kalm, Pehr, 4:315
Kaltbrunner, David, 5:180
KAM theory, 5:197–198
Kamen, Martin D., 4:296–297, 6:42
Kamenev, Lev, 4:83
Kamerlingh Onnes, Heike, 1:280, 304, 4:83
Kames, Lord. *See* Home, Henry, Lord Kames
Kamin, Leon, 2:431
Kaminer, Benjamin, 5:34
Kammerer, Paul, 4:**76–80,** *78*
Kammler, Hans, 7:173, 174
Kan, Daniel, 5:3, 4
Kanam Man, 5:296–297
Kandel, Eric, 5:185
Kandrach, Anne, 6:199
Kangro, Hans, 4:65, 6:417–418
Kannegiser, Eugenia, 6:63
Kant, Immanuel
    epistemology, 6:6
    idealism, 3:421
    influence of, 4:171, 343, 7:282
    influence on algebra, 3:236
    intuition, 2:44
    Kuhn, Thomas Samuel, 4:174
    logic, 3:70
    natural philosophy, 1:433–434
    physics, 3:292
    scientific philosophy, 2:43
Kantrowitz, Arthur, 6:169
Kao, Chung-hsi, 6:323
Kapitsa, Petr Leonidovich, 4:**80–86,** *81,* 5:301
    magnetoresistance, 7:320
    political maneuvering, 4:102
Kapitza, Peter. *See* Kapitsa, Petr Leonidovich
Kaplan, Joseph, 7:174
Kapteyn, Jacobus Cornelius
    galaxies, 5:342–343
    influence of, 5:341, 342
    stellar density, 6:456
Kapur, P. L., 6:64
Kara-Michailova, Elizabeth, 1:301

Karczag, Lázló, 5:251
Karlik, Berta, 1:301
Karlson, Peter, 1:463
Kármán, Theodor von. *See* von Kármán, Theodor
Karmen, Martin David, 7:347
Karplus, Martin, 3:199, 4:260
Karrer, Paul, 4:226
    vitamin A, 7:212
    yellow enzymes, 7:33
Karssen, Albert, 1:280–281
Karsten, Anitra, 4:280
Karsten, Wenceslaus Johann Gustav, 2:231
Kas, Arnold, 4:147
Kataliz v proizvodstve sernoi kisloty (Boreskov), 1:352
Katarchic horoscopy, 7:111
Katayama, Masao, 5:167–168, 288
Kato, S., 3:264
Katsura, Shigehiro, 5:289
Katz, Bernard, 1:122, 4:**86–90,** *88*
    action potentials, 3:331
    colleagues of, 2:330
    neurotransmitters, 7:178
    rivals of, 3:329
Kauffman, George B., 7:310
Kaufmann-Lignac syndrome, 1:2
Kawakami, Hiroshi, 6:333
Kay, Andrew, 5:47
Kedrov, B. M., 5:105–106, 108
Keeling, Charles David, 4:**91–98,** *92, 93, 94, 95, 96*
    carbon dioxide measurement, 4:91–94, 94–95, 6:236, 7:275
    education, 4:91
    recognition, influence, and nonprofessional life, 4:95–97
Keeling, Dave. *See* Keeling, Charles David
Keesom, Willem Hendrik, 1:280, 4:83
Kehrman, Daniel, 1:150–151
Keilin, David, 3:168, 5:159, 6:81
Keim, Franklin D., 1:224, 225
Das Keimplasma (Weismann), 7:258
Keith, Arthur, 2:239, 240, 315, 5:297, 7:116
Kekulé, August. *See* Kekulé von Stradonitz, Friedrich August
Kekulé von Stradonitz, Friedrich August, 2:195, 4:*98,* **98–100,** 6:37
    chemical structure theory, 1:465, 466, 4:149, 7:372
    colleagues of, 3:57
    valence line diagram, 3:403
Keldysh, Mstislav Vsevolodovich, 4:**100–105,** *103,* 5:248
Keller, Andrew, 3:40
Kelley, Harold, 3:15
Kellner, Menachem, 6:7
Kellogg, Chester, 3:267

Kelly, Gregory M., 5:4
Kelly, John L., 6:429
Kelly, Mervin
  electronic switching systems, 6:438
  semiconductors, 6:440
  transistors, 1:180
Kemble, Edwin Crawford, 5:210
Kemeny, John G., 5:187
Kemmer, Nicholas, 6:336, 393
Kendall, Edward, 6:568–569
Kendeigh, Charles, 5:317
Kendrew, John Cowdery, 3:338, 5:202, 6:81–82, *82*
Kennedy, Eugene, 4:72, 75, 239
Kennedy, John F., 2:132
  Apollo Project, 5:262–263
  assassination of, 1:58
  Harvard College Observatory, 5:117
  influence of, 6:485
  petroleum industry, 3:398
Kennedy, John L., 5:255
Kennedy, Joseph William, 6:402, 408
Kennedy, Juliette, 3:131
Kennedy, Robert, 2:132
Kennelly-Heaviside layer, 1:390
Kepler, Johannes, 4:**105–109**
  astronomical tables, 2:179
  Copernicanism, 2:177
  cosmology, 2:149
  education, 1:383
  influence of, 4:133
  solar transit of Mercury, 3:111
  supernovas, 5:176
Kermack, Kenneth A., 6:30
Kern, Stephen, 3:75
Kernel theorem, Schwartz, 6:381
Kerner von Marilaün, Anton, 1:386
Kerr, Frank J., 5:346, 7:129
Kerr, Warwick, 3:230
Kerr solution, 6:399
Ketanserin, 4:32
Ketekaar, Jan, 1:282
Ketoconazole, 4:33
Kettlewell, Bernard. *See* Kettlewell, Henry Bernard Davis
Kettlewell, Henry Bernard Davis, 3:47, 4:**109–111**, 110
Kety, Seymour, 1:120
Key Papers in the Development of Coding Theory (Berlekamp), 3:153
Keynes, John Maynard, 4:**111–114**, *112*
  activism, 6:55
  political economics, 5:14
Keynes, R. D., 3:331
Keynes, Richard. *See* Keynes, R. D.
Keyser, Pieter Dircksz, 6:111
Kezhen, Zhu. *See* Zhu Kezhen

Khan, Ayub, 6:338
Kharasch, Morris, 1:419
Khare, Bishun, 6:314
Kharīdat al-ʿajāʾib (Quṭ al-Dīn), 6:188
Khariton, Yuli B., 4:82, 7:391
al-Khāzinī, 2:121, 6:186
Khimicheskaia fizika, 6:412
Khinchin, Aleksandr Y., 4:151, 6:426
Khorana, Har Gobind
  genetic code, 5:310
  membrane proteins, 5:364
  Nobel Prize, 3:340
  oligonucleotides, 6:480
  students of, 6:478, 479
  in vitro protein synthesis, 1:375
Khrushchev, Nikita, 6:327
Khulāṣat iṣlāḥ al-majisṭī (Quṭ al-Dīn), 6:188
al-Khwārizmī, Abū Jaʿfar Muḥammad ibn Mūsā, 1:14
Kibre, Pearl, 1:309
Kidneys
  metabolism
    glycolysis, 4:72
    renal hypertensions, 4:253
  transplantation, 2:375, 5:87
Kienle, Hans, 6:383
Kieser, Dietrich Georg, 5:331
Kilby, Hilda Blanch, 1:211
Killian, James R., Jr., 1:136, 4:291, 6:182
Killing, Wilhelm, 4:307, 308
Kim, C. W., 6:170
Kimpton, Lawrence, 4:180
Kimura, Motoo, 3:48, 4:**114–118**, *115*
Kin selection, 3:225, 229
Kinble, Gregory A., 3:312
Kincaid, Trevor, 2:354
Die Kindersprache (Stern and Stern), 6:522
al-Kindī, Abū Yūsuf Yaʿqūb ibn Isḥāq al-Ṣabbāḥ
  astrology, 1:145
  colleagues of, 6:212
  students of, 6:215
The Kindly Fruits of the Earth (Hutchinson), 3:410
Kinematics, 1:294, 295
Kinetic Theory of Vehicular Traffic (Prigonine), 6:166
Kinetics
  chemical reactor theory, 1:354
  dense gases, 7:103
  polymerization, 3:38–40
  protein, 1:79–80
King, Ada Augusta, Countess of Lovelace, 1:127–128, 4:**118–120**, *119*
King, Charles Glen, 3:170
King, Clarence Rivers, 4:**120–123**, *121*, 6:150
King, Glen, 6:569
King, Jack, 4:116, 117

King, John G., 5:192
King, Lester S., 6:504
King, Thomas J., 1:398–399, 400
King, William, 4:119
King Solomon's Ring (Lorenz), 4:345
Kingland, Sharon, 2:152, 4:204
Kingsley, Charles, 5:19, 20
Kinoshita, S., 1:299
Kinsey, Alfred Charles, 4:**123–130,** *126, 128*
    controversy, 4:127–128
    education, 4:124
    interview, 4:125–126
    legacy, 4:129
    mission of, 4:127
    sampling, 4:125
    as scholar of sexual science, 4:128–129
    sex research, 4:124–125
    on sexual outlet, 4:126
    taxonomic investigations, 4:124–125
The Kinsey Data (Gebhard), 4:124, 125
Kirch, Gottfried, 7:332–333
Kirch, Maria Margaretha Winkelmann. *See*
    Winkelmann, Maria Margaretha
Kircher, Athanasius, 4:**130–136,** *132*
Kirchhoff, Gustav Robert, 7:105
    crystals, 7:165
    spectral analysis, 1:440
    students of, 3:292
Kirk, Raymond E., 5:31
Kirkeby, John, 4:346, 348
Kirpianov, Andrey I., 5:248
Kirsch, Gerhard, 1:299
Kirwan, Richard, 4:218, 6:97
Kiryushkin, Anatoly, 5:363
Kissen, David, 2:431
Kistemaker, Jaap, 1:315
Kistiakowsky, George, 1:56
    Explosives Research Laboratory, 3:240
    National Laboratory, 1:164
Kita, Gen-itsu, 3:86, 6:330
Kitāab al-Manṣūrī (Rāzī). *See Compendium for al-*
    Manṣūrī (Rāzī)
Kitāb al-Hāwī (Rāzī), 6:212, 291
Kitāb al-tabsira fī al-hay' a (Quṭ al-Dīn), 6:188
Kitāb Hall Shukūk Uqlīdis. See On the Difficulties of
    Euclid (Hero of Alexandria)
Kitāb nuzhat al-ḥukamā' wa-rawḍat al-aṭibbā' (Quṭ al-
    Dīn), 6:188
Kitab al-Taqsīm wa-l-tashjīr (Rāzī), 6:212
Kitching, James, 2:240, 241
Kites, meteorological, 7:18, 19
Kitt Peak National Observatory (KPNO), 3:144, 6:546
Kittel, Charles, 6:169–170
Klacel, Franz Matthaeus, 5:104

Klaiber, G. S., 5:128
Klamroth, Martin, 2:418, 419
Klaproth, M. H., 5:166
Klassen und Ordnungen des Thierreiches (Bronn), 1:416
Klassiker (Ostwald), 5:357
Klau, Christoph. *See* Clavius, Christoph
Klein, Christian Felix, 2:357, 6:489
    correspondence, 6:121
    influence of, 4:158
    relationship with, 4:308–310
Klein, Chuck. *See* Klein, Harold P.
Klein, Felix. *See* Klein, Christian Felix
Klein, Harold P., 4:**136–141**
Klein, Joseph, 1:253
Klein, Martin J., 6:112
Klein, Oscar, 4:55, 7:398
Klein, Ursula, 1:268, 4:311
Klein, Woody, 2:134
Klein-Nishina theory of absorption, 7:398–399
Kleinian groups, 1:21, 23, 263
Kleinzeller, Arnošt, 6:521
Kleist, Karl, 4:143
Die Klimate der geologischen Vorzeit (Köppen), 4:154,
    155, 5:133, 7:247
Klimaty zemnago shara, v osobennosti Rossi (Köppen),
    4:153
Klineberg, Otto, 2:130
Klinkenberg, Adriaan, 7:135
Klipfel, Florence J., 5:283
Klixbüll, Christian. *See* Jørgensen, Axel Christian
    Klixbüll
Klopfer, Peter, 3:411
Klug, Aaron, 2:210
Klüver, Heinrich, 4:**141–144,** 6:12
Klüver-Bucy Syndrome, 4:142–143
Kluyver, Albert Jan, 4:73
Knee joint, 7:113–114
Knight, Goodwin J., 1:235
Knight, J. Brookes, 5:265
Knight, Walter, 3:197
Knipp, Julian K., 7:102
Knipping, Paul, 1:280
Knoblauch, Karl Hermann, 3:326
Knobloch, Eberhard, 2:149
Knoepfel, Margaret. *See* Smagorinsky, Margaret Knoepfel
Knorr, Angelo, 2:206
Knorr, Wilbur R., 1:87, 2:416, 419
Knowledge
    geohistory, 3:422
    geology, 3:419
    scientific method and, 3:421, 5:280
Knowledge systems, 5:257–258
Knuth, Donald, 2:296, 3:51, 52
K'O-Chen Chu. *See* Zhu Kezhen

Koblitz, Ann Hibner, 4:159
Kobunshi Kagaku Kyokai, 6:334
Koch, Christoff, 2:211
Koch, Robert, 2:182, 4:229
    bacteriology, 6:27
    germ theory, 1:209, 454
Koch, Sigmund, 3:409
Kochen, Manfred, 5:140
Kochen, Simon, 1:239
Kochetkov, Nikolai K., 5:246, 247
Kodaira, Kunihiko, 4:**144–147**
Kodama, Shinjiro, 3:86–87
Koebe, Paul, 1:23
Koehler, Derek, 7:95
Koehler, Otto, 4:**147–149**
Koenig, Charles, 3:7
Koenigswald, Gustav Heinrich Ralph von. *See* von
    Koenigswald, Gustav Heinrich Ralph
Koerner, Lisbet, 4:315
Koestler, Arthur, 4:79
Koestler, Johann, 4:134
Koetsier, Teun, 3:236
Koffka, Kurt
    behaviorism, 3:407
    perception, 3:126
Kögl, Fritz, 1:283
Kohlberg, Lawrence, 6:94
Kohler, Elmer Peter, 3:238
Köhler, Georges, 4:50
Kohler, Robert E., 5:184, 185, 7:346
Köhler, Wolfgang, 4:279, 281
    anthropoid apes, 3:294
    stimulus-response connection, 3:407
    students of, 3:295, 296
Kohlhörster, Werner, 6:280–281
Kohlrausch, Friedrich Willem Georg, 1:289
Kohlschütter, Ernst Arnold, 3:274
Kohn, Alan, 3:411, 415
Kohn, David, 2:243, 246
Kohn, Walter, 6:132
Koichiro, Harada, 3:153
Koketsu, Kyozo, 2:331
Kola, 3:272
Kolbe, Adolph Willem Hermann. *See* Kolbe, Hermann
Kolbe, Hermann, 4:**149–150**, *150*
    free radical decarboxylation, 1:199
    structural chemistry, 1:466
Kolhörster, Werner, 5:301
Kolkmeijer, Nicolaas H., 1:280, 281, 284
Kollar, Ianos, 1:345
Kolmogorov, Andrei Nikolaevich, 4:**150–152**
    axiomatics, 3:266
    information theory, 6:426
    stability of solar system, 5:197–198

topology, 7:292
Kölreuter, Joseph, 5:104
Koltun, Walter, 2:202
Komai, Taku, 4:114–115
Kondo, Jun, 2:65
König, Samuel, 5:58
Koninklijke Zout Organon (KZO), 7:138
Koniscope, 1:28
Konnekerk Wilfred R., 6:170
Konopinski, Emil, 1:157
Konsilien (Suchten), 6:552
Koppel, Leopold, 3:204
Köppen, Wladimir Peter, 4:**152–155**
    climatology, 7:39
    colleagues of, 7:247
    curve of insolation, 5:133
    influence of, 4:154–155
Köppen climate classification system, 7:39
Koref, F., 1:311
Korff, Serge Alexander, 4:297
Kornberg, Arthur, 2:374, 5:310, 7:348
Kornberg, Roger, 2:210
Kornilov, Konstantin, 7:193
Korn's inequality, 5:335
Korolev, Sergey P., 4:101, 102, 104
Korsch, Karl, 4:280
Korzhinskii, Dimitri Sergeyevich, 4:**155–158**
Koshiba, Masatoshi, 1:159
Kosmos (Humboldt), 1:206
Kosmos (Sitter), 6:458
Koszegi, Botond, 4:36
Kottler, Malcolm, 2:246, 247
Kovalevskaia, Sofia. *See* Kovalevskaya, Sofya Vasilyevna
Kovalevskaya, Sofya Vasilyevna, 4:**158–160**, *159*
Kovalevsky, Alexsandr Onufrievich, 7:397
Kovalevsky, Sonya. *See* Kovalevskaya, Sofya Vasilyevna
Kováts, Ervin, 5:42
Kövesligethy, Radó, 4:10
Kowalevsky, Sonja. *See* Kovalevskaya, Sofya Vasilyevna
Kowalewski, Gerhard, 4:310
Kox, Lawrence, 1:191
Koyanagi, Bob, 1:32
Koyré, Alexandre, 4:172
Kozyrev, Nikolai Alekseevitch, 1:64, 66, 67, 4:180
KPNO (Kitt Peak National Observatory), 3:144, 6:546
Kraeplin, Emil, 1:408
Kraft, Robert P., 1:277
Kraftheim, Johann Crato von, 6:551
Kramers, Hans, 7:135
Kramers, Hendrik Anthony, 7:127
    quantum electrodynamics, 1:273–274
    Utrecht, 1:304
Krantz, David H., 7:92
Krapina fossils, 3:154, 155–156

Krasner, James, 3:55
Kraus, Paul, 4:19
Krause, Ernst Ludwig, 1:70, 5:260
Krauss, Karl, 2:95
Krebs, Hans Adolf, 4:238, 323, 5:308, 6:569
Krebs cycle, 5:308–309, 6:572
Kreidler, Robert, 6:182
Krein, Mark G., 3:241
Kreitman, Martin, 4:117
Kreplin, Robert, 3:80
Kressley-Mba, Regina, 3:294
Kreuger, Bram, 1:281
Kreuzer, Lloyd, 2:282
Krieckhaus, E. E., 5:151
Krigbaum, William, 3:39
Krishnamurti, Jiddu, 1:325
Krogh, August, 4:71
Krogman, Wilton, 7:236
Krohn, Peter L., 5:87
Krom, Cornelis J., 1:283
Kronecker, Leopold, 2:30–31, 34, 117, 4:309
Krook, Max, 6:499
Kropf, Allen, 5:16
Kropotkin, Petr Alekseyevich, 4:**160–164,** *161*
Kroto, Harold, 6:473–474, 475
Krug, Hans-Jurgen, 5:357
Kruijt, Jaap Pieter, 1:153
Krull, Wolfgang, 2:118
Krumbein, William Christian, 4:**164–167,** 6:467
Krümmel, Otto, 6:371
Krupp, Friedrich Alfred, 7:162
Kruseman Aretz, Frans E. J., 2:296
Krushchev, Leonid I., 5:248, 249
Kruyt, Hugo, 1:282
Krylov, Nikolai Mitrofanovich, 1:316–318
Kū, Abū Sahl Wayjan Ibn Rustam al-. *See* al-Qūhī, Abū Sahl Wayjan ibn Rustam
Kubrick, Stanley, 5:82, 6:312
Küdecke, Karl, 5:252
Kuenen, Philip Henry, 3:375, 7:142
Kuffler, Stephen, 4:87
Kūhī, Abū Sahl Wayjan Ibn Rustam al-. *See* al-Qūhī, Abū Sahl Wayjan ibn Rustam
Kühn, Alfred, 1:463, 464, 3:218
Kuhn, Harold W., 5:227, 7:80–81
Kuhn, Richard, 4:**167–170,** *168*
    acquaintances of, 6:156
    colleagues of, 4:226
    yellow enzymes, 7:33
Kuhn, Thomas Samuel, 2:152, 4:**170–177,** *171*
    influences on, 6:125
    Mertonian paradigm, 5:125
    quantum mechanics, 6:112
    scientific revolution, 6:136

Kuhn, Werner, 3:39, 40, 6:332
Kuhn-Tucker conditions, 7:81
Kuiper, Gerard Peter, 4:**177–181,** *179*
    colleagues of, 7:128
    NASA, 6:444
    students of, 6:310
Kullnig, Rudolf, 4:259
Kumar, Dharma, 7:148
Kumazawa, M., 4:114
Kummel, Bernard, 3:318
Kunckel, Johann, 3:352
Kunitz, Moses, 2:348
Kunkel, Henry, 4:49
Kunsman, Charles Henry, 2:378
Kunstbücher (Ottheinrich), 6:550
Kunstformen der Natur (Haeckel), 3:207
Kuranishi, Masatake, 4:146
Kurchatov, Igor V., 3:34
    acquaintances of, 5:128
    atomic bombs, 1:427
    fusion, 1:426
    nuclear energy, 6:325
Kurchatov, Igor Vasilievich, 3:33
Kurrelmeyer, Bernhard, 3:78
Kursch, Gerhardt, 5:28
Kurt Gödel: Collected Works (Gödel), 3:130
Kurtz, Peter, 1:217–218
Küstner, Karl Friedrich, 3:274
KWG (Kaiser Wilhelm Gesellschaft), 3:212
KWI (Kaiser Wilhelm Institute), 3:210
KWIB (Kaiser Wilhelm Institute for Biochemistry), 1:460–464, 464
Kydland, Finn, 7:151
Kynurenin, 1:463
Kynvyn, James, 2:158
KZO (Koninklijke Zout Organon), 7:138

L
La Mettrie, Julien Offray de, 4:**183–185,** *184*
La Planche, Charles Louis, 4:213
La Ramee, Pierre de. *See* Ramus, Peter
Labor, division of, 1:127
Laboratories, alchemical, 1:231–232
Laboratory manuals, 3:434
Laboratory state of mind, 6:246
Lacaille, Nicolas-Louis de, 4:213
Lacan, Jacques, 3:75
Lack, David, 3:385, 7:377, 379
Ladany, Eugen, 6:156
Ladd, Harry Stephen, 4:**185–187**
Ladenburg, Albert, 4:99
Ladyzhenskaya, Olga Alexandrovna, 4:**187–189,** *188*
Lagalla, Giulio Cesare, 1:442
Lagrange, Joseph-Louis, 2:229, 231, 4:159, 5:197

Laird, John, 5:258
Laird, Wilson M., 6:467
Lakatos, Imre
    influence of, 5:93
        organic chemistry, 6:22
        philosophy of science, 6:135
Lake, Philip, 7:324
The Lake as a Microcosm (Forbes), 7:37
Lake ecosystems, 3:412–414
Lakes. *See* Limnology
Lamarck, Jean-Baptiste, 4:162, **189–193**, *191*, 6:109,
    287
        clouds, 3:386
        influence of, 5:354
        influences on, 4:225
        secularism, 2:221
        transformism, 3:118
Lamarck, Jean-Baptiste Pierre Antoine de Monet de. *See*
    Lamarck, Jean-Baptiste
Lamarckian evolution, 2:243, 3:115, 117, 4:77, 79
Lamb, Hubert Horace, 4:**193–196,** *194*
Lamb, Willis
        hydrogen, 1:275, 6:394
        Lamb shift, 1:273–274
        quantum electrodynamics, 6:196
Lambert, Johann Heinrich, 3:246
LaMettrie, Julien Offray de. *See* La Mettrie, Julien
    Offray de
Land, Edwin, 7:350
Land settlement
        Australia, 6:208–209
        Canada, 7:78–89
Landa, Stanislav, 6:156
Landau, Edmund, 7:156
Landau, Lev Davidovich, 1:318, 319, 2:108, 3:23
        acquaintances of, 4:80, 84, 85
        influence of, 5:129
        Kapitsa Club, 4:82
        students of, 5:127
Landau, Ralph, 4:287
Landauer, Karl, 2:378
Landforms, 6:536–539
Landin, Peter, 6:534
Landriani, Marsilio, 7:170
Landsberg, Helmut Erich, 4:**196–200,** *197*
Landscape analysis
        classical, 1:396
        geomorphology, 6:536–539
Lane, Saunders Mac, 1:287, 366
Lang, Serg, 1:364
Lang, W. D., 3:317
Lange, Carl Georg, 6:11
Lange, Karl, 5:222
Langer, Walter C., 5:217

Langevin, Paul, 1:411, 412
Langfeld, Herbert, 1:358
Langholf, Volker, 3:322
Langlands, Robert, 1:97
Langmuir, Irving, 6:36
        cloud seeding, 1:470, 5:223
        electroconductivity, 6:373–374
        General Electric, 1:310
        tungsten, 1:311
Language
        in animals, 4:148
        anthropology, 7:222–223
        aphasia, 4:350–354, 6:73
        bees, 3:179, 180, 183
        child development, 6:92
        metaphysics, 6:204
        philosophy of, 4:285–286
        psycholinguistics, 7:195
        quantum processes, 1:324–325
        theory of, 2:44–45
Language of arithmetic, 6:265–267
Languages of Art (Goodman), 3:149
Langway, Chester C., 5:328, 329
Lankester, Edwin Ray, 1:209
Lanosterol, 1:198
Lanpo, Jia. *See* Jia Lanpo
Lanz, José María de, 4:**200–203**
Lapicque, Louis, 2:315
Laplace, Pierre-Simon, Marquis de, 2:85
        astronomy, 1:265
        calorimetry, 4:215, 218
        colleagues of, 2:229
        stability of solar system, 5:197
        translations of, 4:119
Laporte, Otto, 7:101
Lapworth, Arthur, 4:14
        acquaintances of, 7:66
        colleagues of, 6:269, 272
Lardner, Dionysius, 3:58
Lardy, Henry, 3:170
*Large-Scale Rotational Flow in a Fixed Cylindrical Volume
    of the Atmosphere* (Saltzman and Pfeffer), 6:342
The Large Scale Structure of Space-Time (Hawking and
    Ellis), 6:399
Lark-Horovitz, Karl, 1:180, 5:202, 6:179, 393–394
Larner, Ken L., 1:31
Larson, Earl R., 2:335
Larson, Richard, 7:59, 60
Lartet, Édouard, 5:298
Lasers
        chemical reactions, 1:259–260
        photochemistry, 6:140
Lash, Jay, 3:187
Lashley, Karl Spencer, 4:141, **203–205,** *204*

animal behavior, 6:367
behavior and perception, 3:269–270
behaviorism, 7:244
colleagues of, 3:268
Harvard neuropsychology, 1:221
learning, 7:241–242
on Murray, Henry Alexander, 5:217
students of, 6:495–496
Lasker, Gabriel W., 7:235
Latimer, Wendell M., 4:295
Latimeria chalumnaie. See coelacanths
Latour, Bruno, 6:21
Lattes, Cesare, 5:303
Laud, William, 3:166
Laue, Max von, 1:280
Laurent, Auguste, 2:323, 324, 4:98, 99, **205–207**
Laurent, Augustin. *See* Laurent, Auguste
Laurent, Goulven, 3:115, 116, 4:190
Laurentianus, 2:121
Lauritsen, Charles Christian, 4:*207,* **207–213,** *210, 211*
  dosimeters, 4:*209*
  NDRC rocket program, 2:167
  nuclear astrophysics, 3:61–62
  solid-propellant rockets, 1:75
  x-ray tubes, 3:59
Lauritsen, Thomas, 7:400
Lauterbur, Paul C., 1:306
Lautman, Albert, 2:120
Lava flows, 3:375–377
Lavochkin, Semyon A., 4:101
Lavoisier, Antoine-Laurent, 2:324–325, 4:**213** **220,** *216*
  chemical revolution, 6:44–45, 7:169
  colleagues of, 1:263, 3:353
  influence of, 3:386, 4:201, 6:513
  oxygen theory, 1:264
  sociology of science and, 5:125
  water synthesis, 7:170
Lavosier, Mme. Marie Anne Pierette. *See* Paulze-
  Lavoisier, Marie-Anne-Pierette
Lavrentev, Mikhail, 1:427
Law, a Liberal Study (Smuts), 6:483
Law, natural
  civil rights, 6:483
  intuition in, 1:146
Law of conservation of energy, 3:307
Law of parsimony, 3:183
Lawrence, Ernest Orlando, 1:55, 56
  Berkeley Radiation Laboratory, 1:322
  colleagues of, 2:15
  conservatism, 6:423
  cyclotrons, 6:179, 7:328
  influence of, 4:296, 328–331, 6:401, 7:329
  MIT Radiation Laboratory, 1:164
  Morse code, 1:390

plutonium, 6:408
radioactivity, 6:407
students of, 7:365
Lawrence, Peter, 2:210
Lawrence Livermore Laboratory, 7:23
The Laws of Disorder (Porter), 6:140
Lawson, James, 7:103
Lawvere, William, 2:362, 5:4
Laycock, Thomas, 2:55–56
Layton, Keith, 4:195
Lazarsfeld, Paul, 5:121
Lazarus, Moritz, 6:522
Le Bel, Joseph Achille, 1:197, 6:154
Le Chatelier, Henry Louis, 2:159, 160
Le Clerc, George-Louis. *See* Buffon, Georges-Louis
  Leclerc, Comte de
Le Gros Clark, Wilfred, 2:240, 7:234
Le Jolis, Auguste, 4:294
Le Rossignol, Robert, 3:203–204
Le Roy, Édouard, 6:109
Le Verrier, Urbain, 4:293–294
Leaci, Antonio, 2:260
Leakey, Louis Seymour Bazett, 2:124, 127, 140,
  4:221–223
  anthropology, 7:116
  influence of, 3:54
  Kanam Man, 5:296–297
Leakey, Mary Douglas Nicol, 2:124, 127, 4:**221–224,**
  222
Learned behavior
  cognitive ethology, 3:182
  foresight and, 5:145
  social contexts and, 5:147
Learning
  animal
    behavior, 6:368–369
    ethology, 7:42–44
    invertebrates, 7:84–86
  behavior and, 3:407–408
  control of autonomic functions, 5:150–151
  history, 6:459–460
  motivation, 3:313
  nervous system, 3:269
  neuropsychology, 3:268
  operationalism, 6:463
  pedagogy, 6:464
  perceptual, 3:120–124, 127–129
  probabilism, 4:36
  reverse, 2:211
  sensory, 3:270
  twin studies, 3:312
Learning and Instinct in Animals (Thorpe), 7:42
Learning and Orientation in Ants (Schneirla), 6:367
Learning disabilities, 7:193–194

Lebanon, excavations, 3:106–107

Leben, Wissenschaft, Klassifikation: Aus dem Nachlass Wilhelm Ostwalds (Niedersen), 5:356

Lebensbilder aus der Tierwelt der Vorzeit (Abel), 7:142

Lebenslinien: Eine Selbstbiographie (Ostwald), 5:356

Lebniewski, Stanislaw, 3:70

Lebour, Marie, 3:259

LeClerc, George-Louis. *See* Buffon, Georges-Louis Leclerc, Comte de

LeConte, Joseph, 4:**224–226**

Lecture Notes for Chemical Students (Frankland), 3:64

Lectures in Celestial Mechanics (Moser), 5:197

Lectures in Statistical Mechanics (Uhlenbeck), 7:103

Lectures on Electricity (Noad), 2:216

Lectures on gas theory (Boltzmann). *See Vorlesungen über Gastheorie* (Boltzmann)

Lectures on number theory (Landau). *See Vorlesungen über Zahlentheorie* (Landau)

Lectures on the Work of the Main Gastric Glands (Pavlov), 6:46

Ledbetter, Myron, 6:146

Lederberg, Joshua, 4:137, 138
  bacterial sex, 7:15
  colleagues of, 7:13
  extraterrestrial life, 3:364
  Nobel Prize, 1:228
  students of, 6:311–312

Lederer, Edgar, 4:**226–230**

Ledingham, J. C. G., 1:454

Ledyard, George. *See* Stebbins, George Ledyard, Jr.

Lee, Richard, 7:237

Lee, Sarah Eglonton Wallis Bowdich, 4:**230–232,** *231*

Lee, Tsung-Dao, 3:23
  beta decay, 7:366
  colleagues of, 3:193
  parity nonconservation problem, 6:337
  superdense matter, 6:170

Lee, William H. K., 1:32

Lee, Yuan T., 6:126

Leegwater, Arie, 5:356

Leeuwenhoek, Antoni van, 4:250

Lefever, René, 6:166

Lefkowitz, Helen, 5:183

Lefschetz, Solomon, 1:317, 2:112
  acquaintances of, 2:360, 7:254
  influence of, 4:145

Lefschetz principle, 3:244

Legem impone subactis (Baldini), 2:150

Legendre, Adrien-Marie, 1:6, 7

Lehman discontinuity, 4:232–235

Lehmann, Bernhard, 5:328

Lehmann, Hermann, 6:83

Lehmann, Inge, 4:**232–236**

Lehmann-Nitsche, Robert, 4:**236–238**

Lehn, Jean-Marie, 2:203

Lehninger, Albert Lester, 3:172, 4:**238–243,** 5:162–163

Lehrbuch der Chemie (Mitscherlich), 5:166

Lehrbuch der kosmischen (Arrhenius), 1:112

Lehrbuch der Naturphilosophie (Oken), 5:332, 333

Lehrbuch der organischen Chemie (Kekulé), 4:98–99

Lehrman, Daniel Sanford, 4:**243–248**
  criticism by, 4:343–344
  ethology, 7:53–54

Leibniz, Gottfried Wilhelm, 3:69, 4:**249–253,** *251*
  Berlin Academy of Sciences, 7:332, 333
  calculus *vs.* geometry, 5:269
  celestial motion, 5:270
  colleagues of, 3:352
  general dynamic relativity, 1:425
  influence of, 3:131
  influences on, 4:65, 134
  metaphysics, 2:171
  motion, 2:273
  on Swineshead, Richard, 6:563
  vis viva controversy, 5:11

Leibowitz, Sarah, 5:151

Leicester, Henry, 1:266

Leiden, Goudsmit, 6:37

Leigh, Egbert, 3:415

Leighly, John, 7:38

Leighton, Robert, 1:75

Leinaas, Jon Magne, 1:237

Lékařské knížky (Prachaticz), 6:153

Leloir, Luis Federico, 4:**253–258,** *254, 255*

Lemaître, Georges, 1:43
  expanding universe, 5:81, 6:457
  positive space curvature, 3:275
  relativistic cosmology, 5:73, 6:456

Lemieux, Raymond Urgel, 4:**258–264**

Lemmon, Richard M., 2:17

Lemniscate curve, 1:5–6

Lenard, Philipp, 2:378

Lengyel, Peter, 5:310

Lenhossék, Mihály, 6:567–568

Lenin, Vladimir Ilich, 7:162

Lennard-Jones, John Edward, 3:254–255, 298, 6:130

Lenses, optical, 1:294–295

Lenz, Fritz, 3:28

Leof, Charlotte. *See* Serber, Charlotte Leof

Leonard, Frederick C., 7:284

Leonardo da Vinci, 1:167

Leonhard, Karl von, 1:415

Leoniceno, Nicolò, 4:**264–267,** *265*
  ancient medicine, 6:120
  medieval medicine, 6:68

Leopold, Aldo, 2:319, 385, 4:*267,* **267–271**

Leopold, Luna B., 1:156

Lepidopterology, 6:379

Leprosy, 6:323

Leptines, 4:**271–272**

Leray, Jean, 2:258, 4:**272–274**
    differential equations, 6:380
    influence of, 4:319
    refinement of work, 4:188

Lerner, I. Michael, 4:**274–278**, 6:515

Lerner, Isadore Michael. *See* Lerner, I. Michael

Lerner, Israel Michael. *See* Lerner, I. Michael

Lesbesgue, Henri-Léon, 3:265

Leske, Nathanael Gottfried, 1:95

Leslie, Patrick, 2:385

Lester, Robert L., 3:171

Lethæa geognostica (Bronn), 1:415

Lettau, Heinz, 6:553

Letter Kappa (Zosimos of Panopolis), 7:406

Letter on Resurrection (Maimonides), 5:8

Letter on the Preservation of Health to Antigonus (Diocles of Carystus), 2:302

Letter Sigma (Zosimos of Panopolis), 7:406

Letter to Colybas of Mitylene (Argyrus), 1:99

Letter to Marcella (Porphyry), 6:137

A Letter to Stalin (Szilard), 6:575

Letters from Jenny (Allport), 1:53

Letters on the English (Voltaire), 5:57

Lettvin, Jerome, 5:77

Leukemia, 2:374–375

Leuschner, Armin Otto, 7:284

Levamisole, 4:32

Levels of Microbiological Investigation (Stephenson), 6:521

Levene, Phoebus A., 1:190

Leverrier, Urbain Jean Joseph, 5:134

Leveson, David J., 3:421

Levi, Giuseppe, 3:220

Levi, Isaac, 4:36

Levi-Città, Tullio, 2:367, 3:192

Levi-Montalcini, Rita, 3:217, 220–221, *221*

Lévi-Strauss, Claude, 7:237, 256

Levin, Gilbert, 3:364, 4:137, 139

Levin, Harry, 3:122

Levine, George, 2:55

Levine, Raphael D., 1:259

Levins, Richard, 2:25, 3:162

Levocabastine, 4:33

Levy, David, 6:446

Levy, Donald, 6:473

Lévy-Bruhl, Lucien, 4:64, 6:92

Lew, Hin, 3:300

Lewin, Kurt, 3:14, 16, 4:**278–284**, *280*

Lewis, Clarence I., 3:408

Lewis, David, 4:**284–287**

Lewis, Edward B., 6:41

Lewis, Gilbert Newton, 6:401
    bonds, 6:36

influence of, 4:295, 331

Lewis, Warren Harmon, 5:17

Lewis, Warren Kendall, 3:383, 4:**287–292**, *288*

Lewontin, Richard C., 2:4
    Spandrels of San Marco, 3:161
    Vietnam War protest, 3:162
    zoology, 6:453

Li, Seung Ki, 6:333

Li-Fu Chiang, 2:111

Liais, Emmanuel-Bernardin, 4:**293–294**

Libau, Andreas. *See* Libavius, Andreas

Libavius, Andreas, 6:418

Libby, Willard Frank, 3:195, 4:**295–300**, *298*, 6:41

Libellus de quinque corporibus reglaribus (Piero Della Francesca), 6:104–105

Liber assumptorum (Archimedes), 1:89

Liber Calculationum (Swineshead), 2:325, 327, 6:562–563

Liber de secretis natura sive de quinta essentia (Lull), 4:347–348

Liber de vita philosophorum (Arnald of Villanova, Pseudo), 1:109

Liber Hermetis, 7:112

Liber Lunae de scientia Abel, 1:14

Liber prestigiorum (Qurra), 1:14

Liberalism against Populism (Riker), 6:254

Libertarianism, 5:286

Libraries, 6:348

Libraries of the Future (Licklider), 4:304, 305

Libya, 1:155–156

Libyan Sands (Bagnold), 1:155

Lichens, 6:389

Lichnérowicz, André, 4:**300–302**

Lichtheim, Ludwig, 4:353

Lick Observatory, 5:112, 113

Licklider, Joseph Carl Robnett, 4:**302–307**

Liddell, Dorothy, 4:221

Liddell, E. G. T., 2:329

Lie, Marius Sophus, 1:344, 2:119, 4:**307–310**, *308*, 6:121

Lie groups (mathematics), 2:119–120
    algebraic topology, 1:344–345
    creation of, 4:307–310
    harmonic analysis, 3:241–244
    Jordan algebra, 3:194
    linear algebraic, 1:343
    quantum mechanics, 7:277–278

Lieberman, Bruce s., 7:225

Liebermann, Carl, 2:358

Liebig, Justus von, 2:323, 4:**310–314**, *311*, 6:359
    controversy with Mitscherlich, Eilhard, 5:166
    influence of, 4:205, 7:371
    periodic law and, 5:107
    students of, 7:45

Liebig, Justus von, *continued*
    theory of derived radicals, 4:206
Life
    extraterrestrial
        genetics, 3:361
        Mars, 3:364–365
        possibility of, 6:309–314, 435, 436, 485–487
        radio astronomy, 3:139
        works on, 6:432
    origin
        comets, 3:391
        genes, 3:363–364
        molecular biology, 2:211
        prebiotic chemistry, 5:154–158
        saltational theory, 5:368
        solar system, 6:310
        spontaneous generation, 1:208–210
    prolongation, 1:139
    Roman philosophy, 6:117
    self-preservation, 2:20
Life: An Introduction to Biology (Simpson et al.), 6:454
Life, Letters, and Labours of Francis Galton (Pearson),
    6:53
Life: The Unfinished Experiment (Luria), 4:359
Life and Letters of Thomas Henry Huxley, 3:429, 430
*Life Cycle of Cyclones and the Polar Front Theory of
    Atmospheric Circulatio*n (Bjerknes and Solberg), 1:247
Life Itself: Its Origin and Nature (Crick), 2:211
Life of Plotinus (Porphyry), 6:137
A Life of Pythagoras (Porphyry), 6:137
Life Science in the Twentieth Century (Morgan), 5:183
Lifton, Robert Jay, 3:28
Light
    absorption
        photosynthesis, 2:14–15
        transition metals, 4:60
        vision, 7:214, *214*
    chromosome banding, 2:299–300
    color, 5:10
    duality, 1:410–411
    dynamics, 1:294–295
    electromagnetism, 6:549
    energy
        quantum hypothesis, 2:364–365
        Smith-Purcell effect, 6:182
    nature of, 4:132–133
    optical phenomena, 3:111–112
    photosynthesis, 2:14–15
    quantum theory, 1:411–412, 2:364–365
    radar, 6:139–140
    radiation, 3:137
    rays, 2:108–109
    scattering, 7:126, 128, 129–130
    solar

        controversies, 5:11
        geometry, 2:233–234
    spectrum, 5:273–274
    sulfur principle, 3:353
    velocity, 2:365–367
    wave theory, 2:78, 3:236
Light Scattering by Small Particles (Van de Hulst),
    7:129–130
Lightfoot, Edwin N., 7:135
Lightman, Bernard, 3:432
Liklider, J. C. R., 6:534
Lilienfeld, Julius E., 1:180
Lilienthal, David E., 1:135–136, 6:196
Liller, William, 1:159
Lillie, Frank Rattray, 2:183
    chicken incubation, 3:223
    colleagues of, 2:389
    students of, 3:218–219
Limb movement, electrophysiology, 1:15, 17–18
Limestone, lithographic, 7:142
*Limit Distributions for Sums of Independent Random
    Variables* (Kolmogorov), 4:151
Limited Test Ban Treaty of 1963, 1:136, 7:24
Limnología (Margalef), 5:24
Limnology
    biogechemistry, 3:413
    biogeochemistry, 3:410
    ecology, 2:355–356
    education, 3:261
    Europe, 7:35–37
    insects, 3:411
    major scientists in, 5:22–26
    oceanography and, 5:172–173
    plankton, 2:353–354
    population biology, 3:412–413
    salmon, 3:260–261
    statistics, 6:256
Limoges, Camille, 2:244
Lindberg, David C., 1:147
Lindblad, Bertil, 5:342
Linde, Justin von, 4:312
Lindeman, Raymond L.
    biogeochemical cycles, 5:317, 322
    education of, 3:411
    influence of, 7:37
    population ecology, 3:416
    radiation ecology, 3:414
Lindemann, Carl Louis Ferdinand von, 2:30
Lindemann, Frederick Alexander, 1:292, 2:307
Linderstrøm-Lang, Kaj Ulrik, 1:76–77, 78
Lindsay, Eric, 5:72
Lindsey, Charles, 2:297
Lindzen, Richard S., 3:264
Linear accelerators, 6:409

Linear algebraic groups, 1:343, 345
Linear Algebraic Groups (Borel), 1:346
Linear astrolabes, 7:88, *88*
Linear programming, 7:80–81
Lingua Aegyptiaca restituta (Kircher), 4:131
Linnaeanism
    animal classification, 5:331
    Buffonianism *vs.*, 1:433–434
Linnaeus, Carl, 4:201, *314*, **314–318,** 5:99–100, 103
Linnaeus: Nature and Nation (Koerner), 4:315
Linné, Carl von. *See* Linnaeus, Carl
Linsen, Hans, 1:314
Linstead, Patrick, 1:198
Lions, Jacques-Louis, 4:273, **318–322**
Liouville, Joseph, 2:30, 3:327
Lipmann, Fritz Albert, 4:**322–327,** *323, 325,* 5:306
    influence of, 4:72, 73, 75
    Klein, Harold P., 4:136
Lipmann, Otto, 6:523, 525
Liposome reconstitution, 6:199–200
Lippens, Ben, 1:314
Lippitt, Ronald, 3:14
Lippmann, Walter, 7:27
Lipson, Carol, 2:270
Lipson, Henry, 3:335
Liquid crystals
    polymers, 3:39
    structure, 2:278
Lissmann, Hans, 1:437
List, Friedrich, 5:332
Listable sets of numbers, 6:265, 266, 267
Listening in the Dark (Griffin), 3:177
Lister, Joseph, 4:150
Lister, Mrs. J.J. *See* Marryat, Dorothea Charlotte Edith
Literacy and the Charlatan in Ancient Greek Medicine (Dean-Jones), 3:324
Lithium Aluminum Hydride, Aluminum Hydride, and Lithium Gallium Hydride, and Some of Their Applications in Organic and Inorganic Chemistry (Schlesinger), 1:421
Lithofacies Map (Krumbein), 4:165
Lithographic limestone, 7:142
Littelwood, John E., 7:414, 415
Little, Arthur D., 4:287
The Little Astronomy (Euclid), 2:416
Little Science, Big Science (Price), 6:162
Littlewood, John Edensor, 7:156, 314
Littré, Émile, 3:322
Liu Xianting, 6:59
Liver cells, 2:*144*, 145, *145*
Lives of the Philosophers (Diogenes Laertius), 2:395
Living on the Third Planet (Alfvén), 1:43
The Living Races of Man (Coon), 2:175

Livingston, Milton Stanley, 1:134, 271, 4:**327–333,** *328,* 7:329
Livingstone, David, 2:124, 125
Livostin, 4:33
Livre d'arithmétique (Mennher), 2:157
Ljubimowa, Militsa, 6:571
Ljungdahl, Lars, 7:347, 348
Lloyd, David P. C., 2:331
Lloyd, G. E. R., 3:322
Lloyd skull, 5:298
Llull, Ramón. *See* Lull, Ramón
Lobachevsky, Nikolai, 3:246
Localisation (Brodmann), 1:408
Lochte-Holtgreven, Walter, 7:106, 107
Lock, Robert Heath, 1:211
Locke, John, 1:432
Locke, S. B., 4:269
Lockley, Ronald M., 3:425
Locks and Beagles (Beach), 1:222–223
Lockyer, Joseph Norman, 3:64, 7:218
Lockyer, William, 7:218
Locomotion, perceptual learning, 3:122–124, 124
Lodestones, magnetism, 3:108–109
Lodge, Oliver, 3:58
Loeb, Jacques, 1:373
    early career of, 5:183
    experimental parthenogenesis, 4:67–68, 69
    physiology, 6:459
    students of, 6:460, 7:239–240
    theoretical opposition, 5:215
Loewi, Otto, 7:178, 179
Löfberg, Jan, 3:370
Logic, 5:178–179
    algebraic, 5:178–179
        axiomatization, 6:134–135
        logicism, 3:70
        set theory and, 5:3–4
    child development, 6:93–94
    education, 6:563–564, 563–564
    inductive, 2:45–46, 6:133–134
    inferences, 2:122–123
    mathematics and, 1:144–145, 3:130–132, 5:3–4
    medieval, 1:35
    natural knowledge, 1:450
    natural philosophy, 5:312–314, 6:562
    pedagogy, 6:205
    propositions, 1:378–379
    rational choice theory, 4:35
    scientific method, 7:388
    symbolic, 2:310–311, 3:69–70
    theory of probability, 4:112
    validity testing, 1:146
The Logic of Collective Action (Olson), 5:336
The Logic of Decision (Jeffrey), 4:35

The Logic of Modern Physics (Bridgman), 1:359
The Logic of Scientific Discovery (Popper), 6:135
Logic Theorist (LT), 5:255, 256
Logica Hamburgensis (Jungius), 4:65
The Logical Structure of Errors in Philosophical Arguments
   (Harsanyi), 3:247
The Logical Structure of the World (Carnap), 2:44
The Logical Syntax of Language (Carnap), 2:44
Logik der Forschung (Popper), 6:134, 135
Loh, Edward, 7:305
Lohmann, Herbert, 5:232
Lohmann, Karl, 4:323
Lohne, J. A., 3:246
Lombard, Peter. *See* Peter Lombard.
Lombroso, Cesare, 3:161
Lomnitz, Cinna, 4:40
London, Fritz, 1:179, 304, 6:37
London, Heinz, 1:179, 304
Long, David, 5:41
Long Island Sound oceanography, 6:256–257
Long Range Desert Group (LRDG), 1:155–156
Longair, Malcolm, 7:130
Longinus, Cassius, 6:137
Longomontanus, Christian Sørenson, 4:107
Lonsdale, Kathleen, 4:16, 5:233
Loomis, Alfred Lee, 1:56
Loomis, Francis Wheeler, 5:210
Loopstra, Bram, 2:295
Loperamide, 4:32
Lords of the Fly (Kohler), 5:185
Lorente de Nó, Rafael, 3:269, 5:77
Lorentz, Hendrik Antoon, 2:366, 4:**333–336**, *334*, 7:99
   colleagues of, 2:365
     local time concept, 2:367
     relativity, 6:122, 123
     Sitter, Willem de, 6:456
     x-ray diffraction, 1:280
Lorenz, Konrad Zacharias, 2:25, 4:*335*, **336–346**, *341*
   animal behavior, 1:150, 151, 6:369, 7:51, 53
   colleagues of, 3:385, 7:182
   comprehensive theory of instinctive behavior,
     4:340–341
   critique of, 4:246
   early scientific development and professional
     contacts, 4:337–340
   ethology, 4:343–344, 7:42
   imprinting, 2:197
   influence of, 3:178, 222
   influences on, 2:198, 5:279
   instinctive behavior patterns, evolution, and
     epistemology, 4:342–343
   life and career, 4:336–337
   meteorology, 6:343
   National Socialism, 4:342
   Nobel Prize, 7:55
   overall significance and influence, 4:344–345
   sociobiology, 1:153
   and Tinbergen, 4:341, 344
   translations of, 4:244
Lorenz transformation, 7:165
Lory, Pierre, 4:19
Los Alamos National Laboratory
   associates, 6:285, 286, 7:21, 22, 23, 328–329
   organization and director, 5:348–349
   See also Manhattan Project
*The Los Alamos Primer: The First Lectures on How to
   Build an Atomic Bomb* (Serber), 6:422
Loschmidt, Josef, 1:338, 4:99
Lotka, Alfred James, 2:384, 385, 3:415, 5:324
Lotka-Volterra equations, 3:415
Louderback, George Davis, 6:234
Loudon, John Claudius, 4:231
Louis Pasteur, Free Lance of Science (Dubos), 2:318
Louise A. Boyd Expedition, 1:395–396
Loukites, Constantine, 2:120–121
Lovelace, Countess. *See* King, Ada Augusta, Countess of
   Lovelace
Loveland, Jeff, 1:433
Lovell, Bernard, 1:292, 6:302
Lovelock, James, 3:364–365
Love's Story Told (Robinson), 5:218
Low, Barbara, 3:336
Low, Frank, 7:289
Low-pressure cyclones, 6:559
Löwdin, Per-Olov, 3:88
Lowe, Clarence van Riet, 2:124
Lowenstam, Heinz, 7:271
Lowry, Dorothy C., 4:275
Lowry, Oliver Howe, 4:73
LRDG (Long Range Desert Group), 1:155–156
LT (Logic Theorist), 5:255, 256
Lu Gwei-Djen, 5:239
Lü Jiong, 7:403
Lub, W. A., 6:76
Lucas, Howard J., 6:37
Lucas, Keith, 1:15, 16–17
Luce, R. Duncan, 7:92
Lüders, Gerhart, 1:237, 238
Ludlow, John M., 5:20
Ludwig, Carl Friedrich Wilhelm, 6:46
Ludwig, George, 7:122
Lugeon, Maurice, 3:393
Luhn, Francis, 7:281
Lukeš, Rudolf, 6:156
Lukoff, Herman, 2:337
Lull, Ramón, 4:**346–349**
Lumley, John, 6:8
Lunar eclipses, 3:283–284

Lunar geochemistry. *See* Moon, geochemistry
Lunar Orbit Rendezvous (LOR), 7:175
Lunar research. *See* Moon
Lundgren, Anders, 1:268
Lundsgaard, Einar, 4:72, 73, 324, 5:306
Lung cancer, automobile emissions, 3:383
Luo Shijun, 7:401
Luria, Alexander Romanovich, 4:**349–355**, *354,* 7:195, 196
Luria, Salvador Edward, 2:269, 270, 4:**355–361**, *358,* 6:318
Luria, Salvatore. *See* Luria, Salvador Edward
Luschan, Felix von, 3:26
Lush, Jay L., 4:115
Lüst, Reimar, 7:130
Luther, Martin
    capitalism and, 6:56
    Protestant Reformation, 6:16
    psychobiography, 2:410
Luttinger, Joaquin, 6:170
Lux. *See* Royer, Clémence-Auguste
Luyten, Willem J., 6:500
Luzin, Nikolai N., 4:151
Lwoff, André, 4:226
Lycan, William, 4:30
Lyell, Charles, 2:57, 85, 243, 5:133
    actualism, 6:248, 249
    catastrophism, 1:395, 7:280
    criticisms of, 5:368
    nonprogressionist paleontology, 3:430
    steady state uniformitarianism, 1:416
Lyman, Theodore, 6:49, 7:73
Lyman alpha line, 7:75
Lynch, Ruth Stocking, 4:45
Lynen, Feodor, 5:309
Lyons, Richard, 3:154
Lyot, Bernard, 2:344
    inventions, 5:113
    Kuiper, Gerard Peter, 4:178
Lysenko, Trofim Denisovich, 4:85
    anti-Mendelianism, 3:364
    Communist Party, 1:371
    critique of work, 4:357
    ecology, 6:510
    genetics, 5:248, 6:493–494
Lysenkoism, 6:493–494
Lysogeny, 1:455
Lysosomes, 5:281, 283
Lyttleton, Raymond
    acquaintances of, 6:499
    comets, 3:391
    electrical cosmology, 1:341
    filament dissipation, 6:500
    interstellar matter, 3:388–389

relativity and astrophysics, 1:342

M

M-F (masculinity-femininity) test, 7:28
Ma, Tsu Sheng, 6:324
Ma Zuscheng. *See* Ma, Tsu Sheng
Maassbestimmungen (Weber), 3:4
Mac Lane, Saunders, 2:361–362, 5:**1–5**
McAdams, William H., 4:288
McAdie, Alexander G., 7:402
MacArthur, Robert, 3:411, 415, 416
Macbride, David, 1:92
MacBride, Ernest William, 4:79
McCall, David, 3:197–198, 199
McCarthy, Joesph Raymond, 1:331
McCarthy, John, 4:304, 5:255, 6:427
McClelland, David, 5:219
McClelland, James L., 1:405
MacClintock, Paul, 4:164
McClintock, Barbara, 1:225, 5:**67–72**, *69,* 6:317
McClung, Clarence Erwin, 2:59
McClung, Leland, 4:356
McClure, Mary Ann, 3:56
McClure, Robert, 3:198, 199
McConnell, Anita, 5:37
McCord, Thomas, 7:271
MacCorquodale, Kenneth, 5:91
McCosh, James, 1:168–169
McCown, Theodore D., 3:106
McCrea, William Hunter, 5:**72–76**
    expanding universe, 5:81
    Newtonian cosmology, 3:275
    on Strömgren, Bengt Georg Daniel, 6:546
MacCullagh, James, 3:236
McCulloch, Warren Sturgis, 5:**76–79**, 255
McCulloch-Pitts networks, 5:*77,* 77–78, *78*
MacDonald, James Ramsay, 1:188
Macdonald, Margaret. *See* Smith, Margaret Macdonald
McDonald, Duncan, 4:114–115
McDougall, William, 2:197, 4:63
    acquaintances of, 7:240
    influence of, 4:340
McElroy, William, 4:75
McEwen, Bruce S., 5:151
McGarvey, Bruce, 3:197–198
MacGillavry, Caroline, 1:282
Mach, Ernst, 2:280, 282
    general relativity, 1:425
    inertia, 6:398
    positivism, 6:55, 7:369
McHenry, James, 1:175
Machina, Mark, 6:350

Machina Carnis: The Biochemistry of Muscular Contraction in Its Historical Development (Needham), 5:232, 233
Machines
    ancient engineering and, 5:175–176
    classification of, 4:201–202
    human cognition and, 1:187
Mach's principle
    cosmological constant, 2:369–370
    influence, 6:398
MacIntyre, Alastair, 4:50
McIntyre, Archibald, 2:330
McKelvey, Vencent E., 3:398
MacKenzie, Chalmers Jack, 7:324
MacKenzie, Donald, 1:211, 6:54
McKenzie, K. R., 6:408
McKinley, J. Charnley, 5:90
Maclaurin, Colin, 2:230, 3:422, 5:10–11
MacLean, Paul, 6:10, 12
McMath, Robert R., 3:142, 5:116
McMillan, Armand, 1:120
McMillan, Edwin Mattison, 1:55, 56
    colleagues of, 6:422
    influence of, 4:332
    phase stability, 6:409
    plutonium, 6:408
    transuranium elements, 6:401, 402, 404
McMillan, Priscilla, 5:349
McMullin, Alister, 1:331
Macnamara, Jean, 6:209
Macquart, Louis Charles Henri, 4:217
Macquer, Pierre Joseph, 6:507, 7:169
Macroeconomics, 7:151
Macroevolution, 6:353–354
Macromolecules, 2:48–50, 6:330–331
McVittie, George Cunliffe, 5:73, **79–85**
Madelung, Erwin, 1:270
Maestlin, Michael, 4:105
Magenes, Enrico, 4:319
Magic, natural, 2:20
Magic squares, 5:196
Magmatology, 6:262
Magnello, Eileen, 6:53
Magnes sive de arte magnetica (Kircher), 4:132
Magnetic fields
    earth
        atmospheric electricity and, 5:51–52
        continental drift and, 1:292–293, 6:298–300
        geophysics, 6:298–301
        radiation, 6:99
        reverse, 3:375–377
        variations in, 5:48–49, *49*
    interstellar, 1:278
The Magnetic Moment of the Proton (Rabi), 6:194

Magnetic moments, protons, 6:194
Magnetic philosophy (Cabeo). *See Philosophia magnetica* (Cabeo)
Magnetic resonance method, 6:194–195
The Magnetic Scattering of Neutrons (Schwinger), 6:392
Magnetism
    Aharonov-Bohm effect, 1:324
    Aristotelian, 2:1–2
    basalt, 5:49, *49*
    continental drift, 2:191–192
    discovery of, 1:146
    electricity and, 2:1–2
    electrodynamics, 3:4
    electromagnetism
        Einstein-Cartan-Sciama-Kibble theory, 6:399
        electrodynamics, 3:3–4
        gauge theory, 6:340
        hadronic SU(6) symmetry, 3:193
        quantum electrodynamics, 6:335
        United Kingdom, 6:549
    experimental procedures, 3:*2*, 2–3
    geophysics, 7:118, 119
    magnetic declination, 4:132
    magnetic reversals, 2:192–193
    measurement of, 4:8
    polarity in, 3:108–109
    solar, 1:131, 3:137–138
    stellar
        hydrodynamics, 2:91
        plasmas, 1:40–42
Magnetographs, 1:131
Magnetohydrohynamics, 6:501
Magnetometers, 7:118, 121
Magnetoresistance, 7:320
Magnetrons
    applications, 6:179–180
    radar, 3:255
    World War II, 6:195
Magnien, Jacques, 6:97
Magulis, Lynn, 6:311
Mahler, Gustav, 4:77
Maienschein, Jane, 5:184
Maier, Norman, 6:367
Maimonides, Rabbi Moses ben Maimon, 5:**5–9**, *6*
Maine de Biran, Marie-François-Pierre, 4:26
Mainer, Edward, 2:244
Mairan, Jean-Jacques Dortous de, 5:**10–13**
Maize, 1:225, 228, 5:68–71, 6:317
Majima, Riko. *See* Majima, Toshiyuki
Majima, Toshiyuki, 5:288, 289, 290–291
Major, Randolph, 3:42–43
Major Features of Evolution (Simpson), 6:454, 455
Majorana, Ettore, 6:170

The Making and Use of the Geometrical Instruction, Called a Sector (Hood), 2:158
Malacology
    genetic assimilation, 7:205
    natural selection, 2:4–5
    taxonomy, 2:3
    See also Mollusks
Malaguti, Faustino Jovita Marianus, 2:324
Malan, Daniel François, 6:477
The Malay Archipelago (Wallace), 7:226
Malcolm, Janet, 3:73
Malcolm, Michael, 3:52
Malde, Harold, 2:192
Malenkov, Georgiǐ, 4:85
Malinowski, Bronislaw, 7:235
Mallet, Lucien, 2:109
Malnutrition, intelligence and, 5:245
Malone, Thomas, 1:470
Malpighi, Marcello, 4:250
Malthus, Thomas Robert, 2:244, 5:**13–15,** *14*
Mammalia, Conchology, Ornithology (Cuvier), 4:231
Mammals, evolution
    creative, 5:354–355
    paleontology, 6:452, 453–455, 453–455
    See also specific mammals
Man Adapting (Dubos), 2:318, 319
Man-Apes or Ape-Men? (Clark), 2:141
Man-computer Interactive Data Access System (McIDAS), 6:556–557
Man in History (Bastian), 1:206
Man on His Nature (Sherrington), 2:332
Man the Tool-Maker (Oakley), 4:221–223, 5:295–296
Manchester differential analyzer, 3:254–255
Mandel, George, 1:120
Mandelbrojt, Szolem, 1:364
Mandelkern, Leo, 3:39
Mandelshtam, Leonid Isaakovich, 1:317, 6:326
Manget, Jean-Jacques, 1:110
Mangold, Hilde, 5:**15–18,** *16*
    dissertation citations, 5:*18*
    embryology, 7:202, 203
    neural induction, 1:373
    organizer experiments, 3:349
Mangold, Otto, 3:349, 4:68, 5:16
Manhattan Engineering District. *See* Manhattan Project.
Manhattan Project
    artillery research, 1:75
    bio-organic chemistry, 2:15
    censorship of uranium publications, 1:392
    chelate chemistry, 2:14
    chemistry, 2:394
    cyclotrons, 1:163
    directors, 2:167, 5:209
    espionage, 6:80

    implosion method research, 1:306
    nuclear weapons, 6:419
    participation, 4:291, 6:573, 7:21, 265–266, 298
    particle physics, 3:19–20
    plutonium, 1:134–135, 5:190, 6:402–403, 408–409
    radiation sickness, 5:242
    recruitment, 6:169
    research, 6:170
    theoretical physics, 1:274
    uranium isotope separation, 1:322
    See also Atomic bombs; Nuclear weapons
Manifolds, 5:229, 7:291–292
Mankind Evolving (Dobzhansky), 7:237
Mann, Alfred K., 6:171
Mann, Frederick George, 2:103
Mann, Thomas, 6:92
Manometry, 4:72 73
Mansfeld, Jaap, 3:323
Mansfield, Charles Blachford, 5:**18–20,** *19*
Mantell, Gideon Algernon, 2:225
Manual du Voyageur (Kaltbrunner), 5:180
Manual of Biochemistry of Men and Animals (Oppenheimer). *See Handbuch der Biochemie des Menschen und der Tiere* (Oppenheimer)
Manual of Experimental Embryology (Hamburger), 3:223
Manual of Sedimentary Petrography (Krumbein), 4:164, 165
Manual of Vascular Plants of Northeastern United States and Adjacent Canada (Cronquist), 2:213
Manuale di economia politica (Pareto), 6:18
Manuel of Trebizond, 2:121
Manufacture of Soda, with Special Reference to the Ammonia Process (Hou Te-Pang), 3:377, 378–379
Manufacturing, 1:127
Manuscript 27 (Galilei), 3:97
Manuscript 72 (Galilei), 3:97, 98, 112
Manuzio, Aldo, 4:264, 265, 6:68
Many-particle systems, 1:318–319
Manzini, Raimondo, 5:37
Map of Prospective Area of Oil Distribution (Huang Jiqing), 3:393
Mapmaking. *See* Cartography
Mapping
    brain, 1:408, 7:161–163
    chromosomes, 1:225
    natural numbers, 6:266
Maps. *See* Cartography
Marbaix, Gerard, 1:375–376
Marcet, Jane Haldimand, 5:**20–22,** *21*
March, Francis Andrew, 2:73
Marchetti, Sandra Citroni. *See* Citroni Marchetti, Sandra
Marcianus graecus 299, 5:339, 7:406
Marcinkiewicz integral, 7:415
Margalef, Ramon, 5:**22–27**

Margoliash, Emmanuel, 4:116
Maricourt, Pierre de. *See* Peter Peregrinus
Marie-Victorin, Frère, 2:235
Marijuana, 2:214
Marilaün, Anton Kerner von. *See* Kerner von Marilaün, Anton
Marine ecosystems
    analytical chemistry, 3:257–259
    tidal flats, 7:142
Marine Geology of the Pacific (Menard), 5:96
Marine science
    analytical chemistry, 3:257–259
    animal behavior, 1:149
    breeding behavior of marine animals, 4:67–68
    ethology, 1:151
    geology, 2:286–288, 5:96–97
    major scientists in, 5:22–26
    Netherlands, 1:148
    research, 7:377
    Tortugas Laboratory, 5:59–60
Mariner, Ruth, 6:312
Mariner space probes, 5:263, 7:124
Marino, Antonio, 2:259
Marinus of Tyre, 5:**27**
Mariotte, Edme, 3:352
Marital adjustment research, 7:28
Mark, Edward L., 5:59
Mark, Herman F., 5:**27–32**, 6:230, 332
Mark-Housing viscosity formula, 6:332
Mark-Houwink equation, 5:29–30
Mark I computers, 3:357–358
Market design, 7:150
Market-oriented scientists, 7:158
Markov, Andrei Andreevich, 7:155
Marks, Pieter, 7:188
Marler, Peter, 7:43
Marolois, Samuel, 5:177
Marquet, Yves, 4:19
Marquis, Donald G., 3:312, 313
Marr, David Courtnay, 2:210, 5:**32–36**
Marryat, Dorothea Charlotte Edith, 1:211
Mars
    atmospheric science, 6:313
    brightness variations, 6:312
    carbon dioxide on, 4:138–139, 178
    life on, 3:364–365, 6:435
    NASA, 5:263–264, 6:486–487
    orbit, 4:107
    organic compounds, 4:139–140
    satellites
        space exploration, 6:100
        Viking Project, 4:137–140, *138*
    solar transit, 2:178
    structure, 4:177

Mars, Pieter
    colleagues of, 7:138
    oxidation, 7:136
    professors of, 1:313
The Mars Project (von Braun), 7:174
Mars-Van Krevelen mechanism, 7:136
Marsh, Adam, 1:143–144
Marsh, Othniel C., 2:314, 4:121
Marshak, Robert, 3:24, 6:169
Marshall, Alfred, 4:112
Marsigli, Luigi. *See* Marsili, Luigi Ferdinando
Marsigli's Europe (Stoye), 5:36
Marsili, Luigi Ferdinando, 5:**36–38**
Martial, René, 7:115
Martianus Capella, 2:412
Martin, Archer John Porter, 2:206, 5:**38–42**, *41*
Martin, Charles, 5:39
Martin, Clyde, 4:125
Martin, Dorothy, 3:15
Martin, James, 6:486
Martin, Paul, 6:395
Martindale, Don, 3:17
Marton, Lucien, 1:374
Martz, Dowell, 7:271
Maruyama, Takeo, 4:116
Marvel, Carl, 3:41
Marxism, 5:281, 284–285
Masculinity and femininity, 7:27–28
Ma'shar, Abu. *See* Abū Ma'shar al-Balkhī, Ja'far ibn Muhammad
Maslov, Victor P., 4:273
Maslow, Abraham, 5:**43–48**, *46*
Mason, Ronald, 7:312
Mason, William, 3:180
Maspin, 6:317, 320
Mass, atomic. *See* Atomic mass
Mass, Ernst, 2:304
Mass-energy equivalency
    light quanta, 2:365
    nuclear isotopes, 1:162–163
Mass extinction, 2:224–226, 5:265, 266
Mass spectrometry, 1:162–163, 165
    in analytical chemistry, 4:229
    industrial science, 2:166
Massachusetts Institute of Technology (MIT)
    associates, 6:285, 286
    neuroscience, 6:360
    radar, 6:195–196
Massini, Peter, 2:16
Massive stars, 5:348
Masson, Jeffrey, 3:73
Masters, Maxwell, 1:211
Masters, William, 4:129
Mästlin, Michael, 2:177

Mataré, Herbert, 1:180–181
Matematicheskaia teoriia optimalnykh protsessov
   (Pontryagin), 6:128
Materialism, 2:80
Materials for the Study of Variation (Bateson), 1:210–211
Materials science, 2:161–163
Maternal genes, 1:399–400
Mathematical analysis
   celestial mechanics, 5:197–198
   computer science, 3:50, 4:319–320
   functions, 2:421–422, 5:198–199
   integrals, 2:76
   Lie groups, 2:119–120
   perimeters, 2:258–259
   rigor in, 1:6–7
   scheme theory, 2:292
   See also specific concepts and branches of Mathematics
*Mathematical Analysis and Numerical Methods for Science
   and Technology* (Lions), 4:320
The Mathematical Analysis of Logic (Frege), 3:70
Mathematical biology, 3:415
Mathematical geology, 4:164
Mathematical logic
   arithmetic, 6:265–267
   computer science, 7:82–84
   development, 7:10–11
Mathematical modeling
   catalysis, 1:354–355
   oceanography, 6:256–257
Mathematical models
   consciousness, 2:382
   visual perception, 2:382
The Mathematical Papers of Isaac Newton (Whiteside),
   5:268–269, 270
Mathematical Psychics (Edgeworth), 5:188
Mathematical psychology, 7:91–96
Mathematical Psychology of War (Richardson), 6:240
The Mathematical Theory of Black Holes
   (Chandrasekhar), 2:92
A Mathematical Theory of Communication (Shannon),
   6:424, 426
A Mathematical Theory of Cryptography (Shannon), 6:426
The Mathematical Theory of Optimal Processes
   (Pontryagin), 6:128
Mathematical Theory of the Differential Analyzer
   (Shannon), 6:425
Mathematico-Deductive Theory of Rote Learning (Hull),
   3:408
Mathematics
   actuarial science, 6:564, 566
   of aerodynamics, 5:335–336
   analysis and synthesis, 3:285
   Arabic, 1:46–47, 4:4–5, 6:185–186, 187
   in Argentina, 4:202

astronomy, 1:85–89, 3:245–246, 320, 6:175–176,
   216–218
atmospheric science, 6:469–472
calculators, 1:128
computer science and, 1:286–288, 3:356–357,
   7:82–84
cosmology and, 5:81
cryptography, 6:426–427
discrete, 2:403–406
dynamic meteorology, 6:558–561
editing and publishing, 1:348–349
education, 2:151–152, 5:1–2, 7:281
Galilean School, 1:349
Greek, 1:83–84, 3:283
history of, 1:166
homology, 2:360–363, 5:2–3
influential textbooks, 5:2
information theory, 6:424, 429
Institutiones mathematicae (Kircher), 4:131
instrumentation, 2:157–158
introductory textbooks, 1:19–21
intuitionistic, 4:150–152
Islamic, 7:87–89
Jesuits, 2:148–149
Judaism, 6:564–565
limits of, 3:278–279
linear programming, 7:80–82
logic and, 1:144–145, 3:130–132, 5:3–4
magic squares, 5:196
meteorology, 6:238–239
natural philosophy and, 1:296–297, 5:313–314,
   351, 6:562–563
Newtonian theory of gravity and, 5:56–57
Paris Problems, 3:308–310
philosophy, 3:435–437, 7:278
physics and, 4:249, 6:489–490, 491
in Portugal, 5:178
professionalization of, 2:34
pure, 2:272
research, 3:326–327
Rudolphine Tables (Kepler), 4:106–107
science and, 5:269
statistical mechanics, 2:356–357
symbolic logic, 2:310–311
theoretical physics, 1:316–318
vision, 1:145–146
   See also specific concepts and branches of Mathematics
Mathematische Analyse des Raumproblems (Weyl), 7:277
Mathematische Begriffsbildungen zur Gravitationstheorie
   (Grossmann and Einstein), 3:192
Mather, Kenneth, 4:276
Mather, Stephen, 2:189
Matijasevič, Iurii Vladimirovich, 6:267
Matilda effect, 7:1–2

Matroid theory, 7:90

Matros, Yuri Shaevich, 1:354

Matter
    alchemy and, 5:273–274
    atomism, 2:80, 3:157–158
    classification of, 2:218, 7:396–397
    cosmology, 2:122
    ecological theory and, 5:24–25
    four-element theory, 2:395
    gravitational attraction, 5:11–12
    interstellar
        accretion, 3:388–389
        comets, 3:391
        field theory, 3:389
        gases, 6:543–544
    mixtures, 2:321–322
    quaternion theory, 1:138–139
    wave theory, 1:409, 410–413

Matter-antimatter colliders. *See* Particle-antiparticle colliders

Matterhorn-S, 6:501

Matters of Health (Diocles of Carystus), 2:302

Matthaei, Johann, 2:210

Matthews, Bryan Harold Cabot, 1:17–18

Matthews, Drummond H., 7:325

Matthews, Paul, 6:336, 339–340

Matthews, Rachel Eckhard, 1:17

Matthiessen, Augustus, 3:57

Mattioli, Pietro Andrea Gregorio, 6:68

Matuyama, Motonori, 5:**48–50**

Mauchly, John William, 2:334–337, *336*, 3:358–359, 5:**50–56**, *55*, 7:315

Mauchly, Sebastian J., 5:51

Maud Committee, 1:164

Mauna Loa Observatory, 7:275

Maupertuis, Pierre Louis Moreau de, 4:183, 5:**56–59**, *57*

Maurolico, Francesco, 1:348–349, 2:148

Maury, Matthew Fontaine, 6:371, 528

Max-Planck-Institut für Verhaltensphysiologie, 7:182

Max Planck Society, 1:464

Maximum power principle, 5:324

Maxwell, Emanuel, 1:181

Maxwell, Graeme, 3:318

Maxwell, James Clerk, 3:4
    electromagnetism, 3:291–292, 6:123, 549
    vector potentials, 1:324

May, Joseph Henry, 4:121

May, Mark, 3:407–408

Mayall, Nicholas Ulrich, 5:343

Mayer, Alfred Goldsborough. *See* Mayor, Alfred Goldsborough

Mayer, Cornell H., 6:310

Maynard, Charles, 1:293

Maynard, William, 1:293

Mayor, Alfred Goldsborough, 5:**59–60**

Mayr, Ernst Walter, 2:4, 62, 5:**61–67**, *65*
    acquaintainces, 7:235
    Australopithecines, 2:139
    biolspecies theory, 6:493
    biospecies theory, 3:159
    on Darwin, Charles, 5:64–65
    evolutionary synthesis, 2:174
    influence of, 4:314, 5:278–279
    influences on, 4:314
    on mathematical population genetics, 4:276
    morphology, 6:353
    on Schindewolf, Otto Heinrich, 6:351
    synthetic theory of evolution, 3:163
    transmutation, 2:243

Mazes, cockroach, 7:*85,* 85–86, *86*

McIDAS (Man-computer Interactive Data Access System), 6:556–557

Mead, Margaret, 3:417

Meaning and Necessity (Carnap), 2:45, 46

Means-end analysis, 5:256–257

Measurement of the Circle (Archimedes), 1:87, 89

Measurement of the Parabola (Ibrāhīm Ibn Sinān Ibn Thābit Ibn Qurra), 4:4, 5

Measurements, electrical, 6:549

Measuring Ethiopia and Flight into Arabia (Coon), 2:173

Measuring Marginal Utility by Reactions to Risk (Vickery), 7:150

Mebendazole, 4:32

Mebenvet, 4:32

Mechanica (Aristotle), 6:540

Mechanical engineering, 7:409–413

A Mechanical Model for Human Attention and Immediate Memory (Broadbent), 1:403

Mechanical philosophy, 1:204–205, 3:111, 4:184

Mechanical Problems (Pseudo-Aristotle), 1:166, 167

Mechanicorum Liber (Monte), 5:175–176

Mechanics
    algebra, 3:236
    architecture and, 1:166
    atomism, 3:109
    biology and, 5:236
    developmental, 4:44
    geometry, 3:292–293
    non-linear, 1:317
    thermodynamics, 1:337–339
    See also Motion; Wave mechanics

Mechanics, quantum. *See* Quantum mechanics

Das mechanische Princip im anatomischen Bau der Monocotylen (Schwendener), 6:390

Mechanischer Kunst-Kammer Erster Theil (Mögling), 1:167

The Mechanism of Action of Solid Catalysts (Boreskov). *See Mekhanism deĭstviia tverdykh katalizatorov* (Boreskov)

The Mechanism of Mendelian Heredity (Hunt et al.), 1:212

The Mechanism of Nervous Action (Adrian), 1:17

The Mechanism of the Assembly of Behavior Segments in Novel Combinations Suitable for Problem Solution (Hull), 3:409

Mechanisms in Bioenergetics (Racker), 6:199

Mechanisms of Biological Oxidation (Green), 3:168

Mechanistic psychology, 7:370–371

Mecke, Rudolf, 5:210

Meckel, Johann Friedrich, 3:118

Medawar, Peter Brian, 5:**85–90,** *87*

Medical ethics, 1:1, 3–4, 3:93
    See also Bioethics; Eugenics

Medical Questions (Rufus of Ephesus), 6:290, 291

Medical Remains (Bacon, Francis), 1:140

Medical Research Council (MRC)
    experimental focus, 1:188
    members of, 6:519, 521

Medical Theories in Hippocrates: Early Texts and the Epidemics (Langholf), 3:322

Les Médications psychologiques (Janet). *See Psychological Healing* (Janet)

Medicina (Campanella), 2:20

Medicina Hydrostatica (Boyle), 1:369

Medicina Plinii (Pliny), 6:119

Medicine
    ancient
        anatomy, 3:91–95
        errors, 6:120
        Galen, 5:280
        Greek, 6:540
        Hippocratic, 3:322–325, 323–325
        history of, 2:301–303
        Islamic, 6:290–291
        philosophy, 6:115–116
        Roman, 6:119–120
        theoretical, 3:325
    medieval
        Arabic, 6:212–215
        diagnostics and pathology, 1:107
        France, 6:68–69
        physicians' philosophy, 5:8–9
        teachers, 2:36
        works, 4:264–266, 6:153
        writers, 2:81–84
    modern
        atomism, 7:342
        dream interpretation, 2:37
        drugs, 4:29–33
        germ theory, 1:209
        military, 1:16
        nanotechnology, 6:475
        natural philosophy, 1:368–369
        pharmacology, 2:375
        social, 7:157–158
        transplantation immunology, 5:85–89
        vitamin C, 6:42–43
    Renaissance, 7:389
        astrology and, 5:280
        atomism, 6:418–419
        criticism of, 6:512
        Germany, 6:504–506
        natural history, 6:551–552
        Paracelsianism and, 1:309
        prolongation of life, 1:139–140
    See also Drugs; *specific fields and specialties of Medicine*

Medicine (Campanella). *See Medicina* (Campanella)

Medina, Pedro de, 2:157

Meditations (Descartes), 2:272

Medusae of the World (Mayor), 5:59, 60

Medvedev, Sergey, 6:509, 510

Medvedev, Zhores A., 4:277

Meehl, Paul Everett, 5:**90–94**

Meerwein, Hans, 1:191, 194–195, 7:336

Mees, C. E. Kenneth, 5:113

Meganthropus palaeojavanicus, 7:187

Mégnié, Pierre Bernard, 4:215

Mehrtens, Herbert, 3:309–310

Mein Lebensgang (Edinger), 2:341

Meinel, Aden, 7:289

Meinzer, Oscar Edward, 3:374

Meissner, Georg, 1:304

Meissner effect, 1:179

Meitner, Lise, 1:55, 2:205, 7:332
    assistants of, 2:268
    fission, 6:408
    radiochemistry, 3:210–211

Mekhanism deĭstviia tverdykh katalizatorov (Boreskov), 1:352

Melanchthon, Philipp, 1:381

Melanism, industrial, 4:109–110

Melatonin, 1:121–122

Melhado, Evan, 1:268

Meliorism, 4:23–24

Meliteniotes, Theodore, 1:98, 2:121, 5:**94–96**

Mellanby, John, 2:329

Mellon, Paul, 3:39–40

Melman, Seymour, 6:317

Melnechuck, Ted, 6:364

Melospiza melodia, 5:277–278

Membranes, cellular
    action potentials, 3:329–332
    cytology, 6:197–202

Membranes, cellular, *continued*
    ion-transporting proteins in, 5:364
Memoir of a Thinking Radish (Medawar), 5:89
Mémoire sur la cause générale du froid en hiver et de la chaleur en été (Mairan), 5:11
Mémoires de physique et chimie (Lavoisier), 4:217, 6:44
Memoirs for the Natural History of Human Blood (Boyle), 1:369
Memoirs of an Effort to Unlock the Mysteries of Severe Storms (Fujita), 3:84
Memoirs of the Analytical Society (Babbage and Herschel), 1:125–126
Memorabilia (Plato), 6:115
Memories, Dreams, Reflections (Jung), 4:63
Memory
    accommodation and, 1:171
    attention and perception, 1:403–404
    nervous system, 3:269
    perception, 1:405
    psychology and, 1:188
    as reconstruction, 1:184
    short-term, 3:145, 146, 147
Men of Mathematics (Bell), 4:158
Menard, Henry William, 2:287, 5:**96–97,** 6:236
Mencke, Otto, 1:255
Mendel, Johann Gregor, 5:**97–105,** *98*
    botany, 5:98–100
    career, 5:97–98
    early Mendelian genetics, 5:101–103
    evolution, 5:104
    influence of, 4:315
    influences on, 2:246, 4:315
Mendeleev, Dmitrii Ivanovich, 1:467, 5:**105–110,** *106*
Mendelian genetics
    botany, 6:317–319, 7:1–2
    diversity and population growth, 3:45–47
    evolution and, 7:189–191
    founding of, 5:101–103
    influence on Darwinism, 2:246
    physiological, 2:399–400, 7:358–360
    protozoans, 4:45
    segregation, 1:211–212
    sickle-cell anemia, 5:242
    theoretical population genetics, 3:29
Mendeloff, John, 3:188–189
Mendel's Principles of Heredity (Bateson), 5:101, 7:190
Menéndez, Eduardo Braun. *See* Braun-Menéndez, Eduardo
Menge, Heinrich, 2:417
Mengele, Josef, 1:463, 3:28
Menger, Karl, 5:186–187
Mengerink, Wilhelmina. *See* Van de Hulst, Wilhemina Mengerink
Mennher, Valentin, 2:157

Menninger, Karl, 5:90
Mental Development in the Child and the Race (Baldwin), 1:169, 171, 172
Mental illness
    hysteria as, 4:25–29
    schizophrenia, 5:91–92
Mental testing. *See* Psychological testing
Mentality of Apes (Köhler), 3:407
Menzel, Donald Howard, 3:141–142, 5:**110–118,** *111, 115,* 6:50, 312
    Goldberg, Leo, 3:144
    Harvard College Observatory, 7:289
    influence of, 7:286
    Smithsonian Astrophysical Observatory, 7:287
    students of, 7:284
Menzies, Alexander, 7:230
Menzies, Robert, 1:331
Mercator, Gerardus, 3:355, *355*
Mercator-Hondius Atlas, 3:355–356
Mercier, Raymond, 2:121
Merck, George W., 3:43
Mercury (element)
    organometallic chemistry, 5:246
    quaternion theory, 1:138, *138*
Mercury (planet)
    orbit, 2:369
        Copernicanism, 2:178
        measured rate of precession, 2:282
    rotation, 3:139
    solar transit, 3:111
Mercury-vapor rectifiers, 6:376
Merian, Maria Sibylla, 5:**118–120**
The Mermaid and the Minotaur (Lehrman), 4:247
Mersenne, Marin, 1:205, 2:46, 4:133
Merton, Robert King, 2:23, 5:**121–126,** *123,* 6:163
Merton mean-speed theorem, 5:314
Merz, Alfred, 2:265, 6:529
    colleagues of, 7:373, 374
    students of, 5:171
Meschkowski, Herbert, 2:29, 30, 33
Mesencephalon, 2:341
Mesons, 1:291, 6:170–171, 282–283, 336, 393, 7:70
Mesotrons. *See* Mesons
Mesozoic Era, 6:453
Messenger RNA. *See* mRNA
Messier, Charles, 3:286
Metabolism
    bacterial, 6:519–520
    coral reefs, 5:318
    drug, 1:118–120
    ecosystems, 5:316, 317, 322–324, *323, 324*
    energy, 6:197–202
    enzymes, 4:322–323
    fatty acids, 3:170, 171, 4:238–241, 253

galactose, 4:74–75
  intermediary, 5:306–309
  microbes, 4:136–137
  muscle, 4:325, 5:231, 232–233, 306
  origin of life, 3:363–364
  phosphates and carbohydrates, 4:72
  vectorial, 5:160–162
Metagenesis, 5:368
Metallurgy
  classification, 2:218
  electron theory of conduction, 1:303–304
  geomorphology and, 1:93
  iron monoxide, 2:160–161
  phlogiston, 6:505
  transmutation, 6:506
Metals
  electron conduction in, 1:303–304, 5:200–201
  mixtures, 6:418–419
  transition, 1:310, 311
    coordination chemistry, 2:102–104
    electronic structure, 4:58–59
    ferrocene, 7:*309, 310*
    nickel, 7:*308*
    organometallic chemistry, 7:308 310
    separation and purification, 1:310
    tungsten, 7:*310*
  transmutation
    chemistry *vs.*, 6:506
    controversy, 3:353
    corpuscular theory, 5:273
    mining, 3:352
    Newton's chemical theory and, 5:274–275
Metamathematics, 7:10
Metamorphism, 4:156–157
Metamorphosis et historia naturalis insectorum (Goedart), 5:120
Metamorphosis insectorum Surinamensium (Merian), 5:118
Metaphysics
  chemistry, 3:158
  cosmology, 6:458
  induction, 3:149
  language, 6:204
  medieval, 6:293
  natural philosophy, 2:272–273, 4:285
  opposition to, 4:184
  personal identity theory, 5:286
  philosophy of, 4:286
  principle of least action and, 5:58
  views on God, 2:412–413
Metaphysics (Aristotle), 1:143, 6:294
Metastatics and Macroeconomics (Vickery), 7:151
Meteor craters, 6:443–444
Meteorological balloons, 7:18–19

Meteorological instruments, 7:18–19
Meteorological Observations (Dalton), 3:386
Meteorologische Zeitschrift, 2:426
Meteorology
  alchemical commentaries on, 5:338
  atmospheric science, 6:2–5
  aviation, 1:468–470
  China, 7:403
  climatology, 6:341–345, 7:39, 40
  clouds, 1:114–117, 3:386–387
  dew, 1:28
  dust, 1:27–29
  dynamic, 2:99
    atmospheric circulation, 7:17–19
    mathematics, 6:558–561
    numerical modeling, 6:469–472
    research, 6:341–342
    tropical cyclones, 3:262–263
    United States, 6:221–223
  earthquakes, 7:199–201
  earth's magnetism, 2:379
  fluid dynamics, 4:39
  forecasting methods, 4:193–195
  growth as a science, 5:221–224
  human impact, 4:199
  hydrodynamics, 1:288–290
  mathematics-based, 2:99–101, 5:52, 6:238–239
  modern, founder of, 4:152–153
  monsoons, 7:216, 217–219
  occlusion process, 1:246–247
  oceanography, 2:264–265
  satellites, 6:554–557
  surface pressure, 2:425–427
  technology, 7:273–276
  tornadoes, 3:82–85
  United States, 6:219–223
  wartime, 6:84, 85–86
  weights and measures in, 5:108–109
  See also Cyclones; Weather forecasting
Meteorology (Aristotle), 2:1, 2, 5:338, 339
Meteorology for Aviators (Sutcliffe), 6:559
Meteorology for Pilots (Haynes), 6:553
Meteors, 7:285–286
Methane
  chemical compounds theory, 2:324
  geophysics, 3:139–140
A Method of Programming (Dijkstra), 2:295
The Method of Trigonometrical Sums in the Theory of Numbers (Vinogradov). *See Metod trigonometricheskikh summ v teorii chisel* (Vinogradov)
Méthode de chimie (Laurent), 4:98, 205
Méthode de nomenclature chimique (Berthollet and Lavoisier), 1:264
Methodist school of medicine, 3:92–93, 6:290

Methodological Foundations of Differential Psychology
(Stern). *See Die Differentielle Psychologie in ihren
methodischen Grundlagen* (Stern)
Methods of Mathematical Physics (Jeffreys), 4:39
Metochites, Theodorus, 5:95, 6:2
Metod trigonometricheskikh summ v teorii chisel
(Vinogradov), 7:156
Metomidate, 4:33
Meton, 6:175
Metrica (Hero of Alexandria), 3:285
Metz, Charles W., 2:59, 60
Meumann, Ernst, 6:524
Mexican axoltols
cranial neural crest development, 3:368–369, 370
maternal genes, 1:399–400
Meyen, Julius, 6:357
Meyenn, Karl von, 6:35
Meyer, Adolf, 6:244
Meyer, Johann Friedrich, 4:214
Meyer, Kurt Heinrich, 5:29, 6:229, 230
Meyer, Leon H., 3:197–198, 198
Meyer, Stephan, 7:305
Meyerhof, Otto, 4:55
antisemitism, 4:168, 169
biochemistry, 5:306
colleagues of, 7:212
enzymology, 3:170
influence of, 4:324
muscle metabolism, 5:231
students of, 6:361
Michael Polányi: Scientist and Philosopher (Scott), 6:126
Michaelis, Leonor, 3:167, 6:568
Michaelis-Stern, Eva, 6:522
Michaud, George, 1:277–278
Michaux, Bernard, 7:225
Michel, K. W., 1:278
Michell, John, 1:294
Michelson, Albert Abraham, 1:295
Michoels, Solomon, 6:447
Mickel, Virgil, 4:187
Miconazole, 4:33
Microbial biochemistry, 6:519–521
Microbial genetics, 6:492–494
Microbiology
antibiotics, 2:318
chemical, 6:519–521
metabolism, 4:136–138
spontaneous generation, 6:24–26
Szilard, Leo, 6:575–576
Microcosms, lakes as, 7:37
Microdensitometry, 1:131
Microeconomics
asymmetric information, 7:149–150
Nash equilibrium, 5:228

Microelectrode recordings, 3:147
Microenvironments for Life on Mars (Sagan and
Legerberg), 6:311–312
Microperoxisomes, 5:281, 283
Microscopes
atoms, 3:110–111
botany, 6:389–390
cytology, 2:70–71
electron, 1:374, 2:*146*
cytology, 2:143, 144–146, 6:143–148
embryology, 2:145–146, *146, 147*
molecular biology, 6:362
transmission, 1:374
homemade, 5:23
light absorption errors, 2:68
Microscopic Technique in Biology and Medicine (Cowdry),
2:185
Microsurgery, 3:*219, 220*
Microtrabecular lattice, 6:147–148
Microtubules, 6:146–147
Microwave Anisotropy Probe, 7:304–305
Microwave radiation, 6:310–311
Microwaves
electronics, 2:166–167
physics
magnetrons, 6:179–180
radiation, 2:280–281, 6:393–394
spectroscopy, 7:101
See also Cosmic Microwave Background (CMB);
Radiation
Mid-Atlantic Ridge Rift Valley, 7:30
Middlemiss, Charles, 7:208
Mie, Gustav, 3:307–308
Migdal, Arkadii. *See* Migdal, Arkady Benediktovich
Migdal, Arkady Benediktovich, 1:425, 5:**127–132**, *129*
Migration
birds, 5:277–278, 322
ethology, 3:177
evolutionary, 2:61–62
salmon, 3:260–261
"Mike" (nuclear weapon), 7:22
Das Mikroskop: Theorie und Anwendung desselben
(Schwendener), 6:390
Milanković, Milutin, 4:155, 5:**132–136**
Milankovitch, Milutin. *See* Milanković, Milutin
Milatz, Jan, 7:229
Miledi, Ricardo, 4:89
Miles, Catharine Cox, 7:28
Miles, Henry, 1:367
Miles, Walter R., 5:145
Milgram, Stanley, 5:**136–143**
The Military and Political Consequences of Atomic Energy
(Blackett), 1:292
Military Information Systems (Licklider), 4:305

Military medicine
    medieval, 2:82
    neurological injuries, 1:16
Military sciences
    air defense systems, 2:110, 4:211–212, 303
    computer science, 4:304–305, 5:53–54
    meteorology research, 6:220, 221
    oceanography, 6:530–531
    operational research, 1:292
    See also Weapons
The Milky Way (Bok), 1:331, 332
Milky Way galaxy
    brightness fluctuations, 1:65
    mapping, 6:181
    microwave radiation, 2:283
    radio astronomy, 5:345
    spiral shape, 1:328 330, 331 332
    stars, 6:50
    structure of, 5:342–343
    thermal radiation, 7:284
    uranography, 2:304–305
Mill, James, 7:369
Mill, John Stuart, 3:70, 5:**143–145,** *144,* 7:282
Miller, David, 2:251, 321
Miller, Donald, 2:319, 320
Miller, George Abram, 4:302, 303, 5:258
Miller, Harry M., 3:170
Miller, Hugh, 4:54
Miller, James Grier, 6:496
Miller, Joseph, 7:272
Miller, Neal Elgar, 5:**145–154**
    autonomic functions, 5:150–151
    education, 5:145
    hunger physiology, 5:*148,* 148–149
    laws of learning and foresight, 5:145
    psychoanalysis and learning, 5:146, 147–148
    reaction formation, 5:146, *146*
    recognitions and high public service, 5:149–150
    research mentor and educator, 5:151–152
    social behavior acquisition, 5:147
    World War II, 5:147
Miller, Stanley Lloyd, 3:364, 5:*154,* **154–158,** 6:310, 315
Miller-Urey experiment, 6:310
Millikan, Max, 6:498–499
Millikan, Robert Andrews, 4:*211,* 5:301
    cloud chambers, 1:72–73
    colleagues of, 2:393
    cosmic rays, 6:280, 282
    influence of, 4:208, 6:99
    kinetics, 6:36
    meteorology, 2:379
    students of, 7:398, 399
    Wu, Chien-Shiung, 7:366

Mills, Bernard, 6:304
Mills, Robert L., 6:337
Mills, William Hobson, 6:476
Milne, Edward Arthur, 2:339
    colleagues of, 5:73–74
    expanding universe, 5:82
    influence of, 5:111
    kinematic relativity, 1:342, 6:458
    Newtonian cosmology, 3:275
    scientific method, 6:542
    theorizing and, 5:112
Milne, Robert, 6:535
Milner, Peter, 5:149
Milnor, John Willard, 5:195, 227
Milstein, César, 4:50
Mimno, Harry, 1:163
A Mind Always in Motion (Segrè), 6:411
Mind and Life: An Essay in Simplification (Tansley), 7:8
Mind-body connection
    brain anatomy, 6:74
    cosmology, 6:15–16
    dualism, 2:332
    evolution, 6:109
    medicine and, 4:184
    personality, 2:428–429
    physicalism, 1:359
    research on, 5:92
Mind-brain connection
    cerebral hemispheres, 6:495–497
    consciousness, 3:305, 6:497–498
    history, 6:458
    research on, 6:363–364
Mind from Matter (Delbrück), 2:270
The Mind of Adolf Hitler (Langer), 5:217
Minds, animal, 3:177, 180–182
Mineralogy
    chemical, 4:213–214, 7:222
    earth's mantle, 6:258–259
    isomorphism, 5:165
    mineral deposits, 3:398
    propaedeutic, 1:281
    stratification, 3:7
    volcanology, 6:262–264
Ming Chen Wang. *See* Wang, Ming Chen
Minimal hypersurfaces, 2:259
Minimax theorem, 5:226–227
Mining, 2:250, 252
    alchemy, 7:335
    China, 2:299
    coal, 2:300
    geomorphology and, 1:93
    See also Mineralogy
Minkowski, Hermann, 3:306, 309
    mathematics, 6:252, 253

Minkowski, Hermann, *continued*
    relativity, 6:122, 123
Minkowski, Rudolf, 6:434
Minnaert, Marcel Gilles Jozef, 7:126, 127
Minnesota Multiphase Personality Inventory (MMPI),
    5:90–91
Minsky, Marvin L., 4:304, 6:427
Minty, George, 4:319
Mirage of Health (Dubos), 2:318
Miranda, Mario, 2:259
Mirecourt, John. *See* John of Mirecourt
Mirror of Princes, 1:146
Mirror of the Soul (Rufus of Cornwall, Richard). *See*
    Speculum animae (Rufus of Cornwall, Richard)
Mirsky, Alfred, 6:38
Misch, Lore, 1:306
Misconduct. *See* Research misconduct
Mises, Richard von, 6:134
Mishchenko, Evgenii F., 6:128
The Mismeasure of Man (Gould), 3:161
Missiles
    ballistic, 7:173–175
    cosmic rays, 7:121
    defense systems, 1:275, 6:327, 7:24
    guided, 5:259–260, 6:99–100
    See also Weapons
The Mission of the Idea (Piaget), 6:92
MIT (Massachusetts Institute of Technology)
    associates, 6:285, 286
    neuroscience, 6:360
    radar, 6:195–196
Mitchell, J. Murray, 4:199
Mitchell, Oscar Howard, 3:70
Mitchell, Peter Dennis, 4:240, 5:**158–165,** *161, 163*
    ATP synthesis, 5:161–163
    chemiosmotic theory, 6:197, 199, 200
    education, 5:159–160
    oxidative phosphorylation, 5:160–163
Mitchison, Graeme, 2:210
Mitochondria
    chemiosmotic theory, 5:162–163
    metabolism and, 4:238–241
    subfractioning, 3:170–172
The Mitochondrion (Lehninger), 4:240
Mitropolsky, Yuri Alekseyevich, 1:318
Mitscherlich, Eilhard, 5:*165,* **165–167**
Mittag-Leffler, Gösta. *See* Mittag-Leffler, Magnus Gustaf
Mittag-Leffler, Magnus Gustaf, 5:197
Mittelstaedt, Horst, 7:183
Mivart, St. George Jackson, 3:432
Mixotrophy, 7:36
Le mixte el la combinaison chimique (Duhem), 2:322
Mixts (Aristotelianism), 6:294
Mixture theory, 6:294, 418–419

Miyatake, Takashi, 1:33
Mizushima, San-Ichirō, 5:**167–171**
MMPI (Minnesota Multiphase Personality Inventory),
    5:90–91
Mobilism, 3:375
Möbius functions, 6:285–286
Modal logic, 3:131
Models
    chemical, 7:33
    climatology, 2:100–101
    crystals, 1:311
    cyclones, 1:289–290
    DNA, 6:40
    earth's motion, 1:31
    energy balance, 4:343
    evolution, 2:62–63
    general circulation, 6:342, 344, 371, 472
    mathematical
        catalysis, 1:354–355
        consciousness, 2:382
        oceanography, 6:256–257
        visual perception, 2:382
    nonlinear chiral sigma, 3:193
    numerical weather forecasting, 6:222, 469–472,
        558–561, 561
    punctuational adaptation, 3:161
    stellar, 2:339, 6:385, 386
    Tolman-Bondi, 2:382
Modern Cosmology (Sciama), 6:399
Modern Mathematics as a Cultural Phenomenon (Gray),
    3:310
Moderne Algebra (Van der Waerden), 1:365, 5:2
Moderne Sprache, Mathematik (Mehrtens), 3:309–310
Modi rerum theory, 5:351, 352
Moerbeke, William of, 3:284
Moerdijk, Ieke, 5:2, 4
Mögling, Daniel, 1:167
Moherwell, William, 1:199
Mohr, Ernst, 1:197
Molding, injection, 2:358, 359
The Molecular Basis of Evolution (Anfinsen), 1:80
Molecular beams
    research, 6:192–194
    scattering techniques, 1:258
Molecular biology
    atomic physics, 2:267–271
    DNA base ratios, 2:93–97
    DNA synthesis, 6:478–482
    electron microscopy, 6:362
    embryology, 1:370–376
    enzymology, 3:340–343
    foundation of, 5:305–311
    genetics and, 1:228, 5:310
    hemoglobin, 6:81–83

protein chemistry, 6:360, 361–365
ribonuclease, 1:79–80
virology, 1:463–464
x-ray crystallography, 2:207–209
See also Biology
Molecular Biology of the Gene (Watson), 5:284
Molecular evolution, 4:116–117
Molecular genetics
    metabolic reactions, 1:225–229
    mutations, 4:56
    Neurospora, 1:*226*
    neutral theory, 4:114–116
    phase research, 2:269–270
    protein production and, 1:224
Molecular Genetics (Stent), 4:357
Molecular physics
    branched chain reactions, 6:411–415, 413–414
    mechanics of molecular collisions, 1:258–259
    orbitals, 5:210–211
Molecular Reaction Dynamics (Levine and Bernstein), 1:259
Molecular Rearrangement of Some O-Acyloxyacetophenones and the Mechanism of the Production of 3-Acylchromones (Baker), 7:144
Molecular Spectra and Molecular Structure (Herzberg), 3:301
Molecular spectroscopy
    atomic theory, 3:298–301
    nuclear magnetic resonance, 3:196
Molecules
    asymmetry
        fermentation, 6:22–23
        induction, 2:201
    atomic theory of, 1:205
    benzene, 2:200–201, 4:14, 15–16
    chain
        graphic formulas, 4:98–99
        polymeric, 3:40
    chirality, 6:*160,* 160–161
    conformational analysis, 4:259–263
    CPD models, 2:201–202
    cyclophane, 2:203–204
    diatomic
        infrared spectrum of, 4:6–9
        spectra analysis, 5:210
    enegy
        Franck-Condon principle, 2:165
        infrared spectrum of, 4:6
    geometry
        change of shape, 4:17
        internal rotation and, 5:169–170
    intermolecular forces, 2:66
    isomerism, 5:169–170
    orbitals

electron states, 3:*402*
organic chemistry, 2:276–278
quantum mechanics, 3:87–88
stereochemistry, 3:400–404
theory, 5:210–211
polarization, 4:14, 5:168–169
structure
    aromatic compounds, 6:272
    bonds, 6:36–40
    fiber research, 5:28–29
    Octant rule, 7:354–355
vibrational motion, 4:6–9
Moler, Cleve B., 3:52
Moleski, Martin X, 6:126
Moll, Jan Willem, 7:1, 2, 191
Molland, George, 1:379
Møller, C., 6:169
Möller, Lotte. *See* Möller, Sophie Carlotte Juliane
Möller, Sophie Carlotte Juliane, 5:**171–174**
Möller, Sophie Charlotte Juliane. *See* Möller, Sophie Carlotte Juliane
Molleson, Theya Ivitsky, 5:299
Mollusks, 5:265, 266
    natural selection, 2:4–5
    taxonomy, 2:3
Molybdenum, 7:310, *310*
Monaghan, Nigel, 1:95
Monarchia di Spagna (Campanella), 2:20
Monarchy of Spain (Campanella). *See Monarchia di Spagna* (Campanella)
Monas hieroglyphica (Dee), 4:133
Mond, Ludwig, 7:309
Le Monde, ou Traité de la lumière (Descartes), 2:272, 273, 274
Monge, Gaspard, 4:201
Mongré, Paul. *See* Hausdorff, Felix
Monism
    evolution, 3:208, 209
    support for, 5:357
Monoclonal antibodies, 4:50
Monod, Jacques, 5:71, 6:82–83, 520
Monophyletic groups, 3:282
Monro, Alexander (Primus), 1:91
Monsanto process, 7:311
Monsoons, 7:216, 217–219
    See also Weather
Montagu, Ashley, 5:297
Montalva, Eduardo Frei. *See* Frei Montalva, Eduardo
Monte, Guidobaldo, Marchese del, 5:**174–178**
Monteiro, António A., 5:**178–180**
Montel, Paul, 2:289
Monteregio, Joannes de. *See* Regiomontanus, Johannes
Montgomery, C. G., 6:180
Monti, Augusto, 4:355

Monti, Maria Teresa, 3:216
Mook, Wilhelm, 4:95
Moon
    Apollo Project, 3:398, 5:262–263
    astronomy, 6:176, 177
    Copernicanism, 2:178
    craters, 2:286, 288, 6:443, 444–445
    eclipses, 3:283–284
    geochemistry, 6:258, 260
    geophysics, 3:138–139
    gravitaional field of, 4:104
    illusion, 1:358–359
    motion, 2:231–232
    orbit, 2:282
        measurement, 7:302–303
        Newton, Isaac and, 5:271
    satellites, 3:80–81, 6:100–101
    surface, 4:180
Moore, Calvin, 2:112, 246
Moore, Eliakim Hastings, 5:1, 3
Moore, George Edward, 1:184
Moore, Gordon B., 1:235, 6:440, 441, 7:239
Moore, Hilbert, 1:180
Moore, James R., 2:14, 244, 3:430
Moore, John C., 1:345
Moore, Raymond, 5:265
Moore, Stanford, 1:78, 79
Moore, Tommy, 5:39
Mooy, Herman, 7:135
The Moral Judgment of the Child (Piaget), 6:92–93, 94
Moralis philosophia (Bacon, Roger), 1:147
Moran, Thomas, 5:257
Mordell, Louis Joel, 7:254–255
Mordente, Fabrizio, 2:158
More, Henry, 2:171, 172
Morell, Virginia, 4:223
Moreno, Francisco Pascasio, 1:453, 4:236, 5:**180–183**
Morgan, Conwy Lloyd, 3:385, 4:44, 340, 6:369
Morgan, Frank, 2:352
Morgan, John, 2:361, 7:244
Morgan, Thomas Hunt, 2:183, 5:**183–186**, *184*
    biology, 6:38
    colleagues of, 7:204
    cytoplasm, 4:69
    Drosophila bredding, 1:212
    fly room, 3:424
    influence of, 2:399, 4:275
    Mendelian genetics, 5:102
    and Stern, Curt, 5:69
    students of, 7:211–212
Morgan, W. Jason, 7:323, 325
Morgan, William W.
    Orion and Perseus, 1:330
    spiral arms of the Milky Way, 1:331, 5:346

stellar classification, 6:544, 546
Morgenau, Henry, 1:392
Morgenstern, Oskar, 5:**186–189**, *188*
    game theory, 3:251, 5:226–227
    rational bargaining, 5:225
    rational choice, 3:248–249
    students of, 5:254
Morino, Yonezō, 5:169
Morowitz, Harold, 6:312
Morphine, 1:198
Morphogenesis of the Behaviour of the Domestic Cat (Baerends), 1:153
Morphological studies of the formative laws of natural bodies generally and organic ones in particular (Bronn). See *Morphologische Studien über die Gestaltungs-Gesetze der Naturkörper überhaupt und der organischen insbesondere* (Bronn)
Morphologische Studien über die Gestaltungs-Gesetze der Naturkörper überhaupt und der organischen insbesondere (Bronn), 1:416–417
Morphology
    animal, 2:313–314, 3:133–134
    cellular
        germ cells, 7:259–260
        infections, 2:182
    descriptive, 3:431
    developmental, 6:356–359
    embryology, 3:207–208
    evolutionary biology, 6:353, 355
    idealist, 5:366–367
    zoology, 1:416–417
    See also Geomorphology
Morrell, Jack, 3:236, 4:312
Morrison, Leslie, 2:148
Morrison, Philip, 5:**189–194**, *192*, 6:310
Morrison, Robert Thornton, 2:200
Morse, Marston, 5:**194–196**
Morse, Philip M., 2:165, 4:332, 6:438
Morton, Newton, 4:115
Morton, Richard A., 3:171, 5:16
Morton, Samuel George, 3:161
Moschopoulos, Manuel, 5:**196**
Moscona, Aaron, 3:187
Moscow Human Rights Commission, 6:327
Moser, Jürgen K., 2:115, 4:151, 5:**197–200**, *198*
Moss, Ralph, 6:571
Mössbauer, Rudolf, 2:281
Mosteller, Frederick, 4:125
Moths, 4:109–110
Motilium, 4:30, 32
Motion
    animals, 1:349
    Aristotelianism, 1:441–443
    elements, 1:362, 442

fire, 7:381–382
fluid, 4:272–273
Galilean Manuscript 72, 3:97, 98, 112
impetus theory, 1:447
laws of, 2:273–274, 5:270–271
machines and, 5:175–176
mathematical description, 5:314
natural, 7:381–382
natural philosophy, 1:378–379, 2:326, 5:313, 351, 352
oscillations, 1:327
planetary
    d'Alembert's principle, 2:230–231
    laws of, 4:105–107
relativity of, 1:424–425
rotational
    Brownian, 7:101
    nuclear and electron spins, 2:64
    vibration, 4:6–7
stellar, 2:89–90
theorem of corresponding states, 4:333–335
tides, 1:361
tonic, 6:506, 507
Motivation
    field theory of, 4:279–280
    learning and, 3:313, 5:147
    mechanisms of, 4:246
    personality and, 4:44–45
    theory of, 5:44–45
Motivation and Personality (Maslow), 5:45
Motor aphasia, 4:352, 353
Motor nerves
    all-or-none principle, 1:16
    electrophysiology, 1:17
Mott, Nevill Francis, 1:271, 5:*200*, **200–204**
    semiconductors, 1:311
    solid-state physics, 2:160, 6:63
Motz, Lloyd, 6:392
Moulin-Quignon jaw, 5:298
Mount Carmel (Palestine), excavations, 3:103, 105–106
Mount Vesuvius, 2:262
The Mountain Gorilla (Schaller), 3:55
Mountains
    building, 6:347–349
    stratigraphy, 6:468
Mousterian culture, 3:106
Movius, Hallam Leonard, 5:299
Mowrer, Orval Hobart, 5:146
Moyle, Jennifer, 4:240, 5:160–164
Moyle-Needham, Dorothy. *See* Needham, Dorothy Moyle
Mozingo, Ralph, 3:43
MRC (Medical Research Council), 1:188, 6:519, 521
mRNA

DNA and, 5:310
    function, 1:370
    isolation, 1:375–376
MSFC (George C. Marshall Space Flight Center), 7:175–176
MSSCC (Multicolor Spin-Scan Cloud Camera), 6:556
Mt. Carmel (Palestine), excavations, 3:103, 105–106
Muchow, Martha, 6:525
Mudgan, Martin, 1:197
Mueller, Ferdinand Jakob Heinrich von, 5:**204–209**
Mueller, George, 7:176
Mugnier, Cécile. *See* Vogt, Cécile Augustine Marie
Muhammad (prophet), 6:214–215
Mu'ayyad al-Dīn al-'Urdī, 6:187
Mühlbach, Elfriede, 2:345
Muir, John, 4:225
al-Mulukhkhuṣ fī ul-huyʾ u al-basīṭa (Jaghmīnī), 4:20
Mulder, Gerardus Johannes, 4:54
Mulders, Gerardus Franciscus Wilhelmus, 7:126
Mulkay, Michael, 5:125
Mullen, George, 6:313
Muller, Christiaan Alexander, 5:346, 7:129
Müller, Ferdinand Jakob Heinrich von. *See* Mueller, Ferdinand Jakob Heinrich von
Muller, Hermann Joseph, 5:185
    Drosophila breeding, 1:212
    genetics, 3:424, 5:242, 6:494
    metabolic reactions, 3:364
    multistep biosynthetic pathways, 3:363
    students of, 6:310
Müller, Johann Christoph, 5:37
Müller, Johannes (von Königsberg). *See* Regiomontanus, Johannes
Müller, K. Alexander, 5:204
Müller, Walther, 5:301
Müller-Freienfels, Richard, 6:525
Müller-Wille, Staffan, 5:99, 103
Mulliken, Robert Sanderson, 5:**209–214**, *211*
    bonds, 6:37
    chemical shifts, 3:198
    electron deficient molecules, 3:196
    influence of, 3:87
    quantum chemistry, 5:211–212
Mulliken, Samuel P., 6:322
Multiattribute decision making, 7:93
Multicolor Spin-Scan Cloud Camera (MSSCC), 6:556
Multiple Light Scattering: Tables, Formulas, and Applications (Van de Hulst), 7:130
Multiple operationalism, 2:25
Multiple regression analysis, 6:256
Multitrait-multimethod matrix, 2:25
Mumford, David, 2:260, 4:147
Mumford, Lewis, 2:236
Munk, Walter, 2:354

Muñoz, Juan M., 4:253
Münsterberg, Hugo, 1:50, 6:524
Müntz, Charles, 6:379
Muons, 1:58, 73, 6:282, 7:367
   See also Mesons
Murchi, Tommaso, 1:110
Murchison, Carl, 7:244
Murchison, Charles, 1:209
Murchison, Roderick Impey, 4:231
Murdoch, Iris, 4:284
Murphy, James, 2:144, 6:143–144, 145
Murphy, Trevor, 6:118
Murray, Bruce, 6:487, 7:270, 271
Murray, Henry Alexander, 2:408, 5:**214–219**, *216*
Murray, John, 6:372
Muscle contraction, 4:324–325
Muscle contractions
   adenosine triphosphate in, 6:571
   biochemistry, 5:231–234, 306
   electricity, 7:170–172
   myosin in, 5:231
Muscular neurophysiology
   end plate potentials, 4:87
   injuries and, 1:16
Museology, 4:43, 5:181, 182
Musgrave, I., 4:110
Musical theory
   commentaries on, 6:137–138
   mathematics, 3:6
   Pythagorean, 2:284–285
   works, 6:172–173, 174–175
Musil, Rudolf, 4:42
Muslims. *See* Islam
Musselman, Elizabeth Green. *See* Green Musselman,
   Elizabeth
Mustard gas, 1:193
   See also Chemical weapons
Müstinger, Georg, 6:153
Musurgia universalis (Kircher), 4:133
Mutation Theory (de Vries). *See Die Mutationstheorie* (de
   Vries)
Mutations
   botany, 7:189–191
   creeper, 3:221–222
   Drosophila, 1:463
   Hagedoorn, 3:30
   induced, 7:13, 14
   introduced, 6:478, 480–482, *481*
   maternal genes, 1:399–400
   metabolic reactions and, 1:225–227
   neutral theory, 4:116–117
   radiation-associated, 5:242–243
   streptomycin, 6:318
Die Mutationstheorie (de Vries), 7:190, 191

Muthukkaruppan, Veerappan, 3:187
Mutual Aid: A Factor in Evolution (Kropotkin), 4:161,
   162
Mutualism, 5:320
My Father's Watch (Morrison), 5:192
Mycobacteria, 4:*228,* 228–229
Mycolic acids, 4:*228*
Myers, Arlo K., 5:149
Myers, Charles, 1:188
Myosin, 5:231, 6:571
Myotonic pupils, 3:345
Mysterium cosmographicum (Kepler), 4:105, 106
Mystery of the Mind (Penfield), 6:74
Mysticism, 3:279
Myxomatosis research, 6:209

N

Naas, Valérie, 6:118
Nachbin, Leopoldo, 5:178
Nachmansohn, David, 4:325
NAD (nicotinamide adenine dinucleotide), 3:171, 5:306
Nader, Ralph, 1:43
Naef, Adolf, 6:354
Naegeli, Carl Wilhelm von. *See* Nägeli, Karl Wilhelm
   von
Nafe, John E., 6:394
Nagasaki bombing, 5:242, 6:422
Nagata, Takeshi, 3:376–377
Nägeli, Karl Wilhelm von, 5:102
   cell theory, 6:358
   microscopes, 6:390
   pleomorphist theory, 1:209
Nairn, A. E. M., 2:191
Nakane, Michiyo, 3:236
Namias, Jerome, 5:**221–225,** *222,* 7:275
Nanos, George, 7:305
Nanotechnology, 6:473–475
   energy consumption, 6:472, 474–475
   microengineering and, 5:41–42
Nansen, Fridtjof, 6:89, 90
Napoléon I, Emperor of France, 1:264, 265
Napp, Cyrill, 5:98, 99
Narrow Roads of Gene Land (Hamilton), 3:234
NASA. *See* National Aeronautics and Space
   Administration (NASA)
Nasar, Sylvia, 5:225
Nash, John Forbes, Jr., 2:258, 5:**225–231,** *226, 230*
   bargaining, 3:249
   cooperative games, 3:251
   game theory, 7:80, 81
   isometric embedding theorem, 5:198
Nash Demand Game, 5:227
Nash equilibrium, 3:250–251, 5:225, 227–228
Nash-Moser theory, 5:198–199

A Nation at Risk: The Imperative for Educational Reform
(National Commission on Excellence in Education),
6:405
National Academy of Sciences
   astronomy, 3:176
   decadal reports, 1:161
   Space Science Board, 5:261–262
National Aeronautics and Space Administration (NASA)
   astronomy, 3:176
   Cosmic Background Explorer, 7:304–305
   establishment, 5:261
   exobiology, 3:364–365
   Hubble Space Telescope, 1:160, 6:502
   instrumentation, 7:75–77
   Jet Propulsion Laboratory, 6:100–103
   key officials in, 5:259
   Microwave Anisotropy Probe, 7:304–305
   planning committee, 6:546
   Ranger Program, 6:444
   rocketry, 7:174–176
   satellites, 6:555–556
   space probes, 6:311, 313
   space science at, 5:261–263
   support for, 7:123–125
National Bureau of Standards, 2:168–169
National Chemical Laboratory (NCL), 7:147
National Commission on Excellence in Education, 6:405
National Education Association, 7:26
National Intelligence Tests, 7:26
National Nanotechnology Initiative (NNI), 6:474
National Radio Astronomy Observatory (NRAO),
   3:143, 176
National Science Foundation (NSF), 3:176
National Socialism (Germany)
   Aryan physics, 4:56–57
   ballistic missiles, 7:173
   biochemistry, 2:94
   biology research, 1:464
   blacklisting, 6:233, 525, 571
   chemical engineering, 3:383
   chemical warfare research, 4:168–170
   companies seized, 2:359
   eugenics, 1:3–4, 3:26–28
   harrassment of non-Jews, 3:350
   indoctrination courses, 2:268
   Jewish scientists and, 3:206, 5:253
   medical experimentation, 1:462–463
   membership in, 4:341–342
   Netherlands, 7:141
   opposition to, 4:86
   pharmacology, 3:247
   racism, 7:250, 251
   radiochemistry, 3:210–212
   rubber, 6:230–232
   science and, 4:341–342, 5:122–123, 6:574
   scientific resistance to, 6:113–114, 352, 7:164
   suicides, 3:266
   university professors, 3:299
   women, 3:294, 5:173
   See also Antisemitism
National Socialist Party. *See* National Socialism
  (Germany)
National Technical Laboratories, 1:234
NATO (North Atlantic Treaty Organization), 1:136
Natua, Walle, 3:146
Natufian culture, 3:105, 107
Natur und Volk (magazine), 6:248
Natura rerum (Royer), 6:288
Natural communities. *See* Ecosystems
The Natural Fit (McCulloch), 5:77
The Natural Geography of Plants (Cronquist), 2:213
Natural Histories (Bacon, Francis), 1:141
Natural history
   Canada, 7:78–79
   classification, 4:314–316
   economics, 4:315–316
   Enlightenment, 1:431–434, 7:220–223
   evolution, 6:109
   human health, 1:368–369
   illustrations, 4:230–232
   museums for, 5:366
   paleontological change, 1:415
   Paracelsianism, 1:308–309
   Renaissance medicine, 6:551–552
   Roman, 6:116–120
   steady state uniformitarianism, 1:416
   systematics, 2:7
   zoology, 3:115
Natural History (Pliny), 4:265, 6:68, 116–120
Natural law
   civil rights, 6:483
   intuition in, 1:146
Natural numbers, mapping of, 6:266
Natural philosophy, 6:115–116
   alchemical commentaries on, 5:338–339
   anti-Aristotelianism, 1:204–205
   Arabic, 1:46–47
   Aristotelianism, 1:361–362, 2:326–327, 6:292–296,
      540, 7:387–390
   atomism, 3:110, 157–158
   Buridan school, 1:34–36
   causation, 1:145
   Christianity, 4:51–52
   civil rights, 6:483
   classification, 4:189–191
   commerce and, 1:230–231
   Copernicanism, 2:178–179
   Darwinism, 3:289

Natural philosophy, *continued*
    Dominicans, 2:19
    education, 5:36, 331–333, 6:563–564
    Empedoclean, 2:396–398
    empiricism, 2:44, 4:65–66
    Enlightenment, 1:431–434
    experimental, 2:2
    Franciscan order, 1:143–144
    heliocentric, 2:20–21
    independent of theology, 1:446–447
    introductory textbooks on, 5:21–22
    limits of natural powers, 5:351–352
    logic, 1:448–450, 5:312–314
    mathematics, 5:351, 6:562–563
    mathematics and, 1:296–297
    mechanical philosophy and, 1:204–205
    mechanics, 1:204–205, 3:111
    motion, 1:441–443, 5:351, 352
    mysticism, 3:277–279
    perspectives on, 4:1–2
    positive, 1:141
    propositions, 1:378–379
    scientific method, 3:287–288, 5:350–351
    speculative, 1:142, 366–369
    theology, 1:444–447
    theory of language, 2:44–45
    translations, 1:13–15
    women, 2:79–80
Natural physics, 1:423–425, 445
Natural powers, 5:351–352
The Natural Regulation of Animal Numbers (Lack), 7:378
Natural resources, 3:395–396, 396–398, *397*
Natural selection, 2:25–26
    adaptation, 7:226–227, *361*
    altruism, 3:226–229
    antibody formation, 4:48
    atomism, 3:289
    consciousness, 3:183
    embryology and, 1:210–211
    epistemology, 2:25–26
    eugenics, 3:234
    first species, 1:417
    flora and fauna, 1:415
    genetical theory, 3:31
    intelligence, 6:91
    mollusks, 2:4–5
    physiological genetics, 7:*358*
    power of struggle, 2:246
    shifting-balance theory, 7:358–362, *359, 360*
    social behavior, 7:376, 377–380
    social environment and, 2:243–247
    territoriality, 3:385
    See also Darwinism; Genetics

The Natural-Selection Theory of Antibody Formation (Jerne), 1:458
Nature
    anthropogenic, 7:4
    Aristotelian theory, 1:101–102
    atomic theory, 6:288
    commerce and, 1:230–231
    laws of motion, 2:273
    mutual aid theory, 4:161–162
    non-separability and nonlocality in, 1:325
    nurture *vs.*
        ethology, 7:53, 54
        gender identity, 7:28–29
        intelligence, 7:26, 27
    philosophy of, 4:190
    Stoicism, 6:117–118
Nature and Man (Carpenter), 2:57
Nature Conservancy, 7:8
Nature conservation. *See* Conservation
The Nature of a Bird's World (Howard), 3:385
The Nature of Human Conflicts (Luria), 4:349–350
Nature of Man (Hippocrates), 3:322, 323
Nature of Matter: Purpose of High Energy Physics (Yuan), 6:396
The Nature of Prejudice (Allport), 1:53
The Nature of the Chemical Bond and the Structure of Molecules and Crystals (Pauling), 5:212, 289, 6:38, 43
The Nature of the Universe (Hoyle), 3:390
Natures Explication and Helmont's Vindication (Starkey), 6:512
Natures Pictures (Cavendish), 2:80
Natürliche Schöpfungsgeschichte (Haeckel), 3:207–208
Die Naturwissenschaften (journal), 7:182
Der Naturwissenschaftler vor der religiösen Frage (Jordan), 4:57
Naudé, Gabriel, 2:38
Nauenberg, Michael, 5:270
Nauert, Charles, 6:120
Naumann, Einar Christian Leonard, 7:36
Naumov, Oleg, 4:160
Naval architecture, 6:470
Naval Research Laboratory (NRL), 5:259–260, 7:74–77
Navier-Stokes equations, 3:263, 4:188–189, 272, 319
Navigation
    almanacs, 1:127, 128–129
    animal, 3:177–178
    Dutch, 6:110–111
    insect, 7:*85,* 85–86
    instrumentation, 2:157–158
an-Nayrīzī, 3:285
The Nazi Doctors (Lifton), 3:28
Nazism. *See* National Socialism (Germany)
NCL (National Chemical Laboratory), 7:147
Neanderthals, 3:155–156, 7:116

Nebulae
  clustering, 3:286–287
  cosmology, 6:456
  Crab Nebula, 5:343
  dark, 1:329–330
  emissions, 6:432, 434
  galaxy as spiral, 5:346
  illumination in, 5:112
  natural history, 3:290
  See also Galaxies
The Necessary and Sufficient Conditions of Therapeutic Personality Change (Rogers), 6:276
Neddermeyer, Seth Henry, 1:56, 73–75, 291, 306
Nederlandse Jeugdbond voor Natuurstudie (NJN), 1:148
Needell, Allan, 6:112
Needham, Dorothy Mary Moyle. *See* Needham, Dorothy Moyle
Needham, Dorothy Moyle, 5:**231–235**, 238, 239, 7:202
Needham, James G., 2:389
Needham, Joseph, 5:**235–241**, *238,* 7:403, 404
  chemical analysis of eggs, 1:372
  embryology, 7:202
  influence of, 4:275
  marriage of, 5:233–234
  United Nations, 3:427
Needs, hierarchy of, 5:45, 46–47
Néel, Eugène-Félix, 3:376–377
Neel, James Van Gundia, 5:**241–246**
Néel, Louis, 2:191–192
Nefrel, Albrecht, 5:328
A Negative Experiment Relating to Magnetism and the Earth's Rotation (Blackett), 1:292
Negretti, Henry, 3:10
Negrín, Juan, 5:305
Neher, Henry Victor, 1:73
Neiburger, Morris, 2:99
Nelson, Edward B., 6:394
Neoplatonism, 6:137
Nephi, Barachias, 4:131
Nepreryvnye gruppy (Pontryagin), 6:127
Neptune
  discovery of, 1:25–26
  moons, 4:177, 178, 179
Neptunium, 6:402
Nernst, Walther Hermann, 3:203–204, 4:288, 6:373
  conflicts with other scientists, 1:113
  courses taught by, 2:205
  reversal potential, 4:88
  students of, 5:167
Nerve gases, 4:169
  See also Chemical weapons
Nerve growth factor (NGF), 3:217, 220–221, *222*
Nerve terminals, 7:180, *180*

Nervous system
  amphibians, 6:495
  autonomic, 3:302–305, 5:150–151
  central
      physiology, 7:183
      psychology, 3:268–269
  chemical mechanisms, 4:86–88
  development, 3:217–224
      gastrulation, 3:350
      genetics, 3:218
      microsurgery, 3:*220*
  diseases, 2:341–342
  drug effects on, 1:119–120
  emotions, 6:11–13
  evolution, 1:438
  muscle fibers, 2:219
  neurons, 1:15–18
  physiology, 7:183
  sympathetic, 7:178–180
  See also Neuroanatomy
Nesmejanov, Aleksandr Nikolaevich, 4:103, 5:**246–250**
Nesting birds, 5:277
Netherlands, 6:110–111, 7:141, 142
Neubauer, Otto, 5:251
Neuberg, Carl Alexander, 4:323, 5:**250–254**
  Kaiser Wilhelm Institute, 1:251
  National Socialists and, 1:462
Neuberg schema, 5:252
Neues Blümenbuch (Merian), 5:120
Neugebauer, Gerry, 7:271
Neugebauer, Otto, 6:518
Neumann, Carl Gottfried, 4:160
Neumann, Franz Ernst, 7:164, 165
Neumann, Johann von. *See* von Neumann, John
Neumayer, Georg von, 4:152, 6:370
The Neural Crest (Hörstadiius), 3:369
Neurath, Otto, 2:44, 4:55, 279
Neuroanatomy
  animal, 1:436–437, 2:340–342
  brain, 1:406–409, 7:161–163
  diseases, 6:69–74
  emotions, 6:10–13
  fish, 7:182
  functional, 6:*71*
  noradrenaline, 7:179–180
  Papez circuit theory, 6:*12*
  See also Neurology
Neurochemistry
  modern medicine, 7:45–46
  sympathomimetic amines, 1:120–122
Neuroembryology, 3:217–224, 218, *219, 220,* 222–223
Neuroethology, 1:436, 438
Neuroleptics, 4:31–32

Neurology, 3:344–347
  See also Neurophysiology
Neuron Doctrine and Electrophysiology (Bullock), 1:437
Neuron Theory or Reticular Theory? (Ramón y Cajal),
  1:437
Neurons
  electrical activity, 2:330–331
  electrophysiology, 1:15–18
  network activity, 5:*77, 77*–78, *78*
Neuropeptides, 7:178
The Neurophysiological Basis of Mind (Eccles), 2:332
Neurophysiology
  behavior and, 4:203–204
  chemical mechanisms in, 4:86–88
  computational neuroscience and, 5:32–36
  cybernetics and, 5:76–79
  electrophysiology, 1:15–18
  muscular
    end plate potentials, 4:87
    injuries, 1:16
  synapses, 2:331–333
  See also Physiology
A Neuropsychological Theory (Hebb), 3:270
Neuropsychology, 3:267–271
Neuroscience
  action potentials, 3:328, *329, 329*–332
  animal, 1:436–438
  cognitive
    cerebral hemispheres, 6:495–497
    computational research in, 5:32–36
    consciousness, 6:498
    prefrontal cortex, 3:145–148
  development, 6:360, 362–365
Neurosciences Research Program Bulletin, 6:364
Neurospora
  genetics, 3:361–363
  mutations, 1:226, *226*
Neurospora crassa, 7:13–14
Neurosurgery, 6:69–71
Neurotransmitters
  regulation at synapses, 1:121
  research, 7:176–180
  role of, 4:89–90
The Neutral Theory of Molecular Evolution (Kimura),
  4:117
Neutrinos
  decaying, 6:400
  solar neutrino problem, 1:157, 158–159
Neutron bombs, 1:392
Neutron stars, 3:139, 5:130–131
Neutrons
  behavior, 3:20
  chain reactions, 6:574
  cyclotrons, 1:304–306

discovery, 1:269
fission, 7:265–266
photographic emulsions, 1:299
positrons and, 1:73
production of, 4:208
scattering, 6:392–393
slow, 6:407
Nevanlinna, Rolf, 1:21, 22
Never at Rest (Westfall), 5:269, 273
Nevill Mott: Reminiscences and Appreciations (Davis),
  5:204
New Atlantis (Bacon, Francis), 1:140
The New Britton and Brown Illustrated Flora (Gleason),
  2:213
*New Developments in the Chemistry of Diborane and
  Borohydrides. I. General Summary* (Brown), 1:421
New General Catalogue (Herschel), 3:287
New History (Zosimus), 5:341
A New Look at Mechanisms in Bioenergetics (Racker),
  6:200
New Patterns in Genetics and Development (Waddington),
  7:203
The New Phytologist, 7:3, 4
The New Psychology and Its Relation to Life (Tansley), 7:5
New Tables (Argyrus), 1:98
*A New Theory of Equilibrium Selection for Games with
  Complete Information* (Harsanyi), 3:251
*A New Theory of Equilibrium Selection for Games with
  Incomplete Information* (Harsanyi), 3:251
New Theory of Parallels (Dodgson), 2:311
*New Yearbook for Mineralogy, Geognosy, Geology, and
  Fossil Sudies* (Bonn). *See Jahrbuch für Mineralogie,
  Geognosie Geologie, and Petrefaktenkunde* (Bronn)
Newbery, John, 2:216
Newcomb problems, 4:35–36
Newcombe, Howard, 6:318
Newcomb's Problem and Two Principles of Choice
  (Nozick), 5:286–287
Newell, Allen, 5:**254–258,** *256,* 6:452
Newell, Homer Edward, Jr., 3:80, 5:*259,* **259–264,**
  6:100, 102
Newell, Norman Dennis, 5:**265–268**
Newell, Robert, 5:254
Newkirk, Gordon, 3:143
Newman, Maxwell Herman Alexander, 3:256
Newman, William, 5:268, 273–277, 6:512, 7:335
Newton, Isaac, 1:28, 5:**268–277,** *274*
  alchemy, 7:335
  atmospheric refraction, 5:352
  calculus, 7:281
  corpuscular theory, 6:512
  gravitational attraction theory of, 5:11–12, 56–57,
    7:282
  infinite mass, 2:92

influence of, 3:408
light, 1:294–295, 295, 5:10
Lullian alchemy, 4:348
magnetism, 4:132
relations of matter, 1:432–433
Newtonian cosmology, 3:275
The Newtonian Philosophy (Newbery), 2:216
Neyman, Jerzy, 7:414
NGF (nerve growth factor), 3:217, 220–221, *222*
Niall, Hugh, 2:352
Nice, Leonard Blaine, 5:277
Nice, Margaret Morse, 5:**277–280,** *278*
Nicephorus Gregoras, 1:98
Niche, ecological, 3:415–416
Nicholas of Autrecourt
    principle of non-contradiction, 1:447
    scientific knowledge, 5:350–351
Nichols, Kenneth D., 1:134
Nicholson, Edward Max, 2:387, 3:385
Nicholson, William, 7:171–172
Nickel, 7:308, *308*
Nicklès, François Joseph Jérôme, 4:205
Nicolaou, K. C., 7:341
Nicomachean Ethics (Aristotle), 1:38
Nicotinamide adenine dinucleotide (NAD), 3:171,
    5:306
Niedersen, Uwe, 5:356, 357
Nielsen, Lauge Olaf, 1:378
Nielsen, Peter E., 5:157
Niemann, Carl, 6:38
Nietzsche, Friedrich Wilhelm
    influence of, 4:64
    transcendent reality, 3:265
*Nieuwe onderwijsinghe op de principaelste puncten der
    zeevaert* (Coignet), 2:157
Nieuwenkamp. Willem, 1:282
Nifo, Agostino, 5:**280–281**
Niggli, Paul, 7:142
Nihāyat al-idrāk fī dirāyat al-aflāk (Quṭb al-Dīn), 6:188
Nijenhuis, Albert, 4:146
Nikodym, Otton, 4:151, 7:415
Nikomachus, 4:51
Nilan, Robert, 5:70
Nilsson, Lars Fredrik, 6:89
Nirenberg, Marshall W., 1:80, 375, 2:210
    DNA, 5:310
    Nobel Prize, 3:340
Nishina, Yoshio, 7:398
Nissl, Franz, 1:407, 408, 2:341
Niter theory, 5:274–275
Nitrogen, dating techniques, 5:298, 299
Nitrogen cycle, marine, 3:259
Nitrogen fertilizers, 3:204
Nitrogen fixation

BET equation, 2:393–394
    biology, 2:104–105
Nixon, Eric, 6:534
Nixon, Richard M., 1:80, 235, 2:170, 3:81, 7:401, 404
Nizoral, 4:33
NJN (Nederlandse Jeugdbond voor Natuurstudie),
    1:148
NMR spectroscopy. *See* Nuclear magnetic resonance
    (NMR)
NNI (National Nanotechnology Initiative), 6:474
No Man Alone (Penfield), 6:69
No More War! (Pauling), 6:41
No Other Gods (Penfield), 6:74
Noad, Henry, 2:216
Noble, G. Kingsley, 4:79, 244
Noble court patronage. *See* Patronage
Noble gases, 3:402
Noël, Yves, 5:357
Noether, Amalie Emmy, 1:287, 2:404, 7:254
Nohl, Hermann, 2:43
Noise, 1:402, 403
Nollet, Jean-Antoine, 4:213
Nomenclature
    binomial, 2:6–7
    botanical, 1:386, 387–388
    chemical
        proposed classification of elements and, 5:19
        reaction to, 4:216
        stereochemistry, 6:158–161
    stratigraphy, 7:62–63
Nominalism
    connotative concepts, 5:312
    logic and semantics, 1:447
Nomological networks, 2:24
Non-Abelian gauge principle, 1:238
Non-Frontal Thunderstorms (Byers), 1:469
Non-linear mechanics, 1:317
Non-Proliferation Treaty, 6:405
Non-zero-sum games, 3:231–232
Nonactin, 6:*158*
Nonbenzenoid Aromatic Compounds (Nozoe), 5:292
The Nonclassical Ion Problem (Brown), 1:421
Nonclassical ions, 1:420–421, *421*
Nonclassical Ions (Bartlett), 1:420–421
Noncooperative games
    incomplete information, 3:250–251
    Nash equilibrium and, 5:227
Nondirective psychotherapy approach, 6:275, 276
Nonlinear elliptical partial differential equations,
    1:261–262
Nonlinear Functional Analysis (Nash), 5:229
Nonlinear programming, 7:81–82
Nonlinear sigma model, 3:192, 193
Nonlocality, 1:325

Nonthermal radiation, 1:41
Noradrenaline, 7:176–180
Norges Pattedyr (Collett), 2:383
Nörlund, Niels Erik. *See* Nørlund, Niels Erik
Nørlund, Niels Erik, 4:233
Normal probability integrals, 1:219
NORPAX (North Pacific Experiment), 5:223
Norris, James Flack, 7:349–350
Norrish, Ronald, 6:139, 140
North, John, 1:142
A North African Story (Coon), 2:175
North American Herpetology (Holbrook), 3:339
North Atlantic Treaty Organization (NATO), 1:136
North Pacific Experiment (NORPAX), 5:223
Northrop, John Howard, 2:348
Notas de Matemática (Monteiro), 5:179
Notes on Bixin (Venkataraman), 7:148
Notes on North America (Johnston), 4:54
Notgemeinschaft der Deutschen Wissenschaft, 3:205
Nothing Is Too Wonderful to Be True (Morrison), 5:193
La Nouvelle alliance (Prigogine), 6:167
Nova, 1:277
Novara, Domenico Maria, 2:177
Noveas, Caterina Dutilh, 6:564
Novgorod, Nizhny, 1:317
Novikoff, Alex Benjamin, 5:**281–286**
Novin, Don, 5:151
Novum lumen chemicum (Sendivogius), 5:274
Novum organum (Bacon, Francis), 1:137, 141
Novum Testamentum (Arnald of Villanova, Pseudo),
   1:109
Noyce, Robert, 1:235, 6:440, 441
Noyes, Arthur Amos, 2:393, 4:287
   recruitment of scientists, 1:234
   thermodynamics, 6:36
Nozick, Robert, 5:*286*, **286–287**
Nozoe, Ju-ichi, 5:288
Nozoe, Tetsuo, 5:**287–293**, *291*
NRAO (National Radio Astronomy Observatory),
   3:143, 176
NRL (Naval Research Laboratory), 5:259–260, 7:74–77
NSF (National Science Foundation), 3:176
De insolubilibus (Bradwardine), 1:378
Nuclear astrophysics
   light nuclei, 4:211
   nuclear magnetic resonance, 6:181
Nuclear chemistry
   plutonium, 6:408–409
   radioactivity, 6:75–78
   transuranium elements, 6:401–406
Nuclear decay, 6:169–171, 7:366
Nuclear energy
   atomic bombs, 6:422
   Australia, 6:260–261

   civilian control over, 1:165
   ecology research and, 5:319
   electricity, 6:401
   explosion, 6:415–416
   fusion, 6:384–385
   Oppenheimer, J. Robert on, 5:348–349
   reactors, 1:314–315
   USSR, 6:325
Nuclear fission. *See* Fission
Nuclear fusion. *See* Fusion
Nuclear magnetic resonance (NMR)
   in analytical chemistry, 4:229
   applications, 7:352
   Bloch equations and, 1:306
   chemical shifts, 3:*198*
   chemistry, 3:195, 196–197
   development, 6:130, 180–182
   dyes, 7:146
   Lemieux, Raymond Urgel, 4:258–261
   nuclear astrophysics, 6:181
   organometallic chemistry, 7:309
   scientific method, 7:312
   spectroscopy, 3:196–201
   World War II, 6:195
Nuclear physics
   alpha particles, 1:290–291
   atomic weapons, 1:269, 327
   beta decay, 7:102
   chain reactions, 6:573–575, 7:295–296
   China, 7:397–402
   Cold War, 2:168–170
   commercial applications, 2:166–167
   cyclotrons, 7:328–329
   experimental, 7:119
   fission, 1:60–62, 257, 7:392
   influential figures, 6:393, 7:391
   magnetic resonance, 6:191, 194–197
   mass spectrography, 1:162–165
   molecular collisions, 1:258–259
   nuclear decay, 6:169–171
   nuclear structure, 2:379
   nuclear weapons, 6:419–424
   particle accelerators, 1:425–428, 4:208–212,
      327–331
   particles, 5:303–304, 6:407–411
   politics, 2:166–167
   quantum electrodynamics, 7:266–267
   quantum mechanics, 1:391–392
   radioactivity, 6:77
   resonance phenomena, 3:60–61
   scattering, 6:499
   scope of, 1:133–135
   solar, 1:157
   spontaneous fission, 3:35–36

steady state theory, 3:388
theoretical, 5:127–131
women scientists, 7:363–368
Nuclear Physics in Photographs (Occhialini and Powell),
5:304
Nuclear quadrupole moments, 6:195
Nuclear reactions
chain reactions, 6:573–575, 7:295–296
stars, 1:157
chemical elements, 3:390
white dwarfs, 3:176
Nuclear reactors, 5:190
Nuclear spin, sodium, 6:193
The Nuclear Spin of Sodium (Rabi), 6:193
Nuclear transplantation, 1:*398*, 398–399, 400
Nuclear waste, 6:530
Nuclear weapons
activism, 6:40–42
Bikini Atoll nuclear tests, 5:254
China, 7:401
development, 6:573, 7:265–266
explosion, 6:415–416
fallout from, 4:295–296
first tests, 1:257
fusion, 6:501–502
genetic effects, 5:242–243
implosion, 1:306, 6:407
mass spectroscopy, 2:166–167
nuclear physics, 6:419–424
Oppenheimer, J. Robert on, 5:348–349
opposition to, 1:292, 6:306, 314–315, 574–575
plutonium, 1:56–57, 6:401, 402–403, 408–409
quantum theory, 1:269
shock waves, 6:170
support for, 7:21–24
test bans, 1:80, 6:405
theoretical physics, 1:274–275, 319
uranium isotope separation, 1:322
USSR, 5:128–129, 6:324–325, 326–329
Weismann Institute, 1:251–253
See also Arms race; Atomic bombs; Hydrogen bombs;
Manhattan Project
Nuclear winter, 6:315
Nucleic acids
measurement, 2:67–69
neural induction, 1:373, *373*
Nucleophilic substitution, 1:*190*, 191, 4:15
Nucleosides, 7:67
Nucleosynthesis in Massive Stars and Supernovae (Fowler),
3:62
Nucleotide sugars, 4:253–256
Nucleotides, 7:67
Nucleus, cell. *See* Cell nucleus
Number counts (radio sources), 6:304

Number theory
analytic, 2:404–405, 7:155–157
arithmetic, 6:265–267
proof theory, 3:309–310
Numbers
cardinal, 2:32–33
complex, 2:63, 229–230
hyperarithmetical sets, 6:266
listable sets, 6:265, 266, 267
natural, 6:266
prime, 2:404–405
real, 2:30–31
Numerical analysis
algebra, 7:255
computer science, 3:50, 256–257, 4:319–320,
7:314, 316–317
cubic equations, 7:87–88
discrete mathematics, 2:403
meteorology, 6:238
theoretical physics, 3:253
wave mechanics, 3:254
Numerical Analysis (Hartree), 3:253
Numerical Archimedes calculators, 6:541
Numerical weather forecasting, 6:222, 469–472,
558–561, 561
Numerische Mathematik (Dijkstra), 2:297
Nur al-Din Abu Ishāq al-Biṭrūjī. *See* al-Biṭrūjī al-Ishbīlī,
Abū Isḥāq
Nüsslein-Volhard, Christiane, 1:400
Nutrition. *See* Diet and nutrition
Nyberg, Alf, 6:3
Nylon, 1:215
development of, 2:50
silk *vs.,* 6:332–333

O

*O nekotorykh problemakh khimicheskoi kinetiki i
reaktsionnoi sposobnosti* (Semenov). *See Some Problems
of Chemical Kinetics and Reactivity* (Semenov)
Oakley, Kenneth Page, 2:140, 241, 4:221, 5:**295–300**,
297
OAO (Orbiting Astronomical Observatory), 6:502
Oath (Hippocrates), 3:324, 325
Obedience psychology, 5:137–140, *138, 139*
Oberth, Hermann, 7:173
Objections to Astrology (Bok), 1:332
An Objectivistic Study of the Innate Behaviour of Animals
(Tinbergen), 7:52
Obligationes (Swyneshed), 6:562, 563
Oblik Biosfer (Margalef), 5:24
O'Brien, Brian, 5:113
O'Brien, Sean, 6:473
*Observational Evidence Confirming Lindblad's Hypothesis
of a Rotation of the Galactic System* (Oort), 5:342

Observations Concerning Evolution (Cockayne), 2:156
Observations upon Experimental Philosophy (Cavendish), 2:80
Observations upon Natural Philosophy (Cavendish), 2:79
Observatories
    in Brazil, 4:293–294
    in Chile, 1:132
    climatology, 1:116–117
    European Sourthern Observatory, 3:273, 276
    galactic spectrography, 1:130–132
    Greenwich Observatory, 3:276
    Harvard College Observatory, 5:115–117,
      7:284–285
    Kitt Peak National Observatory, 6:546
    Lick Observatory, 5:112
    Mauna Loa Observatory, 3:276
    meteorology, 4:293
    national, 3:142–143
    National Radio Astronomy Observatory, 3:276
    Orbiting Astronomic Observatory, 6:502
    Orbiting Solar Observatory, 3:143, 7:76, 77
    radio astronomy research, 5:83–84
    Smithsonian Astrophysical Observatory, 7:287–289
    for solar corona studies, 5:113
    synoptic meteorology, 4:152
    See also Telescopes
Obukhov, Aleksandr Mikhailovch, 7:391
Obyknovennye differentcial'nye uravneniya (Pontryagin),
  6:128
Occhialini, Beppo. *See* Occhialini, Giuseppe Paolo
  Stanislao
Occhialini, Giuseppe Paolo Stanislao, 5:**300–305,** *303*
    Cavendish Laboratory, 5:301–302
    cloud chambers, 1:291
    particle showers, 6:282
    positrons and, 1:73, 7:399
Occlusion process, 1:246–247
Ocean circulation. *See* Ocean currents
Ocean currents, 2:260–264, 5:172, *173,* 329, 6:*528,*
  528–531, *529*
Ocean floor mapping. *See* Seafloor mapping
The Ocean of Truth (Dietz), 2:287, 5:97
Ocean tides, 1:361, 362
Oceanography
    analytical chemistry, 3:257–259
    climate change, 5:329
    ecological modeling, 6:255–257
    ecology, 3:412
    El Niño, 5:223–224
    geophysics, 2:265–266
    Germany, 6:370–373
    hydrodynamics, 1:288–290
    international, 2:262–263
    limnology and, 5:172–173

    major influence in, 5:23
    marine geology, 2:287–288
    meteorology, 6:2–5
    ocean currents, 2:260–264, 5:172, *173,* 6:527–531,
      528, 529
    Pacific atolls, 4:185–187
    physical, 3:8–11, 7:373–376
    physical chemistry, 6:88–90
    radiocarbon dating, 5:326–327
    seafloor mapping, 7:29–31
    space, 3:10–11
    temperature, 6:*528*
    thermohaline finestructures, 3:10
    United States, 6:234–237
    velocity, 6:*528*
    wave height prediction, 2:354
The Oceans (Sverdrup), 2:261, 5:172
Ochoa, Severo, 5:**305–312,** *307*
Ochsenfeld, 1:304
Ockham, William of, 2:327, 5:**312–315**
    indivisibles, 1:449
    influence of, 5:350
    motion, 1:35
    nominalism, 1:447, 450
    propositions, 1:378
    successive entities, 1:379
    truth and falsehood, 1:297
Octant rule, 7:354–355
Oculomotor system, 3:303
Odbert, Henry Sebastian, 1:52
O'Dell, Robert, 1:160
Odling, William, 4:98
O'Donnell, Sean, 3:235–236
Odontornithes (King), 4:121
Odum, Eugene Pleasants, 1:48, 2:390, 5:24, **315–321,**
  316, 322, 323
Odum, Howard Thomas, 5:**322–326**
    biogeochemistry, 3:413, 5:322
    colleagues of, 5:316, 317
    coral reefs, 5:318
    ecosystem ecology, 5:316
    ecosystem energy flow, 5:317, 318, 323
    population ecology, 3:416
    radiation ecology, 3:414
Odum, Howard W., 5:316, 322
Oeconomia Naturae (Linneaus), 4:316
Oedipus Aegyptiacus Mundus subterraneus (Kircher),
  4:130, 133
Oehlkers, Friedrich, 5:69
Oeschger, Hans, 5:**326–331,** *327*
Oeschger counters, 5:326
Oestrogen. *See* Estrogen
Oetker, August, 5:252
Oettinger, Luise, 3:298, 299, 300

Oeuvres complètes (Cauchy), 2:75

Oeuvre (Lavoisier), 4:217

Oeuvres: Collected Papers (Borel), 1:344

Oeuvres Mathématiques (al-Ṭūsī), 7:87, 88

Oeuvres philosophiques de Buffon (Piveteau), 6:109

Of Induction (Whewell), 7:282

Of Molecules and Men (Crick), 2:211

Of Nature's Obvious Laws & Processes in Vegetation (Newton), 5:273, 274

Of the Strength of Acids (Paulze-Lavoisier), 6:44

Office of Naval Research (ONR)
    convexity theory, 7:82
    linear programming, 7:80, 81
    nuclear physics research, 1:193

Office of Scientific Research and Development (OSRD), 7:119

Ogawa, Masataka, 5:288

Oglesby, Ray T., 2:355

Ogston, A. G., 5:159

O'Hara, James G., 3:236

Ohloff, Günther, 4:228

Øhrstrøm, Peter, 3:236

Ohta, Tomoko, 4:116–117

Ohya, Yujiro, 4:273

Oil
    deposits
        China, 3:393–394
        exploration, 3:396–398, *397*
        fluid dynamics, 3:395–396
    refining, 3:380, 381–383
    shale, 7:396
    surveys, 2:299
    See also Petroleum

OIS (Oxygen Isotope Stage), 3:155

Oke, J. Beverly, 6:385

Oken, Lorenz, 5:**331–335,** *332,* 366

Okenfuss, Lorenz. *See* Oken, Lorenz

An Old Palmistry (Price), 6:162

Oldenburg, Henry, 1:350

Oldfield, Eric, 3:200

Olds, James, 5:149

Olefins, 3:240, 7:312

Oleinik, Olga Arsenievna, 4:188, 5:**335–336**

Olfaction, 1:18

Olfactory conditioning, 7:41–42

Olfactory Imprinting and Homing in Salmon (Hasler et al.), 3:261

Oligonucleotides, 6:478–479, 480–482

Oligosaccharides, 4:260–263, *261, 262*

Oligotrophy, 7:36

Oliphant, Marcus Laurence Elwin, 1:55
    atomic bombs, 6:64
    students of, 7:298

The Olivine-Spinel Transition in the Earth's Mantle (Ringwood), 6:258

Ollongren, Alexander, 7:129

Olsen, John W., 7:384

Olson, Mancur, Jr., 5:**336–338**

Olsson, Lennart, 3:370

Olympiodorus, the Younger, of Alexandria, 5:**338–340**

Olympiodorus of Thebes, 5:338, **340–341**

On Abstinence from Eating Food from Animals (Porphyry), 6:137

On Aggression (Lorenz), 2:198, 4:345

On Aims and Methods of Ethology (Tinbergen), 7:54, 56

On Analysis and Synthesis (Ibrāhīm Ibn Sinān Ibn Thābit Ibn Qurra), 4:4, 5

On Animal Locomotion (Aristotle), 1:103

On Bandages (Diocles of Carystus), 2:302

On Burning Mirrors (Diocles of Carystus), 1:83

On Buying Slaves (Rufus of Ephesus), 6:291

On Cellulose and Its substitution Products (Sakurada). *See Über die Cellulose und ihre Substitutionsprodukte* (Sakurada)

On Computable Numbers (Turing), 7:82

On Cookery (Diocles of Carystus), 2:302

On Division and Ramification (Rāzī). *See Kitab al-Taqsīm wa-l-tashjīr* (Rāzī)

On Drawing the Three Sections (Ibrāhīm Ibn Sinān Ibn Thābit Ibn Qurra), 4:4, 5

On Dust, Fogs, and Clouds (Aitken), 1:27

On Excellence (Zosimos of Panopolis), 7:406

On External Remedies (Diocles of Carystus), 2:302

On Floating Bodies (Archimedes), 5:176

On Generation and Corruption (Aristotle), 1:101, 6:294

On Intension and Remission of Forms (Blasius of Parma), 1:297

On Lethal Drugs (Diocles of Carystus), 2:302

On Living in the Biosphere (Hutchinson), 3:413

On Matters of Health to Pleistarchus (Diocles of Carystus). *See Matters of Health* (Diocles of Carystus)

On Melancholy (Rufus of Ephesus), 6:290, 291

On Music (Theophrastus), 6:138

On Mutually Tangent Circles (Archimedes), 1:85, 89

On My Own Books (Galen), 3:92

On Nature (Empedocles of Acragas), 2:395, 396

On Parthenogenesis, or the Successive Production of Procreating Individuals from a Single Ovum (Owen), 5:368

On Prognosis, On Fevers, On Digestions, On Catarrhs, On Matters related to Women (Diocles of Carystus), 2:302

On Prognosis (Galen), 3:92

On Protein Synthesis (Crick), 1:374

On Ptolemy's Approximate Methods for the Anomalies of Mars, Saturn, and Jupiter (Ibrāhīm Ibn Sinān Ibn Thābit Ibn Qurra), 4:4

On Rising Times (al-Qūhī), 6:185

On Rootcutting (Diocles of Carystus), 2:302

On Sects for Beginners (Galen), 3:92

On Seeing the Stars (Orseme), 5:350

On Sexual Activity (Diocles of Carystus), 2:302

On Shadow Instruments (Ibrāhīm Ibn Sinān Ibn Thābit Ibn Qurra), 4:4, 5

On Smallpox and Measles (Rāzī), 6:212

On Social Structure and Science (Merton), 5:123

On Some Applications of the Universal Enveloping Algebra of a Semisimple Lie Algebra (Harish-Chandra), 3:242

On Space (Carnap), 2:44

On Spirals (Archimedes), 1:85

On Tangent Circles (al-Qūhī), 6:186

On Tangent Circles (Ibrāhīm Ibn Sinān Ibn Thābit Ibn Qurra), 4:4, 5

On Temperaments (Galen), 3:93

On the Abyssal Circulation of the World Ocean II (Stommel), 6:530

On the Accuracy of Economic Observations (Morgenstern), 5:187

On the Action (Zosimus), 5:338

On the Anatomy of Vertebrates (Owen), 5:367

On the Archetype and Homologies of the Vertebrate Skeleton (Owen), 5:367

On the Attractive Force of the Electrical Fire and on the Phenomena Depending Thereon (Volta). *See De Vi Attractiva Ignis Electrici ac Phaenomenis inde Pendentibus* (Volta)

On the Causes of the Malignant Fevers (Borelli). *See Delle cagioni delle febbri maligne* (Borelli)

On the Composition of Drugs According to Places (Galen), 3:94

On the Composition of Drugs According to Type (Galen), 3:94

On the Composition of Simple Drugs (Galen), 3:94

On the Criterion (Ptolemy), 6:174

On the Determination of Air Density from a Satellite (Spitzer), 6:502

On the Difference between the Aristoxenians and the Pythagoreans (Ptolemy), 2:284

On the Difficulties of Euclid (Hero of Alexandria), 2:418

On the Distance from the Center of the Earth to the Shooting Stars (al-Qūhī), 6:185

On the Doctrines of Hippocrates and Plato (Galen), 3:95

On the Economy of Machinery and Manufactures (Babbage), 1:127

On the Extent and Aims of a National Museum of Natural History (Owen), 5:366

On the Foundations of Combinatorial Theory I, IV, V and IX (Rota), 6:285

On the Generation of Animals (Aristotle), 1:103, 5:280

On the Great and Sacred Art of Making Gold (Stephanus of Alexandria), 6:517

On the Heavens (Aristotle), 5:350, 351, 7:381–382

On the History of the Psycho-Analytical Movement (Freud), 4:63

On the Hypotheses which Lie at the Basis of Geometry (Riemann), 2:115

On the Influence of Climates on the Discontinuities of Natural Floras (Grisebach). *See Über den Einfluss des Climas auf die Begránzung der Natürlichen Floren* (Grisebach)

On the Interaction between Atomic Nuclei and Electrons (Casimir), 2:65

On the Length of the Year (Hipparchus), 3:321

On the Letter Omega (Zosimos of Panopolis), 7:406

On the Major Tectonic Forms of China (Huang Jiqing), 3:394

On the Method of Healing (Galen), 3:95

On the Modifications of Clouds (Howard), 3:386

On the Motions of the Sun (Ibrāhīm Ibn Sinān Ibn Thābit Ibn Qurra), 4:4

On the Names of Bodily Parts (Rufus of Ephesus), 6:291

On the Natural Faculties (Galen), 3:94

On the Nature of Fear (Hebb), 3:268

On the Nature of Limbs (Owen), 5:367

On the Nature of Man (Hippocrates), 6:290

On the Nature of Things (Lucretius), 2:396

On the Nature of Things According to Its Own Principles (Telesio). *See Dererum natura iuxta propria principia* (Telesio)

On the Nature of Woman (Hippocrates), 3:323

On the Orientation of the Bee Wolf (Tinbergen). *See Über di Orientierung des Bienenwolfes* (Tinbergen)

On the Origin of Species (Darwin), 1:80, 2:242, 243, 246
  consciousness, 3:180
  first species, 1:417
  influence of, 3:208, 4:161, 7:210, 227, 259
  influence on genetic theory, 2:390
  Mendel, Johann Gregor and, 5:104
  naturalism, 3:430–431
  opposing views, 5:206
  philosophy, 3:287
  spontaneous generation and, 1:208
  translations, 6:287, 288

On the Parts of Animals (Aristotle), 1:101, 102, 104, 5:280

On the Plurality of Worlds (Lewis), 4:285

On the Psychology of Individual Differences (Stern). *See Über Psychologie der individuellen Differenzen* (Stern)

On the Pulsation Theory of Delta Cepheid Stars (Schwarzchild). *See Zur Pulsationstheorie der delta Cephei-Sterne* (Schwarzchild)

On the Quantum Theory of Spectral Lines (Sommerfeld), 6:490

On the Ratios of Velocities in Motions (Bradwardine). *See De proportionibus velocitatum in motibus* (Bradwardine)

On the Relations Between Maxwell's Fundamental Electromagnetic Equations and the Fundamental Equations of the Opposing Electromagnetics (Hertz), 3:291

On the Sacred Disease (Hippocrates), 3:323

On the Sense of Things and On Magic (Campanella). *See Desensu rerum et magia* (Campanella)

On the Shoulders of Giants (Merton), 5:124

On the Soul (Aristotle), 1:100, 2:326, 5:351, 6:294, 517, 7:388

On the Soul (Oresme), 5:351

On the Sphere (John of Holywood), 1:296

On the Utility of the Parts (Galen), 3:94

On the Value of Natural Philosophy Especially for the Education of Germans (Oken). *See Über den Wert der Naturgeschichte besonders für die Bildung der Deutschen* (Oken)

On the Volume of the Paraboloid (al-Qūhī), 6:186

On the Westward Intensification of Winddriven Currents (Stommel), 6:528

On Treatments (Diocles of Carystus), 2:302

On Two Lines That Never Meet (al-Ṭūsī), 7:89

On Vegetables (Diocles of Carystus), 2:302

Oncology. *See* Cancer

One gene-one enzyme hypothesis, 7:14

One gene-one polypeptide hypothesis, 1:224, *226,* 227

One-Mile telescopes, 6:305

One World or None (Morrison), 5:191

O'Neill, Eugene, 5:215

O'Neill, John, 3:236

Ong, Walter, 6:205, 206

Onnes, Heike Kamerlingh. *See* Kamerlingh Onnes, Heike

Onomasticon (Bodenstein, Adam of), 1:309

ONR (Office of Naval Research)
    convexity theory, 7:82
    linear programming, 7:80, 81
    nuclear physics research, 1:193

Onsager, Lars, 2:66

Onsager relations, 2:66

Onslow, Muriel Wheldale, 1:211, 5:232

Ontogeny, 3:207

Ontogeny and Phylogeny (Gould), 3:159, 160–161

Ontology, 5:313
    See also Metaphysics

Oort, Abraham, 6:345

Oort, Jan Hendrik, 5:116, **341–347**
    colleagues of, 7:131–132
    Crab Nebula, 6:434
    radio emissions, 7:127, 128
    spectral lines, 7:129

Oort clouds, 5:*344,* 346

The Opacity of Stellar Matter and the Hydrogen Content of the Stars (Strömgren), 6:542

Oparin, Aleksandr, 3:363, 364, 5:155

The Open Society and Its Enemies (Popper), 6:135, 136

Opera logica (Zabarella), 7:387

Operating systems, computer, 2:295–296

Operation Crossroads, 6:235

Operation Overcast, 7:174

Operation Paperclip, 6:229, 232, 7:120, 174

The Operational Analysis of Psychological Terms (Skinner), 6:463

Operational Methods in Mathematical Physics (Jeffreys), 4:40

Operational Research in World War II (Waddington), 7:203

Operationalism, 2:24–25, 6:463

Operations research
    game theory, 7:80–82
    military, 1:292

Opere (Campanella), 2:21

Opere (Galilei). *See Works* (Galilei)

Öpik, Ernst, 7:284–285

Oppenheimer, Carl, 5:252

Oppenheimer, J. Robert, 5:**347–350,** *349*
    acquaintances of, 2:267, 3:193, 7:101
    atomic bombs, 1:56, 162, 3:20, 6:65, 195, 409, 419
    clearance revocation, 1:274
    colleagues of, 2:378, 4:208, 211, 6:328, 336, 393, 420–422, 7:286
    discrediting of, 6:196–197
    energy distribution measurements, 1:306
    Harvard College Observatory, 5:115
    hydrogen bombs, 1:57, 7:21, 22–23
    liberalism, 6:423
    Los Alamos Scientific Laboratory, 6:394, 7:328
    Manhattan Project, 1:75, 4:291, 6:169
    as mentor, 1:321–322
    mesons, 1:291
    National Laboratory, 1:164
    personal crisis of, 5:348
    plutonium implosion research, 1:134–135
    positrons, 7:399
    students of, 1:72, 5:190, 7:264, 365
    temperament and research style, 1:392

Oppenheimer, Katherine, 6:423

Optic aphasia, 4:352

Optical Hypotheses (Damianus of Larissa), 2:233–234

Optical illusions, 1:145–146

Optical interferometers, 7:398

Optical Lectures (Newton), 5:269

Optical lenses, 1:294–295

The Optical Papers of Isaac Newton (Shapiro), 5:269

Optical rotary dispersion, 7:354–355

Opticks (Newton), 1:295, 5:11–12, 269, 6:512

Optics
    atmospheric, 1:131

Optics, *continued*
    chromomictors, 1:28
    color science, 3:133
    Doppler effect, 1:294–295
    ecological, 3:128
    geometry, 2:233–234
    light, 1:25, 3:111–112, 4:1–2, 5:269
    mechanics, 3:236–237
    physiological, 7:74
    quantum, 2:281–283
    rainbow, 6:187–188
    theoretical, 3:275
    See also Visual perception
Optics (Ibn al-Haytham), 4:1
Optics (Euclid), 2:416
Optics of Spherical Particles (Van de Hulst), 7:129
Optimal control, theory of, 6:128
Opus maius (Bacon, Roger), 1:143, 144, 147
Opus Paragranum (Paracelsus), 6:14
Opus Paramirum (Paracelsus), 6:14
Opus tertium (Bacon, Roger), 1:143
Opuscules mathématiques (d'Alembert), 2:231, 232
Orbitals, molecular
    electron states, 3:*402*
    organic chemistry, 2:276–278
    quantum mechanics, 3:87–88
    stereochemistry, 3:400–404
    theory, 5:210–211
Orbiting Astronomical Observatory (OAO), 6:502
Orbiting Solar Observatory (OSO), 3:143, 7:76, 77
Orbits, planetary, 5:270, 271
Order, 1:324–325
Order and Life (Needham), 5:237
The Order of My Own Books (Galen), 3:92
Order Out of Chaos (Prigogine). *See* La Nouvelle alliance
    (Prigogine)
Ordeshook, Peter, 6:254
Ordinary Differential Equations (Pontryagin), 6:128
Ore, Oystein, 3:357
Orel, Vítězslav, 5:99
Oresme, Nicole, 1:448–450, 2:326, 5:**350–354**
    influences on, 5:314
    natural philosophy, 1:34, 35–36
Orfanidis, Sophocles, 3:193
Organelles, 5:283–284, 285
Organic chemistry
    acids, 3:237
    aromatic compounds, 1:250–253
    behavior of matter, 4:205–206
    benzene structure, 4:98–99
    boron, 1:418–423
    carbohydrates, 4:258–263
    chemical shifts, 3:197–200, *198*
    combustion method of analysis, 1:268

    conformational analysis, 1:196–197, 199, *199,* 200
    crystallography, 6:21–22
    cyclohexanes, 1:199, *199*
    dyes, 1:214–218
    flavones, 7:143–148
    France, 7:371–372
    free radical polymerization, 1:*194*
    gravimetric analysis, 4:311–312
    history, 1:194, 195–196
    hydrogenation, 3:41–43
    industrial, 6:228–233
    influential figures, 7:336–341, 349–356
    Japan, 5:287–292
    Kolbe-Frankland theory, 4:149
    molecular orbitals, 2:276–278
    nucleophilic substitution, 1:*191*
    origin of life, 5:156–157
    physical, 1:189, 195–201, 2:199–204, 4:12, 14
    radioactivity, 2:14–15
    reactions, 1:*190,* 190–195, 200
    research, 2:323–324, 6:223–228
    rotenone, 1:459–460
    stereochemistry, 6:154–161
    stoichiometry, 1:268
    structure-reactivity relationships, 3:238–240, *239*
    synthesis, 6:268–273, 321–324, 7:64–68, 396
    water analysis, 3:63–64
Organic Chemistry (Cram and Hammond), 2:200
Organic Chemistry (Thornton, Morrison and Boyd),
    2:200
Organic matter, particulate, 6:257
Organic selection, 1:171, 172
Organic synthesis, 6:268–273, 7:64–68
*Die organische Chemie in ihrer Anwendung auf Agricultur
    und Physiologie* (Liebig), 4:311
Organisers and Genes (Waddington), 7:204
The Organization of Behavior (Hebb), 3:267, 268–270
Organizational behavior, 5:254–255
Organizer effect, 3:349–351, 5:15, 16–17, *17*
Organoboranes, 1:422
Organometallic chemistry
    coordination, 2:102–103
    ferrocene, 7:*309*
    phenyllithium, 7:338–339
    transition metals, 2:102–103, 7:308–310, *310*
    water analysis, 3:63–64
Organometallic compounds, 5:246–247
Orgel, Leslie E., 4:59, 60, 5:157
Orientalism, 3:165–166
The Origin (Kropotkin), 4:161
The Origin of Higher Categories (Kinsey), 4:124
Origin of life
    comets, 3:391
    genes, 3:363–364

metabolism, 3:363–364

molecular biology, 2:211

prebiotic chemistry, 5:154–158

saltational theory, 5:368

solar system, 6:310

spontaneous generation, 1:208–210

The Origin of Races (Coon), 2:174, 175, 7:237

The Origin of Species: A Structuralist Approach (Webster and Goodwin), 6:355

Origin of Species (Darwin). *See On the Origin of Species* (Darwin)

Origin of the Earth and Moon (Ringwood), 6:260, 261

L'origine de l'homme (Piveteau), 6:108

Origine of Formes and Qualities (Newton), 5:274

Les origines humaines et l'évolution de l'intelligence (Le Roy), 6:109

The Origins of Intelligence (Piaget), 6:93

Ornithology

    Anecdotes of the Habits and Instincts of Birds, Reptiles, and Fishes (Lee), 4:232

    cytogenetics, 2:59–61

    ethology, 7:41

    evolution, 2:4

    instinctive behavior, 4:336, 337–338

    natural selection, 7:377–378

    physiology, 5:317

    pigeons, 2:196–197

    ring doves, 4:244–246

    song sparrows, 5:277–279

    songs, 7:42–43

    territoriality, 3:384–385

    zoogeography and, 5:61–62

    See also Birds

Ornstein, Leonard Salomon, 7:101

Orogeny, 6:347–349

Orphika (Homer), 7:112

Ortelius, Abraham, 2:158

Orthner, Ludwig, 1:216

Ortner, Gustav, 1:301

Orton, Kennedy Joseph Previte, 4:15

Ortus Medicinae (van Helmont), 3:278–279

Osborn, Henry Fairfield, 2:138, 239, 5:**354–356,** *355,* 7:117

Osborne, Michael A, 3:115–116

Oscillations

    algebra, 6:127–128

    correspondence principle, 1:327

    non-linear, 1:317

Oseen, Carl Wilhelm, 6:490

Osiander, Andreas, 2:179

Osnovy teorii chisel (Vinogradov), 7:156

OSO (Orbiting Solar Observatory), 3:143, 7:76, 77

Osobye varianty metoda trigonometricheskikh summ (Vinogradov), 7:156

Ospovat, Dov, 2:246

OSRD (Office of Scientific Research and Development), 7:119

Ossemens fossiles (Cuvier), 2:224, 225–226

Ossietsky, Carl von, 1:462

Osteology, 5:366–367

Osterbrock, Donald

    Orion and Perseus, 1:330

    spiral arms of the Milky Way, 5:346

Ostriker, Jeremiah P., 1:159

Ostwald, Carl Wilhelm Wolfgang, 6:330, 331

Ostwald, Friedrich Wilhelm, 1:265, 2:320, 4:288, 5:**356–359,** *357*

    law of substance, 6:6

    linfluence of, 4:287

    students of, 1:112

Ostwald, Grete, 5:356

Otis, Arthur S., 7:26

Ottheinrich, Count Palatinate, 1:308, 6:550

Oudin, Jacques, 4:49

Our Biosphere (Margalef), 5:24

An Outline of Psychology (McDougall), 2:197

Outlines of Astronomy (Herschel), 3:288

Outlines of Comparative Physiology and Morphology of Animals (LeConte), 4:224

Outram, Dorinda, 4:191

Ovchinnikov, Yury Antoloyevich, 5:**359–365,** 6:160

Overbeek, Jan Theodoor Gerard, 2:66

Overfishing, 1:149

Overthrust faults, 3:397

Overton, Charles Ernest, 3:329

Owen, G. E. L., 1:101

Owen, Raymond D., 5:88

Owen, Richard, 2:216, 225, 246, 5:**365–369,** *367*

    alternation of generations, 3:429

    influences on, 5:332

    neuropsychology of humans, 3:430

    spontaneous generation, 1:208

Owen, Robert Dale, 7:226

Oxatomide, 4:33

Oxidation

    biological, 6:569–571

    catalytic, 1:354

    pyruvic acid, 4:325–326

Oxidation enzymes, 7:31–35

Oxidative phosphorylation, 3:170–171

    cellular membranes, 6:199

    chimeric vesicles, 6:200

    cyclophorase, 3:168–169

    enzymology, 5:308

    metabolism and membrane transport, 5:160–163

    research misconduct, 6:201

Oxygen

    in air, 7:169–170

Oxygen, *continued*
 consumption, 4:216
 liquid, 4:84
 in water, 4:215
Oxygen Isotope Stage (OIS), 3:155
Oyama, Vance, 4:137
Ozone
 measurement, 2:306–309
 sufur dioxide, 1:235
 temperature, 2:307–309

P

P-E index, 7:39
Pachymeres, Georges, 5:95, 6:**1–2**
Pachymeres, Georgius. *See* Pachymeres, Georges
Pacific Ocean, 6:372
Pacifism, 6:239–240
Pacini, Franco, 3:139
Pacioli, Luca, 6:105, 106
Packard, David, 3:44
Packard, Martin, 1:306, 3:196, 199
Paeonius, 3:436–437
Pagano, Sergio, 3:96–97
Page, Leigh, 6:499
Page, Lyman, 7:305
Pain, hypnosis for, 3:312
Pais, Abraham, 6:423
Paisley, John, 2:218
Pake, George, 3:196–197
Pakistan, 6:338
Palade, George Emil, 2:331, 4:239, 6:145, 146
 cristae mitochondriales, 3:171
 electron microscopes, 1:374, 2:145
Paladini, Alejandro, 4:254, *254*
Palaeontologia Sinica (Ding Wenjiang), 2:299
Paläontologie, Entwicklungslehre, und Genetik
 (Schindewolf), 6:351, 353
Palay, Sanford, 2:331
Pale Blue Dot: A Vision of the Human Future in Space
 (Sagan), 6:315
Paleoanthropology
 archaeology, 2:123–127
 Argentina, 4:236–237
 australopithecines, 2:237–242
 China, 6:56–61
 dating techniques, 5:299
 evolution, 4:42–43, 6:108–109, 7:115–117
 missing link, 2:313–316
 Neanderthal, 3:155–156
 Olduvai Gorge (Tanzania), 4:221–223
 parallel evolution, 2:138–141
 Sinathropus, 7:250–253
Paleoclimatology, 4:154–155
 experimental physics, 5:327–330

theory of, 6:343–345
Paleoecology
 carbonate sedimentology, 5:266
 limnology, 3:412–413
 Pacific atolls, 4:185–187
Paleoecology (Ladd), 4:186
Paleomagnetism
 continental drift, 6:299–300
 field reversals, 3:375–377
 magnetometers and, 1:292
 Northern Hemisphere, 2:191–192
Paléontologie et Transformisme (Piveteau), 6:109
Paleontology
 actualism, 6:249
 biostratigraphy, 6:351–355
 China, 2:299–300
 cladistics, 6:30–33
 Darwinism, 3:163
 evolutionary biology, 3:159–162
 fossil hominid culture, 5:295–296
 human
  evolution, 2:139–140, 6:108–109
  extinction, 2:226
 invertebrate
  ammonites, 7:62
  classification, 4:190
  education, 5:267
  fossil bivalve mollusks, 5:265, 266
  geology, 3:315–319, 7:15–17
 Neanderthal, 3:154–156
 neuropsychology, 3:430
 Pithecanthropus, 7:184–188
 stratigraphy, 2:299
 unity of plan, 3:116
 vertebrate
  comparative anatomy and, 5:366–367
  creative evolution, 5:354–355
  dinosaurs, 7:383–384
  evolution, 6:452, 453–455
  France, 6:106–108
 zoology, 1:415–417
Paleontology, Development, and Genetics: A Critique and
 Synthesis (Schindewolf). *See Paläontologie,*
 Entwicklungslehre, und Genetik (Schindewolf)
Palestine, excavations, 3:105–106
Paley, Raymond E. A. C., 7:414
Paley, William, 2:245
 theodicies, 5:13
 utilitarianism, 7:282
Palgrave, Richard, 6:512
Palimpsest, Archimedean, 1:87–88
Palmén, Erik Herbert, 6:**2–5**
Palmieri, Paolo, 2:149
Pancake theory, 7:394

Panck, Albrecht, 5:133
Panckoucke, Charles-Joseph, 4:216
Paneth, Friedrich Adolf, 6:**5–7,** 7:307, 308
Panizzi, Anthony, 5:366
Panmixia, 3:230
Pannekoek, Antoine, 7:142
Pannke, Kurt, 7:409, 410
Panofsky, Hans Arnold, 6:**7–10**
Panofsky, Wolfgang, 1:57, 6:424, 7:70
Pantaleoni, Maffeo, 6:17
Pantin, Isabelle, 3:96
Papanicolaou, George, 4:320
Papathanassiou, Maria, 6:517
Paper chromatography
    development of, 5:39–40
    photosynthesis, 2:15–16
Papez, James Wenceslas, 4:143, 6:**10 14**
Papez circuit theory, 6:11–12, *12*
Paracelsus, Theophrastus Philippus Aureolus Bombastus
    von Hohenheim, 6:**14–17,** *15*
        Gassendi, Pierre, 3:111
        natural history, 1:308–309
        Renaissance medicine, 6:552
        salt, 1:141
Paradigms of Personality Assessment (Wiggins), 5:219
Paradis, James G., 3:430
Paradosis tōn Persikōn Kanonōn (Meliteniotes), 1:98
Paramecium aurelia, 6:492–493
Parameters, theory of, 2:258–259
Parasite-host interactions. *See* Host-parasite interactions
Parasitology, antiparasite drugs, 4:32–33
Pardee, Arthur, 6:319
Pardee, Joseph Thomas, 1:394
Parent, Robert, 6:555
Pareto, Vilfredo, 6:**17–21,** *18*
Pariser, Rudolph, 6:131
Parity, 7:366–367
Park, Thomas, 2:390
Parker, Eugene Newman, 2:379
Parker, George, 3:187
Parkes Radio Telescope, 1:336
Parkinson, Sydney, 4:231
Parkinson's disease, 7:196
Parmenides, 2:397
Parr, Robert, 6:130, 131
Parsimony, law of, 3:183
Parsons, Talcott, 5:121
Partacz, James, 3:85
Parthenogenesis, 5:368
Partial differential equations, 5:335–336
    analysis, 2:76
    Cauchy-Kovalevskaya theorem, 4:158–159
    computer science, 3:51
    discrete mathematics, 2:404

elliptic, 2:258–259, 5:335
hyperbolic, 4:273
independent variables, 2:230
integrals, 2:76
nonlinear, 4:319
parabolic and elliptic, 4:187–189
singular integrals, 2:8–9
Partial Differential Equations in Physics (Sommerfeld), 6:491
Partially conserved axial-vector current (PCAC), 1:238
Particle accelerators
    atomic weapons, 2:110, 7:329–331
    betatron, 7:69
    colliding-beam, 1:425–429, *426,* 7:70–72
    development of, 1:237, 4:328–333, 7:69, 70–71
    diagram of, 4:*329, 330*
    field theory and, 1:238
    synchrotron, 2:110
    See also Cyclotrons
Particle-antiparticle colliders, 7:70–72
Particle physics
    cosmic rays, 1:54–55, 62, 5:191, 300, 6:280–283
    dust counter, 1:29
    electrodynamic interactions, 3:19
    influential figures, 7:68–72
    me-mesons, 1:73–75
    unified field theory, 2:370–371
    weak force phenomena, 3:23–25
    women scientists, 7:363–368
Particle showers, 6:282
Particles
    alpha, 1:299
    antiparticles, 6:410
    baryon asymmetry, 6:324, 325–326
    collectivized, 1:318
    colloid, 2:66
    elementary
        Cherenkov radiation, 2:109
        field theory, 1:238–239
        fission, 7:392
        hadronic SU(6) symmetry, 3:193
        nonlinear chiral sigma model, 3:192, 193
        positron, 1:73
        quantum field theory, 1:236, 6:394–396
    energy, 7:263–265, 267–268
    many-particle systems, 1:318–319
    nuclear physics, 5:303, 6:407–411
    quantum optics, 2:281–283
    spin, 1:413, 3:193, 6:336
Particulate organic matter, 6:257
Partie Pittoresque des Voyages de M. de Saussure (Saussure), 6:347
Partington, James R., 6:97

Partition chromatography
  development of, 5:39
  rediscovery of, 4:226
Partridge, R. Bruce, 7:303, 305
Parts of Classes (Lewis), 4:286
Paschen, Friedrich, 2:344, 6:490
Pasteur, Louis, 6:**21–30,** *23,* 154, 7:246–247
  cytology, 6:24
  fermentation, 6:22–24
  organic chemistry, 6:21–22
  scientific method, 6:24–29
Pastor, Rey, 5:179
Patchett, Arthur, 1:198
Paterson, Donald G., 5:90
*A Path Where No Man Thought: Nuclear Winter and the
  End of the Arms Race* (Sagan and Turco), 6:315
Pathoclisis, 7:163
Pathology, Dogmatists, 3:92
Pathos of Power (Clark), 2:135
Pati, Jogesh, 3:193, 6:340
Paton, D. Noel, 5:306
Patronage
  chemistry, 1:229, 232
  Copernicanism, 3:100–101
  France, 6:67–69
The Pattern of Animal Communities (Elton), 2:387
Patterns of Sexual Behavior (Beach and Ford), 1:222
Patterson, A. Lindo, 1:282
Patterson, Colin, 6:**30–34**
Patton, Harry, 2:330
Patton, Robert, 6:496
Pauli, Wolfgang, 3:21, 4:55, 6:**34–36,** *35*
  acquaintances of, 2:271
  chemical bond theory, 3:195
  chemical shifts, 3:198
  colleagues of, 6:192
  communication skills, 3:404
  conductivity of metals, 1:303
  Copenhagen Interpretation, 1:323
  determinism, 2:365
  electron conduction, 5:201
  electron spin, 3:193
  exclusion principle, 2:379, 3:402
  neutrinos, 6:337
  nuclear magnetic resonance, 3:196
  students of, 2:267, 378
  superconductivity, 1:304
  theoretical physics, 1:391, 6:63
Pauli-Gürsey transformation, 3:193
Pauling, Linus Carl, 2:96, 4:296, 6:**36–44,** *41*
  antibody response theories, 4:47
  chemical models, 7:33
  coordination chemistry, 7:310
  CPK models, 2:202

DNA structure, 7:300
  electron transfer, 2:103
  enzymatic catalysis, 3:340
  graduate education, 1:234
  influence of, 2:200, 4:16, 5:289
  influences on, 4:73
  on Mark, Herman F., 5:27
  molecular clock, 4:116
  molecular structure, 5:29, 170, 6:36–40
  nuclear testing concerns, 1:80, 6:40–42, 7:24
  quantum chemistry, 5:211–212
  recruitment of scientists, 1:227
  resonance theory, 5:248
  sickle-cell anemia, 5:242
  stochastic method, 2:208
  on Szent-Györgyi, Albert Imre, 6:571
  transition metal chemistry, 4:58
  vitamin C, 6:42–43
Paulze-Lavoisier, Marie-Anne-Pierette, 6:**44–45,** 97
Pavillard, Jules, 1:387
Pavlov, Ivan Petrovich, 6:**46–49,** *48*
  animal behavior, 7:181
  excitation and inhibition, 2:429
  influence of, 4:350
  reflexes, 6:459
  stimulus-response connection, 3:407
Pavlovian conditioning
  learning, 3:407
  neural activity, 3:267
Payen, Jacques, 1:108
Payne, Cecilia. *See* Payne-Gaposchkin, Cecilia Helena
Payne-Gaposchkin, Cecilia Helena, 6:**49–52,** *50,* 7:105
  colleagues of, 5:112, 7:286
  influence of, 5:72
  students of, 7:284
PCAC (partially conserved axial-vector current), 1:238
Peace research, quantitative methods, 6:240
Peak, Helen, 1:357
Pearl, Raymond, 3:414–415, 6:54
Pearson, Alan, 3:83
Pearson, Gerald, 1:180, 6:438
Pearson, Karl, 6:**52–56,** *53*
Pearson, Ralph G., 2:104
Peat, David, 1:324
Pecher, Maurice, 1:198
Pecking response, 7:53
Pectinacea, 5:266
Pedagogy, 6:205–206, 464
Pedanius Dioscorides of Anazarbus. *See* Dioscorides
Pedersen, Charles J., 2:203
Pedersen, K., 3:239
Peebles, Phillip James Edwin, 2:283, 7:303, 305
Peel, Robert, 5:366
Peerdeman, Antonius, 1:284

Pegram, George, 6:423
Pei Wen-chung. *See* Pei Wenzhong
Pei Wenzhong, 2:239, 6:**56–62,** 7:251
Peierls, Rudolf Ernst, 6:*62,* **62–67**
   colleagues of, 3:388, 7:321
   education, 1:270
   magnetic fields, 7:320
   on Oppenheimer, J. Robert, 5:347
   students of, 1:237
Peiffer, Jeanne, 1:256
Peirce, Charles Sanders, 3:70, 5:143, 6:461
Peiresc, Nicolas Claude Fabri de, 3:110–111, 112,
   4:131–132
Peixoto, José, 6:345
Peking Man. *See Sinathropus*
Péligot, Eugène, 2:323
Pellicier, Guillaume, 6:**67 69**
Pelosi, Anthony, 2:431
Pelouze, Théophile-Jules, 4:205
Pénau, Henri, 4:227
Penck, Albrecht, 1:69
   colleagues of, 7:373
   students of, 5:171, 172
Pender, Harold, 2:333
Penefsky, Harvey, 6:199
Penfield, Wilder Graves, 6:**69–75,** *70*
   colleagues of, 3:347
   intelligence tests, 3:268
Penicillin
   development, 3:43
   mechanism of action research, 5:159–160
   structure, 6:273, 7:66, 353
Penney, William, 7:310
Penrose, Roger, 6:399
El pensamiento de Jean Piaget (Battro), 6:94
Pentose phosphate pathway, 6:198–199
Penzias, Arno Allan, 2:283, 3:390, 7:303, 393
Pepinsky, Ray, 1:284, 3:337
Pepitone, Albert, 3:15
Pepper, Michael, 5:204
Peptides
   chemical reactions, 2:349–351
   conformational analysis, 5:362–363
   proteins, 1:1, 2
   synthesis, 4:*326*
Perception
   behavior, 3:269–270
   cognition and, 1:187
   development of, 3:120–124
   eye movements and, 3:17
   filter theory of attention, 1:403–405
   internal, 2:73
   philosophy and, 4:285–286
   quantitative methods, 6:239
   visual, 1:145–146
      animals, 3:294–297
      birds, 3:*295*
      color, 6:295
      figural quality, 3:*296*
      mathematical modeling, 2:210–211
      object-ground surface relationship, 3:*128*
      optical flow field, 3:*127*
      psychology, 3:125–130
      self-movement, 3:*126*
Perception and Communication (Broadbent), 1:401, 403,
   405
The Perception of the Visual World (Gibson, James
   Jerome), 3:125, 127
Perceptual foundationalism, 2:24
Perceptual Learning: Differentiation or Enrichment?
   (Gibson and Gibson), 3:121
Perceptual learning, theory of, 3:*126, 127,* 3:127–129,
   3:128
Percival, Ian, 1:237
Percy, Walker, 6:314
Peregrinus, Petrus. *See* Peter Peregrinus
Pereira, Michela, 1:109, 4:346, 347
Perey, Marguerite Catherine, 1:163, 6:**75–79,** *76*
Perez y Jorba, Monique, 2:161
Perfect Compass (al-Qūhī), 6:185
Perfetti, Stefano, 1:104
Periodic table, 5:105–108, *107,* 6:*403*
Die Periodicität morphologischer Erscheinungen bei den
   Pflanzen (Tammes), 7:1
The periodicity of morphological phenomena in plants
   (Tammes). *See Die Periodicität morphologischer*
   Erscheinungen bei den Pflanzen (Tammes)
Peripatos, 6:540
Periphyseon (Eriugena), 2:412–413
Perkin, William Henry, 5:19, 6:22
Perkin, William Henry, Jr., 6:269, 271, 272
Perkin-Elmer Corporation, 7:231–232
Permian period
   biostratigraphy, 3:393
   extinction, 5:265, 266
   stratigraphy, 5:265, 266
Pernter, Josef, 2:426
Péron, François, 4:190
Peroxisomes, 5:281, 283
Perrin, Francis Henri Jean Siegfried, 2:*65*
   influence of, 4:227
   radioactivity, 6:77
Perry, John H., 4:289
Perry, Stephen, 7:154
Persian astronomy, 2:120–121
Persian Syntaxis (Chrysococces), 2:121, 5:95
Persian Tables, 1:98, 99
Persico, Enrico, 5:301, 302

Person-centered psychology, 6:278
    See also Client-centered psychology
Person und Sache (Stern), 6:524
Personal Knowledge (Polányi), 6:125
Personalism, critical, 6:522, 523
Personality: A Psychological Interpretation (Allport), 1:49, 52, 53
Personality and Psychotherapy (Dollard), 5:147
Personality change conditions, 6:276–277
Personality in Nature, Society, and Culture (Murray), 5:218
Personality psychology
    cultural anthropology and, 5:44
    development, 5:215–219
    mind-body connection, 2:428–429
    morality and ethics, 1:49–52
    motivation, 5:44–45
    personality development, 2:409–411
    psychotherapy, 5:147–148, 6:276–278
    smoking and physical disease, 2:431
Personhood, 6:524, 525
Perspectiva (Bacon, Roger), 1:145–146, 147
Perspective, 5:176–177, *177*
Perspective Libri Sex (Monte), 5:176
Perspectives in Ecological Theory (Margalef), 5:23, 24
Perthes, Justus, 5:207
Pertz, Dora, 1:211
Perutilis logica (Albert of Saxony), 1:35
Perutz, Max Ferdinand, 3:67, 338, 5:202, 6:**79–84**, *80*, *82*
Peschier, Jacques-Louis, 6:348–349
Pestalozzi, Johann Heinrich, 3:326
Peter Lombard
    commentaries on, 5:313
    contrary qualities, 1:450
    future contingents, 1:378
    lectures, 1:449
Peter of Limoges, 1:146
Peter of Spain, 1:296, 378
Peter Peregrinus
    discovery of magnetism, 1:146
    influence of, 5:273
Peters, James L., 5:61
Peters, Leo J., 1:178–179
Peters, Rudolph Albert, 5:306–307
Peterson, S. W., 1:284
Peterson, William, 7:346
Pethidine, 4:31
Petosiris, rule of, 7:112
Petrography, 6:262–264
Petroleum
    actualistic paleontology, 6:249
    catalysis, 3:380, 381–383
    deposits, 3:395–396, 396–398, *397,* 398

    engineering, 4:289–290
    exploration, 3:393–394
    Fischer-Tropsch process, 2:394
    geology
        geotectonic, 3:392–394
        instrumentation, 7:270–271
    geophysics, 3:139–140
    origins, 7:397
    research, 7:133
Petrology
    geochemistry, 6:259
    high-temperature physics, 2:253–254
    porphyries, 7:142–143
Petrovsky, Ivan, 4:188
Petrucci, Gioseffo, 4:134
Petrus Alphonsus, 1:14
Petrzhak, Konstantin A., 3:33
Petterssen, Sverre, 3:263, 6:**84–88,** 220
Pettersson, Hans, 1:299
Pettersson, Sven Otto, 6:**88–90**
Pettijohn, Francis, 4:164
Pew, Arthur E., Jr., 3:382
Peysonnel, Jean-Andre. *See* Peyssonnel, Jean Andre
Peyssonnel, Jean Andre, 5:37
Pfann, William, 2:161
Pfeffer, Richard, 6:342
Pflanzensoziologie (Braun-Blanquet), 1:387
Pfund, August Herman, 3:78
pH meters, 1:234
Phaedrus (Plato), 3:322
Phaenomenologie en Natuurwetenschap (Van de Hulst), 7:131
Phænomena (Euclid), 2:416
Pharalopes, red-necked, 7:50
Pharmacology
    behavioral, 6:462, 463
    organic chemistry, 6:321–324
    synthesis, 1:198–199
    See also Drugs
Pharmacopoeia, 2:219
Pharmacy, 3:386, 387
Phase and the Origins of Molecular Biology (Watson), 4:358
Phenolic alkaloids, 1:198
Phenomena (Eudoxus), 2:304
Phenomenological theory, 7:165
The Phenomenon of Man (Teilhard de Chardin), 5:89
Phenyllithium, 7:*338,* 338–339
Philalethes, Eiranaeus, 6:511–512
Philanthropy, 1:235–236
Philip Morrison's Long Look at the Literature (Morrison), 5:193
Phillips, David, 3:338, 6:141
Phillips, Dennis, 6:556

Phillips, John, 7:7
Phillips, Norman A., 6:471, 472
Phillips, Richard, 3:6
Phillips, William D., 3:199
Philodemus, 2:284
Philology, 4:264–266
Philoponus, 7:382
The Philosopher Olympiodorus to Petasius, King of Armenia, on the Divine and Sacred Art of the Philosophical Stone (Olympiodorus, the Younger, of Alexandria) , 5:338
Philosophers at War (Hall), 5:269
Philosopher's stone, 1:309, 5:273
The Philosopher's Way of Life (Rāzī), 6:213
Philosophia Botanica (Linnaeus), 4:314, 315
Philosophia magnetica (Niccolò), 2:1, 2
Philosophia naturalis (Basso), 1:204–205
Philosophiae naturalis principia mathematica (Newton). *See Principia Mathematica* (Newton)
Philosophic Fancies (Cavendish), 2:80
Philosophical and Physical Opinions (Cavendish), 2:80
The Philosophical Basis of Biochemistry (Needham), 5:236
Philosophical Explanations (Nozick), 5:286
Philosophical Letters (Cavendish), 2:80
Philosophical Transaction (Johnston), 4:54
Philosophie anatomique (Geoffroy Saint-Hilaire, Étienne), 3:118
Philosophie der Arithmetik (Husserl), 3:70
Philosophy
    Arabic, 6:211–215
    Aristotelianism, 1:100–102, 104–105
    atoms, 3:112
    of biology
        history and, 5:64–66
        mechanist-vitalist debate, 5:236
    Catholicism, 1:38–39
    celestial physics, 7:381–382
    experimental
        Aristotelian theory, 1:102–104
        manual work of artisans and, 1:231
        natural philosophy, 2:2
    health and disease, 2:319
    holism, 6:484
    inductive, 5:143–144
    Islamic, 6:187
    logic, 4:284–286, 6:133–134
    of mathematics, 3:435, 7:278
    mechanics, 1:204–205, 3:111, 4:184
    medicine and, 3:93–94, 5:8–9
    meliorism, 4:23–24
    metaphysics, 2:171–172, 3:292
    of mind, 5:92
    mixtures, 2:322
    natural, 6:115–116
        alchemical commentaries on, 5:338–339
        anti-Aristotelianism, 1:204–205
        Arabic, 1:46–47
        atomism, 3:157–158, 289
        Buridan school, 1:34–36
        causation, 1:145
        Christianity, 4:51–52
        civil rights, 6:483
        classification, 4:189–191
        commerce and, 1:230–231
        Copernicanism, 2:178–179
        Dominicans, 2:19
        education, 5:36, 331–333, 6:563–564
        Empedoclean, 2:396–398
        empiricism, 2:43, 4:65–66
        Enlightenment, 1:431–434
        experimental, 2:2
        Franciscan order, 1:143–144
        heliocentric, 2:20–21
        independent of theology, 1:446–447
        introductory textbooks on, 5:21–22
        limits of natural powers, 5:351–352
        logic, 1:448–450, 5:312–314
        mathematics and, 1:296–297, 5:351, 6:562–563
        mechanics, 1:204–205, 3:111
        motion, 1:441–443, 5:351, 352
        mysticism, 3:277–279
        perspectives on, 4:1–2
        positive, 1:137–138
        propositions, 1:378–379
        scientific method, 3:287–288, 5:350–351
        speculative, 1:141, 142, 366–369
        theology, 1:444–447
        theory of language, 2:44–45
        translations, 1:13–15
        women, 2:79–80
    neoplatonism, 6:137–138
    political, 5:286–287
    positivist, 2:340
    psychology and, 6:522, 525
    quantum mechanics, 1:327
    rational choice theory, 4:35
    religious, 1:20
    of science, 6:135–136
        Aristotelian, 1:99–100
        comparitive theory, 4:278–279
        decision theory, 4:36–37
        elements, 6:6
        empiricism, 6:458
        evolution, 6:288
        Freudian, 3:75
        historiography, 4:172–174, 175–176
        ideology and, 5:122–123
        logic, 6:314

Philosophy, *continued*
  and medicine, 4:183–185
  natural classification, 2:320
  pragmatism, 4:44
  probalistic thinking, 4:35
  progress, 6:123–124
  speculative, 1:140–141
  statistical techniques, 4:39–40
  symbolism, 7:278
  theories, 6:204
  utilitarianism, 7:282
 scientific method, 3:421
 student of, 4:24–29
 subjective, 3:130–132
 Telesian, 2:19–20
 transcendent reality, 3:265
 women's education and, 1:19
 See also specific systems of philosophy
Philosophy and Logical Syntax (Carnap), 4:34
The Philosophy of Karl Popper (Lakatos), 6:135
Philosophy of Mathematics and Natural Science (Weyl),
  7:278
Philosophy to the Athenians (Paracelsus), 6:14
Philpott, Delbert, 6:571
The Phloem (Esau), 2:414
Phlogiston, 6:505, 507, 7:169–170
Phluger, Helmeth, 3:238–239
Phosphate fertilizers, 5:295
Phosphocreatine, 5:306
Phosphoric acid esters, 1:218
Phosphorus, 3:352, 353, 6:413
Phosphorus cycle
  marine, 3:259
  radiation ecology, 3:414
Phosphorylase, 3:168
Phosphorylation, oxidative, 3:168–169, 170–171, 5:308
Photius, 5:340–341
Photocell-astrometry, 6:541
Photochemistry
  instrumentation, 1:234
  interdisciplinary cooperation, 1:440
  laser, 6:140
  photosynthesis, 6:141
  semiconductors, 1:311
Photoelectric effect, 1:410–411
Photoelectric photometry, 6:544, 546
Photographic emulsions, 1:302
  heavy particles, 1:299–301
  nuclear particles, 5:303
Photographic photometry, 6:541
Photographic process, 5:201–202
Photometric Atlas of the Solar Spectrum (Mimmaert et
  al.), 7:126
Photometry

  cosmology, 3:273–274
  photoelectric, 6:544, 546
  photographic, 6:541
  star clusters, 3:276
Photomultipliers, 1:301–302
Photon scattering, 3:21–23, 7:394
Photons, 1:273
Photoreception, 5:13–17
Photosphere, 6:386–387
Photosynthesis
  photochemistry, 6:141
  ratioactivity, 2:14–15
Phthalocyanin, 1:282, 3:334
Phyletic gradualism, 3:159–160
Phylogenetic Systematics (Hennig), 3:281
Phylogeny
  cladistics, 3:281–282
  comparative embryology, 3:207–209
  embryology, 1:210–211, 3:208
  evolutionary biology, 6:353–354
  holism, 6:484
  hominid, 7:113–118
  invertebrate, 3:434–435
  mammals, 6:454
  morphology, 3:435
  ontogeny, 3:160–161
  ontology and, 1:408
Physica (Aristotle). *See Physics* (Aristotle)
Physica Plinii (Pliny), 6:119
Physica subterranea (Becher), 1:229
Physical anthropology
  archaeology, 2:123–127
  Argentina, 5:180–181
  development, 7:234–238
  ethnography, 2:172–175
  ethnology, 4:236–237
  eugenics, 3:26–28
  France, 7:113, 117
  heredity, 3:26–28
The Physical Background of Perception (Adrian), 1:17
Physical chemistry
  acids, 3:237
  atomism, 2:320–322
  catalysis, 2:205–206
  chemical reactions, 6:126
  experimental, 3:57–58
  founding of, 5:356–357
  greenhouse effect, 1:112–113
  molecular structures, 5:167–170
  oceanography, 6:88–90
  organic, 3:86–88
  radar, 6:139–140
  structure-reactivity relationships, 3:238–240
  systematization of, 4:14–15

Physical Chemistry from Ostwald to Pauling: The Making of a Science in America (Servos), 5:356

Physical Chemistry of High Polymeric Systems (Mark), 5:30

Physical Climatology (Landsberg), 4:198

Physical Description of the Argentina (Burmeister), 1:453

The Physical Dimensions of Consciousness (Boring), 1:358, 359

Physical geography, 6:348–349

Physical mathematics, 6:489

Physical-Mineralogical essay of lithogony and orognosy (Arduino). *See Saggio Fisico-Mineralogico di Lythogonia e Orognosia* (Arduino)

Physical oceanography
    geophysics, 2:265–266
    Germany, 7:373–376

Physical Oceanography (Defant), 2:266

Physical Oceanography (Schott). *See Physische Meereskunde* (Schott)

Physical organic chemistry, 2:199–204

Physical Organic Chemistry (Hammett), 3:237, 239–240

Physical Organic Chemistry in Retrospect (Hammett), 3:239

The Physical State of Interstellar Hydrogen (Strömgren), 6:544

Physical symbol systems, 5:258

Physics
    Arabic, 6:188
    Aristotelianism, 1:424, 445–446, 5:7
    Aryan, 4:56–57
    atmospheric, 1:390–391
    atomism, 3:157–158
    axiomatics, 3:306–307
    black hole
        mathematical theory, 2:92
        properties, 7:393–394
        radiation, 2:370
    celestial
        Aristotelianism, 7:381–382
        stellar structure, 2:87–90
    chemical
        bonds, 3:195–196
        branched chain reactions, 6:411–415
        hydrodynamics, 7:391–392
        spectroscopy, 6:473
    Cherenkov effect, 2:107–110
    cloud, 1:470
    computer, 5:51–52
    condensed matter, 6:169
    cosmic rays, 5:300–304
    crystals, 7:164–166
    experimental
        Cherenkov effect, 2:107–110
        climate change, 5:327–330
        nuclear magnetic resonance, 6:178, 179–182

        radiation, 2:108–110
        radiocarbon dating, 5:326–327
        superconductivity, 2:64–65
        telegraphy, 3:58
        United Kingdom, 6:548–549
    gases, 1:202
    geometry relationship
        electromagnetic effects, 2:370
        relativity, 7:277
    gravity
        acceleration, 2:281–282
        affine connection, 2:367–369
        attraction, 1:342
        measurement, 7:302–303
        Newton's law, 5:270–271
        space-time structure, 2:280
    high-energy
        accelerators, 5:304
        antiprotons, 6:410
        colliding-beam accelerators, 1:425
        electron-positron collisions, 1:428–430
        linear accelerators, 6:409
        parity nonconservation problem, 6:337
        relativistic plasmas, 1:426
    high-temperature, 2:253–254
    history of, 4:171–172
    impetus theory, 1:447
    instrumentation, 1:28
    laws of motion and force, 5:270
    low-temperature, 4:80–81
    mathematics and, 6:562–563
    medieval, 6:292–293
    microwave
        magnetrons, 6:179–180
        radiation, 2:280–281
    molecular
        branched chain reactions, 6:411–415, 413–414
        mechanics of collisions, 1:258–259
        orbitals, 5:210–211
    natural, 1:423–425, 445
    networks, 2:269
    Newtonian theory, 5:269–270
    nuclear, 5:200, 7:302
        alpha particles, 1:290–291
        atomic weapons, 1:269, 327
        beta decay, 7:102
        chain reactions, 6:573–575, 7:295–296
        China, 7:397–402
        Cold War, 2:168–170
        commercial applications, 2:166–167
        cyclotrons, 7:328–329
        experimental, 7:119
        fission, 1:60–62, 257, 7:392
        influential figures, 6:393

Physics, *continued*
    magnetic resonance, 6:191, 194–197
    mass spectrography, 1:162–165
    molecular collisions, 1:258–259
    nuclear decay, 6:169–171
    nuclear structure, 2:379
    nuclear weapons, 6:419–424
    particle accelerators, 1:425–428, 4:208–212, 327–331
    particles, 5:303–304, 6:407–411
    politics, 2:166–167
    quantum electrodynamics, 7:266–267
    quantum mechanics, 1:391–392
    quantum theory, 1:269
    radioactivity, 6:77
    resonance phenomena, 3:60–61
    scattering, 6:499
    scope of, 1:133–135
    solar, 1:157
    spontaneous fission, 3:35–36
    stars, 1:157
    steady state theory, 3:388
    theoretical, 5:127–131
    women scientists, 7:363–368
  optical reflection and refraction, 4:1–2
  particle
    cosmic rays, 1:54–55, 62, 5:191, 6:280–283
    dust counter, 1:29
    electrodynamic interactions, 3:19
    influential figures, 7:68–72
    mu-mesons, 1:73–75
    unified field theory, 2:370–371
    weak force phenomena, 3:23–25
    women scientists, 7:363–368
  planetary, 6:300
  plasma
    experimental techniques, 3:59
    fusion, 6:501–502
    magnetism, 1:43
    relativistic, 1:426
    space probes, 6:283
  quantum field theory, 6:34–35
  quantum mechanics, 2:364–371
  radio waves, 3:291–293
  radioactivity, 1:298
  solar
    astronomy, 3:141–144
    spectroscopy, 7:73–77
  solid-state
    conduction electrons, 1:303
    development, 6:437–441
    electron scattering, 3:22–23
    ionics, 2:162
    iron monoxide, 2:160–161
    metals, 6:63–64
    Mott transition, 5:203–204
    pioneering research, 5:200–201
    quantum mechanics, 7:295
    semiconductors, 7:320–321
  space, 1:40–45, 6:283
  theoretical
    as academic discipline, 6:65–66
    astrophysics, 7:105
    baryon asymmetry, 6:324
    conformal groups, 3:193
    crystals, 7:164–166
    development, 6:489–491
    electroconductivity, 6:373–377
    electromagnetism, 6:335–340
    influential figures, 5:347–349, 6:391–397, 7:20–24, 68–72
    light quantum hypothesis, 2:364–365
    many-particle systems, 1:318–319
    mathematics, 6:64
    metals, 5:200–201
    nuclear, 1:391–392
    nuclear physics and, 7:295–296
    numerical analysis, 3:253
    positron, 1:72
    quantum electrodynamics, 7:266–267
    relativity, 4:300–301
    second quantization of fields, 4:55
    United Kingdom, 6:548–549
    University of Michigan, 7:101
    USSR, 6:325
  See also Astrophysics; Biophysics; Geophysics; Quantum mechanics
Physics (Aristotle), 1:35, 100–102, 101
  commentaries on, 4:51, 5:280, 313, 350–352
  expositions, 1:449
  natural knowledge, 1:450
  projectile motion, 6:293
  questions on, 1:143
Physics for Science and Engineering Students (Purcell), 6:182
Physics in the Twentieth Century (Weisskopf), 7:268
The Physics of Blown Sand and Desert Dunes (Bagnold), 1:155
Physics of Climate (Peixoto and Oort), 6:345
The Physics of Sound in the Sea (Spitzer), 6:500
Physik der Atmosphäre (Wegener), 7:246
Physik und das Geheimnis des organischen Lebens (Jordan), 4:56
Physikalische Grundlagen einer Gravitationstheorie (Grossmann and Einstein), 3:192
Physikalisches Denken in der neuen Zeit (Jordan), 4:56
Physiochemical biology, 5:359–364

The Physiographic Ecology of Chicago and Vicinity
  (Cowles), 2:187
Physiographic maps, 7:30
Physiography (Huxley), 3:431
Physiologia Kircheriana experimentalis (Koestler), 4:134
Physiological chemistry. *See* Biochemistry
Physiological genetics
  Drosophila, 2:399–400
  evolution, 7:357–360, *358*
Physiological regulation, 6:244–245, 245–247, 247
Physiology
  behavioral, 6:459, 7:180, 181–183
  biochemistry and, 2:218–219, 5:306
  brain, 5:76–79
  chemical, 4:14–15, 6:447–448
  children's books, 5:284–285
  circulatory and respiratory systems, 3:302–305
  comparative, 6:358
  digestion, 1:1, 6:46–47
  electrophysiology, 1:15
      brain, 1:17–18
      epilepsy, 6:69–74
  eugenics and, 1:3–4
  fish, 3:260–261
  genetics, 7:12–15
  homeostasis, 4:276
  hunger, 5:*148,* 148–149, 151
  Katz, Bernard, 4:88–89
  materialist, 4:183–185
  medical schools, 3:92–95
  modern medicine, 6:567–568
  nerve and muscle fiber, 1:15–18
  nervous system, 7:183
  neuroscience, 3:328–332
  neurotransmitters, 7:176–180
  plants
      botany, 6:389–391
      developmental morphology, 6:356–359
      Mendelian genetics, 7:189–191
  psychology, 2:55–58
  respiration, 4:216
  scientific method, 3:215–216
  synapses, 2:329–333
  vision, 4:224, 7:211–215
  See also Neurophysiology
The Physiology of Synapses (Eccles), 2:332
The Physiology of the Nerve Cell (Eccles), 2:331
Physische Meereskunde (Schott), 6:371
Phytoplankton
  eutrophication, 2:354–355
  growth, 3:257–259
  oceanography, 6:256–257
  study of, 5:22–23, 24, 25
Piaget, Jean, 6:**90–96,** *91*

  egocentric speech, 7:195
  genetic epistemology, 2:25–26
Picard, Charles Émile, 2:117, 289, 4:145
Picard, Jule-Henri, 7:254
Picardet, Claudine, 6:**97–98**
Piccard, Jacques, 2:287
Piccioni, Oreste, 6:410
Piccolomini, Francesco, 7:388
Pick, Anne, 3:123
Pickels, Edward, 2:146
Pickering, Edward Charles, 7:287
Pickering, William Hayward, 6:**98–104,** *100,* 7:123
Pickford, Grace E., 3:411, 412
Pickworth, Jenny, 3:337
Piero della Francesca, 6:**104–106,** *105*
Pierpont, James, 3:357
Pierre of Limoges. *See* Peter of Limoges
Pietism, 6:506
Piezoelectric effect, 7:165
Pigments, chemistry of, 2:14
Pillow Problems (Dodgson), 2:311
Pillsbury, Walter B., 3:406
Pilot ACE computer, 7:314–318
Piltdown Man, 5:295, 296–299, 354, 7:115–117
Pimesons, 5:303
Pinchot, Gifford, 4:267, 268
Pineal gland, 1:121–122
Pines, David, 1:181
Pines, Shlomo, 5:6, 6:6
Pingree, David, 2:121
Pinkava, Jindřich, 5:357
Pinker, Steven, 3:162, 5:35
Pion condensation, 5:130–131
Pioneer space probes, 7:123–124
Pirani, Felix, 1:342
Pit organs, 1:436
Pithecanthropus, 7:184–188, *185, 186*
  hominid fossils, 7:252
  as missing link, 2:313–315
Pithecantropus, 2:313–316
Pitt, Mary, 3:291
Pittendrigh, Colin S., 6:454
Pitts, Walter, 5:77, 255
Pitzer, Kenneth S., 3:195
Piveteau, Jean, 6:**106–110**
Place
  as connotative concept, 5:313
  natural philosophy, 5:352
Plancherel formula, 3:242, 243, 244
Plancius, Petrus, 6:**110–111**
Planck, Max, 2:320, 6:**111–115,** *113*
  Black-Body Theory and the Quantum Discontinuity,
      1894-1912 (Kuhn), 4:175
  booklet on, 7:107

Planck, Max, *continued*
    influence of, 4:335
    quantum mechanics, 6:62
    students of, 6:373, 7:246
    theoretical physics, 6:490
Planck, Max Karl Ernst Ludwig. *See* Planck, Max
Planck constant, 7:398
Planck's law, 1:411–412
Planetary Hypotheses (Ptolemy), 6:174, 177
Planetary motion
    d'Alembert's principle, 2:230–231
    laws of, 4:105–107
Planetary physics, 6:302
Planetary science
    motion, 5:270, 271
    NASA, 5:263–264
    observational astronomy, 3:166
    popular, 6:314
    Venus, 6:310–311
Plankalkül, 7:411–412
Plankton, 3:257–259
Plankton Production and Its Control (Harvey et al.),
    3:259
Plant Anatomy (Esau), 2:413, 415
Plant communities
    ecology, 2:152–154
    sociology, 1:385–388
    See also Ecosystems
Plant ecology, 7:3–8
Plant geography, 7:3–4
Plant pigments
    research, 6:272
    synthesis, 7:64–65
Plant sociology, 1:385–388
Plant Sociology Handbook (Braun-Blanquet and
    Pavillard). *See Vocabulaire de sociologie végétale* (Braun-
    Blanquet and Pavillard)
Plantesamfund (Warming), 2:155, 187
Plants
    anatomy
        botany, 6:389–391
        structure and development, 2:413–415
    classification, 4:316
        Linnaean, 4:316
        relationships, 2:214
        varying approaches to, 5:206
    ecology, 2:152–154, 186–189, 234–237
    evolution, 6:513, 515
    genetics
        chloroplasts, 6:316–319
        cytogenetics, 6:514–515
        evolution, 6:513
        homeostasis, 4:275–276
        hybridization, 1:211–212, 5:98–100

        maize, 5:68–71
    physiology
        botany, 6:389–391
        developmental morphology, 6:356–359
        Mendelian genetics, 7:189–191
    reproduction, 6:356–358
    taxonomy, 2:213–214
Plaskett, Harry Hemley, 5:112, 6:50
Plasma physics
    experimental techniques, 3:59
    fusion, 6:501–502
    magnetic traps, 1:426
    magnetism, 1:43
    space probes, 6:283
Plass, Gilbert, 4:91
Plasticity, 7:182
Plate tectonics
    alpinotype, 1:*71*
    continental drift, 4:40, 41
    development, 6:430–431
    earth expansion, 2:38
    earth's magnetism, 1:292–293, 2:379
    folding, 1:70–71
    geochemistry, 6:259
    geology, 2:38–42
    instruments, 1:243
    marine geology, 2:288
    oceanography, 6:235–236
    paleomagnetism, 2:193
    polycyclic theory, 3:394
    seismicity, 1:244–245
Plate Tectonics: How It Works (Cox), 2:192–193
Plate Tectonics and Geomagnetic Reversals (Cox), 2:193
Platinum, 7:342–343
Plato, 6:*115*, **115–116**
    alchemical commentaries on, 5:338–339
    brain theory, 2:123
    commentaries on, 3:322
    cosmology, 2:122
    Empedoclean, 2:397
    epistemology, 1:14
    influence of, 2:327
    intelligent design, 3:94
    natural classification, 2:320
    neoplatonism and, 6:137
    tripartition and trilocation, 3:95
Plaut, Walter, 6:319
Play, Dreams, and Imitation (Piaget), 6:93
Playfair, John, 3:420
Pleomorphist theory, 1:209
Pliny the Elder, 2:83–84, 6:**116–121**, *118*
    attacks on *Natural History* (Pliny), 4:265
    commentaries on, 6:68
Ploetz, Alfred, 3:26

Ploidy, 1:397–400
Plotz, Harry, 4:226
Plunkett, Roy, 3:38
Plutarch, 3:321
Pluto (planet), 4:179, 7:284
Plutonium
    atomic bombs, 1:274, 5:190, 6:401, 402–403
    discovery, 6:408–409
    implosion in guns, 1:134
Plyler, Earle, 4:7
Pneumatic-attractive model, 7:167–169
Pneumatic chemistry, 6:507
Pneumatica (Hero of Alexandria), 6:540
Pneumatics, 3:353
Pockels, Agnes, 6:549
Pockels, Friedrich, 7:166
Pococke, Edward, 3:166
Podolsky, Boris, 1:240–241, 323, 325, 326–327
Poems and Fancies (Cavendish), 2:80
Poetry, 6:517, 551, 552
Poey y Aguirre, Andrés, 7:153
Poggio, Tomaso, 2:210, 5:35
Pohl, Robert Wichard, 5:201
Pohlmann, Ludwig, 5:357
Poincaré, Henri. *See* Poincaré, Jules Henri
Poincaré, Jules Henri, 1:23, 317, 2:29, 367, 6:**121–125,**
    122
    Bruno, Giordano, 1:425
    gravity, 6:456
    influence of, 5:194
    influences on, 4:335
    Institut Henri Poincaré, 1:410
    stability of solar system, 5:197
Poirier, P. G., 7:114
Poisson, Siméon-Denis, 2:268
Poland, 7:10
Polányi, Michael. *See* Polányi, Mihály
Polányi, Mihály, 2:205–206, 4:172, 6:**125–127**
    colleagues of, 7:66
    Society for Freedom in Science, 7:8
    students of, 7:294
    x-ray diffraction research, 5:28
Polányi-Semenov rule, 6:414
Polar atmosphere, 7:19
*The Polar Front in the Interpretation and Prediction of
    Oklahoma Weather* (Thornthwaite), 7:39
Polar wander
    paleomagnetism, 2:191–192
    Runcorn, Stanley Keith, 6:300
Polare Molekeln (Debye), 5:168
Polarity
    electron, 7:*263*, 263–264
    in magnetism, 3:108–109
    molecular, 4:14, 5:168–169

Polatin, Philip, 5:91
Polder, Dirk, 6:169
Polier, Justine Wise, 2:131
Poliovirus
    evolution, 1:455–456
    vaccines, 3:187
Politia Naturae (Linnaeus), 4:316
Political behavior, 6:254–255
Political coalitions, 6:254
Political economics
    induction, 7:281
    introductory textbooks on, 5:21
    Keynesian, 4:111–113
    population dynamics, 5:13–14
Political Economy (Malthus), 5:13
Political Justice (Godwin), 5:13
Political philosophy, 5:286–287
Political psychology
    belief systems, 1:8–10
    democracy, 6:19–20
    personality and, 2:429–430
Political science, 6:254–255
Politics
    economics and, 5:337
    evolution, 6:484
    planetary exploration, 5:263–264
    science and, 5:234, 6:572, 7:159
    USSR, 7:157
The Politics of Cultural Despair (Stern), 4:150
Politus, Bassanus, 6:563
Poliziano, Angelo, 4:264
Pollack, James B., 6:312
Pollination, 6:357
Pollio, Vitruvius. *See* Vitruvius Pollio, Marcus
Pollister, Arthur, 5:282
Pollution
    air
        automobile emissions, 1:235, 3:383
        industrial melanism, 4:109–110
        ozone, 1:235
    water
        algae, 2:355
        nitrogen analysis, 3:63
        public health, 4:54
Polvani, Giovanni, 7:166
Pólya, George, 2:289, 5:254
Polycyclic aromatic hydrocarbons, 1:251
Polycyclic theory, 3:394
Polygraphia nova et universalis (Kircher), 4:134
Polymer Research Institute, 5:31–32
Polymers
    academic programs in, 5:29–30, 31–32
    advancing the science of, 5:30–31
    free radicals and, 1:189, 192

Polymers, *continued*
 hydrocarbons, 3:87
 kinetics, 3:37, 38–40
 liquid crystalline, 3:39
 molecular structure, 6:330–334
 polyamides, 1:215–217, *216, 217*
 polyethylene, 3:87
 science, 7:133, 138–139
 structure, 2:47–50
 synthesis of, 4:290–291
Polymorphism, genetic, 3:47
 balanced and transient, 3:47
 natural selection, 3:48
 neutral theory, 4:117
Polynomials
 character theory, 3:13
 complex coefficients, 2:229–230
 groups, 2:291
Polynucleotide phosphorylase, 5:310, 6:480
Polypeptides, 1:*77*
 biosynthesis, 4:326–327
 digestion, 1:2
Polyploidy, 6:514–515
Polyurethane, 1:214, 216–217
Polyvinyl acetate (PVA), 6:333
Pomeranchuk, Isaak Yakovlevich, 5:129
Pomeroy, Wardell, 4:125, 129
Pommer, Horst, 7:340
Ponnamperuma, Cyril, 6:312
Pontecorvo, Bruno, 1:159
Pontriagin, Lev Semenovich. *See* Pontryagin, Lev
 Semionovich
Pontryagin, Lev Semionovich, 6:**127–129**
Pool, Ithiel de Sola, 1:9
Pope, William Jackson, 6:476
Popják, George, 5:40
Popkin, Samuel, 1:9
Pople, John Anthony, 6:**129–133**, *130*
Popper, Karl Raimund, 1:342, 2:44, 45, 6:**133–137**,
 134
 criticisms of psychology, 5:93
 electrical excitation and inhibition, 2:330
 inductive philosophy criticism, 5:144
 influence of, 5:88–89
 steady state theory, 5:74
 The Structure of Scientific Revolutions (Kuhn), 4:172
Popularization of science
 astronomy, 6:312–314
 education, 7:159–160
 evolutionary biology, 3:159–162
 influence of Gould, 3:162
 influence of Stephen Jay Gould on, 3:163–164
Population
 biology

Chicago school, 2:390–391
 eugenics, 3:32
dynamics, 5:13–14
ecology
 animals, 3:415–416
 biogeochemistry, 3:413–414
 limnology, 3:412–413
 natural selection, 7:377–380
genetics
 adaptation, 7:*361*
 altruism, 3:226–229
 biological evolution and, 5:62
 diffusion equation approximations, 4:115–116
 diversity, 3:46
 evolution and, 5:63–64, 243–244, 7:353–363
 homeostasis, 4:275–277
 mathematical, 7:356–363
 theoretical, 3:29
growth, 3:414–415
Population Genetics and Animal Improvement (Lerner),
 4:275
The Population Problem (Carr-Saunders), 2:384
Populations, Species, and Evolution (Mayr), 5:63
Porphyries, 7:142–143
Porphyry (philosopher), 2:284, 6:**137–138**, 172
Porter, Arthur, 3:254–255
Porter, George, 6:**139–143**, *141*
Porter, Henry, 7:120
Porter, Keith Roberts, 2:144, 145, 6:**143–149**
Posidonius, 2:304
Positive political theory, 6:254, 255
Positivism
 logical, 6:125
 social Darwinism, 2:244
 sociology, 6:135–136
 The Structure of Scientific Revolutions (Kuhn), 4:172,
 176
Positrons
 cosmic rays and, 1:72–73
 as electrons, 7:399
Post, Emil Leon, 5:257
Posterior Analytics (Aristotle), 1:37, 100, 450
Postgate, John R., 2:104–105
Postma, Henk, 7:142
Postman, Leo Joseph, 1:53
Postscript after Twenty Years (Popper), 6:135
Potato eelworms, 7:66
Potential existence (mixtures), 6:294
Pott, Johann Heinrich, 2:219, 4:214
Potter, David, 2:331
Potter, Van R., 3:169, 170
Pouchet, Félix-Archimède, 6:24–28
Poulter, Thomas, 7:118
Pound, Robert V., 6:180

magnetic resonance, 1:306
    nuclear magnetic resonance, 3:196, 197
Pourciau, Bruce, 5:270
Poverty, 2:132–135
The Poverty of Historicism (Popper), 6:135
Powell, Adam Clayton, 2:134
Powell, Cecil Franck
    mu-mesons, 1:291
    Nobel Prize, 1:302, 5:304
    nuclear particles, 5:303
Powell, Herbert "Tiny," 3:333, 336
Powell, John Wesley, 6:**149–152,** *150*
    Grand Canyon research, 2:186
    National Academy of Sciences, 4:120–123
Power and Prosperity: Outgrowing Communist and Capitalist Dictatorships (Olson), 5:337
Powers, natural, 5:351–352
Powers of Ten (Morrison), 5:193
PR (pyrolytic release) experiment, 3:365
Prachatic, Kristan Z. *See* Prachaticz, Cristannus de
Prachaticz, Cristannus de, 6:**153–154**
Practica arithmetice (Cardano), 2:36
Practical Methods of Organic Chemistry (Woodward), 7:349
Praedicamenta (Aristotle), 5:351
Praelectiones physicae (Jungius), 4:65
Pragmatism, 4:43–44
Pragmatism (James), 4:23
Prandtl, Ludwig, 5:335
Prasad, Gopal, 1:346
Prasad, Jamuna, 3:16
Pratt, Leslie, 7:312
Prebiotic chemistry, origin of life, 5:154–158
Precipitation
    Bergeron-Findeisen process, 1:248, *248*
    cloud physics, 1:245
    effective, 7:39
    seeder-feeder process, 1:249
Predators, 3:183, 184
Predictability of Stock Market Process (Morgenstern), 5:187
Prefatio (Celsus), 2:81
Preference Trees (Tversky and Sattath), 7:93
Preformism, 3:216
Prefrontal cortex, 3:145–148
Pregnancy, Birth and Abortion (Gebhard), 4:124
The Prehistoric Cultures of the Horn of Africa (Clark), 2:124
Preliminary Discourse on the Study of Natural Philosophy (Herschel), 3:287, 289
Prelog, Vladimir, 2:201, 4:17, 5:362, 6:**154–161,** *155,* 7:350
Prelog, Vlado. *See* Prelog, Vladimir
Prelog's rule, 6:158, *159*

Premack, David, 3:183
Premier Discours to the Histoire Naturelle (Buffon), 1:432
Dés premiers vertébrés à l'homme (Piveteau), 6:108
Prepulsid, 4:32
Prescott, Edward, 7:151
Present, Richard D., 2:166
Presidential elections. *See* Elections
President's Science Advisory Committee (PSAC)
    1958 test-ban negotiations, 1:136
    atmospheric nuclear testing, 1:275
Pressure, atmospheric, 6:559–560
Pretree model, 7:93
Prévost, Jean-Louis, Jr., 6:447
Prezent, Isay Izraylovich, 6:510
Pribrum, Karl, 4:354
Price, Derek John Desolla, 6:**162–164**
Price, George, 3:230, 231
Price, public goods, 5:336–337, 7:151
Price, Richard, 1:221
Prichard, James Cowles, 5:368
Pricing in Urban and Suburban Transport (Vickery), 7:151
Priestley, Joseph, 5:125
    air, 7:169
    combustion, 6:507
Prigogine, Ilya, 6:**164–168,** *165*
Primakoff, Henry, 6:**168–172**
Primakoff effect, 6:170
Primakoff waves, 6:170
Primatology
    comparative anatomy, 2:137–139
    conservation, 3:53–56
    development, 7:234–238
    saltational theory, 5:368
Prime numbers, 2:403–405
A Primer of ALGOL 60 Programming (Dijkstra), 2:68
Primitive culture
    archaelogy, 2:173
    archaeology, 2:124–127
    cave art, 4:42–43
    evolution, 2:173–175
    psychology, 1:185
Primordial atmosphere, 5:*155,* 155–156
Prince, Morton, 5:216
Principes de philosophie zoologique (Geoffroy Saint-Hilaire, Étienne), 3:118
Principia Mathematica (Newton), 1:28, 3:408, 5:57, 269–271
Principia Mathematica (Whitehead and Russell), 3:71, 5:255
Principia philosophiae (Descartes), 2:272, 273, 274
Principia philosophiae antiquissimae et recentissimae (Conway), 2:171–172
Principle of least action, 5:58

Principles of Agriculture (Hutton), 3:420

Principles of Animal Ecology (Emerson), 2:390

Principles of Animal Psychology (Schneirla and Maier), 6:367

Principles of Animal Taxonomy (Simpson), 6:454

Principles of Behavior (Hull), 3:408–409

Principles of Chemical Engineering (Lewis), 4:288, 289, 290

Principles of Classification and a Classification of Mammals (Simpson), 6:454

Principles of English University Education (Whewell), 7:281

Principles of General and Comparative Physiology (Carpenter), 2:56

Principles of Mechanics (Hertz), 3:291, 292–293

Principles of Microwave Circuits (Dicke), 2:*281*, 6:180

Principles of Moral and Political Philosophy (Paley), 7:282

Principles of Perceptual Learning and Development (Gibson, Eleanor Jack), 3:121–122

Principles of Physical Geology (Holmes), 2:39

Principles of Polymer Chemistry (Flory), 3:39

Principles of Psychology (James), 2:55, 57–58, 3:405, 4:23

Principles of Stellar Dynamics (Chandrasekhar), 2:89–90

Principles of Topological Psychology (Lewin), 4:282

Pringle, John, 1:92

Printing presses, 6:218

Prinzipienfragen der biologischen Systematik (Schindewolf), 6:353, 354

Prior, Fritz, 2:206

Prisms, 1:295

Prisoner's Dilemma, 3:231–232, 7:81

The Private Life of the Gannet (film), 3:425

The Privilege of Being a Physicist (Weisskopf), 7:268

Probability
    axiomatics, 3:266
    decision theory, 4:35–36
    Enlightenment, 1:432
    epistemology, 4:35
    induction, 1:432, 2:45–46
    integrals, 1:219–220
    logic, 6:134–135
    mathematics, 1:254–256
    notation for, 4:39–40
    representation theory, 6:349
    Schwartz, Laurent, 6:382
    subjective, 2:255–257
    theory of, 4:151
    theory of rationality, 4:111–113
    transcendental, 2:311

Probability and the Art of Judgment (Jeffrey), 4:35

Problem-solving
    cognitive, 3:147
    decision making, 6:449, 452
    heuristics, 5:254, 255–257

Problemi astronomici (Monte), 5:176

Problems of Aging (Cowdry), 2:184

Problems of Astronomy (Monte). *See Problemi astronomici* (Monte)

Problems of Dynamical Theory in Statistical Physics (Bogolubov), 1:318

Problems of Extra-Galactic Research (McVittie), 5:84

Problems of Monopoly and Economic Warfare (Zeuthen), 3:249–250

Problems of Relative Growth (Huxley), 3:425

Procedimenti magico-alchemici (Camplani), 7:407

The Process of Song-Learning in the Chaffinch as Studied by Means of the Spectrograph (Thorpe), 7:43

Processors, computer, 7:410–411

Proctor, Warren, 3:197

Prodi, Giovanni, 4:319

Prodromus Florae Novae Hollandiae (Mueller), 5:206

Producibleness of Chymical Principles (Boyle), 1:367

The Production of Antibodies (Burnet), 1:455, 457, 458

Production systems, 5:257

Productivity, 1:230–231

Proescholdt, Hilde, 3:218

Profession of Faith (Chioniades), 2:121

Professionalization of science, 5:331–333

Progesterone, 1:460

Programming a Computer for Playing Chess (Shannon), 6:428

Programming languages
    ALGOL, 2:296–297
    C, 6:534
    COBOL, 3:356
    cognitive simulations, 5:255–257
    compilers, 2:296–297
    development, 5:254, 6:532–536
    mathematics, 3:358–360
    Plankalkül, 7:411–412
    textbooks, 2:294–295

Programming Research Group, 6:535

Progress, scientific, 1:358, 6:162–163

Proinsulin, 5:364

Project Argus, 7:123

Project Matterhorn, 6:384–385

Project Paperclip. *See* Operation Paperclip

Project Pluvius, 1:249

Project RAND, 6:501, 502

Project Vanguard, 5:261

Project West Ford, 3:143

Projectile motion, 6:292–293

Prony, Gaspard-François-Clair-Marie Riche de, 1:126–127, 4:201

Proof theory, 3:309–310

Proofs and Refutations (Lakatos), 6:135

Proofs from the Book (Erdos), 2:404

Properties of Polymers: Correlations with Chemical Structure (Van Krevelen and Hoftijzer), 7:139
Propiconazole, 4:33
Propionic acid, 7:346–347
A Proposal for Cosmic Ray Observations in Earth Satellites (Van Allen), 7:122
A Proposed Mechanism of Emotion (Papez), 6:11
Propositiones (Suchten), 6:551
Propositiones philosophicae (Agnesi), 1:19
Proscholdt, Hilde. *See* Mangold, Hilde
Proskauer, Eric S., 5:30–31
Prospect theory, 7:94
Prospect Theory (Tversky and Kahneman), 7:94
Prostaglandins, 7:178
Protagon, 7:46
Protagoras (Plato), 3:322
Proteases, 1:1
Protein chemistry, 1:*77*, 2:*349*
    amino acids, 2:348–352
    biosysnthesis, 4:326–327
    chain folding, 1:76–80
    hemoglobin, 6:81–83
    molecular structure, 6:38–40, 360, 361–365
    nucleic acids, 2:68–69
    oligosaccharide recognition, 4:261–263
    peptides, 1:1, 2, 4:326, *326*
    physical chemistry and, 5:170
    synthesis, 2:209–210
Protein sequence, 5:363–364
Protein synthesis, 1:*374*
    instruments, 1:373–376
    molecular genetics and, 1:224, 5:310
    neural induction, 1:373, *373*
    transfer RNA, 3:341–343
Proteins
    biochemistry, 1:1–4
    flaoproteins, 3:168
Proteins and Nucleic Acids (Perutz), 6:83
The Protestant Ethic and the Spirit of Capitalism (Weber), 5:121
Protocol analysis, 5:255, 256
Protogaea (Leibniz), 4:249, 251
Proton beams, 1:428
Proton-neutron isospin, 3:193
Proton synchrocyclotrons, 6:410
Protons
    boost, 1:428–429
    carbon-nitrogen cycle, 3:60–61
    gravitational forces, 2:282
    magnetic moments, 6:194
    photographic emulsions, 1:299–301, 299–301
Protozoans, 6:492–493
Protozoology, 4:44–45
Proust, Joseph Louis, 4:201

Provine, William, 2:63, 246, 3:29, 7:357, 362
Prudhomme, Eugene A., 3:381
Prym, Friedrich Emil, 6:251
Przibram, Hans, 4:77, 78, 79
PSAC (President's Science Advisory Committee), 1:136, 275
Pseudo-Aristotle, 1:166, 167
Pseudoscience, 6:314
Psittacosis, 1:455
Psoriasis, 6:323
Psychasthenia, 4:27, 28
Psychiatric drugs, 1:118–120
Psychiatry
    behavioral therapy, 2:429–430
    and psychoanalysis, 3:73–76, 4:62–64
Psychoanalysis, 7:3, 5–6, 7
    behavioral therapy, 2:429–430
    children, 2:408–409
    Harvard tenureship and, 5:217
    hypnosis, 3:312
    personality change, 1:358
    and psychiatry, 3:73–76, 4:62–64
Psychobiology, 6:243–247
Psychodiagnosis (Meehl), 5:93
Psychogenesis and the History of Science (Piaget), 6:94
Psycholinguistics, 4:350–354, 7:195, 370
Psychological Bulletin, 1:169
Psychological Care of the Infant and Child (Watson), 7:244
Psychological counseling, 6:274–279
Psychological Healing (Janet), 4:28
The Psychological Review, 1:169, 2:74
Psychological testing, 7:25–29
Psychological Types (Jung), 5:215, 216
Psychologie als Wissenschaft (Herbart), 7:370
Psychologie in Biologischer Sicht (Hess), 3:305
Psychologies of 1925 (Murchison), 7:244
Psychology
    analytical
        collective endeavor, 4:62–64
        social change, 2:135–136
    animal
        behaviorism, 7:241–242
        birds, 2:196–198, 4:244–247, 336–342
        experimental, 6:47
        neuroanatomy, 2:341
    autonomic nervous system, 3:305
    behavioral, 3:405–409
        consciousness in, 4:28–29
        development, 6:458–466
        field theory, 4:279–282
        genetics in, 4:203–204
        Klüver-Bucy syndrome, 4:141–143
        Meehl, Paul Everett on, 5:93–94

Psychology, *continued*
    personality psychology and, 5:44–47
    therapy, 2:429–430
  biofeedback, 5:150–151
  British, 1:187–188
  child, 1:169
    behaviorism, 7:243–244
    communication, 6:*93*
    intelligence, 6:91–95
    intelligence quotient, 6:522
    psychoanalysis, 2:408–409
    race and, 2:128–129
  city life, 5:140–141
  client-centered, 6:274–279
  cognitive, 2:55–56
    behavior, 6:466
    behaviorism, 3:267–271
    cerebral hemispheres, 6:495–497
    computer simulations in, 5:254, 255
    education, 7:194–195
    filter theory of attention, 1:403–405
    ideo-motor action, 2:55–56
    noise, 1:402
    unified theory of cognition, 5:257–258
  comparative
    animal behavior, 4:243–244, 6:366–369
    behaviorism, 7:241–242
    biology, 3:294
    figural quality, 3:296–297
    sexual behavior, 1:222–223
  conditioning and learning, 3:310–314
  consciousness
    mechanistic psychology, 7:370–371
    shrinking field of, 4:26–27
  cross-cultural, 2:22
  cultural, 7:192–196
  developmental, 2:409–411, 3:121–124
  differential, 6:522, 524
  ecological
    perception, 3:125–130
    perceptual learning, 3:123–124
  emotional conditioning, 7:243–244
  engineering, 4:304–305
  evolutionary, 3:162, 6:458
  experimental, 1:356–360
    attention and perception, 1:401
    behaviorism, 6:244–247
    computing, 4:302–303
    conditioning and learning, 3:311–312
    consciousness, 7:369
    critical personalism, 6:523
    critique, 6:525
    history of, 1:357–359
    hypnosis, 3:312, 406

    hysteria, 4:25–26
    influential figures, 7:368–371
    laboratory procedures, 2:73–74
    learning research and, 5:145–151
    Miller, Neal Elgar on, 5:151
    obedience research, 5:137–140, *138, 139*
    operationalism, 2:24–25
    primitive culture, 1:185–186
    psychotherapy, 6:274–279
    scientific specialty, 1:405
    tendencies and, 1:185
    twin studies, 3:312
  group
    dynamics, 4:281–282
    social, 3:14–15
  history, 1:358, 6:94–95, 458–459
  humanistic, 5:45–47
  influential figures, 6:522–526
  mathematical, 7:91–96
  mechanistic, 7:370–371
  mental illness, 4:25–29
  moral, 2:57–58
  obedience, 5:137–140, *138, 139*
  perception, 3:125–130
  perceptual learning, 3:121–124
  personality
    cultural anthropology and, 5:44
    development, 2:409–411, 5:215–219
    latent entities and, 5:90–91
    mind-body connection, 2:428–429
    of morality and ethics, 1:49–51
    psychotherapy and, 5:147–148
    smoking and physical disease, 2:431
  physiological, 2:55–58
  political
    belief systems, 1:8–10
    democracy, 6:18–19
    personality and, 2:430
  quantitative methods, 6:239
  social
    belief systems, 1:8–10
    cognitive dissonance, 3:13–17
    cross-cultural, 2:22–27
    experimental, 5:137–142, *138, 139*
    neurocognition, 4:349–350
    of remembering, 1:186–187
  stoic, 2:123
  testing, 7:25–29
  theoretical, 4:22–24, 5:90–94
    scientific specialty, 1:405
  women in, 1:359–360
  See also Psychoanalysis
Psychology and Industrial Efficiency (Münsterberg), 6:524
Psychology and Primitive Culture (Bartlett), 1:185, 187

Psychology for the Armed Services (Boring), 1:359
Psychology for the Fighting Man (Boring), 1:359
Psychology from the Standpoint of a Behaviorist (Watson), 7:240
Psychology in America: An Historical Survey (Hilgard), 3:271, 314
The Psychology of Politics (Eysenck), 2:430
The Psychology of Reading (Gibson, Eleanor Jack and Levin), 3:122
Psychology of Reasoning (Pillsbury), 3:406
The Psychology of Rumor (Allport), 1:53
The Psychology of Science (Maslow), 5:46
Psychoneurology, 7:192, 195–196
Psychopathology
    subconscious, 4:63
    tendencies in, 4:29
Psychotherapy
    behavioral psychology, 2:429–430
    brain mapping, 7:162–163
    client-centered, 6:274–279
    experimental psychology, 4:62–64
    personality psychology and, 5:147–148
    psychoanalysis, 3:73–76
    theories of, 4:26, 27–28
Psychotic disorders, classification, 7:163
Psychrometers, Assmann, 1:114–116, *115*
Ptolemaeus, Claudius. *See* Ptolemy
Ptolemaic astronomy, 6:173–177
    astrolabes, 1:14, 6:153–154
    calendars, 1:98
    The Copernican Revolution (Kuhn), 4:175
    Copernicanism, 2:177
    cosmology, 2:149–150, 4:20–21
    errors and contradictions in, 4:2
    mathematics, 6:2
    Renaissance, 6:216–218
    translations, 1:14
Ptolemais of Cyrene, 6:**172–173**
Ptolemy, 1:85, 89, 2:234, 6:**173–178**, *175*
    applied mathematics, 3:285
    astronomy, 1:82, 3:320–321
    commentaries by, 2:283–284
    commentaries on, 3:436, 5:7, 6:172–173, 216–218, 517, 518, 7:111
    geography, 5:27
    Greek astronomy, 7:47
    Hero of Alexandria, 3:284
    influence of, 4:1
    on Marinus of Tyre, 5:27
    observational astronomy, 3:166
    students of, 6:137–138
    sundials, 2:305
Public goods
    allocation, 7:150
    freerider problem, 5:336–337
Public health, 7:45–46
Public policy
    atomic energy, 6:405
    bioethics, 3:188–189
    environmental, 6:236
    genetics, 5:241
    hydrogen bombs, 7:23–24
    nuclear physics, 1:157
    nuclear weapons, 6:314–315
    oceanography, 6:236–237
    physics, 1:274–275
    sanitation, 4:54
    science and, 1:293, 342–343, 440–441, 5:237–238
    science education, 7:159–160
    space science, 1:160–161, 7:118, 124–125
    unscientific propaganda in, 1:227–228
    USSR, 7:157
    Zionism, 1:253
Publish or perish policy, 7:158
Publishing, 6:218
Pullman, Maynard, 6:199
Pulsars
    discovery, 6:306
    measurement, 7:305
    radio astronomy, 3:139
Pulse-doctrine, 3:94–95
Punched Card Methods in Scientific Computation (Eckert), 3:50
Punctuated equilibria, 3:159–160, 161
Punishment, 6:465
Punnett, Reginald Crundall, 1:211
Pupils (eye), Homes-Adie (myotonic), 3:345
PUR. *See* Polyurethane
Purcell, Edward Mills, 6:**178–183**, *181*
    magnetic resonance, 1:306
    Nobel Prize, 1:303
    nuclear magnetic resonance, 3:196, 197
    radio astronomy, 5:345
    radio signals, 1:330
    spectral lines, 7:129
Purcell, J. D., 7:76
The Purifications (Empedocles of Acragas), 2:395, 396
Puritanism, 5:121–122
Purposive Behavior in Animals and Men (Tolman), 2:197
Pusey, Nathan, 5:116
Putnam, Hilary, 6:267
PVA (polyvinyl acetate), 6:333
Pycior, Helena M., 3:236
Pyke, Geoffrey, 6:80
Pyramidographia (Greaves), 3:166
Pyramids, Egyptian, 3:166
Pyrolite, 6:259
Pyrolytic release (PR) experiment, 3:365

Pyrotechny Asserted and Illustrated (Starkey), 6:512
Pyruvate, 5:251–252
Pyruvic acid, 3:168
Pythagorean Elements of Music (Ptolemais), 6:172
Pythagoreans, 1:46, 2:284, 6:172–173

Q

Q-fever, 1:455
Q-sort, 6:276
Qāḍīzāde al-Rūmī, 4:21
QCD (Quantum chromodynamics), 3:194, 5:130–131
QED. *See* Quantum electrodynamics
Qian Xuesen, 7:401
Quadbeck, Günter, 4:169
Quadratic equations, 7:87–88
Quadrature of Parabola (Archimedes), 1:87
Quadrivium (Pachymeres), 6:1–2
Quaestiones circa logicam (Albert of Saxony), 1: 35
Quaestiones naturales (Adelard of Bath), 1:14
*Quaestiones super libros Physicorum, secundum ultimam
    lecturam* (Buridan), 1:447
Quaestiones super libros Physicorum (Albert of Saxony), 1:
    35–36
Quakers. *See* Society of Friends (Quakers)
Qualitative Methods in Quantum Theory (Migdal), 5:131
Quantification, 3:278–279
Quantitative Aspects of the Evolution of Concepts (Hull),
    3:406
Quantitative geomorphology, 3:371–372
Quantitative methods
    oceanography, 6:255–257
    perception, 6:239
    psychology, 6:239
        psychotherapy, 6:275–279
    war theory, 6:240
Quantitative Seismology (Aki), 1:32
*A Quantitative Treatment of Directive Effects in Aromatic
    Substitution* (Brown and Stock), 1:421
Quantitative Zoology (Simpson and Roe), 6:453
Quantum chemistry
    beginning of, 5:211–212
    computers, 6:129–132
    internationalization of, 5:212–214
    molecular structure, 6:37–40
    resonance theory dispute, 5:248
    wave mechanics, 7:104
Quantum chromodynamics (QCD), 3:194, 5:130–131
Quantum electrodynamics (QED)
    absorption, 7:398–399
    Bloch-Nordsieck method, 7:69
    development, 7:263–268
    electromagnetism, 6:336
    electron-positron emissions, 6:393
    electron scattering, 3:*21*, 21–23, *22*

limit of validity, 1:273
particle collisions, 1:428
refinement, 6:196
renormalization, 6:394–395
synchrotrons, 7:70
theorem of corresponding states, 4:335
thermonuclear reactors, 1:428
Quantum Electrodynamics (Schwinger), 6:395
Quantum field theory
    Bogolubov School, 1:318–319
    elementary particles, 1:236
    gauge theory, 6:339–340
    mesons, 6:393
    particle physics, 1:238–239
    quantum electrodynamics, 6:394
    renormalization, 6:394
    source theory, 6:395–396
    superconductivity, 1:318–319
Quantum mechanics
    absorption, 1:410–413
    astrophysics, 6:541, 7:104–108
    atoms, 6:126
    axiomatics, 3:306–307
    black holes, 2:92
    chemistry, 3:196
    Compton effect, 2:107–108
    Copenhagen Interpretation, 1:326–327
    development, 5:200, 6:35, 111–114
    education, 1:178
    educators, 6:192
    electroconductivity, 6:63
    electrodynamic interactions, 3:19
    electron scattering, 3:*21*, 21–23, *22*
    electron theory of metals, 1:303–304
    experimental, 2:378–379
    ferromagnetism, 6:169–170
    field theory, 1:238–241
    group theory, 7:294
    hidden variables, 1:236–243, 322–323
    history of, 4:172
    influence, 7:319
    influential figures, 6:489–491
    Lie groups, 7:277–278
    mathematical technician in, 4:55
    molecular, 5:210, 213–214
    neutron scattering, 6:392–393
    nuclear physics, 1:269
    nuclear structure, 1:391
    plasma physics, 1:321
    quantum tunneling, 2:165–166
    rotational motion, 2:64
    sodium chloride, 6:437
    solid-state physics, 7:295
    of solids, 1:179

space-time influence, 2:365
spectoscopy, 3:298
statistics, 6:134
stereochemistry, 3:400–404
theoretical physics, 1:270–274
time, 6:167
white dwarf configuration, 2:88–89
See also Physics
Quantum Mechanics: New Approaches to Selected Topics (Lipkin), 2:281
Quantum Mechanics (Condon), 2:165
The quantum mechanics of electrons in crystal lattice (Bloch). *See Über die Quantenmechanik der Elektronen in Kristallgittern* (Bloch)
Quantum optics, 2:281
Quantum physics. *See* Quantum mechanics
Quantum Theory (Bohm), 1:322
The Quantum Theory of Solids (Peierls), 6:65
Quarks, 1:319
Quartermain, David, 5:151
Quarton, Gardner, 6:364
Quartz photoelectric spectrometers, 1:234
Quasars
    black holes and, 1:159
    discovery, 3:173, 6:305
    radio astronomy, 3:176
    steady state theory, 6:399
Quasi geostrophy, 6:559
Quasi-thing groups, 3:153
Quasiconformal mappings, 1:21, 22–23, 262
Quaternions, 1:*138,* 138–139, 3:236
Quay, W. B., 1:122
The Question of Animal Awareness: Evolutionary Continuity of Mental Experience (Griffin, 1976), 3:179–180
A Question of Levels (Broadbent), 1:405
Questions on Aristotle's Physics (Buridan), 1:447
Questions on De anima (Oresme), 5:351
Questions on De generatione et corruptione (Buridan), 1:447
Questions on De spera (Oresme), 5:351
Questions on Logic (Albert of Saxony). *See Quaestiones circa logicam* (Albert of Saxony)
Questions on the Physics (Oresme), 5:351, 352
Quételet, Lambert Adolphe Jacques, 2:244, 4:293, 6:55
al-Qūhī, Abū Sahl Wayjan ibn Rustam, 6:**185–187**
Quignet, Michiel. *See* Coignet, Michiel
Quillen, Daniel G.
    category theory, 5:4
    J-homomorphism, 1:12
Quillen, I. James, 3:314
Quincke, Georg Herman, 3:57
Quine, Willard Van Orman, 3:70, 4:284, 6:461
Quinine, 6:157, *157*

Quinniet, Michiel. *See* Coignet, Michiel
Quintic equation, 1:5
Qurra, Abu 'l Hasan Thabit. *See* Ibrāhīm Ibn Sinān Ibn Thābit Ibn Qurra
al-Qūshjī, Alī. *See* Alī al-Qūshjī
Qūshjī, Alī. *See* Alī al-Qūshjī
Quṭb al-Dīn Maḥmūd Ibn Masʿūd Ibn al-Muṣliḥ al-Shīrāzī, 6:**187–189**
Quṭ al-Dī al-Sh]imacr]rāzī. *See* Quṭb al-Dīn Maḥmūd Ibn Masʿūd Ibn al-Muṣliḥ al-Shīrāzī

R

Rabbits, research on, 6:209
Rabelais, François, 6:68
Rabi, Isidor Isaac, 6:179, **191–197,** *193*
    colleagues of, 6:423
    hydrogen bombs, 7:22, 23
    molecular beams, 1:306
    nuclear decay, 7:366
    scientists as officers, 1:134
    students of, 3:173, 6:392, 393, 394, 7:367
Rabin, Michael, 4:36
Rabinovitz, Mordecai, 1:253
Rabjohn, Norman, 3:39
Racah, Giulio, 6:170
Race
    cranial capacity, 3:161
    intelligence and, 2:131–132, 6:441
    school desegregation, 2:131
    species and, 3:431
Race, Intelligence, and Education (Eysenck), 2:430
Race and constitution (Weidenreich). *See Rasse und Körperbau* (Weidenreich)
Race relations. *See* Civil rights
Races: A Study of the Problems of Race Formation in Man (Coon), 2:174
Les races de l'empire francais (Vallois), 7:115
Les races humaines (Vallois), 7:114, 115
The Races of Europe (Ripley), 2:173
Racial Adaptations (Coon), 2:175
Racial classification
    Darwinism, 3:208–209
    ethnic groups, 7:114–115
Racism
    anthropology, 7:158–159
    South Africa, 6:484
Racker, Efraim, 3:172, 4:72, 5:309, 6:**197–203**
Radar
    air defense, 1:291–292
    altitude determination by, 3:389
    countermeasures, 5:114
    meteorology, 6:222
    microwave, 1:164, 6:393–394
    physical chemistry, 6:139–140

Radar, *continued*
    research, 6:438
    simulation, 5:255
    submarine and aircraft, 1:55–56
    weather forecasting, 1:469
    World War II, 6:195–196, 302–303, 532
Radcliffe-Brown, Alfred, 7:236
Radiation
    accelerators and, 4:208
    black body
        black holes, 6:400
        wave theory, 1:411
    cosmic
        astrophysics, 7:120–125
        cloud chambers, 5:301–303
        particle physics, 5:303–304
    cosmic microwave background
        astronomy, 7:393–394
        measurement, 7:303–305
    damping, 7:105
    ecology, 3:414, 5:318–319
    electromagnetic
        Cherenkov effect, 2:107–210
        cosmic rays, 1:40–41
        energetics, 2:320–321
        geometry, 2:370
        gravity, 2:282
    gamma, 2:108–109, 4:209
    genetic effects, 5:241, 242–243
    gravitational
        bending effect, 2:369
        fossil, 2:283–284
        relativity, 1:342
    illness, 6:78
    Lauritsen dosimeter, 4:208, *209*
    microwave, 2:280–281, 6:310–311
    nonthermal, 1:41
    nuclear, 6:41
    photosynthesis, 2:14–15
    solar, 3:79–80
    synchroton, 6:434
    thermal, 2:281, 7:284
    transfer, 2:90
Radiation and the Origin of the Gene (Sagan), 6:310
Radiation belts, Van Allen, 7:122–123
Radiation ecology, 3:414, 5:318–319
Radiative Transfer (Chandrasekhar), 2:90, 91
Radical behaviorism, 6:458–466
The Radical Reformation (Williams), 6:15
Radicati, Luigi, 3:192, 194
Radio astronomy
    antennae, 1:*334*
    Big bang theory, 3:390
    communications and, 5:114

    galaxies and, 5:343–346
    Milky Way spiral arms, 1:330
    National Astronomy and Ionospheric Center, 3:137
    observatories, 1:292, 3:142–143, 174
    pulsars, 3:139
    quasars, 3:176
    radio source studies, 1:333–336, 5:83–84
    radio star discoveries, 1:332
    Ryle, Martin, 6:302–307
    Sagan, Carl Edward, 6:310–314
    SETI project, 5:192–193
    spectral lines, 7:129
    steady state theory, 6:399
    telescopes, 1:331–332
    USSR, 6:432, 433–436
Radio Astronomy (Ryle), 6:303
Radio emissions, 7:127, 128
Radio interferometry
    radio astronomy, 6:302–304
    telescopes, 1:335–336
Radio proximity fuses, 7:119–120
Radio telescopes, 5:83–84
Radio waves
    discovery, 3:291–293
    geophysics, 1:390–391
    World War II, 5:114
Radioactive decay
    hadrons, 3:193
    nuclear isotopes, 1:162–163
    philosophy of science, 6:6
    quantum tunneling, 2:165–166
Radioactive fallout
    measurement of, 1:165
    nuclear weapons, 6:327
Radioactivity
    carbon
        half-life, 4:296–297
        philosophy of science, 6:6
        photosynthesis, 2:14–15
    effects on living tissues, 1:298–302
    elements, 6:75–78
    measurement, 5:326
    technetium, 6:407–408
Radiocarbon dating, 4:295, 296–298
    atmospheric, 5:326–327
    fossils, 5:298, 299
    ice cores, 5:328
Radiochemistry
    carbon-14, 4:295–298
    inorganic chemistry, 7:306, 307–308
    molecular polarity and, 5:168–169
Radioisotope thermoelectric generators, 7:124
Radioisotopes
    catalysis, 1:354

chemistry, 3:210–211
labeling, 1:374
uranium, 6:408
Radiometers, 6:553, 555, 556
Radiosondes, 6:553, 555
Radium, 3:210–211
Radium E, 7:102
Radke, Marian, 3:14
Radon probability, 6:382
Rafter, George W., 3:372
Raikov, Dmitri A., 3:242
Rainbows
    optics, 6:187–188
    refraction and, 1:146–147
Raine, Derek, 6:398
Rainfall patterns, 7:402
Rajaraman, R., 1:239
Die Rakete zu den Planetenräumen (Oberth), 7:173
Rakic, Pasko, 3:146, 147, 148
RaLa method, 6:422
Rall, Wilfrid, 2:330, 331–332
Raman spectrosopy
    benzene, 1:60, 4:15–16
    molecular structures, 5:169
    scientific method, 7:312
Ramaniz, Zenta, 6:318–319
RaMBaM. *See* Maimonides, Rabbi Moses Ben Maimon
Rambam. *See* Maimonides, Rabbi Moses Ben Maimon
Ramensky, Leonid Grigorievitch, 1:387
Ramism, 6:205, 206–207
Ramón y Cajal, Santiago, 1:437
Ramond, Pierre, 6:171
Ramsay, Robert, 7:220
Ramsey, Frank Plumpton, 2:405, 6:**203–205**, 7:6
Ramsey, Norman F., Jr., 1:164, 3:197, 6:169, 194, 7:330
Ramsey's principle, 6:204
Ramus, Peter, 6:**205–207**, *206*
Ramus and Talon Inventory (Ong), 6:205, 206
Rana pipiens. See Frogs
RAND Corporation
    game theory, 5:228
    Newell, Allen at, 5:254–255
Randall, Harrison M., 4:6
Randall, John Herman, 1:55, 3:67, 7:389
Randall, John Turton, 3:65–66, 7:298
Randers, Gunnar, 6:384
Randolph, Lowell Fitz, 5:68
Random drift, genetic
    neutral theory, 4:116
    population genetics, 3:29–30
Randomization, 3:251, 6:382
Raney nicke reductions, 7:146, *147*
Ranger Program, 6:444
Rango, Albert, 6:8

Ranke, Leopold von, 6:354
Rankine, Alexander Oliver, 6:140
Rankine, William John Macquorn, 1:27
Ranson, S. W., 3:304
Rao, B. C. Subba, 1:422
Rapkine, Louis, 2:398, 5:236
Rapoport, Anatol, 3:231, 232
Ras-el Kelb (Lebanon), 3:106
Rashevsky, Nicolas, 5:78
Rasse und Körperbau (Weidenreich), 7:250
Ratcliffe, Francis Noble, 6:**207–211**
Ratdolt, Erhard, 6:218
Rath, Istvan, 6:572
Ratificationism, 4:35–36
Ratiometric polarity timescale, 3:375, 376–377
Rational bargaining
    cooperative games, 3:249–250
    decision making and, 5:225–226
    Nash equilibrium and, 5:227
Rational Behavior and Bargaining Equilibrium in Games and Social Situations (Harsanyi), 3:252
Rational choice theory, 3:227, 231–232, 4:35
Rational decision making, 5:286–287
Rationalists (medicine). *See* Dogmatists (medicine)
Rationality, Bayesian, 3:248–249, 250
Rats, research on, 5:148, *148*, 6:244–246
Rattlesnakes, 1:436
Ratzel, Friedrich, 1:207, 7:209, 210
Rau, Hans, 3:300
Raup, David, 3:160
Der Raupen wunderbare Verwandlung und sonderbare (Merian), 5:119
Ravens, 3:294–296, *295*
Rawls, John
    bargaining, 3:249
    criticisms of, 5:286
    theory of justice, 5:337
Ray, John
    influence of, 7:221
    influences on, 4:65
Rayleigh, Lord. *See* Strutt, John William, third Baron Rayleigh
Rayleigh, Third Baron. *See* Strutt, John William, Third Baron Rayleigh; Strutt, John William, third Baron Rayleigh
Rayon, 5:28, 30
Rayonnement noir et quanta de lumiére (Broglie), 1:411
al-Rāzī, Abū Bakr Muḥammad Ibn Zakariyyāʾ, 6:**211–216**, 291
al-Rāzī, Abū Ḥātim, 6:212, 213, 214
Reaction formation, 5:146, *146*
Reactions, chemical. *See* Chemical reactions
Das Reafferenzprinzip (von Holst and Mittelstaedt), 7:183

Reagan, Ronald, 1:80
   nuclear weapons, 6:315, 7:24
   strategic defense initiative, 1:275
   White House Science Council, 1:182
Real Algebraic Manifolds (Nash), 5:229
Real numbers, 2:30–31
Reappraising Oppenheimer (Carson and Hollinger), 5:349
Reason-based choice, 7:95
Reason Enough to Hope (Morrison), 5:191
Reasoning
   experimental psychology, 3:406
   knowledge, 3:421
   Pavlovian conditioning, 3:407
Rebel with a Cause (Eysenck), 2:429
Reber, Grote, 1:333, 5:345, 7:127
Recent Advances in Cytology (Darlington), 2:59
Recent Advances in the Chemistry and Biology of Sea Water
   (Harvey), 3:259
Recherche (Piaget), 6:92
Recherches sur de grands Sauriens (Geoffroy Saint-Hilaire,
   Étienne), 3:118–119
Recherches sur différens points importans du systême du
   monde (d'Alembert), 2:231, 232
Recherches sur la théorie des quanta (Broglie), 1:410–413
Recherches sur les fonctions elliptiques (Abel), 1:6
Das Recht auf Gesundheit (Abderhalden), 1:3
Reck, Hans, 4:222
Recollection, testimony, and lying in early childhood (Stern
   and Stern). *See Erinnerung, Aussage, und Lüge in der*
   ersten Kindheit (Stern and Stern)
Reconceiving the Gene (Holmes), 5:185
A Reconsideration of the Harsanyi-Sen Debate on
   Utilitarianism (Weymark), 3:249
Reconstitution, liposomes, 6:200
Reconstitutions of Transporters, Receptors and Pathological
   States (Racker), 6:200
Rectifiers, 6:375–376, 393–394
Red-necked pharalopes, 7:50
Redi, Francesco, 4:134
Redondi, Pietro, 3:98, 100
Redshifts, 5:81, 6:456
The Reduction Potentials of Cysteine, Glutathione, and
   Glycylcysteine (Green), 3:167
Reductionism
   behaviorism, 6:465–466
   genetics, 6:492, 494
   See also Antireductionism (biology)
Reed, Thomas B., 2:161
Rees, Abraham, 3:7
Rees, Graham, 1:137
Rees, Lloyd, 7:231
Rees, Martin, 6:399–400
Rees, Mina, 7:292
Rees-Sciama effect, 6:400

Referat, oder gründliche Beschreibung was in dem Kunst-
   undt Werckhauss àgethan und operirt wirdt (Becher),
   1:231
Reflection
   equal-angle rule, 3:284
   refraction and, 1:146
Reflections on Progress, Peaceful Coexistence and
   Intellectual Freedom (Sakharov), 6:327
Reflections on the Decline of Science (Babbage), 1:127
Reflective equilibrium, 3:151–152
Reflex Activity of the Spinal Cord (Creed), 2:329
Reflexes, 6:459
Réflexions sur la cause générale des vents (d'Alembert),
   2:229, 230
Refocusing method, 6:194
Refraction, 1:295
   atmospheric, 5:352
   conical, 3:236
   reflection and, 1:146
Refraction telescopes
   cost of construction, 3:290–291
   Doppler effect, 1:295
   nebulae, 3:286–287
Refutation of all Heresies (Hippolytus), 1:87
Regener, Erich Rudolph Alexander, 4:178
Regimen (Hippocrates), 3:323
Regiomontanus, Johannes, 2:177, 178, 6:**216–219,** *218*
Regius, Henricus, 3:158
Regulae Solvendi Sophismatum (Heytesbury), 2:325
Regulation, physiological. *See* Physiological regulation
Regulation of respiration (Hess). *See Die Regulierung der*
   Atmung, gleichzeitig ein Beitrag zur Physiologie des
   vegetativen Nervensystems (Hess)
Regulation of the circulatory system (Hess). *See Die*
   Regulierung des Blutkreislaufs, gleichzeitig ein Beitrag
   zur Physiologie des vegetativen Nervensystems (Hess)
Regule Solvendi Sophismatum (Heytesbury), 6:562
Die Regulierung der Atmung, gleichzeitig ein Beitrag zur
   Physiologie des vegetativen Nervensystems (Hess), 3:304
Die Regulierung des Blutkreislaufs, gleichzeitig ein Beitrag
   zur Physiologie des vegetativen Nervensystems (Hess),
   3:304
Die Rehobother Bastards (Fischer), 3:26
Reichelderfer, Francis Wilton, 5:222, 6:**219–223,** *222,*
   470, 471
Reichenbach, Hans, 2:43
   clinical practice criticism, 5:92
   logical empiricism, 4:279
Reichstein, Tadeus, 6:**223–228,** *226*
Reid, Dwight Logan, 6:401
Reik, Thomas, 5:92
Reill, Peter, 1:433
Reilly, Edith, 1:328, 330
Reinforcement (psychology), 3:409, 6:463, *465*

Reinganum, Maximilian, 1:299

Reinke, Johannes, 6:389

Reisen in der Regentschaft Algier in den Jahren (Wagner), 7:209

Reisfeld, Renata, 4:60

Relationship-therapy, 6:275

Relationships, 1:185

Relative dating, 5:296–299

The Relative Value of the Processes Causing Evolution (Hagedoorn), 3:30

Relativistic astrophysics, 2:91–92

Relativistic sociology, 2:23–24

Relativity

    abstract conceptions in, 3:400

    dynamic, 1:425

    general, 1:425

        astrophysics, 1:340

        covariant, 3:307–308

        geometry, 7:278

        hadrons, 3:194

        influential figures, 2:338–339, 367, 6:34, 122, 397, 399

        Mach's principle, 6:398

        radiation, 1:342

        stellar dynamics, 3:274–275

        tensor calculus, 3:190

    Kantian philosophy, 3:131

    mathematical logic, 3:130

    special, 2:365–367

    theory of

        1919 eclipse expedition, 2:338–339

        affine connection, 2:367–369

        astrophysics, 2:91–92

        cosmology and, 5:83–84, 6:456–458

        development, 6:122–123

        gravitational forces, 2:282

        Lichnérowicz, André, 4:300

        quantum mechanics, 3:24–25

Relativity, Thermodynamics and Cosmology (Tolman), 6:169

Relativity and Common Sense (Bondi), 1:342

A Relevant War against Poverty (Clark), 2:134

Religion and science, 6:295–296, 7:57

    anti-Aristotelianism, 1:204–205

    Aristotelian physics and, 5:7

    Catholicism, 1:38, 39

    Christian alchemy, 7:334

    client-centered psychology, 6:278

    conservation, 7:44

    Copernicanism, 3:101

    cosmology, 3:113, 6:15–16

    creationism, 3:162–163

    dualism, 3:214–215

    embryology, 3:216

    ethics, 3:432

    ethnography, 4:251–252

    evolution, 4:224–225, 5:355, 7:63

    geology, 7:280–281

    impact of experiences, 4:22–23

    intelligence, 5:6–7, 6:92

    Islam, 6:213–215

    Judaism, 6:191

    logic and natural philosophy, 5:312–313

    mathematics and, 1:20, 21, 2:33–34

    McCrea, William Hunter on, 5:75

    medical philosophy, 5:8–9

    molecular beams, 6:193

    moral psychology, 2:57–58

    natural history, 1:369

    neuropsychology, 3:430

    nuclear weapons, 6:328–329

    personality psychology, 1:53

    population dynamics, 5:13–14

    positivist, 2:340

    psychoanalysis, 2:410

    Ramism, 6:206–207

    Renaissance medicine, 6:551

    Sandemanian sect, 3:3–4

    skepticism, 6:309

    social gospel, 6:275

    Society of Friends, 7:42

    sociological aspects, 5:121–122

    Telesian philosophy, 2:19–20

    utilitarianism, 7:282

Religious systems

    environment and, 1:207

    geohistory, 3:421–422

    logic and natural philosophy, 5:312–313

    science and, 6:359

Rellich, Franz, 5:197

Remarks on the study of plant groups (Braun-Blanquet and Furrer). *See Remarques sur l'Étude des groupements de plantes* (Braun-Blanquet and Furrer)

Remarques sur l'Étude des groupements de plantes (Braun-Blanquet and Furrer), 1:387

Remembering: A Study in Experimental and Social Psychology (Bartlett), 1:185–186, 188

Renormalization, 6:336, 394–395

Rensch, Bernhard, 5:62, 63

Renshaw, Birdsey, 2:331

Repeated reproduction, 1:186

Report of Norwegian Methods of Weather Analysis (Reichelderfer), 6:220

Report on the Relativity Theory of Gravitation (Eddington), 6:456

Reppe, Julius Walter, 6:**228–234**

Reppe, Walter. *See* Reppe, Julius Walter

Reppe chemistry, 6:230, 231, 232–233

Reproduction
 bacterial, 7:14–15
 plant, 6:356–358
 repeated, 1:186
 serial, 1:186
 sexual, 3:232–233
Reptiles, 4:232
Research misconduct
 oxidative phosphorylation, 6:201
 Wenner-Gren Foundation, 7:35
Researches on the quantum theory (Broglie). *See Recherches sur la théorie des quanta* (Broglie)
Resonance, electron spin, 3:155
Resonance theory
 atmospheric tides, 3:264
 opposition to, 5:248
Respiratory system, 3:304, 4:216
Responsibility, social, 1:293
Retherford, Robert, 1:275, 6:394
Retina, 7:212–213
Retinal, 7:212–215
Rettenmeyer, C. W., 6:367
Reutov, Oleg A., 5:248
Revelle, Roger Randall Dougan, 2:262, 4:91, *92*, 5:326, 6:**234–237**, *235*
Reversals, geomagnetic, 3:375–377
Reviews of Modern Physics 1936-1937, 1:271
The Revision of the Rapid Transit Fare Structure of the City of New York (Vickery), 7:151
Reymond, Arnold, 6:92
Reynafarje, Baltazar, 4:240
Réyni, Alfréd, 2:405–406
Reynolds, Osborne, 6:342
Reynolds, Richard J., 5:321
Rhabdas, Nicolas, 1:99
Rham, Georges de, 6:381–382
Rhazes. *See* al-Rāzī, Abū Bakr Muḥammad Ibn Zakariyyāʾ
Rhetorica (Ramus), 6:206
Rhetorius of Alexandria, 7:112
Rhoades, Marcus, 6:317
Rhodes, Cecil, 6:484
Rhodin, Johannes, 5:283
Rhodium, 7:310–311, *311*
Rhodopsin, 7:212–215
Ribonuclease, 1:78–80
Ribonucleic acid. *See* RNA
Ribot, Théodule, 4:25, 27, 5:92
Ricci, Matteo, 2:151
Ricci-Curbastro, Gregorio, 3:192
Ricci tensor, 2:368–369
Rich, Alexander, 4:137, 138, 6:319
Richard, John H., 3:339–340
Richard de Bury. *See* Bury, Richard de

Richard Rufus de Cornubia. *See* Rufus of Cornwall, Richard
Richardo, David, 7:281
Richards, Evelleen, 3:431
Richards, Henry Caselli, 3:316
Richards, Martin, 6:534
Richards, Paul, 1:32, 7:304
Richards, Robert J., 2:243, 246, 247
Richardson, Lewis Fry, 6:**238–241,** 470, 471
 Forsythe, George Elmer, 3:50
 hydrodynamics, 2:100
 influences on, 4:193
 surface pressure, 2:425
Richardson, Michael K., 3:208
Richardson, Olaf, 4:193
Richardson, Robert S., 6:386–387
Richardson number, 6:239
Richmond, Marsha, 1:211
Richter, Burton, 1:428
Richter, Charles Francis, 1:31, 243, 6:**241–243,** *242,* 7:200
Richter, Curt P., 6:**243–248**
Richter, Emma Hüther, 6:248
Richter, Friedrich, 6:160
Richter, Rudolf, 6:**248–250**
Richter scale, 6:242, 243
Richthofen, Ferdinand Freiherr von, 7:209
Rickettsial diseases, 1:455
Rickover, Hyman, 7:296
Riddel, Robert J., 7:102
Riddle of the Universe (Haeckel). *See Die Welträthsel* (Haeckel)
Rideal, Eric Keightley, 1:312, 5:32
Rideout, Janet, 2:375
Rieck, Gerard, 1:282
Riecken, Henry, 3:15
Rieff, Philip, 3:76
Riehl, Alois, 4:278
Riemann, Bernhard, 2:115, 4:300
Riemann, Georg Friedrich Bernhard, 5:229, 6:**250–254,** *252*
Riemann curvature tensor, 2:368–369
Riemann hypothesis, 6:253
Riemann-Roch theorem, 1:346, 4:144–145
Riemann surface theory, 1:262
 complex manifolds, 4:145
 curves, 7:257
 geometry, 7:254–255
 quasiconformal mappings, 1:22–23
Riemannian manifolds, 5:229
Riemann's mapping theorem for variable metrics (Bers and Ahlfors), 1:262
Riemann's probelm of moduli, 1:262
Riese, W., 2:342

Riesen, Austin, 3:269
The Riffian (Coon), 2:173
Rijkens, Paul, 1:313
Riker, William Harrison, 6:**254–255**
Riley, Gordon Arthur, 3:411, 412, 6:**255–258**
Rilpivirine, 4:33
Rimini, Alberto, 1:241
The Ring of Truth (Morrison), 5:193
Ringwood, Alfred Edward, 6:**258–262**
Ringwood, Ted. *See* Ringwood, Alfred Edward
Ringwoodite, 6:259
Rinia, Herre, 1:313
Rinke, Heinrich, 1:216
Ríos, Joseph de Mendoza, 4:201
Ripley, George, 4:348
Ripley, S. Dillon, 7:289
Ripley, William Z., 2:173
Ris, Hans, 6:319
al-Risāla al-Muhammadiyya fī al-hisāb (Alī al-Qūshjī), 1:46
Risāla dar ïlm al-hay' a (Alī al-Qūshjī), 1:47
Risāla dar ïlm al-hay' āb (Ali al-Qūshjī), 1:46, 47
Risāla fī al-baras (Qut al-Dīn), 6:188
Risāla fī asl al-khārokī yumkinu fī al-sufliyayn (Alī al-Qūshjī), 1:47
Risāla fī bayān al-hāja ila al-tibb (Qut al-Dīn), 6:188
Risāla fī harakat al-dahraja wa-' l-nisba bayn al-mustawī wa-' l-munhanī (Qutb al-Dīn), 6:188
The Rise and Decline of Nations: Economic Growth, Stagflation, and Social Rigidities (Olson), 5:337
The Rise and Fall of T. D. Lysenko (Lerner), 4:277
Risk
    bargaining, 3:249–250
    sure-thing principle, 6:350–351
Risler, Helmut, 7:259
Risperdal, 4:32
Risposta Allegorico Romanzesca (Arduino), 1:94, 95
Ritanserin, 4:32
Rittmann, Alfred Ferdinand, 6:**262–264**
Rittmann, Alfredo. *See* Rittmann, Alfred Ferdinand
Rittmann norm, 6:263
Ritz, Walther, 7:165
Rivadavia, Bernardino, 4:202
River Discharge (Hoyt and Grover), 3:374
Rivers, sediment transport, 1:156
Rivers, W. H. R., 1:184, 185
Rivett, Alvert Cherbury David, 6:208
RNA, 7:67
    cytology, 2:68–70
    DNA, and protein relationships, 1:373–375, *374*
    DNA and protein relationships, 1:*373*
    genetic code and, 5:309–309
    messenger, 1:370, 375–376, 5:310
    origin of life, 5:157

protein synthesis, 2:209–210
    structure, 1:78–80
    transfer, 3:340, 341–343
RNA polymerase, 5:363–364
The Road since Structure (Kuhn), 4:174
The Road to Trinity (Nichols), 1:134
Road use studies, 7:151
Roanoke Settlement, 3:246
Roazen, Paul, 3:73
Robbins, Phillips, 4:257
Robert Grosseteste and the Origins of Modern Science (Crombie), 1:142–143
Robert of Lincoln. *See* Grosseteste, Robert
Robert the Englishman, 6:154
Roberts, John D., 7:338
Roberts, Walter Orr, 5:113, 116
Robertson, E. I., 3:376
Robertson, Howard P., 3:274–275, 5:73
Robertson, James D., 6:362
Robertson, John Monteath
    isomorphic replacement method, 1:282
    phytochemical structure study, 1:198
    plant pigments, 3:334
    SWAC computer, 3:337
Robertus Anglicus. *See* Robert the Englishman
Robeson, Paul, 5:215
Robinson, Arthur, 6:42
Robinson, Forrest, 5:216, 218
Robinson, Gloria, 7:259
Robinson, John, 7:188
Robinson, Julia Bowman, 6:**265–268**
Robinson, Nancy, 2:54
Robinson, Robert, 2:276, 4:14, 6:**268–274,** *273*
    aromatic compounds, 5:290
    cortisone, 7:350
    Fourier synthesis, 1:283
    penicillin, 3:336, 7:353
    plant pigments, 7:64–65
    Robinson-Ingold formulation, 3:87
    scientists recruited by, 1:251
    strychnine, 6:157
    students of, 7:144
    x-ray diffraction, 3:335
Robit, Théodule, 1:169
Robotics, space, 5:262–263
Roch, Gustav, 4:145
Roche, A., 3:376
Rochester, George, 1:291
Rochester, Nathaniel, 6:427
Rock cycle, 3:*419*, 419–420
Rocke, Alan J., 1:268, 466, 4:98, 99, 312
Rocketry
    dynamics, 4:101–103
    early research, 5:259–260

Rocketry, *continued*
  influential figures, 7:173–176
  World War II, 6:99
Rocks, 4:156–157, 6:467–468
Rocks of Ages (Gould), 3:163
Roe, Anne, 6:453
Roger, Jacques, 1:431, 433, 434
Rogers, Carl Ransom, 6:**274–280**, *275*, 464
Rogers, Harry S., 5:31
Roginskiĭ, S. Z., 6:416
The Role of Infiltration in the Hydrologic Cycle (Horton), 3:373
Roll, Peter Guy, 2:283, 7:303
Roman, Nancy, 1:160
Roman Catholicism. *See* Catholicism
Romanes, George John, 7:261
Romani Collegii Societatis Jesu Musaeum celeberrimum (de Sepi), 4:134
Romanticism, English, 2:250
Romer, Robert, 2:281
Rommer, Richard, 6:341
Rommevaux, Sabine, 2:149
Röntgen-analyse van kristallen (Kolkmeijer et al.), 1:281
Roosevelt, Franklin D., 6:65, 81, 421, 574
Rosarius philosophorum (Arnald of Villanova, Pseudo), 1:109, 110, 6:517
Roscoe, Henry Enfield, 1:440
Rose, E. L., 4:291
Rose, Hugh James, 7:280
Rose, Paul Lawrence, 5:177
Rosen, Nathan, 1:240–241, 323, 325, 326–327
Rosen, Peter, 6:170, 171
Rosen, Saul, 2:296
Rosenberg, Milton, 1:9
Rosenblatt, Frank, 5:78
Rosenblatt, Jay, 4:245, 6:368
Rosenbloom, Paul, 5:258
Rosenblueth, Arturo, 5:78
Rosenblum, Salomon, 6:6
Rosenwald, Julius, 4:66
Ross, Mary. *See* Bell, Mary Ross
Ross, Perley, 6:437
Ross, Stephen, 3:63
Rossby, Carl-Gustaf Arvid
  influence of, 6:560
  large-scale atmospheric waves, 2:99–100
  as mentor, 5:221–222
  meteorology, 6:4, 220, 470
  physical oceanography, 2:266
  planetary waves, 3:263
  students of, 7:273
  weather forecasting, 1:468
Rossby-Haurwitz waves, 3:263
Rosseland, Svein, 6:383

Rossi, Bruno Benedetto, 3:80, 6:**280–285**, *281*
  colleagues of, 5:302, 304, 7:400, 401
  cosmic rays, 1:55, 5:301
  Geiger-Müller counters, 1:291, 5:301
  nuclear physics research, 1:61
Rossi, Carlo, 4:240, 241
Rossiter, Margaret, 5:183
Rota, Gian-Carlo, 6:**285–287**
Rotational motion
  Brownian, 7:101
  nuclear and electron spins, 2:64
  vibration, 4:6–7
Rotenone, 1:459–460
Rothe, Edward W., 1:258
Rottenstreich, Yuval, 7:95
Rouelle, Guillaume François, 4:213, 218, 6:506–507
Rounding Errors in Algebraic Processes (Wilkinson), 7:316, 317
Rous, Peyton, 3:328
Rousseau, Jean-Jacques, 4:316
Routh, Edward John, 4:39
Roux, Wilhelm, 4:44
  colleagues of, 3:217, 302–303
  experimental embryology, 3:370
  organizer effect, 5:17
Royal Institution, 6:140–142
Royal Nautical Almanac (Babbage), 1:127, 129
Royal Society, 5:234
Royer, Clémence-Auguste, 6:**287–289**
Rozličná lékařství (Prachaticz), 6:153
Rozynov, Boris, 5:363
Rubber, synthetic
  butadiene, 3:383
  ethynylation reaction, 6:230–231
  isoprene, 1:251
  Soviet, 7:396
Rübel, Eduard, 1:387
Ruben, Samuel, 4:296–297
Rubey, William W., 3:397
Rubinskaya, Margarita I., 5:246
Rubinstein, Ariel, 5:227
Rudge, David, 4:110
Rudolph, Hartmut, 6:15
Rudolphine Tables (Kepler), 4:107
Rudwick, Martin, 2:243, 3:422
Rufus of Cornwall. *See* Rufus of Cornwall, Richard
Rufus of Cornwall, Richard, 1:143, 6:**292–298**
Rufus of Ephesus, 6:**290–292**
Rule, Bruce, 1:335–336
Rule of Petosiris, 7:112
Rules for Solving Sophismata (Heytesbury). *See Regule Solvendi Sophismatum* (Heytesbury)
Rumelhart, David E., 1:405

Runcorn, Stanley Keith, 1:292, 2:191, 3:376, 6:**298–302**
Rundles, Wayne, 2:375
Runge, Friedlieb Ferdinand, 5:40
Runnegar, Bruce, 3:318
Runnström, John, 3:366, 368, 370
Runyan, William McKinley, 5:219
Rupp, Hans, 4:280
Ruse, Michael, 2:242, 243, 244
Ibn Rushd, Abu'l-Walīd Muḥammad ibn Aḥmad ibn Muḥammad
    Buonamici, Francesco, 1:442
    influence on, 6:292
    Rufus of Cornwall, Richard, 6:294–295, 295
Rusinov, Lev I., 3:33
Ruskin, John, 2:289
Ruskin, Steven, 3:288
Russell, Barbara, 7:232
Russell, Bertrand Arthur William, 2:29
    influence of, 4:117
    logic, 2:43
    Logic Theorist, 5:256
    logicism, 3:71
    Moral Sciences Club, 1:184
    Popper, Karl Raimund, 6:134
    on power, 2:135
Russell, Charles, 1:178
Russell, Frederick Stratten, 3:259
Russell, Henry Norris, 7:105
    acquaintances of, 2:344
    astrophysics, 6:50
    colleagues of, 3:389, 6:501
    stellar evolution, 6:385–386, 499, 542
    students of, 5:111, 112
Russia
    antisemitism, 6:224
    hydrogen bombs, 6:196
    professionalization of chemistry, 1:466–467
Rutherford, Ernest, 1:55, 6:79, 103
    astrophysics, 6:49
    atomic physics, 5:200
    Cavendish Laboratory, 1:163, 5:301
    cloud chambers, 1:290
    influence of, 4:80, 83, 7:320
Rutten, Martin G., 3:375
Rutter, William, 3:188
Ruzicka, Leopold, 6:*155,* 156, 158, 225, 226
Ryan, Francis, 6:318, 319, 320
Ryle, Gilbert, 6:463
Ryle, Martin, 3:137, 390, 6:**302–307,** *305*
Ryle telescope, 6:306

S
Sa Bentie. *See* Sah, Adam Pen-tung

Sabatier, Paul, 2:394, 6:92
Sabatini, David, 6:147
Sachs, Hans, 1:358, 2:408
Sachs, Julius von, 4:314, 6:390
Sachse, Hermann, 1:197
Sacks, Oliver, 7:195
Sacro Bosco, Johannes de, 1:296, 445
Sacrobosco, Johannes de. *See* Sacro Bosco, Johannes de
Safety
    aviation, 3:83–84
    lamps, 2:24, 252
Saffrey, H. D., 6:517
Sagan, Carl Edward, 4:179, 181, 6:**309–316,** *311*
    colleagues of, 6:435
    extraterrestrial life, 6:432
    influences on, 5:157
    on Shoemaker, Eugene Merle, 6:446
Sagan, Linda, 6:313
Sager, Ruth, 6:**316–321,** *317*
Saggi sulla Cultura della Compagnia di Gesù (Baldini), 2:150
Saggio Fisico-Mineralogico di Lythogonia e Orognosia (Arduino), 1:93, 94
Sah, Adam Pen-tung, 6:321–322
Sah, Peter P. T., 6:**321–324**
Saha, Meghnad, 5:111, 6:49
Sahara: Histoired de l'Art Rupestre Libyen (Jelínek), 4:42
Saʻīd, Abū, 2:305–306
Saika, Apollo, 3:197, 198, 199
St. John, Charles Edward, 7:105
St. Venant's principle, 5:335
Sakharov, Andrei Dmitrievich. *See* Sakharov, Andrei Dmitriyevich
Sakharov, Andrei Dmitriyevich, 4:85, 6:**324–330,** *328*
    acquaintances of, 6:433, 435
    criticism of Soviet human rights violations, 1:430
    dissertation defense, 5:128
Sakurada, Ichiro, 6:**330–335,** *331*
Sakurai, Jōji, 5:167
Salam, Muhammad Abdus, 6:**335–341,** *336*
    electromagnetic interactions, 3:193
    electroweak theory, 6:396
Salamanders, developmental genetics, 1:399–400, 4:77–78
Salicylic acid, 4:150
Salisbury, Rollin, 2:186, 187
Salk, Jonas, 2:210, 3:187
Salmon, 3:260–261, 6:480
Salmons, Josephine, 2:238
Salpeter, Edwin E., 1:159, 342
Saltpeter, 1:264
Salts
    atomism, 7:344
    classification, 2:218

Salts, *continued*
   microscopy, 3:110–111
Saltzman, Barry, 6:**341–346**
Salzano, Francisco, 5:243–244
Salzman, Linda. *See* Sagan, Linda
Samascius, 3:435
Samelson, Klaus, 2:296
Sample size fallacy, 7:94
Samuel, Arthur, 5:255
Samuel ben Judah Ibn Tibbon. *See* Ibn Tibbon, Samuel
   ben Judah
Samuel, Pierre, 1:364
Samuelson, Paul, 5:336
Sand, drifting, in Australia, 6:208–209
A Sand County Almanac (Leopold), 4:270
Sand dunes, 1:155–156
Sand-reckoner (Archimedes), 1:85, 87
Sandage, Allan Rex, 6:386
Sandemanian community, 3:3–4
Sanderson, Frederick W., 5:236
Sanger, Frederick, 1:78
   gene sequencing, 6:480
   insulin, 3:338
   molecular biology, 6:83
   protein sequencing, 2:348, 349
Sanitation and sewage
   cholera epidemic and, 4:54, 5:20
   eutrophication, 2:355
   water, 3:63
Sanjivi, Krishnasami, 7:144, 145
Sapogenins, 5:288–289
Sapp, Jan, 5:69, 100, 6:389
Sapropels, 7:396, 397
Sarasin, Fritz, 7:261
Sarcoma, 3:220–221, *222*
Sargent, Percy, 3:346
Sarmiento, Domingo, 1:452
Sarton, George Alfred Léon, 4:171, 5:121–122, 7:402
Satellites
   artificial
      communications, 1:331
      cosmic rays, 7:122–123
      development, 7:173, 174–175
      meteorology, 6:554–557
      scientific, 5:260–261
      space exploration, 6:100–101
      Sputnik, 4:180, 6:182
      United States, 6:222
   moon, 3:80–81
   Smithsonian Astrophysical Observatory, 7:287–288
Satir, Peter, 6:146
Sato, Tohru, 1:87
Sattath, Shmuel, 7:93
Saturn, 4:177

Sauer, Carl, 7:38, 39
Saunders, Edith Rebecca, 1:211
Saunders, Percy, 6:461
Saussure, Horace Bénédict de, 6:**346–349**, *348*
Savage, Leonard James, 4:35, 6:**349–351**
Savage, Leonard Jimmie. *See* Savage, Leonard James
Savanna grasses, 6:483
Savile, Henry, 3:165
Saving, economics, 6:203
Sax, Karl, 6:514
Saxon, David, 6:394
Sayings of Hermes and the Philosophers (Olympiodorus,
   the Younger, of Alexandria), 5:338
Sayre, Anne, 3:66
Scablands, 1:393–395, *395*
Scaliger, Julius Caesar, 2:38, 3:157, 6:418
Scarsi, Livio, 7:130
Scattering, anomalous, 1:283–284
Sceptical Chymist (Boyle), 1:367, 6:419, 505
Schaaffhausen, Hermann, 3:156
Schaarschmidt, Alfred, 3:86
Schachter, Stanley, 3:15
Schaefer, H., 2:330
Schaefer, Vincent Julius, 1:469–470
Schaeffer, Howard, 2:376
Schaerf, Carlo, 1:63
Schäfer, Edward Albert, 4:143
Schalén, Dozent Carl, 2:344, 7:128
Schall, Johann Adam, 2:151
Schaller, George, 3:53, 54, 55, 56
Schally, Andrew, 3:44
Schank, Roger, 1:9
Schatz, Albert, 3:43
Schatzman, Evry, 1:278
Schauder, Julius, 4:273
Schedules of Reinforcement (Skinner and Ferster), 6:463
Scheele, Carl Wilhelm, 6:507
Scheffers, Georg, 4:309
Scheidegger, Adrian E., 7:324
Scheiner, Christopher, 1:105
Schelling, Frederick Wilhelm Joseph. *See* Schelling,
   Friedrich von
Schelling, Friedrich von, 2:413, 5:331
Schelling, Thomas, 4:284
Schemata, 1:186
Scheme theory, 2:64, 292
Schepers, Gerrit Willem Hendrik, 2:240
Scheraga, Harold, 3:39
Schering AG, 1:460–461, 462
Scherzer, Karl, 7:209
Scheuer, Peter, 6:304, 305
Scheutz, Edvard, 1:128
Scheutz, Georg, 1:128
Schild, Heinz, 1:216

Schiller, Friedrich von, 4:64
Schilt, Jan, 6:383–384
Schindewolf, Otto Heinrich, 6:**351–356**
Schipperges, Heinrich, 5:331
Schistus, 3:*419,* 419–420
Schizophrenia, 3:147, 5:91–92
Schlack, Paul, 1:217
Schlagdenhauffen, Charles-Frederic, 3:272
Schleicher, August, 3:208, 209
Schleiden, Jacob Mathias. *See* Schleiden, Mathias Jacob
Schleiden, Mathias Jacob, 6:24, **356–360,** *358*
    embryology and cell theory, 5:331
    influence of, 6:389
Schlenk, Wilhelm, 1:250–251, 5:28
Schlesinger, Frank
    assistants to, 5:341
    colleagues of, 6:500
Schlesinger, Hermann I., 1:419, 421
Schlick, Moritz, 2:43
Schlosser, F. C., 5:165
Schlosser, Manfred, 7:340
Schmidt, Bernhard Voldemar, 3:276
Schmidt, Karl Patterson, 2:389, 390
Schmidt, Maarten, 7:272
    quasars, 1:159, 3:176
    spectral lines, 7:129
Schmidt telescopes, 3:276
Schmit, Rudolf, 4:149
Schmithals, Friedemann, 5:357
Schmitt, Charles B., 1:104, 105, 361, 7:388
Schmitt, Francis Otto, 4:88, 6:**360–366,** 361
Schmitt, Harrison, 5:263
Schneider, Walter, 2:145, 4:239
Schneirla, Theodore Christian, 4:243, 244, 247, 6:**366–370,** *368*
Schobinger, Bartholomäus, 6:551
Schoenfeld, Nat, 6:463
Schoenheimer, Rudolf, 2:94
Scholander, P. F., 5:328
Schöllkopf, Ulrich, 7:337, 340
Scholten, Carel, 2:295
Scholten, Jos, 1:313
Scholz, Allan T., 3:261
Scholz, Heinrich, 3:69
Schönberg, Mario, 6:385
Schools. *See* education
Schoone, Jean C., 1:283
Schopenhauer, Arthur, 4:64
Schopf, Thomas, 3:160
Schorr, Richard, 3:276
Schorske, Carl, 3:74
Schott, Kaspar, 4:133
Schott, Paul Gerhard, 6:**370–373**
Schott, Wolfgang, 6:372

Schottky, Walter Hans, 1:311, 5:202, 6:**373–378,** *374*
Schouw, Joakim Frederik, 1:386, 388
Schrader, Gerhard, 1:218
Schramm, Gerhard, 1:374
Schreyer, Helmut, 7:409, 410
Schrieffer, John Robert, 1:178, 181, 182, 318, 5:129
Schröder, Friedrich Wilhelm Karl Ernst, 3:70
Schrödinger, Erwin, 1:65, 2:88, 7:100
    acquaintances of, 6:134
    continuous matter waves, 1:413
    electrons, 1:410, 6:37
    influence of, 7:298
    influences on, 2:268
    nomination of scientists for Nobel Prizes by, 1:302
    orbitals, 3:87
    quantum mechanics, 1:412, 5:200, 7:319
    spinors, 4:301
    students of, 3:298
    wave mechanics, 1:270, 303, 409, 6:62, 7:104
Schrödinger equation, 1:241
Schrot effect, 6:375
Schtern, Lin. *See* Shtern, Lina Solomonovna
Schuchert, Charles, 5:265
Schücking, Engelbert, 3:275
Schuijer, Jan, 7:138
Schull, William J., 5:243, 244
Schuller, Jozef, 4:30
Schultz, Adolph H., 2:51, 7:234
Schultz, Jack, 2:69–70
Schumacker, Heinrich Christian, 6:541
Schumann, Erich, 7:173
Schumpeter, Joseph, 5:187
Schur, Issai, 3:12, 241
Schurz, Carl, 4:121–122
Schwalbe, Gustav, 2:314
Schwann, Theodor Ambrose Hubert, 5:331, 6:24, 357
Schwartz, Laurent, 1:364, 2:290, 291, 6:**378–382,** *380*
    acquaintances of, 4:321
    dissident scientists and, 4:229
Schwartz, Robert, 2:375
Schwartz kernel theorem, 6:381
Schwarzchild, Barbara, 6:386
Schwarzchild, Karl, 7:105
Schwarzchild, Martin, 5:83, 6:**382–389,** *385*
    solar waves, 1:277
    students of, 6:500
Schweber, Silvan, 2:243, 244
Schweitzer, Albert, 4:296, 7:24
Schwenckfeld, Caspar, 6:15
Schwendener, Simon, 6:**389–391**
Schwinger, Julian Seymour, 6:**391–397,** *392,* 7:266
    renormalization, 6:336
    theory of electromagnetic force, 1:428
Schwinner, Robert, 1:70

Sciama, Dennis William, 1:341, 6:**397–401**
Sciara, 2:59–60
Science
 Chinese, 5:235, 238–239
 education
  Atomic Energy Commission, 6:405–406
  critiques of, 1:144
  introductory textbook writers, 5:20–22
  paleontology, 5:267
  popularization of, 7:159–160
  reform and advancement, 5:191–192,
   7:281–282
  teacher training, 3:431–432
 experimental
  Aristotelianism, 7:389–390
  early eighteenth century, 5:36–37
  electricity, 3:2–3
  as hypothetico-deductive enterprise, 5:88–89
  philosophy, 2:171
  zoology, 4:43
 history
  biochemistry, 5:233
  Chinese, 5:235, 239
  The Copernican Revolution (Kuhn), 4:174–175
  education, 6:1–2
  norms of science, 5:123–124
  physics, 6:411
  psychology, 1:358, 6:94–95
  scholarship in, 6:162–164
  USSR, 7:157
 Jesuit, 7:153
 journal editing, 2:74, 6:148
 medieval medicine, 6:68–69
 philosophy of, 6:135–136
  Aristotelian, 1:99–100
  comparative theory, 4:278–279
  decision theory, 4:36–37
  empiricism, 6:458
  Freudian, 3:75
  historiography, 4:172–174, 175–176
  ideology and, 5:122–123
  logic, 6:314
  and medicine, 4:183–185
  natural classification, 2:320
  pragmatism, 4:44
  probalistic thinking, 4:35
  progress, 6:123–124
  speculative, 1:140–141
  statistical techniques, 4:39–40
  symbolism, 7:278
  utilitarianism, 7:282
 popularization of
  astronomy, 6:312–314
  evolutionary biology, 3:159–162
  influence of Gould, 3:162
  influence of Stephen Jay Gould on, 3:163–164
 professionalization of, 5:331–333
 public understanding, 6:142–143
 pure, 7:159
 sociology of
  Merton, Robert King on, 5:121–125
  technological development, 6:162–163
 writing
  alchemy, 1:108–110
  anatomy, 1:91–92
  medicine, 1:107
  microbiology, 2:318–319
  natural history, 4:231–232
  popular, 1:43
  research, 6:83–84
  women authors, 5:20–22
 See also Religion and science
Science, Churchill & Me (Bondi), 1:342
Science: Growth and Change (Menard), 5:97
Science, Order, and Creativity (Bohm and Peat), 1:324
Science and Church Policy (Huxley), 3:430
Science and Civilization in China (Needham), 5:239
Science and Human Behavior (Skinner), 6:464
Science and the Social Order (Barber), 5:124
The Science of Life (Huxley et al.), 1:455, 3:425
Science policy. *See* Public policy
Science since Babylon (Price), 6:162
Les sciences de la vie (Roger), 1:431
Scientific communication, 1:330–331
Scientific concepts, 7:194–195
Scientific Discovery (Simon), 6:452
Scientific humanism, 3:424, 427
Scientific Inference (Jeffreys), 4:40
Scientific method, 1:125
 astronomy, 3:288–289, 6:314
 cosmology, 6:456, 458
 experimental, 1:362, 3:277–279
 experimental psychology, 1:401
 humanistic perspectives, 2:24
 induction, 3:149
 infrared spectroscopy, 7:312
 intuition and, 1:146–147
 knowledge and, 3:421, 5:280
 logic, 7:388
 microbiology, 6:24–29
 Miller, Neal Elgar on, 5:151
 natural philosophy, 3:287, 5:331–333, 350–351
 observation, 1:382, 383
 operationism, 1:359
 ornithology, 5:279
 physical methods, 7:312
 physiology, 3:215–216, 7:183
 primatology, 2:51–54

probability techniques, 4:39–40
psychology and, 1:170, 405
reflective equilibrium, 3:151–152
systems and, 5:11
Scientific misconduct. *See* Research misconduct
Scientific psychology. *See* Experimental psychology
The Scientific Study of Personality (Jung), 2:428
Scintillation (radio sources), 6:306
Scintillation counters, 1:301–302
Scot, Michael, 1:138
Scoto, Ottaviano, 2:36
Scott, Dana, 6:535
Scott, Howard, 3:396
Scott, Ian, 1:198
Scott, Robert Falcon, 2:261, 3:347
Scott, William T., 6:126
Scottus, Ionnes. *See* Eriugena, Johannes Scottus
Scotus, John Duns, 6:418
Scrase, F. J., 7:200
Scripps Institution, 6:234, 235–236
Scripta minora (Euclid), 2:418
Scripts, Plans, Goals, and Understanding (Schank and
    Abelson), 1:9
Sculteri, Alexander, 6:550
Scurvy, 6:569
SDMs (statistical dynamical models), 6:343, 344
SDT (signal detection theory), 1:404–405
Sea birds, 3:425
The Sea Fishes of Southern Africa (Smith, James Leonard
    Brierley), 6:477
Sea urchins, 3:366, *367,* 367–370, *368,* 370
Seaborg, Glenn Theodore, 4:60, 296, 6:**401–407,** *404*
    nuclear taxonomy, 7:308
    plutonium, 6:408, 409
Seaborgium, 6:406
Seabrook, John, 7:40
Seabrook Farms, 7:40
Seafloor mapping, 2:*41,* 42, 7:29–31
Search for extraterrestrial intelligence (SETI), 6:312
Sechenov, Ivan Mikhaylovich, 7:395
The Second Career (Penfield), 6:74
Second-price auctions, 7:150
Secord, James A., 2:244, 3:430, 6:21
Secretum secretorum, 1:146–147
Sectio Canonis (Euclid), 2:417–418
Sedgwick, Adam, 7:280
Sediment analysis
    deep-sea, 5:96
    statistical methodology, 4:164–165
Sedimentary rocks, 7:16
Sedimentology
    carbonate, 5:266
    development, 7:140–143
    Germany, 6:248, 249

rock cycle, 3:419–420
sand dunes, 1:155–156
stratigraphy, 6:467–468
Sée, Germain, 3:272
Seebach, Johann Baptista von, 6:551
Seeding clouds
    Australia, 1:334
    development, 6:222
    ice crystals, 1:249
    weather modification, 1:469–470, 5:223
Seer of Ithaca. *See* Gibson, James Jerome
Segal conjecture, 1:13
Seger, Jon, 3:232
Segrè, Claudio, 6:411
Segrè, Corrado, 4:309
Segrè, Emilio Gino, 6:**407–411,** *408*
    cosmic rays, 1:62
    influence of, 1:60, 4:296
    plutonium, 1:56, 6:402
    students of, 7:365
Segregation, 2:129–131
Séguin, Armand, 4:216, 217
Seidel, Robert, 4:331
Seifert, Karl Johannes Herbert, 7:292
The Seismicity of the Earth (Gutenberg and Richter),
    6:242
Seismology
    broad-band, 1:30–33
    development, 6:241–243
    high-temperature physics, 2:253–254
    Inglada's forumulas, 4:10–11
    Lehmann discontinuity, 4:233
    mountains, 6:348
    oceanography, 7:199–200
    seismographs, 1:243–245, *244*
    statistical techniques, 4:39–40
    stratigraphy, 6:468–469
Seitz, Alfred, 1:151–152
Seitz, Frederick, 1:179, 181
Seizures, 6:69–71
Sela, Michael, 1:79, 81
Selberg, Atle, 2:403
Selbstdarstellung (Stern), 6:525
*Select Extra-Tropical Plants Readily Eligible for Industrial
    Culture or Naturalisation* (Mueller), 5:207
Selected Letters and Documents (Weismann), 7:259
Selected Problems in Geometry; (Ibrāhīm Ibn Sinān Ibn
    Thābit Ibn Qurra), 4:4, 5
Selected Works of Hans A. Bethe (Bethe), 1:272
Selection
    group, 5:319
    organic, 1:171, 172
    sexual, 3:384–385
    species, 3:160, 161

Selection, natural. *See* Natural selection
Selective breeding, 1:211–212
Selenka, Emil, 2:314
Selenka, Margarethe, 2:314
Seler, Eduard, 4:237
The Self and Its Brain (Eccles), 2:332
Self and not-self theory, 1:455–457, 458
Self-determination, 6:274
Self-Organization in Nonequilibrium Systems (Prigogine), 6:166
Self-perception, 6:295
The Selfish Gene (Dawkins), 3:225, 230, 5:228
Selfridge, Oliver, 5:255
Sellars, Wilfrid, 5:92
Sellman, Sven, 3:366, 369
Selten, Reinhard, 3:251, 5:230
Semantic aphasia, 4:352
Semantics
    development, 7:10, 11
    philosophy, 6:204
Semenov, Nikolaï Nickolaevich, 4:81, 6:**411–417,** *415*
Semiconductors, 6:375–377
    Beckman Instruments, 1:235
    development, 6:438–441, 7:318–322
    electrical conduction, 5:203
    electroconductivity, 6:373
    industry, 6:437
    as insulators, 5:202
    molecular orbital theory, 2:278
    photographic process and, 5:201–202
Semiotics, 1:144
Semjonov, Nikolaj N., 2:205
Semper, Karl, 4:163
Sen, Amartya, 3:249, 7:150
Senchkenbergische Naturforschende Gesellschaft. *See* Senckenberg Naturalist Society
Senckenberg am Meer (research station), 6:248–249
Senckenberg Naturalist Society, 6:248, 249
Senckenbergiana, 6:248
Senden, Marius von, 3:269
Sendivogius, Michael, 5:274
Şengör, A. M. C., 3:421–422
Sennert, Daniel, 6:**417–419,** *418*
Senoff, Caesar V., 2:105
Sensation, quantitative methods, 6:239
Sensation and Perception in the History of Experimenta Psychology (Boring), 1:358
The Senses Considered as Perceptual Systems (Gibson, James Jerome), 3:125, 128
Sensorimotor system, 1:437, 6:*71,* 71–72, *72*
Sensory cortex, 6:11–12, *12*
Sensory deprivation, 3:270
Sensory Disturbances from Cerebral Lesions (Holmes and Head), 3:345

Sensory nerves, 1:15–18
Sensory perception. *See* Perception
Sentences (Lombard), 1:378, 449, 450, 5:313
Sententia Oxoniensis (Rufus of Cornwall, Richard), 6:295
Sentiment *vs.* complex, 7:6
Sepkoski, Jack, 3:160
Sequences in the Cratonic Interior of North America (Sloss), 6:468
Serafin, Franz, 2:425
Serber, Charlotte Leof, 6:420, 421, 423
Serber, Robert, 1:291, 6:**419–424,** *420*
Serber-Dancoff method, 6:423
Sergeraert, Francis, 5:198
Serial reproduction, 1:186
Serin, Bernard, 1:181
Serkin, Rudolf, 4:246
Serology, 4:47–48
Serre, Jean-Pierre, 2:361
    Bourbaki group, 1:364
    cohomology, 1:345, 346, 7:257
Serventy, Dominic, 6:210
Servomechanisms, 3:255–256
Servoss, John, 5:356
Set theory
    arithmetic, 3:308–309
    Borel sets, 3:265–266
    infinite series, 2:30–32
    logic, 3:130–132, 5:3–4
SETI (search for extraterrestrial intelligence), 6:312
Settlement. *See* Land settlement
The Seven Caves (Coon), 2:173
Seven Miles Down (Dietz), 2:287
Severi, Francesco, 4:145
Severinus, Petrus, 3:111
Sewall Wright and Evolutionary Biology (Provine), 7:357
Sex and Behavior (Beach), 1:222
Sex and Internal Secretations (Lehrman), 4:245
Sex and Personality: Studies in Masculinity and Femininity (Terman and Miles), 7:28
Sex hormones, 1:459, 460–463
Sex Offenders: an Analysis of Types (Kinsey), 4:124
Sex ratio, 3:230
Sextants, 1:382
Sexual Attractivity, Proceptivity, and Receptivity in Female Mammals (Beach), 1:223
Sexual behavior
    animals, 1:222–223
    in humans, 4:124–129
    humans *vs.* primates, 5:44
    plants, 4:316
    psychoanalysis, 3:73–75
Sexual Behavior in the Human Female (Kinsey), 4:124–126, 128
Sexual Behavior in the Human Male (Kinsey), 4:124–127

Sexual reproduction, evolution, 3:232–233
Sexual selection, 3:384–385
Seyer, Joseph, 5:310
Sezgin, Fuat, 4:19
Shackleton, Nicolas, 5:135
Shadows, Demon-Haunted World (Sagan), 6:315
Shadows of Forgotten Ancestors: A Search for Who We Are (Sagan), 6:314
Shafir, Eldar, 7:95
Shakhparonov, Michael I., 5:248
Shale oil, 7:396
Shane, Charles Donald, 7:284
Shannon, Claude Elwood, 5:255, 6:**424–430,** *428*
Shannon, James, 1:77
The Shape of Threadlike Molecules in Solution and the Relationship Between the Solution Viscosity and the Molecular Weight (Sakurada). *See Yoekichu ni okeru itojo-bunshi no katachi narabini yoeki-nendo to bunshiryo no kankei* (Sakurada)
Shapiro, A. E., 5:269
Shapiro, Monte, 2:429
Shapley, Harlow, 6:49
    Cepheid variable stars, 1:328–329
    colleagues of, 3:389, 5:112–113, 6:383, 7:284, 285
    galaxies, 5:342–343
    Harvard College Observatory, 5:115
    House Committee on Un-American Activities and, 1:331
    management style, 7:286
    on McVittie, George Cunliffe, 5:82
Shapley, Lloyd, 3:250, 5:227
Sharaf al-Dīn. *See* al-Ṭūsī, Sharaf al-Dīn al-Muẓaffar ibn Muḥammad ibn al-Muẓaffar
Sharḥ al-Tadhkira (Quṭ al-Dīn), 6:188
Sharḥ al-Tajrīd (Ali al-Qūshjī), 1:46
Sharḥ al-Urjūza (Quṭ al-Dīn), 6:188
Sharḥ Ḥikmat al-ishrāq (Quṭ al-Dīn), 6:188
Sharh-i Zīj Ulugh Beg (Ali al-Qūshjī), 1:46
Sharp, Lester W., 5:68
Sharples, R. W., 6:540
Sharpless, Steward
    Orion and Perseus, 1:330
    spiral arms of the Milky Way, 5:346
Shatskiy, Nikolay Sergeyevich, 6:**430–432**
Shatsky, Nikolai Sergeevich. *See* Shatskiy, Nikolay Sergeyevich
Shaw, Bernard L., 2:104
Shaw, George Bernard, 5:236
Shaw, J. Cliff, 5:254, 255–256
Shaw, Peter, 1:92
Shaw, Ronald, 6:337
Shaw, William Napier, 1:116, 2:426, 6:238, 239
Sheaves in Geometry and Logic (Mac Lane), 5:2, 4
Sheep, cloning, 1:399

Sheets, Harold, 3:382
Shelford, Victor, 1:47, 3:414, 5:317
    ecological communities study models, 2:382
    Ecological Society of America, 2:188
Shelton, John, 7:229
Shemyakin, Mikhail M., 5:360
Shen Shanjiong, 7:401
Shepard, Francis Parker, 2:286
Shepard, John F., 3:406, 6:367, 368
Shepherd, Ernest S., 2:254
Sheppard, Philip, 2:3, 4–5
Shereshevsky, Solomon, 4:350
Sherman, Albert, 5:210
Sherman, Leroy K., 3:373
Sherrat, Tim, 3:316
Sherrington, Charles Scott, 1:15, 18, 3:267
    mind-body connection, 6:74
    motivational mechanisms, 4:246
    Nobel Prize, 2:329
    students of, 2:332
Sherwood, Martin J., 5:348
Sherwood, Thomas K., 7:136
Sherwood number, 7:136
Shi, Hu. *See* Hu Shi
Shida, Toshi, 7:200
Shifting-balance theory, 7:358–360, *359, 360*
Shiing-Shen Chern. *See* Chern, Shiing-Shen
Shijun, Luo. *See* Luo Shijun
Shils, Edward, 2:23
Shimanouchi, Takehiko, 5:169, 170
Shine, Ian B., 5:185
Shingu, Haruo, 3:86, 87
Shinzo, Shinjyo, 5:48
Shipley, Ruth, 4:359
al-Shīrāzī, Quṭb al-Dīn. *See* Quṭb al-Dīn Maḥmūd Ibn Mas'ūd Ibn al-Musliḥ al-Shīrāzī
Shirkov, Dmitry V., 1:319
Shirley, John, 3:246
Shive, John, 1:181
Shive, William, 3:44
Shklovskii, Iosif Samuilovich, 6:312–313, **432–437**
Shklovsky, Josif. *See* Shklovskii, Iosif Samuilovich
Shock generators, 5:138, *138, 139*
Shockley, William Bradford, 2:131, 6:**437–442,** *439*
    Bell Telephone Laboratories, 1:179
    Nobel Prize, 1:182
    semiconductors, 1:235
    transistors, 1:178, 180
Shoemaker, Carolyn Spellman, 6:443, 446
Shoemaker, Eugene Merle, 6:**442–446,** *445*
Shoemaker-Levy 9, 6:442, 446
Shoppee, Charles W., 4:16
Shorey, Elizabeth, 3:219
Short-term memory, 3:145, 146, 147

Shorter, Edward, 3:75
Shortley, George H., 2:166
Shotland, R. Lance, 5:141
Shriner, Ralph L, 6:322
Shtern, Lina Solomonovna, 6:**447–449**
Shtokman, Vladimir B., 3:8
Shukbah cave (Palestine), 3:105
Shukla, Umeshachandra, 5:4
Siamps the Persian, 2:121
Sickle-cell anemia, 5:242, 6:39, 42
The Sideral Messenger (Galilei). *See Sidereus nuncius* (Galilei)
Sidereus nuncius (Galilei), 3:96, 97
Sidgwick, Eleanor, 6:549
Sidgwick, Henry, 6:548, 549
Siedentopf, Heinrich, 3:274
Siefken, Werner, 1:216
Siegbahn, Manne, 2:343, 344, 6:490
Siegel, Carl Ludwig, 4:146, 5:197
Siekevitz, Philip, 6:146
Sigal, John, 2:429
Sight: An Exposition of the Principles of Monocular and Binocular Vision (LeConte), 4:224
SIGMA (Gébotanique Méditerranéenne et Alpine), 1:388
Signal detection theory (SDT), 1:404–405
Signaling games, 7:150
Signals for Survival (film), 7:54, 56
Signer, Rudolf, 2:68, 3:66, 7:299
Signs of Prophethood (Rāzī), 6:213
Silent Spring (Carson), 2:318, 4:270
Silk, 6:332–333
Silverstein, Abe, 5:261
Ibn Sīnā, Abū ʿAlī al-Ḥusayn, 6:294
Similarity theory, 7:92–93
Simmer, Hans, 5:357
Simon, Herbert Alexander, 5:254, 255
Simon, John, 7:45, 46
Simon, Théodore, 6:92
Simons, James, 2:114, 259
Simplicius, 1:442, 4:52, 7:381
Simplified and extended theory of boundary layer rectifiers (Schottky). *See Vereinfachte und erweiterte Theorie der Randschichtgleichrichter* (Schottky)
Simpson, George E., 5:121
Simpson, George Gaylord, 2:139, 174, 6:351, **452–455**
   evolution, 6:109
   evolutionary biology, 6:354
   group selection, 7:379
Simpson, Thomas, 1:221
Sinathropus, 2:240, 7:249
   discovery, 6:57–58
   hominid fossils, 7:251–253
Šindel, Jan, 6:153–154

Sinel'nikov, Kirill, 4:82
Singer, George John, 2:215, 216
Singer, Isadore, 2:112
Singer, Maxine, 3:342
Singular integral operators, 2:8–9
Sinson, Pierre, 1:204
Sirr-al-ʿasrar, 1:146–147
Sitter, Willem de, 6:**455–458,** *457*
   death of, 5:343
   directorships, 5:341
   positive space curvature, 3:275
Sitterly, Bancroft W., 5:111
Six Books on Perspective (Monte). *See Perspective Libri Sex* (Monte)
Size principle (Riker), 6:254
Sjöquist, John, 2:350, 352
Skeletal system
   anatomy, 7:249–250
   muscle stimulus, 1:16
Skellett, Melvin, 5:113
es-Skhul (Palestine). *See* Es-Skhul (Palestine)
Skinner, B. F. *See* Skinner, Burrhus Frederic
Skinner, Burrhus Frederic, 4:247, 6:**458–467,** *461*
   acquaintances of, 6:279
   students of, 5:90
Skinner, Stuart R., 7:231
Skrinskii, Alexander, 1:429
Skylab program, 7:77
Slansky, Richard, 6:171
Slater, E. C., 5:162
Slater, John Clarke, 3:19
   colleagues of, 3:254
   group theoretical methods, 5:211
   magnetrons, 3:255
   students of, 1:179, 6:437
Slavery
   African American scientists and, 1:175
   ancient medicine, 6:291
   slaveowners, 3:339
Slee, Bruce, 1:333, 6:304
Sleep, 3:305, 6:244
Slichter, Charles P., 3:197, 199
Slin'ko, Michail G., 1:354
Sloan, Philip R., 2:243
Sloane, Richard, 1:237, 239
Slobodkin, Larry, 3:411, 414
Sloss, Laurence Louis, 4:164, 165, 166, 6:**467–469**
Sloss sequences, 6:467–468, *468*
Slotin, Louis, 5:242
Slovic, Paul, 7:94
Smagorinsky, Joseph, 6:**469–472**
Smagorinsky, Margaret Knoepfel, 6:470
Small, Ernest, 2:214
Smalley, Richard Errett, 6:**472–475,** *474*

Smart, John J. C., 4:284
Smeaton, John, 3:6
Smee, Alfred, 2:216
Smekal, Adolph Gustaf Stephan, 1:311
Smell. *See* Olfaction
Smellie, William, 7:220
Smidt, Jaap, 7:138
Smith, Adam, 1:127, 5:46
Smith, Alice Kimball, 5:347
Smith, C. A. B., 7:89, 90
Smith, C. U. M., 3:430
Smith, Cedric, 3:226, 227
Smith, Charles H., 7:225
Smith, Eric, 6:556
Smith, Francis, 4:276
Smith, Fred H., 3:156
Smith, George, 5:268–273
Smith, Gilbert Morgan, 6:318
Smith, Grafton Elliot. *See* Elliot Smith, Grafton
Smith, Henry John Stephen, 2:310, 6:566
Smith, James Edward, 7:221
Smith, James H., 6:182
Smith, James Leonard Brierley, 6:**475–478,** *476*
Smith, John Maynard, 3:162, 7:379
Smith, Lloyd P., 1:271
Smith, Margaret Macdonald, 6:476, 477
Smith, Maynard, 3:230
Smith, Michael, 6:**478–483,** *479*
Smith, Stanley, 3:316–317
Smith, Stephen, 3:153
Smith, Theobald, 2:318
Smith, Wesley, 3:322
Smith, William, 1:177
    colleagues of, 3:6, 7
    stratigraphy, 2:225
Smith-Purcell effect, 6:182
Smithsonian Astrophysical Observatory, 7:287–289
Smits, Andreas, 1:280, 281
Smog
    automobile emissions, 3:383
    ozone, 1:235
Smolarski, Dennis, 2:151
Smuts, Christiaan. *See* Smuts, Jan Christian
Smuts, Jan Christian, 5:237, 6:*483,* **483–484,** 7:7
Snails
    genetic assimilation, 7:205
    natural selection, 2:4–5
The Snark Was a Boojum (Beach), 1:222
Snavely, Parke, D., Jr., 2:192
Snel, Willebrord, 3:246
Snell, Esmond E., 4:325
Snell, Karl, 3:69
Snell, Willebrord, 1:445
Snellius, Willebrord. *See* Snell, Willebrord

Snow, Charles Percy, 5:39, 6:139
Snow samplers, 3:372
Snyder, Hartland, 4:333, 7:329
Snyder, Solomon H., 1:122
So Human an Animal (Dubos), 2:319
Soar (programming language), 5:258
Sobczynska, Danuta, 5:357
Sober, Elliot, 1:48
Sobolev, Sergei Lovich, 6:380, 7:157
Social action, school integration, 2:129–136
The Social and Economic Roots of Newton's Principia
    (Hessen), 5:237
Social and Ethical Interpretations (Baldwin), 1:169, 171,
    172
Social behavior
    adaptation and, 1:171–172
    animals, 1:48
    birds, 2:196–198
    group dynamics, 3:14–15
    humans, 4:127
    natural selection, 7:376, 377–380
    primates, 2:50–54
    psychoanalysis and, 5:146, *146*
    segregation, 2:129–131
    social Darwinism, 2:244–245
Social Choice and Individual Values (Arrow), 7:150
Social confirmation, 1:172
Social control, 6:464
Social ethics
    experimental psychology and, 5:142
    personality and, 1:52
    science and, 4:291–292
Social evolution, 3:226–232, 234
Social justice, 5:236
Social Learning and Imitation (Miller), 5:147
Social medicine, 7:157–158
Social psychology
    belief systems, 1:8–10
    cognitive dissonance, 3:13–17
    cross-cultural, 2:22–27
    experimental, 5:137–142, *138, 139*
    neurocognition, 4:349–350
    of remembering, 1:186–187
Social responsibility, 1:293
Social scripts, 1:9
Social Theory and Social Structure (Merton), 5:123
Socialism
    children's science books, 5:284–285
    science and, 5:237–239
    USSR, 6:326–327
Sociality. *See* Social behavior; Social evolution
Societas Internationalis Limnologiae, 7:36
Society for Freedom in Science, 7:8

Society of Friends (Quakers)
    conservation, 7:44
    pacificism, 6:238
    pacifism, 6:239, 240, 7:42
Socio-cultural anthropology. *See* Ethnology
Sociobiology
    inclusive fitness, 3:225
    insects, 3:230
    opposition, 3:162
Sociobiology: The New Synthesis (Wilson), 3:162, 230
Sociology
    logic, 6:19–20
    plant, 1:385–388
    postivism, 6:137
    relativistic, 2:23–24
    of science
        Merton, Robert King on, 5:121–125
        technological development, 6:162–163
The Sociology of Science (Merton), 5:123
Soda manufacturing, 3:377, 378–379
Söderbaum, Henrik Gustaf, 1:266
Sodium, nuclear spin, 6:193
Sodium borohydride, 1:421–422
Sodium carbonate, 3:377, 378–379
Sodium chloride, 6:437
Sodium-potassium pump, 3:*329,* 329–330
Soffen, Gerald Alan, 6:**484–488**
Software, 2:294–295
Soil
    conservation, 7:39
    erosion, 3:371–374, 6:208, 209
    infiltration capacity, 3:373, 374
Soil Drift in the Arid Pastoral Areas of South Australia (Ratcliffe), 6:209
Sokol, B. J., 3:246
Sokolov, B. S., 3:317
Solar energy
    catalysis, 6:416
    clouds, 6:555
Solar magnetism, 1:131
Solar neutrino problem, 1:157, 158–159
Solar physics
    astronomy, 3:141–144
    spectroscopy, 7:73–77
Solar radiation, 3:79–80
Solar spectrum, 1:277, 7:74–77
Solar system
    origin, 6:499
    stability of, 5:197
    Venus, 6:310–311
The Solar System (Kuiper), 4:180–181
Solar system research, 6:259–260
Solberg, Halvor Skappel, 1:247
Solberg, Thorvald A., 6:234

Solid-state chemistry
    chemical reactions, 6:126
    crystal growth, 2:161–162
Solid-state physics
    conduction electrons, 1:303
    development, 6:437–441
    electron scattering, 3:22–23
    ionics, 2:162
    iron monoxide, 2:160–161
    metals, 6:63–64
    Mott transition, 5:203–204
    pioneering research, 5:200–201
    quantum mechanics, 7:295
    semiconductors, 7:320–321
Solids, 6:490
Sollas, William Johnson, 2:238
Solomon, Arthur K., 1:77
Solomon, Ronald, 3:154
Solutions chemistry, 7:396
Solutions of Electrolytes (Hammett), 3:238
Solvability, 6:265, 266
Solvay, Ernest, 4:7
Solvay process, 3:377, 378–379
Solzhenitzyn, Aleksandre, 6:328
Somatic cells
    hybrids, 2:402
    Mendelian genetics, 7:190
Some Applications of Statistics to Meteorology (Panofsky), 6:8
Some Observations about the Relationship between Theory of Relativity and Kantian Philosophy (Gödel), 3:131
Some Problems of Chemical Kinetics and Reactivity (Semenov), 6:414
Somerville, Mary Fairfax Grieg, 4:119
Somerville, Richard, 5:222
Sommerfeld, Arnold Johannes Wilhelm, 6:**489–492,** *490*
    atomic theory, 2:87–88
    colleagues of, 3:308
    mathematical approach to physics, 1:270
    quantum mechanics, 6:62
    students of, 1:303, 2:165, 378, 7:104, 105
Sonar, 6:500
Sonder, Otto Wilhelm, 5:205
Sondheimer, Franz, 3:404
Soneira, Raymond, 1:159–160
Song learning (birds), 7:42–43
Song sparrows, 5:277–278
Sonneborn, Tracy Morton, 4:45, 6:318, **492–494**
    embryogenesis, 1:457
    soluble RNA, 3:342
Sonoluminescence, 6:397

Sootnoshenie mezhdu molekuliarnosť iu i energiiami aktivatsii v priamom i obratnom napravleniiakh (Boreskov), 1:354
Sophismata (Albert of Saxony), 1:35
Sorabji, Richard, 1:104, 4:51
Sorokin, Pitirim, 5:121, 122
Sorting, species, 3:161
Sound. *See* Acoustics
Sound spectrographs, 7:43
Source theory, 6:395–396
South, James, 3:288
South Africa, 6:475–477, 483–484
The South African Fossil Ape-Men (Broom), 2:240
South America ethnology, 4:237
   See also specific countries
Southern Oscillation, 7:216, 217–219
Space
   biology, 4:137–140, *138*
   cosmic plasmas, 1:40
   Euclidean geometry, 7:291–292
   expanding, 5:81–82
   exploration, 7:287
   nature of
      formal, intuitive, and physical, 2:44
      motion, 2:273
   oceanography, 3:10–11
   rockets, 3:79–80
   Russian exploration, 4:104
   satellites
      cosmic rays, 3:80–81
      Smithsonian Astrophysical Observatory, 7:287–289
      space exploration, 6:100–101
      Sputnik, 4:180, 6:182
   time and
      gravitation, 3:191–192
      Hawking-Penrose singularity theorems, 6:399
      independence, 2:367–369
      Newtonian theory and, 5:269–270
      particle fields, 1:324
      relativity, 1:424–425, 6:122–123
Space, Time, Matter (Weyl), 7:276, 277
Space-based telescopes
   development, 6:498–502
   Hubble, 1:159–161, 6:502, 7:130
   national observatories, 3:142–144
   stratoscopes, 6:387
Space exploration, satellites, 6:100–101
Space probes
   cosmic rays, 7:122–124
   Explorer, 5:261, 7:122–123, 175
   NASA, 5:263–264, 6:311, 313
   plasma physics, 6:283
   scientific, 5:261

Space science
   advocacy, 1:160–161, 7:118, 122–125
   development, 5:259–264
   extraterrestrial life, 6:310–314
   Hubble Space Telescope, 6:502
   influential figures, 6:484–488, 7:173–176
   photometry, 3:274–275
   physics, 5:300
   positive space curvature, 3:275
   spectroscopy, 7:73, 74–77
Space Science and Engineering Center (SSEC), 6:555
Space Science Board (SSB), 5:261–262
Spade, Paul, 6:564
Spagnolo, Sergio, 2:259
Spallanzani, Lazzaro, 1:203
The Spandrels off San Marco and the Panglossian Paradigm: A Critique of the Adaptationist Programme (Gould and Lewontin), 3:161
Sparks, Morgan, 6:439–440
Sparrow, Elizabeth, 5:87, 88
Sparrows, song, 5:277–278
Spawning, 3:260–261
Spearman, Charles Edward, 2:431, 6:55
Special Cytology (Cowdry), 2:183
Special relativity, 2:365–367
Special variants of the method of trigonometric sums (Vinogradov). *See Osobye varianty metoda trigonometricheskikh summ* (Vinogradov)
Speciation
   allopatric, 3:159–160
   Drosophila, 2:62–63
   mammals, 2:86
   Mayr, Ernst Walter on, 5:63–64
Species
   catastrophism, 1:416
   character, 1:387–388
   fixism theory, 1:452, 453
   invasive, 6:515
   selection, 3:160, 161
   sorting, 3:161
Species-being, 6:295
Specific variability, 7:191
Speccker, Ernst P., 1:239
Spector, Mark, 6:201
Spectra of Diatomic Molecules (Herzberg), 3:301
Spectral lines
   galaxies, 7:126–131
   quantum theory, 6:490
   Zeeman effect, 7:165
Spectrography
   astrophysics, 3:174
   atmospheric, 1:131
   electron, 1:165
   mass, 1:162–163, 165

Spectrometers
    design of, 1:440
    diagram, 1:*440*
    quartz photoelectric, 1:234
Spectrophotometry
    development, 7:229–231, *230*
    infrared, 1:234
    ozone, 2:*307,* 307–308
Spectroscopy
    atomic absorption, 7:229–232
    electron
        inorganic chemistry, 2:103
        transition metals, 4:59–60
    infrared
        applications, 7:352
        chemical shifts, 3:*198,* 198–199
        development, 7:228–229
        molecular structures, 5:170
        organic chemistry, 3:197
        protein structure, 5:170
        scientific method, 7:312
    microwave, 7:101
    molecular
        atomic theory, 3:298–301
        quantum chemistry, 3:196
    Raman
        benzene, 1:60, 4:15–16
        molecular structures, 5:169
        scientific method, 7:312
    sound, 7:43
    supersonic bean laser, 6:473
    ultraviolet
        applications, 7:352, 353–354
        astronomy, 2:343–347
        benzene, 4:17
        solar physics, 7:73–77
    x-ray, 3:78–79
    See also Nuclear magnetic resonance (NMR)
Spectrum
    atomic, 1:133–135
    light, 5:273–274
    molecular, 3:298–301
    solar, 1:277
Spectrum analysis, 7:105–107
Specula Melitensis (Kircher), 4:132
Speculum Animae (Rufus of Cornwall, Richard), 6:295
Speculum Orbis Terrarum (de Jode), 2:158
Speech, egocentric, 7:195
Speech: Its Function and Development (de Laguna), 2:197
Speech and Brain Mechanisms (Penfield), 6:73, 74
Speed
    Blasius of Parma, 1:297
    Merton mean-speed theorem, 5:314
Speed, John, 3:356

Speer, Albert, 7:173
Speleology, 1:395–396
Spellman, Carolyn. *See* Shoemaker, Carolyn Spellman
Spemann, Hans, 5:16–17, 7:202, 203
    autobiography, 3:224
    citation frequencies, 5:*18*
    gastrulation, 3:350
    induction theory, 3:220
    microsurgery, 3:219
    neural induction, 1:373
    Nobel Prize, 3:349
    students of, 3:217, 218, 348
Spence, Kenneth, 3:406
Spence, Michael, 7:150
Spencer, Donald, 4:144, 145, 146, 5:229
Spencer, Herbert, 2:152, 4:25
    criticisms of, 5:284
    evolution of the mind, 2:247
    germplasm theory, 7:261
    influence of, 4:340
    progressive evolutionary views, 2:188
    spontaneous generation, 1:208
    Wallace, Alfred Russel, 7:226
    X-Club, 3:327
Spencer, Warren, 5:241
Spenke, Eberhard, 6:376
Sperry, Roger Wolcott, 6:**494–498,** *497*
Sphere (Clavius), 2:148–150
Spheres, 3:246
Spherical geometry, 1:14, 2:113
Spiegelman, Sol, 1:457
Spielmeyer, Walther, 1:408
Spilhaus, Athelstan, 3:10
Spin of particles
    dynamics, 1:413
    electromagnetic interaction, 3:193
Spin-scan cameras, 6:555–556
Spin-spin coupling, 3:199–200
Spin-zero particles, 6:336
Spinal cord, 2:329–333
Spinal cord injuries, 3:345, 346–347
Spinks, John W. T., 3:299
Spinning cup, 2:351, *351*
Spinoza, Baruch (or Benedict de), 1:425
Spirits, inanimate *vs.* vital, 1:139
Spiritualism
    Eucharist, 6:15, 16
    philosophy and, 4:25
    Russian, 1:467
Spitzer, Lyman, Jr., 6:**498–504,** *500*
    acquaintances of, 6:383
    fusion, 6:384–385
    Schwarzschild, Martin, 6:387
    space telescopes, 1:160

Split-brain research, 6:496–498
Spohr, Ulrike, 4:262
Spokane Flood, 1:393–395, *395,* 6:537
Sponer, Hertha, 5:210
Spontaneous behavior, 6:244
Spontaneous generation, 3:391, 6:24–26
    Darwinism and, 1:208–210
    metabolism, 3:363
Sporanox, 4:33
Spores, bacteria, 1:209
Spottiswoode, William, 2:310
Springer, Ferdinand, 5:253
Sputnick, Scientists, and Eisenhower (Killian), 1:136
Sputnik, 4:180, 5:261, 6:182, 7:175
Squares, dissection of, 7:*87,* 89
Squires, Lombard, 4:290
SSB (Space Science Board), 5:261–262
SSEC (Space Science and Engineering Center), 6:555
Stable and Random Motions in Dynamical Systems
    (Moser), 5:197
Stable homotopy theory, 1:11, 12–13
Staden, Heinrich von, 3:325
Stadler, Lewis J., 5:69–70
Stahl, Georg Ernst, 1:229, 2:218, 4:214, 6:*504,*
    504–508
Stalin, Joseph
    antisemitism, 1:426–427
    letter to, 6:575
    science, 7:157
Stalker, Harrison D., 2:60–61
Die Stammesgeschichte der Insekten (Hennig), 3:281
Stampacchia, Guido, 4:319
Stanchinskiy, Vladimir Vladimirovich, 6:**509–511**
Standardized achievement tests, 7:26
Stanford Achievement Test, 7:26
Stanford-Binet intelligence test, 7:25–26
Stanford Hypnotic Susceptibility Scale, 3:312
Stanhope, Philip, 1:221
Stanley, Gordon, 1:333, 334–336
Stanley, Steven, 3:160
Stanley, Wendell Meredith, 1:464, 2:268
    Nobel Prize, 2:348
    origin of life, 3:364
Staphylococcus, 1:80
Star catalogs
    AGK2, 3:274, 275–276
    AGK3, 3:276
    ancient, 3:321
    compilation, 3:287
Star Wars. *See* Strategic Defense Initiative (Star Wars)
Starch Phosphorylase of Potato (Green), 3:168
Starkey, George, 1:367, 6:**511–513,** 7:335
Starr, Victor, 6:342
Stars

binary, 4:177–178
chemical composition of, 7:105–106
contamination, 1:298, 300–301
declinations, 7:47
distribution, 1:329–330
dynamics, 3:274–275
energy production, 6:543
equilibrium, 2:91
evolution, 6:385–386
explanations of, 4:20–21
formation
    catastropic hypotheses, 4:39
    Milky Way galaxy, 1:328
    ongoing process, 1:65–66
    photometry, 6:50–51
    white dwarf configuration, 2:88–90
heliocentrism, 2.21
high velocity, 5:341–342
massive, 5:348
motion
    calculations, 6:384
    gravitational forces, 2:89–91
navigation, 6:110–111
neutron, 3:139, 5:130–131
nuclear reactions, 1:157
    Big bang theory, 3:390
    white dwarfs, 3:176
radiation, 2:90
structure, 1:277–278
    interior, 6:541–542
    models, 6:385–386
variable, 6:383
white dwarfs, 2:92, 3:173, 176
See also Astronomy; Galaxies
Stars and Clusters (Payne-Gaposchkin), 6:51
Stars in the Making (Payne-Gaposchkin), 6:51
The Stars of High Luminosity (Payne-Gaposchkin), 6:50
Starting-Points Leading to the Intelligibles (Porphyry),
    6:137
Stas, Jean-Servais, 2:323
Statement on the Pricing of Urban Street Use (Vickery),
    7:151
Static electricity, 7:166–169
Statistical Account of Scotland (Walker), 7:223
Statistical dynamical models (SDMs), 6:343, 344
Statistical Mechanics of Chain Molecules (Flory), 3:40
Statistics, 6:52–56
    Bayesian, 6:349–351
    of errors, 1:220–221
    genetics, 7:190–191
    limnology, 6:256
    monsoons, 7:217–219
    oceanography, 6:255, 256
    probalistic techniques, 4:39–40

Statistics, *continued*
    psychology, 1:9–10
    quantum mechanics, 6:134
    in social sciences, 1:128
    thermodynamics, 1:338–339
Statistics as Principled Argument (Abelson), 1:10
Statistics of Deadly Quarrels (Richardson), 6:240
Staub, Hans, 1:306
Staudinger, Hermann, 2:48, 3:37
    colleagues of, 7:337
    natural fibers, 5:28
    polymers, 6:330–332
    students of, 6:225
    viscosity, 6:332
Steacie, Edgar William Richard, 4:259
Steady state model. *See* Steady state theory
Steady state theory
    Big bang theory, 3:136–137
    controversies, 5:74–75
    cosmology, 1:339–340, 341–343, 3:139, 388
    galaxies, 6:398–399
    matter creation, 3:389–390
    See also Evolution
Steam engineering, 2:11
Stebbins, George Ledyard, Jr., 4:276, 6:**513–516**
Stebbins, Joel, 6:544
Stebbins, Ledyard. *See* Stebbins, George Ledyard, Jr.
Stebbins-Whitford effect, 1:341, 6:398–399
Stechshulte, V. C., 7:200
Steeg, Karl Ver, 6:536
The Steel Shutter (film), 6:279
Steenrod, Norman, 4:145, 5:2
Steggerda, Jan, 1:313
Steichen, Edward, 6:313, 7:236
Stein, Elias, 7:414
Stein, William Howard, 1:78, 79, 5:270
Steinach, Eugen, 4:79
Steinberger, Jack, 1:238
Steinheil, Carl August von, 1:440
Steinhneil, Karl August von. *See* Steinheil, Carl August von
Steinle, Friedrich, 3:2
Stellar Atmospheres (Payne-Gaposchkin), 6:49
Stellar energy
    chain reactions, 1:271–272
    helium, 1:277–278
Stellar magnetism
    hydrodynamics, 2:91
    plasmas, 1:40–42
Stellar Systems (Kuiper), 4:181
Stellerator, 6:384–385
Stem cell research, 3:186
Stengers, Isabelle, 6:167
Stenglin, Lucas, 6:551

Stent, Gunther, 4:357
Stephanus of Alexandria, 6:**516–519**
Stephanus of Athens. *See* Stephanus of Alexandria
Stephens, William, 1:304–305
Stephenson, E. C., 5:52
Stephenson, F. Richard, 2:148
Stephenson, George, 2:250
Stephenson, Marjorie. *See* Stephenson, Marjory
Stephenson, Marjory, 5:160, 232, 233, 6:**519–521**
Steppes, 6:509, 510
Stereochemie (Wittig), 7:336, 337
Stereochemistry
    configurations, 3:400–404
    conformational analysis, 4:259–263
    development, 6:156–161, *158*
    molecular structure, 6:154–159
    research, 7:341
Stereoisomers, 2:201
Steric effects, 1:259
    enzymes, 7:34–35
    organic compounds, 1:419–421, *420*
Sterility, 3:228–229
Sterilization law, Nazi, 1:3–4
Stern, Clara, 6:522, 525
Stern, Curt
    colleagues of, 3:218, 350–351
    employment, 5:69
    genetics conference, 5:97
    students of, 5:241
Stern, Josef, 5:6–7, 309, 6:6–7
Stern, L. William. *See* Stern, Louis William
Stern, Lina. *See* Shtern, Lina Solomonovna
Stern, Louis William, 1:51, 52, 53, 6:**522–527**
Stern, Moritz Abraham, 6:250
Stern, Otto, 6:192, 194, 195
Stern, Sigismund, 6:522
Stern, William. *See* Stern, Louis William
Steroids
    chemical structure, 1:459
    optical properties, 1:196–199
    synthesis, 6:227, 228
Stetson, R. H., 6:495
Stetter, Georg, 1:300, 301, 302
Stevens, Nettie Maria, 5:183
Stevens, Stanley Smith, 1:359, 4:302, 303
Stevenson, Thomas, 1:28
Stevin, Simon, 5:177
Stewart, John Qunicy, 5:111
Stewart, Kelly, 3:56
Stewart, T. Grainger, 3:345
Stewart, Warren E., 7:135
Stewart-Holmes sign, 3:345
Stibitz, George R., 3:357, 5:52
Stickland, Leonard, 6:520

Stiefel, Eduard, 7:412
Stiegler, Duane, 3:85
Stieglitz, Julius, 1:418
Stigler, Stephen M., 1:219–220
Stiglitz, Joseph, 7:150
Stimulus, signal detection theory, 1:404–405
Stimulus-response model
    adaptive behavior, 3:408–409
    behaviorism, 6:459, 461, 463
    learning, 3:407
    perception, 3:125–129
Stitt, Fred, 3:195
Stochastic cooling, 1:429
Stochastic phylogeny, 3:160–161
Stock, Alfred, 1:418–419
Stock, L. M., 1:421
Stocklöv, Joachim, 5:356
Stockman, Christine. *See* Bondi, Christine Stockman
Stockmayer, Walter, 3:40
Stoddard, George D., 7:27
Stoeckenius, Walther, 6:200
Stoichiometry, 1:268
Stoicism
    elements, 2:122
    mixtures, 2:322
    philosophy, 6:117, 118
    theology and, 1:144
Stoicorum Repugnantiis (Plutarch), 3:321
Stoker, Michael, 6:319
Stoll, Max, 4:228
Stomachion (Archimedes), 1:88
Stommel, Henry Melson, 2:354, 3:10, 5:329, 6:256, **527–532**
Stone, A. H., 7:89
Stone, Marshall Harvey, 2:8, 5:2, 178
Stone, Wilson, 2:61
The Stone Age of Mount Carmel (Garrod), 3:106
Storms, Lowell, 2:429
The Story of Man (Coon), 2:174
The Story of Peking Man (Jia Lanpo), 6:58
Stoy, J. E., 6:535
Stoye, John, 5:36
Straat, Patricia, 4:139
Strabo, 7:381
Strachey, Christopher, 6:**532–536**
Strachey, James, 3:74
Straggs, Suzanne, 7:305
Strahler, Alan H., 6:538
Strahler, Arthur Newell, 6:**536–540**
Straightening algorithms, 6:285–286
Strained Transition States (Brown), 1:420
Strainmeters, 1:245
Strassl, Hans, 3:274
Strassmann, Fritz, 1:55, 2:205, 3:20

fission, 6:408
radio chemistry, 3:210–211
Strategic Defense Initiative (Star Wars)
    opponents, 1:275
    supporters, 7:24
The Strategy of Ecosystem Development (Odum), 5:319
The Strategy of Life (Grobstein), 3:189
Strathdee, John, 6:340
Stratigraphic Code (Yin Zanxun), 7:386
Stratigraphy, 6:467–469
    China, 7:386
    geology, 6:*468*
    nomenclature, 7:62–63
    Permian, 5:265, 266
    plate movement, 1:69–70
    quantitative methods of analysis, 4:164–165
Stratigraphy and Sedimentation (Sloss and Krumbein), 4:164, 165, 6:467–468
Strato of Lampsacus, 6:**540**
Stratoscopes, 6:387
Stratosphere, 1:116, 6:387, 7:19
Straub, Bruno, 6:571
Straus, Werner, 5:283
Strauss, Lewis, 6:196–197
Stream ordering technique, 6:538
Streamflow, 3:373–374
Street, Jabez Curry, 1:162–163, 163, 6:180
Streitwieser, Andrew, 3:403
Streptomycin, 6:318
Stresemann, Erwin, 4:336, 338, 5:61, 63, 278–279
Stress, 7:179
Stricker, Edward, 5:151
Strickland, Catherine Parr. *See* Traill, Catharine Parr
String galvanometers, 1:17
Strogatz, Steven, 5:140
Stromboli volcano, 6:262, *262*
Strömgren, Bengt Georg Daniel, 1:271, 6:**541–547,** *545*
Strontium, 5:322
Structural chemistry, 1:465–467
    advances in, 5:29
    theory, 1:465–466
Structuralism (Piaget), 6:94
Structure and Evolution of the Stars (Schwarzchild), 6:386
Structure and Function in the Nervous Systems of Invertebrates (Bullock and Horridge), 1:437
Structure and Mechanism in Organic Chemistry (Ingold), 4:15
The Structure of Appearance (Goodman), 3:149
The Structure of Atmospheric Turbulence (Panofsky), 6:8
The Structure of Evolutionary Theory (Gould), 3:159
The Structure of Line Spectra (Leiden), 6:37

The Structure of Scientific Revolutions (Kuhn), 4:170,
    172–173, 176
    influenced by, 6:125
    Mertonian paradigm, 5:125
Structure-reactivity relationships, 3:238–240, *239*
Structure Reports, 1:285
Struik, Leen, 7:138
Strum, Shirley, 2:52
Strutt, Evelyn Georgiana Mary Balfour, 6:549
Strutt, John William, Third Baron Rayleigh, 6:**547–550,**
    548
Strutt, Robert John, Fourth Baron Rayleigh, 2:307
Struve, Otto, 4:178
    astronomy, 6:49
    Astrophysical Monographs editor, 1:329
    colleagues of, 3:300
    International Astronomical Union, 3:143
    observatories, 3:174
    stellar emissions, 6:544
Strychnine, 6:157, 7:353
Stryer, Lubert, 5:17
Stuab, Hans, 1:304–305
Stuart, Herbert Arthur, 6:39
Stuart, Patrick Maynard, 2:379
Stubbe, Henry, 2:171
Student Counseling (Hilgard and Edwards), 3:313–314
*Studien über das Gleichgewicht der lebendigen Kraft
    zwischen bewegten materiellen Punkten* (Boltzmann),
    1:338
Studies in Neurology (Head), 3:346
Studies in the Life History of the Song Sparrow (Nice),
    5:279
Studies of Plant Life (Traill), 7:79
Studies of Similarity (Tversky and Gati), 7:92
Studies on Hinokitiol (Nozoe), 5:290
A Study in Avidity (Jerne), 4:47
The Study of Instinct (Tinbergen), 4:244, 7:53, 56
A Study of Qualities (Goodman), 3:149
A Study of Values (Allport), 1:52
Stuhlinger, Ernst, 7:122
Sturtevant, Alfred Henry, 1:212, 2:60–61, 399
Subconscious, 4:26–27
Subjective probability, 2:255–257
Subjective Probability: The Real Thing! (Jeffrey), 4:36, 37
Subjective Probability (Tversky and Kahneman), 7:93
Submarine telegraphy, 1:25
Substance and Function (Lewin), 4:278
Substance P, 7:178
Substitution reactions, 2:324
Subterranean processes, 5:274–275
Succession, ecological, 5:319
The Succession of Life through Geological lTime (Oakley),
    5:295
Suchten, Alexander von, 6:512, **550–553**

Sudarshan, E. C. George, 3:24
Sudhoff, Karl Friedrich Jakob, 6:15
Süe, Jean-Joseph, 1:91
Suess, Eduard, 7:200, 208
Suess, Hans, 4:91, 5:326, 6:236
Sufism, 6:187
Sugano, Satoru, 4:60
Sugar
    colonialism and, 1:230
    configuration of D-glyceraldehyde, 4:*259*
    nucleotides, 4:253–256
    syntheses of trisaccharide antigenic determinants,
        4:*261*
    synthesis, 4:258–263
Sugarbaker, David, 1:183
Sugasawa, Shigehiko, 5:290
*A Suggested Interpretation of the Quantum Theory in
    Terms of Hidden Variables* (Bohm), 1:323
Sugiura, Yohikatse, 6:542
Suicet, Richard. *See* Swineshead, Richard
Suidas (Hypatia), 3:435, 436–437
Suisset. *See* Swineshead, Richard
Suk, Vojtěch, 4:42
Sukachev, Vladimir Nicolayevich, 1:388
Sulfur, 1:138, *138,* 3:353
Sulfuric acid, 1:351–352, 2:216
Sullivan, Dennis, 1:12
Sullivan, John Henry, 7:231, 232
Sulloway, Frank, 2:243, 3:75
Summa de creaturis (Albertus Magnus, Saint), 1:38
Summa logicae (Ockham), 1:378
Summa logicae et philosophiae naturalis (Dumbleton),
    2:325–326, 326–327, 6:562
Summerhayes, Victor, 2:382–383
Summulae de Dialectica (Buridan), 1:447
Sumner, Francis Cecil, 2:128
Sumner, John Bird, 5:13
Sun
    astronomy, 6:176
    comets, 7:286
    Copernican motion, 2:176
    corona
        observation of, 5:113
        spectroscopy, 2:344–346
    gases, 4:39
    interior structure, 1:277
    light
        controversies, 5:11
        geometry, 2:233–234
    orbit, 4:105–106
    physics, 3:141–144
    radiation, 3:79–80
The Sun (Kuiper), 7:128
Sundials

analemma, 2:*305,* 305–306
construction of, 4:4–5, 131–132
Sunyaev, Rashid Alievich, 7:394
Suomi, Verner Edward, 6:**553–558,** *555*
Super (hydrogen bomb), 7:21, 22
Superconductivity
Bose-Einstein gas, 1:307
collectivized particles, 1:318
electron behavior and, 1:179, 181–182
experimental physics, 2:64–65
metals, 1:304
superfluidity and, 5:129–130
theory of, 1:178
Superfluidity
liquid helium, 4:82–83
superconductivity and, 5:129–130
Superheterodyne principle, 6:375
Supernovae
nebulae from, 5:343
observations, 1:382
shock waves and explosions, 1:275
Supersonic bean laser spectroscopy, 6:473
Supplement (Bayes and Price), 1:221
Support theory, 7:95
Support Theory (Tversky and Koehler), 7:95
Sure-thing principle, 6:*350,* 350–351
Surface pressure, earth, 2:*425,* 425–426
Surface runoff, 3:371–374
Surgery
brain, 4:142, 6:69–71
microsurgery, 3:*219, 220*
Survey of Contemporary Knowledge of Biogeochemistry,
3:413
A Survey of Modern Algebra (Birkhoff and Mac Lane),
1:287, 5:2
Survey of Scientists Engaged in Geophysical Researches
(Landsberg), 4:198
A Survey of Statistical-Dynamical Models of the Terrestrial
Climate (Saltzman), 6:343
Sutcliffe, Reginald Cockcroft, 6:86, **558–562**
Sutton, Graham, 4:195
Sutton, Walter Stanborough, 7:261
Suzuki, Michio, 3:12
Svedberg, Theodor, 3:334
Sverdlov, Eugene, 5:364
Sverdrup, Harald Ulrik, 1:468, 2:261
colleagues of, 6:235
oceanography, 5:172, 6:234
Sviberly, Joseph, 6:569
Swales, Peter, 3:73
Swallow, John, 6:529, 531
Swaminathan, Krishnaasami, 7:144
Swammerdam, Jan, 4:250
Swann, Gordon, 6:444

Swann, Michael, 5:160
Swann, William Francis Gray, 1:390, 4:6, 8
Swedenborg, Emanuel, 4:22
Sweeney, Dura, 2:296
Swenson, George W., Jr., 5:83
Swets, John A., 4:303
Swiner, Joseph Sidney, 5:298
Swineshead, Richard, 2:325, 326, 327, 5:314,
6:**562–563**
Swineshead, Roger. *See* Swyneshed, Roger
Swirles, Berta, 4:39
Switching systems, electronic, 6:438
Swoboda, Gustav, 1:248–249
Swyneshed, Richard. *See* Swineshead, Richard
Swyneshed, Roger, 6:562, **563–564**
Sydenham, Thomas, 3:325
Sykes, Lynn, 7:325
Syllabus reform, 6:205
Sylow, Ludwig. *See* Sylow, Peter Ludvig Meidell
Sylow, Peter Ludvig Meidell, 3:213
Sylow groups, 3:153
Sylow theorems, 3:213–214
Sylvester, James Joseph, 6:**564–567,** *565*
Symbiosis, 6:389
Symbol systems, physical, 5:258
Symbolic Analysis of Relay and Switching Circuits
(Shannon), 6:425
Symbolic Logic (Dodgson), 2:310, 311
Symbolism, 7:278
Symbols, mathematical, 1:125, 6:265
Symmetries and Reflections (Wigner), 7:297
Symmetry
hadrons, 3:193, 194
piezoelectric effect, 7:165
Symmetry breaking, particles, 1:238–239
Sympathetic nervous system, neurotransmitters,
7:178–180
Sympathomimetic drugs, 1:119–120
Synapses
Hebb, 3:269, 270
signaling in, 4:89–90
spinal cord transmission, 2:331–332
Synaptic vessicles, 7:179, 180, *180*
Synaptogenesis, 3:147
Synchrocyclotrons, 1:164–165, 6:410
Synchrotons, 6:434
Synchrotrons, 4:332–333, 7:70–72
Synge, Richard Laurence Millington, 2:206, 5:39–40
Synopsis nosologiae methodicae (Cullen), 2:220
Synoptic and Aeronautical Meteorology (Byers), 1:468, 469
SYNROC, 6:258, 260
Syntagma (Gassendi), 3:110, 111, 112, 113
Syntax, 2:45
Synthesis, chemical, 7:64–68, 349, 350–52, 396

Synthesis, organic. *See* Organic synthesis
A Synthesis of Flavones at Room Temperature
  (Venkataraman), 7:144
Synthetic fibers
    cellulose acetate, 2:359
    macromolecules, 2:49–50
    molecular structure research, 5:28–29
    rayon, 5:30
Synthetic rubber
    butadiene, 3:383
    ethynylation reaction, 6:230–231
    isoprene, 1:251
Syrkin, Yakov K., 5:248
System der Naturphilosophie (Oken), 5:331
A System of Chemistry (Thomson), 7:344
System of Logic (Mill), 5:143
Systema fossilium (Walker), 7:222
Systema Naturae (Linnaeus), 4:314, 316
Systematic Census of Australian Plants (Mueller), 5:206
Systematic Geology (King), 4:120
*The Systematic Identification of Organic Compounds: A
  Laboratory Manual* (Shriner and Fuson), 6:322
Systematics, 2:6–7
Systematics and the Origin of Species (Mayr), 2:5, 5:62
Systematische Phylogenie (Haeckel), 3:207, 209
Système de la nature (d'Holbach), 4:185
Le Système du Monde (Duhem), 2:319, 322
Les systèmes socialistes (Pareto), 6:18
Systems ecology. *See* Ecosystems
Szemerédi, Emre, 2:405
Szent-Györgyi, Albert Imre, 6:**567–573**, *570*
Szent-Györgyi, Andrew, 6:571
Szentagothai, John, 2:332
Szilard, Leo, 2:167, 4:296, 6:**573–576**, *575*, 7:267
    Cavendish Laboratory visit, 1:163
    solid-state physics, 6:64
Szily, Kálmán, 1:337

T
T-E index, 7:39
Taba, Hessam, 6:472
Tables of al-Khwārizmī (Adelard translation), 1:14
al-Tabrīzī, Muḥammad bin Abī Bakr, 5:7
Tabula minucionum sanguinis et lunacionum (Prachaticz),
  6:153
et-Tabun (Palestine). *See* Et-Tabun (Palestine)
Tabushi, Iwao, 1:200
Tacconi, Gaetano, 1:202
The Tacit Dimension (Polányi), 6:125
Taderera, Joseph, 3:187
Taḥrīr al-zīj al-jadīd al-riḍwānī (Quṭ al-Dīn), 6:188
Tait's conjecture, 7:89, 90
Takagi, Teiji, 2:117
Takeuchi, Akira, 4:273

Takhtajan, Armen, 2:214
Talbot, William Henry Fox, 7:227
Tallents, Stephen, 6:208
Talmage, David W., 1:458
Tamarkin, Jacob David, 2:356–357, 3:50
Tamm, Igor Evgenievich, 2:108, 109, 110, 6:325, 326
    political maneuvering, 4:102
    quantum mechanics, 6:63
Tammes, Jantina, 7:**1–3**
Tamura, Matsuhei, 4:114
Tanabe, Yukito, 4:60
Tanese, Reiko, 3:232
Tannery, Paul, 2:416, 5:338, 6:2
Tansley, Sir Arthur George, 2:153, 187–188, 7:**3–10**, *7*
    ecosystems, 2:386, 6:510
    influence of, 5:315
    Wild Life Conservation Special Committee, 2:387
Tao, Terence, 2:405
Tapp, Christian, 2:33–34
Target theory, 4:55–56
Tarjamaḥ-i taḥrīr-i uṣūl-i Uqlīdis (Quṭb al-Dīn), 6:188
Tarlo, Lambert Beverly Halstead, 6:33
Tarski, Alfred, 2:44, 45, 7:**10–12**, *11*
    acquaintances of, 6:134
    combinatorics, 2:405
    students of, 6:266, 267
Tartaglia, Niccolò, 5:175
Tartaric acid, 1:284
Taste aversion learning, 6:245–246
Tatevsky, Vladimir, 5:248
Tatlock, Jean, 5:348, 6:421
Tatum, Edward Lawrie, 7:*12,* **12–15**, 346
    amino acids, 6:318
    metabolic reactions, 1:225–226
    Nobel prize, 1:228
Tau Scorpii, 7:106, 107
Taub, Edward, 5:151
Taube, Henry, 3:40
Taurellus, Nicolaus, 3:158
Tausk, Victor, 3:73
Taxation, 6:203, 7:150–151
Taxonomy
    bivalve mollusks, 5:266
    cladistics, 3:281–282
    evolution, 2:5–7, 86
    experimental, 2:153–154
    flatworm, 3:434–435
    gall wasps, 4:124–125
    Linnaean, 5:331
    mammals, 6:454
    natural, 4:315
    plant
        biogeography, 6:514
        biosystematics, 6:515

New York Botanical Garden, 2:213–214
varying approaches to, 5:206
primate, 2:140–141
rules of, 4:315
teratology, 3:119
vertebrates, 5:367
See also Phylogeny
Tayler, R. J., 5:75
Taylor, Brook, 2:423
Taylor, Donald W., 1:358–359
Taylor, Frank Bursley, 7:208, 324
Taylor, Geoffrey Ingram, 2:306–307, 6:170
Taylor, Hugh S., 2:393
Taylor, L. W., 4:275
Taylor, Peter, 5:324
Taylor, William T., 6:81
TCA cycle. *See* Krebs cycle
Te-Kan. *See* Huang Jiqing
Te-Pang, Hou. *See* Hou Te-Pang
Teargas, 4:13
Technocracy, 3:396, 398
Technology, behavioral, 6:464
The Technology of Teaching (Skinner), 6:464
Technology transfer, 6:101–102
Tectonics, plate
alpinotype, 1:*70,* 70–71, *71*
continental drift, 4:41
development, 6:430–431
earth expansion, 2:38
earth's magnetism, 1:292–293, 2:379
folding and, 1:70–71
geochemistry, 6:259
geology, 2:38–42
instruments, 1:243
marine geology, 2:288
oceanography, 6:235–236
paleomagnetism, 2:193
polycyclic theory, 3:394
seismicity, 1:244–245
See also Geotectonics
Teeth, fossil, 5:354–355
Teich, Mikulas, 5:233, 239
Teichert, Curt, 7:**15–17**
Teichmüller, Oswald, 1:22, 262
Teilhard de Chardin, Pierre, 7:184, 384
colleagues of, 3:104
commentaries on, 5:89
evolution, 6:109
influence of, 2:236
metaphysics, 6:108
Piveteau, Jean, 6:106
Teisserenc de Bort, Léon Philippe, 7:**17–20**
TEL (tetraethyllead), 3:382
Telecommunications, wireless, 6:375

Telegraphy, 3:58
Teleology, biological, 3:93–94
Telepathy, 4:25
Telescopes
Airy disk, 1:25
Andromeda Galaxy, 1:130–131
charge-couple device, 7:272
radio, 5:83–84
refraction
cost of construction, 3:290–291
Doppler effect, 1:295
nebulae, 3:286–287
Ryle, 6:306
Schmidt, 3:276
silicon-diode technology, 7:271–272
space-based
development, 6:498–502
Hubble, 1:159–161, 6:502, 7:130
national observatories, 3:142–144
stratoscopes, 6:387
Very Large Array, 3:177
Telesian philosophy, 2:19–20
Telesio, Bernardino, 2:19
Television, 5:141, 142
Telle, Joachim, 6:551
Teller, Edward, 1:43, 135, 7:*20,* **20–25**
acquaintances of, 6:435
atomic bombs, 6:65
catalyst particles, 2:393
colleagues of, 6:328–329
hydrogen bombs, 1:57, 6:421
influence of, 4:16
neutron scattering, 6:392–393
nuclear winter, 6:315
radioactivity, 6:41
students of, 5:155
theory of multilayer adsorption, 2:394
Washington Conferences on Theoretical Physics, 1:271
Teller-Ulam fusion weapon, 7:22, *22*
Telmin, 4:32
Telschow, Ernst, 4:169
Temperature
climatology, 7:39
distribution, 1:117
ocean, 6:*528*
ozone, 2:307–308
Temperley, Neville, 6:398
Tempo and Mode in Evolution (Simpson), 6:454, 7:379
Temporal lobe, brain, 4:142–143, 6:11–12
Tenen, Stan, 5:151
Tennant, Smithson, 1:126, 7:342–343
Tensor calculus, 3:190, 192
Tensor forces, 6:393

Tentamen novae theoriae musicae (Euler), 2:424
Tentamen Theoria Electricitatis et Magnetismi (Aepinus), 7:167
Teoreticheskaia Astrofizika (Ambartsumian), 1:66
La teoría de la información en Ecología (Margalef), 5:24
Teoría de los sistemas ecológicos (Margalef), 5:24
Teoriia sernokislotnogo cataliza (Boreskov), 1:352
Teosinte, 1:228
Ter Meer, Fritz, 6:230, 233
Teratology
    evolution, 3:116
    taxonomy, 3:119
Terkel, Studs, 6:571
Terman, Fred, 3:40, 51
Terman, Lewis Madison, 1:357, 5:47, 145, 7:**25–29**
Termite City (Emerson), 2:391, 392
"Termites" (gifted children), 7:27
Termites (insects), 2:389–391
Terns, black, 1:151
Terpenes, 1:194
Territorial behavior, 7:50
    birds, 3:384–385, 385, 5:278
        British warblers, 5:278
        sexual behavior, 3:384–385
        song sparrows, 5:278
Territorial Imperative (Ardrey), 2:54
Territoriality. *See* Territorial behavior
Territory in Bird Life (Howard), 3:385, 5:278
Terry, Robert J., 2:238
Tesla, Nikola, 3:156
Testamentum (Lull), 4:346–348
Testosterone, 1:460
Tetraethyllead (TEL), 3:382
Tetrahedron, 1:199, 200
Tetrahedron, carbon atoms, 6:*155*
Tetramisole, 4:32
Teutonicus, A. *See* Albertus Magnus, Saint
A Textbook of Histology (Cowdry), 2:185
Textbook of Nature Philosophy (Oken). *See Lehrbuch der Naturphilosophie* (Oken)
A Textbook of Psychology (Hebb), 3:267, 270
Textiles, dyes, 7:143, 145–147
Thābit ibn Qurra, al-Ṣābi' al-Ḥarrānī. *See* Ibrāhīm Ibn Sinān Ibn Thābit Ibn Qurra
Thackray, Arnold, 3:236
Thalamus, 2:332, 341, 6:11–12, *12*
Thallium, 3:333–334
Tharp, Marie, 7:**29–31**, 324
Thayer, Clarence H., 3:382
Theathorn, Henrietta, 3:429
The Theatre of the Empire of Great Britain (Speed), 3:356
Thematic Apperception Test, 5:217
Themistius, 1:442
Thenard, Louis Jacques, 2:325

Theobromine, 3:272
Theology. *See* Religion and science
Theon of Alexandria, 2:418, 3:435, 436
Theophilus, 7:112
Theophrastians, 1:309
Theophrastus, 6:120, 138
Theorell, Axel Hugo Theodor, 2:348, 7:**31–35,** *32*
Theoretical biology
    embryology, 7:201–205
    palingenesis, 4:250–251
    rationality, 2:379–381
    scientific inquiry and, 5:88–89
Theoretical chemistry
    bonds, 6:37
    computers in, 6:131–132
    organic chemistry, 2:277–278, 4:205–206
Theoretical economics, 6:499, 7:149–152
Theoretical geophysics, 3:397
Theoretical Nuclear Physics (Weisskopf), 7:267
Theoretical optics, 3:275
Theoretical physics
    as academic discipline, 6:65–66
    astrophysics, 7:105
    baryon asymmetry, 6:324
    Bogolubov School, 1:318–319
    conformal groups, 3:193
    crystals, 7:164–166
    development, 6:489–491
    electroconductivity, 6:373–377
    electromagnetism, 6:335–340
    influential figures, 5:347–349, 7:20–24, 68–72
    light quantum hypothesis, 2:364–365
    mathematics, 6:64
    metals, 5:200–201
    nuclear, 1:391–392, 7:295–296
    numerical analysis, 3:253–254
    positron, 1:72
    quantum electrodynamics, 7:266–267
    relativity, 4:300–301
    second quantization of fields, 4:55
    United Kingdom, 6:548–549
    University of Michigan, 7:101
    USSR, 6:325
Theoretical psychology, 1:405
Theoria Motus corporum Solidorum seu Rigidorum (Euler), 2:231
Theoria Philosophiae Naturalis (Boscovich), 7:167
Théorie de la Terre (Buffon), 6:109
Theorie der Transformationsgruppen (Engel), 4:310
Théorie mathématique des phénomènes thermiques produits par la radiation solaire (Milanković), 5:133
Theorien der Kosmologie (Heckmann), 3:275
Theories Need Both Essences and Histories (Gould), 3:163
Theories of Learning (Hilgard), 3:312, 313

Theories of Learning and Instruction (edited by Hilgard), 3:314

Theories of the Earth and Universe (Carey), 2:42

The Theory and Applications of Harmonic Integrals (Kodaira), 4:145

Theory and Experiment Relating Psychoanalytic Displacement to Stimulus-Response Generalization (Miller), 5:147

The Theory of Atomic Spectra (Condon), 2:166

A Theory of Cognitive Dissonance (Festinger), 3:15

Theory of convexity. *See* Convexity theory

The Theory of Electrons (Lorentz), 4:334

Theory of Games and Economic Behavior (Neumann and Morgenstern), 3:248–249, 251, 5:187, 188, 225, 226–227

The Theory of Groups and Quantum Mechanics (Weyl), 1:278

Theory of Groups of Finite Order (Burnside), 3:213

Theory of impetus, 1:423–424

A Theory of Justice (Rawls), 3:249

The Theory of Metals (Wilson), 7:321

Theory of mixtures. *See* Mixture theory

The Theory of p-n Junctions in Semiconductors and p-n Junction Transistors (Shockley), 6:439

The Theory of Political Coalitions (Riker), 6:254

Theory of Pressure Curves (Milanković), 5:132

Theory of Probability (Jeffreys), 4:40

A Theory of Programming Language Semantics (Strachey), 6:535

Theory of Salts (Mansfield), 5:19

Theory of similarity. *See* Similarity theory

Theory of sulfuric acid catalysis (Boreskov). *See Teoriia sernokislotnogo cataliza* (Boreskov)

Theory of the Earth (Hutton), 3:419, 422

Theory of the four humors. *See* Humorism

The Theory of the Properties of Metals and Alloys (Mott), 5:201

Therapy, psychological. *See* Psychoanalysis

Thermal explosives, 6:411

Thermal radiation, 2:281, 7:284

Thermal wind, 6:560

Thermionic valve amplifier, 1:15, 17

Thermocline, 6:*529*, 529–530

Thermodynamics
  axiomatics, 3:307
  ecosystems, 5:324
  equilibrium in, 6:164–167
  Fourier synthesis, 1:283
  isentropic analysis, 5:222
  limits, 7:102
  mechanics, 1:337–339
  Onsager relations, 2:66
  protein folding, 1:79–80
  second law of, 6:485
  textbooks, 6:375

Thermodynamics Applied to Air-Mass Analysis (Rossby), 5:221

Thermodynamik (Schottky et al.), 6:375

Thermodynamik der Atmosphäre (Wegener), 4:154, 7:246

Thermohaline Convection with Two Stable Regimes of Flow (Stommel), 6:530

Thermohaline finestructures, 3:10

Thermometry
  boiling apparatus, 2:*253*
  hydrochloric acid, 2:195
  instrumentation, 1:114–116, 3:10
  psychrometers, 1:*115*

Théry, Jeanine, 2:161, 162

These Ruins Are Inhabited (Beadle), 1:228

Thèses de Licence (Chauvon and Hugo), 6:517

Thessalus of Tralles, 3:92

Thiamine, 5:307
  chemical structure, 7:*65*
  in growth, 7:12, 14
  synthesis, 7:65

Thiazolinone, 2:*349*, 349–350

Thibaut, John, 3:15

Thienemann, August Friedrich, 7:**35–38**

Thierry of Chartres, 1:14–15

Thijsse, Jac P., 7:141

Thinking: An Experimental and Social Study (Bartlett), 1:187

The Third Man of the Double Helix (Wilkins), 7:300

Third world countries. *See* Developing countries

Thirring, Hans, 7:262

Thivel, Antoine, 3:324

Thom, René, 7:203, 204

Thom, Taylor, 7:323

Thomae, Carl Johannes, 3:71

Thomas á Kempis, 3:279

Thomas, Alvarus, 6:562

Thomas, H. Deighton, 3:317

Thomas, J. Parnell, 2:169

Thomas, M. B., 5:232

Thomas, Rene, 1:374, 376

Thomas, Robert S. D., 2:416

Thomas Aquinas. *See* Aquinas, Saint Thomas

Thomas Hunt Morgan: Pioneer of Genetics (Shine), 5:185

Thomas Hunt Morgan: The Man and His Science (Allen), 5:183

Thomas of Bradwardine. *See* Bradwardine, Thomas

Thomis, Malcolm, 3:315

Thompson, Gerald L., 5:187

Thompson, Helen, 6:145

Thompson, James B., Jr., 4:157

Thompson, John Griggs, 3:12–13, 153

Thomson, George P., 2:165, 6:64

Thomson, James, 1:29

Thomson, John F., 5:283, 6:507
Thomson, Joseph John, 5:200, 348
Thomson, Thomas, 1:265, 7:344
Thomson, William Sir, 1:27, 29, 3:57
Thoren, Victor E., 1:380, 382
Thorer, Alban, 6:119
Thorium C, 7:398, 399
Thorndike, Edward Lee, 5:44
    behaviorism, 6:459
    individuality, 6:524, 526
    laws of effect and exercise, 3:406
    learning theory, 3:407
Thorndike, Lynn, 1:108, 142
Thorne, Carl B., 5:30, 31
Thorne, Kip, 2:91
Thornthwaite, Charles Warren, 7:**38–41**
Thornthwaite climate classification system, 7:38–40
Thorp, Frank H., 4:287
Thorpe, Charles, 5:349
Thorpe, Joselyn Field, 4:13
Thorpe, William Homan, 2:198, 7:**41–45,** 182
Thorsch, Jennifer, 2:415
Thought and Things (Baldwin), 1:169–170
Thought experiment (EPR), 1:240–241
Thrall, Robert M., 3:12
Three Approaches to Psychotherapy (film), 6:278
Three-dimensionally Combining Synoptic Analysis
    (Bergeron). *See Über die dreidimensional verknüpfende*
    Wetteranalyse (Bergeron)
The Threefold Minimum and the Measure (Bruno), 1:425
Threshold Signals (Uhlenbeck), 7:103
Thrifty genotype, 5:243–244
Through Distant Worlds and Times (Milanković), 5:135
Thudichum, Johann Ludwig Wilhelm, 7:**45–47**
Thudichum nasal speculum, 7:46
Thunderstorms
    aviation and, 1:469
    isentropic analysis, 5:222
    mesoanalysis, 3:82–83
The Thunderstorms (Byers), 1:469
Thurber, Cliff, 1:32
Tibbets, Paul, 6:422
Ibn Tibbon, Samuel ben Judah, 5:9
Tidal flats, 7:142
Tide tables, 1:175–176
Tides
    atmospheric, 3:262, 263, 264
    long-term cycles, 4:95
    ocean, 1:361, 362
    theory of, 3:113
Tieje, Arthur J., 6:453
Tierney, Myles, 5:4
Tierney, Patrick, 5:244
Tiffney, Lewis H., 6:454

Tilak, Bal Dattatreya, 7:147
Tileston, Roland R., 4:328
Timaeus (Plato), 2:122, 123, 6:115–116
Time
    as connotative concept, 5:313
    geologic, 6:468, *468*
    natural philosophy, 5:352
    quantum mechanics, 6:167
    space
        gravitation, 3:191–192
        Hawking-Penrose singularity theorems, 6:399
        independence, 2:367–369
        Newtonian theory, 5:269–270
        particle fields, 1:324
        relativity, 1:424–425, 6:122–123
Time, the Refreshing River (Needham), 5:237
Time reversal, 1:238
Time's Arrow and Evolution (Blum), 6:485
Timescale, ratiometric polarity, 3:375, 376–377
Timocharis, 7:**47**
Timoféeff-Ressovsky, Nicolai. *See* Timofeev-Ressovsky,
    Nikolai Vladimirovich
Timofeev-Ressovsky, Nikolai Vladimirovich, 2:268,
    4:55–56, 7:162
Tinbergen, Elisabeth A., 7:55
Tinbergen, Luuk, 1:148, 150, 151
Tinbergen, Niko. *See* Tinbergen, Nikolaas
Tinbergen, Nikolaas, 4:244, 246, 247, 7:*51*
    animal behavior, 6:369
    bees, 3:297
    colleagues of, 7:42
    ethology, 1:151
    hierarchical organization of behavior, 1:150
    influence of, 3:178, 5:279
    influences on, 3:385
    and Lorenz, 4:341, 344
    sociobiology, 1:153
    students of, 1:148, 149
Tinbergen's four whys, 7:54, 55
Ting, Samuel C. C., 1:428
Ting, V. K. *See* Ding Wenjiang
Tinsley, Beatrice Muriel Hill, 7:**57–61,** *59*
Tinsley, Brian, 7:58, 59–60
Tinsley, Teresa, 7:60
Tintant, Henri, 7:**62–64**
Tishler, Max, 2:199, 3:43
Tit for Tat games, 3:232
Titchener, Edward Bradford, 1:356–357, 359, 7:368,
    369
Titelbaum-Tarski, Alfred. *See* Tarski, Alfred
Tits, Jacques, 1:345
Tizard, Henry T., 1:291
To Gaurus (Porphyry), 6:137
Tobacco mosaic virus, 1:464, 3:68

Tobach, Ethel, 6:369

Tobey, Ronald, 2:152–153

Tobias, Phillip V., 7:188

Todd, Alexander Robertus, 7:**64–68,** *67*
  hexacarboxylic acid, 3:337
  students of, 6:478
  vitamin B12, 3:336

Todes, Daniel, 4:163

Todhunter, Isaac, 2:310

Toellner, Richard, 3:214

Toennies, Jan Friedrich, 2:330

Toepel, Tim, 6:231

Tokamak, 6:325

Tolansky, Samuel, 7:229

Tolbert, Bert M., 2:17

Tolerance, immune, 1:455–457

Tolman, Edward Chace, 2.23, 197, 3:409
  influences on, 4:282
  intelligent behavior, 4:245
  latent learning theory, 5:91

Tolman, Richard C., 2:167
  Manhattan Project, 4:291
  mechanics, 6:36
  relativity, 6:169
  Tolman-Bondi model, 1:342

Tolman-Bondi model, 1:342

Tolstoy, Leo, 4:54, 6:166

Toluene, 1:251

Tomkins, Sylvan, 1:8

Tomlinson, Charles, 1:28

Tomonaga, Sin-itero
  theory of electromagnetic force, 1:428
  Tomonaga-Schwinger equation, 6:395

Tomonaga-Schwinger equation, 6:395

Tomonari, Tsukumo, 6:333

Tonic motion, 6:506, 507

Toolmaking, 5:295–296

Toombs, Harry Ashley, 6:31

Toomer, Gerald, 1:83

Topinard, Paul, 5:181

Topoclimatology (Thornthwaite), 7:40

Topological Groups (Pontryagin), 6:127

Topology
  algebraic, 2:112–115
    Arf invariant, 1:97
    arithmetic properties in, 5:179
    axiomatic method, 5:2–3
    Bourbaki text, 1:364, 2:290–291, 360–362,
      7:255
    cohomology, 4:151, 272–273
    duality law, 6:127
    Lie groups, 1:343–345
    manifold, 5:195, 7:291–292
    Riemann-Roch theorem, 4:144–146

stable homotopy theory, 1:11–13
  differential, 1:12–13, 7:291–292
  differential geometry and, 5:194–195
  Lie groups, 1:344–345

Topology, algebraic. *See* Algebraic topology

Topos theory, 5:4

Torahiko, Terada, 5:48

The Torch (Penfield), 6:74

Tornadoes, 3:82–85

Torrey, Henry C., 1:306, 3:196, 6:180

Torricelli, Evangelista, 3:246

Tort, Patrick, 3:116–117

Tortolini, Barnaba, 3:327

Toshi, Shida, 5:48

Tosques, Mario, 2:259

Tournal, Paul, 2:226

Tournoiement de Turner, 7:85

Touschek, Bruno, 1:427, 7:**68–73**

Touschek effect, 7:71

Tousey, Richard, 3:79, 143, 7:**73–78,** *77*

Toward a Psychology of Being (Maslow), 5:46

Towards a Formal Semantics (Strachey), 6:534

Towards a Theoretical Biology (Waddington), 7:203

Towards the Nuclear Holocaust (Ryle), 6:306

Townes, Philip, 3:351

Toxites, Michael, 1:309, 6:550, 551

Tozzer, Alfred, 7:234

Tracers, radioisotopes
  catalysis, 1:354
  labeling, 1:374

Tracing procedure, 3:251

Tract on Monetary Reform (Keynes), 4:112

Tractatio de praecognitionibus et praecognitis and Tractatio de demonstratione (Galilei). *See Manuscript 27* (Galilei)

Tractatus de proportionibus (Bradwardine), 1:378, 379,
  2:325

Tractatus de suphure (Sendivogius), 5:274

Tractatus logicales (Peter of Spain), 1:296

Tractatus parabolicus (Arnald of Villanova, Pseudo),
  1:109, 110

Tractatus Primus (Burley), 1:449, 450

Tractatus proportionum introductorius ad calculations Suicet (Politus), 6:563

Traill, Catharine Parr, 7:**78–80**

Traité de chimie appliquée aux Arts (Dumas), 4:205

Traité de Géographie Physique (Dansereau), 2:235

Traité de méchanique céleste (Somerville), 4:119

Traité de Paléontologie (Piveteau), 6:106, 108

Traité d'énergétique (Duhem), 2:94, 320

Traité des arts céramiques (Brongniart), 4:205

Traité des caractères extérieurs des fossiles (Werner), 6:97

Traité des systèmes (de Condillac), 5:11

Traité élémentaire de chimie (Lavoisier), 4:216

Traité élémentaire d'électricité (Joubert), 3:58

Trajectories, 6:123–124

Transeau, Edgar Nelson, 6:511

Transfer RNA (tRNA), 3:341–343

Transfinite cardinal numbers, 2:32–33

Transformism
    evolution, 3:117–119
    Lamarckian, 3:117
    paleontology, 3:116
    See also Lamarckian evolution

Transgenic animals, 1:399

Transistors, 6:*439*
    Bell Laboratories, 1:180
    invention of, 1:178, 6:437, 438–441, 442

Transition metals, 1:310, 311
    coordination chemistry, 2:102–104
    electronic structure, 4:58–59
    ferrocene, 7:*309, 310*
    nickel, 7:*308*
    organometallic chemistry, 7:308–310
    tungsten, 7:*310*

Transitivity (choice behavior), 7:92

Transketolase, 6:198–199

Translations
    ancient, 6:120
    of Archimedes, 6:218
    chemistry, 6:97–98
    of Euclid, 1:14, 6:218
    natural philosophy, 1:13
    women scientists, 6:97–98

Transmutation, metals
    chemistry *vs.,* 6:506
    controversy, 3:353
    corpuscular theory, 5:273
    mining, 3:352
    Newton's chemical theory and, 5:274–275
    See also Alchemy

Transplantation medicine, immunosuppression, 2:375, 5:85–89

Transport Phenomena (Van Krevelen), 7:135

Transportation, 7:151

Transuranium elements, 6:401–406

Trasformazione della democrazia (Pareto), 6:18

Trattato d'abaco (Piero Della Francesca), 6:104–105

Trattato di sociologia generale (Pareto), 6:18

Traub, Erich, 1:457

The Travels and Adventures of Serendipity (Merton), 5:124

Travis, Irven, 5:53

Treatise of Anatomy (Poirier), 7:114

Treatise of Invertebrate Palaeontology (Hill), 3:315, 317

Treatise on Analysis (Dieudonné), 2:289

Treatise on Astronomy (Herschel), 3:288

Treatise on Dynamics (Whewell), 7:281

Treatise on Geodesy (Argyrus), 1:99

Treatise on Human Nature (Hume), 5:228

Treatise on Invertebrate Paleontology (Newell), 5:266

Treatise on Limnology (Hutchinson), 3:413

Treatise on Magic Squares (Moschopoulos), 5:196

Treatise on Marine Ecology and Paleoecology (Ladd), 4:185–186

Treatise on Mechanics (Monte). *See Mechanicorum Liber* (Monte)

A Treatise on Money (Keynes), 4:112

Treatise on Probability (Keynes), 4:112

Treatise on Proportions (Bradwardine), 1:297

Treatise on Shadow Instruments (Ibrāhīm Ibn Sinān), 2:305

Treatise on the Astrolabe (Argyrus), 1:98

Treatise on the Construction of the Astrolabe with Proofs (al-Qūhī), 6:185, 186

Treatise on the Date of Easter (Argyrus), 1:98

Treatise on the Hour Lines (Ibrāhīm Ibn Sinān Ibn Thābit Ibn Qurra), 4:5

Treatise on the Square Root (Argyrus), 1:99

Trees, Plants, and Flowers (Lee), 4:232

Trefftz, Eleonore, 1:278

Trehalose, 4:*229*

Treisman, Anne, 1:404

Trendelenburg, Friedrich Adolf, 3:69

Tria prima (Paracelsus), 1:141

Tribes of the Rif (Coon), 2:173

Trifan, Daniel S., 1:420

Trigonometric Series (Zygmund), 2:7, 8, 7:414, 415

Trigonometry
    astronomy, 3:320, 6:185
    continuum hypothesis, 2:30
    Fourier series, 7:414–415
    sums, 7:156
    women in, 4:119

Trinity test, 1:135, 6:422

Triploidy, 1:398

Triumphwagen Antimonii (Valentinus), 6:552

Trivers, Robert, 3:229–230, 231

TRNA, 3:341–343

Tröger's base, 6:157, *157*

Trogus, Carl, 6:332

Trombe, Félix, 2:163

The Trophic-Dynamic Aspect of Ecology (Lindeman), 3:414, 7:37

Tropical atmosphere, 7:19

Tropical cyclones
    formation, 6:559
    height, 3:262–263
    resonance theory, 3:264
    weather forecasting, 7:153–155

A Tropical Rain Forest (Odum), 5:324

Tropinone synthesis, 6:270, *270*

Tropolone, 5:290–291

Troponoid, 5:289–290, 292

Troposphere, 7:19
Trowbridge, Augustus, 5:111
Trucco, Raúl, 4:254, *254*
Trudinger, Neil, 5:199
Trueblood, Kenneth, 3:337
Truman, Harry S., 2:169, 4:211, 5:349
    National Science Foundation, 3:176
    nuclear weapons, 6:422
Trump, John George, 7:400
Trumpler, Robert Julius, 5:342–343, 7:284
Tryon, Robert, 2:23
Tschermak, Armin von, 6:568
Tschermak von Seysenegg, Erich, 5:103
Tschirnhaus, Ehrenfried Walther von, 3:353
Tsepnye reaktsii (Semenov). *See Chemical Kinetics and
    Chain Reactions* (Semenov)
Tsuchida, Ryutaro, 4:59
Tswett, Michael, 4:226, 5:39
Tuberculosis
    cause, 2:318
    mycolic acids in, 4:228–229
    pharmacology, 6:323
Tucker, Albert William, 5:227, 7:**80–82**
Tucker, James, 6:485
al-Tuḥ al-shāhiyya fī al-hayʾa (Quṭ al-Dīn), 6:188
Tukey, John W., 1:8, 9, 4:125, 6:426
Tumors
    neuronal growth rate, 3:220–221, *222*
    suppressors, 6:317, 320
    tissue specific, 1:397
    See also Cancer
Tungsten, 1:311, 7:310, *310*
Tupolev, Andrey Nikolaevich, 4:101
Turan, Paul, 2:405
Turbulence
    atmospheric science, 6:8–9
    hydrodynamics, 2:91, 7:391
Turco, Richard, 6:315
Turing, Alan Mathison, 6:165, 7:**82–84,** *83*
    bombe, 3:357
    colleagues of, 6:533
    computer programming languages, 3:360
    computers, 3:256, 5:255, 7:314, 315
    crytography, 6:426
Turner, Charles Henry, 7:**84–87,** *85*
Turner, Frank M., 2:57, 3:430
Turner, Herbert Hall, 7:200
Turner, Peter, 3:165
Tus Sheng Ma. *See* Ma, Tsu Sheng
al-Ṭūsī, Sharaf al-Dīn al-Muẓaffar ibn Muḥammad ibn
    al-Muẓaffar, 7:**87–89**
Tutt, James W., 4:110
Tutte, Bill. *See* Tutte, William Thomas
Tutte, William Thomas, 7:**89–91**, 292

Tuttle, L. Constance, 4:325
Tuve, Merle Antony, 1:390, 391, 2:166
    colleagues of, 6:543, 7:121
    radio proximity fuses, 7:119–120
Tversky, Amos, 7:**91–97**
Twelve Rules for Graduate Students in Biochemistry
    (Racker), 6:202
Tweney, Ryan D., 3:2
Twinkling (radio sources), 6:306
Two Evolutionary Theories (Grene), 6:354
Two letters on the various natural observations (Arduino).
    See Due Lettere sopra varie osservazioni naturali
    (Arduino)
Two New Sciences (Galilei), 3:97, 98
Two-Person Cooperative Games (Nash), 3:251
2001: A Space Odyssey (film), 5:82, 6:312
Tyndale Biscoe, Hugh, 6:210
Tyndall, Arthur M., 5:200, 202
Tyndall, Edward P. T., 7:119
Tyndall, John, 2:12
    colleagues of, 3:328
    germ theory, 1:209
    scientific method, 6:28
    spontaneous generation, 1:210
    students of, 3:326
    X-Club, 3:327
Types of British Vegetation (Tansley), 7:4
Types of Polyploids: Their Classification and Significance
    (Stebbins), 6:515
Typhoons
    China, 7:402
    Fujita scale, 3:83
Typogenesis, 6:353–354
Tyrrell, H. J. V., 6:142
Tyson, Martha, 1:177
Tzetzes, Joannes, 3:324

U

Über Cyclo-octatetraen (Willstätter and Waster), 3:403
*Über den Einfluss des Climas auf die Begranzung der
    Natürlichen Floren* (Grisebach), 1:386
*Über denʼTypusʼ in morphologischer und phylogenetischer
    Biologie Schindewolf* (Schindewolf), 6:353, 354
*Über den Wert der Naturgeschichte besonders für die
    Bildung der Deutschen* (Oken), 5:332
Über di Orientierung des Bienenwolfes (Tinbergen), 7:49
*Über die Beziehung zwischen dem zweiten Hauptsatze der
    mechanischen Wärmetheorie und der
    Wahrscheinlichkeitsrechnung respektive den Sätzen über
    das Wärmegleichgewicht* (Boltzmann), 1:338
Über die Cellulose und ihre Substitutionsprodukte
    (Sakurada), 6:332
Über die dreidimensional verknüpfende Wetteranalyse
    (Bergeron), 1:249

Über die mechanische Bedeutung des zweiten Hauptsatzes der Wärmetheorie (Boltzmann), 1:337–339

Über die metrischen Eigenschaften Kollinearer Gebilde (Grossmann), 3:191

Über die Quantenmechanik der Elektronen in Kristallgittern (Bloch), 1:303

Über Psychologie der individuellen Differenzen (Stern), 6:524

Uexküll, Jakob Johann von, 4:339

UFOs (Unidentified flying objects)
    debunking, 5:117
    theories, 6:310
    U.S. Air Force investigations, 2:170

Uhle, Max, 4:237

Uhlenbeck, George Eugene, 7:**99–104,** *100*

Ulam, Stanislaw Marcin, 7:22

Ulich, Hermann, 6:375

Ullmann, Manfred, 4:19

Ulstad, Philipp, 1:110

Ultracentrifuges, 1:315, 373–374, 464

Ultraviolet spectroscopy
    applications, 7:352, 353–354
    astronomy, 2:343–347
    benzene, 4:17
    solar physics, 7:73–77

Ulugh Beg, 1:45–46, 47

Ibn Umail, 7:407

UN. *See* United Nations (UN)

Una Juarez, Agustin, 1:449

Unconditional positive regard, 6:276, 277, 278

Unconformities (geology), 6:467–468, 469

Understanding Genetics (Ford), 3:49

Underwater Guideposts (Hasler), 3:261

Unended Quest (Popper), 6:136

UNESCO. *See* United Nations Educational, Scientific and Cultural Organization (UNESCO)

Unger, Franz, 5:98, 104

Unidentified flying objects (UFOs)
    debunking, 5:117
    theories, 6:310
    U. S. Air Force investigations, 2:170

Unified field theory, 2:370–371

Unified theory of nature, 6:288

Union of Soviet Socialist Republics (USSR)
    antisemitism, 1:426–427, 6:447–448
    astrophysics, 1:66, 6:432–436
    biochemistry, 1:122
    chemistry in, 5:247–249
    Chernobyl nuclear accident, 3:36
    ecology, 6:509–511
    experimental science, 6:47–48
    geology, 6:430–432
    mathematics, 7:156–157
    nuclear weapons

        atomic bombs, 6:415–416
        research, 3:33–35, 5:128–129
        test bans, 1:80–81, 6:41–42
    oceanography
        physical, 3:9–11
        World War II, 5:173–174
    physics, 4:80–81, 82–85, 6:324–329
    physiochemical biology, 5:359–362
    psychology, 4:349–350
    radio astronomy, 6:432, 433–436
    rocketry, 4:102–104
    Sputnik, 4:180, 5:261, 6:182, 7:175
    uranium, 6:575
    See also Cold War

Unit hydrographs, 3:373

United Kingdom (U.K.)
    electromagnetism, 6:549
    psychology, 1:187–188
    theoretical physics, 6:548–549

United Nations (UN)
    Atomic Energy Commission, 1:135–136
    theoretical physics, 6:338–339

United Nations Educational, Scientific and Cultural Organization (UNESCO)
    director-generals, 3:423
    directors, 5:238–239
    McCarthyism, 1:330–331
    oceanography, 6:237
    scientific humanism, 3:427

United States (U.S.)
    antisemitism, 5:282
    cartography, 6:149–152
    geology, 6:149–152
    geophysics, 4:197–198
    meteorology, 6:219–223
    oceanography, 6:234–237
    satellites, 6:222
    U.S. Geological Survey, 3:372–373, 398

The Unity of the Universe (Sciama), 6:398

UNIVAC (Universal Automatic Computer), 2:336–337, 3:358–359

Universal algebra, 1:286–287

Universal Automatic Computer (UNIVAC), 2:336–337, 3:358–359

Universalism, 5:123

Universe
    big bang theory, 3:389–390
        helium, 1:277–278
        steady state cosmology, 1:341
    expanding, 6:457
    nuclear astrophysics, 3:61–62
    oscillation, 2:283
    steady state theory, 1:339–340
        cosmology, 3:388

electrical cosmology, 1:341–343
galaxy formation, 6:398–399
matter creation, 3:389–390
theory of impetus, 1:423–424
Universe, Life, Mind (Shlovskii), 6:312–313
The Universe at Large (Bondi), 1:342
University of Basel, 6:226–227
University of California, San Diego, 6:235
University of Michigan, 7:101
University of Pavia, 1:296
Unna-Brachet method, 1:373
Unpacking, Repacking, and Anchoring (Tversky and Rottenstreich), 7:95
Unruh effect, 1:237
Unsöld, Albrecht Otto Johannes, 7:**104–109**
Unsolvability. *See* Solvability
Untersuchungen über die Entwickelungs-Gesetze der organischen Welt während der Bildungs-Zeit unserer Erd-Oberfläche (Bronn), 1:416
Up from the Ape (Washburn), 7:234
The Upper Palaeolithic Age in Britain (Garrod), 3:104
Uraniborg, 1:381–382
Uranium
   Australia, 6:260
   chain reactions, 6:574
   dating techniques, 5:299
   enrichment, 1:315
   isotopes, 3:210–211
   plutonium and, 6:408–409
   Seaborg, Glenn Theodore, 6:402
   USSR, 6:575
   See also Fission
Uranography, 2:304
Uranus, 4:178
Urban VIII, Pope, 2:21
Urban climate, 3:386, 387
The Urban Climate (Landsberg), 4:199
Urban transport, 7:151
Urey, Harold Clayton, 4:179, 296
   colleagues of, 6:313
   Miller-Urey experiment, 6:310
   NASA, 6:444
   nuclear weapons, 6:574
   primordial atmosphere research, 5:155–156
   students of, 5:154, 155
Urine as well as other excretions and bodily fluids in man and animal (Neuberg). *See Der Harn sowie die übrigen Ausscheidungen und Körperflüssigkeiten von Mensch und Tier* (Neuberg)
U.S. Army, intelligence testing, 7:25–26, 27
U.S. Geological Survey (USGS)
   hydrography, 3:372–373
   petroleum exploration, 3:398
U.S. Navy, 6:234–235

See also Naval Research Laboratory (NRL); Office of Naval Research (ONR)
U.S. Weather Bureau, 6:220–222
The Usefulness of Natural Philosophy (Boyle), 1:368–369, 6:512
The Uses of Ecology (Edmondson), 2:354
USGS (U.S. Geological Survey), 3:372–373, 398
Usmani, Ishrat H., 6:338
Uspenskii, Yakov V., 7:155
Usselman, Melvyn C., 4:311
USSR. *See* Union of Soviet Socialist Republics (USSR)
Utilitarianism, 3:247, 248–249, 7:282
Utility
   cardinal, 3:248–249
   decision making, 5:225–226
   marginal, 7:150
   natural history, 1:368–369
   representation theorem, 6:349
   sure-thing principle, 6:350–351
UVBGRI system, 6:544
Uvby system, 6:546
Uvnäs, Börje, 7:178
Uyeda, Seiya, 2:191–192, 3:376–377
Uzman, Betty Geren, 6:362

V

V-2 rockets, 5:259, 7:74–75, 173–174
Vaccari, Ezio, 1:95, 5:37
Vaccines
   diphtheria, 1:454–455
   poliovirus, 3:187
Vacuum tubes
   in computers, 7:409–410, 412
   development, 7:120
   electroconductivity, 6:373–375
Vacuums, 3:353
Vagner, Egor Egorovich, 1:194
Vail, Peter, 6:469
Vail, Richard B., 2:170
Väisälä, Vilho, 6:3
Valdecasas, José, 5:305
Valdivia Expedition, 6:370–371
Valence (Coulson), 5:212, 6:38
Valens, Vettius, 7:**111–113**
Valentinus, Basilius, 6:552
Valiela, Ivan, 5:26
Valinomycin, 5:363, *363*
Valla, Giorgio, 2:177
Vallarta, Manuel, 3:19
Vallois, Henri Victor, 5:299, 7:**113–118**
Valluri, S. R., 5:270
Valoch, Karel, 4:42
Valois, Louis de, 3:112
Value distribution theory, 1:22, 24

A Value for n-Person Games (Shapley), 3:250
Vambutas, Vida, 6:199
van Aken, Jan, 7:134, 138
Van Allen, James A., 6:99, 7:**118–126**
    colleagues of, 6:502, 555, 7:272
    fusion, 6:501–502
    human space missions, 5:262
    stratoscopes, 6:387
    V-2 Upper Atmosphere Panel, 5:260
Van Allen, James Alfred. *See* Van Allen, James A.
Van Allen radiation belts, 7:122–123
van Arkel, Anton E., 1:281, 7:133
van Arkel-De Boer process, 1:310, 311
van Bemmelen, Reinout Willem, 3:375
van Bommel, Adriaan J., 1:283, 284
Van de Graaff, Robert Jemison, 7:400
Van de Hulst, Hendrik Christoffel, 5:345, 346,
    7:**126–132,** *127*
Van de Hulst, Henk C. *See* Van de Hulst, Hendrik
    Christoffel
Van de Hulst, Wilhemina Mengerink, 7:126, 131
van de Water, Marjorie, 1:359
van den Berg, Gerard, 2:65
van der Eijk, Philip, 3:323
van der Meer, Simon, 1:429
van der Poel, Willem, 2:297
van der Waals, Johannes Diderik. *See* Waals, Johannes
    Diderik van der
Van der Waerden, Bartel Leendert, 1:365, 5:2
van Dijck, Willem J. D., 7:135
Van Goorile, David. *See* Gorlaeus, David
Van Goorle, David. *See* Gorlaeus, David
van Heerden, Cor, 1:314
Van Helden, Albert, 3:97
Van Helmont, Francis Mercury, 2:171, 172
Van Helmont, Jean-Baptiste. *See* Helmont, Johannes
    Baptista van
van Helmont, Joan Baptista. *See* Helmont, Johannes
    Baptista van
van Hoesen, H. B., 6:518
van Iersel, Jan, 4:247
van Iterson, F. K. Th., 1:314, 7:134, 135
van Kamp, Franz Gansneb Tengnagel, 4:107
van Krevelen, Dirk Willem, 7:**132–140**
van Krevelen-Hoftyzer diagram, 7:133, 135, 137, 139
van Lansbergen, Philippus, 1:445
van Leeuwen, Willem Storm, 6:568
van Lennap, Daan Ross, 7:134
van Niel, Cornelius Bernardus, 4:73, 7:346
van Ormondt, J., 1:312
van Rhijn, Pieter Johannes, 5:341
van Roon, Jos, 1:149
van Straaten, Lambertus Marius Joannes Ursinus,
    7:**140–143,** *141*

van Tamelen, Eugene, 3:40
van Vleck, John H., 1:178, 4:59
    cohesive energies of metals, 4:172
    colleagues of, 5:200
    Manhattan Project, 4:291
    quantum mechanics, 6:420
    radar waves, 1:306
    visualization of diatomic molecules, 5:210
van Waesberghe, Joannes Jansson, 4:133
van Westen, Hendrik A., 7:137
van Wijngaarden, Adriaan, 2:294
van Woerkom, Adrianus Jan Jasper, 5:346
Vanguard satellites, 7:175
Vanishing point, 5:176–177, *177*
van't Hoff, Henry. *See* van't Hoff, Jacobus Henricus
van't Hoff, Jacobus Henricus, 1:112, 6:154
    dilute solutions, 7:189
    influence of, 1:282–283
    optical chemistry, 1:197
    physical chemistry, 5:356
    stereochemical configurations, 3:400–401
Variability, specific, 7:191
Variability of type theory, 3:115–116
Variable stars, 6:51, 383
Variable Stars and Galactic Structure (Gaposchkin and
    Payne-Gaposchkin), 6:51
Variable time fuses, 7:120
Variables, hidden
    predictions of quantum mechanics, 1:236–237,
        239–241
    quantum level, 1:322–323, 324
    wholeness, 1:325
Varian, Russell, 3:199
Varian, Sigurd, 3:199
Variation, adaptive, 1:210–211
Variation and Evolution in Plants (Stebbins), 6:513, 515
Variational principles, 6:251
Varić, Vladimir, 5:132
Varicella zoster virus, 2:376–377
Varieties of Religious Experience (James), 4:23
Vasari, Giorgio, 6:105
Vascular Plants of the Pacific Northwest (Conquist), 2:214
Vascular system. *See* Circulatory system
Vaticanus, 2:121
Vaughan, Margaret, 6:465
Vauquelin, Louis-Nicolas. *See* Vauquelin, Nicolas Louis
Vauquelin, Nicolas Louis, 4:217
Vavilov, Nikolay Ivanovich, 4:102, 6:510, 511
Vavilov, Sergei Ivanovich, 2:108–110, 4:102
Vavilov, Sergey Ivanovich. *See* Vavilov, Sergei Ivanovich
Veblen, Oswald, 2:112, 115
    acquaintances of, 2:360
    algebraic topology, 5:195
    manifolds, 7:291

students of, 5:111
Vector fields on spheres, 1:11, 12
Die Vegetation der Erde (Engler), 2:156
Vegetation dynamics, 7:4
The Vegetation of New Zealand (Cockayne), 2:154, 156
Veksler, Vladimir Iosifovich, 1:426, 427, 2:110, 4:332
Vekua, Ilia, 1:261
Velikovsky, Immanual, 6:314
Velocity
    Brownian motion, 7:101
    light, 2:365–367
    ocean, 6:*528*
Venel, Gabriel-François, 6:507
Venkataraman, Krishnasami, 7:**143–149**
Venn, John, 2:310
Venus
    atmospheric science, 6:310–311, 315
    Mariner space probes, 7:124
    rotation, 3:139
    Russian expeditions to, 4:104
    solar transit, 2:178
Vénus physique (Maupertuis), 5:58
VEPP1-4, 1:*426*, 428–429
Verati, Giuseppe, 1:202
Verati, Laura Bassi. *See* Bassi Verati, Laura Maria
    Caterina
Verbal behavior, 6:462, 464
Verbal Behavior (Skinner), 6:462, 464
Verbitsky, Mikhail, 6:345
*Vereinfachte und erweiterte Theorie der
    Randschichtgleichrichter* (Schottky), 6:376
Verhandlungen der Naturforschenden Vereines in Brünn
    (Bateson), 1:211
Verhoogen, John, 2:191, 192
Vermox, 4:32
Vernadskiy, Vladimir Ivanovich, 6:509
Vernon, Philip E., 1:52
Verschuer, Otmar von, 1:463
Versiera curve, 1:21
Vertebrate paleontology
    comparative anatomy and, 5:366–367
    creative evolution, 5:354–355
    dinosaurs, 7:383–384
    evolution, 6:452
    France, 6:106–108
    mammals, 6:453–455
Verticity, 3:108–109
Verweel, Herman J., 1:281–282
Verwey, Evert J.W., 1:310, 313, 5:203
Verwey, Jan, 1:149
Verworn, Max, 3:303, 4:44
A Very Decided Preference (Medawar), 5:89
Very Large Array telescope, 3:177

Very Useful Logic (Albert of Saxony). *See Perutilis logica*
    (Albert of Saxony)
Vestal, Arthur, 2:187
Vestiges of the Natural History of Creation (Bastian and
    Chambers), 1:208, 2:84, 85, 86, 216, 3:430, 7:226
Vestine, Ernest Harry, 7:121
Vialleton, Louis, 7:113
Vickrey, William Spencer, 7:*149*, **149–152**
Vickrey-Clarke-Groves mechanism, 7:150
Vienna Circle, 2:43, 44
Viète, François, 3:245, 246
Vietnam War
    napalm, 3:200
    opposition, 3:162
Vijesti geoloskog povjerenstva, 3:156
Viking Program, 5:260, 6:486–487
Viking spacecraft, 4:137–140
Villanova, Arnold of. *See* Arnald of Villanova
Villard, Paul, 1:298
Vincent of Beauvais, 6:119
Vincenz, Stanislaw A., 3:376
Vinci, Leonardo da. *See* Leonardo da Vinci
Vine, Fred, 2:193, 7:325
Viner, Jacob, 5:187
Viñes Martorell, Carlos Benito José, 7:**152–155**
Vinogradov, Ivan Matveevich, 7:**155–157**
Vinyl acetate, 1:192
Vinyl ethers, 6:230
Vinylon, 6:330, 333
Virchow, Rudolf Carl, 7:**157–161**, *158*
    Neanderthals, 3:155
    as Pathological Institute director, 5:250
Virology
    genetics, 4:357–358
    host-parasite interactions, 1:454–458
    molecular biology, 1:463–464
    pharmacology, 2:373–374
    tobacco mosaic virus, 3:68
Viruses
    biological weapons, 1:463
    cancer, 4:358–359
    drug resistance, 6:313
    immune response, 4:456–457
    neuropathology, 6:13
    progeny, 6:480–481, *481*
    See also specific viruses
Vis viva controversy, 5:10–11
Viscosimeters, 3:303
Viscosity, 6:332
Vishik, Mark, 4:319
Vishniac, Wolf, 4:137
Visibility research, 7:74
Visible and Infrared Spin Scan Radiometer (VISSR),
    6:556

Visik, Mark, 4:187–188
Vision
    animal, 3:294–297
    birds, 3:*295*
    color, 7:215
    computational research on, 5:35
    Descartes' theory of, 2:*275*
    figural quality, 3:*296*
    geometry of, 1:145–146
    physiology, 7:211–215
    physiology of, 4:224
    vitamins and, 7:211–215
Vision: A Computational Investigation into the Human
    Representation and Processing of Visual Information
    (Marr), 5:35
Visser, S. W., 7:200
VISSR (Visible and Infrared Spin Scan Radiometer),
    6:556
Vista Project, 1:136
Visual disorders, 3:346
Visual perception
    animals, 3:294–297
    biochemistry, 7:211–215
    birds, 3:*295*
    color, 6:295
    figural quality, 3:*296*
    light, 2:233–234
    mathematical modeling, 2:210–211
    object-ground surface relationship, *3:128*
    optical flow field, *3:127*
    psychology, 3:125–130
    self-movement, *3:126*
Vital spirits, 1:139
Vitalism
    animal behavior, 6:369
    biology and, 5:236
    biostratigraphy, 6:352
    matter theory, 1:229–230
    medicine, 6:505–506
    prolongation of life, 1:139
    religion and, 1:269
Vitamin B complex, 5:306–307
Vitamin B1. *See* Thiamine
Vitamin B12, 3:333, 336–337, *337,* 7:67
Vitamin C
    catalysis, 6:570
    isolation of, 6:567–572, 568–569
    synthesis, 6:225–226, 322, 323
    therapy, 6:42–43
Vitamin C and the Common Cold (Pauling), 6:42
Vitamin E, 5:39, 7:65
Vitamins
    bacteria, 7:12
    conversion of, 5:39
    impact of antivitamin research, 4:169
    medicinal chemistry, 3:42–43
    synthesis, 6:322, 7:352
    vision and, 7:211–215
    See also specific vitamins
Vitruvius Pollio, Marcus, 2:305
Vivanti, Giulio, 2:33
Vivien, Daniel, 2:163
Vivisection, 3:94
Vlugter, Jozef C., 7:137
Vocabulaire de sociologie végétale (Braun-Blanquet and
    Pavillard), 1:387
Vocational counseling, 3:313–314
Voeikov, Alekansandr Ivanovich, 4:153
Voelkel, James, 1:382–383
Voevodskiĭ, V. V., 6:416
Vogeleiland (Tinbergen), 7:49
Vogt, Cécile Augustine Marie, 6:447, 7:**161–164,** *163*
Vogt, Heinrich, 3:321
Vogt, Marguerite, 7:162
Vogt, Marthe Louise, 7:162
Vogt, Oskar Georg Dieckmann, 7:**161–164,** *163*
    acquaintances of, 6:447
    cortex layers, 1:407
    gastrulation, 3:350
    students of, 1:406
Vogt, Volker, 6:201
Voigt, Woldemar, 7:**164–166**
Volcanoes and Their Activity (Rittmann), 6:262, 263
Volcanology
    basalt, 6:348
    glass manufacturing, 2:254
    Italy, 6:262–264
    magnetic fields, 3:375–377
    Mount Etna, 1:350
    paleomagnetism, 2:192
    seismic signals, 1:32–33
    Stromboli volcano, 6:*262*
    Vesuvius, 6:*262*
Voles, Mice, and Lemmings (Elton), 2:386
Volhard, Jakob, 4:311
Vol'kenshtein, F. F., 6:416
Vol'kenstein, Michael V., 5:248
Volta, Alessandro Giuseppe Antonio Anastasio, 1:203,
    4:215, 7:**166–172,** *169*
Voltaire, François Marie Aurouet de
    Bolognese academy, 1:203
    and Maupertuis, Pierre-Louis Moreau de, 5:57
Volterra, Vito, 2:384, 3:415
von Auwers, Karl. *See* Auwers, Karl Friedrich von
von Baer, Karl Ernst. *See* Baer, Karl Ernst von
von Bezold, Wilhelm. *See* Bezold, Johannes Friedrich
    Wilhelm von

von Braun, Wernher Magnus Maximilian Freiherr, 5:259, 7:**172–176,** *175,* 287
von Chauvin, Marie, 7:260
von Euler, Ulf Svante, 1:122, 7:**176–180,** *177*
von Euw, Joseph, 6:225, 227
von Frisch, Karl. *See* Frisch, Karl von
von Gmunden, Johannes. *See* John of Gmunden
von Hohenburg, Johan Georg Herwath. *See* Herwath von Hohenburg, Johann Georg
von Holst, Erich, 1:150, 7:**180–184**
    influence of, 4:340–341
    motivational mechanisms, 4:246
von Humboldt, Alexander. *See* Humboldt, Friedrich Wilhelm Heinrich Alexander von
von Kármán, Theodor, 2:99
    guided missiles, 6:99
    rivals of, 2:379
von Koenigswald, Gustav Heinrich Ralph, 2:315, 7:**184–189,** *185,* 252, 253
von Kövesligethy, Radó. *See* Kövesligethy, Radó
von Kraftheim, Johann Crato. *See* Kraftheim, Johann Crato von
von Leibniz, Gottfried Wilhelm. *See* Leibniz, Gottfried Wilhelm
von Lindemann, Ferdinand. *See* Lindemann, Carl Louis Ferdinand von
von Mises, Richard. *See* Mises, Richard von
von Mueller, Ferdinand Jakob Heinrich. *See* Mueller, Ferdinand Jakob Heinrich von
Von Neumann, John, 2:100, 294, 380, 5:188
    artificial intelligence, 6:427 428
    colleagues of, 7:293, 294
    computer science, 2:335, 7:83, 315, 316
    cryptography, 6:426
    existence theorem, 5:228
    game theory, 3:231, 251, 5:187, 226–227
    general circulation models, 6:471
    hidden variables, 1:323
    Hilbert space, 1:239
    influence of, 4:319
    Jordan algebra, 3:194
    linear programming, 7:80
    meteorology, 6:7
    rational bargaining, 5:225
    students of, 5:73
    utilitarianism, 3:248–249
von Plato, Jan, 2:256
von Ranke, Leopold. *See* Ranke, Leopold von
von Richthofen, Ferdinand Freiherr. *See* Richthofen, Ferdinand Freiherr von
von Sachs, Julius. *See* Sachs, Julius von
von Schelling, Friedrich. *See* Schelling, Friedrich von
von Schiller, Friedrich. *See* Schiller, Friedrich von

von Stradonitz Kekulé, Friedrich August. *See* Kekulé von Stradonitz, Friedrich August
von Traubenberg, Heinrich Rausch, 7:106
von Wassermann, August. *See* Wassermann, August Paul von
Vorlesungen über Gastheorie (Boltzmann), 7:99
Vorlesungen über Himmelsmechanik (Moser), 5:197
Vorlesungen über theoretische Physik (Sommerfeld), 6:491
Vorlesungen über Zahlentheorie (Landau), 7:156
Vorstius, Conrad, 3:158
Vorträge über Descendenztheorie (Weismann), 7:258, 261
Vorzimmer, Peter J., 2:244, 246
Voter behavior, 6:254–255
The Voyage of the Beagle (Kropotkin), 4:161
Voyager space probes, 7:124
Voyages dans les Alpes (Saussure), 6:346, 347
Vrba, Elizabeth, 3:161
Vries, Hugo de, 6:55, 7:**189–192,** *190*
    influence of, 7:1
    Mendelian genetics and, 1:211, 5:103, 104
Vroom, Rob, 7:136
Vues de la nature (Buffon), 1:431
Vulkane und ihre Tätigkeit (Rittmann). *See Volcanoes and Their Activity* (Rittmann)
Vulkollan, 1:217
Vygotsky, Lev Semyonovich, 4:350, 6:95, 7:**192–197,** *194*

W

Waage, Peter, 1:265
Waals, Johannes Diderik van der
    influence of, 5:168
    intermolecular forces, 2:66
    Nobel Prize, 6:124
    statistical mechanics, 1:280
Wacker process, 7:311
el-Wad (Palestine). *See* El-Wad (Palestine)
Wadati, Kiyoo, 7:**199–201**
Wadati-Benioff zone, 7:199–200
Waddington, Conrad Hal, 1:373, 4:114, 276–277, 5:237, 7:**201–207**
Waddington, Guy, 2:199
Wade, Michael, 7:379
Wadia, Darashaw Nosherwan, 7:**207–209**
Waelbroeck, Lucien, 4:273
Waelsch, Heinrich, 6:521
Wagner, Carl, 6:375
Wagner, Moritz, 4:163, 7:**209–211**
Wagschal, Claude, 4:273
Wahl, Arthur Charles, 6:402, 408
Wahrhaftig, Clyde, 2:190, 191
Waiting for the Lord (Allport), 1:53
Wakil, Salih, 3:171
Wakimoto, Roger, 3:84, 85

Waksman, Selman, 2:317, 318, 3:43
Walcott, Charles Doolittle, 4:122, 6:151
Wald, Abraham, 5:186, 6:134
Wald, František, 6:6
Wald, George, 7:**211–216**, *213*
Walden inversion, 4:15
Walden Two (Skinner), 5:90, 6:462–463, 465
Walk, Richard D., 3:121, 127–128
Walker, Arthur Geoffrey, 5:82
Walker, Eric, 6:8
Walker, Gilbert Thomas, 5:221, 7:**216–220**
Walker, John, 2:219, 7:**220–224**, *221*
Walker, William H., 4:287
Walkhoff, Otto, 7:249
Wallace, Alfred Russel, 2:86, 7:**224–228**, *225*
  criticism of Darwinism, 3:384
  influence of, 2:384
  religion, 3:432
  spontaneous generation, 1:208
Wallace, George B., 1:118
Wallace, Henry A., 2:167, 169
Wallace, William, 1:441, 2:150, 3:97
Wallace-Hadrill, Andrew, 6:118
Wallach, Nolan R., 1:346
Waller, C., 5:303
Waller, Ivar, 3:254
Wallerstein, George, 3:176
Wallis, Sarah Eglonton. *See* Lee, Sarah Eglonton Wallis
  Bowdich
Walras, Léon, 6:17, 18
Walsh, Alan, 7:**228–233**
Walshe, Francis M. R., 3:345, 347
Walther, A. F., 6:413
Walton, Ernest Thomas Sinton.
  influence of, 4:208, 331
  x-ray tubes, 3:59
Wambacher, Hertha, 1:299, 300, 301, 302
Wang, Hao, 3:130
Wang, Ming Chen, 7:101
Wang, Sigmund, 5:31
Wang Chang, C. S., 7:103
Wang Ganchang, 7:401
Wangsness, Roald K., 1:306
War research, quantitative methods, 6:240
Warblers, 3:384–385, 415
Warburg, Otto Heinrich, 4:72
  colleagues of, 7:212
  enzymology, 3:170, 7:32–33
  influence of, 4:238
  oxidation, 6:569
Warburton, Henry, 7:344
Ward, James Clifton, 1:186
Ward, Robert DeCourcy, 7:402
Ward, Seth, 3:166

Warhurst, Ernest, 6:126
Waring's problem, 7:156
Warm fronts, 1:247–248
Warming, Johannes Eugenius Bülow, 2:155, 187, 188
Warren, Shields, 6:78
Washburn, Margaret Floy, 7:241
Washburn, Sherwood Larned, 2:125, 174, 7:**233–239**, *234*
Washington State, scablands, 1:393–395, *395*
Wasps, 4:124–125, 7:49–50
Wasserburg, Gerry, 7:272
Wasserman, Edward, 3:183
Wassermann, August Paul von, 4:48, 5:250
Waster, E., 3:403
Wataghin, Gleb, 5:302, 303
Watanabe, Akira, 1:437
Water
  analysis
    inflammable air, 4:215
    nitrogen in, 3:63–64
    wartime projects, 5:31
  bacteria
    algae, 2:354–355
    cholera epidemic and, 5:20
  limnology, 2:353–354, 355–356
  pollution
    eutrophication, 2:355
    nitrogen analysis, 3:63
    public health, 4:54
  sediment transport, 1:155–156
  synthesis, 4:215, 7:170
Water-Supply and Irrigation Paper 200 (Horton), 3:373
A Waterhen's Worlds (Howard), 3:385
Waterhouse, Bruce, 3:317, 318
Waterman, Alan T., 6:499
Waterman, Hein, 7:133, 134, 137
Waterston, John James, 6:549
Waterton, Charles, 2:85
Watkins, James D., 6:405–406
Watkins, Winifred M., 4:256
Watson, James Craig
  base-pairings, 2:93
  criticisms of, 2:96
  DNA discovery, 2:207
  DNA structure, 1:374, 2:208–209, 270, 3:66, 5:202,
    6:40, 478–479, 7:67, 299–300
  influence of, 4:355, 356
  molecular bias, 5:284
  molecular structure, 6:81, 83
  rivals of, 3:67
Watson, John Broadus, 7:**239–245**, *241*
  behaviorism, 3:407, 6:243, 459, 461, 7:50
  definition of personality, 1:51
  influence of, 4:203, 5:43

opinion poll ranking, 5:47
Watson, Kenneth, 5:128
Watson, Maxine, 3:415
Watson, Thomas John, Sr., 6:384
Watson, William George, 1:213
Watt, James, 4:215
Wattenberg, Hermann, 7:375
Watts, Duncan, 5:140
Wave mechanics
    aromatic compounds, 6:38
    influence, 7:100
    Laplace-d'Alember transform, 4:273
    mathematical models, 1:270
    numerical analysis, 3:254
    quantum chemistry, 7:104
Waveguides, 6:394
Wavenumber energetics, 6:342
Waves
    charge density, 1:182–183
    light, 3:236
    matter, 1:409, 410–413
    Primakoff, 6:170
    See also Wave mechanics
*Waves and Vortices at a Quasi-Stationary Frontal Surface
    Over Europe* (Bergeron). *See Wellen und Wirbel an
    einer quasistationären Grenzfläche über Europa*
    (Bergeron)
Waylen, Peter, 6:398
The Ways of Death (Bacon, Francis). *See De vijs mortis*
    (Bacon, Francis)
Ways of Worldmaking (Goodman), 3:149
Weapons
    air defense
        acoustical systems, 2:110
        SAGE system, 4:303
    anti-aircraft
        ballistics, 3:253
        differential analyzers, 3:255
        operational research, 1:292
        research, 6:425
    ballistic missiles, 7:173–175
    biological, 5:361
    chemical
        chlorine gas, 3:204–205
        development of, 4:13, 168–170
    guided missiles, 5:259–260, 6:99–100
    gunpowder, 1:264
    mines, 2:207
    missiles, 7:121
    See also Bombs; Nuclear weapons
Wearn, Joseph Treolar, 7:346
Weather
    almanacs and, 1:176
    clouds, 3:386–387

tornadoes, 3:82–85
    See also Cyclones; Hurricanes; Weather forecasting
Weather Analysis and Forecasting (Petterssen), 6:85, 87
Weather and Health (Landsberg), 4:198
Weather balloons, 7:18–19
Weather Bureau. *See* U.S. Weather Bureau
Weather forecasting, 7:153–155
    aviation, 1:468–470
    Bergeron, Tor Harold Percival, 1:245–249
    cyclones, 1:289–290
    growth as a science, 5:221–224
    hurricanes, 7:153–155
    long-range, 7:274
    mathematics-based, 2:99–101, 6:238–239
    monsoons, 7:217–219
    numerical, 6:469–472, 558–561, 561
    oceanography, 2:264–265
    planetary waves, 3:263
    satellites, 6:554–557
    tropical cyclones, 7:153–155
    United States, 6:220–223
    wartime, 6:84, 85–86
    See also Climatology; Meteorology
*Weather Forecasting: Methods in Scientific Weather Analysis
    and Forecasting. An Outline in the History of Ideas and
    Hints at a Program* (Bergeron), 1:249
Weather modification, 1:469–470, 6:222
Weather prediction. *See* Weather forecasting
Weather Prediction by Numerical Process (Richardson),
    2:100, 3:50, 6:238
Weather satellites, 6:222
Weaver, John, 2:153
Weaver, Thomas, 6:97
Weaver, Warren
    colleagues of, 6:425
    enzymology, 3:170
    information theory, 6:427
Webb, James E., 5:262, 264
Weber, Bruce H., 2:243
Weber, Joseph, 1:63
Weber, Max Wilhelm Carl, 2:95
    energetics, 5:357
    ideal climates, 4:155
    religion and science, 5:121–122
    similitude, 7:135
Weber, Tullio, 1:241
Weber, Wilhelm Eduard, 3:4
Webster, David Locke, 1:306
Webster, George, 6:201
Webster, Gerry, 6:355
Wedekind, Rudolf, 6:351–352, 353
Weekes, William Henry, 2:216
Weeks, C. Andrew, 6:16
Weeldenburg, Jan, 7:138

Wegener, Alfred Lothar, 7:**245–248,** *246,* 324
    Bergeron-Findeisen process, 1:248
    continental drift hypothesis, 1:292
    influence of, 5:133
    influences on, 4:154–155
    paleomagnetism, 2:191
Wei-Liang. *See* Chow, Wei-Liang
Weidenreich, Franz, 7:184, 187, **249–253,** *251*
    acquaintances of, 7:235
    cannibalism, 6:60
    geographical isolation of populations, 2:174
    Neanderthals, 3:156
    Peking Man, 2:239
    Pitecanthropus, 2:315
Weidman, Nadine, 4:203, 204
Weierstrass, Karl Theodor Wilhelm, 2:31
    equations of motion, 4:158, 160
    stability of solar system, 5:197
    students of, 7:254
    theory of continuous groups, 4:309, 310
    variational principles, 6:251–252
Weigert, Carl, 2:341
Weil, André, 7:**254–258**
    Bourbaki group, 1:364, 2:112, 290, 361
    education, 2:117
    Fourier analysis, 3:241
    set theory, 2:291
    textbooks by, 2:118
Weinberg, Alvin, 7:296
Weinberg, Steven, 6:335, 340, 396
Weiner, Charles, 5:347
Weiner, Norbert, 6:532
Weisheipl, James, 6:562
Weiskrantz, Lawrence, 6:12
Weismann, August Friedrich Leopold, 4:78, 7:**258–262,** *260*
    evolution, 7:210
    influence of, 4:147
Weiss, Jay M., 5:151
Weiss, Paul, 6:495
Weissbach, Herbert, 1:121
Weissbach, Oskar, 6:160
Weisskopf, Victor Frederick, 2:267, 6:336, 394, 7:**262–269,** *266*
    Austria, 7:70
    colleagues of, 7:294
    on Morrison, Philip, 5:193
    on Walter Elsasser, 2:378
Weitzenhoffer, Andre M., 3:312
Weiwen, Huang. *See* Huang Weiwen
Weizenbaum, Joseph, 6:279
Weizmann, Chaim
    Weismann Institute, 1:251–252
Weizsäcker, Carl Friedrich von, 4:178

    solar system formation, 6:310
    stellar energy, 1:271, 6:543
    stellar structure, 6:385
Weld, Harry, 1:358
Weldon, T. D., 5:88
Weldon, Walter Frank Raphael, 6:53, 54
Welfare Inequalities and Rawlsian Axiomatics (Sen), 3:249
Welker, Heinrich, 1:180–181, 6:376
Wellen und Wirbel an einer quasistationären Grenzfläche über Europa (Bergeron), 1:249
Wells, G. P., 1:455, 3:425
Wells, George. *See* Wells, G. P.
Wells, Herbert George, 1:455, 3:425, 5:236
Wells, John West, 3:317, *318*
Wells, William Charles, 1:28
Welton, Theodore, 3:19
Die Welträthsel (Haeckel), 3:209
Die Weltseele (Schelling), 5:331
Weng Wenhao, 2:299, 6:57
Wenjian, Ding. *See* Ding Wenjiang
Wenner-Gren, Axel, 3:368, 7:235, 236
Wenner-Gren Foundation, 7:35
Wentzel, Gregor, 7:104
Wenzhong, Pei. *See* Pei Wenzhong
Die Werke von Jakob Bernoulli (Bernoulli), 1:254
Werkman, Chester, 5:308
Werner, Abraham Gottlob, 2:85, 6:97
Werner, Alfred, 2:103, 7:310
Wertheimer, Max, 4:141
    Gestalt theory, 4:279
    visual perception, 3:295
Wessels, Norman, 3:188, 189
West, Andrew Fleming, 1:163
West, Rebecca, 3:417
Westerhout, Gart, 5:346, 7:129
Westerink, Leendert G., 6:517
The Western Mediterranean (Margalef), 5:24
Westfall, Richard S., 5:269, 273, 6:512
Westheimer, Frank, 3:200
Westheimer Report, 3:200
Westphal, James A., 7:**269–273**
Wetlands, 5:325
Wetmore, Ralph, 6:514
Wettstein, Fritz von, 1:464
Wexler, Harry, 4:92, 93, 7:**273–276,** *274*
    carbon dioxide, 6:236
    colleagues of, 6:554–555
    death of, 5:223
    meteorological education, 6:221
    weather forecasting, 6:222
Weyl, Hermann Claus Hugo, 2:112, 289, 7:**276–279,** *278*
    arbitrary compact groups, 3:241, 242
    cosmology, 3:275

electromagnetic field, 2:370
harmonic forms, 4:144, 145
Hilber problems, 3:308
invariant theory, 6:285–286
neutrinos, 6:337
Plancherel formula, 3:244
students of, 6:425
theoretical physics, 3:192
trigonometry, 7:156
Weymark, John, 3:249
Weyssagung Sibylle Tyburtine (Gaurico), 1:309
Whalen, Richard, 1:221
Whaling, Ward, 3:61
Wharton, Lennard, 6:473
What Evolution Is (Mayr), 5:63
What in the World (television program), 2:175
What is Life? (Schrödinger), 2:268, 7:298
What Mad Pursuit (Crick), 2:211
What Makes Biology Unique? (Mayr), 5:66
Whately, Richard, 7:212
Wheatstone, Charles, 3:58
Wheeler, George Montague, 4:120
Wheeler, John Archibald, 2:370, 3:19, 6:326
    on American physicists, 1:389
    on Feza Gürsey, 3:193
    hydrogen bombs, 7:22, 23
    Project Matterhorn, 6:384–385
    on prominent nuclear physicists, 1:392
    xenon, 7:296
Wheeler, Mortimer, 2:123
Wheeler, William Morton, 2:391, 4:124
Wheland, George Willard, 6:38
Wheldale, Muriel. *See* Onslow, Muriel Wheldale
When Prophecy Fails (Festinger), 3:13, 15
Wherry, Edgar T., 6:514
Whewell, William, 2:243, 7:**279–283**, *280*
    colleagues of, 3:288, 289
    on experimental science, 1:142
    inductive philosophy criticism, 5:143, 144
    influence of, 5:366
Whipple, Fred Lawrence, 5:112, 7:**283–291**, *286*
    colleagues of, 6:312
    Harvard College Observatory, 5:117
    icy conglomerate model, 1:278
    postwar opportunities, 5:114–115
    Smithsonian Astrophysical Observatory, 3:144
    space science, 7:174
    students of, 3:173
Whitaker, Andrew, 1:237
White, Errol Ivor, 6:31
White, Frederick H., Jr., 1:79
White, Harvey L., 6:361
White, John, 3:337
White, Paul, 3:429

White, Tim, 2:126
White dwarfs, 2:92, 3:173, 176
White House Science Council (WHSC), 1:182
The White Plague: Tuberculosis, Man, and Society
    (Dubos), 2:90
Whitehead, Alfred North
    colleagues of, 3:408
    Logic Theorist, 5:256
    logicism, 3:71
    metaphysics, 7:201
    students of, 6:179
    verbal behavior, 6:462
Whitehead, Henry. *See* Whitehead, John Henry
    Constantine
Whitehead, John Henry Constantine, 1:11, 7:291
Whiteside, D. T., 5:268–269
Whitford, Albert Edward, 3:176, 6:544
Whitman, Anne, 5:269
Whitman, Charles Otis, 2:196, 3:435
    colleagues of, 2:389
    influence of, 4:337
Whitman, Walt, 6:483
Whitney, Hassler, 7:**291–293**
Whittaker, Edmund Taylor, 5:80
Whitten, E. H. Timothy, 4:166
Whitwell, Charles, 2:158
Whitworth, Joseph, 3:430
Wholeness, 1:325
Whorf, Tim, 4:95
WHSC (White House Science Council), 1:182
Wichura, Max, 5:102
Wick, Gian-Carlo, 1:55
    nuclear fission, 1:60–61
    Primakoff, Henry, 6:170
Wickramasinghe, N. Chandra, 3:391
Wicksteed, Philip, 6:18
Wickström, Mårten, 5:162–163
Wide Field-Planetary Camera, 6:502
Wideröe, Rolf, 4:329
Widmer, Carl, 3:171
Wie die Commercien, auch gemeiner Handel und Wandel,
    gegenwärtig in Ihro Kayl. Mayt. Erblanded, verschaffen
    seye (Becher), 1:230–231
Wiebenga, Eelko, 1:282, 283
Wiegand, Clyde, 6:409, 410
Wieland, Heinrich Otto, 6:569
Wien, Max, 2:43, 6:373
Wien, Wilhelm Carl Werner Otto Fritz Franz, 2:378,
    4:335
Wiener, James, 2:*336*
Wiener, Norbert, 1:30, 186, 7:414
    differential equations, 6:380
    Fourier synthesis, 1:282
    information theory, 5:255, 6:427

Wiener, Norbert, *continued*
    Massachusetts Institute of Technology and, 5:78–79
    purposive behavior, 5:78
Wiener, Otto, 1:289
Wierl, Raimund, 5:29
Wieschaus, Eric, 1:400
Wiesel, Torsten, 2:211, 3:146
Wiggins, Jerry S., 5:219
Wigner, Eugene Paul, 7:**293–297**, *294*
    colleagues of, 3:193
    field quantization, 4:55
    Jordan algebra, 3:194
    nuclear reactions, 6:64
    on Polányi, Mihály, 6:126
    quantum states, 3:242
    students of, 1:179, 6:393
    on Szilard, Leo, 6:574
    theoretical physics, 3:192
Wigner, Jenó Pál. *See* Wigner, Eugene Paul
Wilberforce, Samuel, 3:430
Wilchek, Meir, 1:80
Wild, F., 6:322
Wild Strawberries (film), 2:411
Wilder, Burt Green, 6:10
Wilder, Ray, 2:360
Wildlife conservation, 4:268–269
    Australia, 6:207, 209–210
    evolution, 7:44
Wildlife management, 4:267–270
Wildt, Rupert, 2:90
    negative hydrogen ion, 1:277
    Spitzer, Lyman, Jr., 6:500
    Venus, 6:310–311
Wilhelm Ostwald: Mein Vater (Ostwald), 5:356
Wilhelm-Ostwald-Gesellschaft zu Grossbothen, 5:356
Wilhelm Ostwald und sein schriftlicher Nachlass (Zott), 5:356
Wilkes, Maurice, 2:294, 3:256, 6:534
Wilkins, John, 4:134
Wilkins, Maurice Hugh Frederick, 7:*298*, **298–301**
    DNA, 2:96, 208, 3:66
    helical theory, 3:67
Wilkinson, David Todd, 2:283, 7:**301–306**, *302*
Wilkinson, Geoffrey, 7:**306–314**, *307*
    catalysis chemistry, 7:*311*
    childhood and education, 7:307
    coordination chemistry, 7:*308*, 308–309, *309*, 310–311
    industrial chemistry, 7:311–312, *312*
    organometallic chemistry, 7:*308*, 308–310, *309*, *310*
    publications, 7:312–313
    radiochemistry, 7:307–308
    scientific method, 7:312
Wilkinson, James Hardy, 7:**314–318**, *315*

Wilks, Samuel Stanley, 5:52
Will, Heinrich, 4:312
Willasey, James, 3:63
Willemsen, Rasmus, 7:248
Willet, Hurd C. *See* Willett, Hurd C.
Willett, Hurd C., 7:273
William of Moerbeke. *See* Moerbeke, William of
William of Ockham. *See* Ockham, William of
Williams, Donald C., 4:284
Williams, Evan James, 6:64
Williams, Frederic, 3:256
Williams, Gardner, 3:372, 373
Williams, George Christopher, 1:48, 3:229, 7:379
Williams, George Huntston, 6:15
Williams, Robert Runnels, 3:42, 5:162
Williams, Steven, 1:147
Williamson, Alexander William, 4:98, 5:167
Willis, George, 6:399
Willis, John, 7:231
Willow experiment, 3:278, 279
Willstätter, Richard, 4:226
    aromaticity, 3:403
    Eidgenössische Technische Hochscule, 1:250
Wilson, Alan Herries, 5:202, 6:63, 7:**318–323**, *319*
Wilson, Alex, 2:16
Wilson, Charles Thomson Rees, 1:29, 2:306
Wilson, Curtis, 5:270
Wilson, David Sloan, 1:48, 7:379
Wilson, Edgar Bright, Jr., 3:196, 6:38
Wilson, Edmund Beecher, 2:183, 5:183
Wilson, Edward O.
    altruism theory, 3:230
    ants, 3:229
    biodiversity, 3:416
    criticism of, 3:162
Wilson, James Thomas, 2:238
Wilson, John Tuzo, 7:**323–327**
Wilson, Kinnier, 3:347
Wilson, L. G., 1:103
Wilson, Perry, 3:169
Wilson, Pete, 6:406
Wilson, Robert Rathbun, 2:283, 3:390, 7:303, *327*, **327–332**, 393
Wimperis, Harry, 1:291
Winch, Donald, 5:14
Winckelmann, Maria Margaretha. *See* Winkelmann, Maria Margaretha
Wind
    cyclones, 6:559–560
    distribution, 1:117
    microbursts, 3:83–84
    ocean currents, 6:528–530
    sediment transport, 1:155–156
    thermal, 6:560

velocity, 2:306–307
Wind energy, 6:306
Wind shear, 6:560–561
Windaus, Adolf Otto Reinhold, 1:459
WINDCO system, 6:556
Windelband, Wilhelm, 1:52, 6:354
Winkelmann, Maria Margaretha, 7:**332–333**
Winogradsky, Sergei, 2:317
Winsløw, Jacques Bénigne, 1:91
Winsor, Mary P., 3:429
Winstein, Saul, 1:420, 2:199–200
Winter, Alison, 2:56
Winter, nuclear, 6:315
Winterbourne, Anthony T., 3:236
Winthrop, John, Jr., 7:**333–336**, *334*
Wireless telecommunications, 6:375
Wirth, Louis, 3:314
Wirth, Niklaus, 3:51
The Wisdom of the Body (Cannon), 4:276
Wiseman, Christopher, 5:159
Wissenschaftslehre (Fischte), 5:331
Wittgenstein, Ludwig, 3:75
    animal minds, 3:181
    behaviorism, 6:463
    students of, 6:397
Wittich, Paul, 1:382
Wittig, Georg, 7:*336*, **336–342**
Witting, Rolf, 6:3
Wittke, James Pleister, 2:281
WMO (World Meteorological Organization), 6:223
Wohl, Alfred, 5:250, 251–252
Wöhler, Friedrich, 1:267, 439, 6:21
Wolf, George, 5:151
Wolff, Caspar Friedrich, 6:356
Wolff, Kurt, 2:23, 4:63
Wolfke, Mieczyslaw, 4:83
Wolfrom, Melville, 4:258
Wollaston, William Hyde, 1:268, 7:**342–345**, *343*
Wollman, Eugène, 4:356
Wolpoff, Milford H., 3:156
Wolska-Conus, Wanda, 6:517
The Woman Problem (Boring), 1:360
Women
    discrimination against, 3:431
    education for, 3:103, 6:549
    giftedness, 7:26–27
Women scientists
    by discipline
        anatomy, 1:91–93
        archaeology, 3:103–108
        astronomy, 3:286–287, 7:332–333
        astrophysics, 6:49–52
        biochemistry, 5:231–234, 6:447–448
        botany, 2:413–415, 7:1–2, 78–79

cartography, 7:29–31
        chemical physiology, 6:447–448
        chemistry, 2:205–207, 3:193, 333–338,
            6:44–45
        child pscyhology, 2:128–137
        computer science, 3:356–361
        cosmology, 7:57–61
        cytogenetics, 5:67–71
        developmental biology, 5:15–18
        evolution, 6:287–288
        genetics, 1:211, 2:208
        geology, 3:315–319
        geophysics, 4:232–235
        mathematics, 1:19–21, 2:356–357, 4:118–120,
            158–160, 187–189, 5:335–336, 6:265–268
        microbiology, 6:519–521
        musical theory, 6:172–173
        natural history, 4:230–232, 5:118–120
        natural philosophy, 2:79–81
        neurology, 3:145–148, 7:161–164
        nuclear physics, 7:363–368
        oceanography, 5:171–174
        ornithology, 5:277–280
        paleoanthropology, 4:221–223
        particle physics, 7:363–368
        pharmacology, 2:373–377
        philosophy, 2:171–172, 3:435–437
        physical chemistry, 3:65–68
        physics, 1:202, 298–302
        plant genetics, 6:316–320
        primatology, 3:53–57
        psychology, 1:359–360, 3:120–125, 294–297
        radioactivity, 1:298–302, 6:75–78
        translations, 6:97–98
        writing, 5:20–22
        zoology, 3:434–435
    by name
        Agnesi, Maria Gaetana, 1:19–21
        Arconville, Marie Geneviève Charlotte Thiroux
            d', 1:91–93
        Bassi Verati, Laura Maria Caterina, 1:202
        Blau, Marietta, 1:298–302
        Cavendish, Margaret, Duchess of Newcastle,
            2:79–81
        Clark, Mamie Phipps, 2:128–137
        Conway, Anne, 2:171–172
        Cremer, Erika, 2:205–207
        Ehrenfest-Afanas'eva, Tatiana A., 2:356–357
        Elion, Gertrude Belle, 2:373–377
        Esau, Katherine, 2:413–415
        Fossey, Dian, 3:53–57
        Franklin, Rosalind Elsie, 2:208, 3:65–68
        Garrod, Dorothy Annie Elizabeth, 3:103–108
        Gibson, Eleanor Jack, 3:120–125

Women scientists, *continued*
    Goldman-Rakic, Patricia Shoer, 3:145–148
    Herschel, Caroline Lucretia, 3:286–287
    Hertz, Mathilde Carmen, 3:294–297
    Hill, Dorothy, 3:315–319
    Hisar, Remziye, 3:193
    Hodgkin, Dorothy Mary Crowfoot, 3:333–338
    Hopper, Grace Murray, 3:356–361
    Hyman, Libbie Henrietta, 3:434–435
    Hypatia, 3:435–437
    King, Ada Augusta, Countess of Lovelace, 4:118–120
    Kovalevskaya, Sofya Vasilyevna, 4:158–160
    Ladyzhenskaya, Olga Alexandrovna, 4:187–189
    Leakey, Mary Douglas Nicol, 4:221–223
    Lee, Sarah Eglonton Wallis Bowdich, 4:230–232
    Lehmann, Inge, 4:232–235
    Mangold, Hilde, 5:15–18
    Marcet, Jane Haldimand, 5:20–22
    McClintock, Barbara, 5:67–71
    Merian, Maria Sibylla, 5:118–120
    Möller, Sophie Carlotte Juliane, 5:171–174
    Needham, Dorothy Moyle, 5:231–234
    Nice, Margaret Morse, 5:277–280
    Oleinik, Olga Arsenievna, 5:335–336
    Paulze-Lavoisier, Marie-Anne-Pierette, 6:44–45
    Payne-Gaposchkin, Cecilia Helena, 6:49–52
    Perey, Marguerite Catherine, 6:75–78
    Picardet, Claudine, 6:97–98
    Ptolemais of Cyrene, 6:172–173
    Robinson, Julia Bowman, 6:265–268
    Royer, Clémence-Auguste, 6:287–288
    Sager, Ruth, 6:316–320
    Shtern, Lina Solomonovna, 6:447–448
    Stephenson, Marjory, 6:519–521
    Tammes, Jantina, 7:1–2
    Tharp, Marie, 7:29–31
    Tinsley, Beatrice Muriel Hill, 7:57–61
    Traill, Catharine Parr, 7:78–79
    Vogt, Cécile Augustine Marie, 7:161–164
    Winkelmann, Maria Margaretha, 7:332–333
    Wu, Chien-Shiung, 7:363–368
Wonderful Life (Gould), 3:161–162
Wood, H. O., 6:241, 242
Wood, Harland Goff, 5:308, 7:**345–349**
Wood, Paul B., 1:433
Wood, Roger, 5:99
Woodbury, J. Walter, 2:330
Woodger, Joseph Henri, 5:236, 237
Woodin, W. Hugh, 3:130
Woodruff, Boyd, 3:43
Woods, Donald, 2:374
Woods Hole, Marine Biological Laboratory, 3:223
Woods Hole, Oeanographic Institution, 6:255, 256

Woodward, Arthur Smith, 2:240
Woodward, Ida, 1:282
Woodward, James, 3:278
Woodward, Robert Burns, 7:**349–356**, *354*
    anomalous scattering, 1:283
    colleagues of, 7:68
    early life and career, 7:349–350
    ferrocene, 7:308, 310
    influence of, 1:201
    instruments and structure determination, 7:352–353
    penicillin, 6:273
    research methods, 1:196–197
    rules and generalizations, 7:353–355
    scientific style, 7:355–356
    steroid synthesis, 1:198
    synthesis, 7:349, 350–352
    Tetrahedron board, 1:199
    Woodward-Hoffmann rule, 3:88
Woodward-Hoffman rules, 1:193
Woolard, Edgar W., 2:231
Woolley, Helen B. Thompson, 7:239
Wooster, Warren, 3:8
The Working Brain (Luria), 4:351
Working memory. *See* Short-term memory
Works (Campanella). *See Opere* (Campanella)
Works (Galilei), 3:97
The Works of Robert Boyle (Boyle), 1:367
World Meteorological Organization (WMO), 6:223
World Ocean Floor (map), 7:30
World War I
    aerology, 6:220
    American isolationism during, 1:170
    animal behavior research, 1:48
    anti-aircraft weapons, 3:253
    archaeology, 3:104
    army intelligence testing program, 1:357
    brain injuries, 3:345
    Cavendish laboratory, 4:39
    chemical weapons, 3:204–205
    chemistry, 6:270
    economic consequences, 4:112
    eugenics, 4:45
    evolution, 3:424
    glycerol production, 5:252
    intelligence testing, 7:25–26
    meteorology, 6:238
    nerve damage, 2:342
    neurophysiology, 1:16–17
    service in, 5:28
    teargas, 4:13
    vacuum tubes, 6:374–375
World War II
    air defense, 1:291–292, 2:110
    animal behavior, 7:52

anthropology, 7:115
antisemitism, 7:69
astronomy, 3:142, 174
astrophysics, 1:65–66, 3:388–389
atomic bombs, 6:283, 415–416, 421–422
aviation, 1:469, 2:11–12, 308
ballistic missiles, 7:173–174
biochemistry, 5:307
bomb fuses, 3:61
Canada, 3:350
censorship of publications of uranium studies, 1:392
chemical engineering, 3:380, 383
cholesterol research, 3:335–336
computer science, 3:357–358
cryptography, 7:89–90
cryptology, 5:113–114
differential analyzers, 3:255–256
economics of, 4:113
espionage, 2:173
eugenics, 1:2–3, 3–4
genetics, 2:400–401
geologists, 5:295
German Academy of Natural Sciences, 1:4
heroism, 6:485
hydration of olefins, 3:240
Japanese science, 5:289–290
loyalty and service, 5:282
medical experimentation, 1:462–463
meteorology, 5:82, 6:84, 85–86, 470, 560
microbiology, 6:520–521
microwave electronics, 2:166–167
mines, 2:207
molecular biology, 1:371
Netherlands officer chemists, 1:312
nuclear fission research, 1:60–61
oceanography, 2:354, 6:234–235
organic chemistry, 4:16
paleontology, 6:249
pharmacology, 3:247
physicists, 5:303
plutonium, 6:402–403, 408–409
psychology, 1:53, 359, 3:126, 5:147
radar, 1:340, 6:139, 195–196, 302–303, 438, 532
radar development, 1:55–56
radio astronomy, 5:343–345
radio proximity fuses, 7:119–120
radio wave propagation, 5:114
radiochemistry, 3:211–212
refugees, 6:285
research, 6:425–426, 7:65–66, 321
rocket research, 5:259–260
rocketry, 6:99
rubber, 6:231–232
sedimentology, 1:155–156
semiconductors, 6:376
solar system research, 4:178
sonar, 6:500
theoretical physics, 1:274
undersea warfare, 2:262
weather forecasting, 4:197–198
See also National Socialism (Germany)
Worldmaking, 3:149
Worlds-Antiworlds: Antimatter in Cosmology (Alfvén), 1:43
Wormall, Gillian, 5:267
Worms
earthworms, 7:181
flatworms, 3:434
potato eelworms, 7:66
Worster, Donald, 2:152
Worthington, Valentine, 6:529
Wotiz, John H., 4:99
Wotton, Henry, 1:167
Wright, Almroth Edward, 6:55
Wright, Celeste Turner, 2:415
Wright, Edward, 2:158
Wright, Sewall, 3:29, 30, 46, 48, 227, 5:62, 7:**356–363**
controversies and collaborations, 7:360–362
early years, 7:357
group selection, 7:379
influence of, 4:114, 115
physiological genetics, 7:357–360, *358*
retirement, 7:362–363
USDA, 7:357–358
Wrinch, Dorothy Maud, 4:39–40, 5:237, 6:38
Writing, science
alchemy, 1:108–110
anatomy, 1:91–92
medicine, 1:107
microbiology, 2:318–319
natural history, 4:231–232
popular, 1:43
research, 6:83–84
women authors, 5:20–22
Wrobel, Sylvia, 5:185
Wrubel, Marshall, 1:157
Wu, Chien-Shiung, 6:337, 408, 409, 7:**363–368,** *364*
Wu Jianxiong. *See* Wu, Chien-Shiung
Wu Youxun, 7:400
Wundt, Max, 1:444–445
Wundt, Wilhelm, 2:73, 7:**368–371,** *370*
antipositivism, 1:357
students of, 1:169
Wurtman, Richard J., 1:121
Wurtz, Adolphe, 1:465, 2:194, 195, 321, 7:**371–373,** *372*
influence of, 4:98
students of, 3:57

Wurtz, Charles-Adolphe. *See* Wurtz, Adolphe
Wüst, Georg, 5:172, 6:529, 7:**373–376**
Wyatt, Stanley P., Jr., 5:83
Wylie, Charles Clayton, 7:118
Wylton, Thomas, 1:449
Wyngaard, John, 6:9
Wynne-Edwards, Vero Copner, 3:229, 7:**376–380**

X

X-Club, 3:327
X-ray astronomy
    development, 6:280, 283–284
    stars, 1:159
X-ray crystallography
    biophysics, 7:298–300
    chemical reactions, 6:126
    diffusion, 4:81
    DNA, 2:207–209
    hemoglobin, 6:79–80, 81–83
    insulin, 3:334–335
    molecular configuration, 1:279–285
    protein chemistry, 6:39
    scientific method, 7:312
X-ray diffraction
    cellulose, 6:332
    crystallography, 1:280
    plant pigments, 3:334
X-Ray Investigation of the Crystal Structure of Lithium and Lithiumhydride (Bijvoet), 1:281
X-Ray Photographs of Crystalline Pepsin (Hodgkin and Bernal), 3:334
X-rays
    chemical structures, 3:333–334
    detectors, 3:79–80
    effects on living tissues, 1:298–299
    mutations, 7:13
    spectroscopy, 3:78–79
    tubes, 3:59–60
Xanthopoulos, Basilis, 2:92
Xenarchus, 7:**381–382**
Xenon, 7:296, 365
Xianting, Lu. *See* Liu Xianting

Y

Yagi antenna, 1:333
Yale International Conference on the Evolution of Galaxies and Stellar Populations of 1977, 7:60
Yamaguchi, Shigeto, 5:169
Yamg-Mills Theory, 1:238
Yanagida, Tsutomu, 6:171
Yang, Chen Ning, 3:23, 6:337, 391
    muon capture, 6:170
    parity, 7:366, 367
Yang Zhongjian, 6:57, 61, 7:**383–385**

Yanomamis, 5:244
The Yanomamo: A Multidisciplinary Study (Neel), 5:244
Ye Qisun, 7:398, 400
Yearian, H. J., 6:179
Yeasts
    adaptive mutations, 2:401–402
    drugs for, 4:33
    energy production, 4:324
    fermentation, 6:24
    flaoproteins, 3:168
    in glucose synthesis, 4:255
    scientific method, 6:25–26
Yellow enzymes, 7:33–34
Yerkes, Robert Mearns, 2:51–52, 6:243
Ygobone, Aquiles, 5:182
Yin Tsan-Hsun. *See* Yin Zanxun
Yin Wenying, 7:386
Yin Zanxun, 7:**385–386**
Yoekichu ni okeru itojo-bunshi no katachi narabini yoeki-nendo to bunshiryo no kankei (Sakurada), 6:332
Yonezawa, Teijiro, 3:87
Yoon, Do, 3:40
York, Herbert, 6:182
Yoshizawa, Tóru, 5:17
Young, C. C. *See* Yang Zhongjian
Young, Charles Augustus, 2:344
Young, Chung Chien. *See* Yang Zhongjian
Young, Frank, 5:160
Young, John C., 6:362
Young, M., 4:110
Young, Robert, 2:57, 244, 247
Young, Thomas, 6:141
Young, William C., 1:220, 4:245
Young Man Luther (Erikson), 2:410
Youngner, Julius S., 3:187
Youth in the Ghetto (Clark), 2:134
Youxun, Wu. *See* Wu Youxun
Ypsilantis, Tom, 6:410
Yu, Fu Chun, 3:197, 199
Yuan, Luke Chia-Liu, 6:396, 7:365, 366
Yudkin, John, 6:520
Yukawa, Hideki, 1:291, 302, 4:114
Yule, George Udny, 6:55

Z

Zabarella, Jacopo, 7:**387–390**
Zabell, Sandy L., 2:257
Zacharias, Jerold, 5:191
Zahn process, 3:379
Zambra, Joseph Warren, 3:10
Zamecnik, Paul, 3:341
Zanxun, Yin. *See* Yin Zanxun
Zap! A Hands-on Introduction to Electricity and Magnetism (Morrison), 5:192

Zapp, Alfred D., 3:398

Zariski, Oscar, 3:152

Zarzi cave (Iraq), 3:105

Zavadovsky, Boris, 5:237

Zech, Lore, 2:71–72

Zeeberg, Peter, 1:380, 381–382

Zeeman, Pieter, 6:76, 407

Zeeman effect, 1:131, 7:165

Zeigarnik, Bluma, 4:280

Zeiss, Carl, 6:358

Der Zeitfaktor in Geologie und Paläontologie (Schindewolf), 6:353

Zeitgeist, 1:358

Zeitschrift für angewandte Psychologie, 6:523

Zeitschrift für Ethnologie, 1:206

Zeitschrift für Hypnotismus, Psychotherapie sowie andere psychophysiologische und psychopathologische Forschungen, 7:162

Zeitschrift für Physiologische Chemie, 5:252–253

Zeitschrift für vergleichende Physiologie, 7:182

Zeldovich, Yakov Borisovich, 3:35, 6:325, 7:**391–395**

Zelinskiĭ, Nikolay Dmitrievich, 5:246, 7:**395–397**

Zelinsky, Nikolay Dmitrievich. *See* Zelinskiĭ, Nikolay Dmitrievich

Zemansky, Mark, 6:341

Zener, Clarence, 5:200

Zener, Karl, 3:297

Zernike, Frits, 1:280

Zetzner, Lazarus, 1:110

Die Zeugung (Oken), 5:331

Zeuthen, Frederik, 3:249–250

Zewail, Ahmed, 1:259

Zhabotinsky, Anatol, 6:166

Zhang Hongzhao, 2:299

Zhang Qiyun, 7:403

Zhao, Zhongyao, 7:**397–402**

Zhdanov, Yuri A., 5:248

Zhizneopisanie L'va Semionovicha Pontryagina, matematika, sostavlennoe im samim (Pontryagin), 6:128

Zhongguo diceng guifan (cao'on) (Yin Zanxun), 7:386

Zhongguo diceng zhinan ji diceng zhinan shuomingshu (Yin Zanxun), 7:386

Zhongguo dicengdian: VII shitanxi (Yin Zanxun), 7:386

Zhongguo quyu dicengbiao cao'an (Yin Zanxun), 7:386

Zhongjian, Yang. *See* Yang Zhongjian

Zhu Kezhen, 7:**402–405**

Zhukovski, Nikolai, 4:101

Zhukovsky, Nikolay Egorovich. *See* Zhukovski, Nikolai

Zhurnal fizicheskoi khimii, 6:412

Ziegler, Daniel, 3:171, 172

Ziegler, Karl, 7:139, 336

Ziegner, Erika von, 1:460

al-Zīj al-sulṭānī (Quṭ al-Dīn), 6:188

Zīj as-Sanjārī (al-Khazīnī), 2:121

Zīj ī-Ilkhānī (aṭ-Ṭūsī), 2:121

Zīj i Ulugh Beg (Ulugh Beg), 1:45–46, 47

Zilsel, Edgar, 4:55

Zimmer, Karl Günter, 2:268, 4:56

Zimmerli, William H., 5:31

Zimmerman, Carle Clark, 5:121

Zimmermann, Walter, 6:353

Zimmern, Alfred Eckhard, Sir, 3:427

Zinin, Nikolay Nikolaevich, 1:467

Zisman, Michel, 5:4

Zittel, Karl Alfred von, 3:154, 6:108

Zoogeography, 5:61

Zoology
    animal psychology, 4:336–337
    Australia, 6:207, 208–210
    cladistics, 6:30–33
    commentaries on Aristotle, 5:280–281
    embranchment theory, 2:222–223
    embryology, 3:207–208
    ethology, 7:84–86, 181–183
    evolution, 3:115–119, 133, 4:189–190, 7:259–260
    experimentalism, 4:43–46, 76–78, 147–148
    histology, 2:3–4
    invertebrate, 3:434–435
    jellyfish and ascidian, 3:429
    marine, 5:59
    morphology, 1:416–417
    natural selection, 7:377–378
    paleontology, 6:453
    protozoology, 4:44–45
    taxonomy, 4:314–315
    university-based discipline, 1:415

Zooplankton, 3:258–259

Zootechny, 3:116

Zosimos of Panopolis, 5:338, 339, 340, 341, 7:**405–408**

Zosimos the Alchemist (Giumlia-Mair), 7:407

Zott, Regine, 5:356

Zuckerkandl, Emile, 4:116, 6:42

Zuckerman, Harriet, 5:121, 124

Zuckerman, Solly, 2:140

Zuk, Marlene, 3:232

Zumoffen Rockshelter (Lebanon), 3:106

Zuntz, Nathan, 5:250

Zur Farbenlehre (Goethe), 3:133

Zur Naturgeschichte des Singammers (Nice), 5:279

Zur Pulsationstheorie der delta Cephei-Sterne (Schwarzchild), 6:382

Zur quantitativen Durchführung der Raumladungsund Randschichttheorie der Kristallgleichrichter (Schottsky), 6:376

Zur Theorie der Überlagerungsflächen (Ahlfors), 1:22

Zürich-Montpelier analysis, 1:388

Zuse, Konrad, 3:357, 7:**408–414,** *410*

Zweig, George, 3:194